Basics of **Social Research**

Adapted for FCS380 at California State University, Northridge
by Anne Laurel Marenco and Erin Matthews–Maxwell

Taken from:

Basics of Social Research: Qualitative and Quantitative Approaches, Second Edition
by W. Lawrence Neuman

Elementary Statistics, Tenth Edition
by Mario F. Triola

Taken from:

Basics of Social Research: Qualitative and Quantitative Approaches, Second Edition
by W. Lawrence Neuman
Copyright © 2007 by Pearson Education, Inc.
Published by Allyn and Bacon
Boston, Massachusetts 02116

Elementary Statistics, Tenth Edition
by Mario F. Triola
Copyright © 2007 by Pearson Education, Inc.
Published by Addison Wesley
Boston, Massachusetts 02116

Printed in the United States of America

ISBN 0-536-45184-2

2006540176

KL/JW

Please visit our web site at *www.pearsoncustom.com*

PEARSON CUSTOM PUBLISHING
501 Boylston Street, Suite 900, Boston, MA 02116
A Pearson Education Company

BRIEF CONTENTS

CONTENTS

Many students approach a first course on social research with anxiety and trepidation. Sometimes this is because they associate the course with mathematics and statistics with which they had an unpleasant past experience, sometimes they struggled in natural science courses that used experiments, and sometimes they do not know what to expect but believe it is beyond them and only for advanced, very smart scholars.

Basics of Social Research introduces you to social research and presents "what researchers do and why" in a nonthreatening manner that captures both the excitement and importance of doing "real" research. The "nuts and bolts" of methods for doing research requires disciplined thinking and has rigor, but it is easily within reach of almost all undergraduate students. Once you overcome any anxiety and recognize what research is actually about, you will probably find it fascinating. A course in social research methodology differs from most other social sciences courses. Most courses examine content topics, such as inequality, crime, racial divisions, gender relations, urban society, and so forth. A methodology course is relevant, both in preparing you to think more systematically about the content and in revealing how content findings are created.

This book aims to be easy to understand and very accessible, but accessible does not mean it is "Mickey Mouse" or "fluff." Indeed, proper research is a serious activity and often how well a study was conducted can have real consequences. Also, researchers deal with significant ethical issues, their findings shape policy decisions and service delivery concerns, and ultimately research produces new knowledge, or what we really know about issues of importance. Just as the actual daily work of a nurse, social worker, police officer, teacher, physician, or counselor often involves serious issues that have real implications for people's lives, so does social research.

Basics of Social Research has three goals. First, it seeks to show you that social research is simultaneously a very important enterprise and one that is not beyond you—you *can* understand it. Second, it uses many examples from "real research" in published studies to show you the origins of the findings and information found in textbooks or in the media. Last, it gives you a foundation for further learning about doing research and shows you that this activity requires dedication, creativity, and mature judgment.

Social research is not a matter of simply following a cookbook recipe, looking up the correct formula, or blindly following fixed procedures or routines without thinking. It is a creative process that requires personal integrity, moral choices, and a deep commitment to the free and open inquiry into questions about the social world.

This book is a shortened version of a larger, in-depth textbook on social research that I first wrote 15 years ago and that has been updated many times since then. It was written to provide an uncomplicated introduction to social research for students with less background. It reflects what my students taught me over the 25 years that I have been helping undergraduates understand and appreciate social research methods.

Like most written works, this book reflects its author. From the beginning I have been firmly committed to the value of both quantitative and qualitative approaches to research. I believe each approach offers a distinct and complementary perspective to understanding the social world, and that both are equally important and necessary. Revisions in this second edition include updated examples from the recent literature, rewording for greater clarity, two new charts for emphasis, and a reorganization of material to make the presentation smoother.

Doing Social Research

INTRODUCTION

Social research is all around us. Educators, government officials, business managers, human service providers, and health care professionals regularly use social research methods and findings. People use social research to raise children, reduce crime, improve public health, sell products, or just understand one's life. Reports of research appear on broadcast news programs, in popular magazines, in newspapers, and on the Internet.

Research findings can affect people's daily lives and public policies. For example, I recently heard a debate regarding a U.S. federal government program to offer teenagers sexual abstinence counseling. A high-level government official argued for such counseling and strongly opposed offering teens birth control information. An independent health administrator noted that there is no scientific evidence showing that abstinence-only counseling works. He said that 80 percent of teens are already sexually active by the age of 18, therefore it is essential to provide birth control information. He pointed to many research studies showing that birth control instruction for teens reduces pregnancy rates and the spread of sexually transmitted diseases. The government abstinence-only advocate relied on moral persuasion because he had no research evidence. Ideology, faith, and politics shape many government programs rather than solid research evidence, but good social research can help all of us make informed decisions. The evidence also explains why many programs fail to accomplish much or may do more harm than good.

This book is about social research. In simple terms, research is a way of going about finding answers to questions. Professors, professional researchers, practitioners, and students in many fields conduct research to seek answers to questions about the social world. You probably already have some notion of what social research entails. First, let me end some possible misconceptions.

When I asked students in my classes what they think social research entails, they gave the following answers:

- It is based on facts alone; there is no theory or personal judgment.
- Only experts with a Ph.D. degree or college professors read it or do it.
- It means going to the library and finding a lot of magazine articles or books on a topic.
- It is when someone hangs around a group and observes.
- It means conducting a controlled experiment.
- Social research is drawing a sample of people and giving them questionnaires to complete.
- It is looking up lots of statistical tables and information from official government reports.
- To do it, one must use computers to create statistics, charts, and graphs.

The first two answers are wrong, and the others describe only part of what constitutes social research. It is unwise to confuse one part with the whole.

People conduct social research to learn something new about the social world; or to carefully document guesses, hunches, or beliefs about it; or to refine their understanding of how the social world works. A researcher combines theories or ideas with facts in a careful, systematic way and uses creativity. He or she learns to organize and plan carefully and to select the appropriate technique to address a specific kind of question. A researcher also must treat the people in a study in ethical and moral ways. In addition, a researcher must fully and clearly communicate the results of a study to others.

Social research is a process in which people combine a set of principles, outlooks, and ideas (i.e., methodology) with a collection of specific practices, techniques, and strategies (i.e., a method of inquiry) to produce knowledge. It is an exciting process of discovery, but it requires persistence, personal integrity, tolerance for ambiguity, interaction with others, and pride in doing quality work.

Reading this book cannot transform you into an expert researcher, but it can teach you to be a better consumer of research results, help you to understand how the research enterprise works, and prepare you to conduct small research projects. After studying this book, you will be aware of what research can and cannot do, and why properly conducted research is important.

ALTERNATIVES TO SOCIAL RESEARCH

Unless you are unusual, most of what you know about the social world is not based on doing social research. You probably learned most of what you know using an alternative to social research. It is based on what your parents and other people (e.g., friends, teachers) have told you. You also have knowledge based on your personal experiences, the books and magazines you have read, and the movies and television you have watched. You may also use plain old "common sense."

More than a collection of techniques, social research is a process for producing knowledge. It is a more structured, organized, and systematic process than the alternatives that most of us use in daily life. Knowledge from the alternatives is often correct, but knowledge based on research is more likely to be true and have fewer errors. Although research does not always produce perfect knowledge, compared to the alternatives it is much less likely to be flawed. Let us review the alternatives before examining social research.

Authority

You have acquired knowledge from parents, teachers, and experts as well as from books, television, and other media. When you accept something as being true because someone in a position of authority says it is true or because it is in an authoritative publication, you are relying on authority as a basis for knowledge. Relying on the wisdom of authorities is a quick, simple, and cheap way to learn something. Authorities often spend time and effort to learn something, and you can benefit from their experience and work.

There are also limitations to relying on authority. First, it is easy to overestimate the expertise of other people. You may assume that they are right when they are not. History is full of past experts whom we now see as being misinformed. For example, some "experts" of the past measured intelligence by counting bumps on the skull; other "experts" used bloodletting to try to cure diseases. Their errors seem obvious now, but can you be certain that today's experts will not become tomorrow's fools? Second, authorities may not agree, and all authorities may not be equally dependable. Whom should we believe if authorities disagree? Third, authorities may speak on fields they know little about or be plain wrong. An expert who is very informed about one area may use his or her authority in an unrelated area. Also, using the halo effect (discussed later), expertise in one area may spill over illegitimately to be authority in a totally different area. Have you ever seen television commercials where a movie star uses his or her fame as authority to convince you to buy a car? We need to ask: Who is or is not an authority?

An additional issue is the misuse of authority. Sometimes organizations or individuals give an appearance of authority so they can convince others to agree to something that they might not otherwise agree to. A related situation occurs when a person with little training and expertise is named as a "senior fellow" or "adjunct scholar" in a private "think tank" with an impressive name, such as the Center for the Study of X or the Institute on Y Research. Some think tanks are legitimate research centers, but many are mere fronts created by wealthy special-interest groups to engage in advocacy politics. Think tanks can make anyone a "scholar" to facilitate the mass media accepting the person as an authority on an issue. In reality, the person may not have any real expertise.[1] Also, too much reliance on authorities can be dangerous to a democratic society. Experts may promote ideas that strengthen their own power and position. When we accept the authority of experts, but do not know how they arrived at their knowledge, we lose the ability to evaluate what the experts say and lose control of our destiny.

Tradition

People sometimes rely on tradition for knowledge. Tradition is a special case of authority—the authority of the past. Tradition means you accept something as being true because "it's the way things have always been." For example, my father-in-law says that drinking a shot of whiskey cures a cold. When I asked about his statement, he said that he had learned it from his father when he was a child, and it had come down from past generations. Tradition was the basis of the knowledge for the cure. Here is an example from the social world: Many people believe that children who are raised at home by their mothers grow up to be better adjusted and have fewer personal problems than those raised in other settings. People "know" this, but how did they learn it? Most accept it because they believe (rightly or wrongly) that it was true in the past or is the way things have always been done. Some traditional social knowledge begins as simple prejudice. You might rely on tradition without being fully aware of it with a belief such as "People from that side of the tracks will never amount to anything" or "You never can trust that type of person" or "That's the way men (or women) are." Even if traditional knowledge was once true, it can become distorted as it is passed on, and soon it is no longer true. People may cling to traditional knowledge without real understanding; they assume that because something may have worked or been true in the past, it will continue to be true.

Common Sense

You know a lot about the social world from your everyday reasoning or common sense. You rely on what everyone knows and what "just makes sense." For example, it "just makes sense" that murder rates are higher in nations that do not have a death penalty, because people are less likely to kill if they face execution for doing so. This and other widely held commonsense beliefs, such as that poor youth are more likely to commit deviant acts than those from the middle class or that most Catholics do not use birth control, are false.

Common sense is valuable in daily living, but it allows logical fallacies to slip into thinking. For example, the so-called gambler's fallacy says: "If I have a long string of losses playing a lottery, the next time I play, my chances of winning will be better." In terms of probability and the facts, this is false. Also, common sense contains contradictory ideas that often go unnoticed because people use the ideas at different times, such as "opposites attract" and "birds of a feather flock together." Common sense can originate in tradition. It is useful and sometimes correct, but it also contains errors, misinformation, contradiction, and prejudice.

Media Myths

Television shows, movies, and newspaper and magazine articles are important sources of information. For example, most people have no contact with criminals but learn about crime by watching television shows and movies and by reading newspapers. However, the television portrayals of crime, and of many other things, do not accurately reflect social reality. The writers who create or "adapt" images from life for television shows and movie scripts distort reality either out of ignorance or because they rely on authority, tradition, and common sense. Their primary goal is to entertain, not to represent reality accurately. Although many journalists try to present a realistic picture of the world, they must write stories in short time periods with limited information and within editorial guidelines.

Unfortunately, the media tend to perpetuate the myths of a culture. For example, the media show that most people who receive welfare are Black (actually, most are White), that most people who are mentally ill are violent and dangerous (only a small percentage actually are), and that most people who are elderly are senile and in nursing homes (a tiny minority are). Also, mass media "hype" can create a feeling that a major problem exists when it may not (see Box 1.1). People are misled by visual images more easily than other forms of "lying"; this means that stories or stereotypes that appear on film and television can have a powerful effect on people. For example, television repeatedly shows low-income, inner-city, African American youth using illegal drugs. Eventually, most people "know" that urban Blacks use illegal drugs at a higher rate than other groups in the United States, even though this notion is false.

Competing interests use the media to win public support.[2] Public relations campaigns try to alter what the public thinks about scientific findings, making it difficult for the public to judge research findings. For example, a large majority of scientific research supports the global warming thesis (i.e., pollutants from industrialization and massive deforestation are raising the earth's temperature and will cause dramatic climate change and bring about environmental disasters). The scientific evidence is growing and gets stronger each year. The media give equal attention to a few dissenters who question global warming, creating the impression in the public mind that "no one really knows" or that scientists are undecided about the issue of global warming. The media sources fail to mention that the dissenters represent less than 2 percent of all scientists, or that most dissenting studies are paid for by heavily polluting industries. The industries also spend millions of dollars to publicize the findings because their goal is to deflect growing criticism and delay

Box 1.1 Is Road Rage a Media Myth?

Americans hear a lot about *road rage*. *Newsweek* magazine, *Time* magazine, and newspapers in most major cities have carried headlines about it. Leading national political officials have held public hearings on it, and the federal government gives millions of dollars in grants to law enforcement and transportation departments to reduce it. Today, even psychologists specialize in this disorder.

The term *road rage* first appeared in 1988, and by 1997, the print media were carrying over 4,000 articles per year on it. Despite media attention about "aggressive driving" and "anger behind the wheel," there is no scientific evidence for road rage. The term is not precisely defined and can refer to anything from gunshots from cars, use of hand gestures, running bicyclists off the road, tailgating, and even anger over auto repair bills! All the data on crashes and accidents show declines during the period when road rage reached an epidemic.

Perhaps media reports fueled perceptions of road rage. After hearing or reading about road rage and having a label for the behavior, people began to notice rude driving behavior and engaged in *selective observation*. We will not know for sure until it is properly studied, but the amount of such behavior may be unchanged. It may turn out that the national epidemic of road rage is a widely held myth stimulated by reports in the mass media. (For more information, see Michael Fumento, "Road Rage versus Reality," *Atlantic Monthly* [August 1998].)

environmental regulations, not to advance knowledge.

Newspapers offer horoscopes, and television programs or movies report on supernatural powers, ESP (extrasensory perception), UFOs (unidentified flying objects), and angels or ghosts. Although no scientific evidence exists for such, between 25 and 50 percent of the U.S. public accepts them as true, and the percentage with such beliefs has been growing over time as the entertainment media give the phenomenon more prominence.[3]

Personal Experience

If something happens to you, if you personally see it or experience it, you accept it as true. Personal experience, or "seeing is believing," has a strong impact and is a powerful source of knowledge. Unfortunately, personal experience can lead you astray. Something similar to an optical illusion or mirage can occur. What appears true may actually be due to a slight error or distortion in judgment. The power of immediacy and direct personal contact is very strong. Even knowing that, people fall for illusions. Many people believe what they see or personally experience rather than what very carefully designed research has discovered.

The four errors of personal experience reinforce each other and can occur in other areas, as well. They are a basis for misleading people through propaganda, cons or fraud, magic, stereotyping, and some advertising. The most frequent problem is *overgeneralization;* it occurs when some evidence supports your belief, but you falsely assume that it applies to many other situations, too. Limited generalization may be appropriate; under certain conditions, a small amount of evidence can explain a larger situation. The problem is that many people generalize far beyond limited evidence. For example, over the years, I have known five blind people. All of them were very friendly. Can I conclude that all blind people are friendly? Do the five people with whom I happened to have personal experience with represent all blind people?

The second error, *selective observation,* occurs when you take special notice of some people or events and tend to seek out evidence that confirms what you already believe and ignore contradictory information. People often focus on or observe particular cases or situations, especially when they fit preconceived

ideas. We are sensitive to features that confirm what we think, but ignore features that contradict it. For example, I believe tall people are excellent singers. This may be because of stereotypes, what my mother told me, or whatever. I observe tall people and, without awareness, pay particular attention to their singing. I look at a chorus or top vocalist and notice those who are tall. Without realizing it, I notice and remember people and situations that reinforce my preconceived ideas. Psychologists found that people tend to "seek out" and distort their memories to make them more consistent with what they already think.[4]

A third error is *premature closure.* It often operates with and reinforces the first two errors. Premature closure occurs when you feel you have the answer and do not need to listen, seek information, or raise questions any longer. Unfortunately, most of us are a little lazy or get a little sloppy. We take a few pieces of evidence or look at events for a short while and then think we have it figured out. We look for evidence to confirm or reject an idea and stop when a small amount of evidence is present. In a word, we jump to conclusions. For example, I want to learn whether people in my town support Mary Smith or Jon Van Horn for mayor. I ask 20 people; 16 say they favor Mary, 2 are undecided, and only 2 favor Jon, so I stop there and believe Mary will win.

Another common error is the *halo effect;* it is when we overgeneralize from what we accept as being highly positive or prestigious and let its strong reputation or prestige "rub off" onto other areas. Thus, I pick up a report by a person from a prestigious university, say Harvard or Cambridge University. I assume that the author is smart and talented and that the report will be excellent. I do not make this assumption about a report by someone from Unknown University. I form an opinion and prejudge the report and may not approach it by considering its own merits alone. How the various alternatives to social research might address the issue of laundry is shown in Table 1.1.

TABLE 1.1   Alternatives to Social Research

Alternative Explanation to Social Research	Example Issue: In the division of household tasks by gender, why do women tend to do the laundry?
Authority	Experts say that as children, females are taught to make, select, mend, and clean clothing as part of a female focus on physical appearance and on caring for children or others in a family. Women do the laundry based on their childhood preparation.
Tradition	Women have done the laundry for centuries, so it is a continuation of what has happened for a long time.
Common Sense	Men just are not as concerned about clothing as much as women, so it only makes sense that women do the laundry more often.
Media Myth	Television commercials show women often doing laundry and enjoying it, so they do laundry because they think it's fun.
Personal Experience	My mother and the mothers of all my friends did the laundry. My female friends did it for their boyfriends, but never the other way around. It just feels natural for the woman to do it.

HOW SCIENCE WORKS

Although it builds on some aspects of the alternative ways of developing knowledge, science is what separates social research. Social research involves thinking scientifically about questions about the social world and following scientific processes. This suggests that we examine the meaning of science and how its works.

Science

The term *science* suggests an image of test tubes, computers, rocket ships, and people in white lab coats. These outward trappings are a part of science, especially natural science (i.e., astronomy, biology, chemistry, geology, and physics,), that deals with the physical and material world (e.g., plants, chemicals, rocks, stars, and electricity). The social sciences, such as anthropology, psychology, political science, and sociology, involve the study of people—their beliefs, behavior, interaction, institutions, and so forth. Fewer people associate these disciplines with the word *science.* Science is a social institution and a way to produce knowledge. Not everyone is well informed about science. For example, a 2001 survey found that about only one-third of U.S. adults could correctly explain the basics of science.[5]

Scientists gather data using specialized techniques and use the data to support or reject theories. *Data* are the empirical evidence or information that one gathers carefully according to rules or procedures. The data can be *quantitative* (i.e., expressed as numbers) or *qualitative* (i.e., expressed as words, visual images, sounds, or objects). *Empirical evidence* refers to observations that people experience through the senses—touch, sight, hearing, smell, and taste. This confuses people, because researchers cannot use their senses to directly observe many aspects of the social world about which they seek answers (e.g., intelligence, attitudes, opinions, feelings, emotions, power, authority, etc.). Researchers have many specialized techniques to observe and indirectly measure such aspects of the social world.

The Scientific Community

Science comes to life through the operation of the scientific community, which sustains the assumptions, attitudes, and techniques of science. The *scientific community* is a collection of people who practice science and a set of norms, behaviors, and attitudes that bind them together. It is a professional community—a group of interacting people who share ethical principles, beliefs and values, techniques and training, and career paths. For the most part, the scientific community includes both the natural and social sciences.[6]

Many people outside the core scientific community use scientific research techniques. A range of practitioners and technicians apply research techniques that scientists developed and refined. Many use the research techniques (e.g., a survey) without possessing a deep knowledge of scientific research. Yet, anyone who uses the techniques or results of science can do so better if they also understand the principles and processes of the scientific community.

The boundaries of the scientific community and its membership are defined loosely. There is no membership card or master roster. Many people treat a Ph.D. degree in a scientific field as an informal "entry ticket" to membership in the scientific community. The Ph.D., which stands for doctorate of philosophy, is an advanced graduate degree beyond the master's that prepares one to conduct independent research. Some researchers do not have Ph.D.s and not all those who receive Ph.D.s enter occupations in which they conduct research. They enter many occupations and may have other responsibilities (e.g., teaching, administration, consulting, clinical practice, advising, etc.). In fact, about one-half of the people who receive scientific Ph.D.s do not follow careers as active researchers.

At the core of the scientific community are researchers who conduct studies on a full-time or part-time basis, usually with the help of assistants. Many research assistants are graduate students, and some are undergraduates. Working as a research assistant is the way that most scientists gain a real grasp on the details of doing research. Colleges and universities employ most members of the scientific community's core. Some scientists work for the government or

private industry in organizations such as the National Opinion Research Center and the Rand Corporation. Most, however, work at the approximately 200 research universities and institutes located in a dozen advanced industrialized countries. Thus, the scientific community is scattered geographically, but its members tend to work together in small clusters.

How big is the scientific community? This is not an easy question to answer. Using the broadest definition (including all scientists and those in science-related professions, such as engineers), it includes about 15 percent of the labor force in advanced industrialized countries. A better way to look at the scientific community is to examine the basic unit of the larger community: the discipline (e.g., sociology, biology, psychology, etc.). Scientists are most familiar with a particular discipline because knowledge is specialized. Compared to other fields with advanced training, the numbers are very small. For example, each year, about 500 people receive Ph.D.s in sociology, 16,000 receive medical degrees, and 38,000 receive law degrees.

A discipline such as sociology may have about 8,000 active researchers worldwide. Most researchers complete only two or three studies in their careers, whereas a small number of highly active researchers conduct many dozens of studies. In a specialty or topic area (e.g., study of the death penalty, social movements, divorce), only about 100 researchers are very active and conduct most research studies. Although research results represent what humanity knows and it has a major impact on the lives of many millions of people, only a small number of people are actually producing most new scientific knowledge.

The Scientific Method and Attitude

You have probably heard of the scientific method, and you may be wondering how it fits into all this. The *scientific method* is not one single thing; it refers to the ideas, rules, techniques, and approaches that the scientific community uses. The method arises from a loose consensus within the community of scientists. It includes a way of looking at the world that places a high value on professionalism, craftsmanship, ethical integrity, creativity, rigorous standards, and diligence. It also includes strong professional norms such as honesty and uprightness in doing research, great candor and openness about how one conducted a study, and a focus on the merits of the research itself and not on any characteristics of individuals who conducted the study.

Journal Articles in Science

Consider what happens once a researcher finishes a study. First, he or she writes a detailed description of the study and the results as a research report or a paper using a special format. Often, he or she also gives an oral presentation of the paper before other researchers at a conference or a meeting of a professional association and seeks comments and suggestions. Next, the researcher sends several copies to the editor of a scholarly journal. Each editor, a respected researcher chosen by other scientists to oversee the journal, removes the title page, which is the only place the author's name appears, and sends the article to several reviewers. The reviewers are respected scientists who have conducted studies in the same specialty area or topic. The reviewers do not know who did the study, and the author of the paper does not know who the reviewers are. This reinforces the scientific principle of judging a study on its merits alone. Reviewers evaluate the research based on its clarity, originality, standards of good research methods, and advancing knowledge. They return their evaluations to the editor, who decides to reject the paper, ask the author to revise and resubmit it, or accept it for publication. It is a very careful, cautious method to ensure quality control.

The scholarly journals that are highly respected and regularly read by most researchers in a field receive far more papers than they can publish. They accept only 10 to 15 percent of submitted manuscripts. Even lower-ranked journals regularly reject half of the submissions.

Thus, several experienced researchers screen a journal article based on its merits alone, and publication represents the study's tentative acceptance by the scientific community as a valid contribution to knowledge. Unlike the authors of articles for the popular magazines found at newsstands, scientists are not paid for publishing in scholarly journals. In fact, they may have to pay a small fee to help defray costs just to have their papers considered. Researchers are happy to make their research available to their peers (i.e., other scientists and researchers) through scholarly journals. The article communicates the results of a study that a researcher might have devoted years of his or her life to, and it is the way researchers gain respect and visibility among their professional peers. Likewise, the reviewers are not paid for reviewing papers, but consider it an honor to be asked to conduct the reviews and to carry out one of the responsibilities of being in the scientific community. The scientific community imparts great respect to researchers who publish many articles in the foremost scholarly journals because these researchers are directly advancing the scientific community's primary goal—the accumulation of carefully developed knowledge. A researcher gains prestige and honor and a reputation as an accomplished researcher through such publications.

You may never publish an article in a scholarly journal, but you will probably read many such articles. It is important to see how they are a vital component in the system of scientific research. Researchers actively read what appears in the journals to learn about new research findings and the methods used to conduct a study. Eventually, the new knowledge is disseminated in textbooks, new reports, or public talks.

STEPS IN THE RESEARCH PROCESS

Social research proceeds in a sequence of steps, although various approaches to research suggest slightly different steps. Most studies follow the seven steps discussed here. To begin the process, you select a *topic*—a general area of study or issue, such as domestic abuse, homelessness, or powerful corporate elites. A topic is too broad for conducting a study. This makes the next step crucial. You must then narrow down the topic, or *focus* the topic into a specific research question for a study (e.g., "Are people who marry younger more likely to engage in physical abuse of a spouse under conditions of high stress than those who marry older?"). As you learn about a topic and narrow the focus, you should review past research, or the *literature,* on a topic or question. You also want to develop a possible answer, or hypothesis, and theory can be important at this stage.

After specifying a research question, you have to develop a highly detailed plan on how you will carry out the study. This third step requires that you decide on the many practical details of doing the research (e.g., whether to use a survey or qualitative observing in the field, how many subjects to use, etc.). It is only after completing the design stage that you are ready to *gather the data* or evidence (e.g., ask people the questions, record answers, etc.). Once you have very carefully collected the data, your next step is to manipulate or *analyze the data.* This will help you see any patterns in it and help you to give meaning to or *interpret* the data (e.g., "People who marry young and grew up in families with abuse have higher rates of physical domestic abuse than those with different family histories"). Finally, you must *inform others* by writing a report that describes the study's background, how you conducted it, and what you discovered.

The seven-step process shown in Figure 1.1 is oversimplified. In practice, you will rarely complete one step totally then leave it behind to move to the next step. Rather, the process is interactive in which the steps blend into each other. What you do in a later step may stimulate you to reconsider and slightly adjust your thinking in a previous one. The process is not strictly linear and may flow back and forth before reaching an end. The seven steps are for

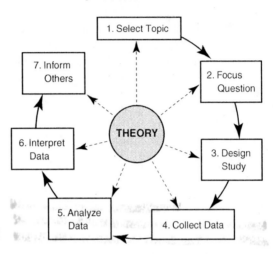

FIGURE 1.1 **Steps in the Research Process**

one research project; it is one cycle of going through the steps in a single study on a specific topic.

Science is an ongoing enterprise that builds on prior research and builds a larger, collectively created body of knowledge. Any one study is a small part of the much larger whole of science. A single researcher may be working on multiple research projects at once, or several researchers may collaborate on one project. Likewise, one project may result in one scholarly article or several, and sometimes several smaller projects are reported in a single article.

DIMENSIONS OF RESEARCH

Three years after they graduated from college, Tim and Sharon met for lunch. Tim asked Sharon, "So, how is your new job as a researcher for Social Data, Inc.? What are you doing?" Sharon answered, "Right now I'm working on an applied research project on day care quality in which we're doing a cross-sectional survey to get descriptive data for an evaluation study." Sharon touched on four dimensions of social research as she described her research on day care.

Social research comes in several shapes and sizes. Before you begin a study, you will need to make several decisions about the specific type of research you are going to conduct. Researchers need to understand the advantages and disadvantages of each type, although most end up specializing in doing one type. We can think of the types as fitting into one of the categories in each of four dimensions of research.

The first dimension is a distinction in how research is used, or between applied and basic research. The next is the purpose of doing research, or its goal, to explore, describe, or explain. The next two dimensions are more specific: how time is incorporated into the study design, and the specific data collection technique used.

The dimensions overlap, in that certain dimensions are often found together (e.g., the goal of a study and a data collection technique). Once you learn the dimensions, you will begin to see how the particular research questions you might want to investigate tend to be more compatible with certain ways of designing a study and collecting data. In addition, being aware of the dimensions of research will make it easier to understand the research reports by others.

Use of Research

For over a century, science has had two wings. Some researchers adopt a detached, purely scientific, and academic orientation; others are more activist, pragmatic, and interventionist oriented. This is not a rigid separation. Researchers in the two wings cooperate and maintain friendly relations. Some individuals move from one wing to another at different stages in their careers. In simple terms, some researchers concentrate on advancing general knowledge over the long term, whereas others conduct studies to solve specific, immediate problems. Those who concentrate on examining the fundamental nature of social reality are engaged in basic research.

Basic Research. *Basic social research* advances fundamental knowledge about the social world. Basic researchers focus on refuting or supporting theories that explain how the social world operates, what makes things happen, why social relations are a certain way, and why society changes. Basic research is the source of most new scientific ideas and ways of thinking about the world. Many nonscientists criticize basic research and ask, "What good is it?" and consider it to be a waste of time and money. Although basic research often lacks a practical application in the short term, it provides a foundation for knowledge that advances understanding in many policy areas, problems, or areas of study. Basic research is the source of most of the tools, methods, theories, and ideas about underlying causes of how people act or think used by applied researchers. It provides the major breakthroughs that significant advances in knowledge; it is the painstaking study of broad questions that has the potential of shifting how we think about a wide range of issues. It may have an impact for the next 50 years or century. Often, the applications of basic research appear many years or decades later. Practical applications may be apparent only after many accumulated advances in basic knowledge build over a long time period. For example, in 1984, Alec Jeffreys, a geneticist at the University of Leicester in England, was engaged in basic research studying the evolution of genes. As an indirect accidental side effect of a new technique he developed, he discovered a way to produce what is now call human DNA "fingerprints" or unique markings of the DNA of individuals. This was not his intent. He even said he would have never thought of the technique if DNA fingerprints had been his goal. Within 10 years applied uses of the technique were developed. Today, DNA analysis is a widely used technique in criminal investigations.

Applied Research. *Applied social research* is designed to address a specific concern or to offer solutions to a problem identified by an employer, club, agency, social movement, or organization. Applied social researchers are rarely concerned with building, testing, or connecting to a larger theory, developing a long-term general understanding, or carrying out a large-scale investigation that might span years. Instead, they usually conduct a quick, small-scale study that provides practical results for use in the short term (i.e., next month or next year). For example, the student government of University X wants to know whether the number of University X students who are arrested for driving while intoxicated or involved in auto accidents will decline if it sponsors alcohol-free parties next year. Applied research would be most applicable for this situation.

People employed in businesses, government offices, health care facilities, social service agencies, political organizations, and educational institutions often conduct applied research and use the results in decision making. Applied research affects decisions such as the following: Should an agency start a new program to reduce the wait time before a client receives benefits? Should a police force adopt a new type of response to reduce spousal abuse? Should a political candidate emphasize his or her stand on the environment instead of the economy? Should a company market a skin care product to mature adults instead of teenagers?

The scientific community is the primary consumer of basic research. The consumers of applied research findings are practitioners such as teachers, counselors, and social workers, or decision makers such as managers, agency administrators, and public officials. Often, someone other than the researcher who conducted the study uses the results.

Applied research results are less likely to enter the public domain in publications and may be available only to few decision makers or practitioners. This means that applied research findings often are not widely disseminated and that well-qualified researchers rarely get to judge the quality of applied studies.

The decision makers who use the results of an applied study may or may not use them

wisely. Sometimes despite serious problems with a study's methodology and cautions from the researchers, politicians use results to justify cutting programs they dislike or to advance programs they favor. Because applied research often has immediate implications or involves controversial issues, it often generates conflict. One famous researcher, William Whyte (1984), encountered conflict over findings in his applied research on a factory in Oklahoma and on restaurants in Chicago. In the first case, the management was more interested in defeating a union than in learning about employment relations; in the other, restaurant owners really sought to make the industry look good and did not want findings on the nitty-gritty of its operations made public.

Applied and basic researchers adopt different orientations toward research methodology (see Table 1.2). Basic researchers emphasize high methodological standards and try to conduct near-perfect research. Applied researchers must make more tradeoffs. They may compromise scientific rigor to get quick, usable results, but compromise is never an excuse for sloppy research. Applied researchers try to squeeze research into the constraints of an applied setting and balance rigor against practical needs. Such balancing requires an in-depth knowledge of research and an awareness of the consequences of compromising standards.

Types of Applied Research. There are many specific types of applied research. Here, you will learn about three major types: evaluation, action, and social impact assessment.

Evaluation Research Study. *Evaluation research study* is applied research designed to find out whether a program, a new way of doing something, a marketing campaign, a policy, and so forth, is effective—in other words, "Does it work?" The most widely used type of applied research is evaluation research.[7] This type of research is widely used in large bureaucratic organizations (e.g., businesses, schools, hospitals, government, large nonprofit agencies) to

TABLE 1.2   Basic and Applied Social Research Compared

Basic	Applied
1. Research is intrinsically satisfying and judgments are by other sociologists.	1. Research is part of a job and is judged by sponsors who are outside the discipline of sociology.
2. Research problems and subjects are selected with a great deal of freedom.	2. Research problems are "narrowly constrained" to the demands of employers or sponsors.
3. Research is judged by absolute norms of scientific rigor, and the highest standards of scholarship are sought.	3. The rigor and standards of scholarship depend on the uses of results. Research can be "quick and dirty" or may match high scientific standards.
4. The primary concern is with the internal logic and rigor of research design.	4. The primary concern is with the ability to generalize findings to areas of interest to sponsors.
5. The driving goal is to contribute to basic, theoretical knowledge.	5. The driving goal is to have practical payoffs or uses for results.
6. Success comes when results appear in a scholarly journal and have an impact on others in the scientific community.	6. Success comes when results are used by sponsors in decision making.

Source: Adapted from Freeman and Rossi (1984:572–573).

demonstrate the effectiveness of what they are doing. An evaluation researcher does not use techniques different from those of other social researchers. The difference lies in the fact that decision makers, who may not be researchers themselves, define the scope and purpose of the research. Also, their objective is to use results in a practical situation.[8]

Evaluation research questions might include: Does a Socratic teaching technique improve learning over lecturing? Does a law-enforcement program of mandatory arrest reduce spouse abuse? Does a flextime program increase employee productivity? Evaluation researchers measure the effectiveness of a program, policy, or way of doing something and often use several research techniques (e.g., survey and field). If it can be used, the experimental technique is usually preferred. Practitioners involved with a policy or program may

conduct evaluation research for their own information or at the request of outside decision makers. The decision makers may place limits on the research by fixing boundaries on what can be studied and by determining the outcome of interest. This often creates ethical dilemmas for a researcher.

Ethical and political conflicts often arise in evaluation research because people can have opposing interests in the findings. The findings of research can affect who gets or keeps a job, it can build political popularity, or it may help promote an alternative program. People who are personally displeased with the findings may attack the researcher or his or her methods.

Evaluation research has several limitations: The reports of research rarely go through a peer review process, raw data are rarely publicly available, and the focus is narrowed to select inputs and outputs more than the full process by which a program affects people's lives. In addition, decision makers may selectively use or ignore evaluation findings.

Action Research Study.   *Action research* is applied research that treats knowledge as a form of power and abolishes the division between creating knowledge and using knowledge to engage in political action. There are several types of action research, but most share five characteristics: (1) the people being studied actively participate in the research process; (2) the research incorporates ordinary or popular knowledge; (3) the research focuses on issues of power; (4) the research seeks to raise consciousness or increase awareness of issues; and (5) the research is tied directly to a plan or program of political action. Action research tends to be associated with a social movement, political cause, or advocacy for an issue. It can be conducted to advance a range of political positions. Some action research has an insurgent orientation with goals of empowering the powerless, fighting oppression and injustice, and reducing inequality. Wealthy and powerful groups or organizations also sponsor and conduct action research to defend their status, position, and privileges in society.

Most action researchers are explicitly political, not value neutral. Because the primary goal is to affect sociopolitical conditions, publishing results in formal reports, articles, or books is secondary. Most action researchers also believe that knowledge develops from direct experience, particularly the experience of engaging in sociopolitical action.

For example, most feminist research is action research. It has a dual mission: to create social change by transforming gender relations and to contribute to the advancement of knowledge. A feminist researcher who studies sexual harassment might recommend policy changes to reduce it as well as to inform potential victims so they can protect themselves and defend their rights. At times, researchers will explain study results in a public hearing to try to modify new policies or laws. The authors of a study on

domestic violence that will be discussed shortly as an explanatory study example (Cherlin et al., 2004) testified in the United States Senate. The study findings and the testimony helped to alter marriage promotion provisions in a 2005 welfare reform law.[9]

Social Impact Assessment Research Study. A researcher who conducts *social impact assessment (SIA)* estimates the likely consequences of a planned intervention or intentional change to occur in the future. It may be part of a larger environmental impact statement required by government agencies and used for planning and making choices among alternative policies. He or she forecasts how aspects of the social environment may change and suggests ways to mitigate changes likely to be adverse from the point of view of an affected population. *Impacts* are the difference between a forecast of the future with the project or policy and without the project or policy. For example, the SIA might estimate the ability of a local hospital to respond to an earthquake, determine how housing availability for the elderly will change if a major new highway is built, or assess the impact on college admissions if students receive interest-free loans. Researchers who conduct SIAs often examine a range of social outcomes and work in an interdisciplinary research team to estimate the social outcomes. The outcomes include measuring "quality of life" issues, such as access to health care, illegal drug and alcohol use, employment opportunities, schooling quality, teen pregnancy rates, commuting time and traffic congestion, availability of parks and recreation facilities, shopping choices, viable cultural institutions, crime rates, interracial tensions, or social isolation. There is an international professional association for SIA research that advances SIA techniques and promotes SIA by governments, corporations, and other organizations.

Social impact assessments are rarely required, but a few governments mandate them. For example, in New South Wales, Australia, a registered club or hotel cannot increase the number of poker machines unless the Liquor Administration Board in the Department Gaming and Racing approves an SIA for the club or hotel. The SIA enables the board to assess the likely local community impact from increasing the number of poker machines. The format includes a matrix that allows the board to identify the social and economic impacts, positive and negative, financial or nonfinancial, quantified or qualitative. In New Zealand, the Gambling Act of 2003 requires an SIA before expanding gambling. In one 2004 study in New Zealand for the Auckland City Council, it noted that 90 percent of New Zealand's adults gamble, 10 percent gamble regularly (once a week or more often), and about 1 percent are problem gamblers, although this varies by age, income, and ethnicity. The SIA recommended limiting the locations of new gambling venues, monitoring their usage, and tracing the amount of gambling revenues that are returned to the community in various ways (e.g., clubs, trusts, etc.). It contained a matrix with social (e.g, arrests, divorce, domestic violence), economic (e.g., unemployment, bankruptcy, tourism expansion), and cultural impacts (e.g., time away from other leisure activity) listed by their effect on all gamblers, problem gamblers, the local community, and the region.[10]

Purpose of a Study

If you ask someone why he or she is conducting a study, you might get a range of responses: "My boss told me to"; "It was a class assignment"; "I was curious"; "My roommate thought it would be a good idea." There are almost as many reasons to do research as there are researchers. Yet, the purposes of social research may be organized into three groups based on what the researcher is trying to accomplish—explore a new topic, describe a social phenomenon, or explain why something occurs. Studies may have multiple purposes (e.g., both to explore and to describe), but one of three major purposes is usually dominant (see Box 1.2).

Box 1.2   Purpose of Research

Exploratory
- Become familiar with the basic facts, setting, and concerns.
- Create a general mental picture of conditions.
- Formulate and focus questions for future research.
- Generate new ideas, conjectures, or hypotheses.
- Determine the feasibility of conducting research.
- Develop techniques for measuring and locating future data.

Descriptive
- Provide a detailed, highly accurate picture.
- Locate new data that contradict past data.
- Create a set of categories or classify types.
- Clarify a sequence of steps or stages.
- Document a causal process or mechanism.
- Report on the background or context of a situation.

Explanatory
- Test a theory's predictions or principle.
- Elaborate and enrich a theory's explanation.
- Extend a theory to new issues or topics.
- Support or refute an explanation or prediction.
- Link issues or topics with a general principle.
- Determine which of several explanations is best.

Exploration. Perhaps you have explored a new topic or issue in order to learn about it. If the issue was new or no researchers had written about it, you began at the beginning. In *exploratory research,* a researcher examines a new area to formulate precise questions that he or she can address in future research. Exploratory research may be the first stage in a sequence of studies. A researcher may need to conduct an exploratory study in order to know enough to design and execute a second, more systematic and extensive study. It addresses the "what?" question: "What is this social activity really about?"

Many higher-education officials are concerned about college students' low retention rates, especially students from minority-disadvantaged social backgrounds. For example, of Latinos who enroll in college, 80 percent leave without receiving a degree. Officials seek ways to reduce dropouts and increase the chances that students who begin college will stay until they earn a degree. Garza and Landeck (2004) conducted an exploratory study of over 500 Latino students at a college along the Texas–Mexico border who had dropped out. They wanted to learn the influencing factors and rationales in student decision making. The authors discovered that the primary factors and rationales were unrelated to teaching quality or university services. Instead, the students who dropped out had been overwhelmed by personal problems or had serious difficulties with family or job responsibilities. Such factors were a major reason given by over 80 percent of the students who dropped out.

Exploratory researchers tend to use qualitative data and not be wedded to a specific theory or research question. Exploratory research rarely yields definitive answers. If you conduct an exploratory study, you may get frustrated and feel it is difficult because there are few guidelines to follow. Everything is potentially important, the steps are not well defined, and the direction of inquiry changes frequently. You need to be creative, open-minded, and flexible; adopt an investigative stance; and explore all sources of information.

Description. Perhaps you have a more highly developed idea about a social phenomenon and want to describe it. *Descriptive research* presents a picture of the specific details of a situation, social setting, or relationship; it focuses on "how?" and "who?" questions: "How did it happen?" "Who is involved?" A great deal of social research is descriptive. Descriptive researchers use most data-gathering techniques—surveys, field research, content analysis, and historical-comparative research. Only experimental research is less often used. Much of the social research found in scholarly journals or used for making policy decisions is descriptive.

Descriptive and exploratory research often blur together in practice. In descriptive research, a researcher begins with a well-defined subject and conducts a study to describe it accurately and the outcome is a detailed picture of the subject. The results may indicate the percentage of people who hold a particular view or engage in specific behaviors—for example, that 8 percent of parents physically or sexually abuse their children. A descriptive study presents a picture of types of people or of social activities.

Stack, Wasserman, and Kern (2004) conducted a descriptive study on pornography use on the Internet by people in the United States. They found that the greatest users were those with weak social bonds. More specifically, the types of people who were adult users of pornography tended to be males with unhappy marriages and weak ties to organized religion. Pornography users were also more likely to have engaged in nonconventional sexual behavior (i.e., had an extramarital affair or engaged in paid sex) but not other forms of deviance, such as illegal drug use.

Explanation. When you encounter an issue that is well recognized and have a description of it, you might begin to wonder why things are the way they are. *Explanatory research* identifies the sources of social behaviors, beliefs, conditions, and events; it documents causes, tests theories, and provides reasons. It builds on exploratory and descriptive research. For example, an exploratory study discovers a new type of abuse by parents; a descriptive researcher documents that 10 percent of parents abuse their children in this new way and describes the kinds of parents and conditions for which it is most frequent; the explanatory researcher focuses on why certain parents are abusing their children in this manner. Cherlin, Burton, Hurt, and Purvin (2004) explained instability in marriage or cohabitation using a woman's past experience with sexual or physical abuse. They tested the hypothesis that women with a history of abuse would be less likely marry than those without such histories. The authors reasoned that those who were abused have fewer social supports and resources to resist or avoid abusive partners, and they are more likely to harbor feelings of self-blame, guilt, and low self-esteem that inhibit the formation of healthy romantic relationships. An abusive experience also creates greater emotional distance and a hesitancy to make long-term commitments. Using quantitative and qualitative data gathered in low-income neighborhoods in three cities—Boston, Chicago, and San Antonio—they found that adult women who had experienced past abuse were less likely to be married, and those with multiple forms of abuse were most likely to remain single. It appears that women without a past history of abuse who found themselves in an abusive relationship as an adult were likely to withdraw from it, but women who had been abused as children were less likely to leave and tended to enter into a series of unstable, transitory relations.

Time Dimension in Research

An awareness of how a study uses the time dimension will help you read or conduct research. This is because different research questions or issues incorporate time differently. Some studies give a snapshot of a single, fixed time point and allow you to analyze it in detail (cross-sectional). Other studies provide a moving picture that lets you follow events, people, or social relations over several time points (longitudinal). Quantitative studies generally look at many cases, people, or units, and measure limited features about them in the form of numbers. By contrast, a qualitative study usually involves qualitative data and examines many diverse features of a small number of cases across either a short or long time period (see Figure 1.2).

Cross-Sectional Research. Most social research studies are *cross-sectional;* they examine a single point in time or take a one-time snapshot approach. Cross-sectional research is usually the simplest and least costly alternative. Its disadvantage is that it cannot capture social processes or change. Cross-sectional research can be exploratory, descriptive, or explanatory, but it is most consistent with a descriptive approach to research. The descriptive study by Stack, Wasserman, and Kern (2004) on pornography use was cross-sectional, based on a national U.S. survey conducted in 2000.

Longitudinal Research. Researchers using *longitudinal research* examine features of people or other units at more than one time. It is usually more complex and costly than cross-sectional research, but it is also more powerful and informative. Descriptive and explanatory researchers use longitudinal approaches. Let us now look at the three main types of longitudinal research: time series, panel, and cohort.

Time-Series Study. A *time-series study* is longitudinal research in which a researcher gathers the same type of information across two or more time periods. Researchers can observe stability or change in the features of the units or can track conditions over time. The specific individuals may change but the overall pattern is clear. For example, there has been a nationwide survey of a large sample of incoming freshman students since 1966. Since it began, over 11 million students at more than 1,800 colleges participated. The fall 2003 survey of 276,449 students found many facts and trends, such as only 34 percent of

FIGURE 1.2   The Time Dimension in Social Research

CROSS-SECTIONAL: Observe a collection of people at one time.

February 2007

TIME SERIES: Observe different people at multiple times.

1950   1970   1990   2010

PANEL: Observe the exact same people at two or more times.

1986   1996   2006

COHORT: Observe people who shared an experience at two or more times.

Married in 1967   1987   2007

CASE STUDY: Observe a small set intensely across time.

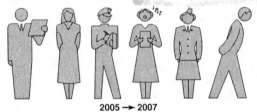

2005 → 2007

entering freshmen studied six or more hours per week. This was the lowest level since the question was asked in 1987 (when it was 47 percent). Yet, alcohol consumption was down. In 2003, 44.8 percent reported drinking beer, which represented a steady decline from 73.7 percent in 1982. In 2003, freshmen were more interested in keeping up with politics. The 33.9 percent who said it was very important to stay politically informed was up from a low of 28.1 percent in 2000, and 22.5 percent said they discussed politics regularly, up from 19.4 percent in 2002 (which had been the highest since a low point in 1993). These figures are still far lower than the 60.3 percent who expressed an interest in politics in 1966, or the one-third who discussed politics regularly in 1968. The importance of family has steadily increased over the years, with 74.8 percent of students calling it essential or very important. This is up from the low point of 58.8 percent in 1977 when the question was first asked. However, religious involvement declined. The percentage of students who attended religious services regularly was at its lowest level in 35 years. In addition, the percent claiming "none" as a religious preference reached a record high of 17.6 percent, compared to a record low of 6.6 percent in 1966. Another trend over the past two decades has been a steady growth in opposition to the death penalty. Nearly one in three incoming students advocated ending capital punishment. This is the highest score since 1980 (when it was 33.2 percent), although the percent withholding an opinion was far higher earlier in time; it exceeded 60 percent in the 1970.[11]

Panel Study. The *panel study* is a powerful type of longitudinal research in which the researcher observes exactly the same people, group, or organization across multiple time points. It is more difficult to conduct than time-series research. Panel research is formidable to conduct and very costly. Tracking people over time is often difficult because some people die or cannot be located. Nevertheless, the results of a well-designed panel study are very valuable.

Even short-term panel studies can clearly show the impact of a particular life event. For example, Oesterle, Johnson, and Mortimer (2004) examined panel data from a longitudinal study that began in 1988 with 1,000 ninth-grade students enrolled in the St. Paul, Minnesota, public school district and looked at volunteering activities during late adolescence and young adulthood, covering nine years from age 18–19 (1992) to age 26–27 (2000). They found that volunteering at an earlier stage strongly affected whether one volunteered at a later stage. Also, people who devoted full time to working or parenting at an earlier stage (18–19 years old) were less likely to volunteer at a later stage (26–27 years old) than those whose major activity was attending school.

Cohort Study. A *cohort study* is similar to a panel study, but rather than observing the exact same people, the study focuses on a category of people who share a similar life experience in a specified time period. Researchers examine the category as a whole for important features and focus on the cohort, or category, not on specific individuals. Commonly used cohorts include all people born in the same year (called *birth cohorts*), all people hired at the same time, and all people who graduate in a given year. Unlike panel studies, researchers do not have to find the exact same people for cohort studies; rather, they need only to identify those who experienced a common life event. In a study of Generation X in the United States, Andolina and Mayer (2003) focused on the cohort of people born between 1967 and 1974. They compared 10 birth cohorts at different time periods over several decades, tracing questions across 24 years. The authors found that White Xers are distinct in their support for school racial integration and for government action to enforce such efforts, compared to other birth cohorts, but not in their attitudes toward employment opportunities or affirmative action. Despite greater general support than other cohorts for equality through integration, it does not extend to issues beyond the schoolyard.

Case Studies. In cross-sectional and longitudinal research, a researcher examines features on many people or units, either at one time period or across time periods, and measures several common features on them, often using numbers. In *case-study research,* a researcher examines, in depth, many features of a few cases over a duration of time with very detailed, varied, and extensive data, often in a qualitative form. The researcher carefully selects a few key cases to illustrate an issue and study it (or them) in detail and considers the specific context of each case. This contrasts with other longitudinal studies in which the researcher gathers data on many units or cases, then looks for general patterns in the mass of numbers.

For example, Snow and Anderson (1992) conducted a case study on homeless people in Austin, Texas. It provided a wealth of details about the lives and conditions of homeless people, identified several types of homeless people, outlined the paths by which they became homeless, and discussed several processes that kept them homeless. This case study used many types of detailed qualitative and quantitative data, with exploratory, descriptive, and explanatory phases to reveal a great amount of unexpected and new information.[12]

Data Collection Techniques

Social researchers collect data using one or more specific techniques. This section gives you a brief overview of the major techniques. In later chapters, you will read about these techniques in detail and learn how to use them. Some techniques are more effective when addressing specific kinds of questions or topics. It takes skill, practice, and creativity to match a research question to an appropriate data collection technique. The techniques fall into two categories based on whether the data being gathered are quantitative or qualitative.

Quantitative Data Collection Techniques. Techniques for quantitative data collection include experiments, surveys, content analyses, and existing statistics.

Experiments. *Experimental research* closely follows the logic and principles found in natural science research; researchers create situations and examine their effects on participants. A researcher conducts experiments in laboratories or in real life with a relatively small number of people and a well-focused research question. Experiments are most effective for explanatory research. In the typical experiment, the researcher divides the people being studied into two or more groups. He or she then treats both groups identically, except that one group but not the other is given a condition he or she is interested in: the "treatment." The researcher measures the reactions of both groups precisely. By controlling the setting for both groups and giving only one group the treatment, the researcher can conclude that any differences in the reactions of the groups are due to the treatment alone.

Surveys. A *survey researcher* asks people questions in a written questionnaire (mailed or handed to people) or during an interview and then records answers. The researcher manipulates no situation or condition; he or she simply asks many people numerous questions in a short time period. Typically, he or she then summarizes answers to questions in percentages, tables, or graphs. Researchers use survey techniques in descriptive or explanatory research. Surveys give the researcher a picture of what many people think or report doing. Survey researchers often use a sample or a smaller group of selected people (e.g., 150 students), but generalize results to a larger group (e.g., 5,000 students) from which the smaller group was selected. Survey research is very widely used in many fields.

Content Analyses. A *content analysis* is a technique for examining information, or content, in written or symbolic material (e.g., pictures, movies, song lyrics, etc.). In content analysis, a researcher first identifies a body of material to analyze (e.g., books, newspapers, films, etc.) and then creates a system for recording specific aspects of it. The system might include counting how often certain words or themes occur. Finally, the researcher records what was found in the material. He or she often measures information in the content as numbers and presents it as tables or graphs. This technique lets a researcher discover features in the content of large amounts of material that might otherwise go unnoticed. Researchers can use content analysis for exploratory and explanatory research, but primarily it is used for descriptive research.

Existing Statistics.   In *existing statistics research,* a researcher locates previously collected information, often in the form of government reports or previously conducted surveys, then reorganizes or combines the information in new ways to address a research question. Locating sources can be time consuming, so the researcher needs to consider carefully the meaning of what he or she finds. Frequently, a researcher does not know whether the information of interest is available when he or she begins a study. Sometimes, the existing quantitative information consists of stored surveys or other data that a researcher reexamines using various statistical procedures. Existing statistics research can be used for exploratory, descriptive, or explanatory purposes, but it is most frequently used for descriptive research.

Qualitative Data Collection Techniques.
Techniques for qualitative data collection include field research and historical-comparative research.

Field Research.   Most field researchers conduct case studies looking at a small group of people over a length of time (e.g., weeks, months, years). A *field researcher* begins with a loosely formulated idea or topic, selects a social group or natural setting for study, gains access and adopts a social role in the setting, and observes in detail. The researcher gets to know personally the people being studied, may conduct open-ended and informal interviews, and takes detailed notes on a daily basis. After leaving the field site, the researcher carefully rereads the notes and prepares written reports. Field research is used most often for exploratory and descriptive studies; it is rarely used for explanatory research.

Historical-Comparative Research.   *Historical-comparative researchers* examine aspects of social life in a past historical era or across different cultures. Researchers who use this technique may focus on one historical period or several, compare one or more cultures, or mix historical periods and cultures. Like field research, a researcher combines theory building/testing with data collection and begins with a loosely formulated question that is refined during the research process. Researchers often gather a wide array of evidence, including existing statistics and documents (e.g., novels, official reports, books, newspapers, diaries, photographs, and maps) for study. In addition, they may make direct observations and conduct interviews. Historical-comparative research can be exploratory, descriptive, or explanatory and can blend types.

CONCLUSION

This chapter gave you an overview of social research. You saw how social research differs from the ordinary ways of learning-knowing about the social world, how doing research is based on science and the scientific community, and about several types of social research based on its dimensions (e.g., its purpose, the technique used to gather data, etc.). The dimensions of research loosely overlap with each other. The dimensions of social research are a kind of "road map" to help you make your way through the terrain of social research. In the next chapter, we turn to social theory. You read about it a little in this chapter. In the next chapter, you will learn how theory and research methods work together and about several types of theory.

Key Terms

action research study
applied social research
basic social research
case study
cohort study
cross-sectional research
data
descriptive research
empirical evidence
evaluation research study
existing statistics research
experimental research
explanatory research
exploratory research
field research
halo effect
historical comparative research
longitudinal research
overgeneralization
panel study
premature closure
qualitative data
quantitative data
scientific community
scientific method
selective observation

social impact assessment study
social research
survey research
time-series study

Endnotes

1. See Rampton and Stauber (2001:247–277 and 305–306).
2. See Best (2001:15) on advocates and media.
3. See National Science Board (2002:735–739).
4. Schacter (2001) provides a summary of memory issues.
5. National Science Board (2002:739).
6. Discussions of the scientific community can be found in Cole and Gordon (1995), Crane (1972), Hagstrom (1965), Merton (1973), Mulkay (1991), and Ziman (1999).
7. See Patton (2001) and Weiss (1997) for a more detailed discussion of recent advances in evaluation research.
8. Beck (1995) provides a useful overview.
9. See Herring and Ebner (2005) on the use of domestic violence study findings.
10. See Adams (2004) for more information on the Auckland City study.
11. See the website at www.gseis.ucla.edu/heri/heri.html.
12. Also see Snow and Anderson (1991) for a discussion of the case-study method in their study of homeless people. Also see George and Bennett (2005) on the case-study method generally.

CHAPTER 2

Foundations of Family and Consumer Sciences

by Erin Matthews-Maxwell

INTRODUCTION

Family and Consumer Sciences is the science of the systematic evaluation of the social, economic, political, biological, physical, and aesthetic environments in which individuals, communities, and families function. This discipline has always operated in the spirit of improving the quality of the environments it is dedicated to studying. The early leaders were converts; women and some men who had been educated in other scientific fields and realized this unique opportunity to start an original field to address problems of their time. The founders had the foresight to see the need for a new academic discipline. This new paradigm was essential to address evolving social and public health issues that resulted from the Industrial Revolution.

This intrepid group quickly sought to establish a prominent place for this discipline in the preexisting structure of human knowledge. Mrs. Ellen Richards, who we will discuss later in this chapter, explained the name in this way, *home* connotes the shelter and nurture of children and the development of self-sacrificing qualities and of strength to meet the world; *economics* suggests the management of this home on economic lines as to time, energy, and money. In this chapter we will see how home economics evolved into what we now know as Family and Consumer Sciences (FCS). This chapter will explore FCS's evolution and growth via an analysis of its history.

THE LAND GRANT ACT

The Land Grant Act of 1862 was originally called the Morrill Act of 1862. President Lincoln signed the act into law on July 2, 1862. It gave 17.4 million acres of land to the senators and state representatives to sell so they could establish funding to create college across the country. The purpose of these colleges was to educate a larger cross-section of the population in academic as well as pragmatic pursuits. Some of the pioneering states were Iowa, Illinois, and Kansas.

Since this act was put into effect during times of segregation, it was acceptable to found a college that did not allow for African Americans or other races. For this reason the second Morrill Act was signed on August 30, 1890 by President Benjamin Harrison. This act ordered states to divide up the new funding equally and create colleges and institutions with the same goals for other races. These colleges became what today are known as Historically Black Colleges. These two important land grant acts allowed for the creation of FCS colleges and for students of all nationalities to be able to learn about Family and Consumer Sciences as well as other academic disciplines.

LAKE PLACID CONFERENCES

Family and Consumer Sciences grew out of a series annual conferences held between 1899 and 1909, which are known as the Lake Placid Conferences. In 1899 the first annual Lake Placid Conference was held at Mr. and Mrs. Melville Dewey's Adirondack Mountain retreat. This would become the historic venue for the conference. The conference began with 11 people in attendance including Mr. and Mrs. Melville Dewey, Martha Van Rensselaer, Isabel Bevier, and Mrs. Ellen Richards the first chairperson of the group. The Deweys, Mrs. Richards, and other conference attendees were in the vanguard of a growing movement towards social change.

The objective of this first conference was to discuss ways in which they could alleviate conditions in the home and lessen the struggles associated with family life in American society at that time. They also directed their attention to the selection of a name for this new field of education, the preparation of women for leadership in this field, and the classification of home economics literature. This little gathering of 11 men and women who met at the Lake Placid Clubhouse in 1899 expanded to thirty members at their second meeting in July 1900.

The tenth Lake Placid conference was held at Chautauqua, New York in July 1908. One of the major accomplishments of the tenth conference was the laying of the plans for a national home economics organization. The recommendation was made that a national organization be created, that home economics groups be started in different states to work for rapid growth and of the new organization, that members pay annual dues to the organization, that a journal be published, and that a name national in character be chosen for the new organization.

The culmination of these conferences was the formation of the American Home Economics Association (AHEA) on New Year's Day, 1909. Each year the interest in the Lake Placid conference grew as indicated by number of attendees. By the tenth conference, in 1908, the number of members had grown to 201, with 74 attending the conference. Each year the conferences included a new set of problems to be discussed in all facets that we now consider Family and Consumer Sciences. It is remarkable that the founders recognized so early the need for an educational and scientific association as a necessary component in formalizing the profession. Also they appreciated what science might do for the homemaker in her daily work, by making both her work easier and

more efficient. In 1973 the AHEA held the Eleventh Lake Placid Conference to develop an agreement among members concerning the future direction of the field. The AHEA commissioned a study to take place to gather the public's view on home economics. Many of the results were contradictory. Some of the public sector believed that home economists were contributors to society and the work force, while others polled believed home economists were traditionalists and did not contribute to an employer's success. The result of these finding lead the AHEA to publish a statement entitled, *New Directions II* in 1975. The statement was a prescription for the future trajectory of home economics focusing on a broader conception of the interrelated aspects of the discipline.

PIONEERS

Ellen H. Swallow Richards

Ellen H. Swallow Richards has been informally called the "patron saint" of home economics. She, more than any other person, may be called the founder of home economics, and her life

FIGURE 2.1   Lake Placid Conference

Courtesy of the American Association of Family and Consumer Sciences.

might be described as home economics in action. Mrs. Richards discussed the problems in home economics, attended meetings, published, was a visionary, and gave future home economists an example to follow. She provided the leadership which reached its point of highest development in the American Home Economics Association and was its first president.

Ellen Henrietta Swallow was born in Dunstable, Massachusetts during mid-December 1842. From her writing, it seems that Ellen considered physical exercise one of life's greatest pleasures and responsibilities. Ellen was educated at home by her parents because they were very critical of the local teachers. Ellen's mother taught her how to do housework and to cook as well as sew. As a result Ellen Swallow was a bright, energetic, and inquisitive child who was given free rein to explore her world. This early freedom to enjoy nature stayed with her throughout her life.

Ellen finished school in 1862. She decided to become a teacher and moved with her family three miles from Littleton, Mass. In June 1864 Ellen began to teach. However, in September Fanny, her mother, became sick and Ellen stopped teaching to stay and care for her. This was a very rough time for Ellen. Her letters in 1868 indicate a period of depression and sadness. Ellen had done what she considered her responsibility, taken care of her ill mother, but it had left her without an ongoing purpose. However, in Fall 1868 everything changed. Ellen enrolled at Vassar, a woman's college. She had found her passion, chemistry. She graduated from Vassar in two years. Those years were exciting, filled with study and new ideas.

Ellen was irritated with the common misconception of the time that women needed to guard their health against too much study. It was thought that females simply could not take the strain of mental work. She pushed to be allowed to study freely without limits. Not only was she an excellent student, she also enjoyed the social life of the school. She seemed to genuinely relish all of life. Later, Ellen said that even though she

loved astronomy, she thought that she chose chemistry because of her concern for social conditions. She felt that chemistry could be more closely related to fields such as nutrition, sanitation, public health and other sciences related to the home.

Ellen attempted to get employment as a chemist's apprentice but no one would hire her. A sympathetic chemist advised her to go to Massachusetts Institute of Technology (MIT) and enroll as a student. This was an extraordinary suggestion because no women were enrolled at the school. When Ellen applied to MIT, the faculty decided they were not yet ready to open their doors to all women. Ellen's application forced their decision; each female would be considered on her own merits. Ellen Swallow was admitted in 1871 because she came highly recommended and the school did not charge her a fee. In this way, if Ellen was not the student MIT hoped she was, the school could say that she was not an actual student.

Again, Ellen threw herself into her work. She relished the chance to learn everything and especially enjoyed chemistry and laboratory work. During her years at MIT, she was a student, then a chemistry assistant, and finally an instructor. In 1873, she received both her bachelor of science in chemistry from MIT and a master's degree from Vassar. Although Ellen wanted to pursue a doctorate in chemistry, she could not get work in pure science and so was not able to do the original work required to earn that degree. Ellen became involved in 1870 in a project headed by Dr. William Nichols of MIT. Massachusetts had formed a State Board of Health in 1869 and one of their first concerns was the water of the state. Dr. Nichols chose Ellen to be his assistant and she analyzed most of the daily water samples taken throughout the state for the next two years.

Unable to continue her doctoral pursuit, she remained at MIT as a research assistant, studying anything that she could put under a microscope. Her particular interests were things involved in the home including air and water quality, ventilation, and sanitation. Ellen even did work without charging fees for her friends and institutions dear to her heart, Vassar and MIT. She often checked the conditions at the schools in an effort to ensure that the students and faculty were safe from contaminants.

In 1875 Ellen became Ellen Richards when she married Dr. Robert Hallowell Richards, head of the department of Mining Engineering at MIT. Two years her junior, Robert shared her enthusiasm for laboratory work and outdoor life. Throughout their lives, they often took trips with students to mines and natural wonders all over the world. The Richards's home was a model of Ellen's education. She cooked with gas instead of coal, had a telephone as soon as they became available, and experimented with vacuum cleaners. Interested in economy of all kind, she discarded her carpets when she discovered that they took so much time to maintain. Unlike many homes of her day, her house was designed with lots of ventilation and natural light. Mrs. Richards's home was a constant experiment.

In 1886, Mrs. Richards instituted a new study, Sanitary Science. This course was concerned with the home and its new conveniences-gas, indoor plumbing, ventilation, electricity, furnaces, hot water heaters, etc. The World's Fair in Chicago took place in 1883. Mrs. Richards was in charge of the Rumford Kitchen (a model house for the workman's family) which sold meals to the public. In addition to preparing meals that the customers enjoyed, the cost of preparation along with the caloric and nutritional content was published on the menus; she tried to educate the public about the economies and nutrition of food.

The last 30 years of her life were spent examining the home. She was convinced that many societal problems could be solved in the family's house and so she wrote and lectured tirelessly on the subject. She described this study as the science of controllable environment and called it *Euthenics*. Housework was drudgework, but housekeeping was science. Education was the key to solving most social ills and everyone deserved that education. Mrs. Richards believed in hands-on learning and industrial education. The labor of the hands was most valuable in her estimation.

In 1899, at Lake Placid in New York, the formal discussion of the field then called Household Science was begun in earnest. Ellen Richards, elected president of the group, drove its philosophical questioning. After a lifetime of work in this field, she had come to believe passionately that the home was linked with society and that the study of that partnership was vital. Her leadership over the next ten years provided the encouragement to see the development of a new name, Home Economics, a new outline for a body of knowledge, a plan for teacher training, new curriculum for all grade levels in public schools, and coordination with new vocational programs instituted by the Federal government. Mrs. Richards was made honorary president in 1910 in hopes that she would still find time to give counsel and guidance. Her ideas about the value of the home had finally been taken up by a larger group of people who would continue to press for more recognition in education after her death in 1911.

FIGURE 2.2   Ellen H. Swallow Richards

Courtesy of the American Association of Family and Consumer Sciences.

Isabel Bevier

Isabel Bevier became the second president of the American Home Economics Association in 1911 and was pioneer in home economics college administration. She came into home economics through her interest in applying scientific knowledge to the improvement of the home. Isabel grew up in an atmosphere somewhat more favorable to the education of women. Isabel received her bachelor's degree in 1885 and her master's degree in 1888 from the University of Wooster. She majored in languages because language was a very respectable field for women of her day. Her first college teaching experience was at the Pennsylvania College for Women, where she was to teach science. To prepare for this work, she took special training at the Case School of Applied Science in Cleveland. Just as Ellen was the first woman to be admitted to MIT, Isabel was the first woman to enter the Case School.

Her interest in science made it possible for her to work with Dr. Wilbur O. Atwater (who many consider the "father of Nutrition") and others in the chemical study of foods. She had the opportunity to participate in some of the earliest dietary studies conducted by Dr. Atwater.

It was at the University of Illinois where Isabel began her real life's work, being a pioneer in teaching home economics to college students. She set out to develop a department of home economics based on scientific principles. Isabel decided through much thought and insight to name the department that she started Household Science because she believed that someday there would be a department where there would be science of the house.

Due to the perception of home economics subject matter as being feminine it was difficult to establish a place within scientific academia. There were people who felt that the practical aspect of education was of paramount importance to the exclusion of anything that provided theory. Almost immediately, applied art was added to the curriculum and in 1908 an experimental house, now known as the home-management house, was established. Research was started early to provide answers to the questions asked in the classrooms and throughout the state about the daily processes and products of the home. Isabel met each new challenge with the same scientific approach. Isabel died in her home in Urbana, IL March 17, 1942.

Catherine Esther Beecher

Catherine Esther Beecher was born in 1800 into the memorable family of the Beechers. Families that have been significant in American culture are often identifiable by their signature names. The Beecher family's deep religious convictions and social principles spanned the nineteenth century and made them prominent historical figures whose impact on education, religion, abolition, literature, reform movements, and public life were extraordinary. Harriet Beecher Stowe wrote *Uncle Tom's Cabin* and for almost 30 years she wrote a book a year. Isabella Beecher Hooker was very active in the National Woman Suffrage Association, and often made speeches. Charlotte Perkins Gilman, daughter of Frederick Beecher Perkins, wrote *Women and Economics* which argues for the socialization of housework through the establishment of community kitchens and child care in order for women to work outside their homes.

Upon the tragic death of Catherine's fiancé in 1823 she decided to devote her life to women's education. That same year she opened a small private school for young ladies in Hartford, Connecticut. The Hartford Female Seminary was known for its advanced curriculum and its excellence of teaching. She spent much of her time and energy on "the securing of professional advantages of education for my sex equal to those bestowed on men."

She was a strong advocate for home economics and she instituted a domestic economy curriculum in every school she founded. In the 1830s

FIGURE 2.3   Catherine Esther Beecher

Courtesy of Hulton-Deutsch Collection/Corbis Images.

Catherine began to write books on domestic economy that fostered favorable public opinion for its inclusion in public schools. The subject of her books fell under six familiar headings (1) family economics and home management, (2) family relations and child development, (3) food and nutrition, (4) health, (5) housing, equipment, and furnishings, and (6) textiles and clothing. Catherine Beecher's *Treatise on Domestic Economy*, published in 1841, was considered the true beginning of the Home Economics Movement. Her second book was *Miss Beecher's Domestic Receipt Book* and was published in 1846. The first book discusses household problems and the second book discusses practical procedures.

Catherine not only was a pioneer for home economics but for women in education. She founded The American Women's Educational Association in 1852, the Western Female Institute in Cincinnati, and The Ladies Society for Promoting Education in the West. Thus, Catherine was one of the early forces which created in this country the opportunity for higher education for women and promoted the belief that a part of this education should help prepare the woman for her responsibilities as a wife, mother, and citizen of the community.

Martha Van Rensselaer

Martha Van Rensselaer, another pioneer in home economics extension work, was born in 1864 in rural New York. Upon graduation from the Chamberlain Institute in 1884, she taught for ten years in the public schools in New York and from 1894 to 1900 was school commissioner in Cattaraugus County. In 1900 she was asked to teach at the State College of Agriculture at Cornell University for an experimental educational adventure, the development of extension work for rural women. The success of this endeavor lead to the first extension courses in homemaking.

Martha's vision of home economics was to help satisfy the needs of the homemaker. In 1903 Martha gave the first course for credit in home economics at Cornell University and the home economics department was established in 1908. Martha had the ability to communicate effectively with others and, with this ability, brought good staff members to the college, teachers who were broadly based and rooted in the advancement of women and the integrity of the home. She conceived of home economics education as a means by which women's minds could be trained, their capacities reached, and their deepest desires found through growth in understanding their own normal social functions.

During her lifetime she gave much of her time and her talents to the development and success of home economics. She was a member of the executive staff of the U.S. Food Administration during World War I; she was active in the Lake Placid Conferences and later in the American Home Economics Association, of which she was a charter member and president from 1914 to 1916. In 1923 a National League of Women Voters committee appointed her as one of the 12 greatest women of the United States.

THE LOGO

The American Home Economics Association (AHEA) chose the Betty Lamp as their logo as the result of a contest in 1926. In colonial days,

FIGURE 2.4   AAFCS Betty Lamp Logo

Reprinted from *AHEA: A History of Excellence* (1980),
American Association of Family and Consumer Sciences.

the Betty Lamp provided light for all household industries. The Betty Lamp symbolizes those pioneers who, in their quest for new horizons of the mind still cherished all that time had tested and found good. To Family and Consumer Sciences professionals the Betty Lamp represents joy, knowledge, fellowship, cooperation, service, achievement, and the light of the home and the mind. The Betty Lamp logo embodies a sense of pride, fellowship, and tradition. This icon has come to represent our discipline from its foundations to the present day.

THE SCOTTSDALE INITIATIVE

In 1992 the American Home Economics Association decided it had to reposition itself for the future. A meeting was held in Scottsdale, Arizona in October 1993. This national meeting was entitled Positioning for the 21st Century. Five major professional home economics organizations selected a joint task force that was charged with creating a process for examining the nature, definition, and focus, and name of the home economics profession and with finding a consensus for a name deemed appropriate for the profession in the years ahead. Many members, professionals, and educators felt that it was necessary to have a new name because it was imperative to move beyond the stereotypic connotations of the term *home economics* that have plagued the field

and to communicate a broader home definition of the discipline. Improvement of individual, family, and community life; how consumer goods were developed, maintained, and consumer services; policy development; and the shaping of societal change, thereby enhancing the human condition, were paths in the right direction towards the improved discipline. Many individuals who attended the conference felt that it had established a new profession that not only added to but also transcended home economics. At their later 1994 annual meetings, all five national associations voted to adopt the conceptual framework and four voted to change their organization's names to accommodate recommendations from the Scottsdale meeting. As a result, the AHEA became the American Association of Family and Consumer Sciences (AAFCS). Members thought this name to be more complimentary to and yet distinct from the agricultural sciences with which home economics in land grant institutions had been connected with since the Morrill Act of 1862.

Family and Consumer Sciences recognizes that individuals are not only educators but also practice in business, industry, government, and human service organizations. The Scottsdale promise is about new beginnings in the profession and these promises are beginning to show. Family and Consumer Sciences will continue to have issues and tensions as in every dynamic changing field encounters new possibilities. The decisions at Scottsdale, their impact, and subsequent actions taken should be seen as positive steps in the ongoing development and evolution of the profession. Being grounded in theory and having a solid research base is relevant to the needs of the future of FCS. However, with a vital and increasingly important mission and enormous opportunities at our fingertips, the profession and its members, without doubt, will continue to meet the challenges of working in coherence with individuals and shared institutions to empower individuals, strengthen families, and build lasting communities.

MEN IN HOME ECONOMICS

Home economics had been stereotyped as a female subject and this conventional model of home economics had been persistent throughout the 20th century. In both absolute and relative terms, the profession has attracted very few males. In the United States, where home economics first developed as a profession, there is a dearth of male home economics teachers at the secondary and post-secondary levels. In the early 1900s men did receive various forms of instruction in what might be considered home economic disciplines however that term was rarely applied. In the first decade of the 20th century no U.S. College offered anything like a complete home economics program for men.

During the 1950s and 1960s home economics came under attack. Administrators, all male, thought that, because home economics was predominately female and mostly single older women with a low proportion of doctorates, it was out of date and due for some changes. The prestigious universities were embarrassed by home economics and wanted action taken. The men did not like the name home economics and took it upon themselves to change the names at several (not all) major universities. Men decided to choose more gender-neutral names; Nutritional Sciences, Human Development, and Human Ecology. The once female-only discipline, taught for decades mostly by single women faculty to women students at all land grant and many other colleges and universities in America, had by the 1960s become unacceptable to many; it was less interesting to female students and intolerable to administrators and many male faculty. This came about not because of any great influx of men into home economics (but because the conservative university presidents and the 20% of home economics faculty, who were males) found their female deans and the school's reputation embarrassing. Consequently, home economics reverted to the more traditional and comfortable hierarchal segregation common in academia with women faculty mostly clustered in the bottom ranks. Unfortunately, for home economics/FCS this has not changed significantly in the last 45 years. Women who are hired in similar positions as their male counterparts are still being paid considerably less but with the same education.

FUTURE

Directions for the Future of Family and Consumer Sciences

A new generation of professionals in Family and Consumer Sciences is getting a new look and a new appreciation from historians, scientists, and scholars. Those who are charged with mentoring future generations and teaching incoming students their first-hand knowledge of their experiences will shape FCS into a field that will enable families and individuals to face their challenges with wisdom and a greater understanding of the world in which they live. Understanding Family and Consumer Science's mission is imperative to the strength of the home. FCS has moved away from the traditional general approach and focused more on the parts of the profession and we have spent very little on the study of the relationship between specialties. Although all of these parts are valuable, the lack of balance between them tends to weaken the interconnected, holistic perspective of the discipline, which is necessary to help people deal with problems as they struggle through them in families. A common goal enabled early thinkers to identify a multitude of factors that could enhance each other, revitalize the whole, contribute to a better home life, and fundamentally improve society. The need for a cohesive profession, with multiple elements unified by underlying themes, is more important than ever before due to the increasing specialization of knowledge and complexity of familial issues.

Many issues facing us today are of a scale never imagined by the founders; technological advances, world hunger, and multiculturalism, to name just a few. Each issue is an opportunity to create new relationships and to help people define their own values, orientations, and problems which, in turn will empower them to arrive at their own solutions. Although Family and Consumer Sciences professionals engage in manifold activities and application of the discipline, one commonality among all practitioners of this discipline is they are all tasked to solve problems of everyday life. Stimulating dialogue among professionals engaged both in the practice and those devoted to the theoretical research help promote and unify the diversity among Family and Consumer Professionals.

Although *family* is being redefined it will continue to be the basic unit in American society. There is a general agreement that there will be a greater variety of lifestyles as well as family variations in the future. Many more women are choosing to remain single as they place more value on their career, and are able to support themselves and enjoy being independent. Individuals appear to have lost or never to have developed the ability to form long-term lasting relationships. Helping people develop this skill is a necessary task for FCS professionals. How individuals live in the present affects how they will live in the future.

"Their persons being cultivated, their families were regulated. Their families being regulated, their States were rightly governed, the whole kingdom was made tranquil and happy."

-Confucius

HISTORICAL HIGHLIGHTS IN FAMILY AND CONSUMER SCIENCES (HOME ECONOMICS MOVEMENT)

1700s – Dame Schools, so-called finishing schools; the earliest schools for girls in the colonies; taught basic housewifery, needlework, and cooking along with reading, spelling, and writing.

1780 – First admission of women to coeducational academies or female seminaries (finishing-type schools).

1780 – Benjamin Thomas, later Count Rumford, emphasized the application of science to problems of the household; called his philosophy Domestic Economy.

1821 – Troy (NY) Female Seminary founded by Emma Willard; theory and practice of housewifery, combined liberal and practical studies.

1822 – Catherine Beecher established a private girls' school in Hartford, CT.

1836 – Mount Holyoke Female Seminary established in Massachusetts by Mary Lyon, a firm believer in educating women for home and family life; developed a cooperative housekeeping plan, the forerunner of home management laboratories.

1837 – Oberlin College became one of the first coeducational institutes to admit women.

1841 – *Treatise on Domestic Economy* was the first textbook on home economics, written by Catherine Beecher.

1852 – Antioch College admitted women.

1857 – *Handbook of Household Science* by Edward Livingston Youmans, a scientific study of food, air, heat, and light from the standpoint of the home worker.

1862 – The Morrill Land-Grant Act passed. Higher education available for the common man, practical pursuits of living; programs for women were included, laying the first foundations for home economics programs. Pioneer states were Iowa, Kansas, and Illinois.
*Vassar initiated the first college program on domestic economy.

1869 – *The American Woman's Home or Principles of Domestic Science* by Catherine Beecher and Harriet Beecher Stowe provided a realistic up-to-date look at women's education for life.

1873 – Winthrop School in Boston appointed first sewing teacher.

1876 – New York Cooking School gave instruction to working and moderate income families and to women who wished to train others.

1880 – 51% of higher education institutions were co-educational.

1888 – Domestic Science was introduced as a discipline in New York City public schools.

1893 – Chicago World's Fair:
  *National Household Economics Association
  *The Rumford Kitchen (Ellen H. Richards)
  *Food exhibits by the United States Department of Agriculture

1894 – First school lunch program established in Boston by Ellen H. Richards.

1899 – The first of ten historical Lake Placid Conferences was held for professionals of diverse disciplines who were interested in education for the home.
  *Initiated by Melville Dewey, based on an interest in the field of household science.
  *Raising the standard of living for American families.

1900 – Second Annual Conference: home economics and education.

1902 – Fourth Annual Conference: proposed the following definition:
  "Home economics in its most comprehensive sense is the study of the laws, conditions, principles, and ideals which are concerned on the one hand with man's immediate physical environment and on the other hand with his nature as a social being, and is the study especially of the relation between those two factors."

1904 – Sixth Annual Conference

1908 – Tenth Annual Conference: American Home Economics Association formed.

1909 – The American Home Economics Association AHEA was formally instituted on January 2, with Ellen H. Richards as the first president. Volume 1, no. 1 of the *Journal of Home Economics*, the official publication of the AHEA was published in February.

1926 – The Betty Lamp, designed by Mildred Chamberlain, was selected as the official logo of the AHEA.

1929 – The depression years found home economists working in other areas to help people extend their resources.

1939 – 1945 – Home economists provided leadership in feeding the masses healthfully, childcare for working mothers, and the conservation and extension of resources.

1950 – The AHEA purchased a permanent headquarters building in Washington, D.C.

1959 – For the 50th birthday of the AHEA, *New Directions*, a statement of philosophy and goals was published. The report reinforced the emphasis on strengthening family life.

1961 – The French Lick Seminar considered identification and articulation of home economics subject matter at all levels.

1967 – The document *Concepts and Generalizations: Their Place in Home Economics Curricular Development* was published.

1971 – Accreditation of higher education programs were authorized.

1972 – Volume I of the *Home Economics Research Journal* was published.

1973 – Eleventh Lake Placid Conference, which was held in October, discussed the definition, focus, role, name, and values of home economics; *New Directions II* was the published outcome.

1975 – *New Directions II* was released. The focus of home economics is family in its various forms. Family is defined as a unit of intimate, transacting, and interdependent persons who share some values and goals, resources, responsibility for decisions, and have committed to one another over time. *New Directions II* lists five new priorities for home economics.
  1. Futuristic thinking
  2. Public policy formation
  3. Creative adaptation to uncertainty and change
  4. Redistribution of resources
  5. Interrelatedness of the professional and the paraprofessional

1978 – 1979 – Home Economics Defined Conferences were conducted to discuss the definitive statement and a conceptual framework developed by Marjorie Brown and Beatrice Paolucci. Their philosophical analysis stated:

"The mission of home economics is to enable families, both as individual units and generally as a social institution, to build and maintain systems of action which lead (1) to maturing in individual self-formation and (2) to enlightened, cooperative participation in the critique and formulation of social goals and means for accomplishing them. To fulfill this mission home economists engage in the provision of services (directly or indirectly) to families."

1993 – Scottsdale Conference proposed the name of the discipline be changed to Family and Consumer Sciences.

The Conference addressed three main issues.

1. Empowering Individuals
2. Strengthening Families
3. Enabling Communities

1994 – Official name change to Family and Consumer Sciences (FCS).

2009 – Centennial anniversary for AHEA/AAFCS.

References

Apple, R. D., & Coleman, J. (2003). "As members of the social whole": A history of social reform as a focus of home economics, 1895–1940. *Family and Consumer Sciences Research Journal 32*(2), 104–126.

Blankenship, M. L., & Moerchen, B. D. (1979). Philosophy of home economics. In *Home economics education.* (pp. 2–18). Boston: Houghton Mifflin.

Couch, S., & Felstehausen, G. (2001) Research in family and consumer sciences education, 1985–2000. *Family and Consumer Sciences Research Journal, 30*(2), 256–270.

Definitive themes in home economics and their impact on families 1909–1984. (1984). Washington, D.C.: American Home Economics Association.

Elias, M. (2006). "Model mamas": The domestic partnership of home economic pioneers Flora Rose and Martha van Rensselaer. *Journal of the History of Sexuality, 15*(1), 65–88.

Kieren, D., Vaines, E., & Badir, D. (1984). In the beginning. In *The home economist as a helping professional.* (pp. 2–22). Winnipeg, Canada: Frye.

Lawson, R. J. (1993). Men and home economics in the U.S.: 1900–1975. *Journal of Home Economics, 85,* 47–52.

Parker, F. J. (1987). *Home economics: An introduction to a dynamic profession* (3rd ed.). New York: Macmillan.

Quigley, E. E. (1974). The history of home economics, with some indications for the future. In *Introduction to home economics* (2nd ed., pp. 14–52). New York: Macmillan.

Rehm, M. L. (2000). Unified diversity in family and consumer sciences: The historic and future significance of aesthetics. *Journal of Family and Consumer Sciences, 92*(1), 95–99.

Richardson, B. (2002). Ellen Swallow Richards: "Humanistic oekologist," "applied sociologist," and the founding of sociology. *The American Sociologist, 33*(3), 21–57.

Simerly, C. B., Ralston, P. A., Harriman, L., & Tayler, B. (2000). The Scottsdale initiative: Positioning the profession for the 21st century. *Journal of Family and Consumer Sciences, 92*(1), 12–17.

Stage, S., & Vincenti, V. B. (Eds.). (1997). *Rethinking home economics: Women and the history of a profession.* Ithaca, NY: Cornell University Press.

Tate, M. T. (1973). The beginning of home economics. In *Home economics as a profession* (2nd ed., pp. 11–37). New York: McGraw-Hill.

Wilensky, J. (2001). The coming of age of home economics. *Human Ecology, (29)*3, 6–8.

Suggested Reading

Matthews, G. (1987). *"Just a housewife:" The rise and fall of domesticity in America.* New York: Oxford University Press.

Pundt, H. (1980). *AHEA: A history of excellence.* Washington, DC: American Home Economics Association.

Rugoff, M. (1981). *The Beechers: An American family in the nineteenth century.* New York: Harper & Row.

Strasser, S. (2000). *Never done: A history of American housework.* New York: Owl Books.

Ethics in Social Research

INTRODUCTION

Ethics include the concerns, dilemmas, and conflicts that arise over the proper way to conduct research. Ethics help to define what is or is not legitimate to do, or what "moral" research procedure involves. This is not as simple as it may appear, because there are few ethical absolutes and only agreed-upon broad principles. These principles require judgment to apply and some may conflict with others in practice. Many ethical issues ask you to balance two values: the pursuit of knowledge and the rights of research participants or of others in society. Social researchers balance potential benefits—such as advancing the understanding of social life, improving decision making, or helping research participants—against potential costs—such as loss of dignity, self-esteem, privacy, or democratic freedoms.

Social researchers confront many ethical dilemmas and must decide how to act. They have a moral and professional obligation to be ethical, even if research participants are unaware of or unconcerned about ethics.

Many areas of professional practice have ethical standards (e.g., journalists, police departments, business corporations, etc.), but the ethical standards for doing social research are often stricter. To do professional social research, you must both know the proper research techniques (e.g., sampling) and be sensitive to ethical concerns. This is not always easy. For centuries, moral, legal, and political philosophers debated the issues researchers regularly face.

It is difficult to appreciate fully the ethical dilemmas experienced by researchers until you actually begin to do research, but waiting until the middle of a study is too late. You need to prepare yourself ahead of time and consider ethical concerns as you design a study so that you can build sound ethical practices into a study's design. In addition, by developing sensitivity to ethical issues, you will be alert to potential ethical concerns that can arise as you make decisions while conducting a study. Also, an ethical awareness will help you better understand the overall research process.

Ethics begin and end with you, the individual social researcher. A strong personal moral code by the researcher is the best defense against unethical behavior. Before, during, and after conducting a study, a researcher has opportunities to, and *should*, reflect on the ethics of research actions and consult his or her conscience. Ultimately, ethical research depends on the integrity of an individual researcher.

WHY BE ETHICAL?

Given that most people who conduct social research are genuinely concerned about others, you might ask, Why would any researcher ever act in an ethically irresponsible manner? Most unethical behavior is due to a lack of awareness and pressures on researchers to take ethical shortcuts. Researchers face pressures to build a career, publish new findings, advance knowledge, gain prestige, impress family and friends, hold on to a job, and so forth. Ethical research will take longer to complete, cost more money, be more complicated, and be less likely to produce unambiguous results. Plus, there are many opportunities in research to act unethically, the odds of getting caught are small, and written ethical standards are in the form of vague, loose principles.

The ethical researcher gets few rewards and wins no praise. The unethical researcher, if caught, faces public humiliation, a ruined career, and possible legal action. The best preparation for ethical behavior is to internalize a sensitivity to ethical concerns, to adopt a serious professional role, and to interact regularly with other researchers. Moreover, the scientific community demands ethical behavior without exceptions.

Scientific Misconduct

The research community and agencies that fund research oppose a type of unethical behavior called scientific misconduct; it includes research fraud and plagiarism. *Scientific misconduct* occurs when a researcher falsifies or distorts the data or the methods of data collection, or plagiarizes the work of others. It also includes significant, unjustified departures from the generally accepted scientific practices for doing and reporting on research. *Research fraud* occurs when a researcher fakes or invents data that he or she did not really collect, or fails to honestly and fully report how he or she conducted a study. Although rare, it is considered a very serious violation. The most famous case of research fraud was that of Sir Cyril Burt, the father of British educational psychology. Burt died in 1971 as an esteemed researcher who was famous for his studies with twins that showed a genetic basis of intelligence. In 1976, it was discovered that he had falsified data and the names of coauthors. Unfortunately, the scientific community had been misled for nearly 30 years. More recently, a social psychologist was discovered to have fabricated data for several experiments on sex bias conducted at Harvard University in the 1990s. *Plagiarism* occurs when a researcher "steals" the ideas or writings of another or uses them without citing the source. Plagiarism also includes stealing the work of another researcher, an assistant, or a student, and misrepresenting it as one's own. These are serious breaches of ethical standards.[1]

Unethical but Legal

Behavior may be unethical but legal (i.e., not break any law). A plagiarism case illustrates the distinction between legal and ethical behavior. The American Sociological Association documented that a 1988 book without any footnotes by a dean from Eastern New Mexico University contained large sections of a 1978 dissertation that a sociology professor at Tufts University wrote. Copying the dissertation was not *illegal;* it did not violate copyright law because the sociologist's dissertation did not have a copyright filed with the U.S. government. Nevertheless, it was

FIGURE 3.1 Typology of Legal and Moral Actions in Social Research

LEGAL	ETHICAL	
	Yes	No
Yes	Moral and Legal	Legal but Immoral
No	Illegal but Moral	Immoral and Illegal

clearly *unethical* according to standards of professional behavior.[2] (See Figure 3.1 for relations between legal and moral actions.)

POWER RELATIONS

A professional researcher and the research participants or employee-assistants are in a relationship of unequal power and trust. An experimenter, survey director, or research investigator has power over participants and assistants, and in turn, they trust his or her judgment and authority. The researcher's credentials, training, professional role, and the place of science in modern society legitimate the power and make it into a form of expert authority. Some ethical issues involve an abuse of power and trust. A researcher's authority to conduct social research and to earn the trust of others is accompanied always by an unyielding ethical responsibility to guide, protect, and oversee the interests of the people being studied.

When looking for ethical guidance, researchers are not alone. They can turn to a number of resources: professional colleagues, ethical advisory committees, institutional review boards or human subjects committees at a college or institution (discussed later), codes of ethics by professional associations (discussed later in this chapter), and writings on ethics in research. The larger research community firmly supports and upholds ethical behavior, even if an individual researcher is ultimately responsible to do what is ethical in specific situations.

ETHICAL ISSUES INVOLVING RESEARCH PARTICIPANTS

Have you ever been a participant in a research study? If so, how were you treated? More attention is focused on the possible negative effects of research on those being studied than any other ethical issue, beginning with concerns about biomedical research. Acting ethically requires that a researcher balance the value of advancing knowledge against the value of noninterference in the lives of others. Either extreme causes problems. Giving research participants absolute rights of noninterference could make empirical research impossible, but giving researchers absolute rights of inquiry could nullify participants' basic human rights. The moral question becomes: When, if ever, are researchers justified in risking physical harm or injury to those being studied, causing them great embarrassment or inconvenience, violating their privacy, or frightening them?

The law and codes of ethics recognize some clear prohibitions: Never cause unnecessary or irreversible harm to subjects; secure prior voluntary consent when possible; and never unnecessarily humiliate, degrade, or release harmful information about specific individuals that was collected for research purposes. In other words, you should always show respect for the research participant. These are minimal standards and are subject to interpretation (e.g., What does *unnecessary* mean in a specific situation?).

Origins of Research Participant Protection

Concern over the treatment of research participants arose after the revelation of gross violations of basic human rights in the name of science. The most notorious violations were "medical experiments" conducted on Jews and others in Nazi Germany, and similar "medical experiments" to test biological weapons by Japan in the 1940s. In these experiments, terrible tortures were committed. For example, people were placed in freezing water to see how long it took them to die, people were purposely starved to death, people were intentionally infected with horrible diseases, and limbs were severed from children and transplanted onto others.[3]

Such human rights violations did not occur only long ago. In a famous case of unethical research, the Tuskegee Syphilis Study, also known as *Bad Blood*, the President of the United States admitted wrongdoing and formally apologized in 1997 to the participant-victims. Until the 1970s, when a newspaper report caused a scandal to erupt, the U.S. Public Health Service sponsored a study in which poor, uneducated African American men in Alabama suffered and died of untreated syphilis, while researchers studied the severe physical disabilities that appear in advanced stages of the disease. The unethical study began in 1929, before penicillin was available to treat the disease, but it continued long after treatment was available. Despite their unethical treatment of the people, the researchers were able to publish their results for 40 years. The study ended in 1972, but a formal apology took another 25 years.[4]

Unfortunately, the Bad Blood scandal is not unique. During the Cold War era, the U.S. government periodically compromised ethical research principles for military and political goals. In 1995, reports revealed that the government authorized injecting unknowing people with radioactive material in the late 1940s. In the 1950s, the government warned Eastman Kodak and other film manufacturers about nuclear fallout from atomic tests to prevent fogged film, but it did not warn nearby citizens of health hazards. In the 1960s, the U.S. army gave unsuspecting soldiers LSD (a hallucinogenic drug), causing serious trauma. Today, researchers widely recognize these to be violations of two fundamental ethical principles: Avoid physical harm and obtain informed consent.[5]

Physical Harm, Psychological Abuse, and Legal Jeopardy

Social research can harm a research participant in several ways: physical, psychological, and legal harm, as well as harm to a person's career, reputation, or income. Different types of harm are more likely in other types of research (e.g., in experiments versus field research). It is a researcher's responsibility to be aware of all types of potential harm and to take specific actions to minimize the risk to participants at all times.

Physical Harm. Physical harm is rare. Even in biomedical research, where the intervention into a person's life is much greater, 3 to 5 percent of studies involved any person who suffered any harm.[6] A straightforward ethical principle is that researchers should never cause physical harm. An ethical researcher anticipates risks before beginning a study, including basic safety concerns (e.g., safe buildings, furniture, and equipment). This means that he or she screens out high-risk subjects (those with heart conditions, mental breakdown, seizures, etc.) if great stress is involved and anticipates possible sources of injury or physical attacks on research participants or assistants. The researcher accepts moral and legal responsibility for injury due to participation in research and terminates a project immediately if he or she can no longer fully guarantee the physical safety of the people involved (see the Zimbardo study in Box 3.1).

Psychological Abuse, Stress, or Loss of Self-Esteem. The risk of physical harm is rare, but social researchers can place people in highly stressful, embarrassing, anxiety-producing, or unpleasant situations. Researchers want to learn about people's responses in real-life, high-anxiety–producing situations, so they might place people in realistic situations of psychological discomfort or stress. Is it unethical to cause discomfort? The ethics of the famous Milgram obedience study are still debated (see Box 3.1). Some say that the precautions taken and the knowledge gained outweighed the stress and

potential psychological harm that research participants experienced. Others believe that the extreme stress and the risk of permanent harm were too great. Such an experiment could not be conducted today because of heightened sensitivity to the ethical issues involved.

Social researchers have created high levels of anxiety or discomfort. They have exposed participants to gruesome photos; falsely told male students that they have strong feminine personality traits; falsely told students that they have failed; created a situation of high fear (e.g., smoke entering a room in which the door is locked); asked participants to harm others; placed people in situations where they face social pressure to deny their convictions; and had participants lie, cheat, or steal.[7] Researchers who study helping behavior often place participants in emergency situations to see whether they will lend assistance. For example, Piliavin and associates (1969) studied helping behavior in subways by faking someone's collapse onto the floor. In the field experiment, the riders in the subway car were unaware of the experiment and did not volunteer to participate in it.

The only researchers who might even consider conducting a study that purposely induces great stress or anxiety in research participants are very experienced and take all necessary precautions before inducing anxiety or discomfort. The researchers should consult with others who have conducted similar studies and mental health professionals as they plan the study. They should screen out high-risk populations (e.g., those with emotional problems or weak hearts), and arrange for emergency interventions or termination of the research if dangerous situations arise. They must always obtain written informed consent (to be discussed) before the research and debrief the people immediately afterward (i.e., explain any deception and what actually happened in the study). Researchers should never create *unnecessary* stress (i.e., beyond the minimal amount needed to create the desired effect) or stress that lacks a very clear, legitimate research purpose. Knowing what "minimal

Box 3.1   Three Cases of Ethical Controversy

Stanley Milgram's *obedience study* (Milgram, 1963, 1965, 1974) attempted to discover how the horrors of the Holocaust under the Nazis could have occurred by examining the strength of social pressure to obey authority. After signing "informed consent forms," subjects were assigned, in rigged random selection, to be a "teacher" while a confederate was the "pupil." The teacher was to test the pupil's memory of word lists and increase the electric shock level if the pupil made mistakes. The pupil was located in a nearby room, so the teacher could hear but not see the pupil. The shock apparatus was clearly labeled with increasing voltage. As the pupil made mistakes and the teacher turned switches, she or he also made noises as if in severe pain. The researcher was present and made comments such as "You must go on" to the teacher. Milgram reported, "Subjects were observed to sweat, tremble, stutter, bite their lips, groan and dig their fingernails into their flesh. These were characteristic rather than exceptional responses to the experiment" (Milgram, 1963:375). The percentage of subjects who would shock to dangerous levels was dramatically higher than expected. Ethical concerns arose over the use of deception and the extreme emotional stress experienced by subjects.

In Laud Humphreys's (Humphreys, 1975) *tearoom trade study* (a study of male homosexual encounters in public restrooms), about 100 men were observed engaging in sexual acts as Humphreys pretended to be a "watchqueen" (a voyeur and lookout). Subjects were followed to their cars, and their license numbers were secretly recorded. Names and addresses were obtained from police registers when Humphreys posed as a market researcher. One year later, in disguise, Humphreys used a deceptive story about a health survey to interview the subjects in their homes. Humphreys was careful to keep names in safety deposit boxes, and identifiers with subject names were burned. He significantly advanced knowledge of homosexuals who frequent "tearooms" and overturned previous false beliefs about them. There has been controversy over the study: The subjects never consented; deception was used; and the names could have been used to blackmail subjects, to end marriages, or to initiate criminal prosecution.

In the *Zimbardo prison experiment* (Zimbardo, 1972, 1973; Zimbardo et al., 1973, 1974), male students were divided into two role-playing groups: guards and prisoners. Before the experiment, volunteer students were given personality tests, and only those in the "normal" range were chosen. Volunteers signed up for two weeks, and prisoners were told that they would be under surveillance and would have some civil rights suspended, but that no physical abuse was allowed. In a simulated prison in the basement of a Stanford University building, prisoners were deindividualized (dressed in standard uniforms and called only by their numbers) and guards were militarized (with uniforms, nightsticks, and reflective sunglasses). Guards were told to maintain a reasonable degree of order and served 8-hour shifts, while prisoners were locked up 24 hours per day. Unexpectedly, the volunteers became too caught up in their roles. Prisoners became passive and disorganized, while guards became aggressive, arbitrary, and dehumanizing. By the sixth day, Zimbardo called off the experiment for ethical reasons. The risk of permanent psychological harm, and even physical harm, was too great.

---

amount" means comes with experience. It is best to begin with too little stress, risking a finding of no effect, than to create too much. It is always wise to work in collaboration with other researchers when the risk to participants is high, because the involvement of several ethically sensitive researchers reduces the chances of making an ethical misjudgment.

Research that induces great stress and anxiety in participants also carries the danger that experimenters will develop a callous or manipulative attitude toward others. Researchers have reported feeling guilt and regret after conducting experiments that caused psychological harm to people. Experiments that place subjects in anxiety-producing situations may produce significant personal discomfort for the ethical researcher.

Legal Harm.   A researcher is responsible for protecting research participants from increased risk of arrest. If participation in research increases the risk of arrest, few individuals will trust researchers or be willing to participate in future research. Potential legal harm is one criticism of Humphreys's 1975 tearoom trade study (see Box 3.1).

A related ethical issue arises when a researcher learns of illegal activity when collecting data. A researcher must weigh the value of protecting the researcher-subject relationship and the benefits to future researchers against potential serious harm to innocent people. The researcher bears the cost of his or her judgment. For example, in his field research on police, Van Maanen (1982:114–115) reported seeing police beat people and witnessing illegal acts and irregular procedures, but said, "On and following these troublesome incidents I followed police custom: I kept my mouth shut."

Field researchers in particular can face difficult ethical decisions. For example, when studying a mental institution, Taylor (1987) discovered the mistreatment and abuse of inmates by the staff. He had two choices: Abandon the study and call for an immediate investigation, or keep quiet and continue with the study for several months, publicize the findings afterwards, and then become an advocate to end the abuse. After weighing the situation, he followed the latter course and is now an activist for the rights of mental institution inmates.

In some studies, observing illegal behavior may be central to the research project. If a researcher covertly observes and records illegal behavior, then supplies the information to law-enforcement authorities, he or she is violating ethical standards regarding research participants and

is undermining future social research. At the same time, a researcher who fails to report illegal behavior is indirectly permitting criminal behavior. He or she could be charged as an accessory to a crime. Cooperation with law-enforcement officials raises the question, Is the researcher a professional scientist who protects research participants in the process of seeking knowledge, or a free-lance undercover informant who is really working for the police trying to "catch" criminals?

Other Harm to Participants

Research participants may face other types of harm. For example, a survey interview may create anxiety and discomfort if it asks people to recall unpleasant or traumatic events. An ethical researcher must be sensitive to any harm to participants, consider precautions, and weigh potential harm against potential benefits.

Another type of harm is a negative impact on the careers, reputations, or incomes of research participants. For example, a researcher conducts a survey of employees and concludes that the supervisor's performance is poor. As a consequence, the supervisor loses her job. Or, a researcher studies homeless people living on the street. The findings show that many engage in petty illegal acts to get food. As a consequence, a city government "cracks down" on the petty illegal acts and the homeless people can no longer eat. What is the researcher's responsibility? The ethical researcher considers the consequences of research for those being studied. The general goal is not to cause any harm simply because someone was a research participant. However, there is no set answer to such questions. A researcher must evaluate each case, weigh potential harm against potential benefits, and bear the responsibility for the decision.

Deception

Has anyone ever told you a half-truth or lie to get you to do something? How did you feel about it? Social researchers follow the ethical *principle of voluntary consent:* Never force anyone to participate in research, and do not lie to anyone unless it is necessary and the only way to accomplish a legitimate research purpose. The people who participate in social research should explicitly agree to participate. A person's right not to participate can be a critical issue whenever the researcher uses deception, disguises the research, or uses covert research methods.

Social researchers sometimes deceive or lie to participants in field and experimental research. A researcher might misrepresent his or her actions or true intentions for legitimate methodological reasons. For example, if participants knew the true purpose, they would modify their behavior, making it impossible to learn of their real behavior. Another situation occurs when access to a research site would be impossible if the researcher told the truth. Deception is never preferable if the researcher can accomplish the same thing without using deception.

Experimental researchers often deceive subjects to prevent them from learning the hypothesis being tested and to reduce "reactive effects" (see Chapter 8). Deception is acceptable only if a researcher can show that it has a clear, specific methodological purpose, and even then, the researcher should use it only to the minimal degree necessary. Researchers who use deception should always obtain informed consent, never misrepresent risks, and always explain the actual conditions to participants afterwards. You might ask, How can a researcher obtain prior informed consent and still use deception? He or she can describe the basic procedures involved and conceal only specific information about hypotheses being tested.

Sometimes field researchers use covert observation to gain entry to field research settings. In studies of cults, small extremist political sects, illegal or deviant behavior, or behavior in a large public area, it may be impossible to conduct research if a researcher announces and discloses her or his true purpose. If a covert stance is not essential, a researcher should not use it. If he or she does not know whether covert access is necessary, then a strategy of gradual disclosure

may be best. When in doubt, it is best to err in the direction of disclosing one's true identity and purpose. Covert research remains controversial, and many researchers feel that all covert research is unethical. Even those who accept covert research as ethical in certain situations say that it should be used only when overt observation is impossible. Whenever possible, the researcher should inform participants of the observation immediately afterwards and give them an opportunity to express concerns.

Deception and covert research may increase mistrust and cynicism as well as diminish public respect for social research. Misrepresentation in field research is analogous to being an undercover agent or government informer in nondemocratic societies. The use of deception has a long-term negative effect. It increases distrust among people who are frequently studied and makes doing social research more difficult in the long term.

Informed Consent

A fundamental ethical principle of social research is: Never coerce anyone into participating; participation *must* be voluntary at all times. Permission alone is not enough; people need to know what they are being asked to participate in so that they can make an informed decision. Participants can become aware of their rights and what they are getting involved in when they read and sign a statement giving *informed consent*— an agreement by participants stating they are willing to be in a study and they know something about what the research procedure will involve.

Governments vary in the requirement for informed consent. The U.S. federal government does not require informed consent in all research involving human subjects. Nevertheless, researchers should get written informed consent unless there are good reasons for not obtaining it (e.g., covert field research, use of secondary data, etc.) as judged by an institutional review board (IRB) (see the later discussion of IRBs).

Informed consent statements provide specific information (see Box 3.2). A general statement about the kinds of procedures or questions involved and the uses of the data are sufficient for informed consent. Studies suggest that participants who receive a full informed consent statement do not respond differently from those who do not. If anything, people who refused to sign such a statement were more likely to guess or answer "no response" to questions.

It is unethical to coerce people to participate, including offering them special benefits that they cannot otherwise attain. For example, it is unethical for a commanding officer to order a soldier to participate in a study, for a professor to require a student to be a research subject in order to pass a course, or for an employer to expect an employee to complete a survey as a condition of continued employment. It is unethical even if someone other than the researcher (e.g., an employer) coerces people (e.g., employees) to participate in research.

Full disclosure with the researcher's identification helps to protect research participants against fraudulent research and to protect legitimate researchers. Informed consent lessens the chance that a con artist in the guise of a researcher will defraud or abuse people. It also reduces the chance that someone will use a bogus researcher identity to market products or obtain personal information on people for unethical purposes.

Legally, a signed informed consent statement is optional for most survey, field, and secondary data research, but it is often mandatory for experimental research. Informed consent is impossible to obtain in existing statistics and documentary research. The general rule is: The greater the risk of potential harm to research participants, the greater the need to obtain a written informed consent statement from them. In sum, there are many sound reasons to get informed consent and few reasons not to get it.

Box 3.2   Informed Consent

Informed consent statements contain the following:

1. A brief description of the purpose and procedure of the research, including the expected duration of the study

2. A statement of any risks or discomfort associated with participation

3. A guarantee of anonymity and the confidentiality of records

4. The identification of the researcher and of where to receive information about subjects' rights or questions about the study

5. A statement that participation is completely voluntary and can be terminated at any time without penalty

6. A statement of alternative procedures that may be used

7. A statement of any benefits or compensation provided to subjects and the number of subjects involved

8. An offer to provide a summary of findings

Special Populations and New Inequalities

Some populations or groups of research participants are not capable of giving true voluntary informed consent. *Special populations* are people who lack the necessary cognitive competency to give valid informed consent or people in a weak position who might cast aside their freedom to refuse to participate in a study. Students, prison inmates, employees, military personnel, the homeless, welfare recipients, children, and the developmentally disabled may not be fully capable of making a decision, or they may agree to participate only because they see their participation as a way to obtain a desired good—such as higher grades, early parole, promotions, or additional services. It is unethical to involve "incompetent" people (e.g., children, mentally disabled, etc.) in research unless a researcher meets two minimal conditions: (1) a legal guardian grants written permission and (2) the researcher follows all standard ethical principles to protect participants from harm. For example, a researcher wants to conduct a survey of high school students to learn about their sexual behavior and drug/alcohol use. If the survey is conducted on school property, school officials must give official permission. For any research participant who is a legal minor (usually under 18 years old), written parental permission is needed. It is best to ask permission from each student, as well.

The use of coercion to participate can be a tricky issue, and it depends on the specifics of a situation. For example, a convicted criminal faces the alternative of imprisonment or participation in an experimental rehabilitation program. The convicted criminal may not believe in the benefits of the program, but the researcher may believe that it will help the criminal. This is a case of coercion. A researcher must honestly judge whether the benefits to the criminal and to society greatly outweigh the ethical prohibition on coercion. This is risky. History shows many cases in which a researcher believed he or she was doing something "for the good of" someone in a powerless position (e.g., prisoners, students, homosexuals), but it turned out that the "good" actually was for the researcher or a powerful organization in society, and it did more harm than good to the research participant.

You may have been in a social science class in which a teacher required you to participate as a subject in a research project. This is a special case of coercion and is usually ethical. Teachers have made three arguments in favor of requiring student participation: (1) it would be difficult and prohibitively expensive to get participants otherwise, (2) the knowledge created from research with students serving as subjects benefits future students and society, and (3) students will learn more about research by experiencing it directly in a realistic research setting. Of the three arguments, only the third justifies limited coercion. This limited coercion is acceptable only as long as it meets three conditions: it is attached to a clear educational objective, the students have a choice of research experience or an alternative activity, and all other ethical principles of research are followed.

Avoid Creating New Inequalities. Another type of harm occurs when one group of people is denied a service or benefit as a result of participating in a research project. For example, a researcher might have a new treatment for people with a terrible disease, such as acquired immune deficiency syndrome (AIDS). To determine the effects of the new treatment, half the group is randomly chosen to receive the treatment, while others receive nothing. The design may clearly show whether the treatment is effective, but participants in the group who receive no treatment may die. Of course, those receiving the treatment may also die, until more is known about whether it is effective. Is it ethical to deny people who have been randomly assigned to a study group the potentially life-saving treatment? What if a clear, definitive test of whether a treatment is effective requires that one study group receive no treatment?

A researcher can reduce creating a new inequality among research participants when the outcome has a major impact on their survival or quality of life in three ways. First, the people who do not receive the "new, improved" treatment continue to receive the best previously acceptable treatment. In other words, instead of denying all assistance, they get the best treatment available prior to the new one being tested. This ensures that people will not suffer in absolute terms, even if they temporarily fall behind in relative terms. Second, researchers can use a *crossover design,* which is when a study group that gets no treatment in the first phase of the experiment becomes the group with the treatment in the second phase, and vice versa. Finally, the researcher continuously monitors results. If it appears early in the study that the new treatment is highly effective, the researcher should offer it to those in the control group. Also, in high-risk experiments with medical treatments or possible physical harm, researchers may use animal or other surrogates for humans.

Privacy, Anonymity, and Confidentiality

How would you feel if private details about your personal life were shared with the public without your knowledge? Because social researchers sometimes transgress the privacy of people in order to study social behavior, they must take several precautions to protect research participants' privacy.

Privacy. Survey researchers invade a person's privacy when they probe into beliefs, backgrounds, and behaviors in a way that reveals intimate private details. Experimental researchers sometimes use two-way mirrors or hidden microphones to "spy" on subjects. Even if people know they are being studied, they are unaware of what the experimenter is looking for. Field researchers may observe private aspects of behavior or eavesdrop on conversations.

In field research, privacy may be violated without advance warning. When Humphreys (1975) served as a "watchqueen" in a public restroom where homosexual contacts took place, he observed very private behavior without informing subjects. When Piliavin and colleagues (1969) had people collapse on subways to study helping behavior, those in the subway car had the privacy of their ride violated. People have been studied in public places (e.g., in waiting rooms, walking down the street, in classrooms, etc.), but some "public" places are more private than others (consider, for example, the use of periscopes to observe people who thought they were alone in a public toilet stall).

Eavesdropping on conversations and observing people in quasi-private areas raises ethical concerns. To be ethical, a researcher violates privacy only to the minimum degree necessary and only for legitimate research purposes. In addition, he or she takes steps to protect the information on participants from public disclosure.

Anonymity. Researchers protect privacy by not disclosing a participant's identity after information is gathered. This takes two forms, both of which require separating an individual's identity from his or her responses: anonymity and confidentiality. *Anonymity* means that people remain anonymous or nameless. For example, a field researcher provides a social picture of a particular individual, but gives a fictitious name and location, and alters some characteristics. The subject's identity is protected, and the individual remains unknown or anonymous. Survey and experimental researchers discard the names or addresses of subjects as soon as possible and refer to participants by a code number only to protect anonymity. If a researcher uses a mail survey and includes a code on the questionnaire to determine which respondents failed to respond, he or she is not keeping respondents anonymous during that phase of the study. In panel studies, researchers track the same individuals over time, so they do not uphold participant anonymity within the study. Likewise, historical researchers use specific names in historical or documentary research. They may do so if the original information was from public sources; if the sources were not publicly available, a researcher must obtain written permission from the owner of the documents to use specific names.

It is difficult to protect research participant anonymity. In one study about a fictitious town, "Springdale," in *Small Town in Mass Society* (Vidich and Bensman, 1968), it was easy to identify the town and specific individuals in it. Town residents became upset about how the researchers portrayed them and staged a parade mocking the researchers. People often recognize the towns studied in community research. Yet, if a researcher protects the identities of individuals with fictitious information, the gap between what was studied and what is reported to others raises questions about what was found and what was made up. A researcher may breach a promise of anonymity unknowingly in small samples. For example, let us say you conduct a survey of 100 college students and ask many questions on a questionnaire, including age, sex, religion, and hometown. The sample contains one 22-year-old Jewish male born in Stratford, Ontario. With this information, you could find out who the specific individual is and how he answered very personal questions, even though his name was not directly recorded on the questionnaire.

Confidentiality.   Even if a researcher cannot protect anonymity, he or she always should protect participant confidentiality. Anonymity means protecting the identity of specific individuals from being known. *Confidentiality* can include information with participant names attached, but the researcher holds it in confidence or keeps it secret from public disclosure. The researcher releases data in a way that does not permit linking specific individuals to responses and presents it publicly only in an aggregate form (e.g., as percentages, statistical means, etc.).

A researcher can provide anonymity without confidentiality, or vice versa, although they usually go together. Anonymity without confidentiality occurs if all the details about a specific individual are made public, but the individual's name is withheld. Confidentiality without anonymity occurs if detailed information is not made public, but a researcher privately links individual names to specific responses.

Attempts to protect the identity of subjects from public disclosure has resulted in elaborate procedures: eliciting anonymous responses, using a third-party custodian who holds the key to coded lists, or using the random-response technique. Past abuses suggest that such measures may be necessary. For example, Diener and Crandall (1978:70) reported that during the 1950s, the U.S. State Department and the FBI requested research records on individuals who had been involved in the famous Kinsey sex study. The Kinsey Sex Institute refused to comply with the government. The institute threatened to destroy all records rather than release any. Eventually, the government agencies backed down. The moral duty and ethical code of the researchers obligated them to destroy the records rather than give them to government officials.

Confidentiality can sometimes protect research participants from legal or physical harm. In a study of illegal drug users in rural Ohio, Draus and associates (2005) took great care to protect the research participants. They conducted interviews in large multiuse buildings, avoided references to illegal drugs in written documents, did not mention of names of drug dealers and locations, and did not affiliate with drug rehabilitation services, which had ties to law enforcement. They noted, "We intentionally avoided contact with local police, prosecutors, or parole officers" and "surveillance of the project by local law enforcement was a source of concern" (p. 169). In other situations, other principles may take precedence over protecting research participant confidentiality. For example, when studying patients in a mental hospital, a researcher discovers that a patient is preparing to kill an attendant. The researcher must weigh the benefit of confidentiality against the potential harm to the attendant.

Social researchers can pay high personal costs for being ethical. Although he was never accused or convicted of breaking any law and he closely followed the ethical principles of the American Sociological Association, Professor Rik Scarce spent 16 weeks in a Spokane jail for contempt of court because he refused to testify before a grand jury and break the confidentiality of social research data. Scarce had been studying radical animal liberation groups and had already published one book on the subject. He had interviewed a research participant who was suspected of leading a group that broke into animal facilities and caused $150,000 damage. Two judges refused to acknowledge the confidentiality of social research data.[8]

A special concern with anonymity and confidentiality arises when a researcher studies "captive" populations (e.g., students, prisoners, employees, patients, and soldiers). Gatekeepers, or those in positions of authority, may restrict access unless they receive information on subjects.[9] For example, a researcher studies drug use and sexual activity among high school students. School authorities agree to cooperate under two conditions: (1) students need parental permission to participate and (2) school officials get the names of all drug users and sexually active students in order to assist the students with counseling and to inform the students' parents. An ethical researcher will refuse to continue rather than meet the second condition. Even though the officials claim to have the participants' best interests in mind, the privacy of participants will be violated and they could be in legal harm as a result of disclosure. If the school officials really want to assist the students and not use researchers as spies, they could develop an outreach program of their own.

Mandated Protections of Research Participants

Many governments have regulations and laws to protect research participants and their rights. In the United States, legal restraint is found in rules and regulations issued by the U.S. Department of Health and Human Services Office for the Protection from Research Risks. Although this is only one federal agency, most researchers and other government agencies look to it for guidance. The National Research Act (1974) established the National Commission for the Protection of Human Subjects in Biomedical and Behavioral Research, which significantly expanded regulations and required informed consent in most social research. The responsibility for safeguarding ethical standards was assigned to research institutes and universities. The Department of Health and Human Services issued regulations in 1981, which are still in force. Federal regulations follow a biomedical model and protect subjects from physical harm. Other rules require institutional review boards (IRBs) at all research institutes, colleges, and universities to review all use of human subjects. An *IRB* is a committee of researchers and community members that oversees, monitors, and reviews the impact of research procedures on human participants and applies ethical guidelines by reviewing research procedures at a preliminary stage when first proposed. Some forms of research, educational tests, normal educational practice, most nonsensitive surveys, most observation of public behavior, and studies of existing data in which individuals cannot be identified are exempt from institutional review boards.

ETHICS AND THE SCIENTIFIC COMMUNITY

Physicians, attorneys, family counselors, social workers, and other professionals have a *code of ethics* and peer review boards or licensing regulations. The codes formalize professional standards and provide guidance when questions arise in practice. Social researchers do not provide a service for a fee, they receive limited ethical training, and rarely are they licensed. They incorporate ethical concerns into research because it is morally and socially responsible, and to protect social research from charges of insensitivity or abusing people. Professional social science associations have codes of ethics that identify proper and improper behavior. They represent a consensus of professionals on ethics. All researchers may not agree on all ethical issues, and ethical rules are subject to interpretation, but researchers are expected to uphold ethical standards as part of their membership in a professional community.

Codes of research ethics can be traced to the Nuremberg code adopted during the Nuremberg Military Tribunal on Nazi war crimes held by the Allied Powers immediately after World War II. The code, developed as a response to the cruelty of concentration camp experiments, outlines ethical principles and rights of human subjects. These include the following:

- The principle of voluntary consent
- Avoidance of unnecessary physical and mental suffering

- Avoidance of any experiment where death or disabling injury is likely
- Termination of research if its continuation is likely to cause injury, disability, or death
- The principle that experiments should be conducted by highly qualified people using the highest levels of skill and care
- The principle that the results should be for the good of society and unattainable by any other method

The principles in the Nuremberg code dealt with the treatment of human subjects and focused on medical experimentation, but they became the basis for the ethical codes in social research. Similar codes of human rights, such as the 1948 Universal Declaration of Human Rights by the United Nations and the 1964 Declaration of Helsinki, also have implications for social researchers. Box 3.3 lists some of the basic principles of ethical social research.

Professional social science associations have committees that review codes of ethics and hear about possible violations, but there is no formal policing of the codes. The penalty for a minor violation rarely goes beyond a letter of complaint. If laws have not been violated, the most extreme penalty is the negative publicity surrounding a well-documented and serious ethical violation. The publicity may result in the loss of employment, a refusal to publish the researcher's findings in scholarly journals, and a prohibition from receiving funding for research—in other words, banishment from the community of professional researchers.

Codes of ethics do more than codify thinking and provide individual researchers with guidance; they also help universities and other institutions defend ethical research against abuses. For example, after interviewing 24 staff members and conducting observations, a researcher in 1994 documented that the staff at the Milwaukee Public Defenders Office were seriously overworked and could not effectively provide legal defense for poor people. Learning of the findings, top officials at the office

---

Box 3.3 | **Basic Principles of Ethical Social Research**

- Ethical responsibility rests with the individual researcher.
- Do not exploit subjects or students for personal gain.
- Some form of informed consent is highly recommended or required.
- Honor all guarantees of privacy, confidentiality, and anonymity.
- Do not coerce or humiliate subjects.
- Use deception only if needed, and always accompany it with debriefing.
- Use the research method that is appropriate to a topic.
- Detect and remove undesirable consequences to research subjects.
- Anticipate repercussions of the research or publication of results.
- Identify the sponsor who funded the research.
- Cooperate with host nations when doing comparative research.
- Release the details of the study design with the results.
- Make interpretations of results consistent with the data.
- Use high methodological standards and strive for accuracy.
- Do not conduct secret research.

---

contacted the university and demanded to know who on their staff had talked to the researcher, with implications that there might be reprisals. The university administration defended the researcher and refused to release the information, citing widely accepted codes that protect human research participants.[10]

ETHICS AND THE SPONSORS OF RESEARCH

Whistle-Blowing

You might find a job where you do research for a sponsor—an employer, a government agency, or a private firm that contracts with a researcher to conduct research. Special ethical problems arise when a sponsor pays for research, especially applied research. Researchers may be asked to compromise ethical or professional research standards as a condition for receiving a contract or for continued employment. Researchers need to set ethical boundaries beyond which they will refuse the sponsor's demands. When confronted with an illegitimate demand from a sponsor, a researcher has three basic choices: loyalty to an organization or larger group, exiting from the situation, or voicing opposition.[11] These present themselves as caving in to the sponsor, quitting, or becoming a whistle-blower. The researcher must choose his or her own course of action, but it is best to consider ethical issues early in a relationship with a sponsor and to express concerns up front. *Whistle-blowing* involves the researcher who sees an ethical wrongdoing, and who cannot stop it after informing superiors and exhausting internal avenues to resolve the issue. He or she then turns to outsiders and informs an external audience, agency, or the media. The whistle-blowing researcher must be convinced that the breach of ethics is serious and approved of in the organization. It is risky. The outsiders may or may not be interested in the problem or able to help. Outsiders often have their own priorities (making an organization look bad, sensationalizing the problem, etc.) that differ from the researcher's primary concern (ending the unethical behavior). Supervisors or managers may try to discredit or punish anyone who exposes problems and acts disloyal. Under the best of conditions, the issue may take a long time to resolve and create great emotional strain. By doing what is moral, a whistle-blower needs to be prepared to make sacrifices—loss of a job or no promo-

tions, lowered pay, an undesirable transfer, abandonment by friends at work, or incurring legal costs. There is no guarantee that doing the ethical-moral thing will stop the unethical behavior or protect the honest researcher from retaliation.

Applied social researchers in sponsored research settings need to think seriously about their professional roles. They may want to maintain some independence from an employer and affirm their membership in a community of dedicated professionals. Many find a defense against sponsor pressures by participating in professional organizations (e.g., the Evaluation Research Society), maintaining regular contacts with researchers outside the sponsoring organization, and staying current with the best research practices. The researcher least likely to uphold ethical standards in a sponsored setting is someone who is isolated and professionally insecure. Whatever the situation, unethical behavior is never justified by the argument that "If I didn't do it, someone else would have."

Arriving at Particular Findings

What should you do if a sponsor tells you, directly or indirectly, what results you should come up with before you do a study? An ethical researcher will refuse to participate if he or she is told to arrive at specific results as a precondition for doing research. Legitimate research is conducted without restrictions on the possible findings that a study might yield.

An example of pressure to arrive at particular findings is in the area of educational testing. Standardized tests to measure achievement by U.S. school children have come under criticism. For example, children in about 90 percent of school districts in the United States score "above average" on such tests. This was called the *Lake Wobegon effect* after the mythical town of Lake Wobegon, where, according to radio show host Garrison Keillor, "all the children are above average." The main reason for this finding was that the researchers compared scores of current students with those of students many years ago. Many teachers, school principals, superintendents, and school boards pressured for a type of result that would allow them to report to parents and voters that their school district was "above average."[12]

Limits on How to Conduct Studies.   Is it ethically acceptable for a sponsor to limit research by defining what a researcher can study or by limiting the techniques used? Sponsors can legitimately set some conditions on research techniques used (e.g., survey versus experiment) and limit costs for research. However, the researcher must follow generally accepted research methods. Researchers must give a realistic appraisal of what can be accomplished for a given level of funding. The issue of limits is common in contract research, when a firm or government agency asks for work on a particular research project. There is often a tradeoff between quality and cost. Plus, once the research begins, a researcher may need to redesign the project, or costs may be higher. The contract procedure makes midstream changes difficult. A researcher may find that he or she is forced by the contract to use research procedures or methods that are less than ideal. The researcher then confronts a dilemma: complete the contract and do low-quality research, or fail to fulfill the contract and lose money and future jobs.

A researcher should refuse to continue a study if he or she cannot uphold generally accepted standards of research. If a sponsor demands a biased sample or leading survey questions, the ethical researcher should refuse to cooperate. If a legitimate study shows a sponsor's pet idea or project to be disaster, a researcher may anticipate the end of employment or pressure to violate professional research standards. In the long run, the sponsor, the researcher, the scientific community, and society in general are harmed by the violation of sound research practice. The researcher has to decide whether he or she is a "hired hand" who always gives the sponsors whatever they want, even if it is ethically wrong, or a professional who is obligated to teach, guide, or even oppose sponsors in the service of higher moral principles.

A researcher should ask: Why would sponsors want the social research conducted if they are not interested in using the findings or in the truth? The answer is that some sponsors are not interested in the truth and have no respect for the scientific process. They see social research only as "a cover" to legitimate a decision or practice that they plan to carry out, but use research to justify their action or deflect criticism. They abuse the researcher's professional status and undermine integrity of science to advance their own narrow goals. They are being deceitful by trying to "cash in" on social research's reputation for honesty. When such a situation occurs, an ethical researcher has a moral responsibility to expose and stop the abuse.

Suppressing Findings

What happens if you conduct a study and the findings make the sponsor look bad, then the sponsor does not want to release the results? This is a common situation for many applied researchers. For example, a sociologist conducted a study for a state government lottery commission on the effects of state government-sponsored gambling. After she completed the report, but before releasing it to the public, the commission asked her to remove sections that outlined the many negative social effects of gambling and to eliminate her recommendations to create social services to help the anticipated increase of compulsive gamblers. The researcher found herself in a difficult position and faced two conflicting values: do what the sponsor requested and paid for, or reveal the truth to the public but then suffer the consequences?[13]

Government agencies may suppress scientific information that contradicts official policy or embarrasses high officials. Retaliation against social researchers employed by government agencies who make the information public also occurs. In 2004, leading scientists, Nobel laureates, leading medical experts, former federal agency directors, and university chairs and presidents signed a statement voicing concern over the misuse of science by the George W. Bush administration. Major accusations included supressing research findings and stacking scientific advisory committees with ideologically committed advocates rather than impartial scientists. Other complaints included limiting the public release studies on auto-saftey data, negative data about pharmaceuticals, and studies on pollution. These involved industries that were major political campaign supporters of the administration. Additional criticisms appeared over removing a government fact sheet citing studies that showed no relationship between abortions and breast cancer, removing study results about positive effects of condom use in pregnancy prevention, holding back information on positive aspects of stem cell research, and requiring researchers to revise their study findings on dangers of arctic oil drilling and endangered species so they would conform to the administration's political agenda. An independent 2005 survey of 460 biologists who worked for Fisheries Service found that about one-third said they were directed to suppress findings for nonscientific reasons or to inappropriately exclude or alter technical information from an official scientific document. In June 2005, it was discovered that a political appointee without scientific training who had previously been an oil industry lobbyist was charged with editing official government reports to play down the research findings that documented linkages between such emissions and global warming.[14]

In sponsored research, a researcher can negotiate conditions for releasing findings *prior to beginning* the study and sign a contract to that effect. It may be unwise to conduct the study without such a guarantee, although competing researchers who have fewer ethical scruples may do so. Alternatively, a researcher can accept the sponsor's criticism and hostility and release the findings over the sponsor's objections. Most researchers prefer the first choice, since the second one may scare away future sponsors.

Social researchers sometimes self-censor or delay the release of findings. They do this to protect the identity of informants, to maintain access to a research site, to hold on to their jobs, or to protect the personal safety of themselves or family members.[15] This is a less disturbing type of censorship because it is not imposed by an outside power. It is done by someone who is close to the research and who is knowledgeable about possible consequences. Researchers shoulder the ultimate responsibility for their research. Often, they can draw on many different resources but they face many competing pressures, as well.

Concealing the True Sponsor

Is it ethical to keep the identity of a sponsor secret? For example, an abortion clinic funds a study on members of religious groups who oppose abortion, but it tells the researcher not to reveal to participants who is funding the study. The researcher must balance the ethical rule that it is usually best to reveal a sponsor's identity to participants against both the sponsor's desire for confidentiality and reduced cooperation by participants in the study. In general, an ethical researcher will tell subjects who is sponsoring a study unless there is a strong methodological reason for not doing so. When reporting or publishing results, the ethical mandate is very clear: A researcher must always reveal the sponsor who provides funds for a study.

POLITICS OF RESEARCH

Ethics largely address moral concerns and standards of professional conduct in research that are under the researcher's control. Political concerns also affect social research, but many are beyond the control of researchers. The politics of research usually involve actions by organized advocacy groups, powerful interests in society, governments, or politicians trying to restrict or control the direction of social research. Historically, the political influence over social research has included preventing researchers from conducting a study, cutting off or redirecting funds for research, harassing individual researchers, censoring the release of research findings, and using social research as a cover or guise for covert government intelligence/military actions. For example, U.S. Congress members targeted and eliminated funding for research projects that independent panels of scientists recommended because Congress did not like the topics that would be studied, and politically appointed officials shifted research funds to support more studies on topics consistent with their political views while ending support for studies on topics that might contradict their views. A large company threatened an individual researcher with a lawsuit for delivering expert testimony in public about research findings that revealed its past bad conduct. Until about a decade ago, social researchers who appeared to be independent were actually conducting covert U.S. government intelligence activities.[16]

Most uses of political or financial influence to control social research share a desire to limit knowledge creation or restrict the autonomous scientific investigation of controversial topics. Attempts at control seem motivated by a fear that researchers might discover something damaging if they have freedom of inquiry. This shows that free scientific inquiry is connected to fundamental political ideals of open public debate, democracy, and freedom of expression.

The attempts to block and steer social research have three main reasons. First, some people defend or advance positions and knowledge that originate in deeply held ideological, political, or religious beliefs, and fear that social researchers might produce knowledge that contradicts them. Second, powerful interests want to protect or advance their political-financial position, and fear social researchers might yield findings showing that their actions are harmful to the public or some sectors of society. And third, some people in society do not respect the ideals of science to pursue truth/knowledge and instead view scientific research only as cover for advancing private interests (see Box 3.4).

VALUE-FREE AND OBJECTIVE RESEARCH

You have undoubtedly heard about "value-free" research and the importance of being "objective" in research. This is not as simple at it might first appear for several reasons. First, there are different meanings of the terms *value free* and *objective*. Second, different approaches to social science (positivism, interpretative, critical) hold different views on the issue. And last, even researchers who agree that social research should be value free and objective do not believe that it needs to be totally devoid of all values.

There are two basic ways the term *value free* is used: research that is free from any prior assumptions, theoretical stand, or value position, and research that is conducted free of influence from an individual researcher's personal prejudices/beliefs. Likewise, *objective* can mean focusing only on what is external or visible, or it can mean following clear and publicly accepted research procedures and not haphazard, personal ones.

The three approaches to social science that you read about in Chapter 2 hold different positions on the importance of value-free, objective research. Positivism puts a high value on such research. An interpretive approach seriously questions whether it is possible, since human values/beliefs pervade all aspects of human activities, including research. Instead of eliminating values and subjective dimension, it suggests a relativist stance—no single value position

---

Box 3.4   What Is Public Sociology?

Michael Burawoy (2004, 2005) distinguished among four ideal types of social research: policy, professional, critical, and public. The aim of public sociology (or social science, more generally) is to enrich public debate over moral and political issues by infusing such debate with social theory and research. Public sociology frequently overlaps with action-oriented research. Burawoy argued that the place of social research in society centers on how one answers two questions: Knowledge for whom? and Knowledge for what? The first question focuses on the sources of research questions and how results are used. The second question looks at the source of research goals. Are they handed down by some external sponsor or agency or are they concerned with debates over larger societal political-moral issues? Public social science tries to generate a conversation or debate between researchers and public. By constrast, policy social science focuses on finding solutions to specific problems as defined by sponsors or clients. Both rely on professional social science for theories, bodies of knowledge, and techniques for gathering and analyzing data. Critical social science, as was discussed in Chapter 2, emphasizes demystifying and raising questioning about basic conditions.

The primary audience for professional and critical social science are members of the scientific community, whereas the main audience for public and policy research are nonexperts and practitioners. Both critical and public social science seek to infuse a moral, value dimension into social research and they try to generate debates over moral-political values. Professional and policy social science are less concerned about debates over moral or value issues and may avoid them. Instead, their focus is more on being effective in providing advances to basic knowledge or specific solutions to practical problems. Both public and policy social science are applied research and have a relevance beyond the community of scientific researchers.

---

is better than any other. A critical approach also questions value-free research, but sees it often as a sham.

Value free means free of everyone's values except those of science, and *objective* means following established rules or procedures that some people created, without considering who they represent and how they created the rules. In other words, a critical approach sees all research as containing some values, so those who claim to be value free are just hiding theirs. Those who follow an interpretive and critical approach and reject value-free research do not embrace sloppy and haphazard research, research procedures that follow a particular researcher's whims, or a study that has a foregone conclusion and automatically supports a specific value position. They believe that a researcher should make his or her own value position explicit, reflect carefully on reasons for doing a study and the procedures used, and communicate in a candid, clear manner exactly how the study was conducted. In this way, other researchers see the role of a researcher's values and judge for themselves whether the values unfairly influenced a study's findings.

Even highly positivist researchers who advocate value-free and objective studies admit a limited place for some personal, moral values. Many hold that a researcher's personal, moral position can enter when it comes to deciding what topic to study and how to disseminate findings. Being value free and objective only refers to actually conducting the study. This means that you can study the issues you believe to be important and after completing a study you can share the results with specific interest groups in addition to making them available to the scientific community.

CONCLUSION

In Chapter 1, we discussed the distinctive contribution of science to society and how social research is a source of knowledge about the social world. The perspectives and techniques of social research can be powerful tools for understanding the world. Nevertheless, with that power to discover comes responsibility—a responsibility to yourself, a responsibility to your sponsors, a responsibility to the community of scientific researchers, and a responsibility to the larger society. These responsibilities can conflict with each other. Ultimately, you personally must decide to conduct research in an ethical manner, to uphold and defend the principles of the social science approach you adopt, and to demand ethical conduct by others. The truthfulness of knowledge produced by social research and its use or misuse depends on individual researchers like you, reflecting on their actions and on the serious role of social research in society. In the next chapter, we examine basic design approaches and issues that appear in both qualitative and quantitative research.

Key Terms

anonymity
confidentiality
crossover design
informed consent
institutional review board (IRB)
plagiarism
principle of voluntary consent
public sociology
research fraud
scientific misconduct
special populations
whistle-blower

Endnotes

1. For a discussion of research fraud, see Broad and Wade (1982), Diener and Crandall (1978), and Weinstein (1979). Hearnshaw (1979) and Wade (1976) discuss the Cyril Burt case, and see Holden (2000) on the social psychologist case. Kusserow (1989) discusses the concept of scientific misconduct.

2. See Blum (1989) and D'Antonio (1989) for details on this case. Also see Goldner (1998) on legal versus scientific views of misconduct. Gibelman (2001) discusses several cases and the changing definition of misconduct.

3. See Lifton (1986) on Nazi experiments, and Williams and Wallace (1989) discuss Japanese experiments. Harris (2002) argues that the Japanese experiments were more horrific, but the United States did not prosecute the Japanese scientists as the Germans were because the U.S. military wanted the results to develop its own biological warfare program.

4. See Jones (1981) and Mitchell (1997) on "Bad Blood."

5. Diener and Crandall (1978:128) discuss examples.

6. A discussion of physical harm to research participants can be found in Kelman (1982), Reynolds (1979, 1982), and Warwick (1982).

7. For a discussion, see Diener and Crandall (1978:21–22) and Kidder and Judd (1986:481–484).

8. See Monaghan (1993a, 1993b, 1993c).

9. Broadhead and Rist (1976) discuss gatekeepers.

10. See "UW Protects Dissertation Sources," *Capital Times* (Madison, Wisconsin), December 19, 1994, p. 4.

11. See Hirschman (1970) on loyalty, exit, or voice.

12. See Edward Fiske, "The Misleading Concept of 'Average' on Reading Test Changes, More Students Fall Below It," *New York Times* (July 12, 1989). Also see Koretz (1988) and Weiss and Gruber (1987).

13. See "State Sought, Got Author's Changes of Lottery Report," *Capital Times* (Madison, Wisconsin), July 28, 1989, p. 21.

14. Andrew Revkin, "Bush Aide Edited Climate Reports," *New York Times* (June 8, 2005). "White House Calls Editing Climate Files Part of Usual Review," *New York Times* (June 9, 2005). Union of Concerned Scientists, "Politics Trumps Science at

U.S. Fish and Wildlife Service" (February 9, 2005)."
Specific Examples of the Abuse of Science
www.ucsusa.org/global_environment/rsi/page.cfm?
pageID=1398, downloaded August 3, 2005. "Sum-
mary of National Oceanic & Atmospheric Adminis-
tration Fisheries Service Scientist Survey" by Union
of Concerned Scientists (June 2005). E. Shogren,
"Researchers Accuse Bush of Manipulating Science,"
Los Angeles Times (July 9, 2004). Jeffrey McCracker,
"Government Bans Release of Auto-Safety Data,"
Detroit Free Press (August 19, 2004). Garddiner
Harris, "Lawmaker Says FDA Held Back Drug Data,"
New York Times (September 10, 2004). James Glanz,
"Scientists Say Administration Distorts Facts," *New
York Times* (February 19, 2004). Dylan O. Krider,
"The Politicization of Science in the Bush Adminis-
tration," *Skeptic* Vol. 11, Number 2 (2004) at www.
Skeptic.com. C. Orstein, "Politics Trumps Science in
Condom Fact Sheet," *New York Times* (December
27, 2002). "Scientist Says Officials Ignored Advice on
Water Levels," *Washington Post* (October 29, 2002).

15. See Adler and Adler (1993).
16. See Neuman (2003, Chapter 16) for a discussion
of political issues in social research.

CHAPTER 4

Reviewing the Scholarly Literature and Planning a Study

INTRODUCTION

In the past three chapters, you have learned about the main principles and types of social research, discovered how researchers use theory in a study, and examined the place of ethics in social research. You are now ready to get into the specifics of how to go about designing a study. Recall from Chapter 1 that a researcher usually begins with a general topic, then narrows the topic down into a specific research question, and then makes decisions about the specifics of designing a study that will address the research question.

Where do topics for study come from? They come from many sources: previous studies, television or film, personal experiences, discussions with friends and family, or something you read about in a book, magazine, or newspaper. A topic often begins as something that arouses your curiosity, about which you hold deep commitments or strong feelings, or that you believe is really wrong and want to change. To apply social research, a topic must be about social patterns that operate in aggregates and be empirically measurable or observable. This rules out topics about one unique situation (e.g., why your boy/girlfriend dumped you yesterday, why your friend's little sister hates her school teacher), or one individual case (e.g., your own family), or something one can never observe, even indirectly (e.g., unicorns, ghosts with supernatural powers, etc.). This may rule out some interesting topics, but many tens of thousands remain to be investigated.

How you proceed differs slightly depending on whether you adopt an inductive or a deductive approach. Compared to an inductive researcher, those who choose a deductive approach and gather quantitative data will devote much more time to specifying the research question very precisely and planning many details of a study in advance. It will take you a while to develop the judgment skills for deciding whether it might be better to conduct a more deductive-quantitative or an inductive-qualitative study to address a

topic and research question. Three things can help you learn what is the most effective type of study to pursue for a question:

1. Reading studies that others have conducted on a topic
2. Grasping issues that operate in qualitative and quantitative approaches to research
3. Understanding how to use various research techniques as well as their strengths and limitations

This chapter introduces you to the first two of these, whereas many of the remaining chapters of the book discuss the third item in the list.

LITERATURE REVIEW

Reading the "literature," or the collection of studies already published on a topic, serves several very important functions. First, it helps you narrow down a broad topic by showing you how others conducted their studies. The studies by others give you a model of how narrowly focused a research question should be, what kinds of study designs others have used, and how to measure variables or analyze data. Second, it informs you about the "state of knowledge" on a topic. From the studies by others, you can learn the key ideas, terms, and issues that surround a topic. You should consider replicating, testing, or extending what others already found. Third, the literature often stimulates your creativity and curiosity. Last, even if you never get to conduct or publish your own research study, a published study offers you an example of what the final report on a study looks like, its major parts, its form, and its style of writing. Another reason is more practical. Just as attentively reading a lot of top-quality writing can help you improve your own writing skills, reading many reports of good-quality social research enables you to grasp better the elements that go into conducting a research study.

It is best to be organized and not haphazard as you locate and read the scholarly or academic literature on a topic and associated research questions. Also, it is wise to plan to prepare a written literature review. There are many specialized types of reviews, but in general a *literature review* is a carefully crafted summary of the recent studies conducted on a topic that includes key findings and methods researchers used while making sure to document the sources. For most purposes, you must first locate the relevant studies; next, read thoroughly to discover the major findings, central issues, and methods of the studies, and take conscientious notes on what you read. While the reading is still fresh in your mind and with the notes in front of you, you need to organize what you have learned and write clearly about the studies in a way that builds a context around a specific research question that is of interest to you.

A literature review is based on the assumption that knowledge accumulates and that people learn from and build on what others have done. Scientific research is a collective effort of many researchers who share their results with one another and who pursue knowledge as a community. Although some studies may be especially important and individual researchers may become famous, a specific research project is just a tiny part of the overall process of creating knowledge. Today's studies build on those of yesterday. Researchers read studies to compare, replicate, or criticize them for weaknesses.

Reviews vary in scope and depth. Different kinds of reviews are stronger at fulfilling one or another of four goals (see Box 4.1). It may take a researcher over a year to complete an extensive professional summary review of all the literature on a broad question. The same researcher might complete a highly focused review in a very specialized area in a few weeks. When beginning a review, a researcher decides on a topic, how much depth to go into, and the kind of review to conduct.

Where to Find Research Literature

Researchers present reports of their research projects in several written forms: periodicals,

Box 4.1 Goals of a Literature Review

1. *To demonstrate a familiarity with a body of knowledge and establish credibility.* A review tells a reader that the researcher knows the research in an area and knows the major issues. A good review increases a reader's confidence in the researcher's professional competence, ability, and background.

2. *To show the path of prior research and how a current project is linked to it.* A review outlines the direction of research on a question and shows the development of knowledge. A good review places a research project in a context and demonstrates its relevance by making connections to a body of knowledge.

3. *To integrate and summarize what is known in an area.* A review pulls together and synthesizes different results. A good review points out areas where prior studies agree, where they disagree, and where major questions remain. It collects what is known up to a point in time and indicates the direction for future research.

4. *To learn from others and stimulate new ideas.* A review tells what others have found so that a researcher can benefit from the efforts of others. A good review identifies blind alleys and suggests hypotheses for replication. It divulges procedures, techniques, and research designs worth copying so that a researcher can better focus hypotheses and gain new insights.

books, dissertations, government documents, or policy reports. They also present them as papers at the meetings of professional societies, but for the most part, you can find them only in a college or university library. This section briefly discusses each type and gives you a simple road map on how to access them.

Periodicals.   You can find the results of social research in newspapers, in popular magazines, on television or radio broadcasts, and in Internet news summaries, but these are not the full, complete reports of research required to prepare a literature review. They are selected, condensed summaries prepared by journalists for a general audience, and they lack many essential details needed for a serious evaluation of the study. Textbooks and encyclopedias also present condensed summaries as introductions to readers who are new to a topic, but, again, these are inadequate for preparing a literature review because many essential details about the study are absent.

It is easy for someone preparing a first literature review to be confused about the many types of periodicals. With skill, you will be able to distinguish among (1) mass market newspapers and magazines written for the general public, (2) popularized social science magazines, (3) opinion magazines in which intellectuals debate and express their views, and (4) scholarly academic journals in which researchers present the findings of studies or provide other communication to the scientific community. Peer-reviewed empirical research findings appear in a complete form only in the last type of publication, although articles in the other types occasionally talk about findings published elsewhere.

Mass market publications (e.g., *McCleans, Time, Newsweek, Economist, The Nation, American Spectator,* and *Atlantic Monthly*) are sold at newsstands and designed to provide the general public with news, opinion, and entertainment. A researcher might occasionally use them as a source on current events, but they do not provide full reports of research studies in the form needed to prepare a literature review.

Popularized social science magazines and professional publications (e.g., *Society* and *Psychology Today*) are sometimes peer reviewed. Their purpose is to provide the interested, educated lay public a simplified version of findings or a commentary, but not to be an outlet for original research findings. At best, popularized social science magazines can supplement to other sources in a literature review.

It is harder to recognize serious opinion magazines (e.g., *American Prospect, Commentary, Dissent,* and *Public Interest*). Larger bookstores in major cities sell them. Leading scholars often write articles for opinion magazines about topics on which they may also conduct empirical research (e.g., welfare reform, prison expansion, voter turnout). They differ in purpose, look, and scope from scholarly journals of social science research findings. The publications are an arena where intellectuals debate current issues, not where researchers present findings of their studies to the broader scientific community.

Scholarly Journals. The primary type of periodical to use for a literature review is the scholarly journal filled with peer-reviewed reports of research (e.g., *American Sociological Review, Social Problems, American Journal of Sociology, Criminology,* and *Social Science Quarterly*). One rarely finds them outside of college and university libraries. Recall from Chapter 1 that researchers disseminate findings of new studies in scholarly journals.

Some scholarly journals are specialized. Instead of reports of research studies, they have only book reviews that provide commentary and evaluations on a book (e.g., *Contemporary Sociology*), or they contain only literature review essays (e.g., *Annual Review of Sociology, Annual Review of Psychology,* and *Annual Review of Anthropology*) in which researchers give a "state of the field" essay for others. Publications that specialize in literature reviews can be helpful if an article was recently published on a specific topic of interest. Many other scholarly journals have a mix of articles that are literature reviews, books reviews, reports on research studies, and theoretical essays.

No simple solution or "seal of approval" distinguishes scholarly journals, the kind of publications on which to build a serious literature review from other periodicals, or instantly distinguishes the report on a research study from other types of articles. One needs to develop judgment or ask experienced researchers or professional librarians. Nonetheless, distinguishing among types of publications is essential to build on a body of research. One of the best ways to learn to distinguish among types of publications is to read many articles in scholarly journals.

The number of journals varies by field. Psychology has over 400 journals, whereas sociology has about 250 scholarly journals, political science and communication have slightly fewer than sociology, anthropology-archaeology and social work have about 100, urban studies and women studies have about 50, and there are about a dozen journals in criminology. Each publishes from a few dozen to over 100 articles a year.

Many, but not all, scholarly journals may be viewed via the Internet. Usually, this is limited to selected years and to libraries that paid special subscription fees. A few Internet services provide full, exact copies of scholarly journal articles over the Internet. For example, JSTOR provides exact copies, but only for a small number of scholarly journals and only for past years. Other Internet services, such as EBSCO HOST, offer a full-text version of recent articles for a limited number of scholarly journals, but they are not in the same format as a print version of an article. This can make it impossible to find a specific page number or see an exact copy of a chart. It is best to visit the library and see what a full-print version of the scholarly article looks like. An added benefit is that it makes it easy for you to browse the Table of Contents of the journals. Browsing can be very useful for generating new ideas for research topics, seeing an established topic in creative ways, or learning how to expand an idea into new areas. Only a tiny handful of new Internet-only scholarly journals, called *e-journals,* present peer-reviewed research studies (e.g., *Sociological Research Online, Current Research in Social Psychology,* and *Journal of World Systems Research*). Eventually, the Internet format may replace print versions. But for now, 99 percent of scholarly journals are available in print form and about one-third of these are also available in a full-text version over the

Internet and only then if a library pays for a special on-line subscription service.

Once you locate a scholarly journal that reports on social science research studies, you need to make sure that a particular article presents the results of a study, since the journal may have other types of articles. It is easier to identify quantitative studies because they usually have a methods or data section and charts, statistical formulas, and tables of numbers. Qualitative research articles are more difficult to identify, and many students confuse them with theoretical essays, literature review articles, idea-discussion essays, policy recommendations, book reviews, and legal case analyses. To distinguish among these types requires a good grasp of the varieties of research as well as experience in reading many articles.

Your college library has a section for scholarly journals and magazines, or, in some cases, they may be mixed with books. Look at a map of library facilities or ask a librarian to find this section. The most recent issues, which look like thin paperbacks or thick magazines, are often physically separate in a "current periodicals" section. This is done to store them temporarily and make them available until the library receives all the issues of a volume. Most often, libraries bind all issues of a volume together as a book before adding them to their permanent collections.

Scholarly journals from many different fields are placed together with popular magazines. All are periodicals, or *serials* in the jargon of librarians. Thus, you will find popular magazines (e.g., *Time, Road and Track, Cosmopolitan,* and *Atlantic Monthly*) next to journals for astronomy, chemistry, mathematics, literature, and philosophy as well as sociology, psychology, social work, and education. Some fields have more scholarly journals than others. The "pure" academic fields usually have more than the "applied" or practical fields such as marketing or social work. The journals are listed by title in a card catalog or a computerized catalog system. Libraries can provide you with a list of the periodicals to which they subscribe.

Scholarly journals are published as rarely as once a year or as frequently as weekly. Most appear four to six times a year. For example, *Sociological Quarterly* appears four times a year. To assist in locating articles, librarians and scholars have developed a system for tracking scholarly journals and the articles in them. Each issue is assigned a date, volume number, and issue number. This information makes it easier to locate an article. Such information—along with details such as author, title, and page number—is called an article's *citation* and is used in bibliographies. When a journal is first published, it begins with volume 1, number 1, and continues increasing the numbers thereafter. Although most journals follow a similar system, there are enough exceptions that you have to pay close attention to citation information. For most journals, each volume is one year. If you see a journal issue with volume 52, for example, it probably means that the journal has been in existence for 52 years. Most, but not all, journals begin their publishing cycle in January.

Most journals number pages by volume, not by issue. The first issue of a volume usually begins with page 1, and page numbering continues throughout the entire volume. For example, the first page of volume 52, issue 4, may be page 547. Most journals have an index for each volume and a table of contents for each issue that lists the title, the author's or authors' names, and the page on which the article begins. Issues contain as few as 1 or 2 articles or as many as 50. Most have 8 to 18 articles, which may be 5 to 50 pages long. The articles often have *abstracts,* short summaries on the first page of the article or grouped together at the beginning of the issue.

Many libraries do not retain physical, paper copies of older journals. To save space and costs, they retain only microfilm versions. There are hundreds of scholarly journals in most academic fields, with each costing $50 to $2,500 per year. Only the large research libraries subscribe to all of them. You may have to borrow a journal or photocopy of an article from a distant library through an *interlibrary loan service,* a system by

which libraries lend books or materials to other libraries. Few libraries allow people to check out recent issues of scholarly journals. You should plan to use these in the library. Some, not all, scholarly journals are available via the Internet.

Once you find the periodicals section, wander down the aisles and skim what is on the shelves. You will see volumes containing many research reports. Each title of a scholarly journal has a call number like that of a regular library book. Libraries often arrange them alphabetically by title. Because journals change titles, it may create confusion if the journal is shelved under its original title.

Citation Formats.   An article's citation is the key to locating it. Suppose you want to read the study by Weitzer and Tuch (2005) on perceptions of police misconduct discussed in Chapter 2. Its citation is as follows:

> Weitzer, Ronald, and Steven Tuch. 2005. "Racially Biased Policing: Determinants of Citizen Perceptions." *Social Forces* 83:1009–1030.

This tells you that you can find the article in an issue of *Social Forces* published in 2005. The citation does not provide the issue or month, but it gives the volume number, 83, and the page numbers, 1009 to 1030.

There are many ways to cite the literature. Formats for citing literature in the text itself vary, with the internal citation format of using an author's last name and date of publication in parentheses being very popular. The full citation appears in a separate bibliography or reference section. There are many styles for full citations of journal articles, with books and other types of works each having a separate style. When citing articles, it is best to check with an instructor, journal, or other outlet for the desired format. Almost all include the names of authors, article title, journal name, and volume and page numbers. Beyond these basic elements, there is great variety. Some include the authors' first names, others use initials only. Some include all authors, others give only the first one. Some include information on the issue or month of publication, others do not (see Figure 4.1).

Citation formats can get complex. Two major reference tools on the topic in social science are *Chicago Manual of Style,* which has nearly 80 pages on bibliographies and reference formats, and *American Psychological Association Publication Manual,* which devotes about 60 pages to the topic. In sociology, the *American Sociological Review* style, with 2 pages of style instructions, is widely followed.

Books. Books communicate many types of information, provoke thought, and entertain. There are many types of books: picture books, textbooks, short story books, novels, popular fiction or nonfiction, religious books, children's books, and others. Our concern here is with those books containing reports of original research or collections of research articles. Libraries shelve these books and assign call numbers to them, as they do with other types of books. You can find citation information on them (e.g., title, author, publisher) in the library's catalog system.

It is not easy to distinguish a book that reports on research from other books. You are more likely to find such books in a college or university library. Some publishers, such as university presses, specialize in publishing them. Nevertheless, there is no guaranteed method for identifying one without reading it.

Some types of social research are more likely to appear in book form than others. For example, studies by anthropologists and historians are more likely to appear in book-length reports than are those of economists or psychologists. Yet, some anthropological and historical studies are articles, and some economic and psychological studies appear as books. In education, social work, sociology, and political science, the results of long, complex studies may appear both in two or three articles and in book form. Studies that involve detailed clinical or ethnographic descriptions and complex theoretical or philosophical discussions usually appear as books. Finally, an author who wants to communicate to scholarly peers and to the educated public may write a book that bridges the scholarly, academic style and a popular nonfiction style.

Locating original research articles in books can be difficult because there is no single source listing them. Three types of books contain collections of articles or research reports. The first is designed for teaching purposes. Such books, called *readers,* may include original research reports. Usually, articles on a topic from scholarly journals are gathered and edited to be easier for nonspecialists to read and understand.

The second type of collection is designed for scholars and may gather journal articles or may contain original research or theoretical essays on a specific topic. Some collections contain articles from journals that are difficult to locate. They may include original research reports organized around a specialized topic. The table of contents lists the titles and authors. Libraries shelve these collections with other books, and some library catalog systems include them.

Citations or references to books are shorter than article citations. They include the author's name, book title, year and place of publication, and publisher's name.

Dissertations. All graduate students who receive the Ph.D. degree are required to complete a work of original research, which they write up as a dissertation thesis. The dissertation is bound and shelved in the library of the university that granted the Ph.D. About half of all dissertations are eventually published as books or articles. Because dissertations report on original research, they can be valuable sources of information. Some students who receive the master's degree conduct original research and write a master's thesis, but fewer master's theses involve serious research, and they are much more difficult to locate than unpublished dissertations.

Specialized indexes list dissertations completed by students at accredited universities. For

FIGURE 4.1   Different Reference Citations for a Journal Article

The oldest journal of sociology in the United States, *American Journal of Sociology*, reports on a study of virginity pledges by Peter Bearman and Hannah Bückner. It appeared on pages 859 to 913 of the January 2001 issue (number 4) of the journal, which begins counting issues in March. It was in volume 106, or the journal's 106th year. Here are ways to cite the article. Two very popular styles are those of *American Sociological Review (ASR)* and *American Psychological Association (APA)*.

ASR Style

Bearman, Peter and Hannah Bückner. 2001. "Promising the Future: Virginity Pledges and First Intercourse."
    American Journal of Sociology 106:859–912.

APA Style

Bearman, P., and Bückner, H. (2001). Promising the future: Virginity pledges and first intercourse. *American
    Journal of Sociology 106*, 859–912.

Other Styles

Bearman, P., and H. Bückner. "Promising the Future: Virginity Pledges and First Intercourse," *American Journal
    of Sociology* 106 (2001), 859–912.
Bearman, Peter and Hannah Bückner, 2001.
    "Promising the future: Virginity pledges and first Intercourse." *Am. J. of Sociol.* 106:859– 912.
Bearman, P. and Bückner, H. (2001). "Promising the Future: Virginity Pledges and First Intercourse." *American Journal of Sociology* 106 (January): 859–912.
Bearman, Peter and Hannah Bückner. 2001.
    "Promising the future: Virginity pledges and first Intercourse." *American Journal of Sociology* 106
    (4):859–912.
Bearman, P. and H. Bückner. (2001). "Promising the future: Virginity pledges and first intercourse." *American
    Journal of Sociology* 106, 859–912.
Peter Bearman and Hannah Bückner, "Promising the Future: Virginity Pledges and First Intercourse," *American
    Journal of Sociology* 106, no. 4 (2001): 859–912.

---

example, *Dissertation Abstracts International* lists dissertations with their authors, titles, and universities. This index is organized by topic and contains an abstract of each dissertation. You can borrow most dissertations via interlibrary loan from the degree-granting university if the university permits this.

Government Documents.   The federal government of the United States, the governments of other nations, state- or provincial-level governments, the United Nations, and other international agencies such as the World Bank, all sponsor studies and publish reports of the

research. Many college and university libraries have these documents in their holdings, usually in a special "government documents" section. These reports are rarely found in the catalog system. You must use specialized lists of publications and indexes, usually with the help of a librarian, to locate these reports. Most college and university libraries hold only the most frequently requested documents and reports.

Policy   Reports   and   Presented   Papers.
A researcher conducting a thorough review of the literature will examine these two sources, which are difficult for all but the trained specialist to

obtain. Research institutes and policy centers (e.g., Brookings Institute, Institute for Research on Poverty, Rand Corporation, etc.) publish papers and reports. Some major research libraries purchase these and shelve them with books. The only way to be sure of what has been published is to write directly to the institute or center and request a list of reports.

Each year, the professional associations in academic fields (e.g., sociology, political science, psychology) hold annual meetings. Thousands of researchers assemble to give, listen to, or discuss oral reports of recent research. Most of these oral reports are available as written papers to those attending the meeting. People who do not attend the meetings but who are members of the association receive a program of the meeting, listing each paper to be presented with its title, author, and author's place of employment. They can write directly to the author and request a copy of the paper. Many, but not all, of the papers are later published as articles. The papers may be listed in indexes or abstract services (to be discussed).

How to Conduct a Systematic Literature Review

Define and Refine a Topic.   Just as a researcher must plan and clearly define a topic and research question when beginning a research project, you need to begin a literature review with a clearly defined, well-focused research question and a plan. A good review topic should be as focused as a research question. For example, "divorce" or "crime" is much too broad. A more appropriate review topic might be "the stability of families with stepchildren" or "economic inequality and crime rates across nations." If you conduct a context review for a research project, it should be slightly broader than the specific research question being tested. Often, a researcher will not finalize a specific research question for a study until he or she has reviewed the literature. The review helps bring greater focus to the research question.

Design a Search.   After choosing a focused research question for the review, the next step is to plan a search strategy. The reviewer needs to decide on the type of review, its extensiveness, and the types of materials to include. The key is to be careful, systematic, and organized. Set parameters on your search: how much time you will devote to it, how far back in time you will look, the minimum number of research reports you will examine, how many libraries you will visit, and so forth.

Also, decide how to record the bibliographic citation for each reference you find and how to take notes (e.g., in a notebook, on 3 × 5 cards, in a computer file). Develop a schedule, because several visits are usually necessary. You should begin a file folder or computer file in which you can place possible sources and ideas for new sources. As the review proceeds, it should become more focused.

Locate Research Reports.   Locating research reports depends on the type of report or "outlet" of research being searched. As a general rule, use multiple search strategies in order to counteract the limitations of a single search method.

Articles in Scholarly Journals.   As discussed earlier, most social research is published in scholarly journals. There are dozens of journals, many going back decades, each containing many articles. The task of searching for articles can be formidable. Luckily, specialized publications make the task easier.

You may have used an index for general publications, such as *Reader's Guide to Periodical Literature.* Many academic fields have "abstracts" or "indexes" for the scholarly literature (e.g., *Psychological Abstracts, Social Sciences Index, Sociological Abstracts,* and *Gerontological Abstracts*). For education-related topics, the Educational Resources Information Center (ERIC) system is especially valuable. There are over 100 such publications. You can usually find them in the reference section of a library. Many abstracts or index services as well as ERIC are available via computer access, which speeds the search process.

Abstracts or indexes are published on a regular basis (monthly, six times a year, etc.) and allow a reader to look up articles by author name or subject. The journals covered by the abstract or index are listed in it, often in the front. An index, such as the *Social Sciences Index,* lists only the citation, whereas an abstract, such as *Sociological Abstracts,* lists the citation and has a copy of the article's abstract. Abstracts do not give you all the findings and details of a research project. Researchers use abstracts to screen articles for relevance, then locate the more relevant articles. Abstracts may also include papers presented at professional meetings.

It may sound as if all you have to do is to go find the index in the reference section of the library or on the Internet and look up a topic. Unfortunately, things are more complicated than that. In order to cover the studies across many years, you may have to look through many issues of the abstracts or indexes. Also, the subjects or topics listed are broad. The specific research question that interests you may fit into several subject areas. You should check each one. For example, for the topic of illegal drugs in high schools, you might look up these subjects: drug addiction, drug abuse, substance abuse, drug laws, illegal drugs, high schools, and secondary schools. Many of the articles under a subject area will not be relevant for your literature review. Also, there is a 3 to 12-month time lag between the publication of an article and its appearance in the abstracts or indexes. Unless you are at a major research library, the most useful article may not be available in your library. You can obtain it only by using an interlibrary loan service, or it may be in a foreign language that you do not read.

The computerized literature search works on the same principle as an abstract or an index. Researchers organize computerized searches in several ways—by author, by article title, by subject, or by keyword. A *keyword* is an important term for a topic that is likely to be found in a title. You will want to use six to eight keywords

in most computer-based searches and consider several synonyms. The computer's searching method can vary and most only look for a keyword in a title or abstract. If you choose too few words or very narrow terms, you will miss a lot of relevant articles. If you choose too many words or very broad terms, you will get a huge number of irrelevant articles. The best way to learn the appropriate breadth and number of keywords is by trial and error.

In a study I conducted on how college students define *sexual harassment* (Neuman, 1992), I used the following keywords: *sexual harassment, sexual assault, harassment, gender equity, gender fairness,* and *sex discrimination.* I later discovered a few important studies that lacked any of these keywords in their titles. I also tried the keywords *college student* and *rape,* but got huge numbers of unrelated articles that I could not even skim.

There are numerous computer-assisted search databases or systems. A person with a computer and an Internet hook-up can search some article index collections, the catalogs of libraries, and other information sources around the globe if they are available on the Internet.

All computerized searching methods share a similar logic, but each has its own method of operation to learn. In my study, I looked for sources in the previous seven years and used five computerized databases of scholarly literature: *Social Science Index, CARL (Colorado Area Research Library), Sociofile, Social Science Citation Index,* and *PsychLit.*

Often, the same articles will appear in multiple scholarly literature databases, but each database may identify a few new articles not found in the others. For example, I discovered several excellent sources not listed in any of the computerized databases that had been published in earlier years by studying the bibliographies of the relevant articles.

The process in my study was fairly typical. Based on my keyword search, I quickly skimmed or scanned the titles or abstracts of over 200 sources. From these, I selected about 80 articles, reports, and books to read. I found about 49 of the 80 sources valuable, and they appear in the bibliography of the published article.

Scholarly Books.   Finding scholarly books on a subject can be difficult. The subject topics of library catalog systems are usually incomplete and too broad to be useful. Moreover, they list only books that are in a particular library system, although you may be able to search other libraries for interlibrary loan books. Libraries organize books by call numbers based on subject matter. Again, the subject matter classifications may not reflect the subjects of interest to you or all the subjects discussed in a book. Once you learn the system for your library, you will find that most books on a topic will share the main parts of the call number. In addition, librarians can help you locate books from other libraries. For example, the *Library of Congress National Union Catalog* lists all books in the U.S. Library of Congress. Librarians have access to sources that list books at other libraries, or you can use the Internet. There is no sure-fire way to locate relevant books. Use multiple search methods, including a look at journals that have book reviews and the bibliographies of articles.

Taking Notes

As you gather the relevant research literature, it is easy to feel overwhelmed by the quantity of information, so you need a system for taking notes. The old-fashioned approach is to write notes onto index cards. You then shift and sort the note cards, place them in piles, and so forth as you look for connections among them or develop an outline for a report or paper. This method still works. Today, however, most people use word-processing software and gather photocopies or printed versions of many articles.

As you discover sources, it is a good idea to create two kinds of files for your note cards or computer documents: a *Source File* and a *Content File*. Record *all* the bibliographic information for each source in the Source File, even

though you may not use some and later erase them. Do not forget anything in a complete bibliographic citation, such as a page number or the name of the second author; you will regret it later. It is far easier to erase a source you do not use than to try to locate bibliographic information later for a source you discover that you need or from which you forgot one detail.

I recommend creating two kinds of Source Files, or divide a master file into two parts: *Have File* and *Potential File*. The Have File is for sources that you have found and for which you have already taken content notes. The Potential File is for leads and possible new sources that you have yet to track down or read. You can add to the Potential File anytime you come across a new source or in the bibliography of something you read. Toward the end of writing a report, the Potential File will disappear while the Have File will become your bibliography.

Your note cards or computer documents go into the Content File. This file contains substantive information of interest from a source, usually its major findings, details of methodology, definitions of concepts, or interesting quotes. If you directly quote from a source or want to take some specific information from a source, you need to record the specific page number(s) on which the quote appears. Link the files by putting key source information, such as author and date, on each content file.

What to Record.   You will find it much easier to take all notes on the same type and size of paper or card, rather than having some notes on sheets of papers, others on cards, and so on. Researchers have to decide what to record about an article, book, or other source. It is better to err in the direction of recording too much rather than too little. In general, record the hypotheses tested, how major concepts were measured, the main findings, the basic design of the research, the group or sample used, and ideas for future study (see Box 4.2). It is wise to examine the report's bibliography and note sources that you can add to your search.

How to Read Journal Articles

1. Read with a clear purpose or goal in mind. Are you reading for basic knowledge or to apply it to a specific question?

2. Skim the article before reading it all. What can you learn from the title, abstract, summary and conclusions, and headings? What are the topic, major findings, method, and main conclusion?

3. Consider your own orientation. What is your bias toward the topic, the method, the publication source, and so on, that may color your reading?

4. Marshal external knowledge. What do you already know about the topic and the methods used? How credible is the publication source?

5. Evaluate as you read the article. What errors are present? Do findings follow the data? Is the article consistent with assumptions of the approach it takes?

6. Summarize information as an abstract with the topic, the methods used, and the findings. Assess the factual accuracy of findings and cite questions about the article.

Source: Adapted from Katzer, Cook, and Crouch (1991: 199–207).

Photocopying all relevant articles or reports will save you time recording notes and will ensure that you will have an entire report. Also, you can make notes on the photocopy. There are several warnings about this practice. First, photocopying can be expensive for a large literature search. Second, be aware of and obey copyright laws. U.S. copyright laws permit photocopying for personal research use. Third, remember to record or photocopy the entire article, including all citation information. Fourth, organizing entire articles can be cumbersome, especially if several different parts of a single article are being used. Finally, unless you highlight carefully or take good notes, you may have to reread the entire article later.

Organize Notes. After gathering a large number of references and notes, you need an organizing scheme. One approach is to group studies or specific findings by skimming notes and creating a mental map of how they fit together. Try several organizing schemes before settling on a final one. Organizing is a skill that improves with practice. For example, place notes into piles representing common themes, or draw charts comparing what different reports state about the same question, noting agreements and disagreements.

In the process of organizing notes, you will find that some references and notes do not fit and should be discarded as irrelevant. Also, you may discover gaps or areas and topics that are relevant but that you did not examine. This necessitates return visits to the library.

There are many organizing schemes. The best one depends on the purpose of the review. Usually, it is best to organize reports around a specific research question or around core common findings of a field and the main hypotheses tested.

Writing the Review

A literature review requires planning and good, clear writing, which requires a lot of rewriting. This step is often merged with organizing notes. All the rules of good writing (e.g., clear organizational structure, an introduction and conclusion, transitions between sections, etc.) apply to writing a literature review. Keep your purposes in mind when you write, and communicate clearly and effectively.

To prepare a good review, read articles and other literature critically. Recall that skepticism is a norm of science. It means that you should not accept what is written simply on the basis of the authority of its having been published. Question what you read, and evaluate it. The first hurdle to overcome is thinking something must be perfect just because it has been published.

Critically reading research reports requires skills that take time and practice to develop. Despite a peer-review procedure and high rejection rates, errors and sloppy logic slip in. Read carefully to see whether the introduction and title really fit with the rest of the article. Sometimes, titles, abstracts, or the introduction are misleading. They may not fully explain the research project's method and results. An article should be logically tight, and all the parts should fit together. Strong logical links should exist between parts of the argument. Weak articles make leaps in logic or omit transitional steps. Likewise, articles do not always make their theory or approach to research explicit. Be prepared to read the article more than once. (See Figure 4.2 on taking notes on an article.)

What a Good Review Looks Like

An author should communicate a review's purpose to the reader by its organization. The *wrong* way to write a review is to list a series of research reports with a summary of the findings of each. This fails to communicate a sense of purpose. It reads as a set of notes strung together. Perhaps the reviewer got sloppy and skipped over the important organizing step in writing the review. The *right* way to write a review is to organize common findings or arguments together. A well-accepted approach is to address the most important ideas first, to logically link statements or findings, and to note discrepancies or weaknesses in the research (see Box 4.3 for an example).

USING THE INTERNET FOR SOCIAL RESEARCH

The Internet (see Box 4.4) has revolutionized how social researchers work. A mere decade ago, it was rarely used; today, most social researchers use the Internet regularly to help them review the literature, to communicate with other researchers, and to search for other information sources. The Internet continues to expand and change at an explosive rate.

The Internet has been a mixed blessing for social research, but it has not proved to be the panacea that some people first thought it might be. It provides new and important ways to find information, but it remains one tool among others. It can quickly make some specific pieces of information accessible. For example, from my home computer, I was able to go to the U.S. Federal Bureau of Prisons and in less than three minutes locate a table showing me that in 1980, 139 people per 100,000 were incarcerated in the United States, whereas in 2004 (the most recent data available), it was 486 per 100,000. The Internet is best thought of as a supplement rather than as a replacement for traditional library research. There are "up" and "down" sides to using the Internet for social research:

The Up Side

1. The Internet is easy, fast, and cheap. It is widely accessible and can be used from many locations. This near-free resource allows people to find source material from almost anywhere— local public libraries, homes, labs or classrooms, or anywhere a computer is connected to the Internet system. Also, the Internet does not close; it operates 24 hours a day, seven days a week. With minimal training, most people can quickly perform searches and get information on their computer screens that would have required them to take a major trip to large research libraries a few years ago. Searching a vast quantity of information electronically has always been easier and faster than a manual search, and the Internet greatly expands the amount and variety of source material. More and more information (e.g., *Statistical Abstract of the United States*) is available on the Internet. In addition, once the information is located, a researcher can often store it electronically or print it at a local site.

2. The Internet has "links" that provide additional ways to find and connect to many

FIGURE 4.2   Example of Notes on an Article

FULL CITATION ON BIBLIOGRAPHY (SOURCE FILE)

Bearman, Peter, and Hannah Bückner. 2001. "Promising the Future: Virginity Pledges and First Intercourse." *American Journal of Sociology* 106:859–912. (January, issue no. 4).

NOTE CARD (CONTENT FILE)

Bearman and Bückner 2001   **Topics:**   Teen pregnancy & sexuality, pledges/promises, virginity, first sexual intercourse, S. Baptists, identity movement

Since 1993, the Southern Baptist Church sponsored a movement among teens whereby the teens make a public pledge to remain virgins until marriage. Over 2.5 million teens have made the pledge. This study examines whether the pledge affected the timing of sexual intercourse and whether pledging teens differ from nonpledging teens. Critics of the movement are uncomfortable with it because pledge supporters often reject sex education, hold an overly romanticized view of marriage, and adhere to traditional gender roles.

Hypothesis

Adolescents will engage in behavior that adults enjoy but that is forbidden to them based on the amount of social controls that constrain opportunities to engage in forbidden behavior. Teens in nontraditional families with greater freedom and less supervision are more likely to engage in forbidden behavior (sex). Teens in traditional families and who are closer to their parents will delay sexual activity. Teens closely tied to "identity movements" outside the family will modify behavior based on norms the movements teach.

Method

Data are from a national health survey of U.S. teens in grades 7–12 who were in public or private schools in 1994–1995. A total of 90,000 students in 141 schools completed questionnaires. A second questionnaire was completed by 20,000 of the 90,000 students. The questionnaire asked about a pledge, importance of religion, and sexual activity.

Findings

The study found a substantial delay in the timing of first intercourse among pledgers. Yet, the effect of pledging varies by the age of the teen. In addition, pledging only works in some social contexts (i.e., where it is at least partially a social norm). Pledgers tend to be more religious, less developed physically, and from more traditional social and family backgrounds.

Box 4.3   Examples of Bad and Good Reviews

Example of Bad Review

Sexual harassment has many consequences. Adams, Kottke, and Padgitt (1983) found that some women students said they avoided taking a class or working with certain professors because of the risk of harassment. They also found that men and women students reacted differently. Their research was a survey of 1,000 men and women graduate and undergraduate students. Benson and Thomson's study in *Social Problems* (1982) lists many problems created by sexual harassment. In their excellent book, *The Lecherous Professor*, Dziech and Weiner (1990) give a long list of difficulties that victims have suffered.

Researchers study the topic in different ways. Hunter and McClelland (1991) conducted a study of undergraduates at a small liberal arts college. They had a sample of 300 students and students were given multiple vignettes that varied by the reaction of the victim and the situation. Jaschik and Fretz (1991) showed 90 women students at a mideastern university a videotape with a classic example of sexual harassment by a teaching assistant. Before it was labeled as *sexual harassment*, few women called it that. When asked whether it was sexual harassment, 98 percent agreed. Weber-Burdin and Rossi (1982) replicated a previous study on sexual harassment, only they used students at the University of Massachusetts. They had 59 students rate 40 hypothetical situations. Reilley, Carpenter, Dull, and Bartlett (1982) conducted a study of 250 female and 150 male undergraduates at the University of California at Santa Barbara. They also had a sample of 52 faculty. Both samples completed a questionnaire in which respondents were presented vignettes of sexual-harassing situations that they were to rate. Popovich and Colleagues (1986) created a nine-item scale of sexual harassment. They studied 209 undergraduates at a medium-sized university in groups of 15 to 25. They found disagreement and confusion among students.

Example of Better Review

The victims of sexual harassment suffer a range of consequences, from lowered self-esteem and loss of self-confidence to withdrawal from social interaction, changed career goals, and depression (Adams, Kottke, and Padgitt, 1983; Benson and Thomson, 1982; Dziech and Weiner, 1990). For example, Adams, Kottke, and Padgitt (1983) noted that 13 percent of women students said they avoided taking a class or working with certain professors because of the risk of harassment.

Research into campus sexual harassment has taken several approaches. In addition to survey research, many have experimented with vignettes or presented hypothetical scenarios (Hunter and McClelland, 1991; Jaschik and Fretz, 1991; Popovich et al., 1987; Reilley, Carpenter, Dull, and Barlett, 1982; Rossi and Anderson, 1982; Valentine-French and Radtke, 1989; Weber-Burdin and Rossi, 1982). Victim verbal responses and situational factors appear to affect whether observers label a behavior as harassment. There is confusion over the application of a sexual harassment label for inappropriate behavior. For example, Jaschik and Fretz (1991) found that only 3 percent of the women students shown a videotape with a classic example of sexual harassment by a teaching assistant initially labeled it as *sexual harassment*. Instead, they called it "sexist," "rude," "unprofessional," or "demeaning." When asked whether it was sexual harassment, 98 percent agreed. Roscoe and colleagues (1987) reported similar labeling difficulties.

---

other sources of information. Many websites, home pages, and other Internet resource pages have "hot links" that can call up information from related sites or sources simply by clicking on the link indicator (usually a button or a highlighted word or phrase). This connects people to more information and provides "instant" access to cross-referenced material. Links make

Box
4.4 **The Internet**

The Internet is not a single thing in one place. Rather, the Internet is a system or interconnected web of computers around the world. It is changing very rapidly. I cannot describe everything on the Internet; many large books attempt to do that. Plus, even if I tried, it would be out of date in six months. The Internet is changing, in a powerful way, how many people communicate and share information.

The Internet provides low-cost (often free), worldwide, fast communication among people with computers or between people with computers and information in the computers of organizations (e.g., universities, government agencies, businesses). There are special hardware and software requirements, but the Internet potentially can transmit electronic versions of text material, up to entire books, as well as photos, music, video, and other information.

To get onto the Internet, a person needs an account in a computer that is connected to the Internet. Most college mainframe computers are connected, many business or government computers are connected, and individuals with modems can purchase a connection from an Internet service provider that provides access over telephone lines, special DSL lines, or cable television lines. In addition to a microcomputer, the person needs only a little knowledge about using computers.

embedding one source within a network of related sources easy.

3. The Internet speeds the flow of information around the globe and has a "democratizing" effect. It provides rapid transmission of information (e.g., text, news, data, and photos) across long distances and international borders. Instead of waiting a week for a report or having to send off for a foreign publication and wait for a month, the information is often available in seconds at no cost. There are virtually no restrictions on who can put material on the Internet or what appears on it, so many people who had difficulty publishing or disseminating their materials can now do so with ease.

4. The Internet is the provider of a very wide range of information sources, some in formats that are more dynamic and interesting. It can send and be a resource for more than straight black and white text, as in traditional academic journals and sources. It transmits information in the form of bright colors, graphics, "action" images, audio (e.g., music, voices, sounds), photos, and video clips. Authors and other creators of information can be creative in their presentations.

The Down Side

1. There is no quality control over what gets on the Internet. Unlike standard academic publications, there is no peer-review process or any review. Anyone can put almost anything on a website. It may be poor quality, undocumented, highly biased, totally made up, or plain fraudulent. There is a lot of real "trash" out there! Once a person finds material, the real work is to distinguish the "trash" from valid information. One needs to treat a webpage with the same caution that one applies to a paper flyer someone hands out on the street; it could contain the drivel of a "nut" or be really valuable information. A less serious problem is that the "glitz" of bright colors, music, or moving images found in sites can distract unsophisticated users. The "glitz" may attract them more than serious content, and they may confuse glitz for high-caliber information. The Internet is better designed for a quick look and short attention spans rather than the slow, deliberative, careful reading and study of content.

2. Many excellent sources and some of the most important resource materials (research studies and data) for social research are *not* available on the Internet (e.g., *Sociofile*, GSS datafiles, and recent journal articles). Much information is available only through special subscription services that can be expensive.

Contrary to popular belief, the Internet has *not* made all information free and accessible to everyone. Often, what is free is limited, and fuller information is available only to those who pay. In fact, because some libraries redirected funds to buy computers for the Internet and cut the purchases for books and paper copies of documents, the Internet's overall impact may have actually reduced what is available for some users.

3. Finding sources on the Internet can be very difficult and time consuming. It is not easy to locate specific source materials. Also, different "search engines" can produce very different results. It is wise to use multiple search engines (e.g., Yahoo, Excite, and Google), since they work differently. Most search engines simply look for specific words in a short description of the webpage. This description may not reveal the full content of the source, just as a title does not fully tell what a book or article is about. In addition, search engines often come up with tens of thousands of sources, far too many for anyone to examine. The ones at the "top" may be there because they were recently added to the Internet or because their short description had several versions of the search word. The "best" or most relevant source might be buried as the 150th item found in a search. Also, one must often wade through a lot of commercials and advertisements to locate "real" information.

4. Internet sources can be "unstable" and difficult to document. After one conducts a search on the Internet and locates webpages with information, it is important to note the specific "address" (usually it starts http://) where it resides. This address refers to an electronic file sitting in a computer somewhere. If the computer file is moved, it may not be at the same address two months later. Unlike a journal article that will be stored on a shelf or on microfiche in hundreds of libraries for many decades to come and available for anyone to read, webpages can quickly vanish. This means it may not be possible to check someone's web references easily, verify a quote in a document, or go back to

original materials and read them for ideas or to build on them. Also, it is easy to copy, modify, or distort, then reproduce copies of a source. For example, a person could alter a text passage or a photo image then create a new webpage to disseminate the false information. This raises issues about copyright protection and the authenticity of source material.

There are few rules for locating the best sites on the Internet—ones that have useful and truthful information. Sources that originate at universities, research institutes, or government agencies usually are more trustworthy for research purposes than ones that are individual home pages of unspecified origin or location, or that a commercial organization or a political/social issue advocacy group sponsors. In addition to moving or disappearing, many webpages or sources fail to provide complete information to make citation easy. Better sources provide fuller or more complete information about the author, date, location, and so on.

As you prepare a review of the scholarly literature and more narrowly focus a topic, you should be thinking about how to design a study. The specifics of design can vary somewhat depending on whether your study will primarily employ a quantitative-deductive-positivist approach or a qualitative-inductive-interpretive/critical approach. The two approaches have a great deal in common and mutually complement one another, but there several places where "branches in the path" of designing a study diverge depending on the approach you adopt.

QUALITATIVE AND QUANTITATIVE ORIENTATIONS TOWARD RESEARCH

Qualitative and quantitative research differ in many ways, but they complement each other, as well. All social researchers systematically collect and analyze empirical data and carefully examine the patterns in them to understand and explain social life. One of the differences between the two styles comes from the nature of the data. *Soft data,* in the form of impressions, words, sentences, photos, symbols, and so forth, dictate different research strategies and data collection techniques than *hard data,* in the form of numbers. Another difference is that qualitative and quantitative researchers often hold different assumptions about social life and have different objectives. These differences can make tools used by the other style inappropriate or irrelevant. People who judge qualitative research by standards of quantitative research are often disappointed, and vice versa. It is best to appreciate the strengths each style offers.

To appreciate the strengths of each style, it is important to understand the distinct orientations of researchers. Qualitative researchers often rely on interpretive or critical social science, follow a nonlinear research path, and speak a language of "cases and contexts." They emphasize conducting detailed examinations of cases that arise in the natural flow of social life. They usually try to present authentic interpretations that are sensitive to specific social-historical contexts.

Almost all quantitative researchers rely on a positivist approach to social science. They follow a linear research path, speak a language of "variables and hypotheses," and emphasize precisely measuring variables and testing hypotheses that are linked to general causal explanations.

Researchers who use one style alone do not always communicate well with those using the other, but the languages and orientations of the styles are mutually intelligible. It takes time and effort to understand both styles and to see how they can be complementary.

Linear and Nonlinear Paths

Researchers follow a path when conducting research. The path is a metaphor for the sequence of things to do: what is finished first or where a researcher has been, and what comes next or where he or she is going. The path may be well worn and marked with signposts where many other researchers have trod. Alternatively, it may be a new path into unknown territory where few others have gone, and without signs marking the direction forward.

In general, quantitative researchers follow a more linear path than do qualitative researchers. A *linear research path* follows a fixed sequence of steps; it is like a staircase leading in one clear direction. It is a way of thinking and a way of looking at issues—the direct, narrow, straight path that is most common in western European and North American culture.

Qualitative research is more nonlinear and cyclical. Rather than moving in a straight line, a *nonlinear research path* makes successive passes through steps, sometimes moving backward and sideways before moving on. It is more of a spiral, moving slowly upward but not directly. With each cycle or repetition, a researcher collects new data and gains new insights.

People who are used to the direct, linear approach may be impatient with a less direct cyclical path. From a strict linear perspective, a cyclical path looks inefficient and sloppy. But the diffuse cyclical approach is not merely disorganized, undefined chaos. It can be highly effective for creating a feeling for the whole, for grasping subtle shades of meaning, for pulling together divergent information, and for switching perspectives. It is not an excuse for doing poor-quality research, and it has its own discipline and rigor. It borrows devices from the humanities (e.g., metaphor, analogy, theme, motif, and irony) and is oriented toward constructing meaning. A cyclical path is suited for tasks such as translating languages, where delicate shades of meaning, subtle connotations, or contextual distinctions can be important.

Preplanned and Emergent Research Questions

Your first step when beginning a research project is to select a topic. There is no formula for this task. Whether you are an experienced researcher or just beginning, the best guide is to conduct research on something that interests you.

All research begins with a topic but a topic is only a starting point that researchers must narrow into a focused research question. Qualitative and quantitative researchers tend to adopt different approaches to turn a topic to a focused research question for a specific study. Qualitative researchers often begin with vague or unclear research questions. The topic emerges slowly during the study. The researchers often combine focusing on a specific question with the process of deciding the details of study design that occurs while they are gathering data. By contrast, quantitative researchers narrow a topic into a focused question as a discrete planning step before they finalize study design. They use it as a step in the process of developing a testable hypothesis (to be discussed later) and to guide the study design before they collect any data.

The qualitative research style is flexible and encourages slowly focusing the topic throughout a study. In contrast to quantitative research, only a small amount of topic narrowing occurs in an early research planning stage, and most of the narrowing occurs after a researcher has begun to collect data.

The qualitative researcher begins data gathering with a general topic and notions of what will be relevant. Focusing and refining continues after he or she has gathered some of the data and started preliminary analysis. Qualitative researchers use early data collection to guide how they adjust and sharpen the research question(s) because they rarely know the most important issues or questions until after they become fully immersed in the data. Developing a focused research question is a part of the data collection process, during which the researcher actively reflects on and develops preliminary interpretations. The qualitative researcher is open to unanticipated data and constantly reevaluates the focus early in a study. He or she is prepared to change the direction of research and follow new lines of evidence.

Typical research questions for qualitative researchers include: How did a certain condition or social situation originate? How is the condition/situation maintained over time? What are the processes by which a condition/situation changes, develops, or operates? A different type of question tries to confirm existing beliefs or assumptions. A last type of question tries to discover new ideas.

Research projects are designed around research problems or questions. Before designing a project, quantitative researchers focus on a specific research problem within a broad topic. For example, your personal experience might suggest labor unions as a topic. "Labor unions" is a topic, not a research question or a problem. In any large library, you will find hundreds of books and thousands of articles written by sociologists, historians, economists, management officials, political scientists, and others on unions. The books and articles focus on different aspects of the topic and adopt many perspectives on it. Before proceeding to design a research project, you must narrow and focus the topic. An example research question is, "How much did U.S. labor unions contribute to racial inequality by creating barriers to skilled jobs for African Americans in the post–World War II period?"

When starting research on a topic, ask yourself: What is it about the topic that is of greatest interest? For a topic about which you know little, first get background knowledge by reading about it. Research questions refer to the relationships among a small number of variables. Identify a limited number of variables and specify the relationships among them.

A research question has one or a small number of causal relationships. Box 4.5 lists some ways to focus a topic into a research question. For example, the question, "What causes divorce?" is not a good research question. A better research question is, "Is age at marriage associated with divorce?" The second question suggests two variables: age of marriage and divorce.

Box 4.5	**Techniques for Narrowing a Topic into a Research Question**

1. *Examine the literature.* Published articles are an excellent source of ideas for research questions. They are usually at an appropriate level of specificity and suggest research questions that focus on the following:

   a. Replicate a previous research project exactly or with slight variations.

   b. Explore unexpected findings discovered in previous research.

   c. Follow suggestions an author gives for future research at the end of an article.

   d. Extend an existing explanation or theory to a new topic or setting.

   e. Challenge findings or attempt to refute a relationship.

   f. Specify the intervening process and consider linking relations.

2. *Talk over ideas with others.*

   a. Ask people who are knowledgeable about the topic for questions about it that they have thought of.

   b. Seek out those who hold opinions that differ from yours on the topic and discuss possible research questions with them.

3. *Apply to a specific context.*

   a. Focus the topic onto a specific historical period or time period.

   b. Narrow the topic to a specific society or geographic unit.

   c. Consider which subgroups or categories of people/units are involved and whether there are differences among them.

4. *Define the aim or desired outcome of the study.*

   a. Will the research question be for an exploratory, explanatory, or descriptive study?

   b. Will the study involve applied or basic research?

Another technique for focusing a research question is to specify the *universe* to which the answer to the question can be generalized. All research questions, hypotheses, and studies apply to some group or category of people, organizations, or other units. The *universe* is the set of all units that the research covers, or to which it can be generalized. For example, your research question is about the effects of a new attendance policy on learning by high school students. The universe, in this case, is all high school students.

When refining a topic into a research question and designing a research project, you also need to consider practical limitations. Designing a perfect research project is an interesting academic exercise, but if you expect to carry out a research project, practical limitations will have an impact on its design.

Major limitations include time, costs, access to resources, approval by authorities, ethical concerns, and expertise. If you have 10 hours a week for five weeks to conduct a research project, but the answer to a research question will take five years, reformulate the research question more narrowly. Estimating the amount of time required to answer a research question is difficult. The research question specified, the research technique used, and the type of data collected all play significant roles. Experienced researchers are the best source of good estimates.

Cost is another limitation. As with time, there are inventive ways to answer a question within limitations, but it may be impossible to answer some questions because of the expense involved. For example, a research question about the attitudes of all sports fans toward their team mascot can be answered only with a great investment of time and money. Narrowing the research question to how students at two different colleges feel about their mascots might make it more manageable.

Access to resources is a common limitation. Resources can include the expertise of others, special equipment, or information. For example, a research question about burglary rates and family income in many different nations is almost impossible to answer because information on burglary and income is not collected or available for most countries. Some questions require the approval of authorities (e.g., to see medical records) or involve violating basic ethical principles (e.g., causing serious physical harm to a person to see the person's reaction). The expertise or background of the researcher is also a limitation. Answering some research questions involves the use of data collection techniques, statistical methods, knowledge of a foreign language, or skills that the researcher may not have. Unless the researcher can acquire the necessary training or can pay for another person's services, the research question may not be practical.

In summary, styles of qualitative and quantitative researchers have much in common, but the researchers often differ on design issues, such as taking a linear or nonlinear research path and developing a research question (see Table 4.1). In addition, researchers tend to adopt a different language and approach to study design, which we will consider next.

QUALITATIVE DESIGN ISSUES

The Language of Cases and Contexts

Qualitative researchers use a language of cases and contexts, examine social processes and cases in their social context, and look at interpretations or the creation of meaning in specific settings. They try look at social life from multiple points of view and explain how people construct identities. Only rarely do they use variables or test hypotheses, or try to convert social life into numbers.

Qualitative researchers see most areas and activities of social life as being intrinsically qualitative. To them, qualitative data are not imprecise or deficient; they are highly meaningful.

TABLE 4.1   Quantitative Research versus Qualitative Research

Quantitative Research	Qualitative Research
Test hypothesis that the researcher begins with.	Capture and discover meaning once the researcher becomes immersed in the data.
Concepts are in the form of distinct variables.	Concepts are in the form of themes, motifs, generalizations, and taxonomies.
Measures are systematically created before data collection and are standardized.	Measures are created in an ad hoc manner and are often specific to the individual setting or researcher.
Data are in the form of numbers from precise measurement.	Data are in the form of words and images from documents, observations, and transcripts.
Theory is largely causal and is deductive.	Theory can be causal or noncausal and is often inductive.
Procedures are standard, and replication is assumed.	Research procedures are particular, and replication is very rare.
Analysis proceeds by using statistics, tables, or charts and discussing how what they show relates to hypotheses.	Analysis proceeds by extracting themes or generalizations from evidence and organizing data to present a coherent, consistent picture.

Instead of trying to convert social life into variables or numbers, qualitative researchers borrow ideas from the people they study and place them within the context of a natural setting. They examine motifs, themes, distinctions, and ideas instead of variables, and they adopt the inductive approach of *grounded theory.*

Some people believe that qualitative data are "soft," intangible, and immaterial. Such data are so fuzzy and elusive that researchers cannot really capture them. This is not necessarily the case. Qualitative data are empirical. They involve documenting real events, recording what people say (with words, gestures, and tone), observing specific behaviors, studying written documents, or examining visual images. These are all concrete aspects of the world. For example, some qualitative researchers take and closely scrutinize photos or videotapes of people or social events. This evidence is just as "hard" and physical as that used by quantitative researchers to measure attitudes, social pressure, intelligence, and the like.

Grounded Theory

A qualitative researcher develops theory during the data collection process. This more inductive method means that theory is built from data or grounded in the data. Moreover, conceptualization and operationalization occur simultaneously with data collection and preliminary data analysis. It makes qualitative research flexible and lets data and theory interact. Qualitative researchers remain open to the unexpected, are willing to change the direction or focus of a research project, and may abandon their original research question in the middle of a project.

A qualitative researcher builds theory by making comparisons. For example, when a researcher observes an event (e.g., a police officer confronting a speeding motorist), he or she immediately ponders questions and looks for similarities and differences. When watching a police officer stop a speeder, a qualitative researcher asks: Does the police officer always radio in the car's license number before proceeding? After radioing the car's location, does the officer ask the motorist to get out of the car sometimes, but in others casually walk up to the car and talk to the seated driver? When data collection and theorizing are interspersed, theoretical questions arise that suggest future observations, so new data are tailored to answer theoretical questions that came from thinking about previous data.

The Context Is Critical

Qualitative researchers emphasize the social context for understanding the social world. They hold that the meaning of a social action or statement depends, in an important way, on the context in which it appears. When a researcher removes an event, social action, answer to a question, or conversation from the social context in which it appears, or ignores the context, social meaning and significance are distorted.

Attention to social context means that a qualitative researcher notes what came before or what surrounds the focus of study. It also implies that the same events or behaviors can have different meanings in different cultures or historical eras. For example, instead of ignoring the context and counting votes across time or cultures, a qualitative researcher asks: What does voting mean in the context? He or she may treat the same behavior (e.g., voting for a presidential candidate) differently depending on the social context in which it occurs. Qualitative researchers place parts of social life into a larger whole. Otherwise, the meaning of the part may be lost. For example, it is hard to understand what a baseball glove is without knowing something about the game of baseball. The whole of the game—innings, bats, curve balls, hits—gives meaning to each part, and each part without the whole has little meaning.

The Case and Process

In quantitative research, cases are usually the same as a unit of analysis, or the unit on which variables are measured (discussed later). Quantitative researchers typically measure variables of their hypotheses across many cases. For example, if a researcher conducts a survey of 450 individuals, each individual is a case or unit on which he or she measures variables. Qualitative researchers tend to use a "case-oriented approach [that] places cases, not variables, center stage" (Ragin, 1992:5). They examine a wide variety of aspects of one or a few cases. Their analyses emphasize contingencies in "messy" natural settings (i.e., the co-occurrence of many specific factors and events in one place and time). Explanations or interpretations are complex and may be in the form of an unfolding plot or a narrative story about particular people or specific events. Rich detail and astute insight into the cases replace the sophisticated statistical analysis of precise measures across a huge number of units or cases found in quantitative research.

The passage of time is integral to qualitative research. Qualitative researchers look at the sequence of events and pay attention to what happens first, second, third, and so on. Because qualitative researchers examine the same case or set of cases over time, they can see an issue evolve, a conflict emerge, or a social relationship develop. The researcher can detect process and causal relations.

In historical research, the passage of time may involve years or decades. In field research, the passage of time is shorter. Nevertheless, in both, a researcher notes what is occurring at different points in time and recognizes that *when* something occurs is often important.

Interpretation

Interpretation means to assign significance or a coherent meaning to something. Quantitative and qualitative researchers both interpret data, but they do so in different ways. A quantitative researcher gives meaning by rearranging, examining, and discussing the numbers by using charts and statistics to explain how patterns in the data relate to the research question. A qualitative researcher gives meaning by rearranging, examining, and discussing textual or visual data in a way that conveys an authentic voice, or that remains true to the original understandings of the people and situations that he or she studied.

Instead of relying on charts, statistics, and displays of numbers, qualitative researchers put a greater emphasis on interpreting the data. Their data are often "richer" or more complex and full of meaning. The qualitative researcher interprets to "translate" or make the originally gathered data understandable to other people. The process of qualitative interpretation moves through three stages or levels.

A researcher begins with the point of view of the people he or she is studying, and the researcher wants to grasp fully how they see the world, how they define situations, or what things mean to them. A *first-order interpretation* contains the inner motives, personal reasons, and point of view of the people who are being studied in the original context. As the researcher discovers and documents this first-order interpretation, he or she remains one step removed from it. The researcher offers a *second-order interpretation,* which is an acknowledgment that however much a researcher tries to get very close and "under the skin" of those he or she is studying, a researcher is still "on the outside looking in." In the second-order interpretation, the researcher tries to elicit an underlying coherence or sense of overall meaning in the data. To reach an understanding of what he or she sees or hears, a researcher often places the data into a context of the larger flow of events and behaviors. A qualitative researcher will often move to the third step and link the understanding that he or she achieved to larger concepts, generalizations, or theories. The researcher can share this broader interpretation with other people who are unfamiliar with the original data, the people and events studied, or the social situations observed by the researcher. This level of meaning translates the researcher's own understanding in a way that facilitates communication with people who are more distant from the original source, and it represents a *third-order interpretation.*

QUANTITATIVE DESIGN ISSUES

The Language of Variables and Hypotheses

Variation and Variables. The *variable* is a central idea in quantitative research. Simply defined, a variable is a concept that varies. Quantitative research uses a language of variables and relationships among variables.

In Chapter 2, you learned about two types of concepts: those that refer to a fixed phenomenon (e.g., the ideal type of bureaucracy) and those that vary in quantity, intensity, or amount (e.g., amount of education). The second type of concept and measures of the concepts are variables. Variables take on two or more values. Once you begin to look for them, you will see variables everywhere. For example, gender is a variable; it can take on two values: male or female. Marital status is a variable; it can take on the values of never married single, married, divorced, or widowed. Type of crime committed is a variable; it can take on values of robbery, burglary, theft, murder, and so forth. Family income is a variable; it can take on values from zero to billions of dollars. A person's attitude toward abortion is a variable; it can range from strongly favoring legal abortion to strongly believing in antiabortion.

The values or the categories of a variable are its *attributes.* It is easy to confuse variables with attributes. Variables and attributes are related, but they have distinct purposes. The confusion arises because the attribute of one variable can itself become a separate variable with a slight change in definition. The distinction is between concepts themselves that vary and conditions within concepts that vary. For example, "male" is not a variable; it describes a category of gender and is an attribute of the variable "gender." Yet, a related idea, "degree of masculinity," is a

variable. It describes the intensity or strength of attachment to attitudes, beliefs, and behaviors associated with the concept of *masculine* within a culture. "Married" is not a variable; it is an attribute of the variable "marital status." Related ideas such as "number of years married" or "depth of commitment to a marriage" are variables. Likewise, "robbery" is not a variable; it is an attribute of the variable "type of crime." "Number of robberies," "robbery rate," "amount taken during a robbery," and "type of robbery" are all variables because they vary or take on a range of values.

Quantitative researchers redefine concepts of interest into the language of variables. As the examples of variables and attributes illustrate, slight changes in definition change a nonvariable into a variable concept. As you saw in Chapter 2, concepts are the building blocks of theory; they organize thinking about the social world. Clear concepts with careful definitions are essential in theory.

Types of Variables. Researchers who focus on causal relations usually begin with an effect, then search for its causes. Variables are classified into three basic types, depending on their location in a causal relationship. The cause variable, or the one that identifies forces or conditions that act on something else, is the *independent variable.* The variable that is the effect or is the result or outcome of another variable is the *dependent variable.* The independent variable is "independent of" prior causes that act on it, whereas the dependent variable "depends on" the cause.

It is not always easy to determine whether a variable is independent or dependent. Two questions help you identify the independent variable. First, does it come before other variables in time? Independent variables come before any other type. Second, if the variables occur at the same time, does the author suggest that one variable has an impact on another variable? Independent variables affect or have an impact on other variables. Research topics are often phrased in terms of the dependent variables because dependent variables are the phenomenon to be explained. For example, suppose a researcher examines the reasons for an increase in the crime rate in Dallas, Texas; the dependent variable is the crime rate.

A basic causal relationship requires only an independent and a dependent variable. A third type of variable, the *intervening variable,* appears in more complex causal relations. It comes between the independent and dependent variables and shows the link or mechanism between them. Advances in knowledge depend not only on documenting cause-and-effect relationships but also on specifying the mechanisms that account for the causal relation. In a sense, the intervening variable acts as a dependent variable with respect to the independent variable and acts as an independent variable toward the dependent variable.

For example, French sociologist Emile Durkheim developed a theory of suicide that specified a causal relationship between marital status and suicide rates. Durkheim found evidence that married people are less likely to commit suicide than single people. He believed that married people have greater social integration (i.e., feelings of belonging to a group or family). He thought that a major cause of one type of suicide was that people lacked a sense of belonging to a group. Thus, his theory can be restated as a three-variable relationship: marital status (independent variable) causes the degree of social integration (intervening variable), which affects suicide (dependent variable). Specifying the chain of causality makes the linkages in a theory clearer and helps a researcher test complex explanations.[1]

Simple theories have one dependent and one independent variable, whereas complex theories can contain dozens of variables with multiple independent, intervening, and dependent variables. For example, a theory of criminal behavior (dependent variable) identifies four independent variables: an individual's economic hardship, opportunities to commit crime easily, membership in a deviant subgroup of society that does not disapprove of crime, and lack of punishment for criminal acts. A multicause explanation usually specifies the independent variable that has the greatest causal effect.

A complex theoretical explanation contains a string of multiple intervening variables that are linked together. For example, family disruption causes lower self-esteem among children, which causes depression, which causes poor grades in school, which causes reduced prospects for a good job, which causes a lower adult income. The chain of variables is: family disruption (independent), childhood self-esteem (intervening), depression (intervening), grades in school (intervening), job prospects (intervening), adult income (dependent).

Two theories on the same topic may have different independent variables or predict different independent variables to be important. In addition, theories may agree about the independent and dependent variables but differ on the intervening variable or causal mechanism. For example, two theories say that family disruption causes lower adult income, but for different reasons. One theory holds that disruption encourages children to join deviant peer groups that are not socialized to norms of work and thrift. Another emphasizes the impact of the disruption on childhood depression and poor academic performance, which directly affect job performance.

A single research project usually tests only a small part of a causal chain. For example, a research project examining six variables may take the six from a large, complex theory with two dozen variables. Explicit links to a larger theory strengthen and clarify a research project. This applies especially for explanatory, basic research, which is the model for most quantitative research.

Causal Theory and Hypotheses

The Hypothesis and Causality.   A *hypothesis* is a proposition to be tested or a tentative statement of a relationship between two variables. Hypotheses are guesses about how the social

Box 4.6	**Five Characteristics of Causal Hypotheses**

1. It has at least two variables.
2. It expresses a causal or cause-effect relationship between the variables.
3. It can be expressed as a prediction or an expected future outcome.
4. It is logically linked to a research question and a theory.
5. It is falsifiable; that is, it is capable of being tested against empirical evidence and shown to be true or false.

world works; they are stated in a value-neutral form.

A causal hypothesis has five characteristics (see Box 4.6). The first two characteristics define the minimum elements of a hypothesis. The third restates the hypothesis. For example, the hypothesis that attending religious services reduces the probability of divorce can be restated as a prediction: Couples who attend religious services frequently have a lower divorce rate than do couples who rarely attend religious services. The prediction can be tested against empirical evidence. The fourth characteristic states that the hypothesis should be logically tied to a research question and to a theory. Researchers test hypotheses to answer the research question or to find empirical support for a theory. The last characteristic requires that a researcher use empirical data to test the hypothesis. Statements that are necessarily true as a result of logic, or questions that are impossible to answer through empirical observation (e.g., What is the "good life"? Is there a God?) cannot be scientific hypotheses.

Testing and Refining Hypothesis. Knowledge rarely advances on the basis of one test of a single hypothesis. In fact, it is easy to get a distorted picture of the research process by focusing on a single research project that tests one hypothesis. Knowledge develops over time as researchers throughout the scientific community test many hypotheses. It grows from shifting and winnowing through many hypotheses. Each hypothesis represents an explanation of a dependent variable. If the evidence fails to support some hypotheses, they are gradually eliminated from consideration. Those that receive support remain in contention. Theorists and researchers constantly create new hypotheses to challenge those that have received support. Figure 4.3 represents an example of the process of shifting through hypotheses over time.

Scientists are a skeptical group. Support for a hypothesis in one research project is not sufficient for them to accept it. The principle of replication says that a hypothesis needs several tests with consistent and repeated support to gain broad acceptance. Another way to strengthen confidence in a hypothesis is to test related causal linkages in the theory from which it comes.

Types of Hypotheses. Hypotheses are links in a theoretical causal chain and can take several forms. Researchers use them to test the direction and strength of a relationship between variables. When a hypothesis defeats its competitors, or offers alternative explanations for a causal relation, it indirectly lends support to the researcher's explanation. A curious aspect of hypothesis testing is that researchers treat evidence that supports a hypothesis differently from evidence that opposes it. They give negative evidence more importance. The idea that negative evidence is critical when evaluating a hypothesis comes from the *logic of disconfirming hypotheses.*[2] It is associated with Karl Popper's idea of falsification and with the use of null hypotheses (see later in this section).

A hypothesis is never proved, but it can be disproved. A researcher with supporting evidence can say only that the hypothesis remains a possibility or that it is still in the running.

FIGURE 4.3   How the Process of Hypotheses Testing Operates over Time

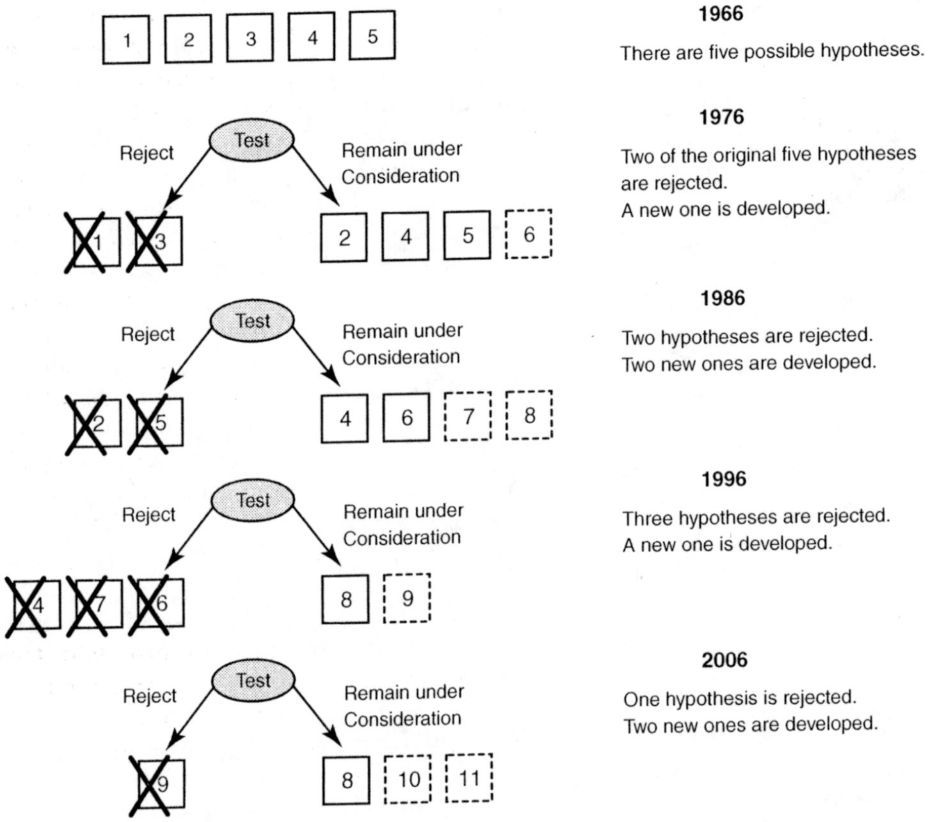

1966

There are five possible hypotheses.

1976

Two of the original five hypotheses
are rejected.
A new one is developed.

1986

Two hypotheses are rejected.
Two new ones are developed.

1996

Three hypotheses are rejected.
A new one is developed.

2006

One hypothesis is rejected.
Two new ones are developed.

In 2006, 3 hypotheses are in contention, but from 1966 to 2006, 11 hypotheses were considered, and over time, 8 of them were rejected in one or more tests.

Negative evidence is more significant because the hypothesis becomes "tarnished" or "soiled" if the evidence fails to support it. This is because a hypothesis makes predictions. Negative and disconfirming evidence shows that the predictions are wrong. Positive or confirming evidence for a hypothesis is less critical because alternative hypotheses may make the same prediction. A researcher who finds confirming evidence for a prediction may not elevate one explanation over its alternatives.

For example, a man stands on a street corner with an umbrella and claims that his umbrella protects him from falling elephants. His hypothesis that the umbrella provides protection has supporting evidence. He has not had a single elephant fall on him in all the time he has had his umbrella open. Yet, such supportive evidence is weak; it also is consistent with an alternative hypothesis—that elephants do not fall from the sky. Both predict that the man will be safe from falling elephants. Negative evidence for the hypothesis—the one elephant that falls on him and his umbrella, crushing both—would destroy the hypothesis for good.

Researchers test hypotheses in two ways: a straightforward way and a null hypothesis way. Many quantitative researchers, especially experimenters, frame hypotheses in terms of a *null hypothesis* based on the logic of the disconfirming hypotheses. They test hypotheses by looking for evidence that will allow them to accept or reject the null hypothesis. Most people talk about a hypothesis as a way to predict a relationship. The null hypothesis does the opposite. It predicts no relationship. For example, Sarah believes that students who live on campus in dormitories get higher grades than students who live off campus and commute to college. Her null hypothesis is that there is no relationship between residence and grades. Researchers use the null hypothesis with a corresponding *alternative hypothesis* or *experimental hypothesis*. The alternative hypothesis says that a relationship exists. Sarah's alternative hypothesis is that students' on-campus residence has a positive effect on grades.

For most people, the null hypothesis approach is a backward way of hypothesis testing. Null hypothesis thinking rests on the assumption that researchers try to discover a relationship, so hypothesis testing should be designed to make finding a relationship more demanding. A researcher who uses the null hypothesis approach only directly tests the null hypothesis. If evidence supports or leads the researcher to accept the null hypothesis, he or she concludes that the tested relationship does not exist. This implies that the alternative hypothesis is false. On the other hand, if the researcher can find evidence to reject the null hypothesis, then the alternative hypotheses remain a possibility. The researcher cannot prove the alternative; rather, by testing the null hypotheses, he or she keeps the alternative hypotheses in contention. When null hypothesis testing is added to confirming evidence, the argument for an alterative hypothesis can grow stronger over time.

Many people find the null hypothesis to be confusing. Another way to think of it is that the scientific community is extremely cautious. It prefers to consider a causal relationship to be false until mountains of evidence show it to be true. This is similar to the Anglo-American legal idea of innocent until proved guilty. A researcher assumes, or acts as if, the null hypothesis is correct until *reasonable doubt* suggests otherwise. Researchers who use null hypotheses generally use it with specific statistical tests (e.g., t-test or F-test). Thus, a researcher may say there is reasonable doubt in a null hypothesis if a statistical test suggests that the odds of it being false are 99 in 100. This is what a researcher means when he or she says that statistical tests allow him or her to "reject the null hypothesis at the .01 level of significance."

Aspects of Explanation

Clarity about Units and Levels of Analysis.   It is easy to become confused at first about the ideas of units and levels of analysis. Nevertheless, they are important for clearly thinking through and planning a research project. All studies have both units and levels of analysis, but few researchers explicitly identify them as such. The levels and units of analysis are restricted by the topic and the research question.

A *level of analysis* is the level of social reality to which theoretical explanations refer. The level of social reality varies on a continuum from micro level (e.g., small groups or individual processes) to macro level (e.g., civilizations or structural aspects of society). The level includes a mix of the number of people, the amount of space, the scope of the activity, and the length of time. For example, an extreme micro-level analysis can involve a few seconds of interaction between two people in the same small room. An extreme macro-level analysis can involve billions of people on several continents across centuries. Most social research uses a level of analysis that lies between these extremes.

The level of analysis delimits the kinds of assumptions, concepts, and theories that a researcher uses. For example, I want to study the topic of dating among college students. I use a micro-level analysis and develop an explanation that uses concepts such as interpersonal contact, mutual friendships, and common interests. I think that students are likely to date someone with whom they have had personal contact in a class, share friends in common, and share common interests. The topic and focus fit with a micro-level explanation because they are targeted at the level of face-to-face interaction among individuals. Another example topic is how inequality affects the forms of violent behavior in a society. Here, I have chosen a more macro-level explanation because of the topic and the level of social reality at which it operates. I am interested in the degree of inequality (e.g., the distribution of wealth, property, income, and other resources) throughout a society and in patterns of societal violence (e.g., aggression against other societies, sexual assault, feuds between families). The topic and research question suggest macro-level concepts and theories.

The *unit of analysis* refers to the type of unit a researcher uses when measuring. Common units in sociology are the individual, the group (e.g., family, friendship group), the organization (e.g., corporation, university), the social category (e.g., social class, gender, race), the social institution (e.g., religion, education, the family), and the society (e.g., a nation, a tribe). Although the individual is the most commonly used unit of analysis, it is by no means the only one. Different theories emphasize one or another unit of analysis, and different research techniques are associated with specific units of analysis. For example, the individual is usually the unit of analysis in survey and experimental research.

As an example, the individual is the unit of analysis in a survey in which 150 students are asked to rate their favorite football player. The individual is the unit because each individual student's response is recorded. On the other hand, a study that compares the amounts different colleges spend on their football programs would use the organization (the college) as the unit of analysis because the spending by colleges is being compared and each college's spending is recorded.

Researchers use units of analysis other than individuals, groups, organizations, social categories, institutions, and societies. For example, a researcher wants to determine whether the speeches of two candidates for president of the United States contain specific themes. The researcher uses content analysis and measures the themes in each speech of the candidates. Here, the speech is the unit of analysis. Geographic units of analysis are also used. A researcher interested in determining whether cities that have a high number of teenagers also have a high rate of vandalism would use the city as the unit of analysis. This is because the researcher measures the percentage of teenagers in each city and the amount of vandalism for each city.

The units of analysis determine how a researcher measures variables or themes. They also correspond loosely to the level of analysis in an explanation. Thus, social-psychological or micro levels of analysis fit with the individual as a unit of analysis, whereas macro levels of analysis fit with the social category or institution as a unit. Theories and explanations at the micro level generally refer to features of individuals or interactions among individuals. Those at the macro level refer to social forces operating across a society or relations among major parts of a society as a whole.

Researchers use levels and units of analysis to design research projects, and being aware of them helps researchers avoid logical errors. For example, a study that examines whether colleges in the North spend more on their football programs than do colleges in the South implies that a researcher gathers information on spending by college and the location of each college. The unit of analysis—the organization or, specifically, the college—flows from the research problem and tells the researcher to collect data from each college.

Researchers choose among different units or levels of analysis for similar topics or research questions. For example, a researcher could conduct a project on the topic of patriarchy and violence with society as the unit of analysis for the research question, "Are patriarchal societies more violent?" He or she would collect data on societies and classify each society by its degree of patriarchy and its level of violence. On the other hand, if the research question was "Is the degree of patriarchy within a family associated with violence against a spouse?" the unit of analysis could be the group or the family, and a more micro level of analysis would be appropriate. The researcher could collect data on families by measuring the degree of patriarchy within different families and the level of violence between spouses in these families. The same topic can be addressed with different levels and units of analysis because patriarchy can be a variable that describes an entire society, or it can describe social relations within one family. Likewise, violence can be defined as general behavior across a society, or as the interpersonal actions of one spouse toward the other.

Ecological Fallacy.   The *ecological fallacy* arises from a mismatch of units of analysis. It refers to a poor fit between the units for which a researcher has empirical evidence and the units for which he or she wants to make statements. It is due to imprecise reasoning and generalizing beyond what the evidence warrants. Ecological fallacy occurs when a researcher gathers data at a *higher* or an *aggregated* unit of analysis but wants to make a statement about a *lower* or *disaggregated* unit. It is a fallacy because what happens in one unit of analysis does not always hold for a different unit of analysis. Thus, if a researcher gathers data for large aggregates (e.g., organizations, entire countries, etc.) and then draws conclusions about the behavior of individuals from those data, he or she is committing the ecological fallacy. You can avoid this error by ensuring that the unit of analysis you use in an explanation is the same as or very

close to the unit on which you collect data (see Box 4.7).

Example.   Tomsville and Joansville each have about 45,000 people living in them. Tomsville has a high percentage of upper-income people. Over half of the households in the town have family incomes of over $200,000. The town also has more motorcycles registered in it than any other town of its size. The town of Joansville has many poor people. Half its households live

Box 4.7   The Ecological Fallacy

Researchers have criticized the famous study *Suicide* ([1897] 1951) by Emile Durkheim for the ecological fallacy of treating group data as though they were individual-level data. In the study, Durkheim compared the suicide rates of Protestant and Catholic districts in nineteenth-century western Europe and explained observed differences as due to differences between people's beliefs and practices in the two religions. He said that Protestants had a higher suicide rate than Catholics because they were more individualistic and had lower social integration. Durkheim and early researchers only had data by district. Since people tended to reside with others of the same religion, Durkheim used group-level data (i.e., region) for individuals.

Later researchers (van Poppel and Day, 1996) reexamined nineteenth-century suicide rates only with individual-level data that they discovered for some areas. They compared the death records and looked at the official reason of death and religion, but their results differed from Durkheim's. Apparently, local officials at that time recorded deaths differently for people of different religions. They recorded "unspecified" as a reason for death far more often for Catholics because of a strong moral prohibition against suicide among Catholics. Durkheim's larger theory may be correct, yet the evidence he had to test it was weak because he used data aggregated at the group level while trying to explain the actions of individuals.

below the poverty line. It also has fewer motor-cycles registered in it than any other town its size. But it is a *fallacy* to say, on the basis of this information alone, that rich people are more likely to own motorcycles or that the evidence shows a relationship between family income and motorcycle ownership. The reason is that we do not know which families in Tomsville or Joans-ville own motorcycles. We only know about the two variables—average income and number of motorcycles—for the towns as a whole. The unit of analysis for observing variables is the town as a whole. Perhaps all of the low- and middle-income families in Tomsville belong to a motor-cycle club, and not a single upper-income family belongs. Or perhaps one rich family and five poor ones in Joansville each own motorcycles. In order to make a statement about the relation-ship between family ownership of motorcycles and family income, we have to collect informa-tion on families, not on towns as a whole.

Reductionism. Another problem involving mismatched units of analysis and imprecise rea-soning about evidence is *reductionism,* also called the *fallacy of nonequivalence* (see Box 4.8). This error occurs when a researcher explains macro-level events but has evidence only about specific individuals. It occurs when a researcher observes a *lower* or *disaggregated* unit of analysis but makes statements about the operations of *higher* or *aggregated* units. It is a mirror image of the mismatch error in the ecological fallacy. A researcher who has data on how individuals behave but makes statements about the dynam-ics of macro-level units is committing the error of reductionism. It occurs because it is often eas-ier to get data on concrete individuals. Also, the operation of macro-level units is more abstract and nebulous. As with the ecological fallacy, you can avoid this error by ensuring that the unit of analysis in your explanation is very close to the one for which you have evidence.

Researchers who fail to think precisely about the units of analysis and those who do not couple data with the theory are likely to commit

the ecological fallacy or reductionism. They make a mistake about the data appropriate for a research question, or they may seriously over-generalize from the data.

You can make assumptions about units of analysis other than the ones you study empiri-cally. Thus, research on individuals rests on assumptions that individuals act within a set of social institutions. Research on social institu-tions is based on assumptions about individual behavior. We know that many micro-level units form macro-level units. The danger is that it is easy to slide into using the causes or behavior of micro units, such as individuals, to explain the actions of macro units, such as social institu-tions. What happens among units at one level does not necessarily hold for different units of analysis. Sociology is a discipline that rests on the fundamental belief that a distinct level of social reality exists beyond the individual. Expla-nations of this level require data and theory that go beyond the individual alone. The causes, forces, structures, or processes that exist among macro units cannot be reduced to individual behavior.

Example. Why did World War I occur? You may have heard that it was because a Serbian shot an archduke in the AustroHungarian Empire in 1914. This is reductionism. Yes, the assassination was a factor, but the macro-political event between nations—war—cannot be reduced to a specific act of one individual. If it could, we could also say that the war occurred because the assassin's alarm clock worked and woke him up that morning. If it had not worked, there would have been no assassination, so the alarm clock caused the war! The event, World War I, was much more complex and was due to many social, political, and economic forces that came together at a point in history. The actions of specific individuals had a role, but only a minor one compared to these macro forces. Individuals affect events, which eventually, in combination with larger-scale social forces and organizations, affect others and move nations,

Box 4.8   Error of Reductionism

Suppose you pick up a book and read the following:

American race relations changed dramatically during the Civil Rights Era of the 1960s. Attitudes among the majority, white population shifted to greater tolerance as laws and court rulings changed across the nation. Opportunities that had been legally and officially closed to all but the white population—in the areas of housing, jobs, schooling, voting rights, and so on—were opened to people of all races. From the Brown vs. Board of Education decision in 1955, to the Civil Rights Act of 1964, to the War on Poverty from 1966 to 1968, a new, dramatic outlook swept the country. This was the result of the vision, dedication, and actions of America's foremost civil rights leader, Dr. Martin Luther King Jr.

This says: *dependent variable* = major change in U.S. race relations over a 10- to 13-year period; *independent variable* = King's vision and actions.

If you know much about the civil rights era, you see a problem. The entire civil rights movement and its successes are attributed to a single individual. Yes, one individual does make a difference and helps build and guide a movement, but the *movement* is missing. The idea of a social-political movement as a causal force is reduced to its major leader. The distinct social phenomenon—a movement—is obscured. Lost are the actions of hundreds of thousands of people (marches, court cases, speeches, prayer meetings, sit-ins, rioting, petitions, beatings, etc.) involved in advancing a shared goal and the responses to them. The movement's ideology,

popular mobilization, politics, organization, and strategy are absent. Related macro-level historical events and trends that may have influenced the movement (e.g., Vietnam War protest, mood shift with the killing of John F. Kennedy, African American separatist politics, African American migration to urban North) are also ignored.

This error is not unique to historical explanations. Many people think only in terms of individual actions and have an individualist bias, sometimes called *methodological individualism*. This is especially true in the extremely individualistic U.S. culture. The error is that it disregards units of analysis or forces beyond the individual. The *error of reductionism* shifts explanation to a much lower unit of analysis. One could continue to reduce from an individual's behavior to biological processes in a person, to micro-level neurochemical activities, to the subatomic level.

Most people live in "social worlds" focused on local, immediate settings and their interactions with a small set of others, so their everyday sense of reality encourages seeing social trends or events as individual actions or psychological processes. Often, they become blind to more abstract, macro-level entities—social forces, processes, organizations, institutions, movements, or structures. The idea that all social actions cannot be reduced to individuals alone is the core of sociology. In his classic work *Suicide*, Emile Durkheim fought methodological individualism and demonstrated that larger, unrecognized social forces explain even highly individual, private actions.

---

but individual actions alone are not the cause. Thus, it is likely that a war would have broken out at about that time even if the assassination had not occurred.

Spuriousness. To call a relationship between variables *spurious* means that it is false, a mirage. Researchers get excited if they think they have found a spurious relationship because they can show that what appears on the surface is false

and a more complex relation exists. Any association between two variables might be spurious, so researchers are cautious when they discover that two variables are associated; upon further investigation, it may not be the basis for a real causal relationship. It may be an illusion, just like the mirage that resembles a pool of water on a road during a hot day.

Spuriousness occurs when two variables appear to be associated but are not causally

Box 4.9   Night-Lights and Spuriousness

For many years, researchers observed a strong positive association between the use of a night-light and children who were nearsighted. Many thought that the night-light was somehow causing the children to develop vision problems (illustrated as **a** below). Other researchers could think of no reason for a causal link between night-light use and developing nearsightedness. A 1999 study provided the answer. It found that nearsighted parents are more likely to use night-lights; they also genetically pass on their vision deficiency to their children. The study found no link between night-light use and nearsightedness once parental vision was added to the explanation (see **b** below). Thus the initial causal link was misleading or spurious (from *New York Times*, May 22, 2001).

a. Initial relationship

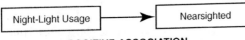

POSITIVE ASSOCIATION

b. Addition of the missing true causal factor

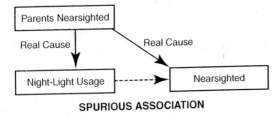

SPURIOUS ASSOCIATION

related because an unseen third factor is the real cause (see Box 4.9). The unseen third or other variable is the cause of both the independent and the dependent variable in the apparent but illusionary relationship and accounts for the observed association. In terms of conditions for causality, the unseen factor is a more powerful alternative explanation.

You now understand that you should be wary of correlations or associations, but how can

you tell whether a relationship is spurious, and how do you find out what the mysterious third factor is? You will need to use statistical techniques (discussed later in this book) to test whether an association is spurious. To use them, you need a theory or at least a guess about possible third factors. Actually, spuriousness is based on commonsense logic that you already use. For example, you already know that there is an association between the use of air conditioners and ice cream cone consumption. If you measured the number of air conditioners in use and the number of ice cream cones sold for each day, you would find a strong correlation, with more cones sold on the days when more air conditioners are in use. But you know that eating ice cream cones does not cause people to turn on air conditioners. Instead, both variables are caused by a third factor: hot days. You could verify the same thing through statistics by measuring the daily temperature as well as ice cream consumption and air conditioner use. In social research, opposing theories help people figure out which third factors are relevant for many topics (e.g., the causes of crime or the reasons for war or child abuse).

Example 1. Some people say that taking illegal drugs causes suicide, school dropouts, and violent acts. Advocates of "drugs are the problem" position point to the positive correlations between taking drugs and being suicidal, dropping out of school, and engaging in violence. They argue that ending drug use will greatly reduce suicide, dropouts, and violence. Others argue that many people turn to drugs because of their emotional problems or high levels of disorder of their communities (e.g., high unemployment, unstable families, high crime, few community services, lack of civility). The people with emotional problems or who live in disordered communities are also more likely to commit suicide, drop out, and engage in violence. This means that reducing emotional problems and community disorder will cause illegal drug use, dropping out, suicide, and violence all to decline greatly. Reducing drug taking alone will have only a limited effect because it ignores the root causes. The "drugs are the problem" argument is spurious because the initial relationship between taking illegal drugs and the problems is misleading. The emotional problems and community disorder are the true and often unseen causal variables.

Example 2.   In the United States and Canada, we observe an empirical association between students classified as being in a non-White racial category and scoring lower academic tests (compared to students classifed as in a White category). The relationship between racial classification and test scores is illusionary, because a powerful and little-recognized variable is the true cause of both the racial classification and the test scores (see Figure 4.4). In this case, the true cause operates directly on the independent variable (racial classification) but indirectly through an intervening process on the dependent variable (test scores). A belief system that is based on classifying people as belonging to racial groups and assigning great significance to superficial physical appearance, such as skin color, is the basis of what people call "race." Such a belief system also is the basis for prejudice and discriminatory behavior. In such a situation, people are seen as belonging to different races and

treated differently because of it, such as having different job opportunities and housing choices. Discriminated-against people who are in some racial categories find limits in their housing choices. This means they get separated or grouped together in undesirable areas. Poor housing gets combined with unequal schooling, such that the lowest-quality schools are located in areas with the least desirable housing. Since the relationship between school quality and test scores is very strong, students from families living in less desirable housing areas with low-quality schools get lower test scores.

We can now turn from the errors in causal explanation to avoid and more to other issues involving hypotheses. Table 4.2 provides a review of the major errors.

From the Research Question to Hypotheses

It is difficult to move from a broad topic to hypotheses, but the leap from a well-formulated research question to hypotheses is a short one. Hints about hypotheses are embedded within a good research question. In addition, hypotheses are tentative answers to research questions (see Box 4.10).

FIGURE 4.4   Example of a Spurious Relationship between Belonging to a Non-White "Race" and Getting Low Academic Test Scores

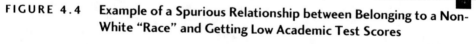
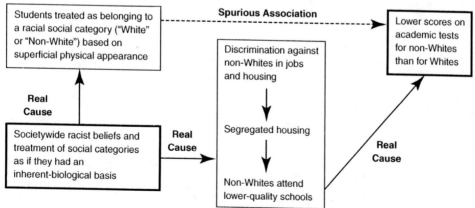

TABLE 4.2   Summary of Errors in Explanation

Type of Error	Short Definition	Example
Ecological Fallacy	The empirical observations are at too high a level for the causal relationship that is stated.	New York has a high crime rate. Joan lives in New York. Therefore, she probably stole my watch.
Reductionism	The empirical observations are at too low a level for the causal relationship that is stated.	Because Steven lost his job and did not buy a new car, the country entered a long economic recession.
Spuriousness	An unseen third variable is the actual cause of both the independent and dependent variable.	Hair length is associated with TV programs. People with short hair prefer watching football; people with long hair prefer romance stories. (*Unseen:* Gender)

 Box 4.10

Examples of Bad and Good Research Questions

Bad Research Questions

Not Empirically Testable, Nonscientific Questions
- Should abortion be legal?
- Is it right to have capital punishment?

General Topics, Not Research Questions
- Treatment of alcohol and drug abuse
- Sexuality and aging

Set of Variables, Not Questions
- Capital punishment and racial discrimination
- Urban decay and gangs

Too Vague, Ambiguous
- Do police affect delinquency?
- What can be done to prevent child abuse?

Need to Be Still More Specific
- Has the incidence of child abuse risen?
- How does poverty affect children?
- What problems do children who grow up in poverty experience that others do not?

Good Research Questions

Exploratory Questions
- Has the actual incidence of child abuse changed in Wisconsin in the past 10 years?

Descriptive Questions
- Is child abuse, violent or sexual, more common in families that have experienced a divorce than in intact, never-divorced families?
- Are the children raised in poverty households more likely to have medical, learning, and social-emotional adjustment difficulties than nonpoverty children?

Explanatory Questions
- Does the emotional instability created by experiencing a divorce increase the chances that divorced parents will physically abuse their children?
- Is a lack of sufficent funds for preventive treatment a major cause of more serious medical problems among children raised in families in poverty?

Consider an example research question: "Is age at marriage associated with divorce?" The question contains two variables: "age at marriage" and "divorce." To develop a hypothesis, a researcher asks, "Which is the independent variable?" The independent variable is "age at marriage" because marriage must logically precede divorce. The researcher also asks, "What is the direction of the relationship?" The hypothesis could be: "The lower the age at time of marriage, the greater the chances that the marriage will end in divorce." This hypothesis answers the research question and makes a prediction. Notice that the research question can be reformulated and better focused now: "Are couples who marry younger more likely to divorce?"

Several hypotheses can be developed for one research question. Another hypothesis from the same research question is: "The smaller the difference between the ages of the marriage partners at the time of marriage, the less likely that the marriage will end in divorce." In this case, the variable "age at marriage" is specified differently.

Hypotheses can specify that a relationship holds under some conditions but not others. For example, a hypothesis states: "The lower the age of the partners at time of marriage, the greater the chances that the marriage will end in divorce,

unless it is a marriage between members of a tight-knit traditional religious community in which early marriage is the norm."

Formulating a research question and a hypothesis do not have to proceed in fixed stages. A researcher can formulate a tentative research question, then develop possible hypotheses; the hypotheses then help the researcher state the research question more precisely. The process is interactive and involves creativity.

You may be wondering: Where does theory fit into the process of moving from a topic to a hypothesis I can test? Recall from Chapter 2 that theory takes many forms. Researchers use general theoretical issues as a source of topics. Theories provide concepts that researchers turn into variables as well as the reasoning or mechanism that helps researchers connect variables into a research question. A hypothesis can both answer a research question and be an untested proposition from a theory. Researchers can express a hypothesis at an abstract, conceptual level or restate it in a more concrete, measurable form.

Examples of specific studies may help to illustrate the parts of the research process. For examples of three quantitative studies, see Table 4.3; for two qualitative studies, see Table 4.4.

TABLE 4.3   Examples of Quantitative Studies

Study Citation (using ASA format style)	Goar, Carla and Jane Sell. 2005. "Using Task Definition to Modify Racial Inequality Within Task Groups" *Sociological Quarterly* 46:525–543.	Musick, Mark, John Wilson, and William Bynum. 2000. "Race and Formal Volunteering: The Differential Effects of Class and Religion" *Social Forces* 78: 1539–70.	Lauzen, Martha M. and David M. Dozier. 2005. "Maintaining the Double Standard: Portrayals of Age and Gender in Popular Films." *Sex Roles* 52: 437–446.
Methodological Technique	Experiment	Survey	Content Analysis

(continued)

TABLE 4.3 *(Continued)*

Topic	Mixed race group working on a task. A test of "expectation states theory"	Rates of volunteering by White and Black adults	Age and Gender Stereotypes in U.S. Mass Media
Research Question	If a group is presented with a task that is complex and requires many diverse skills, does this result in greater equality in participation across racial groups because people believe different racial groups possess different skills?	Do different kinds of resources available to Blacks and Whites explain why Blacks are less likely to volunteer?	Do contemporary films show a double standard, in which males acquire greater status and leadership as they age, while females are not permittted to gain status and leadership with increased age?
Main Hypothesis Tested	Groups exposed to instructions that suggest complex and diverse skills are required to complete a task will show less racial inequality in their operations to complete a task than groups without such instructions.	For Whites and Blacks, social class and religion affect whether a person volunteers in different ways.	As with past popular U.S. films and in other popular mass media, a double standard still exists.
Main Independent Variable(s)	Whether groups were told they were to a complete a complex task that requires diverse skills or not.	Social class, religious attendance, race.	The age and gender of major film characters.
Main Dependent Variable(s)	The amount of time/involvement by people of different races to resolve a group task.	Whether a person said he or she volunteered for any of five organizations (religious, education, political or labor, senior citizen, or local).	Whether a character has a leadership role, high occupational status, and goals.
Unit of Analysis	Mixed race task group	Individual adult	The movie

TABLE 4.3 *(Continued)*

Specific Units in the Study	90 undergraduate females in 3-person groups comprised of one Black and two White students.	Random sample of 2,867 U.S. adults interviewed twice (panel) in 1986 and 1989.	100 top-grossing domestic U.S. films in 2002.
Universe	All task groups that have a diverse set of members.	All adult Whites and Blacks in the United States.	All films.

TABLE 4.4   Examples of Qualitative Studies

Study Citation (using ASA format style)	Lu, Shun and Gary Fine. 1995. "The Presentation of Ethnic Authenticity: Chinese Food as a Social Accomplishment" *Sociological Quarterly* 36:535–53.	Molotch, Harvey, William Freudenburg, and Krista Paulsen. 2000. "History Repeats Itself, but How? City Character, Urban Tradition, and the Accomplishment of Place." *American Sociological Review* 65:791–823.
Methodological Technique	Field Research	Historical-Comparative Research
Topic	The ways ethnic cultures are displayed within the boundaries of being acceptable in the United States and how they deploy cultural resources.	The ways cities develop a distinct urban "character."
Research Question	How do Chinese restaurants present food to balance, giving a feeling of cultural authenticity and yet satisfying non-Chinese U.S. customers?	Why did the California cities of Santa Barbara and Ventura, which appear very similar on the surface, develop very different characters?

(continued)

TABLE 4.4 *(Continued)*

Grounded Theory	Ethnic restaurants Americanize their food to fit local tastes but also construct an impression of authenticity. It is a negotiated process of meeting the customer's expectations/taste conventions and the desire for an exotic and authentic eating experience.	The authors used two concepts—"lash up" (interaction of many factors) and structure (past events create constraints on subsequent ones)—to elaborate on character and tradition. Economic, political, cultural, and social factors combine to create distinct cultural-economic places. Similar forces can have opposite results depending on context.
Social Process	Restaurants make modifications to fit available ingredients, their market niche, and the cultural and food tastes of local customers.	Conditions in the two cities contributed to two different economic development responses to the oil industry and highway development. The city of Ventura formed an industrial-employment base around the oil industry and encouraged new highways. The city of Santa Barbara limited both the oil industry and highway growth. It instead focused on creating a strong tourism industry.
Social Context or Field Site	Chinese restaurants, especially four in Athens, Georgia.	The middle part of California's Pacific coast over the past 100 years.

CONCLUSION

In this chapter, you encountered the groundwork to begin a study. You saw how differences in the qualitative and quantitative styles or approaches to social research direct a researcher to prepare for a study differently. All social researchers narrow their topic into a more specific, focused research question. The styles of research suggest a different form and sequence of decisions, and different answers to when and how to focus the research. The style that a researcher uses will depend on the topic he or she selects, the researcher's purpose and intended use of study results, the orientation toward social science that he or she adopts, and the individual researcher's own assumptions and beliefs.

Quantitative researchers take a linear path and emphasize objectivity. They tend to use explicit, standardized procedures and a causal explanation. Their language of variables and hypotheses is found across many other areas of science. The process is often deductive with a sequence of discrete steps that precede data collection: Narrow the topic to a more focused question, transform nebulous theoretical concepts into more exact variables, and develop one or more hypotheses to test. In actual practice, researchers move back and forth, but the general process flows in a single, linear direction. In addition, quantitative researchers take special care to avoid logical errors in hypothesis development and causal explanation.

Qualitative researchers follow a nonlinear path and emphasize becoming intimate with the details of a natural setting or a particular cultural-historical context. They use fewer standardized procedures or explicit steps, and often devise on-the-spot techniques for one situation or study. Their language of cases and contexts directs them to conduct detailed investigations of particular cases or processes in their search for authenticity. They rarely separate planning and design decisions into a distinct pre–data collection stage, but continue to develop the study design throughout early data collection. The inductive qualitative style encourages a slow, flexible evolution toward a specific focus based on a researcher's ongoing learning from the data. Grounded theory emerges from the researcher's continuous reflections on the data.

Too often, the qualitative and quantitative distinction is overdrawn and presented as a rigid dichotomy. Adherents of one style of social research frequently judge the other style on the basis of the assumptions and standards of their own style. The quantitative researcher demands to know the variables used and the hypothesis tested. The qualitative researcher balks at turning humanity into cold numbers. The challenge for the well-versed, prudent social researcher is to understand and appreciate each style or approach on its own terms, and to recognize the strengths and limitations of each. The ultimate goal is to develop a better understanding and explanation of events in the social world. This comes from an appreciation of the value that each style has to offer.

Key Terms

abstract
alternative hypothesis
attributes
citation
dependent variable
ecological fallacy
first-order interpretation
hypothesis
independent variable
intervening variable
level of analysis
linear research path
literature review
nonlinear research path
null hypothesis
reductionism
second-order interpretation
spuriousness
third-order interpretation
unit of analysis
universe
variable

Endnotes

1. For a discussion of the "logic of the disconfirming hypothesis," see Singleton and associates (1988:456–460).
2. See Bailey (1987:43) for a discussion.

CHAPTER 5

Qualitative and Quantitative Measurement

INTRODUCTION

You may have heard of the Stanford Binet IQ test to measure intelligence, the Index of Dissimilarity to measure racial segregation, the Poverty Line to measure whether one is poor, or Uniform Crime Reports to measure the amount of crime. When social researchers test a hypothesis, evaluate an explanation, provide empirical support for a theory, or systematically study an applied issue or some area of the social world, they measure concepts and variables. How social researchers measure the numerous aspects of the social world—such as intelligence, segregation, poverty, crime, self-esteem, political power, alienation, or racial prejudice—is the focus of this chapter.

Quantitative researchers are far more concerned about measurement issues than are qualitative researchers. They treat measurement as a distinct step in the research process that occurs prior to data collection, and have developed special terminology and techniques for it. Using a deductive approach, they begin with a concept then create empirical measures that precisely and accurately capture it in a form that can be expressed in numbers.

Qualitative researchers approach measurement very differently. They develop ways to capture and express variable and nonvariable concepts using various alternatives to numbers. They often take an inductive approach, so they measure features of social life as part of a process that integrates creating new concepts or theories with measurement.

How people conceptualize and operationalize variables can significantly affect social issues beyond concerns of research methodology. For example, psychologists debate the meaning and measurement of intelligence. Most intelligence tests that people use in schools, on job applications, and in making statements about racial or other inherited superiority measure only analytic reasoning (i.e., one's capacity to think abstractly and to infer logically). Yet, many argue that there are other types of intelligence in addition to analytic. Some say there is practical and creative intelligence. Others suggest more types, such as social-interpersonal, emotional, body-kinesthetic, musical, or spatial. If there are many forms of intelligence but people narrowly limit measurement to one type, it seriously restricts how schools identify and nurture learning; how larger society evaluates, promotes, and recognizes the contributions of people; and how a society values diverse human abilities.

Likewise, different policymakers and researchers conceptualize and operationalize poverty differently. How people measure poverty will determine whether people get assistance from numerous social programs (e.g., subsidized housing, food aid, health care, child care, etc.). For example, some say that people are poor only if they cannot afford the food required to prevent malnutrition. Others say that people are poor if they have an annual income that is less than one-half of the average (median) income. Still others say that people are poor if they earn below a "living wage" based on a judgment about the income needed to meet minimal community standards of health, safety, and decency in hygiene, housing, clothing, diet, transportation, and so forth. Decisions about how to conceptualize and measure a variable—poverty—can greatly influence the daily living conditions of millions of people.

WHY MEASURE?

We use many measures in our daily lives. For example, this morning I woke up and hopped onto a bathroom scale to see how well my diet is working. I glanced at a thermometer to find out whether to wear a coat. Next, I got into my car and checked the gas gauge to be sure I could make it to campus. As I drove, I watched the speedometer so I would not get a speeding ticket. By 8:00 A.M., I had measured weight, temperature, gasoline volume, and speed—all measures about the physical world. Such precise, well-developed measures, which we use in daily life, are fundamental in the natural sciences.

We also measure the nonphysical world in everyday life, but usually in less exact terms. We are measuring when we say that a restaurant is excellent, that Pablo is really smart, that Karen has a negative attitude toward life, that Johnson is really prejudiced, or that the movie last night had a lot of violence in it. However, such everyday judgments as "really prejudiced" or "a lot of violence" are imprecise, vague measures.

Measurement also extends our senses. The astronomer or biologist uses the telescope or the microscope to extend natural vision. In contrast to our senses, scientific measurement is more sensitive, varies less with the specific observer, and yields more exact information. You recognize that a thermometer gives more specific, precise information about temperature than touch can. Likewise, a good bathroom scale gives you more specific, constant, and precise information about the weight of a 5-year-old girl than you get by lifting her and calling her "heavy" or "light." Social measures provide precise information about social reality.

In addition, measurement helps us observe what is otherwise invisible. Measurement extends human senses. It lets us observe things that were once unseen and unknown but were predicted by theory.

Before you can measure, you need a clear idea about what you are interested in. For example, you cannot see or feel magnetism with your natural senses. Magnetism comes from a theory about the physical world. You observe its effects indirectly; for instance, metal flecks move near a magnet. The magnet allows you to "see" or measure the magnetic fields. Natural scientists have invented thousands of measures to "see" very tiny things (molecules or insect organs) or very large things (huge geological land masses or planets) that are not observable through ordinary senses. In addition, researchers are constantly creating new measures.

Some of the things a social researcher is interested in measuring are easy to see (e.g., age, sex, skin color, etc.), but most cannot be directly observed (e.g., attitudes, ideology, divorce rates, deviance, sex roles, etc.). Like the natural scientist who invents indirect measures of the "invisible" objects and forces of the physical world, the social researcher devises measures for difficult-to-observe aspects of the social world.

QUANTITATIVE AND QUALITATIVE MEASUREMENT

Both qualitative and quantitative researchers use careful, systematic methods to gather high-quality data. Yet, differences in the styles of research and the types of data mean they approach the measurement process differently. The two approaches to measurement have three distinctions.

One difference between the two styles involves timing. Quantitative researchers think about variables and convert them into specific actions during a planning stage that occurs before and separate from gathering or analyzing data. Measurement for qualitative researchers occurs during the data collection process.

A second difference involves the data itself. Quantitative researchers develop techniques that can produce quantitative data (i.e., data in the form of numbers). Thus, the researcher moves from abstract ideas to specific data collection techniques to precise numerical information produced by the techniques. The numerical information is an empirical representation of the abstract ideas. Data for qualitative researchers sometimes is in the form of numbers; more often, it includes written or spoken words, actions, sounds, symbols, physical objects, or visual images (e.g., maps, photographs, videos, etc.). The qualitative researcher does not convert all observation into a single medium such as numbers. Instead, he or she develops many flexible, ongoing processes to measure that leaves the data in various shapes, sizes, and forms.

All researchers combine ideas and data to analyze the social world. In both research styles, data are empirical representations of concepts, and measurement links data to concepts. A third difference is how the two styles make such linkages. Quantitative researchers contemplate and reflect on concepts before they gather any data. They construct measurement techniques that bridge concepts and data.

Qualitative researchers also reflect on ideas before data collection, but they develop many, if not most, of their concepts during data collection. The qualitative researcher reexamines and evaluates the data and concepts simultaneously and interactively. Researchers start gathering data and creating ways to measure based what they encounter. As they gather data, they reflect on the process and develop new ideas.

PARTS OF THE MEASUREMENT PROCESS

When a researcher measures, he or she links a concept, idea, or construct[1] to a measure (i.e., a technique, a process, a procedure, etc.) by which he or she can observe the idea empirically. Quantitative researchers primarily follow a deductive route. They begin with the abstract idea, follow with a measurement procedure, and end with empirical data that represent the ideas. Qualitative researchers primarily follow an inductive route. They begin with empirical data, follow with abstract ideas, relate ideas and data, and end with a mixture of ideas and data. Actually, the process is more interactive in both styles of research. As a quantitative researcher develops measures, the constructs become refined and clearer, and as the researcher applies the measures to gather data, he or she often adjusts the measurement technique. As a qualitative researcher gathers data, he or she uses some preexisting ideas to assist in data collection, and will then mix old with new ideas that are developed from the data.

Both qualitative and quantitative researchers use two processes: conceptualization and operationalization in measurement. *Conceptualization* is the process of taking a construct and refining it by giving it a conceptual or theoretical definition. A *conceptual definition* is a definition in abstract, theoretical terms. It refers to other ideas or constructs. There is no magical way to turn a construct into a precise conceptual definition. It involves thinking carefully, observing directly, consulting with others, reading what others have said, and trying possible definitions.

How might I develop a conceptual definition of the construct *prejudice?* When beginning to develop a conceptual definition, researchers often rely on multiple sources—personal experience and deep thinking, discussions with other people, and the existing scholarly literature. I might reflect on what I know about prejudice, ask others what they think about it, and go the library and look up its many definitions. As I gather definitions, the core idea should get clearer, but I have many definitions and need to sort them out. Most definitions state that prejudice is an attitude about another group and involves a prejudgment, or judging prior to getting specific information.

As I think about the construct, I notice that all the definitions refer to prejudice as an attitude, and usually it is an attitude about the members of another group. There are many forms of prejudice, but most are negative views about persons of a different racial-ethnic group. Prejudice could be about other kinds of groups (e.g., people of a religion, of a physical stature, or from a certain region), but it is always about a collectivity to which one does not belong. Many constructs have multiple dimensions or types, so I should consider whether there can be different types of prejudice—racial prejudice, religious prejudice, age prejudice, gender prejudice, nation prejudice, and so forth.

I also need to consider the units of analysis that best fit my definition of the construct. Prejudice is an attitude. Individuals hold and express attitudes, but so might groups (e.g., families, clubs, churches, companies, media outlets). I need to decide, Do I want my definition of prejudice to include only the attitudes of individuals or should it include attitudes held by groups, organizations, and institutions as well? Can I say,

The school or newspaper was prejudiced? I also must distinguish my construct from closely related ones. For example, I must ask, How is prejudice similar to or different from ideas such as discrimination, stereotype, or racism?

Conceptualization is the process of carefully thinking through the meaning of a construct. At this stage, I believe that *prejudice* means an inflexible negative attitude that an individual holds and is directed toward a race or ethnic group that is an out-group. It can, but does not always, lead to behavior, such as treating people unequally (i.e., discrimination), and it generally relies on a person's stereotypes of out-group members. Thus, my initial thought, "Prejudice is a negative feeling," has become a precisely defined construct. Even with all my conceptualization, I need to be even more specific. For example, if prejudice is a negative attitude about a race or an ethnic group of which one is not a member, I need to consider the meaning of *race* or *ethnic group*. I should not assume everyone sees racial-ethnic categories the same. Likewise, it is possible to have a positive prejudgment, and if so is that a kind of prejudice? The main point is that conceptualization requires that I become very clear and state what I mean very explicitly for others to see.

Operationalization links a conceptual definition to a specific set of measurement techniques or procedures, the construct's *operational definition* (i.e., a definition in terms of the specific operations of actions a researcher carries out). An operational definition could be a survey questionnaire, a method of observing events in a field setting, a way to measure symbolic content in the mass media, or any process carried out by the researcher that reflects, documents, or represents the abstract construct as it is expressed in the conceptual definition.

There are usually multiple ways to measure a construct. Some are better or worse and more or less practical than others. The key is to fit your measure to your specific conceptual definition, to the practical constraints within which you must operate (e.g., time, money, available subjects, etc.),

Box 5.1 Five Suggestions for Coming Up with a Measure

1. *Remember the conceptual definition.* The underlying principle for any measure is to match it to the specific conceptual definition of the construct that will be used in the study.

2. *Keep an open mind.* Do not get locked into a single measure or type of measure. Be creative and constantly look for better measures.

3. *Borrow from others.* Do not be afraid to borrow from other researchers, as long as credit is given. Good ideas for measures can be found in other studies or modified from other measures.

4. *Anticipate difficulties.* Logical and practical problems often arise when trying to measure variables of interest. Sometimes a problem can be anticipated and avoided with careful forethought and planning.

5. *Do not forget your units of analysis.* Your measure should fit with the units of analysis of the study and permit you to generalize to the universe of interest.

and to the research techniques you know or can learn. You can develop a new measure from scratch, or it can be a measure that is already being used by other researchers (see Box 5.1).

Operationalization links the language of theory with the language of empirical measures. Theory is full of abstract concepts, assumptions, relationships, definitions, and causality. Empirical measures describe how people concretely measure specific variables. They refer to specific operations or things people use to indicate the presence of a construct that exists in observable reality.

Quantitative Conceptualization and Operationalization

The measurement process for quantitative research flows in a straightforward sequence: first conceptualization, followed by operationalization, followed by applying the operational definition or measuring to collect the data. Quantitative researchers developed several ways to rigorously link abstract ideas to measurement procedures that will produce precise quantitative information about empirical reality.

Figure 5.1 illustrates the measurement process for two variables that are linked together in a theory and a hypothesis. There are three levels to consider: conceptual, operational, and empirical. At the most abstract level, the researcher is interested in the causal relationship between two constructs, or a *conceptual hypothesis.* At the level of operational definitions, the researcher is interested in testing an *empirical hypothesis* to determine the degree of association between indicators. This is the level at which correlations, statistics, questionnaires, and the like are used. The third level is the concrete empirical world. If the operational indicators of variables (e.g., questionnaires) are logically linked to a construct (e.g., racial discrimination), they will capture what happens in the empirical social world and relate it to the conceptual level.

The measurement process links together the three levels, moving deductively from the abstract to the concrete. A researcher first conceptualizes a variable, giving it a clear conceptual definition. Next, he or she operationalizes it by developing an operational definition or set of indicators for it. Last, he or she applies the indicators in the empirical world. The links from abstract constructs to empirical reality allow the researcher to test empirical hypotheses. Those tests are logically linked back to a conceptual hypothesis and causal relations in the world of theory.

A hypothesis has at least two variables, and the processes of conceptualization and operationalization are necessary for each variable. In the preceding example, prejudice is not a hypothesis. It is one variable. It could be a dependent variable caused by something else, or it could be an independent variable causing something else. It depends on my theoretical explanation.

We can return to the quantitative study by Weitzer and Tuch on perceptions of police bias and misconduct for an example of how

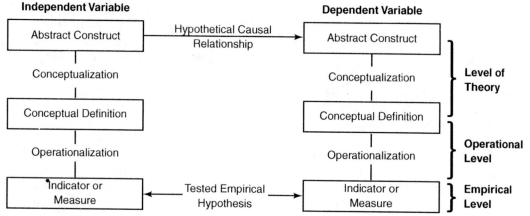

FIGURE 5.1   Conceptualization and Operationalization

Abstract Construct to Concrete Measure

researchers conceptualize and operationalize variables. It is an explanatory study with two main variables in a causal hypothesis. The researchers began with the *conceptual hypothesis:* Members of a nondominant racial group are more likely than a dominant racial group to believe that policing is racially biased, and their experience with policing and exposure to media reports on police racial bias increase the perception of racial bias. They *conceptualized* the independent variable, dominant racial group, as White and the nondominant group as non-White subdivided into Black and Hispanic. The researchers *conceptualized* the dependent variable, racially biased policing, as unequal treatment by the police of Whites and non-Whites and racial prejudice by police officers. The researchers *operationalized* the independent variable by self-identification to a survey question about race. They *operationalized* the dependent variable by using four sets of survey questions: (1) questions about whether police treat Blacks better, the same, or worse than Whites, and the same question with Hispanics substituted for Blacks; (2) questions about whether police treat Black neighborhoods better, the same, or worse than Whites ones, with the same question asked for Hispanic neighborhoods; (3) a question about whether there is racial-ethnic prejudice among police officers in the city; and (4) a question about whether police are more likely to stop some drivers because they are Black or Hispanic.

Qualitative Conceptualization and Operationalization

Conceptualization. The conceptualization process in qualitative research also differs from that in quantitative research. Instead of refining abstract ideas into theoretical definitions early in the research process, qualitative researchers refine rudimentary "working ideas" during the data collection and analysis process. Conceptualization is a process of forming coherent theoretical definitions as one struggles to "make sense" or organize the data and one's preliminary ideas.

As the researcher gathers and analyzes qualitative data, he or she develops new concepts, formulates definitions for the concepts, and considers relationships among the concepts. Eventually, he or she links concepts to one another to create theoretical relationships that may or may not be causal. Qualitative researchers form the concepts as they examine their qualitative data (i.e., field notes, photos and maps, historical documents, etc.). Often, this involves a researcher asking theoretical questions about the data (e.g., Is this a case of class conflict? What is the sequence of events and could it be different? Why did this happen here and not somewhere else?).

A qualitative researcher conceptualizes by developing clear, explicit definitions of constructs. The definitions are somewhat abstract and linked to other ideas, but usually they are also closely tied to specific data. They can be expressed in the words and concrete actions of the people being studied. In qualitative research, conceptualization is largely determined by the data.

Operationalization. The operationalization process for qualitative research significantly differs from that in quantitative research and often precedes conceptualization. A researcher forms conceptual definitions out of rudimentary "working ideas" that he or she used while making observations or gathering data. Instead of turning refined conceptual definitions into a set of measurement operations, a qualitative researcher operationalizes by describing how specific observations and thoughts about the data contributed to working ideas that are the basis of conceptual definitions and theoretical concepts.

Operationalization in qualitative research is an after-the-fact description more than a before-the-fact preplanned technique. Almost in a reverse of the quantitative process, data gathering occurs with or prior to full operationalization.

Just as quantitative operationalization deviates from a rigid deductive process, the process followed by qualitative researchers is one of mutual interaction. The researcher draws on ideas from beyond the data of a specific research setting. Qualitative operationalization describes how the researcher collects data, but it includes the researcher's use of preexisting techniques and concepts that were blended with those that emerged during the data collection process. In qualitative research, ideas and evidence are mutually interdependent.

We can see an example of qualitative operationalization in the study on managerialization of law by Edelman and associates (2001). It is a descriptive study that developed one main construct. The researchers began with an interest in how major U.S. corporations came to accept legal mandates from the late 1970s to early 1990s. The mandates stated that firms must institute policies to equalize and improve the hiring and promotion of racial minorities and women, something the firms initially opposed. The researcher's *empirical data* consisted of articles in magazines written for and by corporate managers, or "managerial rhetoric" (i.e., debates and discussion within the community of leading professional managers on important issues). After gathering numerous articles, the rese-archers *operationalized* the data by developing working ideas and concepts from an inductive examination of the data. The researchers discovered that as managers discussed and deliberated, they had created a set of new nonlegal terms, ideas, and justifications. The operationalization moved inductively from looking at articles to creating working ideas based on what resea-rchers found in the rhetoric. The researchers *conceptualized* their working ideas into the abstract construct "managerialization of law." The researchers saw that that corporate managers had altered and reformulated the original legal terms and mandates, and created new ones that were more consistent with the values and views of major corporations. The researchers documented a

historical process that moved from resistance to reformulation to acceptance, and with acceptance came new corporate policy. The researchers also drew on past studies to argue that the "managerialization of law" illustrates one role of top corporate managers—they innovate and alter internal operations by creating new terms, justifications, and maneuvers that help firms adjust to potential "disruptions" and requirements originating in the corporation's external political-legal environment.

RELIABILITY AND VALIDITY

Reliability and validity are central issues in all measurement. Both concern how concrete measures are connected to constructs. Reliability and validity are salient because constructs in social theory are often ambiguous, diffuse, and not directly observable. Perfect reliability and validity are virtually impossible to achieve. Rather, they are ideals for which researchers strive.

All social researchers want their measures to be reliable and valid. Both ideas are important in establishing the truthfulness, credibility, or believability of findings. Both terms also have multiple meanings. Here, they refer to related, desirable aspects of measurement.

Reliability means dependability or consistency. It suggests that the same thing is repeated or recurs under the identical or very similar conditions. The opposite of reliability is a measurement that yields erratic, unstable, or inconsistent results.

Validity suggests truthfulness and refers to the match between a construct, or the way a researcher conceptualizes the idea in a conceptual definition, and a measure. It refers to how well an idea about reality "fits" with actual reality. The absence of validity occurs if there is poor fit between the constructs a researcher uses to describe, theorize, or analyze the social world and what actually occurs in the social world. In simple terms, validity addresses the question of how well the social reality being measured through research matches with the constructs researchers use to understand it.

Qualitative and quantitative researchers want reliable and valid measurement, but beyond an agreement on the basic ideas at a general level, each style sees the specifics of reliability and validity in the research process differently.

Reliability and Validity in Quantitative Research

Reliability.   As just stated, reliability means dependability. It means that the numerical results produced by an indicator do not vary because of characteristics of the measurement process or measurement instrument itself. For example, I get on my bathroom scale and read my weight. I get off and get on again and again. I have a reliable scale if it gives me the same weight each time—assuming, of course, that I am not eating, drinking, changing clothing, and so forth. An unreliable scale will register different weights each time, even though my "true" weight does not change. Another example is my car speedometer. If I am driving at a constant slow speed on a level surface, but the speedometer needle jumps from one end to the other, my speedometer is not a reliable indicator of how fast I am traveling.

How to Improve Reliability.   It is rare to have perfect reliability. There are four ways to increase the reliability of measures: (1) clearly conceptualize constructs, (2) use a precise level of measurement, (3) use multiple indicators, and (4) use pilot-tests.

Clearly Conceptualize All Constructs.   Reliability increases when a single construct or subdimension of a construct is measured. This means developing unambiguous, clear theoretical definitions. Constructs should be specified to eliminate "noise" (i.e., distracting or interfering information) from other constructs. Each measure should indicate one and only one concept.

Otherwise, it is impossible to determine which concept is being "indicated." For example, the indicator of a pure chemical compound is more reliable than one in which the chemical is mixed with other material or dirt. In the latter case, it is difficult to separate the "noise" of other material from the pure chemical.

Increase the Level of Measurement.   Levels of measurement are discussed later. Indicators at higher or more precise levels of measurement are more likely to be reliable than less precise measures because the latter pick up less detailed information. If more specific information is measured, then it is less likely that anything other than the construct will be captured. The general principle is: Try to measure at the most precise level possible. However, it is more difficult to measure at higher levels of measurement. For example, if I have a choice of measuring prejudice as either high or low, or in 10 categories from extremely low to extremely high, it would be better to measure it in 10 refined categories.

Use Multiple Indicators of a Variable.   A third way to increase reliability is to use multiple indicators, because two (or more) indicators of the same construct are better than one. Figure 5.2 illustrates the use of multiple indicators in hypothesis testing. Three indicators of the one independent variable construct are combined into an overall measure, A, and two indicators of a dependent variable are combined into a single measure, B.

For example, I create three indicators of the variable, racial-ethnic prejudice. My first indicator is an attitude question on a survey. I ask research participants their beliefs and feelings about many different racial and ethnic groups. For a second indicator, I observe research participants from various races and ethnic groups interacting together over the course of three days. I look for those who regularly either (1) avoid eye contact, appear to be tense, and sound cool and distant; or (2) make eye contact,

FIGURE 5.2   Measurement Using Multiple Indicators

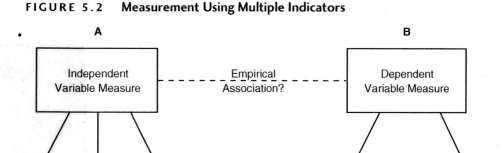

appear relaxed, and sound warm and friendly as they interact with people of their same or with people of a different racial-ethnic group. Last, I create an experiment. I ask research participants to read the grade transcripts, resumes, and interview reports on 30 applicants for five jobs—youth volunteer coordinator, office manager, janitor, clothing store clerk, and advertising account executive. The applicants have many qualifications, but I secretly manipulate their racial or ethnic group to see whether a research participant decides on the best applicant for the jobs based on an applicant's race and ethnicity.

Multiple indicators let a researcher take measurements from a wider range of the content of a conceptual definition. Different aspects of the construct can be measured, each with its own indicator. Also, one indicator (e.g., one question on a questionnaire) may be imperfect, but several measures are less likely to have the same (systematic) error. Multiple indicator measures tend to be more stable than measures with one item.

Use Pretests, Pilot Studies, and Replication. Reliability can be improved by using a pretest or pilot version of a measure first. Develop one or more draft or preliminary versions of a measure and try them before applying the final version in a hypothesis-testing situation. This takes more time and effort.

The principle of using pilot-tests extends to replicating the measures other researchers have used. For example, I search the literature and find measures of prejudice from past research. I may want to build on and use a previous measure if it is a good one, citing the source, of course. In addition, I may want to add new indicators and compare them to the previous measure.

Validity.   *Validity* is an overused term. Sometimes, it is used to mean "true" or "correct." There are several general types of validity. Here, we are concerned with *measurement validity.* There are also several types of measurement validity. Nonmeasurement types of validity are discussed later.

When a researcher says that an indicator is valid, it is valid for a particular purpose and definition. The same indicator can be valid for one purpose (i.e., a research question with units of analysis and universe) but less valid or invalid for others. For example, the measure of prejudice discussed here might be valid for measuring prejudice among teachers but invalid for measuring the prejudice of police officers.

At its core, measurement validity refers to how well the conceptual and operational definitions mesh with each other. The better the fit, the greater the measurement validity. Validity is more difficult to achieve than reliability. We cannot have absolute confidence about validity, but some measures are *more valid* than others. The reason we can never achieve absolute validity is that constructs are abstract ideas, whereas indicators refer to concrete observation. This is the gap between our mental pictures about the world and the specific things we do at particular times and places. Validity is part of a dynamic process that grows by accumulating evidence over time. Without it, all measurement becomes meaningless.

Three Types of Measurement Validity

Face Validity. The easiest to achieve and the most basic kind of validity is *face validity*. It is a judgment by the scientific community that the indicator really measures the construct. It addresses the question, On the face of it, do people believe that the definition and method of measurement fit? It is a consensus method. For example, few people would accept a measure of college student math ability using a question that asked students: $2 + 2 = ?$ This is not a valid measure of college-level math ability on the face of it. Recall that in the scientific community, aspects of research are scrutinized by others. See Table 5.1 for a summary of types of measurement validity.

TABLE 5.1 **Summary of Measurement Validity Types**

Validity (True Measure)

Face—in the judgment of others

Content—captures the entire meaning

Criterion—agrees with an external source

• Concurrent—agrees with a preexisting measure

• Predictive—agrees with future behavior

Content Validity. *Content validity* is a special type of face validity. It addresses the question, Is the full content of a definition represented in a measure? A conceptual definition holds ideas; it is a "space" containing ideas and concepts. Measures should represent all ideas or areas in the conceptual space. Content validity involves three steps. First, specify fully the entire content in a construct's definition. Next, sample from all areas of the definition. Finally, develop an indicator that taps all of the parts of the definition.

An example of content validity is my definition of *feminism* as a person's commitment to a set of beliefs creating full equality between men and women in areas of the arts, intellectual pursuits, family, work, politics, and authority relations. I create a measure of feminism in which I ask two survey questions: (1) Should men and women get equal pay for equal work and (2) Should men and women share household tasks? My measure has low content validity because the two questions ask only about pay and household tasks. They ignore the other areas (intellectual pursuits, politics, authority relations, and other aspects of work and family). For a content-valid measure, I must either expand the measure or narrow the definition.

Criterion Validity. *Criterion validity* uses some standard or criterion to indicate a construct accurately. The validity of an indicator is verified by comparing it with another measure of the same construct that is widely accepted. There are two subtypes of this kind of validity.

Concurrent Validity. To have *concurrent validity*, an indicator must be associated with a preexisting indicator that is judged to be valid (i.e., it has face validity). For example, you create a new test to measure intelligence. For it to be concurrently valid, it should be highly associated with existing IQ tests (assuming the same definition of intelligence is used). This means that most people who score high on the old measure should also score high on the new one, and vice versa. The two measures may not be perfectly associated, but if they measure the same or a similar construct, it is logical for them to yield similar results.

Predictive Validity. Criterion validity whereby an indicator predicts future events that are logically related to a construct is called *predictive validity*. It cannot be used for all measures. The measure and the action predicted must be distinct from but indicate the same construct. Predictive measurement validity should not be confused with prediction in hypothesis testing, where one variable predicts a different variable in the future. For example, the Scholastic Assessment Test (SAT) that many U.S. high school students take measures scholastic aptitude—the ability of a student to perform in college. If the SAT has high predictive validity, then students who get high SAT scores will subsequently do well in college. If students with high scores perform the same as students with average or low scores, then the SAT has low predictive validity.

Another way to test predictive validity is to select a group of people who have specific characteristics and predict how they will score (very high or very low) vis-à-vis the construct. For example, I have a measure of political conservatism. I predict that members of conservative groups (e.g., John Birch Society, Conservative Caucus, Daughters of the American Revolution, Moral Majority) will score high on it, whereas members of liberal groups (e.g., Democratic Socialists, People for the American Way, Americans for Democratic Action) will score low. I "validate" the measure with the groups—that is, I pilot-test it by using it on members of the groups. It can then be used as a measure of political conservatism for the general public.

Reliability and Validity in Qualitative Research

Most qualitative researchers accept the principles of reliability and validity, but use the terms infrequently because of their close association with quantitative measurement. In addition,

qualitative researchers apply the principles differently in practice.

Reliability. *Reliability* means dependability or consistency. Qualitative researchers use a variety of techniques (e.g., interviews, participation, photographs, document studies, etc.) to record their observations consistently. Qualitative researchers want to be consistent (i.e., not vacillating and erratic) in how, over time, they make observations, similar to the idea of stability reliability. One difficulty is that they often study processes that are not stable over time. Moreover, they emphasize the value of a changing or developing interaction between the researcher and what he or she studies.

Qualitative researchers believe that the subject matter and a researcher's relationship to it should be a growing, evolving process. The metaphor for the relationship between a researcher and the data is one of an evolving relationship or living organism (e.g., a plant) that naturally matures. Most qualitative researchers resist the quantitative approach to reliability, which they see as a cold, fixed mechanical instrument that one repeatedly injects into or applies to some static, lifeless material.

Qualitative researchers consider a range of data sources and employ multiple measurement methods. They accept that different researchers or that researchers using alternative measures will get distinctive results. This is because qualitative researchers see data collection as an interactive process in which particular researchers operate in an evolving setting and the setting's context dictates using a unique mix of measures that cannot be repeated. The diverse measures and interactions with different researchers are beneficial because they can illuminate different facets or dimensions of a subject matter. Many qualitative researchers question the quantitative researcher's quest for standard, fixed measures. They fear that such measures ignore the benefits of having a variety of researchers with many approaches and may neglect key aspects of diversity that exist in the social world.

Validity.   *Validity* means truthful. It refers to the bridge between a construct and the data. Qualitative researchers are more interested in authenticity than validity. *Authenticity* means giving a fair, honest, and balanced account of social life from the viewpoint of someone who lives it everyday. Qualitative researchers are less concerned with trying to match an abstract concept to empirical data and more concerned with giving a candid portrayal of social life that is true to the experiences of people being studied. Most qualitative researchers concentrate on ways to capture an inside view and provide a detailed account of how those being studied feel about and understand events.

Qualitative researchers have developed several methods that serve as substitutes for the quantitative approach to validity. These emphasize conveying the insider's view to others. Historical researchers use internal and external criticisms to determine whether the evidence they have is real or they believe it to be. Qualitative researchers adhere to the core principle of validity, to be truthful (i.e., avoid false or distorted accounts). They try to create a tight fit between their understanding, ideas, and statements about the social world and what is actually occurring in it.

Relationship between Reliability and Validity

Reliability is necessary for validity and is easier to achieve than validity. Although reliability is necessary in order to have a valid measure of a concept, it does not guarantee that a measure will be valid. It is not a sufficient condition for validity. A measure can produce the same result over and over (i.e., it has reliability), but what it measures may not match the definition of the construct (i.e., validity).

A measure can be reliable but invalid. For example, I get on a scale and get weighed. The weight registered by the scale is the same each time I get on and off. But then I go to another scale—an "official" one that measures true weight—and it says that my weight is twice as great. The first scale yielded reliable (i.e., dependable and consistent) results, but it did not give a valid measure of my weight.

A diagram might help you see the relationship between reliability and validity. Figure 5.3 illustrates the relationship between the concepts by using the analogy of a target. The bull's-eye represents a fit between a measure and the definition of the construct.

Validity and *reliability* are usually complementary concepts, but in some situations they

FIGURE 5.3   Illustration of Relationship between Reliability and Validity

A Bull's-Eye = A Perfect Measure

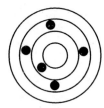 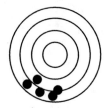 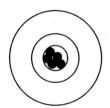

Low Reliability and Low Validity   High Reliability but Low Validity   High Reliability and High Validity

Source: Adapted from Babbie (2004:145).

conflict with each other. Sometimes, as validity increases, reliability is more difficult to attain, and vice versa. This occurs when the construct has a highly abstract and not easily observable definition. Reliability is easiest to achieve when the measure is precise and observable. Thus, there is a strain between the true essence of the highly abstract construct and measuring it in a concrete manner. For example, "alienation" is a very abstract, highly subjective construct, often defined as a deep inner sense of loss of one's humanity that diffuses across many aspects of one's life (e.g., social relations, sense of self, orientation toward nature). Highly precise questions in a questionnaire give reliable measures, but there is a danger of losing the subjective essence of the concept.

Other Uses of the Terms *Reliable* and *Valid*

Many words have multiple definitions, including *reliability* and *validity*. This creates confusion unless we distinguish among alternative uses of the same word.

Reliability.   We use *reliability* in everyday language. A reliable person is one who is dependable, stable, and responsible; a reliable car is dependable and trustworthy. This means the person responds in similar, predictable ways in different times and conditions; the same can be said for the car. In addition to measurement reliability, researchers sometimes say a study or its results are reliable. By this, they mean that the method of conducting a study or the results from it can be reproduced or replicated by other researchers.

Internal Validity.   *Internal validity* means there are no errors internal to the design of the research project. It is used primarily in experimental research to talk about possible errors or alternative explanations of results that arise despite attempts to institute controls. High internal validity means there are few such errors. Low internal validity means that such errors are likely.

External Validity.   *External validity* is used primarily in experimental research. It is the ability to generalize findings from a specific setting and small group to a broad range of settings and people. It addresses the question, If something happens in a laboratory or among a particular group of subjects (e.g., college students), can the findings be generalized to the "real" (nonlaboratory) world or to the general public (nonstudents)? High external validity means that the results can be generalized to many situations and many groups of people. Low external validity means that the results apply only to a very specific setting.

Statistical Validity.   *Statistical validity* means that the correct statistical procedure is chosen and its assumptions are fully met. Different statistical tests or procedures are appropriate for different conditions, which are discussed in textbooks that describe the statistical procedures.

All statistics are based on assumptions about the mathematical properties of the numbers being used. A statistic will be invalid and its results nonsense if the major assumptions are violated. For example, to compute an average (actually the mean, which is discussed in a later chapter), one cannot use information at the nominal level of measurement (to be discussed). For example, suppose I measure the race of a class of students. I give each race a number: White = 1, African American = 2, Asian = 3, others = 4. It makes no sense to say that the "mean" race of a class of students is 1.9 (almost African American?). This is a misuse of the statistical procedure, and the results are invalid even if the computation is correct. The degree to which statistical assumptions can be violated or bent (the technical term is *robustness*) is a topic in which professional statisticians take great interest.

A GUIDE TO QUANTITATIVE MEASUREMENT

Thus far, you have learned about the principles of measurement, including the principles of reliability and validity. Quantitative researchers have developed ideas and specialized measures to help them in the process of creating operational definitions that will be reliable and valid measures and yield numerical data for their variable constructs. This section of the chapter is a brief guide to these ideas and a few of the measures.

Levels of Measurement

Levels of measurement is an abstract but important and widely used idea. Basically, it says that some ways a researcher measures a construct are at a higher or more refined level, and others are crude or less precisely specified. The level of measurement depends on the way in which a construct is conceptualized—that is, assumptions about whether it has particular characteristics. The level of measurement affects the kinds of indicators chosen and is tied to basic assumptions in a construct's definition. The way in which a researcher conceptualizes a variable limits the levels of measurement that he or she can use and has implications for how measurement and statistical analysis can proceed.

Continuous and Discrete Variables. Variables can be thought of as being either continuous or discrete. *Continuous variables* have an infinite number of values or attributes that flow along a continuum. The values can be divided into many smaller increments; in mathematical theory, there is an infinite number of increments. Examples of continuous variables include temperature, age, income, crime rate, and amount of schooling. *Discrete variables* have a relatively fixed set of separate values or variable attributes. Instead of a smooth continuum of values, discrete variables contain distinct categories. Examples of discrete variables include gender (male or female), religion (Protestant, Catholic, Jew, Muslim, atheist), and marital status (never married single, married, divorced or separated, widowed). Whether a variable is continuous or discrete affects its level of measurement.

Four Levels of Measurement

Precision and Levels. The idea of levels of measurement expands on the difference between continuous and discrete variables and organizes types of variables for their use in statistics. The four *levels of measurement* categorize the degree of precision of measurement.

Deciding on the appropriate level of measurement for a construct often creates confusion. The appropriate level of measurement for a variable depends on two things: (1) how a construct is conceptualized and (2) the type of indicator or measurement that a researcher uses.

The way a researcher conceptualizes a construct can limit how precisely it can be measured. For example, some of the variables listed earlier as continuous can be reconceptualized as discrete. Temperature can be a continuous variable (e.g., degrees, fractions of degrees) or it can be crudely measured with discrete categories (e.g., hot or cold). Likewise, age can be continuous (how old a person is in years, months, days, hours, and minutes) or treated as discrete categories (infancy, childhood, adolescence, young adulthood, middle age, old age). Yet, most discrete variables cannot be conceptualized as continuous variables. For example, sex, religion, and marital status cannot be conceptualized as continuous; however, related constructs *can* be conceptualized as continuous (e.g., femininity, degree of religiousness, commitment to a marital relationship, etc.).

The level of measurement limits the statistical measures that can be used. A wide range of powerful statistical procedures are available for the higher levels of measurement, but the types of statistics that can be used with the lowest levels are very limited.

There is a practical reason to conceptualize and measure variables at higher levels of measurement. You can collapse higher levels of measurement to lower levels, but the reverse is not true. In other words, it is possible to measure a construct very precisely, gather very specific information, and then ignore some of the precision. But it is not possible to measure a construct with less precision or with less specific information and then make it more precise later.

Distinguishing among the Four Levels. The four levels from lowest to greatest or highest precision are nominal, ordinal, interval, and ratio. Each level gives a different type of information (see Table 5.2). *Nominal* measures indicate only that there is a difference among categories (e.g., religion: Protestant, Catholic, Jew, Muslim; racial heritage: African, Asian, Caucasian, Hispanic, other). *Ordinal* measures indicate a difference, *plus* the categories can be ordered or ranked (e.g., letter grades: A, B, C, D, F; opinion measures: Strongly Agree, Agree, Disagree, Strongly Disagree). *Interval* measures everything the first two do, *plus* it can specify the amount of distance between categories (e.g., Fahrenheit or Celsius temperature: 5°, 45°, 90°; IQ scores: 95, 110, 125). Arbitrary zeroes may be used in interval measures; they are just there to help keep score. *Ratio* measures do everything all the other levels do, *plus* there is a true zero, which makes it possible to state relations in terms of proportion or ratios (e.g., money income: $10, $100, $500; years of formal schooling: 1 year, 10 years, 13 years).

In most practical situations, the distinction between interval and ratio levels makes little difference. The arbitrary zeroes of some interval measures can be confusing. For example, a rise in temperature from 30 to 60 degrees is not really a doubling of the temperature, although the numbers double, because zero degrees is not the absence of all heat.

Discrete variables are nominal and ordinal, whereas continuous variables can be measured at the interval or ratio level. A ratio-level measure can be turned into an interval, ordinal, or nominal level. The interval level can always be turned into an ordinal or nominal level, but the process does not work in the opposite way!

In general, use at least five ordinal categories and obtain many observations. This is because the distortion created by collapsing a continuous construct into a smaller number of ordered categories is minimized as the number of categories and the number of observations increase.

The ratio level of measurement is rarely used in the social sciences. For most purposes, it is indistinguishable from interval measurement. The only difference is that ratio measurement has a "true zero." This can be confusing because some measures, like temperature, have zeroes that are not true zeroes. The temperature can be zero, or below zero, but zero is an arbitrary number when it is assigned to temperature. This can be illustrated by comparing zero degrees Celsius with zero degrees Fahrenheit—they are different temperatures. In addition, doubling the degrees in one system does not double the degrees in the other. Likewise, it does not make sense to say that it is "twice as warm," as is possible with ratio measurement, if the temperature rises from 2 to 4 degrees, from 15 to 30 degrees, or from 40 to 80 degrees. Another common

TABLE 5.2 Characteristics of the Four Levels of Measurement

Level	Different Categories	Ranked	Distance between Categories Measured	True Zero
Nominal	Yes			
Ordinal	Yes	Yes		
Interval	Yes	Yes	Yes	
Ratio	Yes	Yes	Yes	Yes

example of arbitrary—not true—zeroes occurs when measuring attitudes where numbers are assigned to statements (e.g., −1 = disagree, 0 = no opinion, +1 = agree). True zeroes exist for variables such as income, age, or years of education. Examples of the four levels of measurement are shown in Table 5.3.

Specialized Measures: Scales and Indexes

Researchers have created thousands of different scales and indexes to measure social variables. For example, scales and indexes have been developed to measure the degree of formalization in bureaucratic organizations, the prestige of occupations, the adjustment of people to a marriage, the intensity of group interaction, the level of social activity in a community, the degree to which a state's sexual assault laws reflect feminist values, and the level of socioeconomic development of a nation. I cannot discuss the thousands of scales and indexes. Instead, I will focus on principles of scale and index construction and explore some major types.

Keep two things in mind. First, virtually every social phenomenon can be measured. Some constructs can be measured directly and produce precise numerical values (e.g., family income). Other constructs require the use of surrogates or proxies that indirectly measure a variable and may not be as precise (e.g., predisposition to commit a crime). Second, a lot can be learned from measures used by other researchers. You are fortunate to have the work of thousands of researchers to draw on. It is not always necessary to start from scratch. You can use a past scale or index, or you can modify it for your own purposes.

Indexes and Scales. You might find the terms *index* and *scale* confusing because they are often used interchangeably. One researcher's scale is another's index. Both produce ordinal- or interval-level measures of a variable. To add to the confusion, scale and index techniques can be combined in one measure. Scales and indexes give a researcher more information about variables and make it possible to assess the quality of measurement. Scales and indexes increase

TABLE 5.3   Example of Levels of Measurement

Variable (Level of Measurement)	How Variable Measured
Religion (nominal)	Different religious denominations (Jewish, Catholic, Lutheran, Baptist) are not ranked, just different (unless one belief is conceptualized as closer to heaven).
Attendance (ordinal)	"How often do you attend religious services? (0) Never, (1) less than once a year, (3) several times a year, (4) about once a month, (5) two or three times a week, or (8) several times a week?" This might have been measured at a ratio level if the exact number of times a person attended was asked instead.
IQ Score (interval)	Most intelligence tests are organized with 100 as average, middle, or normal. Scores higher or lower indicate distance from the average. Someone with a score of 115 has somewhat above average measured intelligence for people who took the test, while 90 is slightly below. Scores of below 65 or above 140 are rare.
Age (ratio)	Age is measured by years of age. There is a true zero (birth). Note that a 40-year-old has lived twice as long as a 20-year-old.

<table>
<tr><td>

Box 5.2

Scales and Indexes: Are They Different?

</td></tr>
</table>

For most purposes, you can treat scales and indexes as interchangeable. Social researchers do not use a consistent nomenclature to distinguish between them.

A *scale* is a measure in which a researcher captures the intensity, direction, level, or potency of a variable construct. It arranges responses or observations on a continuum. A scale can use a single indicator or multiple indicators. Most are at the ordinal level of measurement.

An *index* is a measure in which a researcher adds or combines several distinct indicators of a construct into a single score. This composite score is often a simple sum of the multiple indicators. It is used for content and convergent validity. Indexes are often measured at the interval or ratio level.

Researchers sometimes combine the features of scales and indexes in a single measure. This is common when a researcher has several indicators that are scales (i.e., that measure intensity or direction). He or she then adds these indicators together to yield a single score, thereby creating an index.

---

reliability and validity, and they aid in data reduction; that is, they condense and simplify the information that is collected (see Box 5.2).

Mutually Exclusive and Exhaustive Attributes.
Before discussing scales and indexes, it is important to review features of good measurement. The attributes of all measures, including nominal-level measures, should be mutually exclusive and exhaustive.

Mutually exclusive attributes means that an individual or case fits into one and only one attribute of a variable. For example, a variable measuring type of religion—with the attributes Christian, non-Christian, and Jewish—is not mutually exclusive. Judaism is both a non-Christian religion and a Jewish religion, so a Jewish person fits into both the non-Christian and

the Jewish category. Likewise, a variable measuring type of city, with the attributes river port city, state capital, and interstate highway exit, lacks mutually exclusive attributes. One city could be all three (a river port state capital with an interstate exit), any one of the three, or none of the three.

Exhaustive attributes means that all cases fit into one of the attributes of a variable. When measuring religion, a measure with the attributes Catholic, Protestant, and Jewish is not exclusive. The individual who is a Buddhist, a Moslem, or an agnostic does not fit anywhere. The attributes should be developed so that every possible situation is covered. For example, Catholic, Protestant, Jewish, or other is an exclusive and mutually exclusive set of attributes.

Unidimensionality.
In addition to being mutually exclusive and exhaustive, scales and indexes should also be unidimensional, or one dimensional. *Unidimensionality* means that all the items in a scale or index fit together, or measure a single construct. Unidimensionality was suggested in discussions of content and concurrent validity. Unidimensionality says: If you combine several specific pieces of information into a single score or measure, have all the pieces work together and measure the same thing. Researchers use a statistical measure called Cronbach's alpha to assess unidimenionality. Alpha ranges from a maximum of 1.0 for a perfect score to zero. To be considered a good measure, the alpha should be .70 or higher.

There is an apparent contradiction between using a scale or index to combine parts or subparts of a construct into one measure and the criteria of unidimensionality. It is only an apparent contradiction, however, because constructs are theoretically defined at different levels of abstraction. General, higher-level or more abstract constructs can be defined as containing several subparts. Each subdimension is a part of the construct's overall content.

For example, I define the construct "feminist ideology" as a general ideology about gender. Feminist ideology is a highly abstract and general construct. It includes specific beliefs and attitudes toward social, economic, political, family, and sexual relations. The ideology's five belief areas are parts of the single general construct. The parts are mutually reinforcing and together form a system of beliefs about the dignity, strength, and power of women.

If feminist ideology is unidimensional, then there is a unified belief system that varies from very antifeminist to very profeminist. We can test the validity of the measure that includes multiple indicators that tap the construct's subparts. If one belief area (e.g., sexual relations) is consistently distinct from the other areas in empirical tests, then we question its unidimensionality.

It is easy to become confused: A specific measure can be an indicator of a unidimensional construct in one situation and indicate a part of a different construct in another situation. This is possible because constructs can be used at different levels of abstraction.

For example, a person's attitude toward gender equality with regard to pay is more specific and less abstract than feminist ideology (i.e., beliefs about gender relations throughout society). An attitude toward equal pay can be both a unidimensional construct in its own right and a subpart of the more general and abstract unidimensional construct, *ideology toward gender relations*.

INDEX CONSTRUCTION

The Purpose

You hear about indexes all the time. For example, U.S. newspapers report the Federal Bureau of Investigation (FBI) crime index and the consumer price index (CPI). The FBI index is the sum of police reports on seven so-called index crimes (criminal homicide, aggravated assault, forcible rape, robbery, burglary, larceny of $50 or more, and auto theft). It began with the Uniform Crime Report in 1930. The CPI, which is a measure of inflation, is created by totaling the cost of buying a list of goods and services (e.g., food, rent, and utilities) and comparing the total to the cost of buying the same list in the previous year. The consumer price index has been used by the U.S. Bureau of Labor Statistics since 1919; wage increases, union contracts, and social security payments are based on it. An *index* is a combination of items into a single numerical score. Various components or subparts of a construct are each measured, then combined into one measure.

There are many types of indexes. For example, if you take an exam with 25 questions, the total number of questions correct is a kind of index. It is a composite measure in which each question measures a small piece of knowledge, and all the questions scored correct or incorrect are totaled to produce a single measure.

Indexes measure the most desirable place to live (based on unemployment, commuting time, crime rate, recreation opportunities, weather, and so on), the degree of crime (based on combining the occurrence of different specific crimes), the mental health of a person (based on the person's adjustment in various areas of life), and the like.

One way to demonstrate that indexes are not very complicated is to use one. Answer yes or no to the seven questions that follow on the characteristics of an occupation. Base your answers on your thoughts regarding the following four occupations: long-distance truck driver, medical doctor, accountant, telephone operator. Score each answer 1 for yes and 0 for no.

1. Does it pay a good salary?
2. Is the job secure from layoffs or unemployment?
3. Is the work interesting and challenging?
4. Are its working conditions (e.g., hours, safety, time on the road) good?
5. Are there opportunities for career advancement and promotion?
6. Is it prestigious or looked up to by others?
7. Does it permit self-direction and the freedom to make decisions?

Total the seven answers for each of the four occupations. Which had the highest and which had the lowest score? The seven questions are my operational definition of the construct *good occupation*. Each question represents a subpart of my theoretical definition. A different theoretical definition would result in different questions, perhaps more than seven.

Creating indexes is so easy that it is important to be careful that every item in the index has face validity. Items without face validity should be excluded. Each part of the construct should be measured with at least one indicator. Of course, it is better to measure the parts of a construct with multiple indicators.

Weighting

An important issue in index construction is whether to weight items. Unless it is otherwise stated, assume that an index is unweighted. Likewise, unless you have a good theoretical reason for assigning different weights, use equal weights. An *unweighted index* gives each item equal weight. It involves adding up the items without modification, as if each were multiplied by 1 (or −1 for items that are negative).

In a weighted index, a researcher values or weights some items more than others. The size of weights can come from theoretical assumptions, the theoretical definition, or a statistical technique such as factor analysis. Weighting changes the theoretical definition of the construct.

Weighting can produce different index scores, but in most cases, weighted and unweighted indexes yield similar results. Researchers are concerned with the relationship between variables, and weighted and unweighted indexes usually give similar results for the relationships between variables.

Missing Data

Missing data can be a serious problem when constructing an index. Validity and reliability are threatened whenever data for some cases are missing. There are four ways to attempt to resolve the problem, but none fully solve it.

For example, I construct an index of the degree of societal development in 1975 for 50 nations. The index contains four items: life expectancy, percentage of homes with indoor plumbing, percentage of population that is literate, and number of telephones per 100 people. I locate a source of United Nations statistics for my information. The values for Belgium are 68 + 87 + 97 + 28; for Turkey, the scores are 55 + 36 + 49 + 3; for Finland, however, I discover that literacy data are unavailable. I check other sources of information, but none has the data because they were not collected.

Rates and Standardization

You have heard of crime rates, rates of population growth, and the unemployment rate. Some indexes and single-indicator measures are expressed as rates. Rates involve standardizing the value of an item to make comparisons possible. The items in an index frequently need to be standardized before they can be combined.

Standardization involves selecting a base and dividing a raw measure by the base. For example, City A had 10 murders and City B had 30 murders in the same year. In order to compare murders in the two cities, the raw number of murders needs to be standardized by the city population. If the cities are the same size, City B is more dangerous. But City B may be safer if it is much larger. For example, if City A has 100,000 people and City B has 600,000, then the murder rate per 100,000 is 10 for City A and 5 for City B.

Standardization makes it possible to compare different units on a common base. The process of standardization, also called *norming*, removes the effect of relevant but different characteristics in order to make the important differences visible. For example, there are two classes of students. An art class has 12 smokers and a biology class has 22 smokers. A researcher can compare the rate or incidence of smokers by standardizing the number of smokers by the size of the classes. The art class has 32 students and the biology class has 143 students. One method of standardization that you already know is the use of percentages, whereby measures are standardized to a common base of 100. In terms of percentages, it is easy to see that the art class has more than twice the rate of smokers (37.5 percent) than the biology class (15.4 percent).

A critical question in standardization is deciding what base to use. In the examples given, how did I know to use city size or class size as the base? The choice is not always obvious; it depends on the theoretical definition of a construct.

Different bases can produce different rates. For example, the unemployment rate can be defined as the number of people in the work force who are out of work. The overall unemployment rate is:

$$\text{Unemployment rate} = \frac{\text{Number of unemployed people}}{\text{Total number of people working}}$$

We can divide the total population into subgroups to get rates for subgroups in the population such as White males, African American females, African American males between the ages of 18 and 28, or people with college degrees. Rates for these subgroups may be more relevant to the theoretical definition or research problem. For example, a researcher believes that unemployment is an experience that affects an entire household or family and that the base should be households, not individuals. The rate will look like this:

$$\text{New Unemployment rate} = \frac{\text{Number of households with at least one unemployed person}}{\text{Total number of households}}$$

Different conceptualizations suggest different bases and different ways to standardize.

When combining several items into an index, it is best to standardize items on a common base (see Box 5.3).

SCALES

The Purpose

Scaling, like index construction, creates an ordinal, interval, or ratio measure of a variable expressed as a numerical score. Scales are common in situations where a researcher wants to measure how an individual feels or thinks about something. Some call this the hardness or potency of feelings.

Scales are used for two related purposes. First, scales help in the conceptualization and operationalization processes. Scales show the fit between a set of indicators and a single construct. For example, a researcher believes that there is a single ideological dimension that underlies people's judgments about specific policies (e.g., housing, education, foreign affairs, etc.). Scaling can help determine whether a single construct— for instance, "conservative/ liberal ideology"—underlies the positions people take on specific policies.

Second, scaling produces quantitative measures and can be used with other variables to test hypotheses. This second purpose of scaling is our primary focus because it involves scales as a technique for measuring a variable.

Logic of Scaling

As stated before, scaling is based on the idea of measuring the intensity, hardness, or potency of a variable. Graphic rating scales are an elementary form of scaling. People indicate a rating by checking a point on a line that runs from one extreme to another. This type of scale is easy to construct and use. It conveys the idea of a continuum, and assigning numbers helps people think about quantities. A built-in assumption of scales is that people with the same subjective feeling mark the graphic scale at the same place.

| Box 5.3 | **Standardization and the Real Winners at the Olympics** |

Sports fans in the United States were jubilant about "winning" at the 2000 Olympics by carrying off the most gold medals. However, because they failed to *standardize*, the "win" is an illusion. Of course, the world's richest nation with the third largest population does well in one-on-one competition among all nations. To see what really happened, one must standardize on a base of the population or wealth. Standardization yields a more accurate picture by adjusting the results as if the nations had equal populations and wealth. The results show that the Bahamas, with less than 300,000 citizens (smaller than a medium-sized U.S. city), proportionately won the most gold. Adjusted for its population size or wealth, the United States is not even near the top; it appears to be the leader only because of its great size and wealth. Sports fans in the United States can perpetuate the illusion of being at the top only if they ignore the comparative advantage of the United States.

TOP TEN GOLD MEDAL WINNING COUNTRIES AT THE 2000 OLYMPICS IN SYDNEY

Unstandardized Rank			Standardized Rank*			
Rank	Country	Total	Country	Total	Population	GDP
1	USA	39	Bahamas	1	33.3	20.0
2	Russia	32	Slovenia	2	10	10.0
3	China	28	Cuba	11	9.9	50.0
4	Australia	16	Norway	4	9.1	2.6
5	Germany	14	Australia	16	8.6	4.1
6	France	13	Hungry	8	7.9	16.7
7	Italy	13	Netherlands	12	7.6	3.0
8	Netherlands	12	Estonia	1	7.1	20.0
9	Cuba	11	Bulgaria	5	6.0	41.7
10	Britain	11	Lithuania	2	5.4	18.2
	EU15**	80	EU15	80	2.1	0.9
			USA	39	1.4	0.4

Note: *Population is gold medals per 10 million people and GDP is gold medals per $10 billion;
**EU15 is the 15 nations of the European Union treated as a single unit.
Source: Adapted from *The Economist,* October 7, 2000, p. 52.

Figure 5.4 is an example of a "feeling thermometer" scale that is used to find out how people feel about various groups in society (e.g., the National Organization of Women, the Ku Klux Klan, labor unions, physicians, etc.). This type of measure has been used by political scientists in the National Election Study since 1964 to measure attitudes toward candidates, social groups, and issues.

Commonly Used Scales

Likert Scale. You have probably used *Likert scales;* they are widely used and very common in

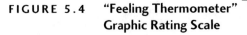

FIGURE 5.4 "Feeling Thermometer" Graphic Rating Scale

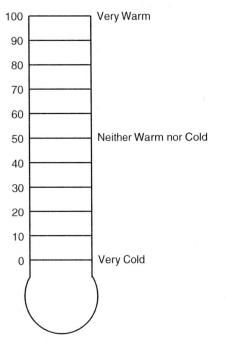

100 — Very Warm
90 —
80 —
70 —
60 —
50 — Neither Warm nor Cold
40 —
30 —
20 —
10 —
0 — Very Cold

survey research. They were developed in the 1930s by Rensis Likert to provide an ordinal-level measure of a person's attitude. Likert scales usually ask people to indicate whether they agree or disagree with a statement. Other modifications are possible; people might be asked whether they approve or disapprove, or whether they believe something is "almost always true." Box 5.4 presents several examples of Likert scales.

Likert scales need a minimum of two categories, such as "agree" and "disagree." Using only two choices creates a crude measure and forces distinctions into only two categories. It is usually better to use four to eight categories. A researcher can combine or collapse categories after the data are collected, but data collected with crude categories cannot be made more precise later.

You can increase the number of categories at the end of a scale by adding "strongly agree," "somewhat agree," "very strongly agree," and so

forth. Keep the number of choices to eight or nine at most. More distinctions than that are probably not meaningful, and people will become confused. The choices should be evenly balanced (e.g., "strongly agree," "agree" with "strongly disagree," "disagree").

Researchers have debated about whether to offer a neutral category (e.g., "don't know," "undecided," "no opinion") in addition to the directional categories (e.g., "disagree," "agree"). A neutral category implies an odd number of categories.

A researcher can combine several Likert scale questions into a composite index if they all measure a single construct. Consider the Social Dominance Index that van Laar and colleagues (2005) used in their study of racial-ethnic attitudes among college roommates (see Box 5.5). As part of a larger survey, they asked four questions about group inequality. The answer to each question was a seven-point Likert scale with choices from Strongly Disagree to Strongly Agree. They created the index by adding the answers for each student to create scores that ranged from 4 to 28. Notice that they worded question number four in a reverse direction from the other questions. The reason for switching directions in this way is to avoid the problem of the *response set*. The response set, also called *response style* and *response bias,* is the tendency of some people to answer a large number of items in the same way (usually agreeing) out of laziness or a psychological predisposition. For example, if items are worded so that saying "strongly agree" always indicates self-esteem, we would not know whether a person who always strongly agreed had high self-esteem or simply had a tendency to agree with questions. The person might be answering "strongly agree" out of habit or a tendency to agree. Researchers word statements in alternative directions, so that anyone who agrees all the time appears to answer inconsistently or to have a contradictory opinion.

Researchers often combine many Likert-scaled attitude indicators into an index. The scale and indexes have properties that are associated

Box 5.4 Examples of Types of Likert Scales

The Rosenberg Self-Esteem Scale

All in all, I am inclined to feel that I am a failure:
1. Almost always true
2. Often true
3. Sometimes true
4. Seldom true
5. Never true

A Student Evaluation of Instruction Scale

Overall, I rate the quality of instruction in this course as:

    Excellent   Good   Average   Fair   Poor

A Market Research Mouthwash Rating Scale

Brand	Dislike Completely	Dislike Somewhat	Dislike a Little	Like a Little	Like Somewhat	Like Completely
X	____	____	____	____	____	____
Y	____	____	____	____	____	____

Work Group Supervisor Scale

My supervisor:

	Never	Seldom	Sometimes	Often	Always
Lets members know what is expected of them	1	2	3	4	5
Is friendly and approachable	1	2	3	4	5
Treats all unit members as equals	1	2	3	4	5

with improving reliability and validity. An index uses multiple indicators, which improves reliability. The use of multiple indicators that measure several aspects of a construct or opinion improves content validity. Finally, the index scores give a more precise quantitative measure of a person's opinion. For example, each person's opinion can be measured with a number from 10 to 40, instead of in four categories: "strongly agree," "agree," "disagree," and "strongly disagree."

Instead of scoring Likert items, as in the previous example, the scores $-2, -1, +1, +2$ could be used. This scoring has an advantage in that a zero implies neutrality or complete ambiguity, whereas a high negative number means an attitude that opposes the opinion represented by a high positive number.

The numbers assigned to the response categories are arbitrary. Remember that the use of a zero does not give the scale or index a ratio level of measurement. Likert scale measures are at the

Box 5.5   Examples of Creating Indexes

Example 1

In a study of college roommates and racial–ethnic groups, van Laar and colleagues (2005) measured Social Dominance (i.e., a feeling that groups are fundamentally unequal) with the following four-item index that used a Likert scale, from 1 (Strongly Disagree) to 7 (Strongly Agree).

1. It is probably a good thing that certain groups are at the top and other groups are at the bottom.
2. Inferior groups should stay in their place.
3. We should do all we can to equalize the conditions of different groups.
4. We should increase social equality.*

*NOTE: This item was reverse scored.

The scores for the Likert responses (1 to 7) for items 1 to 4 were added to yield an index that ranged from 4 to 28 for each respondent. They report a Cronbach's alpha for this index as .74.

Example 2

In a study of perceptions of police misconduct, Weitzer and Tuch (2004) measured a respondent's experiences with police by asking seven questions that had yes or no answers to create two composite indexes. The index for vicarious experiences was the sum of items 2, 4, and 6, with "yes" scored as 1 and "no" scored as zero. An index of personal experience was the sum of answers to items 1, 3, 5, and 7, with "yes" scored as 1 and "no" scored as zero.

1. Have you ever been stopped by police on the street without a good reason?
2. Has anyone else in your household been stopped by police on the street without a good reason?
3. Have the police ever used insulting language toward you?
4. Have the police ever used insulting language toward anyone else in your household?
5. Have the police ever used excessive force against you?
6. Have the police ever used excessive force against anyone else in your household?
7. Have you ever seen a police officer engage in any corrupt activities (such as taking bribes or involvement in drug trade)?

Weitzer and Tuch (2004) report a Cronbach's alpha for the personal experiences index as .78 and for vicarious experience index as .86.

---

ordinal level of measurement because responses indicate a ranking only. Instead of 1 to 4 or −2 to +2, the numbers 100, 70, 50, and 5 would have worked. Also, do not be fooled into thinking that the distances between the ordinal categories are intervals just because numbers are assigned. Although the number system has nice mathematical properties, the numbers are used for convenience only. The fundamental measurement is only ordinal.

The simplicity and ease of use of the Likert scale is its real strength. When several items are combined, more comprehensive multiple indicator measurement is possible. The scale has two limitations: Different combinations of several scale items can result in the same overall score or result, and the response set is a potential danger.

Bogardus Social Distance Scale. The *Bogardus social distance scale* measures the social distance separating ethnic or other groups from each other. It is used with one group to determine how much distance it feels toward a target or "out-group."

The scale has a simple logic. People respond to a series of ordered statements; those that are most threatening or most socially distant are at one end, and those that might be least threatening or socially intimate are at the other end. The logic of the scale assumes that a person who refuses contact or is uncomfortable with the socially distant items will refuse the socially closer items (see Box 5.6).

Researchers use the scale in several ways. For example, people are given a series of statements: People from Group X are entering your country,

---

Box 5.6 Replication of the Original Bogardus Social Distance Scale Study

In 1993, Kleg and Yamamoto (1998) replicated the original 1925 study by Emory Bogardus that first used the social distance scale. The original study had 110 subjects from the Pacific Coast. Participants included 107 White Americans of non-Jewish European ancestry, 1 Jewish White, 1 Chinese, and 1 Japanese (about 70 percent were female). In their 1993 replication, Kleg and Yamamoto selected 135 middle school teachers from an affluent school district in a Colorado metropolitan area. There were 119 non-Jewish Whites, 7 Jewish Whites, 6 African Americans, 1 American Indian, 1 Asian, and 1 unknown (65 percent were female). There were three minor deviations from the 1925 study. First, the original Bogardus respondents were given a list of 39 groups. Those in the replication had a list of 36 groups. The two lists shared 24 groups in common. Three target groups were renamed: Negroes in 1925 versus African Americans in 1993; Syrians versus Arabs; and German-Jews and Russian-Jews vs. Jews. Second, both studies contained seven

categories, but they were worded slightly differently (see below). Third, both studies had seven categories (called anchor points) printed left to right at the top. In the Bogardus original it said: "According to my first feeling reactions I would willingly admit members of each race (as a class, and not the best I have known, nor the worst members) to one or more of the classifications under which I have placed a cross (x)." In the 1993 replication it said: "Social distance means the degree that individuals desire to associate with others. This scale relates to a special form of social distance known as person to group distance. You are given a list of groups. Across from each group there are boxes identified by the labels at the top. Place an "x" in the boxes that indicate the degree of association you would desire to have with each group. Give your first reaction." The main finding was that although the average social distance declined a great deal over over 68 years, the ranking of the 25 groups changed very little (see below).

Instructions

Original 1925 Study	1993 Replication
I would willingly admit members of each race:	*The degree of association I would desire to have with members of each group is:*
1. To close kinship by marriage	To marry into group
2. To my club as personal chums	To have as best friend
3. To my street as neighbors	To have as next-door neighbors
4. To employment in my occupation in my country	To work in the same office
5. To citizenship in my country	To have as speaking acquaintances only
6. As visitors only to my country	To have as visitors to my country
7. Would exclude from my country	To keep out of my country

BOX 5.6 Continued

Results

Group	1925 Original		1993 Replication	
	Mean Score	Rank	Mean Score	Rank
English	1.27	1	1.17	2
Scottish	1.69	2	1.22	6
Irish	1.93	3	1.14	1
French	2.04	4	1.20	4
Dutch	2.12	5	1.25	9
Swedish	2.44	6	1.21	5
Danish	2.48	7	1.23	7
Norwegian	2.67	8	1.25	8
German	2.89	9	1.27	10
Spanish	3.28	10	1.29	11
Italian	3.98	11	1.19	3
Hindu	4.35	12	1.95	23
Polish	4.57	13	1.30	12
Russian	4.57	14	1.33	13
Native American	4.65	15	1.44	16
Jewish	4.83*	16	1.42	15
Greek	4.89	17	1.38	14
Arab	5.00*	18	2.21	24
Mexican	5.02	19	1.56	18
Black American	5.10*	20	1.55	17
Chinese	5.28	21	1.68	20
Japanese	5.30	22	1.62	19
Korean	5.55	23	1.72	21
Turk	5.80	24	1.77	22
Grand Mean	3.82		1.43	

*Slight change in name of group.

are in your town, work at your place of employment, live in your neighborhood, become your personal friends, and marry your brother or sister. People are asked whether they feel comfortable with the statement or if the contact is acceptable. It is also possible to ask whether they feel uncomfortable with the relationship. People may be asked to respond to all statements, or they may keep reading statements until they are not comfortable with a relationship. There is no set number of statements required; the number usually ranges from five to nine. The measure of social distance can be used as either an independent or a dependent variable.

A researcher can use the Bogardus scale to see how distant people feel from one out-group versus another. In addition to studying racial–ethnic groups, it has been used to examine doctor–patient distance. For example, Gordon and associates (2004) found that college students reported different social distance toward people with different disabilities. Over 95 percent would be willing to be a friend with someone with arthritis, cancer, diabetes, or a heart condition. Fewer than 70 percent would ever consider being a friend to someone with mental retardation. The social distance scale is a convenient way to determine how close a respondent feels toward a social group. It has two potential limitations. First, a researcher needs to tailor the categories to a specific out-group and social setting. Second, it is not easy for a researcher to compare how a respondent feels toward several different groups unless the respondent completes a similar social distance scale for all out-groups at the same time. Of course, how a respondent completes the scale and the respondent's actual behavior in specific social situations may differ.

Semantic Differential. *Semantic Differential* provides an indirect measure of how a person feels about a concept, object, or other person. The technique measures subjective feelings toward something by using adjectives. This is because people communicate evaluations through adjectives in spoken and written language. Because most adjectives have polar opposites (e.g., *light/dark, hard/soft, slow/fast*), it uses polar opposite adjectives to create a rating measure or scale. The Semantic Differential captures the connotations associated with whatever is being evaluated and provides an indirect measure of it.

The Semantic Differential has been used for many purposes. In marketing research, it tells how consumers feel about a product; political advisers use it to discover what voters think about a candidate or issue; and therapists use it to determine how a client perceives himself or herself (see Box 5.7).

To use the Semantic Differential, a researcher presents subjects with a list of paired opposite adjectives with a continuum of 7 to 11 points between them. The subjects mark the spot on the continuum between the adjectives that expresses their feelings. The adjectives can be very diverse and should be well mixed (e.g., positive items should not be located mostly on either the right or the left side). Studies of a wide variety of adjectives in English found that they fall into three major classes of meaning: evaluation *(good–bad)*, potency *(strong–weak)*, and activity *(active–passive)*. Of the three classes of meaning, evaluation is usually the most significant. The analysis of results is difficult, and a researcher needs to use statistical procedures to analyze a subject's feelings toward the concept.

Results from a Semantic Differential tell a researcher how one person perceives different concepts or how different people view the same concept. For example, political analysts might discover that young voters perceive their candidate as traditional, weak, and slow, and as halfway between good and bad. Elderly voters perceive the candidate as leaning toward strong, fast, and good, and as halfway between traditional and modern.

Guttman Scaling. *Guttman scaling,* or cumulative scaling, differs from the previous scales or indexes in that researchers use it to evaluate data after they are collected. This means that researchers must design a study with the Guttman scaling technique in mind.

Guttman scaling begins with measuring a set of indicators or items. These can be questionnaire items, votes, or observed characteristics. Guttman scaling measures many different phenomena (e.g., patterns of crime or drug use, characteristics of societies or organizations, voting or political participation, psychological disorders). The indicators are usually measured in a simple yes/no or present/absent fashion. From 3 to 20 indicators can be used. The researcher

Box
5.7   **Example of Using the Semantic Differential**

As part of her undergraduate thesis, Daina Hawkes studied attitudes toward women with tattoos using the semantic differential (Hawkes, Senn, and Thorn, 2004). The researchers had 268 students at a medium-sized Canadian university complete a semantic differential form in response to several scenarios about a 22-year-old woman college student with a tattoo. They had five scenarios in which they varied the size of the tattoo (small versus large) and whether or not it was visible, and one with no details about the tattoo. The authors also varied features of the senario: weight problem or not; part-time job at restaurant, clothing store, or grocery store; boyfriend or not; average grades or failing grades. They used a semantic differential with 22 adjective pairs. They also had participants complete two scales: Feminist and Women's Movement scale and Neosexism scale. The semantic differential terms were selected to indicate three factors: evaluative, activity, and potency (strong/weak). Based on statistical analysis three adjectives were dropped. The 19 items used are listed below. Among other findings, the authors found that there were more negative feelings toward a woman with a visible tattoo.

Good								Bad*
Beautiful								Ugly
Clean								Dirty
Kind								Cruel*
Rich								Poor*
Honest								Dishonest*
Pleasant								Unpleasant*
Successful								Unsuccessful
Reputable								Disreputable
Safe								Dangerous
Gentle								Violent*
Feminine								Masculine
Weak								Powerful*
Passive								Active*
Cautious								Rash*
Soft								Hard
Weak								Strong
Mild								Intense
Delicate								Rugged*

*These items were presented in reverse order.

selects items on the belief that there is a logical relationship among them. He or she then places the results into a Guttman scale and determines whether the items form a pattern that corresponds to the relationship. (See Box 5.8 for an example of a study using Guttman scaling.)

Once a set of items is measured, the researcher considers all possible combinations of responses for the items. For example, three items are measured: whether a child knows her age, her telephone number, and three local elected political officials. The little girl may know her

<table>
<tr><td>Box 5.8</td><td colspan="5">Guttman Scale Example</td></tr>
</table>

Crozat (1998) examined public responses to various forms of political protest. He looked at survey data on the public's acceptance of forms of protest in Great Britain, Germany, Italy, Netherlands, and the United States in 1974 and 1990. He found that the pattern of the public's acceptance formed a Guttman scale. Those who accepted more intense forms of protest (e.g., strikes and sit-ins) almost always accepted more modest forms (e.g., petitions or demonstrations), but not all who accepted modest forms accepted the more intense forms. In addition to showing the usefulness of the Guttman scale, Crozat also found that people in different nations saw protest similarly and the degree of Guttman scalability increased over time. Thus, the pattern of acceptance of protest activities was Guttman "scalable" in both time periods, but it more closely followed the Guttman pattern in 1990 than 1974.

FORM OF PROTEST

	Petitions	Demonstrations	Boycotts	Strike	Sit-In
Guttman Patterns					
	N	N	N	N	N
	Y	N	N	N	N
	Y	Y	N	N	N
	Y	Y	Y	N	N
	Y	Y	Y	Y	N
	Y	Y	Y	Y	Y
Other Patterns (examples only)					
	N	Y	N	Y	N
	Y	N	Y	Y	N
	Y	N	Y	N	N
	N	Y	Y	N	N
	Y	N	N	Y	Y

age but no other answer, or all three, or only her age and telephone number. In fact, for three items there are eight possible combinations of answers or patterns of responses, from not knowing any through knowing all three. There is a mathematical way to compute the number of combinations (e.g., 2^3), but you can write down all the combinations of yes or no for three questions and see the eight possibilities.

The logical relationship among items in Guttman scaling is hierarchical. Most people or cases have or agree to lower-order items. The smaller number of cases that have the higher-order items also have the lower-order ones, but not vice versa. In other words, the higher-order items build on the lower ones. The lower-order items are necessary for the appearance of the higher-order items.

An application of Guttman scaling, known as *scalogram analysis,* lets a researcher test whether a hierarchical relationship exists among the items. For example, it is easier for a child to know her age than her telephone number, and to know her telephone number than the names of political leaders. The items are called *scalable,* or capable of forming a Guttman scale, if a hierarchical pattern exists.

The patterns of responses can be divided into two groups: scaled and errors (or nonscalable). The scaled patterns for the child's knowledge example would be as follows: not knowing any item, knowing only age, knowing only age plus phone number, knowing all three. Other combinations of answers (e.g., knowing the political leaders but not her age) are possible but are nonscalable. If a hierarchical relationship exists among the items, then most answers fit into the scalable patterns.

The strength or degree to which items can be scaled is measured with statistics that measure whether the responses can be reproduced based on a hierarchical pattern. Most range from zero to 100 percent. A score of zero indicates a random pattern, or no hierarchical pattern. A score of 100 percent indicates that all responses to the answer fit the hierarchical or scaled pattern.

Alternative statistics to measure scalability have also been suggested.

CONCLUSION

In this chapter, you learned about the principles and processes of measurement in quantitative and qualitative research. All researchers conceptualize—or refine and clarify their ideas into conceptual definitions. All researchers operationalize—or develop a set of techniques or processes that will link their conceptual definitions to empirical reality. Qualitative and quantitative researchers differ in how they approach these processes, however. The quantitative researcher takes a more deductive path, whereas the qualitative researcher takes a more inductive path. The goal remains the same: to establish unambiguous links between a reseacher's abstract ideas and empirical data.

You also learned about the principles of reliability and validity. Reliability refers to the dependability or consistency of a measure; validity refers to its truthfulness, or how well a construct and data for it fit together. Quantitative and qualitative styles of research significantly diverge in how they understand these principles. Nonetheless, both quantitative and qualitative researchers try to measure in a consistent way, and both seek a tight fit between the abstract ideas they use to understand social world and what occurs in the actual, empirical social world. In addition, you saw how quantitative researchers apply the principles of measurement when they create indexes and scales, and you read about some major scales they use.

Beyond the core ideas of reliability and validity, good measurement requires that you create clear definitions for concepts, use multiple indicators, and, as appropriate, weigh and standardize the data. These principles hold across all fields of study (e.g., family, criminology, inequality, race relations, etc.) and across the many research techniques (e.g., experiments, surveys, etc.).

As you are probably beginning to realize, research involves doing a good job in each phase of a study. Serious mistakes or sloppiness in any one phase can do irreparable damage to the results, even if the other phases of the research project were conducted in a flawless manner.

Key Terms

- Bogardus Social Distance Scale
- conceptual definition
- conceptual hypothesis
- conceptualization
- concurrent validity
- content validity
- continuous variables
- criterion validity
- discrete variables
- empirical hypothesis
- exhaustive attributes
- external validity
- face validity
- Guttman scaling
- index
- internal validity
- interval-level measurement
- levels of measurement
- Likert scale
- measurement validity
- multiple indicators
- mutually exclusive attributes
- nominal-level measurement
- operational definition
- operationalization
- ordinal-level measurement
- predictive validity
- ratio-level measurement
- reliability
- scale
- Semantic Differential
- standardization
- unidimensionality
- validity

Endnote

1. The terms *concept, construct,* and *idea* are used more or less interchangeably, but there are differences in meaning between them. An *idea* is any mental image, belief plan, or impression. It refers to any vague impression, opinion, or thought. A *concept* is a thought, a general notion, or a generalized idea about a class of objects. A *construct* is a thought that is systematically put together, an orderly arrangement of ideas, facts, and impressions. The term *construct* is used here because its emphasis is on taking vague concepts and turning them into systematically organized ideas.

CHAPTER 6

Qualitative and Quantitative Sampling

INTRODUCTION

Qualitative and quantitative researchers approach sampling differently. Most discussions of sampling come from researchers who use the quantitative style. Their primary goal is to get a representative sample, or a small collection of units or cases from a much larger collection or population, such that the researcher can study the smaller group and produce accurate generalizations about the larger group. They tend to use sampling based on theories of probability from mathematics (called probability sampling).

Researchers have two motivations for using probability or random sampling. The first motivation is saving time and cost. If properly conducted, results from a sample may yield results at 1/1,000 the cost and time. For example, instead of gathering data from 20 million people, a researcher may draw a sample of 2,000; the data from those 2,000 are equal for most purposes to the data from all 20 million. The second purpose of probability sampling is accuracy. The results of a well-designed, carefully executed probability sample will produce results that are equally if not more accurate than trying to reach every single person in the whole population. A census is usually an attempt to count everyone. In 2000, the U.S. Census Bureau tried to count everyone in the nation, but it would have been more accurate if it used very specialized statistical sampling.

Qualitative researchers focus less on a sample's representativeness or on detailed techniques for drawing a probability sample. Instead, they focus on how the sample or small collection of cases, units, or activities illuminates key features of social life. The purpose of sampling is to collect cases, events, or actions that clarify and deepen understanding. Qualitative researchers' concern is to find cases that will enhance what the researchers learn about the processes of social life in a specific context. For this reason, qualitative researchers tend to collect a second type of sampling: nonprobability sampling.

NONPROBABILITY SAMPLING

Qualitative researchers rarely draw a representative sample from a huge number of cases to intensely study the sampled cases—the goal in quantitative research. Instead, they use nonprobability or *nonrandom samples*. This means they rarely determine the sample size in advance and have limited knowledge about the larger group or population from which the sample is taken. Unlike the quantitative researcher who uses a preplanned approach based on mathematical theory, the qualitative researcher selects cases gradually, with the specific content of a case determining whether it is chosen. Table 6.1

TABLE 6.1   Types of Nonprobability Samples

Type of Sample	Principle
Haphazard	Get any cases in any manner that is convenient.
Quota	Get a preset number of cases in each of several predetermined categories that will reflect the diversity of the population, using haphazard methods.
Purposive	Get all possible cases that fit particular criteria, using various methods.
Snowball	Get cases using referrals from one or a few cases, and then referrals from those cases, and so forth.
Deviant Case	Get cases that substantially differ from the dominant pattern (a special type of purposive sample).
Sequential	Get cases until there is no additional information or new characteristics (often used with other sampling methods).

shows a variety of nonprobability sampling techniques.

Haphazard, Accidental, or Convenience Sampling

Haphazard sampling can produce ineffective, highly unrepresentative samples and is not recommended. When a researcher haphazardly selects cases that are convenient, he or she can easily get a sample that seriously misrepresents the population. Such samples are cheap and quick; however, the systematic errors that easily occur make them worse than no sample at all. The person-on-the-street interview conducted by television programs is an example of a haphazard sample. Television interviewers go out on the street with camera and microphone to talk to a few people who are convenient to interview. The people walking past a television studio in the middle of the day do not represent everyone (e.g., homemakers, people in rural areas, etc.). Likewise, television interviewers often select people who look "normal" to them and avoid people who are unattractive, poor, very old, or inarticulate.

Another example of a haphazard sample is that of a newspaper that asks readers to clip a questionnaire from the paper and mail it in. Not everyone reads the newspaper, has an interest in the topic, or will take the time to cut out the questionnaire and mail it. Some people will, and the number who do so may seem large (e.g., 5,000), but the sample cannot be used to generalize accurately to the population. Such haphazard samples may have entertainment value, but they can give a distorted view and seriously misrepresent the population.

Quota Sampling

Quota sampling is an improvement over haphazard sampling. In quota sampling, a researcher first identifies relevant categories of people (e.g., male and female; or under age 30, ages 30 to 60, over age 60, etc.), then decides how many to get in each category. Thus, the number of people in various categories of the sample is fixed. For example, a researcher decides to select 5 males and 5 females under age 30, 10 males and 10 females aged 30 to 60, and 5 males and 5 females over age 60 for a 40-person sample. It is difficult to represent all population characteristics accurately (see Figure 6.1).

Quota sampling is an improvement because the researcher can ensure that some differences are in the sample. In haphazard sampling, all those interviewed might be of the same age, sex, or race. But once the quota sampler fixes the categories and number of cases in each category, he or she uses haphazard sampling. For example, the researcher interviews the first five males under age 30 he or she encounters, even if all five just walked out of the campaign headquarters of a political candidate. Not only is misrepresentation possible because haphazard sampling is used within the categories, but nothing prevents the researcher from selecting people who "act friendly" or who want to be interviewed.

A case from the history of sampling illustrates the limitations of quota sampling. George Gallup's American Institute of Public Opinion, using quota sampling, successfully predicted the outcomes of the 1936, 1940, and 1944 U.S. presidential elections. But in 1948, Gallup predicted the wrong candidate. The incorrect prediction had several causes (e.g., many voters were undecided, interviewing stopped early), but a major reason was that the quota categories did not accurately represent all geographical areas and all people who actually cast a vote.

Purposive or Judgmental Sampling

Purposive sampling is used in situations in which an expert uses judgment in selecting cases with a specific purpose in mind. It is inappropriate if it is used to pick the "average housewife" or the "typical school." With purposive sampling, the researcher never knows whether the cases selected represent the population. It is often used in exploratory research or in field research.

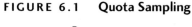

FIGURE 6.1   Quota Sampling

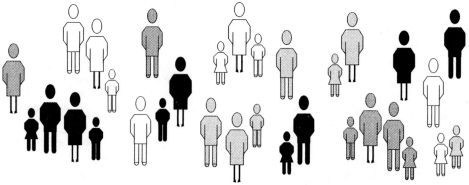

Of 32 adults and children in the street scene, select 10 for the sample:

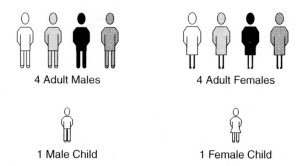

4 Adult Males   4 Adult Females

1 Male Child   1 Female Child

Purposive sampling is appropriate in three situations. First, a researcher uses it to select unique cases that are especially informative. For example, a researcher wants to use content analysis to study magazines to find cultural themes. He or she selects a specific popular women's magazine to study because it is trend setting.

Second, a researcher may use purposive sampling to select members of a difficult-to-reach, specialized population (see Hidden Populations later in this chapter). For example, the researcher wants to study prostitutes. It is impossible to list all prostitutes and sample randomly from the list. Instead, he or she uses subjective information (e.g., locations where prostitutes solicit, social groups with whom prostitutes associate, etc.) and experts (e.g., police who work on vice units, other prostitutes,

etc.) to identify a "sample" of prostitutes for inclusion in the research project. The researcher uses many different methods to identify the cases, because his or her goal is to locate as many cases as possible.

Another situation for purposive sampling occurs when a researcher wants to identify particular types of cases for in-depth investigation. The purpose is less to generalize to a larger population than it is to gain a deeper understanding of types. For example, Gamson (1992) used purposive sampling in a focus group study of what working-class people think about politics. (Chapter 11 discusses focus groups.) Gamson wanted a total of 188 working-class people to participate in one of 37 focus groups. He sought respondents who had not completed college but who were diverse in terms of age, ethnicity, religion, interest in politics, and type of occupation. He recruited people from 35 neighborhoods in the Boston area by going to festivals, picnics, fairs, and flea markets and posting notices on many public bulletin boards. In addition to explaining the study, he paid the respondents well so as to attract people who would not traditionally participate in a study.

Snowball Sampling

Snowball sampling (also called *network, chain referral,* or *reputational sampling*) is a method for identifying and sampling (or selecting) the cases in a network. It is based on an analogy to a snowball, which begins small but becomes larger as it is rolled on wet snow and picks up additional snow. Snowball sampling is a multistage technique. It begins with one or a few people or cases and spreads out on the basis of links to the initial cases.

One use of snowball sampling is to sample a network. Social researchers are often interested in an interconnected network of people or organizations. The network could be scientists around the world investigating the same problem, the elites of a medium-sized city, the members of an organized crime family, persons who sit on the boards of directors of major banks and corporations, or people on a college campus who have had sexual relations with each other. The crucial feature is that each person or unit is connected with another through a direct or indirect linkage. This does not mean that each person directly knows, interacts with, or is influenced by every other person in the network. Rather, it means that, taken as a whole, with direct and indirect links, they are within an interconnected web of linkages.

Researchers represent such a network by drawing a *sociogram*—a diagram of circles connected with lines. For example, Sally and Tim do not know each other directly, but each has a good friend, Susan, so they have an indirect connection. All three are part of the same friendship network. The circles represent each person or

case, and the lines represent friendship or other linkages (see Figure 6.2).

Researchers also use snowball sampling in combination with purposive sampling as in the case of Kissane (2003) in a descriptive field research study of low-income women in Philadelphia. The U.S. policy to provide aid and services to low-income people changed in 1996 to increase assistance (e.g., food pantries, domestic violence shelters, drug rehabilitation services, clothing distribution centers) delivered by nonpublic as opposed to government/public agencies. As frequently occurs, the policy change was made without a study of its consequences in advance. No one knew whether the affected low-income people would use the assistance provided by nonpublic agencies as much as that provided by public agencies. One year after the new policy, Kissane studied whether low-income women were equally likely to use non-public aid. She focused on the Kensington area of Philadelphia. It had a high (over 30 percent)

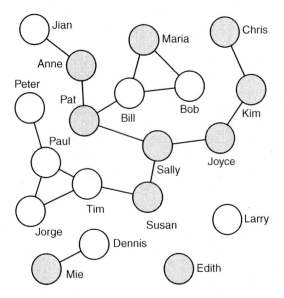

FIGURE 6.2   Sociogram of Friendship Relations

poverty rate and was a predominately White (85 percent) section of the city. First, she identified nonpublic service providers by using telephone books, the Internet, referral literature, and walking down every street of the area until she identified 50 nonpublic social service providers. She observed that a previous study found low-income women in the area distrusted outsiders and intellectuals. Her snowball sample began asking service providers for the names of a few low-income women in the area. She then asked those women to refer her to others in a similar situation, and asked those respondents to refer her to still others. She identified 20 low-income women aged 21 to 50, most who had received public assistance. She conducted in-depth, open-ended interviews about their awareness and experience with nonpublic agencies. She learned that the women were less likely to get nonpublic than public assistance. Compared to public agencies, the women were less aware of nonpublic agencies. Nonpublic agencies created more social stigma, generated greater administrative hassles, were in worse locations, and involved more scheduling difficulties because of limited hours.

Deviant Case Sampling

A researcher uses *deviant case sampling* (also called *extreme case sampling*) when he or she seeks cases that differ from the dominant pattern or that differ from the predominant characteristics of other cases. Similar to purposive sampling, a researcher uses a variety of techniques to locate cases with specific characteristics. Deviant case sampling differs from purposive sampling in that the goal is to locate a collection of unusual, different, or peculiar cases that are not representative of the whole. The deviant cases are selected because they are unusual, and a researcher hopes to learn more about the social life by considering cases that fall outside the general pattern or including what is beyond the main flow of events.

For example, a researcher is interested in studying high school dropouts. Let us say that previous research suggested that a majority of dropouts come from families that have low income, are single parent or unstable, have been geographically mobile, and are racial minorities. The family environment is one in which parents and/or siblings have low education or are themselves dropouts. In addition, dropouts are often engaged in illegal behavior and have a criminal record prior to dropping out. A researcher using deviant case sampling would seek majority-group dropouts who have no record of illegal activities and who are from stable two-parent, upper-middle–income families who are geographically stable and well educated.

Sequential Sampling

Sequential sampling is similar to purposive sampling with one difference. In purposive sampling, the researcher tries to find as many relevant cases as possible, until time, financial resources, or his or her energy is exhausted. The goal is to get every possible case. In sequential sampling, a researcher continues to gather cases until the amount of new information or diversity of cases is filled. In economic terms, information is gathered until the marginal utility, or incremental benefit for additional cases, levels off or drops significantly. It requires that a researcher continuously evaluate all the collected cases. For example, a researcher locates and plans in-depth interviews with 60 widows over 70 years old who have been living without a spouse for 10 or more years. Depending on the researcher's purposes, getting an additional 20 widows whose life experiences, social backgrounds, and worldviews differ little from the first 60 may be unnecessary.

PROBABILITY SAMPLING

A specialized vocabulary or jargon has developed around terms used in probability sampling. Before examining probability sampling, it is important to review its language.

Populations, Elements, and Sampling Frames

A researcher draws a sample from a larger pool of cases, or *elements*. A *sampling element* is the unit of analysis or case in a population. It can be a person, a group, an organization, a written document or symbolic message, or even a social action (e.g., an arrest, a divorce, or a kiss) that is being measured. The large pool is the *population*, which has an important role in sampling. Sometimes, the term *universe* is used interchangeably with *population*. To define the population, a researcher specifies the unit being sampled, the geographical location, and the temporal boundaries of populations. Consider the examples of populations in Box 6.1. All the examples include the elements to be sampled (e.g., people, businesses, hospital admissions,

Box 6.1   Examples of Populations

1. All persons aged 16 or older living in Singapore on December 2, 1999, who were not incarcerated in prison, asylums, and similar institutions

2. All business establishments employing more than 100 persons in Ontario Province, Canada, that operated in the month of July 2005

3. All admissions to public or private hospitals in the state of New Jersey between August 1, 1988, and July 31, 1993

4. All television commercials aired between 7:00 A.M. and 11:00 P.M. Eastern Standard Time on three major U.S. networks between November 1 and November 25, 2006

5. All currently practicing physicians in Australia who received medical degrees between January 1, 1960, and the present

6. All African American male heroin addicts in the Vancouver, British Columbia, or Seattle, Washington, metropolitan areas during 2003

commercials, etc.) and geographical and time boundaries.

A researcher begins with an idea of the population (e.g., all people in a city) but defines it more precisely. The term *target population* refers to the specific pool of cases that he or she wants to study. The ratio of the size of the sample to the size of the target population is the *sampling ratio*. For example, the population has 50,000 people, and a researcher draws a sample of 150 from it. Thus, the sampling ratio is $150/50,000 = 0.003$, or 0.3 percent. If the population is 500 and the researcher samples 100, then the sampling ratio is $100/500 = 0.20$, or 20 percent.

A population is an abstract concept. How can population be an abstract concept, when there are a given number of people at a certain time? Except for specific small populations, one can never truly freeze a population to measure it. For example, in a city at any given moment, some people are dying, some are boarding or getting off airplanes, and some are in cars driving across city boundaries. The researcher must decide exactly who to count. Should he or she count a city resident who happens to be on vacation when the time is fixed? What about the tourist staying at a hotel in the city when the time is fixed? Should he or she count adults, children, people in jails, those in hospitals? A population, even the population of all people over the age of 18 in the city limits of Milwaukee, Wisconsin, at 12:01 A.M. on March 1, 2006, is an abstract concept. It exists in the mind but is impossible to pinpoint concretely.

Because a population is an abstract concept, except for small specialized populations (e.g., all the students in a classroom), a researcher needs to estimate the population. As an abstract concept, the population needs an operational definition. This process is similar to developing operational definitions for constructs that are measured.

A researcher operationalizes a population by developing a specific list that closely approximates all the elements in the population. This list is a *sampling frame.* He or she can choose from many types of sampling frames: telephone directories, tax records, driver's license records, and so on. Listing the elements in a population sounds simple. It is often difficult because there may be no good list of elements in a population.

A good sampling frame is crucial to good sampling. A mismatch between the sampling frame and the conceptually defined population can be a major source of error. Just as a mismatch between the theoretical and operational definitions of a variable creates invalid measurement, so a mismatch between the sampling frame and the population causes invalid sampling. Researchers try to minimize mismatches. For example, you would like to sample all people in a region of the United States, so you decide to get a list of everyone with a driver's license. But some people do not have driver's licenses, and the lists of those with licenses, even if updated regularly, quickly go out of date. Next, you try income tax records. But not everyone pays taxes; some people cheat and do not pay, others have no income and do not have to file, some have died or have not begun to pay taxes, and still others have entered or left the area since the last time taxes were due. You try telephone directories, but they are not much better; some people are not listed in a telephone directory, some people have unlisted numbers, and others have recently moved. With a few exceptions (e.g., a list of all students enrolled at a university), sampling frames are almost always inaccurate.

A sampling frame can include some of those outside the target population (e.g., a telephone directory that lists people who have moved away) or might omit some of those inside it (e.g., those without telephones).

Any characteristic of a population (e.g., the percentage of city residents who smoke cigarettes, the average height of all women over the age of 21, the percent of people who believe in UFOs) is a population *parameter*. It is the true characteristic of the population. Parameters are determined when all elements in a population are measured. The parameter is never known with absolute accuracy for large populations (e.g., an entire nation), so researchers must estimate it on the basis of samples. They use information from the sample, called a *statistic,* to estimate population parameters (see Figure 6.3).

A famous case in the history of sampling illustrates the limitations of the technique. The *Literary Digest,* a major U.S. magazine, sent postcards to people before the 1920, 1924, 1928, and 1932 U.S. presidential elections. The magazine took the names for the sample from automobile registrations and telephone directories— the sampling frame. People returned the postcards indicating whom they would vote for. The magazine correctly predicted all four election outcomes. The magazine's success with predictions was well known, and in 1936, it increased the sample to 10 million. The magazine predicted a huge victory for Alf Landon over

FIGURE 6.3   A Model of the Logic of Sampling

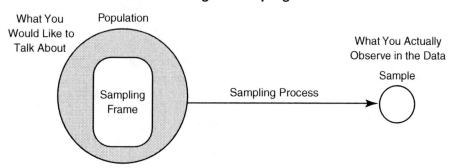

Franklin D. Roosevelt. But the *Literary Digest* was wrong; Franklin D. Roosevelt won by a landslide.

The prediction was wrong for several reasons, but the most important were mistakes in sampling. Although the magazine sampled a large number of people, its sampling frame did not accurately represent the target population (i.e., all voters). It excluded people without telephones or automobiles, a sizable percentage of the population in 1936, during the worst of the Great Depression of the 1930s. The frame excluded as much as 65 percent of the population and a segment of the voting population (lower income) that tended to favor Roosevelt. The magazine had been accurate in earlier elections because people with higher and lower incomes did not differ in how they voted. Also, during earlier elections, before the Depression, more lower-income people could afford to have telephones and automobiles.

You can learn two important lessons from the *Literary Digest* mistake. First, the sampling frame is crucial. Second, the size of a sample is less important than whether or not it accurately represents the population. A representative sample of 2,500 can give more accurate predications about the U.S. population than a nonrepresentative sample of 1 million or 10 million.

Why Random?

The area of applied mathematics called probability theory relies on random processes. The word *random* has a special meaning in mathematics. It refers to a process that generates a mathematically random result; that is, the selection process operates in a truly random method (i.e., no pattern), and a researcher can calculate the probability of outcomes. In a true random process, each element has an equal probability of being selected.

Probability samples that rely on random processes require more work than nonrandom ones. A researcher must identify specific sampling elements (e.g., person) to include in the sample. For example, if conducting a telephone survey, the researcher needs to try to reach the specific sampled person, by calling back four or five times, to get an accurate random sample.

Random samples are most likely to yield a sample that truly represents the population. In addition, random sampling lets a researcher statistically calculate the relationship between the sample and the population—that is, the size of the *sampling error*. A nonstatistical definition of the sampling error is the deviation between sample results and a population parameter due to random processes.

Random sampling is based on a great deal of sophisticated mathematics. This chapter focuses on the fundamentals of how sampling works, the difference between good and bad samples, how to draw a sample, and basic principles of sampling in social research. This does not mean that random sampling is unimportant. It is essential to first master the fundamentals. If you plan to pursue a career using quantitative research, you should get more statistical background than space permits here.

Types of Probability Samples

Simple Random.   The *simple random sample* is both the easiest random sample to understand and the one on which other types are modeled. In simple random sampling, a researcher develops an accurate sampling frame, selects elements from the sampling frame according to a mathematically random procedure, then locates the exact element that was selected for inclusion in the sample.

After numbering all elements in a sampling frame, a researcher uses a list of random numbers to decide which elements to select. He or she needs as many random numbers as there are elements to be sampled; for example, for a sample of 100, 100 random numbers are needed. The researcher can get random numbers from a *random-number table,* a table of numbers chosen in a mathematically random way. Random-number tables are available in most statistics and research methods books. The numbers are generated by a pure random process so that any number has an equal probability of appearing in any position. Computer programs can also produce lists of random numbers.

You may ask, Once I select an element from the sampling frame, do I then return it to the sampling frame or do I keep it separate? The common answer is that it is not returned. Unrestricted random sampling is random sampling with replacement—that is, replacing an element after sampling it so it can be selected again. In simple random sampling without replacement, the researcher ignores elements already selected into the sample.

The logic of simple random sampling can be illustrated with an elementary example—sampling marbles from a jar. I have a large jar full of 5,000 marbles, some red and some white. The 5,000 marbles are my population, and the parameter I want to estimate is the percentage of red marbles in it. I randomly select 100 marbles (I close my eyes, shake the jar, pick one marble, and repeat the procedure 99 times). I now have a random sample of marbles. I count the number of red marbles in my sample to estimate the percentage of red versus white marbles in the population. This is a lot easier than counting all 5,000 marbles. My sample has 52 white and 48 red marbles.

Does this mean that the population parameter is 48 percent red marbles? Maybe not. Because of random chance, my specific sample might be off. I can check my results by dumping the 100 marbles back in the jar, mixing the marbles, and drawing a second random sample of 100 marbles. On the second try, my sample has 49 white marbles and 51 red ones. Now I have a problem. Which is correct? How good is this random sampling business if different samples from the same population can yield different results? I repeat the procedure over and over until I have drawn 130 different samples of 100 marbles each (see Box 6.2 for results). Most people might empty the jar and count all 5,000, but I want to see what is going on. The results of my

130 different samples reveal a clear pattern. The most common mix of red and white marbles is 50/50. Samples that are close to that split are more frequent than those with more uneven splits. The population parameter appears to be 50 percent white and 50 percent red marbles.

Mathematical proofs and empirical tests demonstrate that the pattern found in Box 6.2 always appears. The set of many random samples is my *sampling distribution*. It is a distribution of different samples that shows the frequency of different sample outcomes from many separate random samples. The pattern will appear if the sample size is 1,000 instead of 100; if there are 10 colors of marbles instead of 2; if the population has 100 marbles or 10 million marbles instead of 5,000; and if the population is people, automobiles, or colleges instead of marbles. In fact, the pattern will become clearer as more and more independent random samples are drawn from the population.

The pattern in the sampling distribution suggests that over many separate samples, the true population parameter (i.e., the 50/50 split in the preceding example) is more common than any other result. Some samples deviate from the population parameter, but they are less common. When many different random samples are plotted as in the graph in Box 6.2, then the sampling distribution looks like a normal or bell-shaped curve. Such a curve is theoretically important and is used throughout statistics.

The *central limit theorem* from mathematics tells us that as the number of different random samples in a sampling distribution increases toward infinity, the pattern of samples and the population parameter become more predictable. With a huge number of random samples, the sampling distribution forms a normal curve, and the midpoint of the curve approaches the population parameter as the number of samples increases.

Perhaps you want only one sample because you do not have the time or energy to draw many different samples. You are not alone. A researcher rarely draws many samples. He or she

Box 6.2 Example of Sampling Distribution

Red	White	Number of Samples
42	58	1
43	57	1
45	55	2
46	54	4
47	53	8
48	52	12
49	51	21
50	50	31
51	49	20
52	48	13
53	47	9
54	46	5
55	45	2
57	43	1
	Total	130

Number of red and white marbles that were randomly drawn from a jar of 5,000 marbles with 100 drawn each time, repeated 130 times for 130 independent random samples.

Number of Samples

```
31                                   *
30                                   *
29                                   *
28                                   *
27                                   *
26                                   *
25                                   *
24                                   *
23                                   *
22                                   *
21                              *    *
20                              *    *    *
19                              *    *    *
18                              *    *    *
17                              *    *    *
16                              *    *    *
15                              *    *    *
14                              *    *    *
13                              *    *    *    *
12                         *    *    *    *    *
11                         *    *    *    *    *
10                         *    *    *    *    *
 9                         *    *    *    *    *    *    *
 8                    *    *    *    *    *    *    *    *
 7                    *    *    *    *    *    *    *    *
 6                    *    *    *    *    *    *    *    *
 5                    *    *    *    *    *    *    *    *    *
 4               *    *    *    *    *    *    *    *    *
 3               *    *    *    *    *    *    *    *    *
 2          *    *    *    *    *    *    *    *    *    *    *
 1     *  * *    *    *    *    *    *    *    *    *    *    *    *              *
      42 43 44  45   46   47   48   49   50   51   52   53   54   55  56   57
```

Number of Red Marbles in a Sample

usually draws only one random sample, but the central limit theorem lets him or her generalize from one sample to the population. The theorem is about many samples, but lets the researcher calculate the probability of a particular sample being off from the population parameter.

Random sampling does not guarantee that every random sample perfectly represents the population. Instead, it means that most random samples will be close to the population most of the time, and that one can calculate the probability of a particular sample being inaccurate. A researcher estimates the chance that a particular sample is off or unrepresentative (i.e., the size of the sampling error) by using information from the sample to estimate the sampling distribution. He or she combines this information with knowledge of the central limit theorem to construct *confidence intervals.*

The confidence interval is a relatively simple but powerful idea. When television or newspaper polls are reported, you may hear about something called the margin of error being plus or minus 2 percentage points. This is a version of confidence intervals. A confidence interval is a range around a specific point used to estimate a population parameter. A range is used because the statistics of random processes do not let a researcher predict an exact point, but they let the researcher say with a high level of confidence (e.g., 95 percent) that the true population parameter lies within a certain range.

The calculations for sampling errors or confidence intervals are beyond the level of this discussion, but they are based on the idea of the sampling distribution that lets a researcher calculate the sampling error and confidence interval. For example, I cannot say, "There are precisely 2,500 red marbles in the jar based on a random sample." However, I can say, "I am 95 percent certain that the population parameter lies between 2,450 and 2,550." I can combine characteristics of the sample (e.g., its size, the variation in it) with the central limit theorem to predict specific ranges around the parameter with a great deal of confidence.

Systematic Sampling. *Systematic sampling* is simple random sampling with a shortcut for random selection. Again, the first step is to number each element in the sampling frame. Instead of using a list of random numbers, a researcher calculates a *sampling interval,* and the interval becomes his or her quasi-random selection method. The sampling interval (i.e., 1 in *k*, where *k* is some number) tells the researcher how to select elements from a sampling frame by skipping elements in the frame before selecting one for the sample.

For instance, I want to sample 300 names from 900. After a random starting point, I select every third name of the 900 to get a sample of 300. My sampling interval is 3. Sampling intervals are easy to compute. I need the sample size and the population size (or sampling frame size as a best estimate). You can think of the sampling interval as the inverse of the sampling ratio. The sampling ratio for 300 names out of 900 is 300/900 = .333 = 33.3 percent. The sampling interval is 900/300 = 3.

In most cases, a simple random sample and a systematic sample yield virtually equivalent results. One important situation in which systematic sampling cannot be substituted for simple random sampling occurs when the elements in a sample are organized in some kind of cycle or pattern. For example, a researcher's sampling frame is organized by married couples with the male first and the female second (see Table 6.2). Such a pattern gives the researcher an unrepresentative sample if systematic sampling is used. His or her systematic sample can be nonrepresentative and include only wives because of how the cases are organized. When his or her sample frame is organized as couples, even-numbered sampling intervals result in samples with all husbands or all wives.

Table 6.3 illustrates simple random sampling and systematic sampling. Notice that different names were drawn in each sample. For example, H. Adams appears in both samples, but C. Droullard is only in the simple random sample. This is because it is rare for any two random samples to be identical.

TABLE 6.2   Problems with Systematic Sampling of Cyclical Data

Case	
1	Husband
2[a]	Wife
3	Husband
4	Wife
5	Husband
6[a]	Wife
7	Husband
8	Wife
9	Husband
10[a]	Wife
11	Husband
12	Wife

Random start = 2; Sampling interval = 4.
[a]Selected into sample.

The sampling frame contains 20 males and 20 females (gender is in parenthesis after each name). The simple random sample yielded 3 males and 7 females, and the systematic sample yielded 5 males and 5 females. Does this mean that systematic sampling is more accurate? No. To check this, draw a new sample using different random numbers; try taking the first two digits and beginning at the end (e.g., 11 from 11921, then 43 from 43232). Also draw a new systematic sample with a different random start. The last time the random start was 18. Try a random start of 11. What did you find? How many of each sex?

Stratified Sampling.   In *stratified sampling,* a researcher first divides the population into subpopulations (strata) on the basis of supplementary information. After dividing the population into strata, the researcher draws a random sample from each subpopulation. He or she can sample randomly within strata using simple

TABLE 6.3   How to Draw Simple Random and Systematic Samples

1. Number each case in the sampling frame in sequence. The list of 40 names is in alphabetical order, numbered from 1 to 40.

2. Decide on a sample size. We will draw two 25 percent (10-name) samples.

3. For a *simple random sample,* locate a random-number table (see excerpt). Before using random-number table, count the largest number of digits needed for the sample (e.g., with 40 names, two digits are needed; for 100 to 999, three digits; for 1,000 to 9,999, four digits). Begin anywhere on the random number table (we will begin in the upper left) and take a set of digits (we will take the last two). Mark the number on the sampling frame that corresponds to the chosen random number to indicate that the case is in the sample. If the number is too large (over 40), ignore it. If the number appears more than once (10 and 21 occurred twice in

the example), ignore the second occurrence. Continue until the number of cases in the sample (10 in our example) is reached.

4. For a *systematic sample,* begin with a random start. The easiest way to do this is to point blindly at the random number table, then take the closest number that appears on the sampling frame. In the example, 18 was chosen. Start with the random number, then count the sampling interval, or 4 in our example, to come to the first number. Mark it, and then count the sampling interval for the next number. Continue to the end of the list. Continue counting the sampling interval as if the beginning of the list was attached to the end of the list (like a circle). Keep counting until ending close to the start, or on the start if the sampling interval divides evenly into the total of the sampling frame.

TABLE 6.3 *Continued*

No.	Name (Gender)	Simple Random	Systematic	No.	Name (Gender)	Simple Random	Systematic
01	Abrams, J. (M)			21	Hjelmhaug, N. (M)	Yes*	
02	Adams, H. (F)	Yes	Yes (6)	22	Huang, J. (F)	Yes	Yes (1)
03	Anderson, H. (M)			23	Ivono, V. (F)		
04	Arminond, L. (M)			24	Jaquees, J. (M)		
05	Boorstein, A. (M)			25	Johnson, A. (F)		
06	Breitsprecher, P. (M)	Yes	Yes (7)	26	Kennedy, M. (F)		Yes (2)
07	Brown, D. (F)			27	Koschoreck, L. (F)		
08	Cattelino, J. (F)			28	Koykkar, J. (M)		
09	Cidoni, S. (M)			29	Kozlowski, C. (F)	Yes	
10	Davis, L. (F)	Yes*	Yes (8)	30	Laurent, J. (M)		Yes (3)
11	Droullard, C. (M)	Yes		31	Lee, R. (F)		
12	Durette, R. (F)			32	Ling, C. (M)		
13	Elsnau, K. (F)	Yes		33	McKinnon, K. (F)		
14	Falconer, T. (M)		Yes (9)	34	Min, H. (F)	Yes	Yes (4)
15	Fuerstenberg, J. (M)			35	Moini, A. (F)		
16	Fulton, P. (F)			36	Navarre, H. (M)		
17	Gnewuch, S. (F)			37	O'Sullivan, C. (M)		
18	Green, C. (M)		START, Yes (10)	38	Oh, J. (M)		Yes (5)
19	Goodwanda, T. (F)	Yes		39	Olson, J. (M)		
20	Harris, B. (M)			40	Ortiz y Garcia, L. (F)		

Excerpt from a Random-Number Table (for Simple Random Sample)

15010	18590	00102	42210	94174	22099
90122	38221	21529	00013	04734	60457
67256	13887	94119	11077	01061	27779
13761	23390	12947	21280	44506	36457
81994	66611	16597	44457	07621	51949
79180	25992	46178	23992	62108	43232
07984	47169	88094	82752	15318	11921

* Numbers that appeared twice in random numbers selected.

random or systematic sampling. In stratified sampling, the researcher controls the relative size of each stratum, rather than letting random processes control it. This guarantees representativeness or fixes the proportion of different strata within a sample. Of course, the necessary supplemental information about strata is not always available.

In general, stratified sampling produces samples that are more representative of the population than simple random sampling if the stratum information is accurate. A simple example illustrates why this is so. Imagine a population that is 51 percent female and 49 percent male; the population parameter is a sex ratio of 51 to 49. With stratified sampling, a researcher draws random samples among females and among males so that the sample contains a 51 to 49 percent sex ratio. If the researcher had used simple random sampling, it would be possible for a random sample to be off from the true sex ratio in the population. Thus, he or she makes fewer errors representing the population and has a smaller sampling error with stratified sampling.

Researchers use stratified sampling when a stratum of interest is a small percentage of a population and random processes could miss the stratum by chance. For example, a researcher draws a sample of 200 from 20,000 college students. He or she gets information from the college registrar indicating that 2 percent of the 20,000 students, or 400, are divorced women with children under the age of 5. This group is important to include in the sample. There would be 4 such students (2 percent of 200) in a representative sample, but the researcher could miss them by chance in one simple random sample. With stratified sampling, he or she obtains a list of the 400 such students from the registrar and randomly selects 4 from it. This guarantees that the sample represents the population with regard to the important strata (see Box 6.3).

In special situations, a researcher may want the proportion of a stratum in a sample to differ from its true proportion in the population. For example, the population contains 0.5 percent Aleuts, but the researcher wants to examine Aleuts in particular. He or she oversamples so that Aleuts make up 10 percent of the sample. With this type of disproportionate stratified sample, the researcher cannot generalize directly from the sample to the population without special adjustments.

In some situations, a researcher wants the proportion of a stratum or subgroup to differ from its true proportion in the population. For example, Davis and Smith (1992) reported that the 1987 General Social Survey (explained in a later chapter) oversampled African Americans. A random sample of the U.S. population yielded 191 Blacks. Davis and Smith conducted a separate sample of African Americans to increase the total number of Blacks to 544. The 191 Black respondents are about 13 percent of the random sample, roughly equal to the percentage of Blacks in the U.S. population. The 544 Blacks are 30 percent of the disproportionate sample. The researcher who wants to use the entire sample must adjust it to reduce the number of sampled African Americans before generalizing to the U.S. population. Disproportionate sampling helps the researcher who wants to focus on issues most relevant to a subpopulation. In this case, he or she can more accurately generalize to African Americans using the 544 respondents than using a sample of only 191. The larger sample is more likely to reflect the full diversity of the African American subpopulation.

Cluster Sampling. *Cluster sampling* addresses two problems: Researchers lack a good sampling frame for a dispersed population and the cost to reach a sampled element is very high. For example, there is no single list of all automobile mechanics in North America. Even if a researcher got an accurate sampling frame, it would cost too much to reach the sampled mechanics who are geographically spread out. Instead of using a single sampling frame, researchers use a sampling design that involves multiple stages and clusters.

A *cluster* is a unit that contains final sampling elements but can be treated temporarily as a sampling element itself. A researcher first samples clusters, each of which contains elements, then draws a second sample from within the clusters selected in the first stage of sampling. In other words, the researcher randomly samples clusters, then randomly samples elements from within the selected clusters. This has a big practical advantage. He or she can create a good sampling frame of clusters, even if it is impossible to create one for sampling elements. Once the researcher gets a sample of clusters, creating a

Box 6.3	Illustration of Stratified Sampling

SAMPLE OF 100 STAFF OF GENERAL HOSPITAL, STRATIFIED BY POSITION

Position	Population		Simple Random Sample	Stratified Sample	Errors Compared to the Population
	N	Percent	n	n	
Administrators	15	2.88	1	3	−2
Staff physicians	25	4.81	2	5	−3
Intern physicians	25	4.81	6	5	+1
Registered nurses	100	19.23	22	19	+3
Nurse assistants	100	19.23	21	19	+2
Medical technicians	75	14.42	9	14	+5
Orderlies	50	9.62	8	10	−2
Clerks	75	14.42	5	14	+1
Maintenance staff	30	5.77	3	6	−3
Cleaning staff	25	4.81	3	5	−2
Total	520	100.00	100	100	

Randomly select 3 of 15 administrators, 5 of 25 staff physicians, and so on.

Note: Traditionally, N symbolizes the number in the population and n represents the number in the sample.

The simple random sample overrepresents nurses, nursing assistants, and medical technicians, but underrepresents administrators, staff physicians, maintenance staff, and cleaning staff. The stratified sample gives an accurate representation of each type of position.

sampling frame for elements within each cluster becomes more manageable. A second advantage for geographically dispersed populations is that elements within each cluster are physically closer to one another. This may produce a savings in locating or reaching each element.

A researcher draws several samples in stages in cluster sampling. In a three-stage sample, stage 1 is random sampling of big clusters; stage 2 is random sampling of small clusters within each selected big cluster; and the last stage is sampling of elements from within the sampled small clusters. For example, a researcher wants a sample of individuals from Mapleville. First, he or she randomly samples city blocks, then households within blocks, then individuals within households (see Box 6.4). Although there is no accurate list of all residents of Mapleville, there is an accurate list of blocks in the city. After selecting a random sample of blocks, the researcher counts all households on the selected blocks to create a sample frame for each block. He or she then uses the list of households to draw a random sample at the stage of sampling households. Finally, the researcher chooses a specific individual within each sampled household.

Box 6.4 **Illustration of Cluster Sampling**

Goal: Draw a random sample of 240 people in Mapleville.

Step 1: Mapleville has 55 districts. Randomly select 6 districts.

1 2 3* 4 5 6 7 8 9 10 11 12 13 14 15* 16 17 18 19 20 21 22 23 24 25 26
27* 28 29 30 31* 32 33 34 35 36 37 38 39 40* 41 42 43 44 45 46 47 48
49 50 51 52 53 54* 55

* = Randomly selected.

Step 2: Divide the selected districts into blocks. Each district contains 20 blocks. Randomly select 4 blocks from the district.

Example of District 3 (selected in step 1):

1 2 3 4* 5 6 7 8 9 10* 11 12 13* 14 15 16 17* 18 19 20

* = Randomly selected.

Step 3: Divide blocks into households. Randomly select households.

Example of Block 4 of District 3 (selected in step 2):

Block 4 contains a mix of single-family homes, duplexes, and four-unit apartment buildings. It is bounded by Oak Street, River Road, South Avenue, and Greenview Drive. There are 45 households on the block. Randomly select 10 households from the 45.

1	#1 Oak Street	16	"	31*	"	
2	#3 Oak Street	17*	#154 River Road	32*	"	
3*	#5 Oak Street	18	#156 River Road	33	"	
4	"	19*	#158 River Road	34	#156 Greenview Drive	
5	"	20*	"	35*	"	
6	"	21	#13 South Avenue	36	"	
7	#7 Oak Street	22	"	37	"	
8	"	23	#11 South Avenue	38	"	
9*	#150 River Road	24	#9 South Avenue	39	#158 Greenview Drive	
10*	"	25	#7 South Avenue	40	"	
11	"	26	#5 South Avenue	41	"	
12	"	27	#3 South Avenue	42	"	
13	#152 River Road	28	#1 South Avenue	43	#160 Greenview Drive	
14	"	29*	"	44	"	
15	"	30	#152 Greenview Drive	45	"	

* = Randomly selected.

Step 4: Select a respondent within each household.

Summary of cluster sampling:

1 person randomly selected per household
10 households randomly selected per block
4 blocks randomly selected per district
6 districts randomly selected in the city
1 × 10 × 4 6 = 240 people in sample

Cluster sampling is usually less expensive than simple random sampling, but it is less accurate. Each stage in cluster sampling introduces sampling errors. This means a multistage cluster sample has more sampling errors than a one-stage random sample.

A researcher who uses cluster sampling must decide the number of clusters and the number of elements within each cluster. For example, in a two-stage cluster sample of 240 people from Mapleville, the researcher could randomly select 120 clusters and select 2 elements from each, or randomly select 2 clusters and select 120 elements in each. Which is best? The general answer is that a design with more clusters is better. This is because elements within clusters (e.g., people living on the same block) tend to be similar to each other (e.g., people on the same block tend to be more alike than those on different blocks). If few clusters are chosen, many similar elements could be selected, which would be less representative of the total population. For example, the researcher could select two blocks with relatively wealthy people and draw 120 people from each. This would be less representative than a sample with 120 different city blocks and 2 individuals chosen from each.

When a researcher samples from a large geographical area and must travel to each element, cluster sampling significantly reduces travel costs. As usual, there is a tradeoff between accuracy and cost.

For example, Alan, Ricardo, and Barbara each plan to visit and personally interview a sample of 1,500 students who represent the population of all college students in North America. Alan obtains an accurate sampling frame of all students and uses simple random sampling. He travels to 1,000 different locations to interview one or two students at each. Ricardo draws a random sample of three colleges from a list of all 3,000 colleges, then visits the three and selects 500 students from each. Barbara draws a random sample of 300 colleges. She visits the 300 and selects 5 students at each. If travel costs average $250 per location, Alan's travel bill is

$250,000, Ricardo's is $750, and Barbara's is $75,000. Alan's sample is highly accurate, but Barbara's is only slightly less accurate for one-third the cost. Ricardo's sample is the cheapest, but it is not representative at all.

Probability Proportionate to Size (PPS). There are two methods of cluster sampling. The method just described is proportionate or unweighted cluster sampling. It is proportionate because the size of each cluster (or number of elements at each stage) is the same. The more common situation is for the cluster groups to be of different sizes. When this is the case, the researcher must adjust the probability or sampling ratio at various stages in sampling (see Box 6.5).

The foregoing cluster sampling example with Alan, Barbara, and Ricardo illustrates the problem with unweighted cluster sampling. Barbara drew a simple random sample of 300 colleges from a list of all 3,000 colleges, but she made a mistake—unless every college has an identical number of students. Her method gave each college an equal chance of being selected—a 300/3,000 or 10 percent chance. But colleges have different numbers of students, so each student does not have an equal chance to end up in her sample.

Barbara listed every college and sampled from the list. A large university with 40,000 students and a small college with 400 students had an equal chance of being selected. But if she chose the large university, the chance of a given student at that college being selected was 5 in 40,000 (5/40,000 = 0.0125 percent), whereas a student at the small college had a 5 in 400 (5/400 = 1.25 percent) chance of being selected. The small-college student was 100 times more likely to be in her sample. The total probability of being selected for a student from the large university was 0.125 percent (10 × 0.0125), while it was 12.5 percent (10 × 1.25) for the small-college student. Barbara violated a principle of random sampling—that each element has an equal chance to be selected into the sample.

Box 6.5 Example Sample

Sampling has many terms for the different parts of samples or types of samples. A complex sample illustrates how researchers use them. Look at the 1980 sample for the best-known national U.S. survey in sociology, the General Social Survey.

The *population* is defined as all resident adults (18 years or older) in the U.S. for the *universe* of all Americans. The *target population* consists of all English-speaking adults who live in households, excluding those living in institutional settings such as college dormitories, nursing homes, or military quarters. The researchers estimated that 97.3 percent of all resident adults lived in households and that 97 percent of the household population spoke sufficient English to be interviewed.

The researchers used a complex multistage probability sample that is both a *cluster sample* and a *stratified sample*. First, they created a national *sampling frame* of all U.S. counties, independent cities, and Standard Metropolitan Statistical Areas (SMSAs), a Census Bureau designation for larger cities and surrounding areas. Each *sampling element* at this first level had about 4,000 households. They divided these elements into strata. The strata were the four major geographic regions as defined by the Census Bureau, divided into metropolitan and nonmetropolitan areas. They then sampled from each strata using *probability proportionate to size (PPS)* random selection, based on the number of housing units in each county or SMSA. This gave them a sample of 84 counties or SMSAs.

For the second stage, the researchers identified city blocks, census tracts, or the rural equivalent in each county or SMSA. Each *sampling element* (e.g., city block) had a minimum of 50 housing units. In order to get an accurate count of the number of housing units for some counties, a researcher counted addresses in the field. The researchers selected 6 or more blocks within each county or SMSA using PPS to yield 562 blocks.

In the third stage, the researchers used the household as a *sampling element*. They randomly selected households from the addresses in the block. After selecting an address, an interviewer contacted the household and chose an eligible respondent from it. The interviewer looked at a selection table for possible respondents and interviewed a type of respondent (e.g., second oldest) based on the table. In total, 1,934 people were contacted for interviews and 75.9 percent of interviews were completed. This gave a final sample size of 1,468. We can calculate the *sampling ratio* by dividing 1,468 by the total number of adults living in households, which was about 150 million, which is 0.01 percent. To check the representativeness of their sample, the researchers also compared characteristics of the sample to census results (see Davis and Smith, 1992: 31–44).

If Barbara uses *probability proportionate to size (PPS)* and samples correctly, then each final sampling element or student will have an equal probability of being selected. She does this by adjusting the chances of selecting a college in the first stage of sampling. She must give large colleges with more students a greater chance of being selected and small colleges a smaller chance. She adjusts the probability of selecting a college on the basis of the proportion of all students in the population who attend it. Thus, a college with 40,000 students will be 100 times more likely to be selected than one with 400 students. (See Box 6.6 for another example.)

Random-Digit Dialing. *Random-digit dialing (RDD)* is a special sampling technique used in research projects in which the general public is interviewed by telephone. It differs from the traditional method of sampling for telephone interviews because a published telephone directory is not the sampling frame.

<table>
<tr><td>Box
6.6</td><td>Cluster Sample Example</td></tr>
</table>

Vaquera and Kao (2005) studied displays of affection among adolescent couples in which the couple were either from the same or different racial groups. Their data were from a national longitudinal study of adolescent health given to students in grades 7 through 12 in 80 randomly selected U.S. high schools. There were over 90,000 students in these schools. After the schools were sampled, approximately 200 students were sampled for interviews from within those schools. Thus, the first cluster was the school, and students were sampled from within the school. Because the schools were not of the same size, ranging from 100 to 3,000 students, the authors adjusted using probabilities proportionate to size (PPS). They found that 53 percent of respondents had a relationship with someone of the opposite sex in the previous 18 months. Whites and Blacks were more likely to have same-race relationships (90 percent) compared to Asians and Hispanics (70 percent). The authors found that same- and mixed-race couples differed little in showing intimate affection, but the interracial couples were less likely to do so in public than the same-race couples.

Three kinds of people are missed when the sampling frame is a telephone directory: people without telephones, people who have recently moved, and people with unlisted numbers. Those without phones (e.g., the poor, the uneducated, and transients) are missed in any telephone interview study, but the proportion of the general public with a telephone is nearly 95 percent in advanced industrialized nations. As the percentage of the public with telephones has increased, the percentage with unlisted numbers has also grown. Several kinds of people have unlisted numbers: people who want to avoid collection agencies; the very wealthy; and those who want privacy and want to avoid obscene calls, salespeople, and prank calls. In some urban areas, the percentage of unlisted numbers is as high as

50 percent. In addition, people change their residences, so directories that are published annually or less often have numbers for people who have left and do not list those who have recently moved into an area. Plus, directories do not list cell phone numbers. A researcher using RDD randomly selects telephone numbers, thereby avoiding the problems of telephone directories. The population is telephone numbers, not people with telephones. Random-digit dialing is not difficult, but it takes time and can frustrate the person doing the calling.

Here is how RDD works in the United States. Telephone numbers have three parts: a three-digit area code, a three-digit exchange number or central office code, and a four-digit number. For example, the area code for Madison, Wisconsin, is 608, and there are many exchanges within the area code (e.g., 221, 993, 767, 455); but not all of the 999 possible three-digit exchanges (from 001 to 999) are active. Likewise, not all of the 9,999 possible four-digit numbers in an exchange (from 0000 to 9999) are being used. Some numbers are reserved for future expansion, are disconnected, or are temporarily withdrawn after someone moves. Thus, a possible U.S. telephone number consists of an active area code, an active exchange number, and a four-digit number in an exchange.

In RDD, a researcher identifies active area codes and exchanges, then randomly selects four-digit numbers. A problem is that the researcher can select any number in an exchange. This means that some selected numbers are out of service, disconnected, pay phones, or numbers for businesses; only some numbers are what the researcher wants—working residential phone numbers. Until the researcher calls, it is not possible to know whether the number is a working residential number. This means spending a lot of time getting numbers that are disconnected, for businesses, and so forth.

Remember that the sampling element in RDD is the phone number, not the person or the household. Several families or individuals can share the same phone number, and in other situations each person may have a separate phone number or more than one phone number. This means that after a working residential phone is reached, a second stage of sampling is necessary, within household sampling, to select the person to be interviewed.

Box 6.5 presents an example of how the many sampling terms and ideas can be used together in a specific real-life situation.

Hidden Populations

In contrast to sampling the general population or visible and accessible people, sampling *hidden populations* (i.e., people who engage in concealed activities) is a recurrent issue in the studies of deviant or stigmatized behavior. It illustrates the creative application of sampling principles, mixing qualitative and quantitative styles of research and often using nonprobability techniques. Examples of hidden populations include illegal drug users, prostitutes, homosexuals, people with HIV/AIDS, homeless people, and others.

Tyldum and Brunovskis (2005) described ways to measure the hidden population of women and children victims of sex trafficking in Norway. They suggested using multiple sampling approaches and thinking of in terms of several overlapping populations in which victims are a subset. One population is all working prostitutes. By telephoning all identifiable escort and massage services, then calculating response rates and the number of women per phone, the authors estimated that 600 female prostitutes worked in the Oslo metro area in October 2003. Based on number of months most women work in prostitution and their turnover rate each year, they estimated that 1,100 different women work as prostitutes in Oslo in a year. Of these, about 80 percent of them are of non-Norwegian origin. Victims of sex trafficking are a subset among the roughly 800 non-Norwegians who work as prostitutes who are being exploited by others and working involuntary. A second population is the women law-enforcement officials or

nongovernment service agencies identified as victims. Law-enforcement estimates depend on the specific level of enforcement efforts and are most likely to identify a small percent of the most visible and serious cases. Similar difficulties exist with nongovernment service agencies that provide aid to victims. Thus, during the first 10 months of 2004, Norwegian police detected 42 sex trafficking victims. This is subset of all possible trafficking victims. For this population Tyldum and Brunovskis suggested using a capture-recapture method borrowed from biology. In capture-recapture, a percentage of the same cases will reappear across multiple attempts to "capture" cases (with a release after past capture). This percentage recaptured allows researchers to estimate the size of the total population. A third population is that of migrants who have returned to their country of origin. By surveying returnees and estimating the proportion of them who are former trafficking victims, researchers have another way to estimate the size of the hidden population.

Draus and associates (2005) described their sampling a hidden population in a field research study of illicit drug users in four rural Ohio counties. They used respondent-driven sampling (RDS), which is a version of snowball sampling and appropriate when members of a hidden population are likely to maintain contact with one another. This type of sampling begins by identifying an eligible case or participant. This person, called a "seed," is given referral coupons to distribute among other eligible people who engage in the same activity. For each successful referral, the "seed" receives some money. This process is repeated with several waves of new recuits until the a point of saturation (see Sequential Sampling earlier in this chapter). In the study by Draus and associates, each interviewed drug-using participant was paid $50 for an initial two-hour interview and $35 for an hour-long follow-up interview. The participants received three referral coupons at the end of the initial interview and got $10 for each eligible participant they referred who completed an initial interview. No participant received more than three referral coupons. Sometimes this yielded no new participants, but at other times more than the three people with referral coupons were recruited. In one case, a young man heard about the study at a local tatoo parlor and called the study office in July 2003. He (participant 157) had been a powder cocaine user and in his interview said he knew many other drug users. He referred two new participants (participants 161 and 146) who came in about one month later. Participant 161 did not refer anyone new, but participant 146 referred four new people, and two of the four (154 and 148) referred still others. Participant 154 referred four new people and 146 referred one new person, and that one person, (participant 158) referred four others. This sampling process that took place in different geographic locations produced 249 users of cocaine or methanmphetamine between June 2002 and February 2004.

You are now familiar with several major types of probability samples (see Table 6.4) and supplementary techniques used with them (e.g., PPS, within-household, RDD, and RDS) that may be appropriate. In addition, you have seen how researchers combine nonprobability and probability sampling for special situations, such as hidden populations. Next, we turn to determining a sample size for probability samples.

TABLE 6.4   Types of Probability Samples

Type of Sample	Technique
Simple Random	Create a sampling frame for all cases, then select cases using a purely random process (e.g., random-number table or computer program).
Stratified	Create a sampling frame for each of several categories of cases, draw a random sample from each category, then combine the several samples.
Systematic	Create a sampling frame, calculate the sampling interval 1/k, choose a random starting place, then take every 1/k case.
Cluster	Create a sampling frame for larger cluster units, draw a random sample of the cluster units, create a sampling frame for cases within each selected cluster unit, then draw a random sample of cases, and so forth.

How Large Should a Sample Be?

Students and new researchers often ask, "How large does my sample have to be?" The best answer is, "It depends." It depends on the kind of data analysis the researcher plans, on how accurate the sample has to be for the researcher's purposes, and on population characteristics. As you have seen, a large sample size alone does not guarantee a representative sample. A large sample without random sampling or with a poor sampling frame is less representative than a smaller one with random sampling and an excellent sampling frame. Good samples for qualitative purposes can be very small.

The question of sample size can be addressed in two ways. One is to make assumptions about the population and use statistical equations about random sampling processes. The calculation of sample size by this method requires a statistical discussion that is beyond the level of this text. The researcher must make assumptions about the degree of confidence (or number of errors) that is acceptable and the degree of variation in the population.

A second and more frequently used method is a rule of thumb—a conventional or commonly accepted amount. Researchers use it because they rarely have the information required by the statistical method and because it gives sample sizes close to those of the statistical method. Rules of thumb are not arbitrary but are based on past experience with samples that have met the requirements of the statistical method.

One principle of sample sizes is, the smaller the population, the bigger the sampling ratio has to be for an accurate sample (i.e., one with a high probability of yielding the same results as the entire population). Larger populations permit smaller sampling ratios for equally good samples. This is because as the population size grows, the returns in accuracy for sample size shrink.

For small populations (under 1,000), a researcher needs a large sampling ratio (about 30 percent). For example, a sample size of about 300 is required for a high degree of accuracy. For moderately large populations (10,000), a smaller sampling ratio (about 10 percent) is needed to be equally accurate, or a sample size of around 1,000. For large populations (over 150,000), smaller sampling ratios (1 percent) are possible, and samples of about 1,500 can be very accurate. To sample from very large populations (over 10 million), one can achieve accuracy using tiny sampling ratios (0.025 percent) or samples of about 2,500. The size of the population ceases to be relevant once the sampling ratio is very small, and samples of about 2,500 are as accurate for populations of 200 million as for 10 million. These are approximate sizes, and practical limitations (e.g., cost) also play a role in a researcher's decision.

A related principle is that for small samples, small increases in sample size produce big gains in accuracy. Equal increases in sample size produce more of an increase in accuracy for small than for large samples.

A researcher's decision about the best sample size depends on three things: (1) the degree of accuracy required, (2) the degree of variability or diversity in the population, and (3) the number of different variables examined simultaneously in data analysis. Everything else being equal, larger samples are needed if one wants high accuracy, if the population has a great deal of variability or heterogeneity, or if one wants to examine many variables in the data analysis simultaneously. Smaller samples are sufficient when less accuracy is acceptable, when the population is homogeneous, or when only a few variables are examined at a time.

The analysis of data on subgroups also affects a researcher's decision about sample size. If the researcher wants to analyze subgroups in the population, he or she needs a larger sample. For example, I want to analyze four variables for males between the ages of 30 and 40 years old. If this sample is of the general public, then only a small proportion (e.g., 10 percent) of sample cases will be males in that age group. A rule of thumb is to have about 50 cases for each subgroup to be analyzed. Thus, if I want to analyze a group that is only 10 percent of the population, then I should have 10 × 50 or 500 cases in the sample to be sure I get enough for the subgroup analysis.

Drawing Inferences

A researcher samples so he or she can draw inferences from the sample to the population. In fact, a subfield of statistical data analysis that concerns drawing accurate inferences is called *inferential statistics*. The researcher directly observes variables using units in the sample. The sample stands for or represents the population. Researchers are not interested in samples in themselves; they want to infer to the population. Thus, a gap exists between what the researcher concretely has (a sample) and what is of real interest (a population) (see Figure 6.4).

In the last chapter, you saw how the logic of measurement could be stated in terms of a gap between abstract constructs and concrete indicators. Measures of concrete, observable data are approximations for abstract constructs. Researchers use the approximations to estimate what is of real interest (i.e., constructs and causal laws). Conceptualization and operationalization

FIGURE 6.4   Model of the Logic of Sampling and of Measurement

A Model of the Logic of Sampling

What You
Would Like to
Talk About

Population

Sampling
Frame

Sampling Process

What You Actually
Observe in the Data

Sample

A Model of the Logic of Measurement

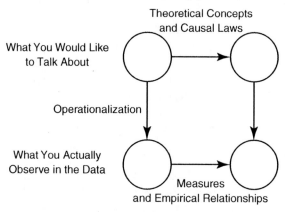

Theoretical Concepts
and Causal Laws

What You Would Like
to Talk About

Operationalization

What You Actually
Observe in the Data

Measures
and Empirical Relationships

A Model Combining Logics of Sampling and Measurement

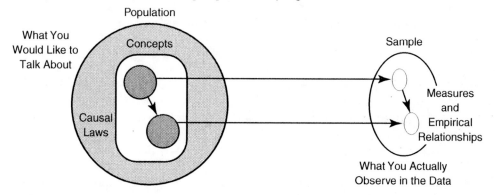

Population

What You
Would Like to
Talk About

Concepts

Causal
Laws

Sample

Measures
and
Empirical
Relationships

What You Actually
Observe in the Data

bridge the gap in measurement just as the use of sampling frames, the sampling process, and inference bridge the gap in sampling.

Researchers put the logic of sampling and the logic of measurement together by directly observing measures of constructs and empirical relationships in samples (see Figure 6.4). They infer or generalize from what they can observe empirically in samples to the abstract causal laws and constructs in the population.

Validity and sampling error have similar functions, as can be illustrated by the analogy between the logic of sampling and the logic of measurement—that is, between what is observed and what is discussed. In measurement, a researcher wants valid indicators of constructs— that is, concrete indicators that accurately represent abstract constructs. In sampling, he or she wants samples that have little sampling error— concrete collections of cases that accurately represent unseen and abstract populations. A valid measure deviates little from the construct it represents. A sample with little sampling error permits estimates that deviate little from population parameters.

Researchers try to reduce sampling errors. The calculation of the sampling error is not presented here, but it is based on two factors: the sample size and the amount of diversity in the sample. Everything else being equal, the larger the sample size, the smaller the sampling error. Likewise, the greater the homogeneity (or the less the diversity) in a sample, the smaller its sampling error.

Sampling error is also related to confidence intervals. If two samples are identical except that one is larger, the one with more cases will have a smaller sampling error and narrower confidence intervals. Likewise, if two samples are identical except that the cases in one are more similar to each other, the one with greater homogeneity will have a smaller sampling error and narrower confidence intervals. A narrow confidence interval means more precise estimates of the population parameter for a given level of confidence. For example, a researcher wants to estimate

average annual family income. He or she has two samples. Sample 1 gives a confidence interval of $30,000 to $36,000 around the estimated population parameter of $33,000 for an 80 percent level of confidence. For a 95 percent level of confidence, the range is $23,000 to $43,000. A sample with a smaller sampling error (because it is larger or is more homogeneous) might give a $30,000 to $36,000 range for a 95 percent confidence level.

CONCLUSION

In this chapter, you learned about sampling. Sampling is widely used in social research. You learned about types of sampling that are not based on random processes. Only some are acceptable, and their use depends on special circumstances. In general, probability sampling is preferred by quantitative researchers because it produces a sample that represents the population and enables the researcher to use powerful statistical techniques. In addition to simple random sampling, you learned about systematic, stratified, and cluster sampling. Although this book does not cover the statistical theory used in random sampling, from the discussion of sampling error, the central limit theorem, and sample size, it should be clear that random sampling produces more accurate and precise sampling.

Before moving on to the next chapter, it may be useful to restate a fundamental principle of social research: Do not compartmentalize the steps of the research process; rather, learn to see the interconnections between the steps. Research design, measurement, sampling, and specific research techniques are interdependent. Unfortunately, the constraints of presenting information in a textbook necessitate presenting the parts separately, in sequence. In practice, researchers think about data collection when they design research and develop measures for variables. Likewise, sampling issues influence research design, measurement of variables, and data collection strategies. As you will see in future chapters, good social research depends on simultaneously controlling quality at several different steps—research design, conceptualization, measurement, sampling, and data collection and handling. The researcher who makes major errors at any one stage may make an entire research project worthless.

Key Terms

- central limit theorem
- cluster sampling
- confidence intervals
- deviant case sampling
- haphazard sampling
- hidden populations
- inferential statistics
- nonrandom sample
- parameter
- population
- probability proportionate to size (PPS)
- purposive sampling
- quota sampling
- random-digit dialing (RDD)
- random-number table
- random sample
- sample
- sampling distribution
- sampling element
- sampling error
- sampling frame
- sampling interval
- sampling ratio
- sequential sampling
- simple random sampling
- snowball sampling
- sociogram
- statistic
- stratified sampling
- systematic sampling
- target population

Survey Research

INTRODUCTION

Someone hands you a sheet of paper full of questions. The first reads: "I would like to learn your opinion of the Neuman research methods textbook. Would you say it is (a) well organized, (b) adequately organized, or (c) poorly organized?" You probably would not be shocked by this. It is a kind of survey, and most of us are accustomed to surveys by the time we reach adulthood.

The survey is the most widely used data-gathering technique in sociology, and it is used in many other fields, as well. In fact, surveys are almost too popular. People sometimes say, "Do a survey" to get information about the social world, when they should be asking, "What is the most appropriate research design?" Despite the popularity of surveys, it is easy to conduct a survey that yields misleading or worthless results. Good surveys require thought and effort.

All surveys are based on the professional social research survey. In this chapter, you will learn the main ingredients of good survey research, as well as the limitations of the survey method.

Research Questions Appropriate for a Survey

Survey research developed within the positivist approach to social science. The survey asks many people (called *respondents*) about their beliefs, opinions, characteristics, and past or present behavior.

Surveys are appropriate for research questions about self-reported beliefs or behaviors. They are strongest when the answers people give to questions measure variables. Researchers usually ask about many things at one time in surveys, measure many variables (often with multiple indicators), and test several hypotheses in a single survey.

Although the categories overlap, the following can be asked in a survey:

1. *Behavior.* How frequently do you brush your teeth? Did you vote in the last city election? When did you last visit a close relative?
2. *Attitudes/beliefs/opinions.* What kind of job do you think the mayor is doing? Do you think other people say many negative things about you when you are not there? What is the biggest problem facing the nation these days?
3. *Characteristics.* Are you married, never married, single, divorced, separated, or widowed? Do you belong to a union? What is your age?
4. *Expectations.* Do you plan to buy a new car in the next 12 months? How much schooling do you think your child will get? Do you think the population in this town will grow, shrink, or stay the same?
5. *Self-classification.* Do you consider yourself to be liberal, moderate, or conservative? Into which social class would you put your family? Would you say you are highly religious or not religious?
6. *Knowledge.* Who was elected mayor in the last election? About what percentage of the people in this city are non-White? Is it legal to own a personal copy of Karl Marx's *Communist Manifesto* in this country?

Researchers warn against using surveys to ask "why?" questions (e.g., Why do you think crime occurs?). "Why?" questions are appropriate, however, if a researcher wants to discover a respondent's subjective understanding or informal theory (i.e., the respondent's own view of "why" he or she acts a certain way). Because few respondents are fully aware of the causal factors that shape their beliefs or behavior, such questions are not a substitute for the researcher developing a consistent causal theory of his or her own that builds on the existing scientific literature.

An important limitation of survey research is that it provides data only of what a person or organization says, and this may differ from what he or she actually does. This is illustrated by Pager and Quillian (2005), who compared telephone survey responses from Milwaukee-area employers about their willingness to hire ex-offenders of different races with an "audit." In the audit, a trained pair of young males with specific characteristics applied for 350 job openings in December 2001. Employers agreed to hire 34 percent of White and 14 percent of Black applicants. The applicants had identical job experience and credentials and no criminal records. The same employers agreed to hire 17 percent of Whites and 5 percent of Blacks with identical job experience and credentials but also with a criminal record for illegal drug use. The employers were telephoned a few months later. Pager and Quillian found in the telephone survey far more employers expressed a willingness to hire an ex-offender (67 percent) and there were no differences in the offender's race. Also, certain employers said they were more willing to hire an ex-offender, but in the audit all employers acted the same. The authors said, "Survey responses have very little connection to the actual behaviors exhibited by these employers" (2005:367).

THE LOGIC OF SURVEY RESEARCH

What Is a Survey?

Survey researchers sample many respondents who answer the same questions. They measure many variables, test multiple hypotheses, and infer temporal order from questions about past behavior, experiences, or characteristics. For example, years of schooling or a respondent's race are prior to current attitudes. An association among variables is measured with statistical techniques. Survey researchers think of alternative explanations when planning a survey, measure variables that represent alternative explanations (i.e., control variables), then statistically examine their effects to rule out alternative explanations.

Survey research is often called *correlational*. Survey researchers use questions as control variables to approximate the rigorous test for causality that experimenters achieve with their physical control over temporal order and alternative explanations.

Steps in Conducting a Survey

The survey researcher follows a deductive approach. He or she begins with a theoretical or applied research problem and ends with empirical measurement and data analysis. Once a researcher decides that the survey is an appropriate method, basic steps in a research project can be divided into the substeps outlined in Figure 7.1.

In the first phase, the researcher develops an instrument—a survey questionnaire or interview schedule—that he or she uses to measure variables. Respondents read the questions themselves and mark answers on a *questionnaire*. An *interview schedule* is a set of questions read to the respondent by an interviewer, who also records responses. To simplify the discussion, I will use only the term *questionnaires*.

A survey researcher conceptualizes and operationalizes variables as questions. He or she writes and rewrites questions for clarity and completeness, and organizes questions on the questionnaire based on the research question, the respondents, and the type of survey. (The types of surveys are discussed later.)

When preparing a questionnaire, the researcher thinks ahead to how he or she will record and organize data for analysis. He or she pilot-tests the questionnaire with a small set of respondents similar to those in the final survey. If interviewers are used, the researcher trains them with the questionnaire. He or she asks respondents in the pilot-test whether the questions were clear and explores their interpretations to see if his or her intended meaning was clear. The researcher also draws the sample during this phase.

FIGURE 7.1 **Steps in the Process of Survey Research**

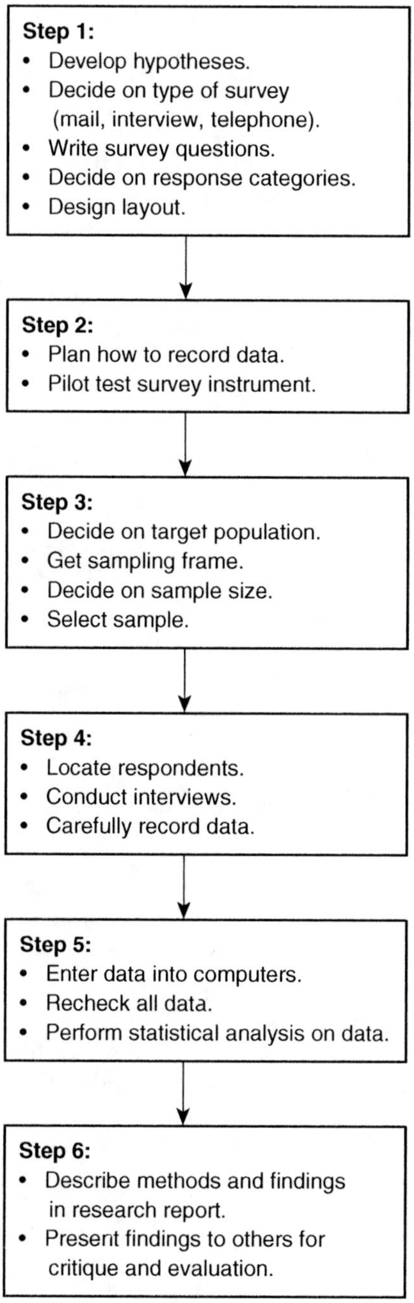

Step 1:
- Develop hypotheses.
- Decide on type of survey (mail, interview, telephone).
- Write survey questions.
- Decide on response categories.
- Design layout.

Step 2:
- Plan how to record data.
- Pilot test survey instrument.

Step 3:
- Decide on target population.
- Get sampling frame.
- Decide on sample size.
- Select sample.

Step 4:
- Locate respondents.
- Conduct interviews.
- Carefully record data.

Step 5:
- Enter data into computers.
- Recheck all data.
- Perform statistical analysis on data.

Step 6:
- Describe methods and findings in research report.
- Present findings to others for critique and evaluation.

After the planning phase, the researcher is ready to collect data. This phase is usually shorter than the planning phase. He or she locates sampled respondents in person, by telephone, or by mail. Respondents are given information and instructions on completing the questionnaire or interview. The questions follow, and there is a simple stimulus/response or question/answer pattern. The researcher accurately records answers or responses immediately after they are given. After all respondents complete the questionnaire and are thanked, he or she organizes the data and prepares them for statistical analysis.

Survey research can be complex and expensive and it can involve coordinating many people and steps. The administration of survey research requires organization and accurate record keeping. The researcher keeps track of each respondent, questionnaire, and interviewer. For example, he or she gives each sampled respondent an identification number, which also appears on the questionnaire. He or she then checks completed questionnaires against a list of sampled respondents. Next, the researcher reviews responses on individual questionnaires, stores original questionnaires, and transfers information from questionnaires to a format for statistical analysis. Meticulous bookkeeping and labeling are essential. Otherwise, the researcher may find that valuable data and effort are lost through sloppiness.

CONSTRUCTING THE QUESTIONNAIRE

Principles of Good Question Writing

A good questionnaire forms an integrated whole. The researcher weaves questions together so they flow smoothly. He or she includes introductory remarks and instructions for clarification and measures each variable with one or more survey questions.

Three principles for effective survey questions are: Keep it clear, keep it simple, and keep the respondent's perspective in mind. Good survey questions give the researcher valid and reliable measures. They also help respondents feel that they understand the question and that their answers are meaningful. Questions that do not mesh with a respondent's viewpoint or that respondents find confusing are not good measures. A survey researcher must exercise extra care if the respondents are heterogeneous or come from different life situations than his or her own.

Researchers face a dilemma. They want each respondent to hear exactly the same questions, but will the questions be equally clear, relevant, and meaningful to all respondents? If respondents have diverse backgrounds and frames of reference, the exact same wording may not have the same meaning. Yet, tailoring question wording to each respondent makes comparisons almost impossible. A researcher would not know whether the wording of the question or the differences in respondents accounted for different answers.

Question writing is more of an art than a science. It takes skill, practice, patience, and creativity. The principles of question writing are illustrated in the following 12 things to avoid when writing survey questions. The list does not include every possible error, only the more frequent problems.

1. *Avoid jargon, slang, and abbreviations.* Jargon and technical terms come in many forms. Plumbers talk about *snakes*, lawyers about a contract of *uberrima fides*, psychologists about the *Oedipus complex*. Slang is a kind of jargon within a subculture—for example, the homeless talk about a *snowbird* and skiers about a *hotdog*. Also avoid abbreviations. *NATO* usually means North Atlantic Treaty Organization, but for a respondent, it might mean something else (National Auto Tourist Organization, Native Alaskan Trade Orbit, or North African Tea Office). Avoid slang and jargon unless a specialized population is being surveyed. Target the vocabulary and grammar to the respondents

sampled. For the general public, this is the language used on television or in the newspaper (about an eighth-grade reading vocabulary). Survey researchers have learned that some respondents may not understand basic terminology.

2. *Avoid ambiguity, confusion, and vagueness.* Ambiguity and vagueness plague most question writers. A researcher might make implicit assumptions without thinking of the respondents. For example, the question, "What is your income?" could mean weekly, monthly, or annual; family or personal; before taxes or after taxes; for this year or last year; from salary or from all sources. The confusion causes inconsistencies in how different respondents assign meaning to and answer the question. The researcher who wants before-tax annual family income for last year must explicitly ask for it.[1]

Another source of ambiguity is the use of indefinite words or response categories. For example, an answer to the question, "Do you jog regularly? Yes _____ No _____," hinges on the meaning of the word *regularly*. Some respondents may define *regularly* as every day, others as once a week. To reduce respondent confusion and get more information, be specific—ask whether a person jogs "about once a day," "a few times a week," "once a week," and so on. (See Box 7.1 on improving questions.)

3. *Avoid emotional language.* Words have implicit connotative as well as explicit denotative meanings. Words with strong emotional connotations can color how respondents hear and answer survey questions.

Use neutral language. Avoid words with emotional "baggage," because respondents may react to the emotionally laden words rather than to the issue. For example, the question, "What do you think about a policy to pay murderous terrorists who threaten to steal the freedoms of peace-loving people?" is full of emotional words (*murderous, freedoms, steal,* and *peace*).

4. *Avoid prestige bias.* Titles or positions in society (e.g., president, expert, etc.) carry

Box 7.1 Improving Unclear Questions

Here are three survey questions written by experienced professional researchers. They revised the original wording after a pilot test revealed that 15 percent of respondents asked for clarification or gave inadequate answers (e.g., don't know). As you can see, question wording is an art that may improve with practice, patience, and pilot testing.

Original Question	Problem	Revised Question
Do you exercise or play sports regularly?	What counts as exercise?	Do you do any sports or hobbies, physical activities, or exercise, including walking, on a regular basis?
What is the average number of days each week you have butter?	Does margarine count as butter?	The next question is just about butter—not including margarine. How many days a week do you have butter?
[Following question on eggs] What is the number of servings in a typical day?	How many eggs is a serving? What is a typical day?	On days when you eat eggs, how many eggs do you usually have?

	Responses to Question		Percentage Asking for Clarification	
	Original	Revision	Original	Revision
Exercise question (% saying "yes")	48%	60%	5%	0%
Butter question (% saying "none")	33%	55%	18%	13%
Egg question (% saying "one")	80%	33%	33%	0%

Source: Adapted from Fowler (1992).

prestige or status. Issues linked to people with high social status can color how respondents hear and answer survey questions. Avoid associating a statement with a prestigious person or group. Respondents may answer on the basis of their feelings toward the person or group rather than addressing the issue. For example, saying, "Most doctors say that cigarette smoke causes lung disease for those near a smoker. Do you agree?" affects people who want to agree with doctors. Likewise, a question such as, "Do you support the president's policy regarding Kosovo?" will be answered by respondents who have never heard of Kosovo on the basis of their view of the president.

5. *Avoid double-barreled questions.* Make each question about one and only one topic. A *double-barreled question* consists of two or more questions joined together. It makes a

respondent's answer ambiguous. For example, if asked, "Does this company have pension and health insurance benefits?" a respondent at a company with health insurance benefits only might answer either yes or no. The response has an ambiguous meaning, and the researcher cannot be certain of the respondent's intention. A researcher who wants to ask about the joint occurrence of two things—for example, a company with both health insurance and pension benefits—should ask two separate questions.

6. *Do not confuse beliefs with reality.* Do not confuse what a respondent believes with what you, the researcher, measures. A respondent may think that a relationship exists between two variables but this is not an empirical measurement of variables in a relationship. For example, a researcher wants to find out if students rate teachers higher who tell many jokes in class. The two variables are "teacher tells jokes" and "rating the teacher." The *wrong* way to approach the issue is to ask students, "Do you rate a teacher higher if the teacher tells many jokes?" This measures whether or not students *believe* that they rate teachers based on joke telling; it does not measure the empirical relationship. The *correct* way is to ask two separate empirically based questions: "How do you rate this teacher?" and "How many jokes does the teacher tell in class?" Then the researcher can examine answers to the two questions to determine if there is an association between them. People's beliefs about a relationship among variables are distinct from an actual empirical relationship.

7. *Avoid leading questions.* Make respondents feel that all responses are legitimate. Do not let them become aware of an answer that the researcher wants. A *leading* (or *loaded*) *question* is one that leads the respondent to choose one response over another by its wording. There are many kinds of leading questions. For example, the question, "You don't smoke, do you?" leads respondents to state that they do not smoke.

Loaded questions can be stated to get either positive or negative answers. For example,

"Should the mayor spend even more tax money trying to keep the streets in top shape?" leads respondents to disagree, whereas "Should the mayor fix the pot-holed and dangerous streets in our city?" is loaded for agreement.

8. *Avoid asking questions that are beyond respondents' capabilities.* Asking something that few respondents know frustrates respondents and produces poor-quality responses. Respondents cannot always recall past details and may not know specific factual information. For example, asking an adult, "How did you feel about your brother when you were 6 years old?" is probably worthless. Asking respondents to make a choice about something they know nothing about (e.g., a technical issue in foreign affairs or an internal policy of an organization) may result in an answer, but one that is unreliable and meaningless. When many respondents are unlikely to know about an issue, use a full-filter question form (to be discussed).

Phrase questions in the terms in which respondents think. For example, few respondents will be able to answer, "How many gallons of gasoline did you buy last year for your car?" Yet, respondents may be able to answer a question about gasoline purchases for a typical week, which the researcher can multiply by 52 to estimate annual purchases.[2]

9. *Avoid false premises.* Do not begin a question with a premise with which respondents may not agree, then ask about choices regarding it. Respondents who disagree with the premise will be frustrated and not know how to answer. For example, the question, "The post office is open too many hours. Do you want it to open four hours later or close four hours earlier each day?" leaves those who either oppose the premise or oppose both alternatives without a meaningful choice.

A better question explicitly asks the respondent to assume a premise is true, then asks for a preference. For example, "Assuming the post office has to cut back its operating hours, which would you find more convenient, opening four hours later or closing four hours earlier each day?" Answers to a hypothetical situation are not very reliable, but being explicit will reduce frustration.

10. *Avoid asking about intentions in the distant future.* Avoid asking people about what they might do under hypothetical circumstances far in the future. Responses are poor predictors of behavior removed far from their current situation or far in the future. Questions such as, "Suppose a new grocery store opened down the road in three years. Would you shop at it?" are usually a waste of time. It is better to ask about current or recent attitudes and behavior. In general, respondents answer specific, concrete questions that relate to their experiences more reliably than they do those about abstractions that are beyond their immediate experiences.

11. *Avoid double negatives.* Double negatives in ordinary language are grammatically incorrect and confusing. For example, "I ain't got no job" logically means that the respondent does have a job, but the second negative is used in this way for emphasis. Such blatant errors are rare, but more subtle forms of the double negative are also confusing. They arise when respondents are asked to agree or disagree with a statement. For example, respondents who *dis*agree with the statement, "Students should *not* be required to take a comprehensive exam to graduate" are logically stating a double negative because they *disagree* with *not* doing something.

• 12. *Avoid overlapping or unbalanced response categories.* Make response categories or choices mutually exclusive, exhaustive, and balanced. *Mutually exclusive* means that response categories do not overlap. Overlapping categories that are numerical ranges (e.g., 5–10, 10–20, 20–30) can be easily corrected (e.g., 5–9, 10–19, 20–29). The ambiguous verbal choice is another type of overlapping response category—for example, "Are you satisfied with your job or are there things you don't like about it?" *Exhaustive* means that every respondent has a choice—a

place to go. For example, asking respondents, "Are you working or unemployed?" leaves out respondents who are not working but do not consider themselves unemployed (e.g., full-time homemakers, people on vacation, students, people with disabilities, retired people, etc.). A researcher first thinks about what he or she wants to measure and then considers the circumstances of respondents. For example, when asking about a respondent's employment, does the researcher want information on the primary job or on all jobs? On full-time work only or both full- and part-time work? On jobs for pay only or on unpaid or volunteer jobs as well?

Keep response categories *balanced*. A case of unbalanced choices is the question, "What kind of job is the mayor doing: outstanding, excellent, very good, or satisfactory?" Another type of unbalanced question omits information—for example, "Which of the five candidates running for mayor do you favor: Eugene Oswego or one of the others?" Researchers can balance responses by offering bipolar opposites. It is easy to see that the terms *honesty* and *dishonesty* have different meanings and connotations. Asking respondents to rate whether a mayor is highly, somewhat, or not very *honest* is not the same as asking them to rate the mayor's level of *dishonesty*. Unless there is a specific purpose for doing otherwise, it is better to offer respondents equal polar opposites at each end of a continuum.[3] For example, "Do you think the mayor is: very honest, somewhat honest, neither honest nor dishonest, somewhat dishonest, or very dishonest?" (see Table 7.1).

Aiding Respondent Recall

Recalling events accurately takes more time and effort than the five seconds that respondents have to answer survey questions. Also, one's ability to recall accurately declines over time. Studies in hospitalization and crime victimization show that although most respondents can recall significant events that occurred in the past several weeks, half are inaccurate a year later.

TABLE 7.1 Summary of Survey Question Writing Pitfalls

Things to Avoid	Not Good	A Possible Improvement
1. Jargon, slang, abbreviations	Did you drown in brew until you were totally blasted last night?	Last night, about how much beer did you drink?
2. Vagueness	Do you eat out often?	In a typical week, about how many meals do you eat away from home, at a restaurant, cafeteria, or other eating establishment?
3. Emotional language 4. Prestige bias	"The respected Grace Commission documents that a staggering $350 BILLION of our tax dollars are being completely wasted through poor procurement practices, bad management, sloppy bookkeeping, 'defective' contract management, personnel abuses and other wasteful practices. Is cutting pork barrel spending and eliminating government waste a top priority for you?"*	How important is it to you that Congress adopt measures to reduce government waste? Very Important Somewhat Important Neither Important or Unimportant Somewhat Unimportant Not Important At All
5. Double-barreled questions	Do you support or oppose raising social security benefits and increased spending for the military?	Do you support or oppose raising social security benefits? Do you support or oppose increasing spending on the military?
6. Beliefs as real	Do you think more educated people smoke less?	What is your education level? Do you smoke cigarettes?
7. Leading questions	Did you do your patriotic duty and vote in the last election for mayor?	Did you vote in last month's mayoral election?
8. Issues beyond respondent capabilities	Two years ago, how many hours did you watch TV every month?	In the past two weeks, about how many hours do you think you watched TV on a typical day?
9. False premises	When did you stop beating your girl/boyfriend?	Have you ever slapped, punched, or hit your girl/boyfriend?
10. Distant future intentions	After you graduate from college, get a job, and are settled, will you invest a lot of money in the stock market?	Do you have definite plans to put some money into the stock market within the coming two months?
11. Double negatives	Do you disagree with those who do not want to build a new city swimming pool?	There is a proposal to build a new city swimming pool. Do you agree or disagree with the proposal?
12. Unbalanced responses	Did you find the service at our hotel to be, Outstanding, Excellent, Superior, or Good?	Please rate the service at our hotel: Outstanding, Very Good, Adequate, or Poor.

*Actual question taken from a mail questionnaire that was sent to me in May 1998 by the National Republican Congressional Committee. It is also a double-barreled question.

Survey researchers recognize that memory is less trustworthy than was once assumed. It is affected by many factors—the topic, events occurring simultaneously and subsequently, the significance of an event for a person, situational conditions (question wording and interview style), and the respondent's need to have internal consistency.

The complexity of respondent recall does not mean that survey researchers cannot ask about past events; rather, they need to customize questions and interpret results cautiously. Researchers should provide respondents with special instructions and extra thinking time. They should also provide aids to respondent recall, such as a fixed time frame or location references. Rather than ask, "How often did you attend a sporting event last winter?" they should say, "I want to know how many sporting events you attended last winter. Let's go month by month. Think back to December. Did you attend any sporting events for which you paid admission in December? Now, think back to January. Did you attend any sporting events in January?"

Types of Questions and Response Categories

Threatening Questions. Survey researchers sometimes ask about sensitive issues or issues that respondents may believe threaten their presentation of self, such as questions about sexual behavior, drug or alcohol use, mental health problems, or deviant behavior. Respondents may be reluctant to answer the questions or to answer completely and truthfully. Survey researchers who wish to ask such questions must do so with great care and must be extra cautious about the results[4] (see Table 7.2).

Threatening questions are part of a larger issue of self-presentation and ego protection. Respondents often try to present a positive image of themselves to others. They may be ashamed, embarrassed, or afraid to give truthful answers, or find it emotionally painful to confront their own actions honestly, let alone admit

TABLE 7.2 Threatening Questions and Sensitive Issues

Topic	Percentage Very Uneasy
Masturbation	56
Sexual intercourse	42
Use of marijuana or hashish	42
Use of stimulants and depressants	31
Getting drunk	29
Petting and kissing	20
Income	12
Gambling with friends	10
Drinking beer, wine, or liquor	10
Happiness and well-being	4
Education	3
Occupation	3
Social activities	2
General leisure	2
Sports activity	1

Source: Adapted from Bradburn and Sudman (1980:68).

them to other people. They may underreport or self-censor reports of behavior or attitudes they wish to hide or believe to be in violation of social norms. Alternatively, they may overreport positive behaviors or generally accepted beliefs (social desirability bias is discussed later).

People are likely to underreport having an illness or disability (e.g., cancer, mental illness, venereal disease), engaging in illegal or deviant behavior (e.g., evading taxes, taking drugs, consuming alcohol, engaging in uncommon sexual practices), or revealing their financial status (e.g., income, savings, debts) (see Table 7.3).

Survey researchers have created several techniques to increase truthful answers to threatening questions. Some techniques involve the context and wording of the question itself. Researchers should ask threatening questions only after a warm-up, when an interviewer has developed rapport and trust with the respondents, and they should tell respondents that they

TABLE 7.3   **Over- and Underreporting Behavior on Surveys**

	Percentage Distorted or Erroneous Answers		
	Face to Face	*Phone*	*Self-Administered*
Low Threat/Normative			
Registered to vote	+15	+17	+12
Voted in primary	+39	+31	+36
Have own library card	+19	+21	+18
High Threat			
Bankruptcy	−32	−29	−32
Drunk driving	−47	−46	−54

Source: Adapted from Bradburn and Sudman (1980:8).

want honest answers. They can phrase the question in an "enhanced way" to provide a context that makes it easier for respondents to give honest answers. For example, the following enhanced question was asked of heterosexual males: "In past surveys, many men have reported that at some point in their lives they have had some type of sexual experience with another male. This could have happened before adolescence, during adolescence, or as an adult. Have you ever had sex with a male at some point in your life?" In contrast, a standard form of the question would have asked, "Have you ever had sex with another male?"

Also, by embedding a threatening response within more serious activities, it may be made to seem less deviant. For example, respondents might hesitate to admit shoplifting if it is asked first, but after being asked about armed robbery or burglary, they may admit to shoplifting because it appears less serious.

Socially Desirable Questions.   *Social desirability bias* occurs when respondents distort answers to make their reports conform to social norms. People tend to overreport being cultured (i.e., reading, attending high-culture events), giving

money to charity, having a good marriage, loving their children, and so forth. For example, one study found that one-third of people who reported in a survey that they gave money to a local charity really did not. Because a norm says that one should vote in elections, many report voting when they did not. In the United States, those under the greatest pressure to vote (i.e., highly educated, politically partisan, highly religious people who had been contacted by an organization that urged them to vote) are the people most likely to overreport voting.

Questionnaire writers try to reduce social desirability bias by phrasing questions in ways that make norm violation appear less objectionable and that presents a wider range of behavior as acceptable. They can also offer multiple response categories that give respondents "face-saving" alternatives.

Knowledge Questions.   Studies suggest that a large majority of the public cannot correctly answer elementary geography questions or identify important political documents (e.g., the Declaration of Independence). Researchers sometimes want to find out whether respondents know about an issue or topics, but knowledge questions can be threatening because respondents do not want to appear ignorant. Surveys may measure opinions better if they first ask about factual information, because many people have inaccurate factual knowledge.

Some simple knowledge questions, such as the number of people living in a household, are not always answered accurately in surveys. In some households, a marginal person—the boyfriend who left for a week, the adult daughter who left after an argument about her pregnancy, or the uncle who walked out after a dispute over money—may be reported as not living in a household, but he or she may not have another permanent residence and consider himself or herself to live there.[5]

Others have found that many Americans oppose foreign aid spending. Their opposition is based on extremely high overestimates of the cost of the programs. When asked what they would prefer to spend on foreign aid, most give an amount much higher than what now is being spent.

A researcher pilot-tests questions so that questions are at an appropriate level of difficulty. Little is gained if 99 percent of respondents cannot answer the question. Knowledge questions can be worded so that respondents feel comfortable saying they do not know the answer—for example, "How much, if anything, have you heard about . . . ."

Skip or Contingency Questions. Researchers avoid asking questions that are irrelevant for a respondent. Yet, some questions apply only to specific respondents. A *contingency question* is a two- (or more) part question. The answer to the first part of the question determines which of two different questions a respondent next receives. Contingency questions select respondents for whom a second question is relevant. Sometimes they are called *screen* or *skip questions.* On the basis of the answer to the first question, the respondent or an interviewer is instructed to go to another or to skip certain questions.

The following example is a contingency question, adapted from deVaus (1986:79).

1. Were you born in Australia?
   [ ] Yes (GO TO QUESTION 2)
   [ ] No _____
      (a) What country were you born in? _____
      (b) How many years have you lived in Australia? _____
      (c) Are you an Australian citizen?
          [ ] Yes [ ] No
   NOW GO TO QUESTION 2

Open versus Closed Questions

There has long been a debate about open versus closed questions in survey research. An *open-ended* (unstructured, free response) *question* asks a question (e.g., "What is your favorite television program?") to which respondents can give any answer. A *closed-ended* (structured, fixed response) *question* both asks a question and gives the respondent fixed responses from which to choose (e.g., "Is the president doing a very good, good, fair, or poor job, in your opinion?").

Each form has advantages and disadvantages (see Box 7.2). The crucial issue is not which form is best. Rather, it is under what conditions a form is most appropriate. A researcher's choice to use an open- or closed-ended question depends on the purpose and the practical limitations of a research project. The demands of using open-ended questions, with interviewers writing verbatim answers followed by time-consuming coding, may make them impractical for a specific project.

Large-scale surveys have closed-ended questions because they are quicker and easier for both respondents and researchers. Yet something important may be lost when an individual's beliefs and feelings are forced into a few fixed categories that a researcher created. To learn how a respondent thinks, to discover what is really important to him or her, or to get an answer to a question with many possible answers (e.g., age),

Box 7.2 Closed versus Open Questions

Advantages of Closed

- It is easier and quicker for respondents to answer.
- The answers of different respondents are easier to compare.
- Answers are easier to code and statistically analyze.
- The response choices can clarify question meaning for respondents.
- Respondents are more likely to answer about sensitive topics.
- There are fewer irrelevant or confused answers to questions.
- Less articulate or less literate respondents are not at a disadvantage.
- Replication is easier.

Disadvantages of Closed

- They can suggest ideas that the respondent would not otherwise have.
- Respondents with no opinion or no knowledge can answer anyway.
- Respondents can be frustrated because their desired answer is not a choice.
- It is confusing if many (e.g., 20) response choices are offered.
- Misinterpretation of a question can go unnoticed.
- Distinctions between respondent answers may be blurred.
- Clerical mistakes or marking the wrong response is possible.
- They force respondents to give simplistic responses to complex issues.
- They force people to make choices they would not make in the real world.

Advantages of Open

- They permit an unlimited number of possible answers.
- Respondents can answer in detail and can qualify and clarify responses.
- Unanticipated findings can be discovered.
- They permit adequate answers to complex issues.
- They permit creativity, self-expression, and richness of detail.
- They reveal a respondent's logic, thinking process, and frame of reference.

Disadvantages of Open

- Different respondents give different degrees of detail in answers.
- Responses may be irrelevant or buried in useless detail.
- Comparisons and statistical analysis become very difficult.
- Coding responses is difficult.
- Articulate and highly literate respondents have an advantage.
- Questions may be too general for respondents who lose direction.
- Responses are written verbatim, which is difficult for interviewers.
- A greater amount of respondent time, thought, and effort is necessary.
- Respondents can be intimidated by questions.
- Answers take up a lot of space in the questionnaire.

open questions may be best. In addition, sensitive topics (e.g., sexual behavior, liquor consumption) may be more accurately measured with closed questions.

The disadvantages of a question form can be reduced by mixing open-ended and closed-ended questions in a questionnaire. Mixing them also offers a change of pace and helps interviewers establish rapport. Periodic probes (i.e., follow-up questions by interviewers) with closed-ended questions can reveal a respondent's reasoning.

Having interviewers periodically use probes to ask about a respondent's thinking is a way to check whether respondents are understanding the questions as the researcher intended. However, probes are not substitutes for writing clear questions or creating a framework of understanding for the respondent. Unless carefully stated, probes might shape the respondent's answers or force answers when a respondent does not have an opinion or information. Yet, flexible or conversational interviewing in which interviewers use many probes can improve accuracy on questions about complex issues on which respondents do not clearly understand basic terms or about which they have difficulty expressing their thoughts. For example, to the question, "Did you do any work for money last week?" a respondent might hesitate then reply, "Yes." An interviewer probes, "Could you tell me exactly what work you did?" The respondent may reply, "On Tuesday and Wednesday, I spent a couple hours helping my buddy John move into his new apartment. For that he gave me $40, but I didn't have any other job or get paid for doing anything else." If the researcher's intention was only to get reports of regular employment, the probe revealed a misunderstanding. Researchers also use *partially open questions* (i.e., a set of fixed choices with a final open choice of "other"), which allows respondents to offer an answer that the researcher did not include.

Open-ended questions are especially valuable in early or exploratory stages of research. For large-scale surveys, researchers use open questions in pilot-tests, then develop closed-question

responses from the answers given to the open questions.

Researchers writing closed questions have to make many decisions. How many response choices should be given? Should they offer a middle or neutral choice? What should be the order of responses? What types of response choices? How will the direction of a response be measured?

Answers to these questions are not easy. For example, two response choices are too few, but more than five response choices are rarely effective. Researchers want to measure meaningful distinctions and not collapse them. More specific responses yield more information, but too many specifics create confusion. For example, rephrasing the question, "Are you satisfied with your dentist?" (which has a yes/no answer) to "How satisfied are you with your dentist: very satisfied, somewhat satisfied, somewhat dissatisfied, or not satisfied at all?" gives the researcher more information and a respondent more choices.

Nonattitudes and the Middle Positions. Survey researchers debate whether to include choices for neutral, middle, and nonattitudes (e.g., "not sure," "don't know," or "no opinion").[6] Two types of errors can be made: accepting a middle choice or "no attitude" response when respondents hold a nonneutral opinion, or forcing respondents to choose a position on an issue when they have no opinion about it.

Many fear that respondents will choose nonattitude choices to evade making a choice. Yet, it is usually best to offer a nonattitude choice, because people will express opinions on fictitious issues, objects, and events. By offering a nonattitude (middle or no opinion) choice, researchers identify those holding middle positions or those without opinions.

The issue of nonattitudes can be approached by distinguishing among three kinds of attitude questions: standard-format, quasi-filter, and full-filter questions (see Box 7.3). The *standard-format question* does not offer a "don't know"

Box 7.3 Standard-Format, Quasi-Filter, and Full-Filter Questions

Standard Format

Here is a question about an other country. Do you agree or disagree with this statement? "The Russian leaders are basically trying to get along with America."

Quasi-Filter

Here is a statement about an other country: "The Russian leaders are basically trying to get along with America." Do you agree, disagree, or have no opinion on that?

Full Filter

Here is a statement about an other country. Not everyone has an opinion on this. If you do not have an opinion, just say so. Here's the statement: "The Russian leaders are basically trying to get along with America." Do you have an opinion on that? If yes, do you agree or disagree?

Example of Results from Different Question Forms

	Standard Form (%)	Quasi-Filter (%)	Full Filter (%)
Agree	48.2	27.7	22.9
Disagree	38.2	29.5	20.9
No opinion	13.6*	42.8	56.3

*Volunteered
Source: Adapted from Schuman and Presser (1981:116–125). Standard format is from Fall 1978; quasi- and full-filter are from February 1977.

choice; a respondent must volunteer it. A *quasi-filter question* offers respondents a "don't know" alternative. A *full-filter question* is a special type of contingency question. It first asks if respondents have an opinion, then asks for the opinion of those who state that they do have an opinion.

Many respondents will answer a question if a "no opinion" choice is missing, but they will choose "don't know" when it is offered, or say that they do not have an opinion if asked. Such respondents are called *floaters* because they "float" from giving a response to not knowing. Their responses are affected by minor wording changes, so researchers screen them out using

quasi-filter or full-filter questions. Filtered questions do not eliminate all answers to nonexistent issues, but they reduce the problem.

Agree/Disagree, Rankings or Ratings? Survey researchers who measure values and attitudes have debated two issues about the responses offered.[7] Should questionnaire items make a statement and ask respondents whether they agree or disagree with it, or should it offer respondents specific alternatives? Should the questionnaire include a set of items and ask respondents to rate them (e.g., approve, disapprove), or should it give them a list of items and force them to rank-order items (e.g., from most favored to least favored)?

It is best to offer respondents explicit alternatives. For example, instead of asking, "Do you agree or disagree with the statement, 'Men are better suited to. . . .' " instead ask, "Do you think men are better suited, women are better suited, or both are equally suited?" Less well educated respondents are more likely to agree with a statement, whereas forced-choice alternatives encourage thought and avoid the *response set* bias—a tendency of some respondents to agree and not really decide.

Researchers create bias if question wording gives respondents a reason for choosing one alternative. For example, respondents were asked whether they supported or opposed a law on energy conservation. The results changed when respondents heard, "Do you support the law or do you oppose it because the law would be difficult to enforce?" instead of simply, "Do you support or oppose the law?"

It is better to ask respondents to choose among alternatives by ranking instead of rating items along an imaginary continuum. Respondents can rate several items equally high, but will place them in a hierarchy if asked to rank them.[8]

Wording Issues

Survey researchers face two wording issues. The first, discussed earlier, is to use simple vocabulary and grammar to minimize confusion. The second issue involves effects of specific words or phrases. This is trickier because it is not possible to know in advance whether a word or phrase affects responses.

The well-documented difference between *forbid* and *not allow* illustrates the problem of wording differences. Both terms have the same meaning, but many more people are willing to "not allow" something than to "forbid" it. In general, less well educated respondents are most influenced by minor wording differences.

Certain words seem to trigger an emotional reaction, and researchers are just beginning to learn of them. For example, Smith (1987) found large differences (e.g., twice as much support) in U.S. survey responses depending on whether a question asked about spending "to help the poor" or "for welfare." He suggested that the word *welfare* has such strong negative connotations for Americans (lazy people, wasteful and expensive programs, etc.) that it is best to avoid it.

Many respondents are confused by words or their connotations. For example, respondents were asked whether they thought television news was impartial. Researchers later learned that large numbers of respondents had ignored the word *impartial*—a term the middle-class, educated researchers assumed everyone would know. Less than half the respondents had interpreted the word as intended with its proper meaning. Over one-fourth ignored it or had no idea of its meaning. Others gave it unusual meanings, and one-tenth thought it was directly opposite to its true meaning. Researchers need to be cautious, because some wording effects (e.g., the difference between *forbid* and *not allow*) remain the same for decades, while other effects may appear.[9]

Questionnaire Design Issues

Length of Survey or Questionnaire.   How long should a questionnaire be or an interview last? Researchers prefer long questionnaires or interviews because they are more cost effective. The cost for extra questions—once a respondent has been sampled, has been contacted, and has completed other questions—is small. There is no absolute proper length. The length depends on the survey format (to be discussed) and on the respondent's characteristics. A 5-minute telephone interview is rarely a problem and may be extended to 20 minutes. A few researchers stretched this to beyond 30 minutes. Mail questionnaires are more variable. A short (3- or 4-page) questionnaire is appropriate for the general population. Some researchers have had success with questionnaires as long as 10 pages (about 100 items) with the general public, but responses drop significantly for longer questionnaires. For highly educated respondents and a salient topic, using questionnaires of 15 pages may be possible. Face-to-face interviews lasting an hour are not uncommon. In special situations, face-to-face interviews as long as three to five hours have been conducted.

Question Order or Sequence. A survey researcher faces three question sequence issues: organization of the overall questionnaire, question order effects, and context effects.

Organization of Questionnaire. In general, you should sequence questions to minimize the discomfort and confusion of respondents. A questionnaire has opening, middle, and ending questions. After an introduction explaining the survey, it is best to make opening questions pleasant, interesting, and easy to answer to help a respondent feel comfortable about the questionnaire. Avoid asking many boring background questions or threatening questions first. Organize questions into common topics. Mixing questions on different topics causes confusion. Orient respondents by placing questions on the same topic together and introduce the section with a short introductory statement (e.g., "Now I would like to ask you questions about housing"). Make question topics flow smoothly and logically, and organize them to assist respondents' memory or comfort levels. Do not end with highly threatening questions, and always end with a "thank you."

Order Effects. Researchers are concerned that the order in which they present questions may influence respondent answers. Such "order effects" appear to be strongest for people who lack strong views, for less educated respondents, and for older respondents or those with memory loss.[10] For example, support for an unmarried woman having an abortion rises if the question is preceded by a question about abortion being acceptable when a fetus has serious defects, but not when the question is by itself or before a question about fetus defects. A classic example of order effects is presented in Box 7.4.

Respondents may not perceive each issue of a survey as isolated and separate. They respond to survey questions based on the set of issues and their order of presentation in a questionnaire. Previous questions can influence later ones in two ways: through their content (i.e., the issue) and through the respondent's response. For example, a student respondent is asked, "Do you support or favor an educational contribution for students?" Answers vary depending on the topic of the preceding question. If it comes after, "How much tuition does the average U.S. student pay?" respondents interpret "contribution" to mean support for what students will pay. If it comes after "How much does the Swedish government pay to students?" respondents interpret it to mean a contribution that the government will pay. Responses can be also influenced by previous answers, because a respondent having already answered one part will assume no overlap. For example, a respondent is asked, "How is your wife?" The next question is, "How is your family?" Most respondents will assume that the second question means family members other than the wife because they already gave an answer about the wife.[11]

Context Effects. Researchers found powerful context effects in surveys. As a practical matter, two things can be done regarding context effects. Use a *funnel sequence* of questions—that is, ask more general questions before specific ones (e.g., ask about health in general before asking about specific diseases). Or, divide the number of respondents in half and give half of the questions in one order and the other half in the alternative order, then examine the results to see whether question order mattered. If question order effects are found, which order tells you what the respondents really think? The answer is that you cannot know for sure.

For example, a few years ago, a class of my students conducted a telephone survey on two

Box 7.4   Question Order Effects

Question 1

"Do you think that the United States should let Communist newspaper reporters from other countries come in here and send back to their papers the news as they see it?"

Question 2

"Do you think a Communist country like Russia should let American newspaper reporters come in and send back to America the news as they see it?"

	Percentage Saying Yes	
Heard First	*Yes to #1* *(Communist Reporter)*	*Yes to #2* *(American Reporter)*
#1	54%	75%
#2	64%	82%

The context created by answering the first question affects the answer to the second question.

Source: Adapted from Schuman and Presser (1981:29).

topics: concern about crime and attitudes toward a new anti–drunk-driving law. A random half of the respondents heard questions about the drunk-driving law first; the other half heard about crime first. I examined the results to see whether there was any *context effect*—a difference by topic order. I found that respondents who were asked about the drunk-driving law first expressed less fear about crime than did those who were asked about crime first. Likewise, they were more supportive of the drunk-driving law than were those who first heard about crime. The first topic created a context within which respondents answered questions on the second topic. After they were asked about crime in general and thought about violent crime, drunk driving may have appeared to

be a less important issue. By contrast, after they were asked about drunk driving and thought about drunk driving as a crime, they may have expressed less concern about crime in general.

Respondents answer all questions based on a context of preceding questions and the interview setting. A researcher needs to remember that the more ambiguous a question's meaning, the stronger the context effects, because respondents will draw on the context to interpret and understand the question. Previous questions on the same topic and heard just before a question can have a large context effect. For example, Sudman and associates (1996:90–91) contrasted three ways of asking how much a respondent followed politics. When they asked the question alone, about 21 percent of respondents said they followed politics "now and then" or "hardly at all." When they asked the question after asking what the respondent's elected representative recently did, the percentage who said they did not follow nearly doubled, going to 39 percent. The knowledge question about the representative made many respondents feel that they did not really know much. When a question about the amount of "public relations work" the elected representative provided to the area came between the two questions, 29 percent of respondents said they did not follow politics. This question gave respondents an excuse for not knowing the first question—they could blame their representative for their ignorance. The context of a question can make a difference and researchers need to be aware of it at all times.

Format and Layout. There are two format or layout issues: the overall physical layout of the questionnaire and the format of questions and responses.

Questionnaire Layout. Layout is important, whether a questionnaire is for an interviewer or for the respondent. Questionnaires should be clear, neat, and easy to follow. Give each question a number and put identifying information (e.g., name of organization) on questionnaires. Never cramp questions together or create a confusing appearance. A few cents saved in postage or printing will ultimately cost more in terms of lower validity due to a lower response rate or of confusion of interviewers and respondents. Make a *cover sheet* or face sheet for each interview, for administrative use. Put the time and date of interview, the interviewer, the respondent identification number, and the interviewer's comments and observations on it. A professional appearance with high-quality graphics, space between questions, and good layout improves accuracy and completeness and helps the questionnaire flow.

Give interviewers or respondents instructions on the questionnaire. Print instructions in a different style from the questions (e.g., in a different color or font or in all capitals) to distinguish them. This is so an interviewer can easily distinguish between questions for respondents and instructions intended for the interviewer alone.

Layout is crucial for mail questionnaires because there is no friendly interviewer to interact with the respondent. Instead, the questionnaire's appearance persuades the respondent. In mail surveys, include a polite, professional cover letter on letterhead stationery, identifying the researcher and offering a telephone number for questions. Details matter. Respondents will be turned off if they receive a bulky brown envelope with bulk postage addressed to Occupant or if the questionnaire does not fit into the return envelope. Always end with "Thank you for your participation." Interviewers and questionnaires should leave respondents with a positive feeling about the survey and a sense that their participation is appreciated.

Question design matters. One study of college students asked how many hours they studied per day. Some students saw five answer choices ranging from 0.5 hour to more than 2.5 hours; others saw five answer choices ranging from less than 2.5 hours to more than 4.5 hours. Of students who saw the first set, 77 percent said they studied under 2.5 hours versus 31 percent of those receiving the second set. When the mail questionnaire and telephone interview were compared, 58 percent of students hearing the first set said under 2.5 hours, but there was no change among those hearing the second set. More than differences in response categories were involved, because when students were asked about hours of television watching per day with similar response categories and then the alternative response categories made no difference. What can we learn from this? Respondents without clear answers tend to rely on questionnaire response categories for guidance and more anonymous answering formats tend to yield more honest responses (see Dillman 2000:32–39 for more details).

Question Format.   Survey researchers decide on a format for questions and responses. Should respondents circle responses, check boxes, fill in dots, or put an $\times$ in a blank? The principle is to make responses unambiguous. Boxes or brackets to be checked and numbers to be circled are usually clearest. Also, listing responses down a page rather than across makes them easier to see (see Box 7.5). As mentioned before, use arrows and instructions for contingency questions. Visual aids are also helpful. For example, hand out thermometer-like drawings to respondents

---

Box 7.5   Question Format Examples

Example of Horizontal versus Vertical Response Choices

Do you think it is too easy or too difficult to get a divorce, or is it about right?

☐ Too Easy   ☐ Too Difficult   ☐ About Right

Do you think it is too easy or too difficult to get a divorce, or is it about right?

☐ Too Easy

☐ Too Difficult

☐ About Right

Example of a Matrix Question Format

	Strongly Agree	Agree	Disagree	Strongly Disagree	Don't Know
The teacher talks too fast.	☐	☐	☐	☐	☐
I learned a lot in this class.	☐	☐	☐	☐	☐
The tests are very easy.	☐	☐	☐	☐	☐
The teacher tells many jokes.	☐	☐	☐	☐	☐
The teacher is organized.	☐	☐	☐	☐	☐

Examples of Some Response Category Choices

Excellent, Good, Fair, Poor
Approve/Disapprove
Favor/Oppose
Strongly Agree, Agree, Somewhat Agree, Somewhat Disagree, Disagree, Strongly Disagree
Too Much, Too Little, About Right
Better, Worse, About the Same
Regularly, Often, Seldom, Never
Always, Most of Time, Some of Time, Rarely, Never
More Likely, Less Likely, No Difference
Very Interested, Interested, Not Interested

when asking about how warm or cool they feel toward someone. A *matrix question* (or grid question) is a compact way to present a series of questions using the same response categories. It saves space and makes it easier for the respondent or interviewer to note answers for the same response categories.

Nonresponse. The failure to get a valid response from every sampled respondent weakens a survey. Have you ever refused to answer a survey? In addition to research surveys, people are asked to respond to many requests from charities, marketing firms, candidate polls, and so forth. Charities and marketing firms get low response rates, whereas government organizations get much higher cooperation rates. Nonresponse can be a major problem for survey research because if a high proportion of the sampled respondents do not respond, researchers may not be able to generalize results, especially if those who do not respond differ from those who respond.

Public cooperation in survey research has declined over the past 20 to 30 years across many countries, with the Netherlands having the highest refusal rate, and with refusal rates as high as 30 percent in the United States.[12] There is both a growing group of "hard core" refusing people and a general decline in participation because many people feel there are too many surveys. Other reasons for refusal include a fear of crime and strangers, a more hectic life-style, a loss of privacy, and a rising distrust of authority or government. The misuse of the survey to sell products or persuade people, poorly designed questionnaires, and inadequate explanations of surveys to respondents also increase refusals for legitimate surveys.

Survey researchers can improve eligibility rates by careful respondent screening, better sample-frame definition, and multilingual interviewers. They can decrease refusals by sending letters in advance of an interview, offering to reschedule interviews, using small incentives (i.e., small gifts), adjusting interviewer behavior

and statements (i.e., making eye contact, expressing sincerity, explaining the sampling or survey, emphasizing importance of the interview, clarifying promises of confidentiality, etc.). Survey researchers can also use alternative interviewers (i.e., different demographic characteristics, age, race, gender, or ethnicity), use alternative interview methods (i.e., phone versus face to face), or accept alternative respondents in a household.

A critical area of nonresponse or refusal to participate occurs with the initial contact between an interviewer and a respondent. A face-to-face or telephone interview must overcome resistance and reassure respondents.

Research on the use of incentives found that prepaid incentives appear to increase respondent cooperation in all types of surveys. They do not appear to have negative effects on survey composition or future participation.

There is a huge literature on ways to increase response rates for mail questionnaires (see Box 7.6).[13] Heberlein and Baumgartner (1978, 1981) reported 71 factors affecting mail questionnaire response rates.

TYPES OF SURVEYS: ADVANTAGES AND DISADVANTAGES

Mail and Self-Administered Questionnaires

Advantages.   Researchers can give questionnaires directly to respondents or mail them to respondents who read instructions and questions, then record their answers. This type of survey is by far the cheapest, and it can be conducted by a single researcher. A researcher can send questionnaires to a wide geographical area. The respondent can complete the questionnaire when it is convenient and can check personal records if necessary. Mail questionnaires offer anonymity and avoid interviewer bias. They can be effective, and response rates may be high for an educated target population that has a strong interest in the topic or the survey organization.

Box 7.6	**Ten Ways to Increase Mail Questionnaire Response**

1. Address the questionnaire to specific person, not "Occupant," and send it first class.

2. Include a carefully written, dated cover letter on letterhead stationery. In it, request respondent cooperation, guarantee confidentiality, explain the purpose of the survey, and give the researcher's name and phone number.

3. *Always* include a postage-paid, addressed return envelope.

4. The questionnaire should have a neat, attractive layout and reasonable page length.

5. The questionnaire should be professionally printed and easy to read, with clear instructions.

6. Send two follow-up reminder letters to those not responding. The first should arrive about one week after sending the questionnaire, the second a week later. Gently ask for cooperation again and offer to send another questionnaire.

7. Do not send questionnaires during major holiday periods.

8. Do not put questions on the back page. Instead, leave a blank space and ask the respondent for general comments.

9. Sponsors that are local and are seen as legitimate (e.g., government agencies, universities, large firms, etc.) get a better response.

10. Include a small monetary inducement ($1) if possible.

Disadvantages. Since people do not always complete and return questionnaires, the biggest problem with mail questionnaires is a low response rate. Most questionnaires are returned within two weeks, but others trickle in up to two months later. Researchers can raise response rates by sending nonrespondents reminder letters, but this adds to the time and cost of data collection.

A researcher cannot control the conditions under which a mail questionnaire is completed. A questionnaire completed during a drinking party by a dozen laughing people may be returned along with one filled out by an earnest respondent. Also, no one is present to clarify questions or to probe for more information when respondents give incomplete answers. Someone other than the sampled respondent (e.g., spouse, new resident, etc.) may open the mail and complete the questionnaire without the researcher's knowledge. Different respondents can complete the questionnaire weeks apart or answer questions in a different order than that intended by researchers. Incomplete questionnaires can also be a serious problem.

Researchers cannot visually observe the respondent's reactions to questions, physical characteristics, or the setting. For example, an impoverished 70-year-old White woman living alone on a farm could falsely state that she is a prosperous 40-year-old Asian male doctor living in a town with three children. Such extreme lies are rare, but serious errors can go undetected.

The mail questionnaire format limits the kinds of questions that a researcher can use. Questions requiring visual aids (e.g., look at this picture and tell me what you see), open-ended questions, many contingency questions, and complex questions do poorly in mail questionnaires. Likewise, mail questionnaires are ill suited for the illiterate or near-illiterate in English. Questionnaires mailed to illiterate respondents are not likely to be returned; if they are completed and returned, the questions were probably misunderstood, so the answers are meaningless (see Table 7.4).

Web Surveys

Access to the Internet and e-mail has become widespread since the late-1990s across most advanced nations. For example, 3 percent of the U.S. population had e-mail in 1994; only 10 years later about 75 percent of households had Internet connections.

TABLE 7.4   Types of Surveys and Their Features

Features	Type of Survey			
	Mail Questionnaire	Web Survey	Telephone Interview	Face-to-Face Interview
Administrative Issues				
Cost	Cheap	Cheapest	Moderate	Expensive
Speed	Slowest	Fastest	Fast	Slow to moderate
Length (number of questions)	Moderate	Moderate	Short	Longest
Response rate	Lowest	Moderate	Moderate	Highest
Research Control				
Probes possible	No	No	Yes	Yes
Specific respondent	No	No	Yes	Yes
Question sequence	No	Yes	Yes	Yes
Only one respondent	No	No	Yes	Yes
Visual observation	No	No	No	Yes
Success with Different Questions				
Visual aids	Limited	Yes	None	Yes
Open-ended questions	Limited	Limited	Limited	Yes
Contingency questions	Limited	Yes	Yes	Yes
Complex questions	Limited	Yes	Limited	Yes
Sensitive questions	Some	Yes	Limited	Limited
Sources of Bias				
Social desirability	Some	Some	Some	Most
Interviewer bias	None	None	Some	Most
Respondent's reading skill	Yes	Yes	No	No

Advantages. Web-based surveys over the Internet or by e-mail are very fast and inexpensive. They allow flexible design and can use visual images, or even audio or video in some Internet versions. Despite great flexibility, the basic principles for question writing and for paper questionnaire design generally apply.

Disadvantages. Web surveys have three areas of concern: coverage, privacy and verification, and design issues. The first concern involves sampling and unequal Internet access or use. Despite high coverage rates, older, less-educated, lower-income, and more rural people are less likely to have good Internet access. In addition, many people have multiple e-mail addresses, which limits using them for sampling purposes. Self-selection is a potential problem with web surveys. For example, a marketing department could get very distorted results of the population of new car buyers. Perhaps half of the new car buyers for a model are over age 55, but 75 percent of respondents to a web survey are under age 32 and only 8 percent are over age 55. Not only would the results be distorted by age but the relatively small percentage of over-55 respondents may not be representative of all over-55 potential new car buyers (e.g., they may be higher income or more educated).

A second concern is protecting respondent privacy and confidentiality. Researchers should encrypt collected data, only use secure websites and erase nonessential respondent identification or linking information on a daily or weekly basis. They should develop a system of respondent verification to ensure that only the sampled respondent participates and does so only once. This may involve a system such as giving each respondent a unique PIN number to access the questionnaire.

A third concern involves the complexity of questionnaire design. Researchers need to check and verify the compatibility of various web software and hardware combinations for respondents using different computers. Researchers are

still learning what is most effective for web surveys. It is best to provide screen-by-screen questions and make an entire question visible on the screen at one time in a consistent format with drop-down boxes for answer choices. It is best to include a progress indicator (as motivation), such as a clock or waving hand. Visual appearance of a screen, such as the range of colors and fonts, should be kept simple for easy readability and consistency. Be sure to provide very clear instructions for all computer actions (e.g., use of drop-down screens) where they are needed and include "click here" instructions. Also, make it easy for respondents to move back and forth across questions. Researchers using web surverys need to avoid technical glitches at the implementation stage by repeated pretesting, having a dedicated server, and obtaining sufficient broadband to handle high demand.

Telephone Interviews

Advantages. The telephone interview is a popular survey method because about 95 percent of the population can be reached by telephone. An interviewer calls a respondent (usually at home), asks questions, and records answers. Researchers sample respondents from lists, telephone directories, or random digit dialing, and can quickly reach many people across long distances. A staff of interviewers can interview 1,500 respondents across a nation within a few days and, with several callbacks, response rates can reach 90 percent. Although this method is more expensive than a mail questionnaire, the telephone interview is a flexible method with most of the strengths of face-to-face interviews but for about half the cost. Interviewers control the sequence of questions and can use some probes. A specific respondent is chosen and is likely to answer all the questions alone. The researcher knows when the questions were answered and can use contingency questions effectively, especially with computer-assisted telephone interviewing (CATI) (to be discussed).

Disadvantages. Higher cost and limited interview length are among the disadvantages of telephone interviews. In addition, respondents without telephones are impossible to reach, and the call may come at an inconvenient time. The use of an interviewer reduces anonymity and introduces potential interviewer bias. Open-ended questions are difficult to use, and questions requiring visual aids are impossible. Interviewers can only note serious disruptions (e.g., background noise) and respondent tone of voice (e.g., anger or flippancy) or hesitancy.

Face-to-Face Interviews

Advantages. Face-to-face interviews have the highest response rates and permit the longest questionnaires. Interviewers also can observe the surroundings and can use nonverbal communication and visual aids. Well-trained interviewers can ask all types of questions, can ask complex questions, and can use extensive probes.

Disadvantages. High cost is the biggest disadvantage of face-to-face interviews. The training, travel, supervision, and personnel costs for interviews can be high. Interviewer bias is also greatest in face-to-face interviews. The appearance, tone of voice, question wording, and so forth of the interviewer may affect the respondent. In addition, interviewer supervision is less than for telephone interviews, which supervisors monitor by listening in.[14]

INTERVIEWING

The Role of the Interviewer

Interviews to gather information occur in many settings. Survey research interviewing is a specialized kind of interviewing. As with most interviewing, its goal is to obtain accurate information from another person.[15]

The survey interview is a social relationship. Like other social relationships, it involves social roles, norms, and expectations. The interview is a short-term, secondary social interaction between two strangers with the explicit purpose of one person's obtaining specific information from the other. The social roles are those of the interviewer and the interviewee or respondent. Information is obtained in a structured conversation in which the interviewer asks prearranged questions and records answers, and the respondent answers. It differs in several ways from ordinary conversation (see Table 7.5).

An important problem for interviewers is that many respondents are unfamilar with the survey respondents' role. As a result, they substitute another role that may affect their responses. Some believe the interview is an intimate conversation or thearpy session, some see it as a bureaucratic exercise in completing forms, some view it as a citizen referendum on policy choices, some view it as a testing situation, and some consider it as a form of deceit in which interviewers are trying to trick or entrap respondents. Even in a well-designed, professional survey, follow-up research found that only about half the respondents understand questions exactly as intended by researchers. Respondents reinterpreted questions to make them applicable to their ideosynactic, personal situations or to make them easy to answer.[16]

The role of interviewers is difficult. They obtain cooperation and build rapport, yet remain neutral and objective. They encroach on the respondents' time and privacy for information that may not directly benefit the respondents. They try to reduce embarrassment, fear, and suspicion so that respondents feel comfortable revealing information. They may explain the nature of survey research or give hints about social roles in an interview. Good interviewers monitor the pace and direction of the social interaction as well as the content of answers and the behavior of respondents.

Survey interviewers are nonjudgmental and do not reveal their opinions, verbally or nonverbally (e.g., by a look of shock). If a respondent asks for an interviewer's opinion, he or she

TABLE 7.5   Differences between Ordinary Conversation and a Structured Survey Interview

Ordinary Conversation	The Survey Interview
1. Questions and answers from each participant are relatively equally balanced.	1. Interviewer asks and respondent answers most of the time.
2. There is an open exchange of feelings and opinions.	2. Only the respondent reveals feelings and opinions.
3. Judgments are stated and attempts made to persuade the other of a particular points of view.	3. Interviewer is nonjudgmental and does not try to change respondent's opinions or beliefs.
4. A person can reveal deep inner feelings to gain sympathy or as a therapeutic release.	4. Interviewer tries to obtain direct answers to specific questions.
5. Ritual responses are common (e.g., "Uh huh," shaking head, "How are you?" "Fine").	5. Interviewer avoids making ritual responses that influence a respondent and also seeks genuine answers, not ritual responses.
6. The participants exchange information and correct the factual errors that they are aware of.	6. Respondent provides almost all information. Interviewer does not correct a respondent's factual errors.
7. Topics rise and fall and either person can introduce new topics. The focus can shift directions or digress to less relevant issues.	7. Interviewer controls the topic, direction, and pace. He or she keeps the respondent "on task," and irrelevant diversions are contained.
8. The emotional tone can shift from humor, to joy, to affection, to sadness, to anger, and so on.	8. Interviewer attempts to maintain a consistently warm but serious and objective tone throughout.
9. People can evade or ignore questions and give flippant or noncommittal answers.	9. Respondent should not evade questions and should give truthful, thoughtful answers.

Source: Adapted from Gorden (1980:19–25) and Sudman and Bradburn (1983:5–10).

politely redirects the respondent and indicates that such questions are inappropriate. For example, if a respondent asks, "What do you think?" the interviewer may answer, "Here, we are interested in what *you* think; what I think doesn't matter." Likewise, if the respondent gives a shocking answer (e.g., "I was arrested three times for beating my infant daughter and burning her with cigarettes"), the interviewer does not show shock, surprise, or disdain but treats the answer in a matter-of-fact manner. He or she helps respondents feel that they can give any truthful answer.

You might ask, "If the survey interviewer must be neutral and objective, why not use a robot or machine?" Machine interviewing has not been successful because it lacks the human warmth, sense of trust, and rapport that an interviewer creates. An interviewer helps define the situation and ensures that respondents have the information sought, understand what is expected, give relevant answers, are motivated to cooperate, and give serious answers.

Interviewers do more than interview respondents. Face-to-face interviewers spend only about 35 percent of their time interviewing. About 40 percent is spent in locating the correct respondent, 15 percent in traveling, and 10 percent in studying survey materials and dealing with administrative and recording details.[17]

Stages of an Interview

The interview proceeds through stages, beginning with an introduction and entry. The interviewer gets in the door, shows authorization, and reassures and secures cooperation from the respondent. He or she is prepared for reactions such as, "How did you pick me?" "What good will this do?" "I don't know about this," "What's this about, anyway?" The interviewer can explain why the specific respondent is interviewed and not a substitute.

The main part of the interview consists of asking questions and recording answers. The interviewer uses the exact wording on the questionnaire—no added or omitted words and no rephrasing. He or she asks all applicable questions in order, without returning to or skipping questions unless the directions specify this. He or she goes at a comfortable pace and gives nondirective feedback to maintain interest.

In addition to asking questions, the interviewer accurately records answers. This is easy for closed-ended questions, where interviewers just mark the correct box. For open-ended questions, the interviewer's job is more difficult. He or she listens carefully, must have legible writing, and must record what is said verbatim without correcting grammar or slang. More important, the interviewer never summarizes or paraphrases. This causes a loss of information or distorts answers. For example, the respondent says, "I'm really concerned about my daughter's heart problem. She's only 10 years old and she has trouble climbing stairs. I don't know what

she'll do when she gets older. Heart surgery is too risky for her and it costs so much. She'll have to learn to live with it." If the interviewer writes, "concerned about daughter's health," much is lost.

The interviewer knows how and when to use probes. A *probe* is a neutral request to clarify an ambiguous answer, to complete an incomplete answer, or to obtain a relevant response. Interviewers recognize an irrelevant or inaccurate answer and use probes as needed.[18] There are many types of probes. A three- to five-second pause is often effective. Nonverbal communication (e.g., tilt of head, raised eyebrows, or eye contact) also works well. The interviewer can repeat the question or repeat the reply and then pause. She or he can ask a neutral question, such as, "Any other reasons?" "Can you tell me more about that?" "How do you mean?" "Could you explain more for me?" (see Box 7.7).

The last stage is the exit, when the interviewer thanks the respondent and leaves. He or she then goes to a quiet, private place to edit the questionnaire and record other details such as the date, time, and place of the interview; a thumbnail sketch of the respondent and interview situation; the respondent's attitude (e.g., serious, angry, or laughing); and any unusual circumstances (e.g., "Telephone rang at question 27 and respondent talked for four minutes before the interview started again"). He or she notes anything disruptive that happened during the interview (e.g., "Teenage son entered room, sat at opposite end, turned on television with the volume loud, and watched a music video"). The interviewer also records personal feelings and anything that was suspected (e.g., "Respondent became nervous and fidgeted when questioned about his marriage").

Training Interviewers

A large-scale survey requires hiring multiple interviewers. Few people appreciate the difficulty of the interviewer's job. A professional-quality interview requires the careful selection of

Box **7.7**	**Example of Probes and Recording Full Responses to Closed Questions**

Interviewer Question: What is your occupation?

Respondent Answer: I work at General Motors.
　Probe: What is your job at General Motors? What type of work do you do there?

Interviewer Question: How long have you been unemployed?

Respondent Answer: A long time.
　Probe: Could you tell me more specifically when your current period of unemployment began?

Interviewer Question: Considering the country as a whole, do you think we will have good times during the next year, or bad times, or what?

Respondent Answer: Maybe good, maybe bad, it depends, who knows?
　Probe: What do you expect to happen?

Record Response to a Closed Question

Interviewer Question: On a scale of 1 to 7, how do you feel about capital punishment or the death penalty, where 1 is strongly in favor of the death penalty, and 7 is strongly opposed to it?
(Favor) 1 __   2 __   3 __   4 __   5 __   6 __   7 __   (Oppose)

Respondent Answer: About a 4. I think that all murderers, rapists, and violent criminals should get death, but I don't favor it for minor crimes like stealing a car.

---

interviewers and extensive training. As with any employment situation, adequate pay and good supervision are important for consistent high-quality performance. Unfortunately, professional interviewing has not always paid well or provided regular employment. In the past, interviewers were largely drawn from a pool of middle-aged women willing to accept irregular part-time work.

Good interviewers are pleasant, honest, accurate, mature, responsible, moderately intelligent, stable, and motivated. They have a non-threatening appearance, have experience with many different types of people, and possess poise and tact. Researchers may consider interviewers' physical appearance, age, race, sex, languages spoken, and even the sound of their voice.

Professional interviewers will receive a two-week training course. It includes lectures and reading, observation of expert interviewers, mock interviews in the office and in the field that are recorded and critiqued, many practice interviews, and role-playing. The interviewers learn about survey research and the role of the interviewer. They become familiar with the questionnaire and the purpose of questions, although not with the answers expected.

The importance of carefully selecting and training interviewers was evident during the 2004 U.S. presidential election. Exit polls are quick, very short surveys conducted outside a polling place for people immediately after they voted. On Election Day of 2004 exit polls showed candidate John Kerry well ahead, but after final votes were counted he lost to his opponent, George W. Bush. A major cause of the mistake was that the research organization, paid $10 million by six major news organizations to conduct the exit polls, had hired many young inexperienced interviewers and gave them only minimal training. Younger voters tended to support John Kerry, whereas older voters tended to support George Bush. The young inexperienced interviewers were less successful in gaining cooperation from older voters and felt more comfortable handing the questionnaire to someone of a similar age. As a result, exit poll participants did not reflect the composition of all voters and poll results showed greater support for Kerry than actually existed among all voters.[19]

Although interviewers largely work alone, researchers use an interviewer supervisor in large-scale surveys with several interviewers. Supervisors are familiar with the area, assist with problems, oversee the interviewers, and ensure that work is completed on time. For telephone interviewing, this includes helping with calls, checking when interviewers arrive and leave, and monitoring interview calls. In face-to-face interviews, supervisors check to find out whether the interview actually took place. This means calling back or sending a confirmation postcard to a sample of respondents. They can also check the response rate and incomplete questionnaires to see whether interviewers are obtaining cooperation, and they may reinterview a small subsample, analyze answers, or observe interviews to see whether interviewers are accurately asking questions and recording answers.

Interviewer Bias

Survey researchers proscribe interviewer behavior to reduce bias. This goes beyond reading each question exactly as worded. Ideally, the actions of a particular interviewer will not affect how a respondent answers, and responses will not vary from what they would be if asked by any other interviewer.

Survey researchers know that interviewer expectations can create significant bias. Interviewers who expect difficult interviews have them, and those who expect certain answers are more likely to get them (see Box 7.8). Proper interviewer behavior and exact question reading may be difficult, but the issue is larger.

The social setting in which the interview occurs can affect answers, including the presence of other people. For example, students answer differently depending on whether they are asked questions at home or at school. In general, survey researchers do not want others present because they may affect respondent answers. It may not always make a difference, however, especially if the others are small children.[20]

An interviewer's visible characteristics, including race and gender, often affect interviews and respondent answers, especially for questions about issues related to race or gender. For example, African American and Hispanic American respondents express different policy positions on race- or ethnic-related issues depending on the apparent race or ethnicity of the interviewer. This occurs even with telephone interviews when a respondent has clues about the interviewer's race or ethnicity. In general, interviewers of the same ethnic-racial group get more accurate answers.[21] Gender also affects interviews both in terms of obvious issues, such as sexual behavior, as well as support for gender-related collective action or gender equality.[22] Survey researchers need to note the race and gender of both interviewers and respondents.

Computer-Assisted Telephone Interviewing

Advances in computer technology and lower computer prices have enabled professional survey research organizations to install *computer-assisted telephone interviewing (CATI)* systems.[23] With CATI, the interviewer sits in front of a computer and makes calls. Wearing a

Box 7.8 Interviewer Characteristics Can Affect Responses

Example of Interviewer Expectation Effects

Asked by Female Interviewer Whose Own	Female Respondent Reports That Husband Buys Most Furniture
Husband buys most furniture	89%
Husband does not buy most furniture	15%

Example of Race or Ethnic Appearance Effects

Interviewer	Percentage Answering Yes to:	
	"Do you think there are too many Jews in government jobs?"	"Do you think that Jews have too much power?"
Looked Jewish with Jewish-sounding name	11.7	5.8
Looked Jewish only	15.4	15.6
Non-Jewish appearance	21.2	24.3
Non-Jewish appearance and non-Jewish-sounding name	19.5	21.4

Note: Racial stereotypes held by respondents can affect how they respond in interviews.
Source: Adapted from Hyman (1975:115, 163).

headset and microphone, the interviewer reads the questions from a computer screen for the specific respondent who is called, then enters the answer via the keyboard. Once he or she enters an answer, the computer shows the next question on the screen.

Computer-assisted telephone interviewing speeds interviewing and reduces interviewer errors. It also eliminates the separate step of entering information into a computer and speeds data processing. Of course, CATI requires an investment in computer equipment and some knowledge of computers. The CATI system is valuable for contingency questions because the computer can show the questions appropriate for a specific respondent; interviewers do not have to turn pages looking for the next question. In addition, the computer can check an answer immediately after the interviewer enters it. For example, if an interviewer enters an answer that is impossible or clearly an error (e.g., an *H* instead of an *M* for "Male"), the computer will request another answer. Innovations with computers and web surveys also help to gather data on sensitive issue (see Box 7.9).

Several companies have developed software programs for personal computers that help researchers develop questionnaires and analyze survey data. They provide guides for writing questions, recording responses, analyzing data,

<table>
<tr><td>Box 7.9</td><td>**Computer-Aided Surveys and Sensitive Topics**</td></tr>
</table>

The questioning format influences how respondents answer questions about sensitive topics. Formats that permit the greater respondent anonymity, such as a self-administered questionnaire or the web survey, are more likely to elicit honest responses than one that requires interaction with another person, such as in a face-to-face interview or telephone interview. One of a series of computer-based technological innovations is called *computer-assisted self-administered interviews (CASAI)*. It appears to improve respondent comfort and honesty in answering questions on sensitive topics. In CASAI, respondents are "interviewed" with questions that are asked on a computer screen or heard over earphones. The respondents answer by moving a computer mouse or entering information using a computer keyboard. Even when a researcher is present in the same room, the respondent is semi-insulated from human contact and appears to feel comfortable answering questions about sensitive issues.

and producing reports. The programs may speed the more mechanical aspects of survey research—such as typing questionnaires, organizing layout, and recording responses—but they cannot substitute for a good understanding of the survey method or an appreciation of its limitations. The researcher must still clearly conceptualize variables, prepare well-worded questions, design the sequence and forms of questions and responses, and pilot-test questionnaires. Communicating unambiguously with respondents and eliciting credible responses remain the most important parts of survey research.

THE ETHICAL SURVEY

Like all social research, people can conduct surveys in ethical or unethical ways. A major

ethical issue in survey research is the invasion of privacy. Survey researchers can intrude into a respondent's privacy by asking about intimate actions and personal beliefs. People have a right to privacy. Respondents decide when and to whom to reveal personal information. They are likely to provide such information when it is asked for in a comfortable context with mutual trust, when they believe serious answers are needed for legitimate research purposes, and when they believe answers will remain confidential. Researchers should treat all respondents with dignity and reduce anxiety or discomfort. They are also responsible for protecting the confidentiality of data.

A second issue involves voluntary participation by respondents. Respondents agree to answer questions and can refuse to participate at any time. They give "informed consent" to participate in research. Researchers depend on respondents' voluntary cooperation, so researchers need to ask well-developed questions in a sensitive way, treat respondents with respect, and be very sensitive to confidentiality.

A third ethical issue is the exploitation of surveys and pseudosurveys. Because of its popularity, some people use surveys to mislead others. A *pseudosurvey* is when someone who has little or no real interest in learning information from a respondent uses the survey format to try to persuade someone to do something. Charlatans use the guise of conducting a survey to invade privacy, gain entry into homes, or "suggle" (sell in the guise of a survey). I personally experienced a type of pseudosurvey known as a "suppression poll" in the 1994 U.S. election campaign. In this situation, an unknown survey organization telephoned potential voters and asked whether the voter supported a given candidate. If the voter supported the candidate, the interviewer next asked whether the respondent would still support the candidate if he or she knew that the candidate had an unfavorable characteristic (e.g., had been arrested for drunk driving, used illegal drugs, raised the wages of convicted criminals in prison, etc.). The goal of the interview was not to measure candidate support; rather, it was to identify a candidate's supporters then attempt to suppress voting. Although they are illegal, no one has been prosecuted for using this campaign tactic.

Another ethical issue is when people misuse survey results or use poorly designed or purposely rigged surveys. Why does this occur? People may demand answers from surveys that surveys cannot provide and not understand a survey's limitations. Those who design and prepare surveys may lack sufficient training to conduct a legitimate survey. Unfortunately, policy decisions are sometimes made based on careless or poorly designed surveys. They often result in waste or human hardship. This is why legitimate researchers conducting methodologically rigorous survey research are important.

The media report more surveys than other types of social research, yet sloppy reporting of survey results permits abuse.[24] Few people reading survey results may appreciate it, but researchers should include details about the survey (see Box 7.10) to reduce the misuse of survey research and increase questions about surveys that lack such information. Survey researchers urge the media to include such information, but it is rarely included. Over 88 percent of reports on surveys in the mass media fail to reveal the researcher who conducted the survey, and only 18 percent provide details on how the survey was conducted.[25] Currently, there are no quality-control standards to regulate the opinion polls or surveys reported in the U.S. media. Researchers have made unsuccessful attempts since World War II to require adequate samples, interviewer training and supervision, satisfactory questionnaire design, public availability of results, and controls on the integrity of survey organizations.[26] As a result, the mass media report both biased and misleading survey results and rigorous, professional survey results without making any distinction. It is not surprising that public confusion and a distrust of all surveys occur.

Box 7.10 Ten Items to Include When Reporting Survey Research

1. The sampling frame used (e.g., telephone directories)
2. The dates on which the survey was conducted
3. The population that the sample represents (e.g., U.S. adults, Australian college students, housewives in Singapore)
4. The size of the sample for which information was collected
5. The sampling method (e.g., random)
6. The exact wording of the questions asked
7. The method of the survey (e.g., face to face, telephone)
8. The organizations that sponsored the survey (paid for it and conducted it)
9. The response rate or percentage of those contacted who actually completed the questionnaire
10. Any missing information or "don't know" responses when results on specific questions are reported

---

CONCLUSION

In this chapter, you learned about survey research. You also learned some principles of writing good survey questions. There are many things to avoid and to include when writing questions. You learned about the advantages and disadvantages of three types of survey research: mail, telephone interviews, and face-to-face interviews. You saw that interviewing, especially face-to-face interviewing, can be difficult.

Although this chapter focused on survey research, researchers use questionnaires to measure variables in other types of quantitative research (e.g., experiments). The survey, often called the sample survey because random sampling is usually used with it, is a distinct technique. It is a process of asking many people the same questions and examining their answers.

Survey researchers try to minimize errors, but survey data often contain them. Errors in surveys can compound each other. For example, errors can arise in sampling frames, from nonresponse, from question wording or order, and from interviewer bias. Do not let the existence of errors discourage you from using the survey, however. Instead, learn to be very careful when designing survey research and cautious about generalizing from the results of surveys.

Key Terms

- closed-ended question
- computer-assisted telephone interviewing (CATI)
- context effect
- contingency question
- cover sheet
- double-barreled question
- floaters
- full-filter question
- funnel sequence
- interview schedule
- matrix question
- open-ended question
- order effects
- partially open question
- prestige bias
- probe
- quasi-filter question
- response set
- social desirability bias
- standard-format question
- threatening questions
- wording effects

Endnotes

1. Sudman and Bradburn (1983:39) suggested that even simple questions (e.g., "What brand of soft drink do you usually buy?") can cause problems.

Respondents who are highly loyal to one brand of traditional carbonated sodas can answer the question easily. Other respondents must implicitly address the following questions to answer the question as it was asked: (a) What time period is involved—the past month, the past year, the last 10 years? (b) What conditions count—at home, at restaurants, at sporting events? (c) Buying for oneself alone or for other family members? (d) What is a "soft drink"? Do lemonade, iced tea, mineral water, or fruit juices count? (e) Does "usually" mean a brand purchased as 51 percent or more of all soft drink purchases, or the brand purchased more frequently than any other? Respondents rarely stop and ask for clarification; they make assumptions about what the researcher means.

2. See Dykema and Schaeffer (2000) and Sudman and colleagues (1996:197–226).

3. See Ostrom and Gannon (1996).

4. See Bradburn (1983), Bradburn and Sudman (1980), and Sudman and Bradburn (1983) on threatening or sensitive questions. Backstrom and Hursh-Cesar (1981:219) and Warwick and Lininger (1975:150–151) provide useful suggestions as well.

5. On how "Who knows who lives here?" can be complicated, see Martin (1999) and Tourangeau et al. (1997).

6. For a discussion of the "don't know," "no opinion," and middle positions in response categories, see Backstrom and Hursh-Cesar (1981:148–149), Bishop (1987), Bradburn and Sudman (1988: 154), Brody (1986), Converse and Presser (1986:35–37), Duncan and Stenbeck (1988), and Sudman and Bradburn (1983:140–141).

7. The disagree/agree versus specific alternatives debate can be found in Bradburn and Sudman (1988:149–151), Converse and Presser (1986:38–39), and Schuman and Presser (1981:179–223).

8. The ranking versus ratings issue is discussed in Alwin and Krosnick (1985) and Krosnick and Alwin (1988). Also see Backstrom and Hursh-Cesar (1981:132–134) and Sudman and Bradburn (1983:156–165) for formats of asking rating and ranking questions.

9. See Foddy (1993) and Presser (1990).

10. Studies by Krosnick (1992) and Narayan and Krosnick (1996) show that education reduces response-order (primacy or recency) effects, but

Knäuper (1999) found that age is strongly associated with response-order effects.

11. This example comes from Strack (1992).
12. For a discussion, see Couper, Singer et al. (1998), de Heer (1999), Keeter et al. (2000), Sudman and Bradburn (1983:11), and "Surveys Proliferate, but Answers Dwindle," *New York Times,* October 5, 1990, p. 1. Smith (1995) and Sudman (1976:114–116) also discuss refusal rates.
13. Bailey (1987:153–168), Church (1993), Dillman (1978, 1983), Fox and colleagues (1988), Goyder (1982), Heberlein and Baumgartner (1978, 1981), Hubbard and Little (1988), Jones (1979), and Willimack and colleagues (1995) discuss increasing return rates in surveys
14. For a comparison among types of surveys, see Backstrom and Hursh-Cesar (1981:16–23), Bradburn and Sudman (1988:94–110), Dillman (1978:39–78), Fowler (1984:61–73), and Frey (1983:27–55).
15. For more on survey research interviewing, see Brenner and colleagues (1985), Cannell and Kahn (1968), Converse and Schuman (1974), Dijkstra and van der Zouwen (1982), Foddy (1993), Gorden (1980), Hyman (1975), and Moser and Kalton (1972:270–302).
16. See Turner and Martin (1984:262–269, 282).
17. From Moser and Kalton (1972:273).
18. The use of probes is discussed in Backstrom and Hursh-Cesar (1981:266–273), Gorden (1980:368–390), and Hyman (1975:236–241).
19. Report by Jacques Steinberg (2005). "Study Cites Human Failings in Election Day Poll System," *New York Times* (January 20, 2005).
20. See Bradburn and Sudman (1980), Pollner and Adams (1997), and Zane and Matsoukas (1979).
21. The race or ethnicity of interviewers is discussed in Anderson and colleagues (1988), Bradburn (1983), Cotter and colleagues (1982), Davis (1997), Finkel and colleagues (1991), Gorden (1980:168–172), Reese and colleagues (1986), Schaffer (1980), Schuman and Converse (1971), and Weeks and Moore (1981).
22. See Catania and associates (1996) and Kane and MacAulay (1993).
23. CATI is discussed in Bailey (1987:201–202), Bradburn and Sudman (1988:100–101), Frey (1983:24–25, 143–149), Groves and Kahn (1979:226), Groves and Mathiowetz (1984), and Karweit and Meyers (1983).
24. On reporting survey results in the media, see Channels (1993) and MacKeun (1984).
25. See Singer (1988).
26. From Turner and Martin (1984:62).

CHAPTER 8

Experimental Research

INTRODUCTION

Experimental research builds on the principles of a positivist approach more directly than do the other research techniques. Researchers in the natural sciences (e.g., chemistry and physics), related applied fields (e.g., agriculture, engineering, and medicine), and the social sciences conduct experiments. The logic that guides an experiment on plant growth in biology or testing a metal in engineering is applied in experiments on human social behavior. Although it is most widely used in psychology, the experiment is found in education, criminal justice, journalism, marketing, nursing, political science, social work, and sociology. This chapter focuses first on the experiment conducted in a laboratory under controlled conditions, then looks at experiments conducted in the field.

The experiment's basic logic extends commonsense thinking. Commonsense experiments are less careful or systematic than scientifically based experiments. In commonsense language, an *experiment* is when you modify something in a situation, then compare an outcome to what existed without the modification. For example, I try to start my car. To my surprise, it does not start. I "experiment" by cleaning off the battery connections, then try to start it again. I modified something (cleaned the connections) and compared the outcome (whether the car started) to the previous situation (it did not start). I began with an implicit "hypothesis"—a buildup of crud on the connections is the reason the car is not starting, and once the crud is cleaned off, the car will start. This illustrates three things researchers do in experiments: (1) begin with a hypothesis, (2) modify something in a situation, and (3) compare outcomes with and without the modification.

Compared to the other social research techniques, experimental research is the strongest for testing causal relationships because the three conditions for causality (temporal order, association, and no alternative explanations) are best met in experimental designs.

Research Questions Appropriate for an Experiment

The Issue of an Appropriate Technique. Some research questions are better addressed using certain techniques. New researchers often ask, Which technique (e.g., experiments and surveys) best fits which research question? There is no easy answer, because the match between a research question and technique is not fixed but depends on informed judgment. You can develop judgment from reading research reports, understanding the strengths and weaknesses of different techniques, assisting more experienced researchers with their research, and gaining practical experience.

Research Questions for Experimental Research. The experiment allows a researcher to focus sharply on causal relations, and it has practical advantages over other techniques, but it also has limitations. The research questions most appropriate for an experiment fit its strengths and limitations.

The questions appropriate for using an experimental logic confront ethical and practical limitations of intervening in human affairs for research purposes. It is immoral and impossible to manipulate many areas of human life for research purposes. The pure logic of an experiment has an experimenter intervene or induce a change in some focused part of social life, then examine the consequences that result from the change or intervention. This usually means that the experiment is limited to research questions in which a researcher is able to manipulate conditions. Experimental research cannot answer questions such as, Do people who complete a college education increase their annual income more than people who do not? Do children raised with younger siblings develop better leadership skills than children without siblings? Do people who belong to more organizations vote more often in elections? This is because an experimenter often cannot manipulate conditions or intervene. He or she cannot randomly assign thousands to attend college and prevent others from attending to discover who later earns more income. He or she cannot induce couples to have either many children or a single child so he or she can examine how leadership skills develop in children. He or she cannot compel people to join or quit organizations then see whether they vote. Experimenters are highly creative in simulating such interventions or conditions, but they cannot manipulate many of the variables of interest to fit the pure experimental logic.

The experiment is usually best for issues that have a narrow scope or scale. This strength allows experimenters to assemble and "run" many experiments with limited resources in a short period. Some carefully designed experiments require assembling only 50 or 60 volunteers and can be completed in one or two months. In general, the experiment is better suited for micro-level (e.g., individual or small-group phenomena) than for macro-level concerns or questions. Experiments can rarely address questions that require looking at conditions across an entire society or across decades. The experiment also limits one's ability to generalize to larger settings (see External Validity and Field Experiments later in this chapter).

Experiments encourage researchers to isolate and target the impact that arises from one or a few causal variables. This strength in demonstrating causal effects is a limitation in situations where a researcher tries to examine numerous variables simultaneously. The experiment is rarely appropriate for research questions or issues that require a researcher to examine the impact of dozens of diverse variables all together. Although the accumulated knowledge from many individual experiments, each focused on one or two variables, advances understanding, the approach of experimental research differs from doing research on a highly complex situation in which one examines how dozens of variables operate simultaneously.

Often, researchers study closely related topics using either an experimental or a nonexperimental method. For example, a researcher may wish to study attitudes toward people in wheelchairs. An experimenter might ask people to respond (e.g., Would you hire this person? How comfortable would you be if this person asked you for a date?) to photos of some people in wheelchairs and some people not in wheelchairs. A survey researcher might ask people their opinions about people in wheelchairs. The field researcher might observe people's reactions to someone in a wheelchair, or the researcher himself or herself might be in wheelchair and carefully note the reactions of others.

RANDOM ASSIGNMENT

Social researchers frequently want to compare. For example, a researcher has two groups of 15 students and wants to compare the groups on the basis of a key difference between them (e.g., a course that one group completed). Or a researcher has five groups of customers and wants to compare the groups on the basis of one characteristic (e.g., geographic location). The cliché, "Compare apples to apples, don't compare apples to oranges," is not about fruit; it is about comparisons. It means that a valid comparison depends on comparing things that are fundamentally alike. Random assignment facilitates comparison in experiments by creating similar groups.

When making comparisons, researchers want to compare cases that do not differ with regard to variables that offer alternative explanations. For example, a researcher compares two groups of students to determine the impact of completing a course. In order to be compared, the two groups must be similar in most respects except for taking the course. If the group that completed the course is also older than the group that did not, for example, the researcher cannot determine whether completing the course or being older accounts for differences between the groups.

Why Randomly Assign?

Random assignment is a method for assigning cases (e.g., individuals, organizations, etc.) to groups for the purpose of making comparisons. It is a way to divide or sort a collection of cases into two or more groups in order to increase one's confidence that the groups do not differ in a systematic way. It is a mechanical method; the assignment is automatic, and the researcher cannot make assignments on the basis of personal preference or the features of specific cases.

Random assignment is random in a statistical or mathematical sense, not in an everyday sense. In everyday speech, *random* means unplanned, haphazard, or accidental, but it has a specialized meaning in mathematics. In probability theory, *random* describes a process in which each case has a known chance of being selected. Random selection lets a researcher calculate the odds that a specific case will be sorted into one group over another. Random means a case has an exactly equal chance of ending up in one or the other group. The great thing about a random process is that over many separate random occurrences, predictable things happen. Although the process itself is entirely due to chance and does not allow predicting a specific outcome at one specific time, it obeys mathematical laws that makes very accurate predictions possible when conducted over a large number of situations.

Random assignment or randomization is unbiased because a researcher's desire to confirm a hypothesis or a research subject's personal interests do not enter into the selection process. *Unbiased* does not mean that groups with identical characteristics are selected in each specific situation of random assignment. Instead, it says that the probability of selecting a case can be mathematically determined, and, in the long run, the groups will be identical.

Sampling and random assignment are processes of selecting cases for inclusion in a study. When a researcher randomly assigns, he or she sorts a collection of cases into two or more groups using a random process. In random sampling, he or she selects a smaller subset of cases from a larger pool of cases (see Figure 8.1). Ideally, a researcher will both randomly sample and randomly assign. He or she can first sample to obtain a smaller set of cases (e.g., 150 people out of 20,000) and then use random assignment to divide the sample into groups (e.g., divide the 150 people into three groups of 50). Unfortunately, few social science experimenters use random samples. Most begin with a convenience sample then randomly assign.

How to Randomly Assign

Random assignment is very simple in practice. A researcher begins with a collection of cases (individuals, organizations, or whatever the unit of analysis is), then divides it into two or more groups by a random process, such as asking people to count off, tossing a coin, or throwing dice. For example, a researcher wants to divide 32 people into two groups of 16. A random method is writing each person's name on a slip of paper, putting the slips in a hat, mixing the slips with eyes closed, then drawing the first 16 names for group 1 and the second 16 for group 2.

Matching versus Random Assignment

You might ask, If the purpose of random assignment is to get two (or more) equivalent groups, would it not be simpler to match the characteristics of cases in each group? Some researchers match cases in groups on certain characteristics, such as age and sex. Matching is an alternative to random assignment, but it is an infrequently used one.

Matching presents a problem: What are the relevant characteristics to match on, and can one locate exact matches? Individual cases differ in thousands of ways, and the researcher cannot know which might be relevant. For example, a researcher compares two groups of 15 students. There are 8 males in one group, which means there should be 8 males in the other group. Two males in the first group are only children; one is from a divorced family, one from an intact family. One is tall, slender, and Jewish; the other is short, heavy, and Methodist. In order to match groups, does the researcher have to find a tall Jewish male only child from a divorced home and a short Methodist male only child from an intact home? The tall, slender, Jewish male only child is 22 years old and is studying to become a physician. The short, heavy Methodist male is 20 years old and wants to be an accountant. Does the researcher also need to match the age and career aspirations of the two males? True matching soon becomes an impossible task.

EXPERIMENTAL DESIGN LOGIC

The Language of Experiments

Experimental research has its own language or set of terms and concepts. You already encountered the basic ideas: random assignment and independent and dependent variables. In experimental research, the cases or people used in research projects and on whom variables are measured are called the *subjects.*

Parts of the Experiment.   We can divide the experiment into seven parts. Not all experiments

FIGURE 8.1   Random Assignment and Random Sampling

Random Sampling

Population (Sampling Frame)   Sample

Random Process

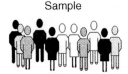

Random Assignment

Step 1: Begin with a collection of subjects.

Step 2: Devise a method to randomize that is purely mechanical (e.g., flip a coin).

Step 3: Assign subjects with "Heads" to one group   and "Tails" to the other group.

Control Group

Experimental Group

have all these parts, and some have all seven parts plus others. The following seven, to be discussed here, make up a true experiment:

1. Treatment or independent variable
2. Dependent variable
3. Pretest
4. Posttest
5. Experimental group
6. Control group
7. Random assignment

In most experiments, a researcher creates a situation or enters into an ongoing situation, then modifies it. The *treatment* (or the stimulus or manipulation) is what the researcher modifies. The term comes from medicine, in which a physician administers a treatment to patients; the physician intervenes in a physical or psychological condition to change it. It is the independent variable or a combination of independent variables. In earlier examples of measurement, a researcher developed a measurement instrument or indicator (e.g., a survey question), then applied it to a person or case. In experiments, researchers "measure" independent variables by creating a condition or situation. For example, the independent variable is "degree of fear or anxiety"; the levels are high fear and low fear. Instead of asking subjects whether they are fearful, experimenters put subjects into either a high-fear or a low-fear situation. They measure the independent variable by manipulating conditions so that some subjects feel a lot of fear and others feel little.

Researchers go to great lengths to create treatments. Some are as minor as giving different groups of subjects different instructions. Others can be as complex as putting subjects into situations with elaborate equipment, staged physical settings, or contrived social situations to manipulate what the subjects see or feel. Researchers want the treatment to have an impact and produce specific reactions, feelings, or behaviors.

Dependent variables or outcomes in experimental research are the physical conditions, social behaviors, attitudes, feelings, or beliefs of subjects that change in response to a treatment. Dependent variables can be measured by paper-and-pencil indicators, observation, interviews, or physiological responses (e.g., heartbeat or sweating palms).

Frequently, a researcher measures the dependent variable more than once during an experiment. The *pretest* is the measurement of the dependent variable prior to introduction of the treatment. The *posttest* is the measurement of the dependent variable after the treatment has been introduced into the experimental situation.

Experimental researchers often divide subjects into two or more groups for purposes of comparison. A simple experiment has two groups, only one of which receives the treatment. The *experimental group* is the group that receives the treatment or in which the treatment is present. The group that does not receive the treatment is called the *control group*. When the independent variable takes on many different values, more than one experimental group is used.

We can review the variables in the three experiments used as examples in previous chapters. In Chapter 2 you read about an experiment by Brase and Richmond (2004) about doctor–patient interactions and perceptions. After random assignment, subjects saw same- and opposite-gender models identified as being medical doctors but who wore either informal or formal/traditional attire (independent variable). The experimenters then measured the subjects' judgments about trust in the physician and the physician's abilities (dependent variable). In Goar and Sell's (2005) experiment about mixed race task groups described in Chapter 4, randomly assigned three-person groups were told they were either to a complete complex task requiring diverse skills or not (independent variable). The experimenters measured the time it took the group to complete a task and involvement by group members of different races (dependent variable). In the study on college women with tattoos discussed in Chapter 5 by

Hawkes, Senn, and Thorn (2004), randomly assigned subjects were asked to read one of five scenarios about a 22-year-old college student woman who had a tattoo (independent variable). The experimenters then measured the subjects' feelings about the woman and tattoo using a semantic differential, a Feminist scale, and a Women's Movement and Neosexisms scale (dependent variables).

Steps in Conducting an Experiment.   Following the basic steps of the research process, experimenters decide on a topic, narrow it into a testable research problem or question, then develop a hypothesis with variables. Once a researcher has the hypothesis, the steps of experimental research are clear.

A crucial early step is to plan a specific experimental design (to be discussed). The researcher decides the number of groups to use, how and when to create treatment conditions, the number of times to measure the dependent variable, and what the groups of subjects will experience from beginning to end. He or she also develops measures of the dependent variable and pilot-tests the experiment (see Box 8.1).

The experiment itself begins after a researcher locates subjects and randomly assigns them to groups. Subjects are given precise, preplanned instructions. Next, the researcher measures the dependent variable in a pretest before the treatment. One group is then exposed to the treatment. Finally, the researcher measures the dependent variable in a posttest. He or she also interviews subjects about the experiment before they leave. The researcher records measures of the dependent variable and examines the results for each group to see whether the hypothesis receives support.

Control in Experiments.   Control is crucial in experimental research. A researcher wants to control all aspects of the experimental situation to isolate the effects of the treatment and eliminate alternative explanations. Aspects of an experimental situation that are not controlled by

Box 8.1	Steps in Conducting an Experiment

1. Begin with a straightforward hypothesis appropriate to the experimental research.
2. Decide on an experimental design that will test the hypothesis within practical limitations.
3. Decide how to introduce the treatment or create a situation that induces the independent variable.
4. Develop a valid and reliable measure of the dependent variable.
5. Set up an experimental setting and conduct a pilot test of the treatment and dependent variable measures.
6. Locate appropriate subjects or cases.
7. Randomly assign subjects to groups (if random assignment is used in the chosen research design) and give careful instructions.
8. Gather data for the pretest measure of the dependent variable for all groups (if a pretest is used in the chosen design).
9. Introduce the treatment to the experimental group only (or to relevant groups if there are multiple experimental groups) and monitor all groups.
10. Gather data for posttest measure of the dependent variable.
11. *Debrief* the subjects by informing them of the true purpose and reasons for the experiment. Ask subjects what they thought was occurring. Debriefing is crucial when subjects have been deceived about some aspect of the experiment.
12. Examine data collected and make comparisons between different groups. Where appropriate, use statistics and graphs to determine whether or not the hypothesis is supported.

the researcher are alternatives to the treatment for change in the dependent variable and undermine his or her attempt to establish causality definitively.

Experimental researchers use deception to control the experimental setting. *Deception* occurs when the researcher intentionally misleads subjects through written or verbal instructions, the actions of others, or aspects of the setting. It may involve the use of *confederates* or stooges—people who pretend to be other subjects or bystanders but who actually work for the researcher and deliberately mislead subjects. Through deception, the researcher tries to control what the subjects see and hear and what they believe is occurring. For example, a researcher's instructions falsely lead subjects to believe that they are participating in a study about group cooperation. In fact, the experiment is about male/female verbal interaction, and what subjects say is being secretly tape recorded. Deception lets the researcher control the subjects' definition of the situation. It prevents them from altering their cross-sex verbal behavior because they are unaware of the true research topic. By focusing their attention on a false topic, the researcher induces the unaware subjects to act "naturally." For realistic deception, researchers may invent false treatments and dependent variable measures to keep subjects unaware of the true ones. The use of deception in experiments raises ethical issues (to be discussed).

Types of Design

Researchers combine parts of an experiment (e.g., pretests, control groups, etc.) together into an *experimental design*. For example, some designs lack pretests, some do not have control groups, and others have many experimental groups. Certain widely used standard designs have names.

You should learn the standard designs for two reasons. First, in research reports, researchers give the name of a standard design instead of
• describing it. When reading reports, you will be able to understand the design of the experiment if you know the standard designs. Second, the standard designs illustrate common ways to combine design parts. You can use them for experiments you conduct or create your own variations.

The designs are illustrated with a simple example. A researcher wants to learn whether wait staff (waiters and waitresses) receive more in tips if they first introduce themselves by first name and return to ask "Is everything fine?" 8 to 10 minutes after delivering the food. The dependent variable is the size of the tip received. The study occurs in two identical restaurants on different sides of a town that have had the same types of customers and average the same amount in tips.

Classical Experimental Design. All designs are variations of the *classical experimental design*, the type of design discussed so far, which has random assignment, a pretest and a posttest, an experimental group, and a control group.

Example. The experimenter gives 40 newly hired wait staff an identical two-hour training session and instructs them to follow a script in which they are not to introduce themselves by first name and not to return during the meal to check on the customers. They are next randomly divided into two equal groups of 20 and sent to the two restaurants to begin employment. The experimenter records the amount in tips for all subjects for one month (pretest score). Next, the experimenter "retrains" the 20 subjects at restaurant 1 (experimental group). The experimenter instructs them henceforth to introduce themselves to customers by first name and to check on the customers, asking, "Is everything fine?" 8 to 10 minutes after delivering the food (treatment). The group at restaurant 2 (control group) is "retained" to continue without an introduction or checking during the meal. Over the second month, the amount of tips for both groups is recorded (posttest score).

Preexperimental Designs. Some designs lack random assignment and are compromises or shortcuts. These *preexperimental designs* are used in situations where it is difficult to use the classical design. They have weaknesses that make inferring a causal relationship more difficult.

One-Shot Case Study Design. Also called the one-group posttest-only design, the *one-shot case study design* has only one group, a treatment, and a posttest. Because there is only one group, there is no random assignment.

Example. The experimenter takes a group of 40 newly hired wait staff and gives all a two-hour training session in which they are instructed to introduce themselves to customers by first name and to check on the customers, asking, "Is everything fine?" 8 to 10 minutes after delivering the food (treatment). All subjects begin employment, and the experimenter records the amount in tips for all subjects for one month (posttest score).

One-Group Pretest-Posttest Design. This design has one group, a pretest, a treatment, and a posttest. It lacks a control group and random assignment.

Example. The experimenter takes a group of 40 newly hired wait staff and gives all a two-hour training session. They are instructed to follow a script in which they are not to introduce themselves by first name and not to return during the meal to check on the customers. All begin employment, and the experimenter records the amount in tips for all subjects for one month (pretest score). Next, the experimenter "retrains" all 40 subjects (experimental group). The experimenter instructs the subjects henceforth to introduce themselves to customers by first name and to check on the customers, asking, "Is everything fine?" 8 to 10 minutes after delivering the food (treatment). Over the second month, the amount of tips is recorded (posttest score).

This is an improvement over the one-shot case study because the researcher measures the dependent variable both before and after the treatment. But it lacks a control group. The researcher cannot know whether something other than the treatment occurred between the pretest and the posttest to cause the outcome.

Static Group Comparison. Also called the posttest-only nonequivalent group design, *static group comparison* has two groups, a posttest, and treatment. It lacks random assignment and a pretest. A weakness is that any posttest outcome difference between the groups could be due to group differences prior to the experiment instead of to the treatment.

Example. The experimenter gives 40 newly hired wait staff an identical two-hour training session and instructs them to follow a script in which they are not to introduce themselves by first name and not to return during the meal to check on the customers. They can choose one of the two restaurants to work at, so long as each restaurant ends up with 20 people. All begin employment. After one month, the experimenter "retrains" the 20 subjects at restaurant 1 (experimental group). The experimenter instructs them henceforth to introduce themselves to customers by first name and to check on the customers, asking, "Is everything fine?" 8 to 10 minutes after delivering the food (treatment). The group at restaurant 2 (control group) is "retained" to continue without an introduction or checking during the meal. Over the second month, the amount of tips for both groups is recorded (posttest score).

Quasi-Experimental and Special Designs. These designs, like the classical design, make identifying a causal relationship more certain than do preexperimental designs. *Quasi-experimental designs* help researchers test for causal relationships in a variety of situations where the classical design is difficult or inappropriate. They are called *quasi* because they are variations of the classical experimental design. Some have randomization but lack a pretest, some use more than two groups, and others substitute many observations of one group over time for a control group. In general, the researcher has less control over the independent variable than in the classical design (see Table 8.1).

TABLE 8.1   A Comparison of the Classical Experimental Design with Other Major Designs

Design	Random Assignment	Pretest	Posttest	Control Group	Experimental Group
Classical	Yes	Yes	Yes	Yes	Yes
One-Shot Case Study	No	No	Yes	No	Yes
One-Group Pretest Postest	No	Yes	Yes	No	Yes
Static Group Comparison	No	No	Yes	Yes	Yes
Two-Group Posttest Only	Yes	No	Yes	Yes	Yes
Time Series Designs	No	Yes	Yes	No	Yes

Two-Group Posttest-Only Design.   This is identical to the static group comparison, with one exception: The groups are randomly assigned. It has all the parts of the classical design except a pretest. The random assignment reduces the chance that the groups differed before the treatment, but without a pretest, a researcher cannot be as certain that the groups began the same on the dependent variable.

In a study using a two-group posttest-only design with random assignment, Rind and Strohmetz (1999) examined messages about a upcoming special written on the back of customers' checks. The subjects were 81 dining parties eating at an upscale restaurant in New Jersey. The treatment was whether a female server wrote a message about an upcoming restaurant special on the back of a check and the dependent variable was the size of tips. The server with two years' experience was given a randomly shuffled stack of cards, half of which said No Message and half of which said Message. Just before she gave a customer his or her check, she randomly pulled a card from her pocket. If it said Message, she wrote about an upcoming special on the back of the customer's check. If it said No Message, she wrote nothing. The experimenters recorded the amount of the tip and the number of people at the table. They instructed the server to act the same toward all customers. The results showed that higher tips came from customers who received the message about upcoming specials.

Interrupted Time Series.   In an *interrupted time series* design, a researcher uses one group and makes multiple pretest measures before and after the treatment. For example, after remaining level for many years, in 1995, cigarette taxes jumped 35 percent. Taxes remained relatively constant for the next 10 years. The hypothesis is that increases in taxes lower cigarette consumption. A researcher plots the rate of cigarette consumption for 1985 through 2005. The researcher notes that cigarette consumption was level during the 10 years prior to the new taxes, then dropped in 1995 and stayed about the same for the next 10 years.

Equivalent Time Series.   An *equivalent time series* is another one-group design that extends over a time period. Instead of one treatment, it has a pretest, then a treatment and posttest, then treatment and posttest, then treatment and posttest, and so on. For example, people who drive motorcycles were not required to wear helmets before 1985, when a law was passed requiring helmets. In 1991, the law was repealed because of pressure from motorcycle clubs. The helmet law was reinstated in 2003. The researcher's hypothesis is that wearing protective helmets lowers the number of head injury deaths in motorcycle accidents. The researcher plots head injury death rates in motorcycle accidents over time. The rate was very high prior to 1985, dropped sharply between 1985 and 1991, then returned to pre-1985 levels between 1991 and 2003, then dropped again from 2003 to the present.

Latin Square Designs.   Researchers interested in how several treatments given in different sequences or time orders affect a dependent variable can use a *Latin square design.* For example, a junior high school geography instructor has three units to teach students: map reading, using a compass, and the longitude/latitude (LL) system. The units can be taught in any order, but the teacher wants to know which order most helps students learn. In one class, students first learn to read maps, then how to use a compass, then the LL system. In another class, using a compass comes first, then map reading, then the LL system. In a third class, the instructor first teaches the LL system, then compass usage, and ends with map reading. The teacher gives tests after each unit, and students take a comprehensive exam at the end of the term. The students were randomly assigned to classes, so the instructor can see whether presenting units in one sequence or another resulted in improved learning.

Solomon Four-Group Design.   A researcher may believe that the pretest measure has an influence on the treatment or dependent variable. A pretest can sometimes sensitize subjects to the treatment or improve their performance on the posttest (see the discussion of testing effect to come). Richard L. Solomon developed the *Solomon four-group design* to address the issue of pretest effects. It combines the classical experimental design with the two-group posttest-only design and randomly assigns subjects to one of four groups. For example, a mental health worker wants to determine whether a new training method improves clients' coping skills. The worker measures coping skills with a 20-minute test of reactions to stressful events. Because the clients might learn coping skills from taking the test itself, a Solomon four-group design is used. The mental health worker randomly divides clients into four groups. Two groups receive the pretest; one of them gets the new training method and the other gets the old method. Another two groups receive no pretest; one of them gets the new method and the other the old method. All four groups are given the same posttest and the posttest results are compared. If the two treatment (new method) groups have similar results, and the two control (old method) groups have similar results, then the mental health worker knows pretest learning is not a problem. If the two groups with a pretest (one treatment, one control) differ from the two groups without a pretest, then the worker concludes that the pretest itself may have an effect on the dependent variable.

Factorial Designs.   Sometimes, a research question suggests looking at the simultaneous effects of more than one independent variable. A *factorial design* uses two or more independent variables in combination. Every combination of the categories in variables (sometimes called *factors*) is examined. When each variable contains several categories, the number of combinations grows very quickly. The treatment or manipulation is not each independent variable; rather, it is each combination of the categories.

The treatments in a factorial design can have two kinds of effects on the dependent variable: main effects and interaction effects. Only *main effects* are present in one-factor or single-treatment designs. In a factorial design, specific combinations of independent variable categories can also have an effect. They are called *interaction effects* because the categories in a combination interact to produce an effect beyond that of each variable alone.

FIGURE 8.2   Blame, Resistance, and Schema: Interaction Effect

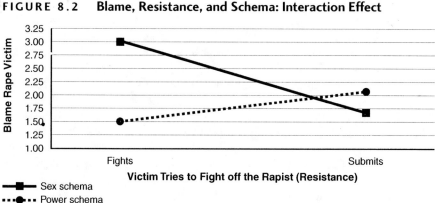

Interaction effects are illustrated in Figure 8.2, which uses data from a study by Ong and Ward (1999). As part of a study of 128 female undergraduates at the National University of Singapore, Ong and Ward measured which of two major ways subjects understood the crime of rape. Some of the women primarily understood it as sex and due to the male sex drive (sex schema); others understood it as primarily an act of male power and domination of a woman (power schema). The researchers asked the subjects to read a realistic scenario about the rape of a college student at their university. One randomly selected group of subjects read a scenario in which the victim tried to fight off the rapist. In the other set, she passively submitted. The researchers next asked the subjects to evaluate the degree to which the rape victim was at blame or responsible for the rape.

Results showed that the women who held the sex schema (and who also tended to embrace traditionalist gender role beliefs) more strongly blamed the victim when she resisted. Blame decreased if she submitted. The women who held a power schema (and who also tended to be nontraditionalists) were less likely to blame the victim if she fought. They blamed her more if she passively submitted. Thus, the subjects' responses to the victim's act of resisting the attack varied by, or interacted with, their understanding of the crime

of rape (i.e., the rape schema held by each subject). The researchers found that two rape schemas caused subjects to interpret victim resistance in opposite ways for the purpose of assigning responsibility for the crime.

Researchers discuss factorial design in a shorthand way. A "two by three factorial design" is written 2 × 3. It means that there are two treatments, with two categories in one and three categories in the other. A 2 × 3 × 3 design means that there are three independent variables, one with two categories and two with three categories each.

The previously discussed experiment by Hawkes, Seen, and Thorn (2004) on tattoos among college women used a 3 × 2 × 2 × 2 × 2 factorial design. The full study considered four independent variables, one with three categories, the rest having two categories, and it had three measures of the dependent variable. The dependent variable measures included a Semantic Differential measure (which contained three dimensions). In addition, experimenters had subjects complete a Neosexism measure (an 11-item, 5-point Likert Scale statements summed into an index) and a measure of Feminism and Women's Movement Support (a 10-item, 5-point Likert Scale summed into an index). The experimenters manipulated two independent variables in the descriptions of the tattoo read by subjects: (1) whether the woman had no tattoo, a tattoo smaller than a Canadian $1 coin, or larger than a $1 coin; and (2) the tattoo's visiblity as always hidden versus always hidden. Two independent variables were not manipulated but were preexisting characteristics of researcher subjects, (3) whether the subject him/herself had a tattoo or not, and (4) the subject's gender. The study included 268 subjects, 122 males and 146 females, of them 43 (or 16 percent) had a tattoo.

The study results showed that subjects viewed college women without a tattoo more positivity and female subjects were more positive toward a college woman having a tattoo than male subjects. There was also a significant effect for visibility, with more favorable attitudes for a nonvisible tattoo. Generally, subjects who had tattoos themselves were more favorable toward the woman having a tattoo. Size of tattoo had little effect. Men and women with a tattoo were more favorable, regardless of tattoo size, while those without a tattoo were negative. In addition, gender made no difference toward size of tattoo. The experiment had many specific findings for each combination of the five independent variables. One specific finding was that female subjects who had a tattoo themselves were least likely to react negatively to a larger tattoo. Results from the attitude measures suggest that "the tattooed woman may be seen by some as flaunting her freedom from gender norms or as threatening women's traditional place in society" (Hawkes, Seen, and Thorn 2004:603).

Design Notation

Experiments can be designed in many ways. *Design notation* is a shorthand system for symbolizing the parts of experimental design. Once you learn design notation, you will find it easier to think about and compare designs. For example, design notation expresses a complex, paragraph-long description of the parts of an experiment in five or six symbols arranged in two lines. It uses the following symbols: O = observation of dependent variable; X =

treatment, independent variable; R = random assignment. The Os are numbered with subscripts from left to right based on time order. Pretests are O_1, posttests O_2. When the independent variable has more than two levels, the Xs are numbered with subscripts to distinguish among them. Symbols are in time order from left to right. The R is first, followed by the pretest, the treatment, and then the posttest. Symbols are arranged in rows, with each row representing a group of subjects. For example, an experiment with three groups has an R (if random assignment is used), followed by three rows of Os and Xs. The rows are on top of each other because the pretests, treatment, and posttest occur in each group at about the same time. Table 8.2 gives the notation for many standard experimental designs.

INTERNAL AND EXTERNAL VALIDITY

The Logic of Internal Validity

Internal validity means the ability to eliminate alternative explanations of the dependent variable. Variables, other than the treatment, that affect the dependent variable are threats to internal validity. They threaten the researcher's ability to say that the treatment was the true causal factor producing change in the dependent variable. Thus, the logic of internal validity is to rule out variables other than the treatment by controlling experimental conditions and through experimental designs. Next, we examine major threats to internal validity.

Threats to Internal Validity

The following are nine common threats to internal validity.[1]

Selection Bias. *Selection bias* is the threat that research participants will not form equivalent groups. It is a problem in designs without

TABLE 8.2   Summary of Experimental Designs with Notation

Name of Design	Design Notation
Classical experimental design	$R \begin{array}{l} \longrightarrow O \quad\quad X \quad\quad O \\ \longrightarrow O \quad\quad\quad\quad\quad\quad O \end{array}$
Preexperimental Designs	
One-shot case study	$\quad\quad\quad\quad\quad\quad\quad X \quad\quad O$
One-group pretest-posttest	$\quad\quad\quad\quad\quad O \quad X \quad\quad O$
Static group comparison	$\quad\quad\quad\quad\quad\quad\quad X \quad\quad O$ $\quad\quad\quad\quad\quad\quad\quad\quad\quad\quad O$
Quasi-Experimental Designs Two-group posttest only	$R \begin{array}{l} \longrightarrow X \quad\quad\quad\quad O \\ \longrightarrow \quad\quad\quad\quad\quad O \end{array}$
Interrupted time series	$O \quad O \quad\quad O \quad O \quad X \quad O \; O \; O$
Equivalent time series	$O \quad X \quad\quad O \quad X \quad O \; X \; O \; X \; O$
Latin square designs	$R \begin{array}{llllll} O & X_a & O & X_b & O & X_c \; O \\ O & X_b & O & X_a & O & X_c \; O \\ O & X_c & O & X_b & O & X_a \; O \\ O & X_a & O & X_c & O & X_b \; O \\ O & X_b & O & X_c & O & X_a \; O \\ O & X_c & O & X_a & O & X_b \; O \end{array}$
Solomon four-group design	$R \begin{array}{l} \longrightarrow O \quad\quad X \quad\quad O \\ \longrightarrow O \quad\quad\quad\quad\quad\quad O \\ \longrightarrow \quad\quad\quad X \quad\quad O \\ \longrightarrow \quad\quad\quad\quad\quad\quad\quad O \end{array}$
Factorial designs	$R \begin{array}{lll} X_1 & Z_1 & O \\ X_1 & Z_2 & O \\ X_2 & Z_1 & O \\ X_2 & Z_2 & O \end{array}$

random assignment. It occurs when subjects in one experimental group have a characteristic that affects the dependent variable. For example, in an experiment on physical aggressiveness, the treatment group unintentionally contains subjects who are football, rugby, and hockey players, whereas the control group is made up of musicians, chess players, and painters. Another example is an experiment on the ability of people to dodge heavy traffic. All subjects assigned to one group come from rural areas, and all subjects in the other grew up in large cities. An examination of pretest scores helps a researcher detect this threat, because no group differences are expected.

History. This is the threat that an event unrelated to the treatment will occur during the *experiment and influence the dependent variable.* *History effects* are more likely in experiments that continue over a long time period. For example, halfway through a two-week experiment to evaluate subjects' attitudes toward space travel, a spacecraft explodes on the launch pad, killing the astronauts. The history effect can occur in the cigarette tax example discussed earlier (see the discussion of interrupted time-series design). If a public antismoking campaign or reduced cigarette advertising also began in 1989, it would be hard to say that higher taxes caused less smoking.

Maturation. This is the threat that some biological, psychological, or emotional process within the subjects and separate from the treatment will change over time. *Maturation* is more common in experiments over long time periods. For example, during an experiment on reasoning ability, subjects become bored and sleepy and, as a result, score lower. Another example is an experiment on the styles of children's play between grades 1 and 6. Play styles are affected by physical, emotional, and maturation changes that occur as the children grow older, instead of or in addition to the effects of a treatment. Designs with a pretest and control group help researchers determine whether maturation or history effects are present, because both experimental and control groups will show similar changes over time.

Testing. Sometimes, the pretest measure itself affects an experiment. This *testing effect* threatens internal validity because more than the treatment alone affects the dependent variable. The Solomon four-group design helps a researcher detect testing effects. For example, a researcher gives students an examination on the first day of class. The course is the treatment. He or she tests learning by giving the same exam on the last day of class. If subjects remember the pretest questions and this affects what they learned (i.e., paid attention to) or how they answered questions on the posttest, a testing effect is present. If testing

effects occur, a researcher cannot say that the treatment alone has affected the dependent variable.

Instrumentation. This threat is related to reliability. It occurs when the *instrument* or dependent variable measure changes during the experiment. For example, in a weight-loss experiment, the springs on the scale weaken during the experiment, giving lower readings in the posttest. Another example might have occurred in an experiment by Bond and Anderson (1987) on the reluctance to transmit bad news. The experimenters asked subjects to tell another person the results of an intelligence test and varied the test results to be either well above or well below average. The dependent variable was the length of time it took to tell the test taker the results. Some subjects were told that the session was being videotaped. During the experiment, the video equipment failed to work for one subject. If it had failed to work for more than one subject or had worked for only part of the session, the experiment would have had instrumentation problems. (By the way, subjects took longer to deliver bad news only if they thought they were doing so publicly—that is, being videotaped.)

Mortality. *Mortality,* or attrition, arises when some subjects do not continue throughout the experiment. Although the word *mortality* means death, it does not necessarily mean that subjects have died. If a subset of subjects leaves partway through an experiment, a researcher cannot know whether the results would have been different had the subjects stayed. For example, a researcher begins a weight-loss program with 50 subjects. At the end of the program, 30 remain, each of whom lost 5 pounds with no side effects. The 20 who left could have differed from the 30 who stayed, changing the results. Maybe the program was effective for those who left, and they withdrew after losing 25 pounds. Or perhaps the program made subjects sick and forced them to quit. Researchers should notice and report the number of subjects in each group during pretests and posttests to detect this threat to internal validity.

Statistical Regression. *Statistical regression* is not easy to grasp intuitively. It is a problem of extreme values or a tendency for random errors to move group results toward the average. It can occur in two ways.

One situation arises when subjects are unusual with regard to the dependent variable. Because they begin as unusual or extreme, subjects are unlikely to respond further in the same direction. For example, a researcher wants to see whether violent films make people act violently. He or she chooses a group of violent criminals from a high-security prison, gives them a pretest, shows violent films, then administers a posttest. To the researcher's shock, the prisoners are slightly less violent after the film, whereas a control group of prisoners who did not see the film are slightly more violent than before. Because the violent criminals began at an extreme, it is unlikely that a treatment could make them more violent; by random chance alone, they appear less extreme when measured a second time.[2]

A second situation involves a problem with the measurement instrument. If many research participants score very high (at the ceiling) or very low (at the floor) on a variable, random chance alone will produce a change between the pretest and the posttest. For example, a researcher gives 80 subjects a test, and 75 get perfect scores. He or she then gives a treatment to raise scores. Because so many subjects already had perfect scores, random errors will reduce the group average because those who got perfect scores can randomly move in only one direction—to get some answers wrong. An examination of scores on pretests will help researchers detect this threat to internal validity.

Diffusion of Treatment or Contamination. *Diffusion of treatment* is the threat that research participants in different groups will communicate with each other and learn about the other's treatment. Researchers avoid it by isolating groups or having subjects promise not to reveal anything to others who will become subjects. For example, subjects participate in a day-long experiment on a new way to memorize words. During a break, treatment-group subjects tell those in the control group about the new way to memorize, which control-group subjects then use. A researcher needs outside information, such as postexperiment interviews, with subjects to detect this threat.

Experimenter Expectancy. Although it is not always considered a traditional internal validity problem, the experimenter's behavior, too, can threaten causal logic.[3] A researcher may threaten internal validity, not by purposefully unethical behavior but by indirectly communicating *experimenter expectancy* to subjects. Researchers may be highly committed to the hypothesis and indirectly communicate desired findings to the subjects. For example, a researcher studies the effects of memorization training on student learning ability, and also sees the grade transcripts of subjects. The researcher believes that students with higher grades tend to do better at the training and will learn more. Through eye contact, tone of voice, pauses, and other nonverbal communication, the researcher unconsciously trains the students with higher grades more intensely; the researcher's nonverbal behavior is the opposite for students with lower grades.

Here is a way to detect experimenter expectancy. A researcher hires assistants and teaches them experimental techniques. The assistants train subjects and test their learning ability. The researcher gives the assistants fake transcripts and records showing that subjects in one group are honor students and the others are failing, although in fact the subjects are identical. Experimenter expectancy is present if the fake honor students, as a group, do much better than the fake failing students.

The *double-blind experiment* is designed to control researcher expectancy. In it, people who have direct contact with subjects do not know the details of the hypothesis or the treatment. It is *double* blind because both the subjects and those in contact with them are blind to details of the experiment (see Figure 8.3). For example, a researcher wants to see if a new drug is effective. Using pills of three colors—green, yellow, and pink—the researcher puts the new drug in the yellow pill, puts an old drug in the pink one, and makes the green pill a *placebo*—a false treatment that appears to be real (e.g., a sugar pill without any physical effects). Assistants who give the pills and record the effects do not know which color

contains the new drug. Only another person who does not deal with subjects directly knows which colored pill contains the drug and it is he or she who examines the results.

External Validity and Field Experiments

Even if an experimenter eliminates all concerns about internal validity, external validity remains a potential problem. *External validity* is the ability to generalize experimental findings to events and settings outside the experiment itself. If a

FIGURE 8.3   Double-Blind Experiments: An Illustration of Single-Blind, or Ordinary, and Double-Blind Experiments

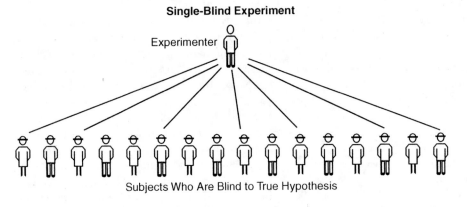

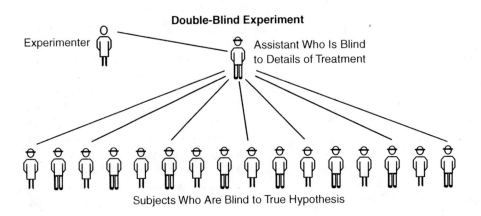

study lacks external validity, its findings hold true only in experiments, making them useless to both basic and applied science.

Reactivity.   Research participants might react differently in an experiment than they would in real life because they know they are in a study; this is called *reactivity*. The *Hawthorne effect* is a specific kind of reactivity.[4] The name comes from a series of experiments by Elton Mayo at the Hawthorne, Illinois, plant of Westinghouse Electric during the 1920s and 1930s. Researchers modified many aspects of working conditions (e.g., lighting, time for breaks, etc.) and measured productivity. They discovered that productivity rose after each modification, no matter what it was. This curious result occurred because the workers did not respond to the treatment but to the additional attention they received from being part of the experiment and knowing that they were being watched. Later research questioned whether this occurred, but the name is used for an effect from the attention of researchers. A related effect is the effect of something new, which may wear off over time.

Field Experiments.   So far, this chapter has focused on experiments conducted under the controlled conditions of a laboratory. Experiments are also conducted in real-life or field settings where a researcher has less control over the experimental conditions. The amount of control varies on a continuum. At one end is the highly controlled *laboratory experiment*, which takes place in a specialized setting or laboratory; at the opposite end is the *field experiment*, which takes place in the "field"—in natural settings such as a subway car, a liquor store, or a public sidewalk. Subjects in field experiments are usually unaware that they are involved in an experiment and react in a natural way. For example, researchers have had a confederate fake a heart attack on a subway car to see how the bystanders react.[5]

Dasgupta and Asgari (2004) tested the hypothesis that stereotypical beliefs weaken when a person encounters people who contradict the stereotype, especially if the others are respected. They used both a laboratory experiment (with a two-group, posttest-only design) and a field experiment. Past studies focused on out-group stereotypes, but the authors wanted to examine the hypothesis for an in-group, women. In the laboratory experiment, experimenters randomly assigned female subjects to view either (1) a set photographs and biographies of 16 famous women leaders or (2) photos and descriptions of 16 flowers. The experimenters used deception and told subjects the study was about testing memory. The dependent variable was attitudes and beliefs about women and was measured with a Implicit Association Test (IAT). The results showed that subjects associated gendered first names (e.g., John vs. Emily) with leadership or follower traits (e.g., assertive and sympathetic). A high IAT score indicated that a subject viewed women more than men as having leadership more than supportive traits. The researchers also used a scale on beliefs about women. They found support for the hypothesis that exposure to famous women in leadership positions increased IAT scores, compared to exposure to neutral information about flowers. The field experiment had a pretest and a posttest but no random assignment. Subjects were females who attended two colleges in the same town. One was a coeducational college and the other had all female students. Subjects were recruited from first-year classes at the beginning of the academic year and completed the IAT measure, the beliefs about women scale, and a general campus questionnaire. The experimenters documented that the all-female college had more females in administrative and faculty leadership positions. Pretest IAT scores were very similar, with subjects from coeducational college having slightly lower scores. This helped the experimenters to check for possible selection bias. Subjects were contacted one year later and asked to complete the same measures as presented in the posttest. Experimenters watched very carefully for experimental mortality since some students stopped attending college or did not complete later surveys. The IAT scores for subjects at the coeducational college declined (i.e., they were less likely to see females as having leadership traits), whereas the IAT scores for subjects at the all-female college greatly increased. In addition, the experimenters found that the more female teachers a student had at either college, the higher the posttest IAT scores, and this was especially the case for math and sciences courses. Thus, exposure to women in leadership positions caused the IAT scores to increase, whereas the absence of such exposure, if anything, lowered the scores.

Von Larr and colleagues (2005) used a field experiment to test the well-known *contact hypothesis* that says intergroup contact reduces racial–ethnic prejudice as people replace their stereotypes with personal experience, although this happens so long as the contact involves people of equal status pursuing common goals in a cooperative setting and is approved by authorities. In addition, informal contact in which people get to know about out-group members as acquaintances also reduces out-group prejudice. The experiment took place at UCLA, where the student body is very racially and ethnically diverse. Unless they preselect a roommate, incoming students are randomly assigned roommates. About 20 percent of students choose a roommate and the rest are randomly assigned. The authors measured student background and attitudes among nearly 3,800 new incoming students using a panel design across five time periods—before college entry (summer 1996) and during the spring of each of the next four years (1997–2000) with surveys (20-minute telephone interviews). The dependent variable was the students' racial–ethnic attitudes and included questions about roommates, other friends, interracial dating, multiculturalism, symbolic racism, and feelings about various racial–ethnic groups. These were the experiment's pretest and multiple posttest measures. Experimenters

watched very carefully for experimental mortality, since some students stopped attending college, left college dormitories, or did not complete the later surveys. They tested the hypotheses that students who were randomly assigned to live with an out-group member (the independent variable) developed less prejudicial attitudes toward members of that out-group. They found that compared to pretest measures, prejudicial attitudes declined as predicted by the contact hypothesis with one exception. Apparently having an Asian American roommate worked in the opposite way and actually increased prejudice, especially among the White students.

Experimenter control relates to internal and external validity. Laboratory experiments tend to have greater internal validity but lower external validity; that is, they are logically tighter and better controlled, but less generalizable. Field experiments tend to have greater external validity but lower internal validity; that is, they are more generalizable but less controlled. Quasi-experimental designs are common in field experiments. Table 8.3 summarizes threats to internal and external validity.

TABLE 8.3   Major Internal and External Validity Concerns

Internal Validity	External Validity and Reactivity
Selection bias	Hawthorne effect
History effect	
Maturation	
Testing	
Instrumentation	
Experimental mortality	
Statistical regression	
Diffusion of treatment	
Experimenter expectancy	

PRACTICAL CONSIDERATIONS

Every research technique has informal tricks of the trade. These are pragmatic, commonsense ideas that account for the difference between the successful research projects of an experienced researcher and the difficulties a novice researcher faces. Three are discussed here.

Planning and Pilot-Tests

All social research requires planning, and most quantitative researchers use pilot-tests. During the planning phase of experimental research, a researcher thinks of alternative explanations or threats to internal validity and how to avoid them. The researcher also develops a neat and well-organized system for recording data. In addition, he or she devotes serious effort to pilot-testing any apparatus (e.g., computers, video cameras, tape recorders, etc.) that will be used in the treatment situation, and he or she must train and pilot-test confederates. After the pilot-tests, the researcher should interview the pilot subjects to uncover aspects of the experiment that need refinement.

Instructions to Subjects

Most experiments involve giving instructions to subjects to set the stage. A researcher should word instructions carefully and follow a prepared script so that all subjects hear the same thing. This ensures reliability. The instructions are also important in creating a realistic cover story when deception is used.

Postexperiment Interview

At the end of an experiment, the researcher should interview subjects, for three reasons. First, if deception was used, the researcher needs to debrief the research participants, telling them the true purpose of the experiment and answering questions. Second, he or she can learn what the subjects thought and how their definitions of the situation affected their behavior. Finally, he or she can explain the importance of not revealing the true nature of the experiment to other potential participants.

RESULTS OF EXPERIMENTAL RESEARCH: MAKING COMPARISONS

Comparison is the key to all research. By carefully examining the results of experimental research, a researcher can learn a great deal about threats to internal validity, and whether the treatment has an impact on the dependent variable. For example, in the Bond and Anderson (1987) experiment on delivering bad news, discussed earlier, it took an average of 89.6 and 73.1 seconds to deliver favorable versus 72.5 or 147.2 seconds to deliver unfavorable test scores in private or public settings, respectively. A comparison shows that delivering bad news in public takes the longest, whereas good news takes a bit longer in private.

A more complex illustration of such comparisons is shown in Figure 8.4 on the results of a series of five weight-loss experiments using the classical experimental design. In the example, the 30 research participants in the experimental group at Enrique's Slim Clinic lost an average of 50 pounds, whereas the 30 in the control group did not lose a single pound. Only one person dropped out during the experiment. Susan's Scientific Diet Plan had equally dramatic results, but 11 people in her experimental group dropped out. This suggests a problem with experimental mortality. People in the experimental group at Carl's Calorie Counters lost 8 pounds, compared to 2 pounds for the control group, but the control group and the experimental group began with an average of 31 pounds difference in weight. This suggests a problem with selection bias. Natalie's Nutrition Center had no experimental mortality or selection bias problems, but those in the experimental group lost no more weight than those in the control group.

FIGURE 8.4 Comparisons of Results, Classical Experimental Design, Weight-Loss Experiments

Enrique's Slim Clinic				Natalie's Nutrition Center		
	Pretest	*Posttest*			*Pretest*	*Posttest*
Experimental	190 (30)	140 (29)		Experimental	190 (30)	188 (29)
Control group	189 (30)	189 (30)		Control group	192 (29)	190 (28)

Susan's Scientific Diet Plan				Pauline's Pounds Off		
	Pretest	*Posttest*			*Pretest*	*Posttest*
Experimental	190 (30)	141 (19)		Experimental	190 (30)	158 (30)
Control group	189 (30)	189 (28)		Control group	191 (29)	159 (28)

Carl's Calorie Counters		
	Pretest	*Posttest*
Experimental	160 (30)	152 (29)
Control group	191 (29)	189 (29)

It appears that the treatment was not effective. Pauline's Pounds Off also avoided selection bias and experimental mortality problems. People in her experimental group lost 32 pounds, but so did those in the control group. This suggests that the maturation, history, or diffusion of treatment effects may have occurred. Thus, the treatment at Enrique's Slim Clinic appears to be the most effective one. See Box 8.2 for a practical application of comparing experimental results.

Box 8.2 A "Natural" Field Experiment on Law Compliance in New Orleans

Occasionally, a "natural" experiment is possible due to public policy changes or a government intervention, and researchers are able to measure, participate, and learn from it and conduct a field experiment with high *external validity*. This occurred in New Orleans, Lousiana. Until the mid-1990s, laws on selling liquor to underage customers were barely enforced in New Orleans. If caught, the offending liquor retailer met privately with the liquor commission and paid a small fine. Enforcing liquor laws was low priority for state and local government, so only three enforcement officers monitored 5,000 alcohol outlets in the New Orleans area. When public officials planned to shift enforcement priorities, Scribner and Cohen (2001) examined its impact. They had several people who clearly looked under 18 years old attempt to purchase alcoholic beverages illegally (the law required being at least 21 years of age) at 143 randomly selected liquor outlets between November 1995 and January 1996 (Time 0). The percentage who could buy liquor illegally was the *pretest measure*. After assessing the rate of illegal sales, the *dependent variable*, the police issued citations to 51 of the sales outlets, the primary *independent variable* or treatment.

BOX
8.2 **Continued**

About the same time, government officials initiated a media campaign urging better law compliance. There were *two posttest measures*, first in March to April 1996 (Time 1) and again in November 1996 to January 1997 (Time 2), during which the experimenters checked the 143 outlets.

DEPENDENT VARIABLE: PERCENTAGE WHO OBEY THE LAW

	Pretest (Time 0)	Media Campaign	Posttest 1 (Time 1)	Posttest 2 (Time 2)	No. of Retail Liquor Outlets
Experimental (citation)	6.7%		51%	29%	45
Control (no citation)	13.3%		35%	17%	98
Total	11.1%		40%	21%	143

The results allow us to compare rates of illegal selling activity before and after citations plus media campaign (*pretest* and *posttest* measures) and to compare outlets that received citations (*experimental group*) with those that did not receive citations and only had media exposure (*control group*). We see that the citations and campaign did not stop the illegal activity, but it had some effect. The impact was greater on outlets that experienced direct punishment. In addition, by adding a later follow-up (Time 2), we see how the law-enforcement impact slowly decayed over time. As frequently happens in a natural experiment, internal validity is threatened: First, the pretest measure shows a difference in the two sets of outlets, with outlets that received the treatment showing higher rates of illegal behavior; this is potential *selection bias*. Second, the media campaign occurred for all outlets, so the treatment is really a citation plus the media campaign. The authors noted that they had intended to compare the New Orleans area with another area with neither the media nor the citation campaign, but were unable to do so. Since outlets that did not receive the treatment (i.e., a citation for law violation) probably learned about it from others in the same business, a form of *diffusion of the treatment* could be operating. Third, the researchers report that they began with 155 outlets, but studied only 143 because 12 outlets went out of business during the study. The authors noted that none of the outlets that stopped selling alcohol closed due to new law enforcement, but if those outlets that received citations had more problems and were more likely to go out of business, it suggests *experimental mortality*. The experimenters did not mention any external events in New Orleans that happened during the time of the study (e.g., a publicized event such as underage drinker dying of alcohol poisoning from overdrinking). Researchers need to be aware of potential external events when a study continues for a long time and consider possible *history effects*.

A WORD ON ETHICS

Ethical considerations are a significant issue in experimental research because experimental research is intrusive (i.e., it interferes). Treatments may involve placing people in contrived social settings and manipulating their feelings or behaviors. Dependent variables may be what subjects say or do. The amount and type of intrusion is limited by ethical standards.

Researchers must be very careful if they place research participants in physical danger or in embarrassing or anxiety-inducing situations. They must painstakingly monitor events and control what occurs.

Deception is common in social experiments, but it involves misleading or lying to subjects. Such dishonesty is not condoned unconditionally and is acceptable only as the means to achieve a goal that cannot be achieved otherwise. Even for a worthy goal, deception can be used only with restrictions. The amount and type of deception should not go beyond what is minimally necessary, and research participants should be debriefed.

CONCLUSION

In this chapter, you learned about random assignment and the methods of experimental research. Random assignment is an effective way to create two (or more) groups that can be treated as equivalent and hence compared. In general, experimental research provides precise and relatively unambiguous evidence for a causal relationship. It follows the positivist approach, produces quantitative results that can be analyzed with statistics, and is often used in evaluation research (see Box 8.2).

This chapter also examined the parts of an experiment and how they can be combined to produce different experimental designs. In addition to the classical experimental design, you learned about preexperimental and quasi-experimental designs. You also learned how to express them using design notation.

You learned that internal validity—the internal logical rigor of an experiment—is a key idea in experimental research. Threats to internal validity are possible alternative explanations to the treatment. You also learned about external validity and how field experiments maximize external validity.

The real strength of experimental research is its control and logical rigor in establishing evidence for causality. In general, experiments tend to be easier to replicate, less expensive, and less time consuming than the other techniques. Experimental research also has limitations. First, some questions cannot be addressed using experimental methods because control and experimental manipulation are impossible. Another limitation is that experiments usually test one or a few hypotheses at a time. This fragments knowledge and makes it necessary to synthesize results across many research reports. External validity is another potential problem because many experiments rely on small nonrandom samples of college students.[6]

You learned how a careful examination and comparison of results can alert you to potential problems in research design. Finally, you saw some practical and ethical considerations in experiments.

In the next chapters, you will examine other research techniques. The logic of the nonexperimental methods differs from that of the experiment. Experimenters focus narrowly on a few hypotheses. They usually have one or two independent variables, a single dependent variable, a few small groups of subjects, and an independent variable that the researcher induces. By contrast, other social researchers test many hypotheses at once. For example, survey researchers measure a large number of independent and dependent variables and use a larger number of randomly sampled subjects. Their independent variables are usually preexisting conditions in research participants.

Key Terms

- classical experimental design
- control group
- debrief
- deception
- demand characteristics
- design notation
- diffusion of treatment
- double-blind experiment

- equivalent time series
- experimental design
- experimental group
- factorial design
- field experiment
- Hawthorne effect
- history effects
- interaction effect
- interrupted time series
- laboratory experiment
- Latin square design
- maturation
- mortality
- one-shot case study
- placebo
- posttest
- preexperimental designs
- pretest
- quasi-experimental designs
- random assignment
- reactivity
- selection bias
- Solomon four-group design

- static group comparison
- treatment

Endnotes

1. For additional discussions of threats to internal validity, see Cook and Campbell (1979:51–68), Kercher (1992), Smith and Glass (1987), Spector (1981:24–27), and Suls and Rosnow (1988).
2. This example is borrowed from Mitchell and Jolley (1988:97).
3. Experimenter expectancy is discussed in Aronson and Carlsmith (1968:66–70), Dooley (1984:151–153), and Mitchell and Jolley (1988:327–329).
4. The Hawthorne effect is described in Roethlisberger and Dickenson (1939), Franke and Kaul (1978), and Lang (1992). Also see the discussion in Cook and Campbell (1979:123–125) and Dooley (1984:155–156). Gillespie (1988, 1991) discussed the political context of the experiments.
5. See Piliavin and associates (1969).
6. See Graham (1992) and Sears (1986).

CHAPTER 9

Nonreactive Research and Secondary Analysis

INTRODUCTION

Experiments and survey research are both *reactive;* that is, the people being studied are aware of that fact. The techniques in this chapter address a limitation of reactive measures. You will learn about four research techniques that are *nonreactive;* that is, the people being studied are not aware that they are part of a research project. Nonreactive techniques are largely based on positivist principles but are also used by interpretive and critical researchers.

The first technique we will consider is less a distinct technique than a loose collection of inventive nonreactive measures. It is followed by content analysis, which builds on the fundamentals of quantitative research design and is a well-developed research technique. Existing statistics and secondary analysis, the last two techniques, refer to the collection of already existing information from government documents or previous surveys. Researchers examine the existing data in new ways to address new questions. Although the data may have been reactive when first collected, a researcher can address new questions without reactive effects.

NONREACTIVE MEASUREMENT

The Logic of Nonreactive Research

Nonreactive measurement begins when a researcher notices something that indicates a variable of interest. The critical thing about nonreactive or *unobtrusive measures* (i.e., measures that are not obtrusive or intrusive) is that the people being studied are not aware of it but leave evidence of their social behavior or actions "naturally." The observant researcher infers from the evidence to behavior or attitudes without disrupting the people being studied. Unnoticed observation is also a type of nonreactive measure. For example, McKelvie and Schamer (1988) unobtrusively observed whether drivers stopped at stop signs. They made observations during both daytime and nighttime. Observers noted whether the driver was male or female; whether the driver was alone or with passengers; whether other traffic was present; and whether the car came to a complete stop, a slow stop, or no stop. Later, we will contrast this type of observation to a slightly different type used in field research.

Varieties of Nonreactive or Unobtrusive Observation

Nonreactive measures are varied, and researchers have been creative in inventing indirect ways to measure social behavior (see Box 9.1). Because the measures have little in common except being nonreactive, they are best learned through examples. Some are *erosion measures,* where selective wear is used as a measure, and some are *accretion measures,* where the measures are deposits of something left behind.[1]

Researchers have examined family portraits in different historical eras to see how gender relations within the family are reflected in seating patterns. Urban anthropologists have examined the contents of garbage dumps to learn about life-styles from what is thrown away (e.g., liquor bottles indicate level of alcohol consumption). Based on garbage, people underreport their

Box 9.1   Finding Data on Tombstones

Foster and colleagues (1998) examined the tombstones in 10 cemeteries in an area of Illinois for the period from 1830 to 1989. They retrieved data on birth and death dates and gender from over 2,000 of the 2,028 burials. The researchers learned the area differed from some national trends. They found that conceptions had two peaks (spring and winter), females aged 10 to 64 had a higher death rate than males, and younger people died in late summer but older people in late winter.

liquor consumption by 40 to 60 percent (Rathje and Murphy, 1992:71). Researchers have studied the listening habits of drivers by checking what stations their radios are tuned to when cars are repaired. They have measured interest in different exhibits by noting worn tiles on the floor in different parts of a museum. They have studied differences in graffiti in male versus female high school restrooms to show gender differences in themes. Some have examined high school yearbooks to compare the high school activities of

those who had psychological problems in latter life versus those who did not. (Also see Box 9.2.)

Recording and Documentation

Creating nonreactive measures follows the logic of quantitative measurement. A researcher first conceptualizes a construct, then links the construct to nonreactive empirical evidence, which is its measure. The operational definition of the variable includes how the researcher systematically notes and records observations.

 Box 9.2   Examples of Nonreactive Measures

Physical Traces

Erosion: Wear suggests greater use.
Example: A researcher examines children's toys at a day care that were purchased at the same time. Worn-out toys suggest greater interest by the children.

Accretion: Accumulation of physical evidence suggests behavior.
Example: A researcher examines the brands of aluminum beverage cans in trash or recycling bins in male and female dormitories. This indicates the brands and types of beverages favored by each sex.

Archives

Running Records: Regularly produced public records may reveal much.
Example: A researcher examines marriage records for the bride and groom's ages. Regional differences suggest that the preference for males marrying younger females is greater in certain areas of the country.

Other Records: Irregular or private records can reveal a lot.

Example: A researcher finds the number of reams of paper purchased by a college dean's office for 10 years when student enrollment was stable. A sizable increase suggests that bureaucratic paperwork has increased.

Observation

External Appearance: How people appear may indicate social factors.
Example: A researcher watches students to see whether they are more likely to wear their school's colors and symbols after the school team won or lost.

Count Behaviors: Counting how many people do something can be informative.
Example: A researcher counts the number of men and women who come to a full stop and those who come to a rolling stop at a stop sign. This suggests gender difference in driving behavior.

Time Duration: How long people take to do things may indicate their attention.
Example: A researcher measures how long men and women pause in front of the painting of a nude man and in front of a painting of a nude woman. Time may indicate embarrassment or interest in same or cross-sex nudity by each sex.

Because nonreactive measures indicate a construct indirectly, the researcher needs to rule out reasons for the observation other than the construct of interest. For example, a researcher wants to measure customer walking traffic in a store. The researcher's measure is dirt and wear on floor tiles. He or she first clarifies what the customer traffic means (e.g., Is the floor a path to another department? Does it indicate a good location for a visual display?) Next, he or she systematically measures dirt or wear on the tiles, compares it to that in other locations, and records results on a regular basis (e.g., every month). Finally, the researcher rules out other reasons for the observations (e.g., the floor tile is of lower quality and wears faster, or the location is near an outside entrance).

CONTENT ANALYSIS

What Is Content Analysis?

Content analysis is a technique for gathering and analyzing the content of text. The *content* refers to words, meanings, pictures, symbols, ideas, themes, or any message that can be communicated. The *text* is anything written, visual, or spoken that serves as a medium for communication. It includes books, newspaper and magazine articles, advertisements, speeches, official documents, films and videotapes, musical lyrics, photographs, articles of clothing, and works of art.

The content analysis researcher uses objective and systematic counting and recording procedures to produce a quantitative description of the symbolic content in a text.[2] There are also qualitative or interpretive versions of content analysis, but in this chapter the emphasis is on quantitative data about a text's content.

Content analysis is nonreactive because the process of placing words, messages, or symbols in a text to communicate to a reader or receiver occurs without influence from the researcher who analyzes its content. For example, I, as

author of this book, wrote words and drew diagrams to communicate research methods content to you, the student. The way the book was written and the way you read it are without any knowledge or intention of its ever being content analyzed.

Content analysis lets a researcher reveal the content (i.e., messages, meanings, etc.) in a source of communication (i.e., a book, article, movie, etc.). It lets him or her probe into and discover content in a different way from the ordinary way of reading a book or watching a television program.

With content analysis, a researcher can compare content across many texts and analyze it with quantitative techniques (e.g., charts and tables). In addition, he or she can reveal aspects of the text's content that are difficult to see. For example, you might watch television commercials and feel that non-Whites rarely appear in commercials for expensive consumer goods (e.g., luxury cars, furs, jewelry, perfume, etc.). Content analysis can document—in objective, quantitative terms—whether your vague feelings based on unsystematic observation are true. It yields repeatable, precise results about the text.

Content analysis involves random sampling, precise measurement, and operational definitions for abstract constructs. Coding turns aspects of content that represent variables into numbers. After a content analysis researcher gathers the data, he or she analyzes them with statistics in the same way that an experimenter or survey researcher would.

Topics Appropriate for Content Analysis

Researchers have used content analysis for many purposes: to study themes in popular songs and religious symbols in hymns, trends in the topics that newspapers cover and the ideological tone of newspaper editorials, sex-role stereotypes in textbooks or feature films, how often people of different races appear in television commercials and programs, answers to open-ended survey questions, enemy propaganda during wartime, the covers of popular magazines, personality characteristics from suicide notes, themes in advertising messages, gender differences in conversations, and so on.

Generalizations that researchers make on the basis of content analysis are limited to the cultural communication itself. Content analysis cannot determine the truthfulness of an assertion or evaluate the aesthetic qualities of literature. It reveals the content in text but cannot interpret the content's significance. Researchers should examine the text directly.

Content analysis is useful for three types of research problems. First, it is helpful for problems involving a large volume of text. A researcher can measure large amounts of text (e.g., years of newspaper articles) with sampling and multiple coders. Second, it is helpful when a topic must be studied "at a distance." For example, content analysis can be used to study historical documents, the writings of someone who has died, or broadcasts in a hostile foreign country. Finally, content analysis can reveal messages in a text that are difficult to see with casual observation. The creator of the text or those who read it may not be aware of all its themes, biases, or characteristics. For example, authors of preschool picture books may not consciously intend to portray children in traditional stereotyped sex roles, but a high degree of sex stereotyping has been revealed through content analysis.[3]

Measurement and Coding

General Issues. Careful measurement is crucial in content analysis because a researcher converts diffuse and murky symbolic communication into precise, objective, quantitative data. He or she carefully designs and documents procedures for coding to make replication possible. The researcher operationalizes constructs in content analysis with a coding system. A *coding*

system is a set of instructions or rules on how to systematically observe and record content from text. A researcher tailors it to the specific type of text or communication medium being studied (e.g., television drama, novels, photos in magazine advertisements, etc.). The coding system also depends on the researcher's unit of analysis. For example, in the study by Lauzen and Dozier (2005) on gender stereotypes in the most popular U.S. films in 2002 (discussed in Chapter 4), the authors developed a coding system based on prior studies of prime-time television shows and film.

Units.   The unit of analysis can vary a great deal in content analysis. It can be a word, a phrase, a theme, a plot, a newspaper article, a character, and so forth. In addition to units of analysis, researchers use other units in content analysis that may or may not be the same as units of analysis: recording units, context units, and enumeration units. There are few differences among them, and they are easily confused, but each has a distinct role. In simple projects, all three are the same.

What Is Measured?   Measurement in content analysis uses *structured observation*: systematic, careful observation based on written rules. The rules explain how to categorize and classify observations. As with other measurement, categories should be mutually exclusive and exhaustive. Written rules make replication possible and improve reliability. Although researchers begin with preliminary coding rules, they often conduct a pilot study and refine coding on the basis of it.

Coding systems identify four characteristics of text content: frequency, direction, intensity, and space. A researcher measures from one to all four characteristics in a content analysis research project.

Frequency.   Frequency simply means counting whether or not something occurs and, if it occurs, how often. For example, how many elderly people appear on a television program within a given week? What percentage of all characters are they, or in what percentage of programs do they appear?

Direction.   *Direction* is noting the direction of messages in the content along some continuum (e.g., positive or negative, supporting or opposed). For example, a researcher devises a list of ways an elderly television character can act. Some are positive (e.g., friendly, wise, considerate) and some are negative (e.g., nasty, dull, selfish).

Intensity.   *Intensity* is the strength or power of a message in a direction. For example, the characteristic of forgetfulness can be minor (e.g., not remembering to take your keys when leaving home, taking time to recall the name of someone you have not seen in years) or major (e.g., not remembering your name, not recognizing your children).

Space.   A researcher can record the size of a text message or the amount of space or volume allocated to it. *Space* in written text is measured by counting words, sentences, paragraphs, or space on a page (e.g., square inches). For video or audio text, space can be measured by the amount of time allocated. For example, a TV character may be present for a few seconds or continuously in every scene of a two-hour program.

Coding, Validity, and Reliability

Manifest Coding.   Coding the visible, surface content in a text is called *manifest coding*. For example, a researcher counts the number of times a phrase or word (e.g., *red*) appears in written text, or whether a specific action (e.g., a kiss) appears in a photograph or video scene. The coding system lists terms or actions that are then located in text. A researcher can use a computer program to search for words or phrases in text and have a computer do the counting work. To do this, he or she learns about the computer program, develops a comprehensive list of

relevant words or phrases, and puts the text into a form that computers can read.[4]

Manifest coding is highly reliable because the phrase or word either is or is not present. Unfortunately, manifest coding does not take the connotations of words or phrases into account. The same word can take on different meanings depending on the context. The possibility that there are multiple meanings of a word limits the measurement validity of manifest coding.

For example, I read a book with a *red* cover that is a real *red* herring. Unfortunately, its publisher drowned in *red* ink because the editor could not deal with the *red* tape that occurs when a book is *red* hot. The book has a story about a *red* fire truck that stops at *red* lights only after the leaves turn *red*. There is also a group of *Reds* who carry *red* flags to the little *red* schoolhouse. They are opposed by *red*-blooded *red*necks who eat *red* meat and honor the *red*, white, and blue. The main character is a *red*-nosed matador who fights *red* foxes, not bulls, with his *red* cape. *Red*-lipped little *Red* Riding Hood is also in the book. She develops *red* eyes and becomes *red*-faced after eating a lot of *red* peppers in the *red* light district. She is given a *red* backside by her angry mother, a *red*head.

In the study of gender stereotypes in films in 2002, Lauzen and Dozier (2005) largely used manifest coding. Coders coded each character in a film as male or female, the estimated age of each character in one of 7 categories, the occupation of each character, and whether a character was formally appointed to provide guidance or direction in a group or informally emerged in such a function.

Latent Coding.   A researcher using *latent coding* (also called *semantic analysis*) looks for the underlying, implicit meaning in the content of a text. For example, a researcher reads an entire paragraph and decides whether it contains erotic themes or a romantic mood. The researcher's coding system has general rules to guide his or her interpretation of the text and for determining whether particular themes or moods are present.

Latent coding tends to be less reliable than manifest coding. It depends on a coder's knowledge of language and social meaning.[5] Training, practice, and written rules improve reliability, but still it is difficult to consistently identify themes, moods, and the like. Yet, the validity of latent coding can exceed that of manifest coding because people communicate meaning in many implicit ways that depend on context, not just in specific words.

A researcher can use both manifest and latent coding. If the two approaches agree, the final result is strengthened; if they disagree, the researcher may want to reexamine the operational and theoretical definitions.

Intercoder Reliability. Content analysis often involves coding information from a very large number of units. A research project might involve observing the content in dozens of books, hundreds of hours of television programming, or thousands of newspaper articles. In addition to coding the information personally, a researcher may hire assistants to help with the coding. He or she teaches coders the coding system and trains them to fill out a recording sheet. Coders should understand the variables, follow the coding system, and ask about ambiguities. A researcher records all decisions he or she makes about how to treat a new specific coding situation after coding begins so that he or she can be consistent.

A researcher who uses several coders must *always* check for consistency across coders. He or she does this by asking coders to code the same text independently and then checking for consistency across coders. The researcher measures *intercoder reliability* with a statistical coefficient that tells the degree of consistency among coders. The coefficient is *always* reported with the results of content analysis research. There are several intercoder reliability measures that range from 0 to 1, with 1.0 signifying perfect agreement among coders. An interreliability coefficent of .80 or better is generally required, although .70 may be acceptable for exploratory research. When the coding process stretches over a considerable time period (e.g., more than three months), the researcher also checks reliability by having each coder independently code samples of text that were previously coded. He or she then checks to see whether the coding is stable or changing. For example, six hours of television episodes are coded in April and coded again in July without the coders looking at their original coding decisions. Large deviations in coding necessitate retraining and coding the text a second time.

In the study of the 100 most popular U.S. films of 2002 by Lauzen and Dozier (2005), three graduate students worked as coders. During an initial training period they studied the coding system and variable definitions. Next, the coders practiced by coding independent of one another several films that were not in the study then comparing and discussing results. For coding of study films, 10 percent of all films were double coded to calculate intercoder reliability measures. Intercorder reliability measures were calculated for each variable. For the gender of the major character in the film it was .99, for occupation of the chacters it was .91, and for the age of characters it was .88.

Content Analysis with Visual Material. Using content analysis to study visual "text," such as photographs, paintings, statues, buildings, clothing, and videos and film, is difficult. It communicates messages or emotional content indirectly through images, symbols, and metaphors. Moreover, visual images often contain mixed messages at multiple levels of meaning.

To conduct content analysis on visual text, the researcher must "read" the meaning(s) within visual text. He or she must interpret signs and discover the meanings attached to symbolic images. Such "reading" is not mechanical (i.e., image X always means G); it depends heavily on the cultural context because the meaning of an image is culture bound. For example, a red light does not inevitably mean "stop"; it means "stop" only in cultures where people have given it that meaning. People construct cultural meanings that they attach to symbolic images, and the meanings can change over time. Some meanings are clearer and more firmly attached to symbols and images than others.

Most people share a common meaning for key symbols of the dominant culture, but some people may read a symbol differently. For example, one group of people may "read" a national flag to mean patriotism, duty to nation, and honor of tradition. For others, the same flag evokes fear, and they read it to indicate government oppression, abuse of power, and military aggression. A researcher pursuing the content analysis of images needs to be aware of divergent readings of symbols for people in different situations or who may have diverse beliefs and experiences.

Sociopolitical groups may invent or construct new symbols with attached meanings (e.g., a pink triangle came to mean gay pride). They may wrestle for control of the meaning of major existing symbols. For example, some people want to assign a Christian religious meaning to the Christmas tree; others want it to represent a celebration of tradition and family values without specific religious content; others see its origins as an anti-Christian pagan symbol; and still others want it to mean a festive holiday season for commercial reasons. Because images have symbolic content with complex, multilayer meaning, researchers often combine qualitative judgments about the images with quantitative data in content analysis.

For example, Chavez (2001) conducted a content analysis of the covers of major U.S. magazines that dealt with the issue of immigration into the United States. Looking at the covers of 10 magazines from the mid-1970s to the mid-1990s, he classified the covers as having one of three major messages: affirmative, alarmist, or neutral or balanced. Beyond his classification and identifying trends in messages, he noted how the mix of people (i.e., race, gender, age,

and dress) in the photographs and the recurrent use of major symbols, such as the Statute of Liberty or the U.S. flag, communicated messages.

Chavez argued that magazine covers are a site, or location, where cultural meaning is created. Visual images on magazine covers have multiple levels of meaning, and viewers construct specific meanings as they read the image and use their cultural knowledge. Collectively, the covers convey a worldview and express messages about a nation and its people. For example, a magazine cover that displayed the icon of the Statute of Liberty as strong and full of compassion (message: welcome immigrants) was altered to have strong Asian facial features (message: Asian immigrants distorted the national culture and altered the nation's racial make-up), or holding a large stop sign (message: go away immigrants). Chavez (2001: 44) observed that "images on magazines both refer to, and in the process, help to structure and construct contemporary 'American' identity." (See Box 9.3 for another content analysis example.)

How to Conduct Content Analysis Research

Question Formulation.   As in most research, content analysis researchers begin with a research question. When the question involves variables that are messages or symbols, content analysis may be appropriate. For example, I want to study how newspapers cover a political campaign. My construct "coverage" includes the amount of coverage, the prominence of the coverage, and whether the coverage favors one candidate over another. I could survey people about what they think of the newspaper coverage, but a better strategy is to examine the newspapers directly using content analysis.

Units of Analysis.   A researcher decides on the units of analysis (i.e., the amount of text that is assigned a code). For example, for a political campaign, each issue (or day) of a newspaper is the unit of analysis.

Box 9.3 Advertising and Race–Ethnicity in America

Two studies that examined race–ethnicity and advertising in the United States illustrate how content analysis is conducted. Mastro and Stern (2003) wanted to see whether television advertising represents major racial–ethnic groups proportionate to their presence in U.S. society. They examined a one-week random sample of prime-time television programming for six U.S. television networks (ABC, CBS, NBC, Fox, UPN, and WB) drawn from a three-week period in February 2001. Prime time was Monday through Saturday 8:00 P.M. to 11:00 P.M. EST and Sunday 7:00–11:00 P.M. Four undergraduate students were trained as coders. They used two units of analysis: a commercial (excluding local commercials, political advertisements, and trailers for upcoming programs) and the first three speaking characters in a commercial. Variables included product type based on a 30-product coding scheme, setting (e.g., work, outdoors), relation to product (e.g., endorse, use, neither or both), job authority, family status, social authority, sexual gazing, and affective state (e.g., cry, show anger, laugh). Other variables included respect shown for a character, character's age, and affability (friendly or hostile). The study coded 2,880 commercials with 2,315 speaking characters, among whom 2,290 had a race–ethnicity identified. Data analysis found that African American characters were most often shown advertising financial services (19 percent) or food (17 percent), Asians were associated with technology products (30 percent), and Latinos were shown selling soap (40 percent). In general, Whites were slightly overrepresented, Blacks equally represented, but Asians, Latinos, and Native Americans underrepresented. For example, Latinos are 12 percent of the population but had 1 percent of speaking parts, and were usually scantly clad young people with noticeable accents. The authors said that African Americans appear in commercials in a way that approximates their proportion in the United States, but other racial minorities are underrepresented or limited to specific products.

In another study, Mastro and Atkin (2002) examined whether alcohol advertising to promote brands and make drinking appear glamorous influenced high school students who are too young to drink legally. They looked at alcohol signs and billboards in a Mexican-American Chicago neighborhood. They first photographed all outdoor billboards and signs concerning alcohol in the neighborhood over a two-day period in March 1999. After a period of coder training, two female graduate students content-analyzed the photographs, coding the following variables: product type, product name, number of human models, and the race, age, gender of each model. More subjective-latent aspects of models coded included attractiveness, sexiness, stylishness, friendliness, and activity level. In addition, placement of products and colors in the billboard were coded. Coders also classified an overall theme of the billboard as romance, individuality, relaxation, sports, adventure, or tradition. Next, a questionnaire was developed for students at a high school in the neighborhood where 89 percent of the students were Mexican American. Students in grades 10, 11, and 12 were asked to volunteer to complete the survey across a three-day period and 123 completed it. Questionnaire items asked about attention, exposure, recall, and brand exposure to the outdoor signs and billboards as well as drinking intention, approval of underage drinking, and pro-drinking beliefs. Results showed that a student's recall of billboard images did not affect his or her drinking attitudes. However, brand exposure and accepting the themes in the billboards were associated with greater approval of underage drinking. The general impact on the students was present but not strong. The authors suggested that the weak impact was because there were few Mexican American models and the models were older. Also, survey measures of family beliefs suggested that the influence of the student's family and culture may have weakened the billboard's impact on pro-drinking attitudes.

Sampling. Researchers often use random sampling in content analysis. First, they define the population and the sampling element. For example, the population might be all words, all sentences, all paragraphs, or all articles in certain types of documents over a specified time period. Likewise, it could include each conversation, situation, scene, or episode of certain types of television programs over a specified time period. For example, I want to know how women and minorities are portrayed in U.S. weekly newsmagazines. My unit of analysis is the article. My population includes all articles published in *Time, Newsweek,* and *U.S. News and World Report* between 1985 and 2005. I first verify that the three magazines were published in those years and define precisely what is meant by an "article." For instance, do film reviews count as articles? Is there a minimum size (two sentences) for an article? Is a multipart article counted as one or two articles?

Second, I examine the three magazines and find that the average issue of each contains 45 articles and that the magazines are published 52 weeks per year. With a 20-year time frame, my population contains over 140,000 articles (3 × 45 × 52 × 20 = 140,400). My sampling frame is a list of all the articles. Next, I decide on the sample size and design. After looking at my budget and time, I decide to limit the sample size to 1,400 articles. Thus, the sampling ratio is 1 percent. I also choose a sampling design. I avoid systematic sampling because magazine issues are published cyclically according to the calendar (e.g., an interval of every 52nd issue results in the same week each year). Because issues from each magazine are important, I use stratified sampling. I stratify by magazine, sampling 1,400/3 = 467 articles from each. I want to ensure that articles represent each of the 20 years, so I also stratify by year. This results in about 23 articles per magazine per year.

Finally, I draw the random sample using a random-number table to select 23 numbers for the 23 sample articles for each magazine for each year. I develop a sampling frame worksheet to keep track of my sampling procedure. See Table 9.1 for a sampling frame worksheet in which 1,398 sample articles are randomly selected from 140,401 articles.

Variables and Constructing Coding Categories.
In my example, I am interested in the construct of an African American or Hispanic American woman portrayed in a significant leadership role. I must define "significant leadership role" in operational terms and express it as written rules for classifying people named in an article. For example, if an article discusses the achievements of someone who is now dead, does the dead person have a significant role? What is a significant role—a local Girl Scout leader or a corporate president?

I must also determine the race and sex of people named in the articles. What if the race and sex are not evident in the text or accompanying photographs? How do I decide on the person's race and sex?

Because I am interested in positive leadership roles, my measure indicates whether the role was positive or negative. I can do this with either latent or manifest coding. With manifest coding, I create a list of adjectives and phrases. If someone in a sampled article is referred to with one of the adjectives, then the direction is decided. For example, the terms *brilliant* and *top performer* are positive, whereas *drug kingpin* and *uninspired* are negative. For latent coding, I create rules to guide judgments. For example, I classify stories about a diplomat resolving a difficult world crisis, a business executive unable to make a firm profitable, or a lawyer winning a case into positive or negative terms. (Relevant questions for coding each article are in Box 9.4.)

In addition to written rules for coding decisions, a content analysis researcher creates a *recording sheet* (also called a *coding form* or *tally sheet*) on which to record information (see Box 9.5). Each unit should have a separate recording sheet. The sheets do not have to be pieces of paper; they can be 3″ × 5″ or 4″ × 6″ file cards, or lines in a computer record or file. When a lot of

TABLE 9.1   Excerpt from Sampling Frame Worksheet

Magazine	Issue	Article	Number	Article In Sample?*	Sampled Article ID
Time	January 1–7, 1985	pp. 2–3	000001	No	
Time	"	p. 4, bottom	000002	No	
Time	"	p. 4, top	000003	Yes—1	0001
•					
•					
•					
Time	March 1–7, 2005	pp. 2–5	002101	Yes—10	0454
Time	"	p. 6, right column	002102	No	
Time	"	p. 6, left column	002103	No	
Time	"	p. 7	002104	No	
•					
•					
•					
Time	December 24–31, 2005	pp. 4–5	002201	Yes—22	0467
Time	"	p. 5, bottom	002202	No	
Time	"	p. 5, top	002203	Yes—23	0468
Newsweek	January 1–7, 1985	pp. 1–2	010030	No	
Newsweek	"	p. 3	010031	Yes—1	0469
•					
•					
•					
U.S. News	December 25–31, 2005	p. 62	140401	Yes—23	1389

*"Yes" means the number was chosen from a random number table. The number after the dash is a count of the number of articles selected for a year.

Box 9.4   Example of Latent Coding Questions, Magazine Article Leadership Role Study

1. *Characteristics of the article.* What is the magazine? What is the date of the article? How large is the article? What was its topic area? Where did it appear in the issue? Were photographs used?

2. *People in the article.* How many people are named in the article? Of these, how many are significant in the article? What is the race and sex of each person named?

3. *Leadership roles.* For each significant person in the article, which ones have leadership roles? What is the field of leadership or profession of the person?

4. *Positive or negative roles.* For each leadership or professional role, rate how positively or negatively it is shown. For example, 5 = highly positive, 4 = positive, 3 = neutral, 2 = negative, 1 = highly negative, 0 = ambiguous.

Box 9.5	Example of Recording Sheet

Blank Example

Professor Neuman, Sociology Department   Coder:____

Minority/Majority Group Representation in Newsmagazines Project

ARTICLE #____   MAGAZINE:____   DATE:____   SIZE:____ col. in.

Total number of people named ____   Number of Photos ____

No. people with significant roles: ____   Article Topic: _____

Person____:	Race:____	Gender:____	Leader?:____	Field?____	Rating:____
Person____:	Race:____	Gender:____	Leader?:____	Field?____	Rating:____
Person____:	Race:____	Gender:____	Leader?:____	Field?____	Rating:____
Person____:	Race:____	Gender:____	Leader?:____	Field?____	Rating:____
Person____:	Race:____	Gender:____	Leader?:____	Field?____	Rating:____
Person____:	Race:____	Gender:____	Leader?:____	Field?____	Rating:____
Person____:	Race:____	Gender:____	Leader?:____	Field?____	Rating:____
Person____:	Race:____	Gender:____	Leader?:____	Field?____	Rating:____

Example of Completed Recording Sheet for One Article

Professor Neuman, Sociology Department   Coder: Susan J.

Minority/Majority Group Representation in Newsmagazines Project

ARTICLE # 0454   MAGAZINE: Time   DATE: March 1–7, 2005   SIZE: 14 col. in.

Total number of people named 5   Number of Photos 0

No. people with significant roles: 4   Article Topic: Foreign Affairs

Person 1 :	Race: White	Gender: M	Leader?: Y	Field? Banking	Rating: 5
Person 2 :	Race: White	Gender: M	Leader?: N	Field? Government	Rating: NA
Person 3 :	Race: Black	Gender: F	Leader?: Y	Field? Civil Rights	Rating: 2
Person 4 :	Race: White	Gender: F	Leader?: Y	Field? Government	Rating: 0
Person ____:	Race: ____	Gender: ____	Leader?: ____	Field? ____	Rating: ____
Person ____:	Race: ____	Gender: ____	Leader?: ____	Field? ____	Rating: ____
Person ____:	Race: ____	Gender: ____	Leader?: ____	Field? ____	Rating: ____
Person ____:	Race: ____	Gender: ____	Leader?: ____	Field? ____	Rating: ____

information is recorded for each recording unit, more than one sheet of paper can be used. When planning a project, researchers calculate the work required. For example, during my pilot-test, I find that it takes an average of 15 minutes to read and code an article. This does not include sampling or locating magazine articles. With approximately 1,400 articles, that is 350 hours of coding, not counting time to verify the accuracy of coding. Because 350 hours is about nine weeks of nonstop work at 40 hours a week, I should consider hiring assistants as coders.

Each recording sheet has a place to record the identification number of the unit and spaces for information about each variable. I also put identifying information about the research project on the sheet in case I misplace it or it looks similar to other sheets I have. Finally, if I use multiple coders, the sheet reminds the coder to check intercoder reliability and, if necessary, makes it possible to recode information for inaccurate coders. After completing all recording sheets and checking for accuracy, I can begin data analysis.

Inferences

The inferences a researcher can or cannot make on the basis of results is critical in content analysis. Content analysis describes what is in the text. It cannot reveal the intentions of those who created the text or the effects that messages in the text have on those who receive them. For example, content analysis shows that children's books contain sex stereotypes. That does not necessarily mean that children's beliefs or behaviors are influenced by the stereotypes; such an inference requires a separate research project on how children's perceptions develop.

EXISTING STATISTICS/ DOCUMENTS AND SECONDARY ANALYSIS

Appropriate Topics

Many types of information about the social world have been collected and are available to the researcher. Some information is in the form of statistical documents (books, reports, etc.) that contain numerical information. Other information is in the form of published compilations available in a library or on computerized records. In either case, the researcher can search through collections of information with a research question and variables in mind, and

then reassemble the information in new ways to address the research question.

It is difficult to specify topics that are appropriate for existing statistics research because they are so varied. Any topic on which information has been collected and is publicly available can be studied. In fact, existing statistics projects may not fit neatly into a deductive model of research design. Rather, researchers creatively reorganize the existing information into the variables for a research question after first finding what data are available.

Experiments are best for topics where the researcher controls a situation and manipulates an independent variable. Survey research is best for topics where the researcher asks questions and learns about reported attitudes or behavior. Content analysis is best for topics that involve the content of messages in cultural communication.

Existing statistics research is best for topics that involve information routinely collected by large bureaucratic organizations. Public or private organizations systematically gather many types of information. Such information is gathered for policy decisions or as a public service. It is rarely collected for purposes directly related to a specific research question. Thus, existing statistics research is appropriate when a researcher wants to test hypotheses involving variables that are also in official reports of social, economic, and political conditions. These include descriptions of organizations or the people in them. Often, such information is collected over long time periods. For example, existing statistics can be used by a researcher who wants to see whether unemployment and crime rates are associated in 150 cities across a 20-year period.

Downey (2005) conducted an existing statistics study on racial inequality (Black/White) and living near a toxic pollution site in Detroit. He used census data on the population/housing and manufacturing directories of manufacturing facilities. He also identified highly polluting industries and used the Environmental Protection Agency's inventory of toxic chemicals. His unit of analysis was the census tract. Downey tested competing models of environmental inequality: (1) racist siting policy: toxic sites were placed in Black residential areas, (2) economic inequality: low-income people who are disproportionately Black move into areas near toxic sites because they find low-cost housing there, and (3) residential segregation: Whites move into specific areas and keep out non-Whites. He found greatest support for the residential segregation model. Paradoxically, it meant that Blacks were less likely than Whites to live close to a toxic pollution site. This was because Whites had obtained housing near the factories where they worked and kept Blacks from moving in but those factories were the major sources of toxic pollution.

Social Indicators

During the 1960s, some social scientists, dissatisfied with the information available to decision makers, spawned the "social indicators' movement" to develop indicators of social well-being. Many hoped that information about social well-being could be combined with widely used indicators of economic performance (e.g., gross national product) to better inform government and other policymaking officials. Thus, researchers wanted to measure the quality of social life so that such information could influence public policy.[6]

Today, there are many books, articles, and reports on social indicators, and even a scholarly journal, *Social Indicators Research,* devoted to the creation and evaluation of social indicators. The U.S. Census Bureau produced a report, *Social Indicators,* and the United Nations has many measures of social well-being in different nations.

A *social indicator* is any measure of social well-being used in policy. There are many specific indicators that are operationalizations of well-being. For example, social indicators have been developed for the following areas: population, family, housing, social security and welfare,

health and nutrition, public safety, education and training, work, income, culture and leisure, social mobility, and public participation.

A more specific example of a social indicator is the FBI's uniform crime index. It indicates the amount of crime in U.S. society. Social indicators can measure negative aspects of social life, such as the infant mortality rate (the death rate of infants during the first year of life) or alcoholism, or they can indicate positive aspects, such as job satisfaction or the percentage of housing units with indoor plumbing. Social indicators often involve implicit value judgments (e.g., which crimes are serious or what constitutes a good quality of life).

Locating Data

Locating Existing Statistics. The main sources of existing statistics are government or international agencies and private sources. An enormous volume and variety of information exists. If you plan to conduct existing statistics research, it is wise to discuss your interests with an information professional—in this case, a reference librarian, who can point you in the direction of possible sources.

Many existing documents are "free"—that is, publicly available at libraries—but the time and effort it takes to search for specific information can be substantial. Researchers who conduct existing statistics research spend many hours in libraries or on the Internet. After the information is located, it is recorded on cards, graphs, or recording sheets for later analysis. Often, it is already available in a format for computers to read. For example, instead of recording voting data from books, a researcher could use a social science data archive at the University of Michigan (to be discussed).

There are so many sources that only a small sample of what is available is discussed here. The single-most valuable source of statistical information about the United States is the *Statistical Abstract of the United States,* which has been published annually (with a few exceptions) since

1878. The *Statistical Abstract* is available in all public libraries and on the Internet and can be purchased from the U.S. Superintendent of Documents. It is a selected compilation of the many official reports and statistical tables produced by U.S. government agencies. It contains statistical information from hundreds of more detailed government reports. You may want to examine more specific government documents. (The detail of what is available in government documents is mind boggling. For example, you can learn that there were two African American females over the age of 75 in Tucumcari City, New Mexico, in 1980.)

The *Statistical Abstract* has over 1,400 charts, tables, and statistical lists from over 200 government and private agencies. It is hard to grasp all that it contains until you skim through the tables. A two-volume set summarizes similar information across many years; it is called *Historical Statistics of the U.S.: Colonial Times to 1970.*

Most governments publish similar statistical yearbooks. Australia's Bureau of Statistics produces *Yearbook Australia,* Statistics Canada produces *Canada Yearbook,* New Zealand's Department of Statistics publishes *New Zealand Official Yearbook,* and in the United Kingdom, the Central Statistics Office publishes *Annual Abstract of Statistics.*[7] Many nations publish books with historical statistics, as well.

Locating government statistical documents is an art in itself. Some publications exist solely to assist the researcher. For example, the *American Statistics Index: A Comprehensive Guide* and *Index to the Statistical Publications of the U.S. Government and Statistics Sources: A Subject Guide to Data on Industrial, Business, Social Education, Financial and Other Topics for the U.S. and Internationally* are two helpful guides for the United States.[8] The United Nations and international agencies such as the World Bank have their own publications with statistical information for various countries (e.g., literacy rates, percentage of the labor force working in agriculture, birth rates)—for example, the *Demographic Yearbook,*

UNESCO Statistical Yearbook, and *United Nations Statistical Yearbook.*

In addition to government statistical documents, there are dozens of other publications. Many are produced for business purposes and can be obtained only for a high cost. They include information on consumer spending, the location of high-income neighborhoods, trends in the economy, and the like.[9]

Over a dozen publications list characteristics of businesses or their executives. These are found in larger libraries. Three such publications are as follows:

Dun and Bradstreet Principal Industrial Businesses is a guide to approximately 51,000 businesses in 135 countries with information on sales, number of employees, officers, and products.

Who Owns Whom comes in volumes for nations or regions (e.g., North America, the United Kingdom, Ireland, and Australia). It lists parent companies, subsidiaries, and associated companies.

Standard and Poor's Register of Corporations, Directors and Executives lists about 37,000 U.S. and Canadian companies. It has information on corporations, products, officers, industries, and sales figures.

Many biographical sources list famous people and provide background information on them. These are useful when a researcher wants to learn about the social background, career, or other characteristics of famous individuals. The publications are compiled by companies that send out questionnaires to people identified as "important" by some criteria. They are public sources of information, but they depend on the cooperation and accuracy of individuals who are selected.

Politics has its own specialized publications. There are two basic types. One has biographical information on contemporary politicians. The other type has information on voting, laws enacted, and the like. Here are three examples of political information publications for the United States:

> *Almanac of American Politics* is a biannual publication that includes photographs and a short biography of U.S. government officials. Committee appointments, voting records, and similar information are provided for members of Congress and leaders in the executive branch.
>
> *America Votes: A Handbook of Contemporary American Election Statistics* contains detailed voting information by county for most statewide and national offices. Primary election results are included down to the county level.
>
> *Vital Statistics on American Politics* provides dozens of tables on political behavior, such as the campaign spending of every candidate for Congress, their primary and final votes, ideological ratings by various political organizations, and a summary of voter registration regulations by state.

Another source of public information consists of lists of organizations (e.g., business, educational, etc.) produced for general information purposes. A researcher can sometimes obtain membership lists of organizations. There are also publications of public speeches given by famous people.

Secondary Survey Data. Secondary analysis is a special case of existing statistics; it is the reanalysis of previously collected survey or other data that were originally gathered by others. As opposed to primary research (e.g., experiments, surveys, and content analysis), the focus is on analyzing rather than collecting data. Secondary analysis is increasingly used by researchers. It is relatively inexpensive; it permits comparisons across groups, nations, or time; it facilitates replication; and it permits asking about issues not thought of by the original researchers.

Large-scale data collection is expensive and difficult. The cost and time required for a major national survey that uses rigorous techniques are prohibitive for most researchers. Fortunately, the organization, preservation, and dissemination of major survey data sets have improved. Today, there are archives of past surveys that are open to researchers.

The Inter-University Consortium for Political and Social Research (ICPSR) at the University of Michigan is the world's major archive of social science data. Over 17,000 survey research and related sets of information are stored and made available to researchers at modest costs. Other centers hold survey data in the United States and other nations.[10]

A widely used source of survey data for the United States is the *General Social Survey (GSS)*, which has been conducted annually in most years by the National Opinion Research Center at the University of Chicago. In recent years, it has covered other nations as well. The data are made publicly available for secondary analysis at a low cost (see Box 9.6).

Limitations

Despite the growth and popularity of secondary data analysis and existing statistics research, there are limitations in their use. The use of such techniques is not trouble free just because a government agency or research organization gathered the data. One danger is that a researcher may use secondary data or existing statistics that are inappropriate for his or her research question. Before proceeding, a researcher needs to consider units in the data (e.g., types of people, organizations), the time and place of data collection, the sampling methods used, and the specific issues or topics covered in the data (see Box 9.7). For example, a researcher wanting to examine racial–ethnic tensions between Latinos and Anglos in the United States uses secondary data that includes only the Pacific Northwest and New England states should reconsider the question or the use of data.

Box 9.6   The General Social Survey

The General Social Survey (GSS) is the best-known set of survey data used by social researchers for secondary analysis. The mission of the GSS is "to make timely, high quality, scientifically relevant data available to the social science research community" (Davis and Smith, 1992:1). It is available in many computer-readable formats and is widely accessible for a low cost. Neither datasets nor codebooks are copyrighted. Users may copy or disseminate them without obtaining permission. You can find results using the GSS in over 2,000 research articles and books.

The National Opinion Research Center (NORC) has conducted the GSS almost every year since 1972. A typical year's survey contains a random sample of about 1,500 adult U.S. residents. A team of researchers selects some questions for inclusion, and individual researchers can recommend questions. They repeat some questions and topics each year, include some on a four- to six-year cycle, and add other topics in specific years. For example, in 1998, the special topic was job experiences and religion,

and in 2000, it was intergroup relations and multiculturalism.

Interviewers collect the data through face-to-face interviews. The NORC staff carefully selects interviewers and trains them in social science methodology and survey interviewing. About 120 to 140 interviewers work on the GSS each year. About 90 percent are women, and most are middle aged. The NORC recruits bilingual and minority interviewers. Interviewers with respondents are race-matched with respondents. Interviews are typically 90 minutes long and contain approximately 500 questions. The response rate has been 71 to 79 percent. The major reason for nonresponse is a refusal to participate.

The International Social Survey Program conducts similar surveys in other nations. Beginning with the German ALLBUS and British Social Attitudes Survey, participation has grown to include 33 nations. The goal is to conduct on a regular basis large-scale national general surveys in which some common questions are asked across cooperating nations.

A second danger is that the researcher does not understand the substantive topic. Because the data are easily accessible, researchers who know very little about a topic could make erroneous assumptions or false interpretations about results. Before using any data, a researcher needs to be well informed about the topic. For example, if a researcher uses data on high school graduation rates in Germany without understanding the Germany secondary education system with its distinct academic and vocational tracks, he or she may make serious errors in interpreting results.

A third danger is that a researcher may quote statistics in great detail to give an impression of scientific rigor. This can lead to the *fallacy of misplaced concreteness,* which occurs when someone gives a false impression of precision by quoting

statistics in greater detail than warranted and "overloading" the details. For example, existing statistics report that the population of Australia is 19,169,083, but it is better to say that it is a little over 19 million. One might calculate the percentage of divorced people as 15.65495 in a secondary data analysis of the 2000 General Social Survey, but it is better to report that about 15.7 percent of people are divorced.[11]

Units of Analysis and Variable Attributes.

A common problem in existing statistics is finding the appropriate units of analysis. Many statistics are published for aggregates, not the individual. For example, a table in a government document has information (e.g., unemployment rate, crime rate, etc.) for a state, but the unit of analysis for the research question is the individual

Almost every country conducts a census, or a regular count of its population. For example, Australia has done so since 1881, Canada since 1871, and the United States since 1790. Most nations conduct a census every 5 or 10 years. In addition to the number of people, census officials collect information on topics such as housing conditions, ethnicity, religious affiliation, education, and so forth.

The census is a major source of high-quality existing statistical data, but it can be controversial. In Canada, an attempt to count the number of same-sex couples living together evoked public debate about whether the government should document the changes in society. In Great Britain, the Muslim minority welcomed questions about religion in the 2001 census because they felt that they had been officially ignored. In the United States, the measurement of race and ethnicity was hotly debated, so in the 2000 census, people could place themselves in multiple racial/ethnic categories.

The U.S. 2000 census also generated a serious public controversy because it missed thousands of people, most from low-income areas with concentrations of recent immigrants and racial minorities. Some double counting also occurred of people in high income areas where many owned second homes. A contentious debate arose among politicians to end miscounts by using scientific sampling and adjusting the census. The politicians proved to be less concerned about improving the scientific accuracy of the census than retaining traditional census methods that would benefit their own political fortunes or help their constituencies, because the government uses census data to draw voting districts and allocate public funds to areas.

raw information on each respondent from archives.

A related problem involves the categories of variable attributes used in existing documents or survey questions. This is not a problem if the initial data were gathered in many highly refined categories. The problem arises when the original data were collected in broad categories or ones that do not match the needs of a researcher. For example, a researcher is interested in people of Asian heritage. If the racial and ethnic heritage categories in a document are "White," "Black," and "Other," the researcher has a problem. The "Other" category includes people of Asian and other heritages. Sometimes information was collected in refined categories but is published only in broad categories. It takes special effort to discover whether more refined information was collected or is publicly available.

Validity.   Validity problems occur when the researcher's theoretical definition does not match that of the government agency or organization that collected the information. Official policies and procedures specify definitions for official statistics. For example, a researcher defines a *work injury* as including minor cuts, bruises, and sprains that occur on the job, but the official definition in government reports only includes injuries that require a visit to a physician or hospital. Many work injuries, as defined by the researcher, would not be in official statistics. Another example occurs when a researcher defines people as *unemployed* if they would work if a good job were available, if they have to work part time when they want full-time work, and if they have given up looking for work. The official definition, however, includes only those who are now actively seeking work (full or part time) as unemployed. The official statistics exclude those who stopped looking, who work part time out of necessity, or who do not look because they believe no work is available. In both cases, the researcher's definition differs from that in official statistics (see Box 9.8).

(e.g., "Are unemployed people more likely to commit property crimes?"). The potential for committing the ecological fallacy is very real in this situation. It is less of a problem for secondary survey analysis because researchers can obtain

Box 9.8   Official Unemployment Rates versus the Nonemployed

In most countries, the official unemployment rate measures only the unemployed (see below) as a percent of all working people. It would be 50 percent higher if two other categories of nonemployed people were added: involuntary part-time workers and discouraged workers (see below). In some countries (e.g., Sweden and United States), it would be nearly double if it included these people. This does not consider other nonworking people, transitional self-employed, or the underemployed (see below). What a country measures is a theoretical and conceptual definition issue: What construct should an unemployment rate measure and why measure it?

An economic policy or labor market perspective says the rate should measure those ready to enter the labor market immediately. It defines nonworking people as a supply of high-quality labor, an input for use in the economy available to employers. By contrast, a social policy or human resource perspective says the rate should measure those who are not currently working to their fullest potential. The rate should represent people who are not or cannot fully utilize their talents, skills, or time to the fullest. It defines nonworking people as a social problem of individuals unable to realize their capacity to be productive, contributing members of society.

Categories of Nonemployed/Fully Utilized

Unemployed people	People who meet three conditions: lack a paying job outside the home, are taking active measures to find work, can begin work immediately if it is offered.
Involuntary part-time workers	People with a job, but work irregularly or fewer hours than they are able and willing.
Discouraged workers	People able to work and who actively sought it for some time, but being unable to find it, have given up looking.
Other nonworking	Those not working because they are retired, on vacation, temporarily laid off, semidisabled, homemakers, full-time students, or in the process of moving.
Transitional self-employed	Self-employed who are not working full time because they are just starting a business or are going through bankruptcy.
Underemployed	Persons with a temporary full-time job for which they are seriously overqualified. They seek a permanent job in which they can fully apply their skills and experience.

Source: Adapted from *The Economist,* July 22, 1995, p. 74.

Another validity problem arises when official statistics are a surrogate or proxy for a construct in which a researcher is really interested. This is necessary because the researcher cannot collect original data. For example, the researcher wants to know how many people have been robbed, so he or she uses police statistics on robbery arrests as a proxy. But the measure is not entirely valid because many robberies are not reported to the police, and reported robberies do not always result in an arrest.

A third validity problem arises because the researcher lacks control over how information is collected. All information, even that in official government reports, is originally gathered by people in bureaucracies as part of their jobs. A researcher depends on them for collecting, organizing, reporting, and publishing data accurately. Systematic errors in collecting the initial information (e.g., census people who avoid poor neighborhoods and make up information, or people who put a false age on a driver's license); errors in organizing and reporting information (e.g., a police department that is sloppy about filing crime reports and loses some); and errors in publishing information (e.g., a typographical error in a table) all reduce measurement validity.

This kind of problem happened in U.S. statistics on the number of people permanently laid off from their jobs. A university researcher reexamined the methods used to gather data by the U.S. Bureau of Labor Statistics and found an error. Data on permanent job losses come from a survey of 50,000 people, but the government agency failed to adjust for a much higher survey nonresponse rate. The corrected figures showed that instead of a 7 percent decline in the number of people laid off between 1993 and 1996, as had been first reported, there was no change.[12]

Reliability.   Problems with reliability can plague existing statistics research. Reliability problems develop when official definitions or the method of collecting information changes over time. Official definitions of work injury, disability, unemployment, and the like change periodically. Even if a researcher learns of such changes, consistent measurement over time is impossible. For example, during the early 1980s, the method for calculating the U.S. unemployment rate changed. Previously, the unemployment rate was calculated as the number of unemployed persons divided by the number in the civilian work force. The new method divided the number of unemployed by the civilian work force plus the number of people in the military. Likewise, when police departments computerize their records, there is an apparent increase in crimes reported, not because crime increases but due to improved record keeping.

Reliability can be a serious problem in official government statistics. This goes beyond recognized problems, such as the police stopping poorly dressed people more than well-dressed people, hence poorly dressed, lower-income people appear more often in arrest statistics. For example, the U.S. Bureau of Labor Statistics found a 0.6 percent increase in the female unemployment rate after it used gender-neutral measurement procedures. Until the mid-1990s, interviewers asked women only whether they had been "keeping house or something else?" The women who answered "keeping house" were categorized as housewives, and not unemployed. Because the women were not asked, this occurred even if the women had been seeking work. Once women were asked the same question as men, "Were you working or something else?" more women said they were not working but doing "something else" such as looking for work. This shows the importance of methodological details in how government statistics get created.

Researchers often use official statistics for international comparisons but national governments collect data differently and the quality of data collection varies. For example, in 1994, the official unemployment rate reported for the United States was 7 percent, Japan's was 2.9 percent, and France's was 12 percent. If the nations defined and gathered data the same way, including discouraged workers and involuntary part-time workers rates, the rates would have been 9.3 percent for the United States, 9.6 percent for Japan, and 13.7 percent for France. To evaluate the quality of official government statistics, *The Economist* magazine asked a team of 20 leading statisticians to evaluate the statistics of 13 nations based on freedom from political interference, reliability, statistical methodology, and coverage of topics. The top five nations in order were Canada, Australia, Holland, France, and Sweden. The United States was tied for sixth with Britain and Germany. The United States spent more per person gathering its statistics than all nations except Australia and it released data the fastest. The quality of U.S. statistics suffered from being highly decentralized, having fewer statisticians employed than any nation, and politically motivated cutbacks on the range of data collected.[13]

Missing Data.   One problem that plagues researchers who use existing statistics and documents is that of missing data. Sometimes, the data were collected but have been lost. More frequently, the data were never collected. The decision to collect official information is made within government agencies. The decision to ask questions on a survey whose data are later made publicly available is made by a group of researchers. In both cases, those who decide what to collect may not collect what another researcher needs in order to address a research question. Government agencies start or stop collecting information for political, budgetary, or other reasons. For example, during the early 1980s, cost-cutting measures by the U.S. federal government stopped the collection of much information that social researchers had found

valuable. Missing information is especially a problem when researchers cover long time periods. For instance, a researcher interested in the number of work stoppages and strikes in the United States can obtain data from the 1890s to the present, except for a five-year period after 1911 when the federal government did not collect the data. (See Box 9.9 for an existing statistics example.)

ISSUES OF INFERENCE AND THEORY TESTING

Inferences from Nonreactive Data

A researcher's ability to infer causality or test a theory on the basis of nonreactive data is limited. It is difficult to use unobtrusive measures to establish temporal order and eliminate alternative explanations. In content analysis, a researcher cannot generalize from the content to its effects on those who read the text, but can only use the correlation logic of survey research

---

 Box 9.9   Existing Statistics, Androgynous First Names, and Collective Behavior

An androgynous first name is one that can be for either a girl or boy without clearly marking the child's gender. Some argue that the feminist movement decreased gender marking in a child's name as part of its broader societal influence to reduce gender distinctions and inequality. Others observe that gender remains the single-most predominant feature of naming in most societies. Even when racial groups or social classes invent distinctive new first names, the gender distinctions are retained.

Lieberson and colleagues (2000) examined existing statistical data in the form of computerized records from the birth certificates of 11 million births of White children in the state of Illinois from 1916 to 1989. They found that androgynous first names are

rare (about 3 percent) and that there has been a very slight historical trend toward androgyny, but only in very recent years. In addition, parents give androgynous names to girls more than to boys, and gender segregation in naming is unstable (i.e., a name tends to lose its androgynous meaning over time). The authors noted that the way parents name children mimics a pattern of collective behavior found to operate in another research area: the racial segregation of neighborhoods. Change in residence is unequal among races with less movement by the dominant group; the less powerful group moves to occupy areas that the dominant group has abandoned; and integration is unstable, with new segregation reappearing after some time.

to show an association among variables. Unlike the ease of survey research, a researcher does not ask respondents direct questions to measure variables, but relies on the information available in the text.

Ethical Concerns

Ethical concerns are not at the forefront of most nonreactive research because the people being studied are not directly involved. The primary ethical concern is the privacy and confidentiality of using information gathered by someone else. Another ethical issue is that official statistics are social and political products. Implicit theories and value assumptions guide which information is collected and the categories used when gathering it. Measures or statistics that are defined as official and collected on a regular basis are objects of political conflict and guide the direction of policy. By defining one measure as official, public policy is shaped toward outcomes that would be different if an alternative, but equally valid, measure had been used. For example, the collection of information on many social conditions (e.g., the number of patients who died while in public mental hospitals) was stimulated by political activity during the Great Depression of the 1930s. Previously, the conditions were not defined as sufficiently important to warrant public attention. Likewise, information on the percentage of non-White students enrolled in U.S. schools at various ages is available only since 1953, and for specific non-White races only since the 1970s. Earlier, such information was not salient for public policy.

The collection of official statistics stimulates new attention to a problem, and public concern about a problem stimulates the collection of new official statistics. For example, drunk driving became a bigger issue once statistics were collected on the number of automobile accidents and on whether alcohol was a factor in an accident.

Political and social values influence decisions about which existing statistics to collect. Most official statistics are designed for top-down bureaucratic or administrative planning purposes. They may not conform to a researcher's purposes or the purposes of people opposed to bureaucratic decision makers. For example, a government agency measures the number of tons of steel produced, miles of highway paved, and average number of people in a household. Information on other conditions such as drinking-water quality, time needed to commute to work, stress related to a job, or number of children needing child care may not be collected because officials say it is unimportant. In many countries, the gross national product (GNP) is treated as a critical measure of societal progress. But GNP ignores noneconomic aspects of social life (e.g., time spent playing with one's children) and types of work (e.g., housework) that are not paid. The information available reflects the outcome of political debate and the values of officials who decide which statistics to collect.[14]

CONCLUSION

In this chapter, you have learned about several types of nonreactive research techniques. They are ways to measure or observe aspects of social life without affecting those who are being studied. They result in objective, numerical information that can be analyzed to address research questions. The techniques can be used in conjunction with other types of quantitative or qualitative social research to address a large number of questions.

As with any form of quantitative data, researchers need to be concerned with measurement issues. It is easy to take available information from a past survey or government document, but what it measures may not be the construct of interest to the researcher.

You should be aware of two potential problems in nonreactive research. First, the availability of existing information restricts the questions that a researcher can address. Second, the nonreactive variables often have weaker validity because they do not measure the construct of interest. Although existing statistics and secondary data analysis are low-cost research techniques, the researcher lacks control over, and substantial knowledge of, the data collection process. This introduces a potential source of errors about which researchers need to be especially vigilant and cautious.

In the next chapter, we move from designing research projects and collecting data to analyzing data. The analysis techniques apply to the quantitative data you learned about in the previous chapters. So far, you have seen how to move from a topic, to a research design and measures, to collecting data. Next, you will learn how to look at data and see what they can tell you about a hypothesis or research question.

Key Terms

accretion measures
coding
coding system
content analysis
erosion measures
fallacy of misplaced concreteness
General Social Survey (GSS)
latent coding
manifest coding
nonreactive
recording sheet
Statistical Abstract of the United States
structured observation
text
unobtrusive measures

Endnotes

1. See Webb and colleagues (1981:7–11).
2. For definitions of content analysis, see Holsti (1968:597), Krippendorff (1980:21–24), Markoff and associates (1974:5–6), Stone and Weber (1992), and Weber (1983, 1984, 1985:81, note 1).
3. Weitzman and colleagues (1972) is a classic in this type of research.

4. Stone and Weber (1992) and Weber (1984, 1985) summarized computerized content analysis techniques.
5. See Andren (1981:58–66) for a discussion of reliability. Coding categorization in content analysis is discussed in Holsti (1969:94–126).
6. A discussion of social indicators can be found in Carley (1981). Also see Bauer (1966), Duncan (1984:233–235), Juster and Land (1981), Land (1992), and Rossi and Gilmartin (1980).
7. Many non-English yearbooks are also produced; for example, *Statistiches Jahrbuch* for the Federal Republic of Germany, *Annuaire Statistique de la France* for France, *Year Book Australia* for Australia, and Denmark's *Statiskisk Ti Arsoversigt*. Japan produces an English version of its yearbook called the *Statistical Handbook of Japan*.
8. Guides exist for the publications of various governments—for example, the *Guide to British Government Publications, Australian Official Publications,* and *Irish Official Publications.* Similar publications exist for most nations.
9. See Churchill (1983:140–167) and Stewart (1984) for lists of business information sources.
10. Other major U.S. archives of survey data include the National Opinion Research Center, University of Chicago; the Survey Research Center, University of California–Berkeley; the Behavioral Sciences Laboratory, University of Cincinnati; Data and Program Library Service, University of Wisconsin–Madison; the Roper Center, University of Connecticut–Storrs; and the Institute for Research in Social Science, University of North Carolina–Chapel Hill. Also see Kiecolt and Nathan (1985) and Parcel (1992).
11. For a discussion of these issues, see Dale and colleagues (1988:27–31), Maier (1991), and Parcel (1992). Horn (1993:138) gives a good discussion with examples of the fallacy of misplaced concreteness.
12. See Stevenson (1996).
13. See *The Economist,* "The Good Statistics Guide" (September 11, 1993), "The Overlooked Housekeeper" (February 5, 1994), and "Fewer Damned Lies?" (March 30, 1996).
14. See Block and Burns (1986), Carr-Hill (1984), Hindess (1973), Horn (1993), Maier (1991), and Van den Berg and Van der Veer (1985).

CHAPTER 10

Analysis of Quantitative Data

by Anne Laurel Marenco

INTRODUCTION

After collecting quantitative data, the next step is the analysis. Whether you ever analyze data after this class or not, you will always be exposed to research findings. A good consumer of research is skeptical about research.

CODING DATA

After you collect your completed surveys, you need to code them so that you can process the data. You need to assign numbers to variables that are not numerical in nature, such as a Likert type question about agreement to the comfort of a living room design. Your question is "How much do you agree that the living room seen in this photo would be comfortable for your family to live in?" The response choices, or attributes, are strongly agree, slightly agree, slightly disagree, and strongly disagree. When coding or assigning numbers to the attributes of an ordinal level variable such as this one, we generally assign greater numbers to more of the variable. Since this variable is measuring agreement, we want higher numbers to be more agreement. So, strongly disagree should equal a value, or score, of 1, slightly disagree = 2, slightly agree = 3, and strongly agree = 4.

If we use, as we usually do, a computer to analyze our data, we need to assign a number to every attribute of a variable. For nominal level variables, assign a number at random. For example it does not matter if we assign male = 1 and female = 2 or female = 1 and male = 2. Remember that nominal level variables are just categories; one is not more of the other. This is true of many demographic variables such as religion, ethnicity, major in school, and geographic locale to name a few. Now that you know how to code nominal and ordinal level variables, what about interval and ratio level variables? Remember that these variables are those where numbers are the attributes such as number of children, dress size, square footage of a room, calories consumed at a meal, and mortgage amount. Since they are numerical in nature we don't need to code them.

UNIVARIATE DESCRIPTIVE STATISTICS

Uni as in unicycle means one; variate means variable, so univariate statistics look at one variable. Descriptive statistics are those that describe your data. This is always the starting point in data analysis.

FREQUENCY DISTRIBUTIONS

A frequency distribution is the first step in any quantitative analysis. How many people chose each attribute of the variable? Suppose you have the variable "employment status." A frequency distribution of this variable might reveal that 626 of your respondents work full time, 448 work part time, and 102 are unemployed. These numbers may be represented in a table similar to Table 10.1. If we look at the number of part time workers, 448, we don't really know much about them, if they are typical of our respondents or not, so we calculate what percentage they represent by dividing this number by the total number of respondents (N) and multiplying by 100 ($448/1176 * 100 = 38.0952381$). We can round this number to one decimal place and call it 38.1%.

With any chart or graph, you must label the X and Y axes and include a descriptive caption. If you are using APA format, the caption for a figure goes below the figure.

MEASURES OF CENTRAL TENDENCY

Measures of central tendency are measures of the average. In statistics there are three ways to measure the average and each is appropriate for different levels of measurement. For nominal level data the only average you can use is the *mode*. For ordinal level data you can use the mode or the *median*. For interval or ratio level data you can use the mode, median, or the *mean*. Use the most sophisticated level of central tendency that is appropriate.

TABLE 10.1   Employment Status, $N = 1176$.

Employment Status	N	%
Full-time	626	53.2
Part-time	448	38.1
Unemployed	102	8.7

Mode

The mode is simply the most frequently occurring value. Looking back at our employment status variable, the modal value is full-time. So the "average" employment status is fulltime. However, that doesn't tell us much so in general with nominal level data we report the number and percentage of each attribute as seen in Table 10.1.

Median

The median is the middle value. Half of the respondents' values are above the median and half are below. So if I have an ordinal level variable such as letter grades (A+, A, A–, B+, B, B–, C+, C, C–, D+, D, D–, F) I can take all of the grades and line them up in order from highest to lowest (or lowest to highest) and find the middle value by adding N (total number of respondents) plus 1 and dividing by 2. I have 13 values, so $13 + 1/2 = 7$. So the 7th score (after lining up highest to lowest) is the median value, C+ is the median grade possible. Now what if I have actual students with the following grades: A, C+, B–, C+, A–, B+, B. What is the median grade? Well, let's line them up: A, A–, B+, B, B–, C+, C+. If $7 + 1/2 = 4$, then B is the median grade. If you have an even number of scores there is just one more step. The result of $N+1/2$ will be something point 5. Let's say we also had a student with an A+ in the above example, so now we have eight scores (A+, A, A–, B+, B, B–, C+, C+). $8 + 1/2 = 4.5$. This just means that the median is half way between the 4th and 5th values. If your level of measurement is interval or ratio you can just take the 4th and 5th values

and add them together and divide by two, but for an ordinal variable, you just have to say that the median is halfway between B and B+ in our case.

Mean

The mean is what most people think of when asked about the average. To calculate the mean you add up all the scores and divide by N (the total number of respondents). If I have respondents with the following ages 18, 22, 17, 23, 20, 22, 21, what is their mean age? $18 + 22 + 17 + 23 + 20 + 22 + 21 = 143/7 = 20.4$ years.

Now compare the mode, median, and mean for these ages. What is the median age? Line up all of the ages in order from lowest to highest: 17 18 20 21 22 22 23. $7+1/2 = 4$, the 4th value (the median) is 21. How about the mode? Only the value 22 shows up more than once, so 22 is the modal age. The mean, median, and mode are 20.4, 21, and 22. They are all good measures of central tendency in this case, so we would use the most sophisticated measure, the mean.

Let's compare the three measures of central tendency for the variable income. You have five respondents with incomes of $1,000,000, $40,000, $30,000, $20,000, and $10,000. What are the mean, median, and modal income? The mean is $220,000, the median is $30,000, and there is no mode. Which is more descriptive of these data? The mean is no where near the person who earns $1,000,000 and also no where near anyone else. But the median is a value that seems to represent the average of most of the data; it's not influenced by the million dollar earner, so it's the best measure of central tendency for these particular data.

SKEWNESS

The million dollar earner *skews* the data or pulls it to one end. The top panel of Figure 10.1 shows a normal distribution of interval/ratio level data where the mean, median, and mode all are the same value and the curve is symmetrical. The two lower frequency distributions in Figure 10.1 show skewed data. The left diagram

FIGURE 10.1   Measures of Central Tendency

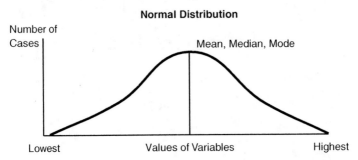

Normal Distribution

Number of
Cases

Mean, Median, Mode

Lowest   Values of Variables   Highest

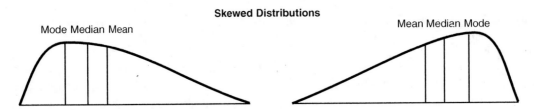

Skewed Distributions

Mode Median Mean

Mean Median Mode

Taken from: *Basics of Social Research: Qualitative and Quantitative Approaches*, Second Edition,
by W. Lawrence Neuman.

is skewed to the right which results in the mean being pulled up to a higher value. The right diagram is skewed to the left which results in the mean being pulled down to a lower value. If your data are skewed look critically at the mean and median and choose the median if it's more descriptive of the data as in our income example income above.

VARIATION OR DISPERSION

It is interesting to know the average value, but how far do your data spread out? Are the bell shaped curves we saw in Figure 10.1 tall and skinny or really spread out and relatively flat?

RANGE

The *range* is one way we look at variation in ordinal, interval, or ratio level data. The range looks at the difference between the highest and lowest values. In our age example above the highest age is 23 and the lowest is 17, so the range is 6. Let's say you had a survey where

people's ages were 16–31, the range is 15. If we made graphs of these two groups of data the second curve would be more spread out.

VARIANCE AND STANDARD DEVIATION

Variance (S^2) and standard deviation (S) are important to understand for two reasons. It tells us how much distance is between scores. A higher standard deviation value means greater distance or variability and a lower value means less variability for interval or ratio level data. It is also used as a stepping stone for other more sophisticated statistics. Calculating standard deviation by hand is very easy, but you probably would not want to do it for more than twenty cases or so. Some calculators and of course computer programs can calculate this for you in seconds. Statisticians know that when data are normally distributed, about 68% of cases will be within one standard deviation greater or less than the mean, about 95% of cases will be within two standard deviations, and about 99% of cases will be within three standard deviations. To calculate standard deviation, use the following formula:

$$S^2 = \frac{\sum (X-\overline{X})^2}{N-1}$$

Σ = sum of $(X-\overline{X})^2$
X = individual scores
$\overline{X}$ = mean of all scores
N = the number of scores

To calculate standard deviation (S) take the square root of your answer for variance (S^2).

Let's say we have nine respondents with the following number of credit cards: 4, 5, 4, 6, 9, 5, 11, 3, 7. What is the standard deviation of these scores? Well the formula above asks for some numbers: the individual scores, we have that, that's our data we collected about number of credit cards as signified by X; the mean of the scores, we can calculate that; N, we have that, that's how many respondents we have. The rest of the formula just tells us to add, subtract, square, or take the square root. If we put our data into a table, it makes it easier to keep track. Let's take it step by step.

Step 1. Enter your data into a table with the headings below; be sure to look at what the headings ask for.

Respondent #	X	$\overline{X}$	$(X-\overline{X})$	$(X-\overline{X})^2$
1	4			
2	5			
3	4			
4	6			
5	9			
6	5			
7	11			
8	3			
9	7			
Total	54			

Step 2. Calculate the mean (add up all the scores, as signified by X, and divide by the total number of scores, as signified by N, to calculate a mean of 6).

Now enter the mean (6) into each cell in the column labeled as the mean (as signified by $(\overline{X})$).

Respondent #	X	$\overline{X}$	$(X-\overline{X})$	$(X-\overline{X})^2$
1	4	6		
2	5	6		
3	4	6		
4	6	6		
5	9	6		
6	5	6		
7	11	6		
8	3	6		
9	7	6		
Total	54			

Step 3. Subtract the mean from each individual score (be sure to put in the sign, positive or negative). Then add up these values. They should equal zero. If not you have either calculated the mean incorrectly, subtracted incorrectly, or added them up incorrectly. Or perhaps you have rounded your values, in that case you want the sum of $X - \overline{X}$ to be as close to zero as possible to accurately calculate your standard deviation. Using more decimal places will yield a sum closer to zero.

Respondent #	X	$\overline{X}$	$(X-\overline{X})$	$(X-\overline{X})^2$
1	4	6	-2	
2	5	6	-1	
3	4	6	-2	
4	6	6	-0	
5	9	6	3	
6	5	6	-1	
7	11	6	5	
8	3	6	-3	
9	7	6	1	
Total	54		0	

Step 4. Now square the $X - \overline{X}$ values and add them up. You have done the top of the formula for variance, now all you need to do is the bottom half, divide, and take the square root.

Respondent #	X	$\bar{X}$	$(X-\bar{X})$	$(X-\bar{X})^2$
1	4	6	–2	4
2	5	6	–1	1
3	4	6	–2	4
4	6	6	–0	0
5	9	6	3	9
6	5	6	–1	1
7	11	6	5	25
8	3	6	–3	9
9	7	6	1	1
Total	54		0	54

Step 5. $N-1 = 9-1 = 8$.
Step 6. $54/8 = 6.75$

Step 7. The square root of 6.75 is 2.598076211. The standard deviation of your data on credit card ownership is 2.6 cards. The mean number of credit cards is six cards, so 68% of the people you asked will have one standard deviation more or less cards. Sixty-eight percent of your respondents have from 3.4 to 8.6 cards. Ninety-five percent of your respondents have two standard deviations plus or minus of the mean or .8 to 11.2 cards. If you noticed, all of your respondents have from 4 to 11 credit cards, that's because your data are not normally distributed. Are they skewed to the right or the left? The mean is six and the median is five, so it's skewed to the right, remember right skewed pulls the mean above the median.

Bivariate Descriptive Statistics

Bivariate statistics look at two variables. You may have univariate data that tell you how many men and women you have in your department, and univariate data that tell you how many are apparel design majors and how many are apparel merchandising majors. Until you look at these two variables together you don't know if men or women tend to be one or the other.

Crosstabulation

We looked at frequencies, or tabulations, with univariate statistics, a crosstabulation looks at

TABLE 10.2 Crosstabulation of Major by Sex.

Sex	Major	
	Design	Merchandising
Male	47	13
Female	16	82

two variables (or more) and how they intersect. Draw yourself a grid with enough rows and columns to accommodate the number of attributes each variable has. We have the variable sex, with two attributes, male and female. Our other variable is major with two attributes, apparel design and apparel merchandising. Now you would look at each of your surveys and enter the number of males who are design majors, etc. You end up with something like Table 10.2. If we look at it, we notice that males tend to be design majors and females tend to be merchandising majors.

Percentaging

These numbers may be interesting to you, but we can go one step further in describing these data, let's calculate some percentages.

Step 1, first we need to calculate the totals.

Sex	Major		Total
	Design	Merchandising	
Male	47	13	60
Female	16	82	98
Total	63	95	158

Step 2, now calculate what percentage of each sex are each major. Among the males in this sample what percentage are design majors = 47/60 * 100 = 78.3%. Males who are merchandising majors = 13/60 * 100 = 21.7%. We refer to these as row percentages.

	Major		Total
Sex	Design	Merchandising	
Male	47 78.3%	13 21.7%	60
Female	16 16.3%	82 83.7%	98
Total	63	95	158

Step 3, now do the same thing for the majors (column percentages). Of those who are design majors, what percentage are male? 47/63*100 = 74.6%. So of males, 78.3% are design majors, and of the design majors, 74.6% are male. In this example males tend to be design majors and design majors tend to be male. If we had variables with more attributes we may not have such a clear cut distribution. For example, if we had a representation of all of the subspecialties in the FCS discipline and data about what level in college they were, we may have data that reveal that most graduate level students are nutrition majors, but most nutrition majors are seniors.

	Major		Total
Sex	Design	Merchandising	
Male	47 74.6%	13 13.7%	60
Female	16 25.4%	82 86.1%	98
Total	63	95	158

Multivariate Descriptive Statistics

Multivariate is the term used for any statistical procedure that uses more than two variables.

Factorial Designs

Factorial designs allow for two independent variables. These variables can be nominal level or higher. Let's say you have a variable called marital status with married and single as the attributes (a nominal level variable). You also have a variable called sex with male and female as the attributes

(a nominal level variable). You further have a dependent variable (see chapter 4) called life satisfaction score which is an interval level variable ranging from 1–8. In a factorial design the dependent variable must be interval or ratio level. You are interested in the combined affect of marital status (independent variable 1 or $X1$) and sex (independent variable 2 or $X2$) on life satisfaction (dependent variable or Y). Let's set this up with a grid that looks a bit like the grid we used in the crosstabulation.

Step 1, enter the mean life satisfaction score for all married males. You can sort your surveys into four piles, married men, married women, unmarried men, and unmarried women. Now add up the life satisfaction score for each married male and divide by the number of married males. Now enter the mean life satisfaction score for all married females. Finally enter the mean scores for all unmarried males and females.

		Married	
		Yes	No
Sex	Male	8.0	6.0
	Female	7.0	9.5

Step 2, calculate the marginal means; the effect of each independent variable alone regardless of the other independent variable. For males the marginal mean is the mean for married males plus the mean for unmarried males divided by two.

		Married		Marginal means
		yes	no	
Sex	Male	8.0	6.0	7.0
	Female	7.0	9.5	8.25
Marginal means		7.5	7.75	

Step 3, interpret the means, marginals first. When looking at the effect sex has on life satisfaction, females have greater life satisfaction (8.25) than males (7.00). Marital status does little to predict life satisfaction (7.5 and 7.75). When the two variables are combined, we find that unmarried females have the highest life satisfaction score (9.5) followed by married males (8.0). We don't know if these scores are significantly different from each other, we would need a *t*–Test to establish that (discussed later in this chapter).

Descriptive vs. Inferential Statistics

The goal of research is often more than just describing data. You may want to predict something or investigate if relationships you observe are due to chance or are real relationships. When you choose a random sample from a larger population, you want to draw inferences about that population, hence you use inferential statistics. When using inferential statistics, we state a hypothesis and a null hypothesis. Then we set a significance level. Then we calculate the desired statistic.

Statistical Significance
If our result is significant that means that the result we found is not likely due to chance. If the result is significant it tells us that the relationship is *likely*; it doesn't *prove* anything with 100% certainty.

Levels of Significance
The most common level of significance for the FCS discipline is .05 which means the result will be found by chance only 5% of the time. So 95% of the time this result reflects a real relationship. If our results are significant we can reject the null hypothesis (the hypothesis of no relationship) and accept the alternative hypothesis.

Type I and Type II Errors
Remember that with a significance level of .05 we have a 5% chance of being incorrect. Sometimes it is not that bad to be wrong, but at other times it might be life threatening as in drug therapy research. Let's look at an example from FCS.

Null hypothesis: There is no difference between the visual appeal of maroon and burgundy fabric.

Alternative hypothesis: Maroon fabric is more visually appealing than burgundy fabric.

I calculate my statistic and find that it is significant so I reject the null hypothesis and accept the alternative hypothesis, but I could be wrong 5% of the time and let's say this is one of those times. I have made a Type I Error (false alarm)-rejected the null hypothesis when it is really true. Ok, so let's play this out. I *think* there is a difference and I assume maroon is more appealing so I make dresses in maroon. Probably not a big deal because people buy these dresses anyway, they don't really care if maroon or burgundy; remember the null hypothesis was really true, there is no difference in the visual appeal of maroon and burgundy.

What about the reverse? My statistical calculation tells me my finding is not significant, so I accept the null hypothesis that there is no difference in visual appeal. I buy burgundy fabric since it's less expensive, but people buy the other company's dresses that they made in maroon; I lose money. A Type II error (a miss) is usually worse than a Type I error. I have lost money. I can lower the chance of a Type I error by lowering the significance level, but that increases the chance of Type II error. I can lower the chance of a Type II error by increasing my sample size. Below we'll put the significance level into practice.

Bivariate Inferential Statistics

This is not a statistics class so the coverage of inferential statistics will be brief: Chi Square, correlatio n, and *t*–test.

Chi Square
Chi square (X^2) is used to examine whether the frequencies that are observed differ from the expected frequencies. Think back to the crosstabulation, is the distribution among the two variables a chance distribution or is there some real relationship there? This statistic can be used with nominal or higher level data. Let's examine the formulas.

$$\chi^2 = \sum \frac{(O - E)^2}{E}$$
$$df = (R - 1)(C - 1)$$

O = observed frequency
E = expected frequency = row total * column total / N
N = total number of participants
R = # of rows
C = # of columns
df = degrees of freedom

Step 1, start with a crosstabulation of your data. These are your observed frequencies from your data collection.

Divorced			
Religious	**No**	**Yes**	**Total**
Not at all	85	25	
Somewhat	520	120	
Very	220	30	
Total			**N = 1000**

Step 2, calculate row and column totals and expected frequencies. I put the observed frequencies at the top left and the expected frequencies on the bottom right of each cell to keep them straight. For not at all religious, non divorced participants, expected is calculated as 110 * 825/1000 = 90.75.

Divorced			
Religious	**No**	**Yes**	**Total**
Not at all	85 / 90.75	25 / 19.25	110
Somewhat	520 / 528	120 / 112	640
Very	220 / 206.25	30 / 43.75	250
Total	825	175	**N = 1000**

Step 3, next I make a similar grid to enter the $(O - E)^2/E$ values. For not at all religious, non divorced individuals the calculation is $(85–90.75)^2/90.75 = .364325068$.

Divorced		
Religious	**No**	**Yes**
Not at all	.3643	1.7175
Somewhat	.1212	.5714
Very	.9167	4.3214

Step 4, add up all these values. So, for these data, $\chi 2 = .3643 + 1.7175 + .1212 + .5714 + .9167 + 4.3214 = 8.012$. Now calculate the degrees of freedom. $df = (r–1)(c–1) = (3 \text{ rows} – 1)(2 \text{ cols} – 1) = (2)(1) = 2$. Degrees of freedom refers to the number of values that are free to vary once you know the marginal totals.

Take a look at the critical values of $\chi 2$ table in Appendix A1. The critical value for 2 degrees of freedom and .05 probability level is 5.991. The obtained value from above is 8.012 which is greater than the critical value so it is significant. The frequencies we observed in these data would not have occurred by chance. There is a relationship between religiousness and divorce. We can't say for sure exactly what this relationship is but we can look at the crosstabulation and make some general statements such as people who are more religious are less likely to be divorced in this sample. However we don't know if they are *significantly* less likely to be divorced, we need other statistics to determine that.

t-Test

A *t*-Test is used to test whether two groups (a nominal dichotomous variable) are statistically different from each other on a certain measure (interval or ratio level; i.e., diet results in pounds lost of males and females; aggression scores of boys and girls; visual appeal scores of maroon and burgundy).

The *t*-value is derived from the between group difference divided by the within groups variability.

Between group difference: how are the two groups different from each other? What is the difference between the groups? What makes them distinct?

Within group variability: the variability about the mean. How does each group alone vary? Let's take a look at the formula.

$$t = \frac{\overline{X}_1 - \overline{X}_2}{\sqrt{\frac{S_1^2}{N_1} + \frac{S_2^2}{N_2}}}$$

df = total # of participants − # of groups

Nothing new here except the group number as designated by the subscript 1 or 2.

$\overline{X}_1$ = mean for group 1

$\overline{X}_2$ = mean for group 2

S^2_1 = variance for group 1

S^2_2 = variance for group 2

N_1 = number of respondents for group 1

N_2 = number of respondents for group 2

The two groups in our example each have 10 respondents, 20 total respondents, but you may not have an equal number in your two groups

Let's say we have data for life satisfaction scores for married men and women. Your hypothesis is that their scores will be significantly different.

Step 1, yes another grid; it is somewhat similar to the grid we used for variance. Fill in your data.

Step 2, calculate the mean and subtract the mean from each individual score and square it. Add up these two columns and be sure that the sum of X−$\overline{X}$ equals zero, or as close to it as possible. Calculate the variance for groups 1 and 2.

Step 3, now plug these values in to the formula.

$$\text{So, } t = \frac{\overline{X}_1 - \overline{X}_2}{\sqrt{\frac{S_1^2}{N_1} + \frac{S_2^2}{N_2}}}$$

$$t = \frac{3.1 - 5.2}{\sqrt{\frac{1.4333}{10} + \frac{1.2889}{10}}}$$

and,

$$t = \frac{-2.1}{\sqrt{.1433 + .1289}}$$

Therefore,

$$t = \frac{-2.1}{\sqrt{.2722}}$$

Thus,

$$t = \frac{-2.1}{.5217}$$

$$t = -4.0253$$

The degrees of freedom = the total number of participants (N) minus the number of groups = 20 − 2 = 18. Take a look at Appendix A2 at the critical values of t table. You would use the first line of significance values if you stated a 1-tailed hypothesis (directional; i.e., married males will have significantly higher life satisfaction scores than married females) and the second line if you stated a 2-tailed hypothesis (no direction stated; i.e., married males and females will have significantly different life satisfaction scores). Our hypothesis was 2-tailed; life satisfaction scores would be different for married men and women. The critical value is 2.101 and our calculated value is .025. Now don't be confused by the negative sign, when deciding if the value is significant or not, we look at the absolute value (disregard any sign). So our −4.023 IS significant. Now we can consider the sign. A positive sign means that the scores for group one were higher and a negative sign means the scores for group two were higher.

So we reject the null hypothesis that there is no difference and accept the alternate hypothesis that there is a difference in life satisfaction scores for married males and females. Because the t–value is negative, we know that the scores for married males (group 2) were higher than for

Subject#	Females	$(X-\bar{X})$	$(X-\bar{X})^2$	Males	$(X-\bar{X})$	$(X-\bar{X})^2$
1	1			3		
2	2			4		
3	2			5		
4	3			5		
5	3			5		
6	3			5		
7	4			6		
8	4			6		
9	4			6		
10	5			7		
Total						
$\bar{X}$						
S^2						
N						
t						

Subject #	Females	$(X-\bar{X})$	$(X-\bar{X})^2$	Males	$(X-\bar{X})$	$(X-\bar{X})^2$
1	1	-2.1	4.41	3	-2.2	4.84
2	2	-1.1	1.21	4	-1.2	1.44
3	2	-1.1	1.21	5	-0.2	.04
4	3	-0.1	.01	5	-0.2	.04
5	3	-0.1	.01	5	-0.2	.04
6	3	-0.1	.01	5	-0.2	.04
7	4	.9	.81	6	.8	.64
8	4	.9	.81	6	.8	.64
9	4	.9	.81	6	.8	.64
10	5	1.9	3.61	7	1.8	3.24
Total	31	0	12.9	52	0	11.6
$\bar{X}$	3.1			5.2		
s^2			1.4333			1.2899
N			10			10
t						-4.025

married females (group 1); married males are more satisfied than married females. Well you've done the easy part, now the hard part. Why? What might be an explanation for this difference? Is it that married women take care of others in the family? They work for eight hours at their paid jobs and then work the rest of the 24 hours at home? I can't say for sure, but this might have something to do with it.

PEARSON PRODUCT MOMENT CORRELATION COEFFICIENT (r)

You may be interested in how strongly two interval or ratio level variables are related to each other. Related, associated, correlated are used interchangeably in this context. If they are related, they vary together. As one variable changes in value, so does the other. A correlation can only look at linear relationships, is used with interval or ratio level data, and ranges from –1 to +1.

Direction

Figure 10.2 illustrates four types of relationships. Panel A shows no correlation. As the variable plotted on the X-axis (horizontal axis) increases, the variable plotted on the Y-axis (vertical axis) stays the same; they don't vary together, one increases and the other does not change. This would result from an r value of .00. In Panel B, as variable X increases, so does variable Y. They both increase (same direction) so they are positively correlated. Panel C shows a negative correlation. Variable X increases and variable Y decreases (opposite direction). Panel B illustrates an r value of 1.00 and Panel C illustrates an r value of –1.00; both are perfect correlations. Panel D shows a curvilinear relationship, when X is low, Y is high; when X is at a medium value, Y is lowest; when X is high, Y is high. The Pearson Product Moment Correlation is not able to detect this type of relationship and it is beyond the scope of this class.

FIGURE 10.2

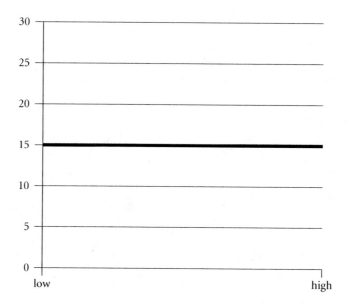

Panel A

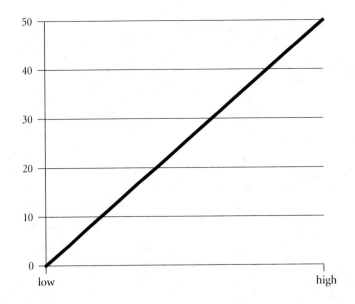

Panel B

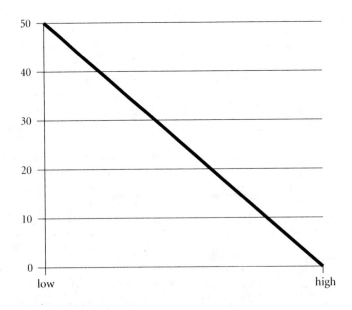

Panel C

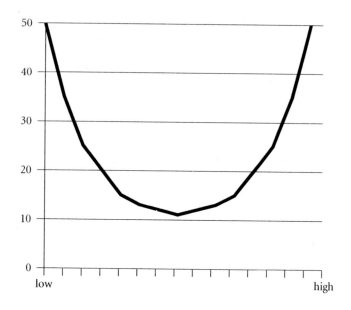

Panel D

Strength

The r value indicates how strong the relationship is. An r of .00 indicates no correlation; .01–.30 indicates a weak correlation; .31–.70 is a moderate correlation; .71–.99 indicates a strong correlation; and 1.00 is a perfect correlation. So when you have a significant r value you need to look at the strength and the direction to interpret it. Let's take a look at the formulas for r.

$$r = \frac{N(\Sigma XY) - (\Sigma X)(\Sigma Y)}{\sqrt{[N(\Sigma X^2) - (\Sigma X)^2] \times [N(\Sigma Y^2) - (\Sigma Y)^2]}}$$

$df = N–2$
X = individual scores of variable X
Y = individual scores of variable Y
N = number of respondents

It's easier than you think. Dissect it. It's just individual scores for X and Y, adding, multiplying, dividing, squaring, and taking the square root. Let's take it step by step in the example of Credit Card Ownership and Shopping Frequency. You have ten subjects and have asked how many credit cards they own and also how many times they went shopping for clothing or accessories in the past 30 days.

Step 1, draw yourself a grid and enter the scores for each variable. We call them X to signify the independent or cause variable and Y to signify the dependent or outcome variable. If you cannot determine which is which, it doesn't really matter in the calculation of a correlation; just put one in the X column and the other in the Y column. In this example, does it make sense that the number of times a person went shopping in the past 30 days influenced the number of credit cards he owns? Probably not. Does it make sense that the number of credit cards a person owns influences the frequency he goes shopping? Well, maybe because I own a large number of credit cards I feel free to shop because I can spread out the debt among several cards. Then again, maybe they are related, but one doesn't cause the other, some other variable I didn't consider caused both of them; then this relationship between number of credit cards and shopping frequency would be a spurious relationship. So let's say number of credit cards is the independent variable (x) and frequency of shopping is the dependent variable (Y).

Subject#	X	X²	Y	Y²	XY
1	4		10		
2	6		15		
3	7		8		
4	8		9		
5	8		7		
6	12		10		
7	14		15		
8	15		13		
9	15		15		
10	17		14		

Step 2, square each X score and each Y score. Multiply X by Y.

Subject#	X	X²	Y	Y²	XY	
1	4	16	10	100	40	
2	6	36	15	225	90	
3	7	49	8	64	56	
4	8	67	9	81	72	
5	8	64	7	79	56	
6	12	144	10	100	120	
7	14	196	27	725	378	
8	15	225	23	529	345	
9	15	225	25	625	375	
10	17	289	19	361	323	
$\sum X$	106	$\sum Y$	155	$\sum XY$	1855	A
$(\sum X^2)$	11236	$(\sum Y^2)$	24025			B
	$\sum X^2$	1308	$\sum Y^2$	2860		C

Step 3, add up all the X values ($\sum X$), Y values ($\sum Y$), and XY values ($\sum XY$)(see row A). Take the sum of X ($\sum X$) and square it [$(\sum X)^2$]. Do the same for Y (see row B). Now add up the squared X and Y values ($\sum X^2$ and (Y^2) (see row C). Now you're ready to plug the values into the formula.

$$r = \frac{10(1855)-(106)(155)}{\sqrt{[10(1308)-11236]\times[10(2860)-24025]}}$$

Remember the order of operations, PEMDAS. Do what is in parentheses or brackets first, then exponents, then multiplication and division in the order they appear left to right, then addition and subtraction in the order they appear left to right.

So,

$$r = \frac{18550-16430}{\sqrt{[13080-11236]\times[28600-24025]}}$$

Then,

$$r = \frac{2120}{\sqrt{[1844]\times[4575]}}$$

And,

$$r = \frac{2120}{843630}$$

Further,

$$r = \frac{2120}{2904.531}$$

S = .729894086

r = .730

Now calculate the degrees of freedom

df = n–2 = 10–2 = 8

Turn to Appendix A3 to the critical values of r table. Look down the degrees of freedom column on the left for 8 and then move two columns to the right to the .05 level of significance column and where 8 df and .05 probability intersect you will find .632. If the value obtained in your calculation is equal to or greater than this critical value, your finding is significant. Our obtained value of .730 is greater than the critical value of .632 so this is a significant result. Now remember that we have to take a look at the strength and direction. This is a strong positive correlation.

To illustrate our finding we can use a scatter plot. The X-axis is the horizontal axis at the

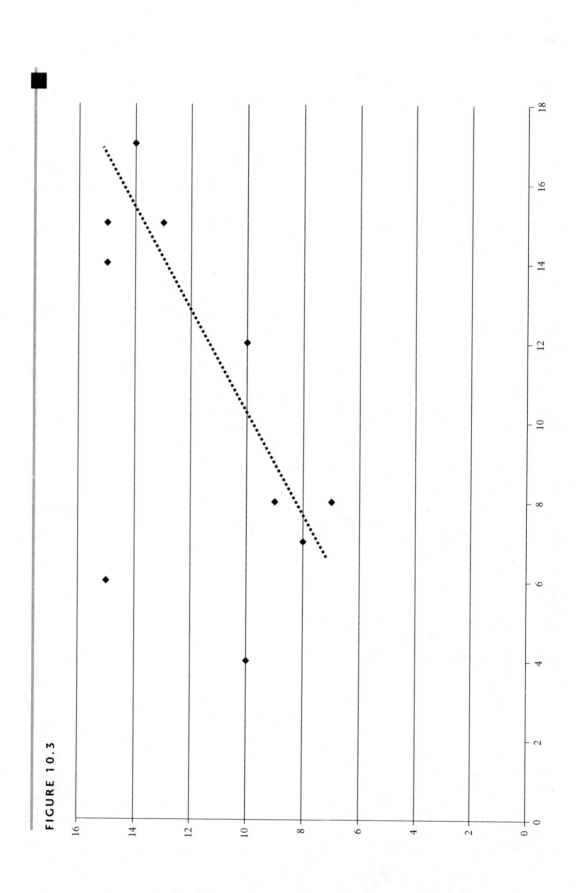

FIGURE 10.3

bottom and the Y-axis is the vertical axis on the left. Plot each set of scores on a scatter plot as shown in Figure 10.3. As you can see the plot points are roughly gathered around the imaginary line that is drawn on the scatter plot.

So what kind of a statement can you make about this relationship? People who own more credit cards shop more frequently than those who own fewer credit cards. That's not to say that one causes the other. Remember that correlation does not mean causation.

CONCLUSION

We have looked at the tip of the iceberg with regard to statistics and calculated some of the most basic. Whether you ever conduct research outside of this class or not, you will be lifelong consumers of research and this fundamental understanding will enable you to be skeptical consumers. Every time you hear that a certain percentage of Americans approve of the president you are consuming research. When you hear these "facts" ask yourself who they asked the questions of, how many respondents there were, and if they calculated the correct statistic.

Key Terms

Bar chart
Bivariate statistics
Chi Square
Codebook
Crosstabulation
Correlation coefficient
Curvilinear relationship
Descriptive statistics
Factorial design
Figures
Frequency distribution
Linear relationship
Marginals
Mean
Median
Mode
Normal distribution
Range
Scatter plot
Skewed distribution
Standard deviation
Statistical significance
Tables
t–Test
Type I error
Type II error
Univariate statistics
Variance

Field Research

INTRODUCTION

This chapter and the two that follow shift from the quantitative style of the past several chapters to the qualitative research style. The qualitative and the quantitative styles can differ a great deal. This chapter describes field research, also called *ethnography* or *participant-observation research.* It is a qualitative style in which a researcher directly observes and participates in small-scale social settings in the present time and in the researcher's home culture.

Many students are excited by field research because it involves hanging out with some exotic group of people. There are no cold mathematics or complicated statistics, and no abstract deductive hypotheses. Instead, there is direct, face-to-face social interaction with "real people" in a natural setting.

In field research, the individual researcher directly talks with and observes the people being studied. Through interaction over months or years, the researcher learns about them, their life histories, their hobbies and interests, and their habits, hopes, fears, and dreams. Meeting new people, developing friendships, and discovering new social worlds can be fun. It is also time consuming, emotionally draining, and sometimes physically dangerous.

Research Questions Appropriate for Field Research

Field research is appropriate when the research question involves learning about, understanding, or describing a group of interacting people. It is usually best when the question is: How do people do Y in the social world? or What is the social world of X like? It can be used when other methods (e.g., survey, experiments) are not practical, as in studying street gangs.

Field researchers study people in a location or setting. It has been used to study entire communities. Beginning field researchers should start with a relatively small group (30 or fewer) who interact with each other on a regular basis in a relatively fixed setting (e.g., a street corner, church, bar, beauty salon, baseball field, etc.).

In order to use consistent terminology, we can call the people who are studied in a field setting *members.* They are insiders or natives in the field and belong to a group, subculture, or social setting that the "outsider" field researcher wants to penetrate and learn about.

Field researchers have explored a wide variety of social settings, subcultures, and aspects of social life[1] (see Figure 11.1). Places my students have conducted successful short-term, small-scale field research studies include a beauty salon, day-care center, bakery, bingo parlor, bowling alley, church, coffee shop, laundromat, police dispatch office, nursing home, tattoo parlor, and weight room.

Ethnography and Ethnomethodology. Two modern extensions of field research, ethnography and ethnomethodology, build on the social constructionist perspective. Each is redefining how field research is conducted. They are not yet the core of field research, so they are discussed only briefly here.

Ethnography comes from cultural anthropology.[2] *Ethno* means people or folk, and *graphy* refers to describing something. Thus *ethnography* means describing a culture and understanding another way of life from the native point of view. Ethnography assumes that people make inferences—that is, go beyond what is explicitly seen or said to what is meant or implied. People display their culture (what people think, ponder, or believe) through behavior (e.g., speech and actions) in specific social contexts. Displays of behavior do not give meaning; rather, meaning is inferred, or someone figures out meaning. Moving from what is heard or observed to what is actually meant is at the center of ethnography. For example, when a student is invited to a "kegger," the student infers that it is an informal party with other student-aged people at which beer will be served, based on his or her cultural knowledge. Cultural knowledge includes symbols, songs, sayings, facts, ways of behaving, and

---

FIGURE 11.1   Examples of Field Research Sites/Topics

Small-Scale Settings

Passengers in an airplane
Bars or taverns
Battered women's shelters
Camera clubs
Laundromats
Social movement organizations
Social welfare offices
Television stations
Waiting rooms

Community Settings

Retirement communities
Small towns
Urban ethnic communities
Working-class neighborhoods

Children's Activities

Children's playgrounds
Little League baseball
Youth in schools
Junior high girl groups

Occupations

Airline attendants
Artists
Cocktail waitresses
Dog catchers

Door-to-door salespersons
Factory workers
Gamblers
Medical students
Female strippers
Police officers
Restaurant chefs
Social workers
Taxi drivers

Deviance and Criminal Activity

Body/genital piercing and branding
Cults
Drug dealers and addicts
Hippies
Nude beaches
Occult groups
Prostitutes
Street gangs, motorcycle gangs
Street people, homeless shelters

Medical Settings and Medical Events

Death
Emergency rooms
Intensive care units
Pregnancy and abortion
Support groups for Alzheimer's caregivers

---

objects (e.g., telephones, newspapers, etc.). We learn the culture by watching television, listening to parents, observing others, and the like.

Cultural knowledge includes both explicit knowledge, what we know and talk about, and tacit knowledge, what we rarely acknowledge. For example, *explicit knowledge* includes the social event (e.g., a "kegger"). Most people can easily describe what happens at one. *Tacit knowledge* includes the unspoken cultural norm for the proper distance to stand from others. People are generally unaware that they use this norm.

They feel unease or discomfort when the norm is violated, but it is difficult to pinpoint the source of discomfort. Ethnographers describe the explicit and tacit cultural knowledge that members use. Their detailed descriptions and careful analysis take what is described apart and put it back together.

Ethnomethodology is a distinct approach developed in the 1960s, with its own unique terminology. It combines theory, philosophy, and method. Some do not consider it a part of sociology.

A simple definition of *ethnomethodology* is the study of commonsense knowledge. Ethnomethodologists study common sense by observing its creation and use in ongoing social interaction in natural settings. Ethnomethodology is a radical or extreme form of field research, based on phenomenological philosophy and a social constructionist approach. It involves the specialized, highly detailed analysis of micro-situations (e.g., transcripts of short conversations or videotapes of social interactions). Compared to other field research, it is more concerned about method and argues that research findings result as much from the method used as from the social life studied.

Ethnomethodology assumes that social meaning is fragile and fluid, not fixed, stable, or solid. Meaning is constantly being created and re-created in an ongoing process. For this reason, ethnomethodologists analyze language, including pauses and the context of speech. They assume that people "accomplish" commonsense understanding by using tacit social-cultural rules, and social interaction is a process of reality construction. People interpret everyday events by using cultural knowledge and clues from the social context. Ethnomethodologists examine how ordinary people in everyday settings apply tacit rules to make sense of social life (e.g., to know whether or not someone is joking).

Ethnomethodologists examine ordinary social interaction in great detail to identify the rules for constructing social reality and common sense, how these rules are applied, and how new rules are created. For example, they argue that standardized tests or survey interviews measure a person's ability to pick up implicit clues and apply common sense more than measuring objective facts.

THE LOGIC OF FIELD RESEARCH

What Is Field Research?

It is difficult to pin down a specific definition of *field research* because it is more of an orientation toward research than a fixed set of techniques to apply.[3] A field researcher uses various methods to obtain information. A *field researcher* is a resourceful, talented individual who has ingenuity and an ability to think on her or his feet while in the field.

Field research is based on naturalism, which is also used to study other phenomena (e.g., oceans, animals, plants, etc.). *Naturalism* involves observing ordinary events in natural settings, not in contrived, invented, or researcher-created settings. Research occurs in the field and outside the safe settings of an office, laboratory, or classroom.

A field researcher's goal is to examine social meanings and grasp multiple perspectives in natural social settings. He or she wants to get inside the meaning system of members and then return to an outside or research viewpoint. To do this, the researcher switches perspectives and looks at the setting from multiple points of view simultaneously.

Field research is usually conducted by a single individual, although small teams have been effective (see Box 11.1). The researcher is directly involved in and part of the social world studied, so his or her personal characteristics are relevant in research. The researcher's direct involvement in the field often has an emotional impact. Field research can be fun and exciting, but it can also disrupt one's personal life, physical security, or mental well-being. More than other types of social research, it reshapes friendships, family life, self-identity, and personal values.

Steps in a Field Research Project

Naturalism and direct involvement mean that field research is less structured than quantitative research. This makes it essential for a researcher to be well organized and prepared for the field. It also means that the steps of a project are not entirely predetermined but serve as an approximate guide or road map (see Box 11.2).

Box 11.1 What Do Field Researchers Do?

A field researcher does the following:

1. Observes ordinary events and everyday activities as they happen in natural settings, in addition to any unusual occurrences

2. Becomes directly involved with the people being studied and personally experiences the process of daily social life in the field setting

3. Acquires an insider's point of view while maintaining the analytic perspective or distance of an outsider

4. Uses a variety of techniques and social skills in a flexible manner as the situation demands

5. Produces data in the form of extensive written notes, as well as diagrams, maps, or pictures to provide very detailed descriptions

6. Sees events holistically (e.g., as a whole unit, not in pieces) and individually in their social context

7. Understands and develops empathy for members in a field setting, and does not just record "cold" objective facts

8. Notices both explicit (recognized, conscious, spoken) and tacit (less recognized, implicit, unspoken) aspects of culture

9. Observes ongoing social processes without upsetting, disrupting, or imposing an outside point of view

10. Copes with high levels of personal stress, uncertainty, ethical dilemmas, and ambiguity

Box 11.2 Steps in Field Research

1. Prepare oneself, read the literature, and defocus.
2. Select a field site and gain access to it.
3. Enter the field and establish social relations with members.
4. Adopt a social role, learn the ropes, and get along with members.
5. Watch, listen, and collect quality data.
6. Begin to analyze data and to generate and evaluate working hypotheses.
7. Focus on specific aspects of the setting and use theoretical sampling.
8. Conduct field interviews with member informants.
9. Disengage and physically leave the setting.
10. Complete the analyses and write the research report.

Note: There is no fixed percentage of time needed for each step. For a rough approximation, Junker (1960:12) suggested that, once in the field, the researcher should expect to spend approximately one-sixth of his or her time observing, one-third recording data, one-third of the time analyzing data, and one-sixth reporting results. Also see Denzin (1989:176) for eight steps of field research.

Flexibility. Field researchers rarely follow fixed steps. In fact, flexibility is a key advantage of field research, which lets a researcher shift direction and follow leads. Good field researchers recognize and seize opportunities, "play it by ear," and rapidly adjust to fluid social situations.

A field researcher does not begin with a set of methods to apply or explicit hypotheses to test. Rather, he or she chooses techniques on the basis of their value for providing information. In the beginning, the researcher expects little control over data and little focus. Once socialized to the setting, however, he or she focuses the inquiry and asserts control over the data.

Getting Organized in the Beginning. Human and personal factors can play a role in any research project, but they are crucial in field research. Field projects often begin with chance occurrences or a personal interest. Field researchers can begin with their own experiences, such as working at a job, having a hobby, or being a patient or an activist.

Field researchers use the skills of careful looking and listening, short-term memory, and regular writing. Before entering the field, a new researcher practices observing the ordinary details of situations and writing them down. Attention to details and short-term memory can improve with practice. Likewise, keeping a daily diary or personal journal is good practice for writing field notes.

As with all social research, reading the scholarly literature helps the researcher learn concepts, potential pitfalls, data collection methods, and techniques for resolving conflicts. In addition, a field researcher finds diaries, novels, journalistic accounts, and autobiographies useful for gaining familiarity and preparing emotionally for the field.

Field research begins with a general topic, not specific hypotheses. A researcher does not get locked into any initial misconceptions. He or she needs to be well informed but open to discovering new ideas. Finding the right questions to ask about the field takes time.

A researcher first empties his or her mind of preconceptions. The researcher should move outside his or her comfortable social niche to experience as much as possible in the field without betraying a primary commitment to being a researcher.

Another preparation for field research is self-knowledge. A field researcher needs to know himself or herself and reflect on personal experiences. He or she can expect anxiety, self-doubt, frustration, and uncertainty in the field. Especially in the beginning, the researcher may feel that he or she is collecting the wrong data and may suffer emotional turmoil, isolation, and confusion. He or she often feels doubly marginal: an outsider in the field setting and also distant from friends, family, and other researchers.[4] The relevance of a researcher's emotional make-up, personal biography, and cultural experiences makes it important to be aware of his or her personal commitments and inner conflicts (see Box 11.3). Fieldwork can have a strong impact on a researcher's identity and outlook. Researchers

may be personally transformed by the field experience. Some adopt new values, interests, and moral commitments, or change their religion or political ideology.[5]

CHOOSING A SITE AND GAINING ACCESS

Although a field research project does not proceed by fixed steps, some common concerns arise in the early stages. These include selecting a site and gaining access to the site, entering the field, learning the ropes, and developing rapport with members in the field.

Selecting a Site and Entering

Where to Observe.   Field researchers talk about doing research on a setting, or *field site*, but this term is misleading. A site is the context in which events or activities occur, a socially defined territory with shifting boundaries. A social group may interact across several physical sites. For example, a college football team may interact on the playing field, in the locker room, in a dormitory, at a training camp, or at a local hangout. The team's field site includes all five locations.

The field site and research question are bound together, but choosing a site is not the same as focusing on a case for study. A *case* is a social relationship or activity; it can extend beyond the boundaries of the site and have links to other social settings. A researcher selects a site, then identifies cases to examine within it—for example, how football team members relate to authority figures.

Selecting a field site is an important decision, and researchers take notes on the site selection processes. Three factors are relevant when choosing a field research site: richness of data, unfamiliarity, and suitability.[6] Some sites are more likely than others to provide rich data. Sites that present a web of social relations, a variety of activities, and diverse events over time provide richer, more interesting data. Beginning

Box 11.3	Field Research at a Country and Western Bar

Eliasoph (1998) conducted field research on several groups in a California community to understand how Americans avoid political expression. One was a social club. Eliasoph describes herself as an "urban, bicoastal, bespectacled, Jewish, Ph.D. candidate from a long line of communists, atheists, liberals, book-readers, ideologues, and arguers" (p. 270). The social club's world was very foreign to her. The social club, the Buffalos, centered on country and western music at a bar, the Silverado Club. She describes it:

The Silverado huddled on a vast, rutted parking lot on what was once wetlands and now was a truck stop, a mile and a half from Amargo's [town name] nuclear battleship station. Occasional gulleys of salt water cattails poked through the wide flat miles of paved malls and gas stations. Giant four-wheeled-drive vehicles filled the parking lot, making my miniature Honda look like a toy. . . . Inside the windowless Silverado, initial blinding darkness gave way to a huge Confederate flag pinned up behind the bandstand, the standard collection of neon beer signs and beer mirrors, men in cowboys hats, cow-

boys shirts and jeans, women in curly perms and tiered flounces of lace or denim skirts, or jeans, and belts with their names embroidered in glitter on the back. (1998:92)

Eliasoph introduced herself as a student. During her two years of research, she endured smoke-filled rooms as well as expensive beer and bottled-water prices; attended a wedding and many dance lessons; and participated in countless conversations and heard many abusive sexist/racist jokes. She listened, asked questions, observed, and took notes in the bathroom. When she returned home after hours with club members, it was to a university crowd who had little understanding of the world she was studying. For them, witty conversation was central and being bored was to be avoided. The club members used more nonverbal than verbal communication and being bored, or sitting and doing nothing, was just fine. The research forced Eliasoph to reexamine her own views and tastes, which she had taken for granted.

---

field researchers should choose an unfamiliar setting. It is easier to see cultural events and social relations in a new site. When "casing" possible field sites, one must consider such practical issues as the researcher's time and skills, serious conflicts among people in the site, the researcher's personal characteristics and feelings, and access to parts of a site.

A researcher's ascriptive characteristics (e.g., age, gender, race) can limit access. Physical access to a site can be an issue. Sites are on a continuum, with open and public areas (e.g., public restaurants, airport waiting areas, etc.) at one end and closed and private settings (e.g., private firms, clubs, activities in a person's home, etc.) at the other. A researcher may find that he or she is not welcome or not allowed on the site, or there are legal and political barriers to access. Laws

and regulations in institutions (e.g., public schools, hospitals, prisons, etc.) restrict access. In addition, institutional review boards may limit field research on ethical grounds.

Level of Involvement. Field roles can be arranged on a continuum by the degree of detachment or involvement a researcher has with members. At one extreme is a detached outsider; at the other extreme is an intimately involved insider.

The field researcher's level of involvement depends on negotiations with members, specifics of the field setting, the researcher's personal comfort, and the particular role adopted in the field. Many move from outsider to insider levels with more time in the field. Each level has its advantages and disadvantages.

Different field researchers advocate different levels of involvement.

Roles at the outsider end of the continuum reduce the time needed for acceptance, make overrapport less an issue, and can sometimes help members open up. They facilitate detachment and protect the researcher's self-identity. A researcher feels marginal. Although there is less risk of "going native," he or she is also less likely to know an insider's experience and misinterpretation is more likely. To really understand social meaning for those being studied, the field researcher must participate in the setting, as others do.

By contrast, roles at the insider end of the continuum facilitate empathy and sharing of a member's experience. The goal of fully experiencing the intimate social world of a member is achieved. Nevertheless, a lack of distance from, too much sympathy for, or overinvolvement with members is likely. A researcher's reports may be questioned, data gathering is difficult, there can be a dramatic impact on the researcher's self, and the distance needed for analysis may be hard to attain.

Gatekeepers. A *gatekeeper* is someone with the formal or informal authority to control access to a site.[7] It can be the thug on the corner, an administrator of a hospital, or the owner of a business. Informal public areas (e.g., sidewalks, public waiting rooms, etc.) rarely have gatekeepers; formal organizations have authorities from whom permission must be obtained.

Field researchers expect to negotiate with gatekeepers and bargain for access. The gatekeepers may not appreciate the need for conceptual distance or ethical balance. The researcher must set nonnegotiable limits to protect research integrity. If there are many restrictions initially, a researcher can often reopen negotiations later, and gatekeepers may forget their initial demands as trust develops. It is ethically and politically astute to call on gatekeepers. Researchers do not expect them to listen to research concerns or care about the findings, except insofar as these findings might provide evidence for someone to criticize them.

Dealing with gatekeepers is a recurrent issue as a researcher enters new levels or areas. In addition, a gatekeeper can shape the direction of research. In some sites, gatekeeper approval creates a stigma that inhibits the cooperation of members. For example, prisoners may not be cooperative if they know that the prison warden gave approval to the researcher.

Strategy for Entering

Entering a field site requires having a flexible strategy or plan of action, negotiating access and relations with members, and deciding how much to disclose about the research to field members or gatekeepers.

Planning. Entering and gaining access to a field site is a process that depends on common-sense judgment and social skills. Field sites usually have different levels or areas, and entry is an issue for each. Entry is more analogous to peeling the layers of an onion than to opening a door. Moreover, bargains and promises of entry may not remain stable over time. A researcher needs fallback plans or may have to return later for renegotiation. Because the specific focus of research may not emerge until later in the research process or may change, it is best to avoid being locked into specifics by gatekeepers.

Negotiation. Social relations are negotiated and formed throughout the process of fieldwork.[8] Negotiation occurs with each new member until a stable relationship develops to gain access, develop trust, obtain information, and reduce hostile reactions. The researcher expects to negotiate and explain what he or she is doing over and over in the field (see Normalizing Social Research later in the chapter).

Deviant groups and elites often require special negotiations for gaining access. To gain access to deviant subcultures, field researchers have used contacts from the researcher's private life, gone to social welfare or law-enforcement agencies where the deviants are processed, advertised for volunteers, offered a service (e.g., counseling) in exchange for access, or gone to a location where deviants hang out and joined a group.

Disclosure. A researcher must decide how much to reveal about himself or herself and the research project. Disclosing one's personal life, hobbies, interests, and background can build trust and close relationships, but the researcher will also lose privacy, and he or she needs to ensure that the focus remains on events in the field.

A researcher also decides how much to disclose about the research project. Disclosure ranges on a continuum from fully covert research, in which no one in the field is aware that research is taking place, to the opposite end, where everyone knows the specifics of the research project. The degree and timing of disclosure depends on a researcher's judgment and particulars in the setting. Disclosure may unfold over time as the researcher feels more secure.

Researchers disclose the project to gatekeepers and others unless there is a good reason for not doing so, such as the presence of gatekeepers who would seriously limit or inhibit research for illegitimate reasons (e.g., to hide graft or corruption). Even in these cases, a researcher may disclose his or her identity as a researcher, but may pose as one who seems submissive, harmless, and interested in nonthreatening issues.

Learning the Ropes

After a field site is selected and access obtained, researchers must learn the ropes, develop rapport with members, adopt a role in the setting, and maintain social relations. Before confronting such issues, the researcher should ask: How will I present myself? What does it mean for me to be a "measurement instrument"? How can I assume an "attitude of strangeness"?

Presentation of Self. People explicitly and implicitly present themselves to others. We display who we are—the type of person we are or would like to be—through our physical appearance, what we say, and how we act. The presentation of self sends a symbolic message. It may be, "I'm a serious, hard-working student," "I'm a warm and caring person," "I'm a cool jock," or "I'm a rebel and party animal." Many selves are possible, and presentations of selves can differ depending on the occasion.

A field researcher is conscious of the presentation of self in the field. For example, how should he or she dress in the field? The best guide is to respect both oneself and those being studied. Do not overdress so as to offend or stand out, but copying the dress of those being studied is not always necessary. A professor who studies street people does not have to dress or act like one; dressing and acting informally is sufficient. Likewise, more formal dress and professional demeanor are required when studying corporate executives or top officials.

A researcher must be aware that self-presentation will influence field relations to some degree. It is difficult to present a highly deceptive front or to present oneself in a way that deviates sharply from the person one is ordinarily.

Researcher as Instrument. The researcher is the instrument for measuring field data. This has two implications. First, it puts pressure on the researcher to be alert and sensitive to what happens in the field and to be disciplined about recording data. Second, it has personal consequences. Fieldwork involves social relationships and personal feelings. Field researchers are flexible about what to include as data and admit their own subjective insights and feelings. Personal, subjective experiences are part of field data. They are valuable both in themselves and for interpreting events in the field. Instead of trying to be objective and eliminate personal reactions, field researchers treat their feelings toward field events as data.

Field research can heighten a researcher's awareness of personal feelings. For example, a researcher may not be fully aware of personal feelings about nudity until he or she is in a nudist colony, or about personal possessions until he or she is in a setting where others "borrow" many items. The researcher's own surprise, indignation, or questioning then may become an opportunity for reflection and insight.

An Attitude of Strangeness.   It is hard to recognize what we are very close to. The everyday world we inhabit is filled with thousands of details. If we paid attention to everything all the time, we would suffer from severe information overload. We manage by ignoring much of what is around us and by engaging in habitual thinking. Unfortunately, we fail to see the familiar as distinctive, and assume that others experience reality just as we do. We tend to treat our own way of living as natural or normal.

Field research in familiar surroundings is difficult because of a tendency to be blinded by the familiar. By studying other cultures, researchers encounter dramatically different assumptions about what is important and how things are done. This confrontation of cultures, or culture shock, has two benefits: It makes it easier to see cultural elements and it facilitates self-discovery. Researchers adopt the attitude of strangeness to gain these benefits. The *attitude of strangeness* means questioning and noticing ordinary details or looking at the ordinary through the eyes of a stranger. Strangeness helps a researcher overcome the boredom of observing ordinary details. It helps him or her see the ordinary in a new way, one that reveals aspects of the setting of which members are not consciously aware. A field researcher adopts both a stranger's and an insider's point of view.

People rarely recognize customs they take for granted. For example, when someone gives us a gift, we say thank you and praise the gift. By contrast, gift-giving customs in many cultures include complaining that the gift is inadequate. The attitude of strangeness helps make the tacit culture visible—for example, that gift givers expect to hear "Thank you" and "The gift is nice," and become upset otherwise.

Strangeness also encourages a researcher to reconsider his or her own social world. Immersion in a different setting breaks old habits of thought and action. He or she finds reflection and introspection easier and more intense when encountering the unfamiliar, whether it is a different culture or a familiar culture seen through a stranger's eyes.

Building Rapport

A field researcher builds rapport by getting along with members in the field. He or she forges a friendly relationship, shares the same language, and laughs and cries with members. This is a step toward obtaining an understanding of members and moving beyond understanding to empathy—that is, seeing and feeling events from another's perspective.

It is not always easy to build rapport. The social world is not all in harmony, with warm, friendly people. A setting may contain fear, tension, and conflict. Members may be unpleasant, untrustworthy, or untruthful; they may do things that disturb or disgust a researcher. An experienced researcher is prepared for a range of events and relationships. He or she may find, however, that it is impossible to penetrate a setting or get really close to members. Settings where cooperation, sympathy, and collaboration are impossible require different techniques.[9]

Charm and Trust.   A field researcher needs social skills and personal charm to build rapport. Trust, friendly feelings, and being well liked facilitate communication and help him or her to understand the inner feelings of others. There is no magical way to do this. Showing a genuine concern for and interest in others, being honest, and sharing feelings are good strategies, but they are not foolproof. It depends on the specific setting and members.

Many factors affect trust and rapport—how a researcher presents himself or herself; the role he or she chooses for the field; and the events that encourage, limit, or make it impossible to achieve trust. Trust is not gained once and for all. It is a developmental process built up over time through many social nuances (e.g., sharing of personal experiences, story telling, gestures, hints, facial expressions). It is constantly re-created and seems easier to lose once it has been built up than to gain in the first place.

Establishing trust is important, but it does not ensure that all information will be revealed. It may be limited to specific areas. For example, trust can be built up regarding financial matters but not to disclose intimate dating behavior. Trust may have to be created anew in each area of inquiry; it requires constant reaffirmation.

Understanding.   Rapport helps field researchers understand members, but understanding is a precondition for greater depth, not an end in itself. It slowly develops in the field as the researcher overcomes an initial bewilderment with a new or unusual language and system of social meaning. Once he or she attains an understanding of the member's point of view, the next step is to learn how to think and act within a member's perspective. This is *empathy,* or adopting another's perspective. Empathy does not necessarily mean sympathy, agreement, or approval; it means feeling things as another does. Rapport helps create understanding and ultimately empathy, and the development of empathy facilitates greater rapport.

RELATIONS IN THE FIELD

You play many social roles in daily life—daughter/son, student, customer, sports fan—and maintain social relations with others. You choose some roles and others are structured for you. Few have a choice but to play the role of son or daughter. Some roles are formal (e.g., bank teller, police chief, etc.), others are informal (flirt, elder statesperson, buddy, etc.). You can switch roles, play multiple roles, and play a role in a particular way. Field researchers play roles in

the field. In addition, they learn the ropes and maintain relations with members.

Roles in the Field

Preexisting versus Created Roles.   At times, a researcher adopts an existing role. Some existing roles provide access to all areas of the site, the ability to observe and interact with all members, the freedom to move around, and a way to balance the requirements of researcher and member. At other times, a researcher creates a new role or modifies an existing one. Duneier (1999), in his four-year study of New York City street vendors, assumed the role of browser, customer, and even magazine vendor.

Limits on the Role Chosen.   The field roles open to a researcher are affected by ascriptive factors and physical appearance. He or she can change some aspects of appearance, such as dress or hairstyle, but not ascriptive features such as age, race, gender, and attractiveness. Nevertheless, such factors can be important in gaining access and can restrict the available roles. For example, Gurney (1985) reported that being a female in a male-dominated setting required extra negotiations and "hassles." Nevertheless, her gender provided insights and created situations that would have been absent with a male researcher.

Since many roles are sex-typed, gender is an important consideration. Female researchers often have more difficulty when the setting is perceived as dangerous or seamy and where males are in control (e.g., police work, fire fighting, etc.). They may be shunned or pushed into limiting gender stereotypes (e.g., "sweet kid," "mascot," "loud mouth," etc.).

New researchers face embarrassment, experience discomfort, and are overwhelmed by the details in the field. For example, in her study of U.S. relocation camps for Japanese Americans during World War II, respected field researcher Rosalie Wax (1971) reported that she endured the discomfort of 120-degree Fahrenheit temperatures, filthy and dilapidated living conditions, dysentery, and mosquitoes. She felt isolated, she cried a lot, and she gained 30 pounds from compulsive eating. After months in the field, she thought she was a total failure; she was distrusted by members and got into fights with the camp administration.

Maintaining a "marginal" status is stressful; it is difficult to be an outsider who is not fully involved, especially when studying settings full of intense feelings (e.g., political campaigns, religious conversions, etc.). The loneliness and isolation of fieldwork may combine with the desire to develop rapport and empathy to cause overinvolvement. A researcher may "go native" and drop the professional researcher's role to become a full member of the group being studied. Or the researcher may feel guilt about learning intimate details as members drop their guard, and may come to overidentify with members.

Normalizing Social Research. A field researcher not only observes and investigates members in the field but is observed and investigated by members as well. In overt field research, members are usually initially uncomfortable with the presence of a researcher. Most are unfamiliar with field research and fail to distinguish between sociologists, psychologists, counselors, and social workers. They may see the researcher as an outside critic or spy, or as a savior or all-knowing expert.

An overt field researcher must *normalize social research*—that is, help members redefine social research from something unknown and threatening to something normal and predictable. He or she can help members manage research by presenting his or her own biography, explaining field research a little at a time, appearing nonthreatening, or accepting minor deviance in the setting (e.g., minor violations of official rules).

Maintaining Relations

Social Relations. With time, a field researcher develops and modifies social relationships. Members who are cool at first may warm up later. Or they may put on a front of initial friendliness, and their fears and suspicions surface only later. A researcher is in a delicate position. Early in a project, when not yet fully aware of everything about a field site, the researcher does not form close relationships because circumstances may change. Yet, if he or she does develop close friends, they can become allies who will defend the researcher's presence and help him or her gain access.

A field researcher monitors how his or her actions or appearance affects members. For example, a physically attractive researcher who interacts with members of the opposite sex may encounter crushes, flirting, and jealousy. He or she develops an awareness of these field relations and learns to manage them.

In addition to developing social relationships, a field researcher must be able to break or withdraw from relationships as well. Ties with one member may have to be broken in order to forge ties with others or to explore other aspects of the setting. As with the end of any friendly relationship, the emotional pain of social withdrawal can affect both the researcher and the member. The researcher must balance social sensitivity and the research goals.

Small Favors. *Exchange relationships* develop in the field, in which small tokens or favors, including deference and respect, are exchanged. A researcher may gain acceptance by helping out in small ways. Exchange helps when access to sensitive issues is limited. A researcher may offer small favors but not burden members by asking for return favors. As the researcher and members share experiences and see each other again, members recall the favors and reciprocate by allowing access. For example, Duneier (1999) used the small favor of watching the tables of street vendors when they had to leave for a short time, such as to use the bathroom.

Conflicts in the Field. Fights, conflict, and disagreements can erupt in the field, or a researcher may study groups with opposing positions. In such situations, the researcher will feel pressure to take sides and will be tested to see if he or she can be trusted. In such occasions, a researcher usually stays on the neutral sidelines and walks a tightrope between opposing sides. This is because once he or she becomes aligned with one side, the researcher will cut off access to the other side. In addition, he or she will see the situation from only one point of view.

Appearing Interested. Field researchers maintain an *appearance of interest* in the field. An experienced researcher appears to be interested in and involved with field events by statements and behaviors (e.g., facial expression, going for coffee, organizing a party, etc.) even if he or she is not truly interested. This is because field relations may be disrupted if the researcher appears to be bored or distracted. Putting up such a temporary front of involvement is a common small deception in daily life and is part of being polite.

Of course, selective inattention (i.e., not staring or appearing not to notice) is also part of acting polite. If a person makes a social mistake (e.g., accidentally uses an incorrect word, passes gas, etc.), the polite thing to do is to ignore it. Selective inattention is used in fieldwork, as well. It gives an alert researcher an opportunity to learn by casually eavesdropping on conversations or observing events not meant to be public.

OBSERVING AND COLLECTING DATA

This section looks at how to get good qualitative field data. Field data are what the researcher experiences and remembers, and what are recorded in field notes and become available for systematic analysis.

Watching and Listening

Observing. In the field, researchers pay attention, watch, and listen carefully. They use all the senses, noticing what is seen, heard, smelled, tasted, or touched. The researcher becomes an instrument that absorbs all sources of information.

A field researcher carefully scrutinizes the physical setting to capture its atmosphere. He or she asks: What is the color of the floor, walls, ceiling? How large is the room? Where are the windows and doors? How is the furniture arranged, and what is its condition (e.g., new or old and worn, dirty or clean)? What type of lighting is there? Are there signs, paintings, plants? What are the sounds or smells?

Why bother with such details? You may have noticed that stores and restaurants often plan lighting, colors, and piped-in music to create a certain atmosphere. Maybe you know that used-car sales people spray a new-car scent into cars or that shops in shopping malls intentionally send out the odor of freshly made cookies. These subtle, unconscious signals influence human behavior.

Observing in field research is often detailed, tedious work. Instead of the quick flash, motivation arises out of a deep curiosity about the details. Good field researchers are intrigued about details that reveal "what's going on here" through careful listening and watching. Field researchers believe that the core of social life is communicated through the mundane, trival, everyday minutia. This is what people often overlook, but field researchers need to learn how to notice.

In addition to physical surroundings, a field researcher observes people and their actions, noting each person's observable physical characteristics: age, sex, race, and stature. People socially interact differently depending on whether another person is 18, 40, or 70 years old; male or female; White or non-White; short and frail or tall, heavyset, and muscular. When noting such characteristics, the researcher is included. For example, an attitude of strangeness heightens sensitivity to a group's racial composition. A researcher who ignores the racial composition of a group of Whites in a multiracial society because he or she too is White is being racially insensitive.

The researcher records such details because something of significance *might* be revealed. It is better to err by including everything than to ignore potentially significant details. For example, "The tall, White muscular 19-year-old male sprinted into the brightly lit room just as the short, overweight Black woman in her sixties eased into a battered chair" says much more than "One person entered, another sat down."

A field researcher notes aspects of physical appearance such as neatness, dress, and hairstyle because they express messages that can affect social interactions. People spend a great deal of time and money selecting clothes, styling and combing hair, grooming with make-up, shaving, ironing clothes, and using deodorant or perfumes. These are part of their presentation of self. Even people who do not groom, shave, or wear deodorant present themselves and send a symbolic message by their appearance. No one dresses or looks "normal." Such a statement suggests that a researcher is not seeing the social world through the eyes of a stranger or is insensitive to social signals.

Behavior is also significant. A field researcher notices where people sit or stand, the pace at which they walk, and their nonverbal communication. People express social information, feelings, and attitudes through nonverbal communication, including gestures, facial expressions, and how one stands or sits (standing stiffly, sitting in a slouched position, etc.). People express relationships by how they position themselves in a group and through eye contact. A researcher may read the social communication of people by noting that they are standing close together, looking relaxed, and making eye contact.

A field researcher also notices the context in which events occur: Who was present? Who just arrived or left the scene? Was the room hot and stuffy? Such details may help the researcher assign meaning and understand why an event occurred. If they are not noticed, the details are lost, as is a full understanding of the event.

Serendipity is important in field research. Many times, a field researcher does not know the relevance of what he or she is observing until later. This has two implications. First is the importance of keen observation and excellent notes at all times, even when "nothing seems to be happening." Second is the importance of looking back over time and learning to appreciate wait time. Most field researchers say that they spend a lot of time "waiting." Novice field researchers get frustrated with the amount of time they seem to "waste," either waiting for other people or waiting for events to occur.

A field researcher needs must be attuned to the rhythms of the setting, operate on other people's schedules, and observe how events occur within their own flow of time. Wait time is not always wasted time. Wait time is time for reflection, for observing details, for developing social relations, for building rapport, and for becoming a familiar sight to people in the field setting. Wait time also displays that a researcher is committed and serious; perseverance is a significant trait field researchers need to cultivate. The researcher may be impatient to get in, get the research over, and get on with his or her "real life" but for the people in the field site, this *is* real life. The researcher should subordinate his or her personal wants to the demands of the field site.

Listening. A field researcher listens carefully to phrases, accents, and incorrect grammar, listening both to *what* is said and *how* it is said or what was implied. For example, people often use phrases such as "you know" or "of course" or "et cetera." A field researcher knows the meaning behind such phrases. He or she can try to hear everything, but listening is difficult when many conversations occur at once or when eavesdropping. Luckily, significant events and themes usually recur.

Taking Notes

Most field research data are in the form of field notes. Full field notes can contain maps, diagrams, photographs, interviews, tape recordings, videotapes, memos, artifacts or objects from the field, notes jotted in the field, and detailed notes written away from the field. A field researcher expects to fill many notebooks, or the equivalent in computer memory. He or she may spend more time writing notes than being in the field. Some researchers produce 40 single-spaced pages of notes for three hours of observation. With practice, even a new field researcher can produce several pages of notes for each hour in the field.

Writing notes is often boring, tedious work that requires self-discipline. The notes contain extensive descriptive detail drawn from memory. A researcher makes it a daily habit or compulsion to write notes immediately after leaving the field. The notes must be neat and organized because the researcher will return to them over and over again. Once written, the notes are private and valuable. A researcher treats them with care and protects confidentiality. Field notes may be of interest to hostile parties, blackmailers, or legal officials, so some researchers write field notes in code.

A researcher's state of mind, level of attention, and conditions in the field affect note taking. He or she will usually begin with relatively short one- to three-hour periods in the field before writing notes.

Types of Field Notes.   Field researchers take notes in many ways.[10] The recommendations here (also see Box 11.4) are suggestions. Full field notes have several types or levels. Five levels will be described. It is usually best to keep all the notes for an observation period together and to distinguish types of notes by separate pages. Some researchers include inferences with direct observations if they are set off by a visible device such as brackets or colored ink. The quantity of notes varies across types. For example, six hours in the field might result in 1 page of jotted notes, 40 pages of direct observation, 5 pages of researcher inference, and 2 pages total for methodological, theoretical, and personal notes.

Jotted Notes.   It is nearly impossible to take good notes in the field. Even a known observer

in a public setting looks strange when furiously writing. More important, when looking down and writing, the researcher cannot see and hear what is happening. The attention given to note writing is taken from field observation where it belongs. The specific setting determines whether any notes in the field can be taken. The researcher may be able to write, and members may expect it, or he or she may have to be secretive (e.g., go to the restroom).

Jotted notes are written in the field. They are short, temporary memory triggers such as words, phrases, or drawings taken inconspicuously, often scribbled on any convenient item (e.g., napkin, matchbook). They are incorporated into direct observation notes but are never substituted for them.

Direct Observation Notes.   The basic source of field data are notes a researcher writes immediately after leaving the field, which he or she can add to later. The notes should be ordered chronologically with the date, time, and place on each entry. They serve as a detailed description of what the researcher heard and saw in concrete, specific terms. To the extent possible, they are an exact recording of the particular words, phrases, or actions.

A researcher's memory improves with practice. A new researcher can soon remember exact phrases from the field. Verbatim statements should be written with double quote marks to distinguish them from paraphrases. Dialogue accessories (nonverbal communication, props, tone, speed, volume, gestures) should be recorded as well. A researcher records what was actually said and does not clean it up; notes include ungrammatical speech, slang, and misstatements (e.g., write, "Uh, I'm goin' home, Sal," not "I am going home, Sally").

A researcher puts concrete details in notes, not summaries. For example, instead of, "We talked about sports," he or she writes, "Anthony argued with Sam and Jason. He said that the Cubs would win next week because they traded for a new shortstop, Chiappetta. He also said

Box 11.4 Recommendations for Taking Field Notes

1. Record notes as soon as possible after each period in the field, and do not talk with others until observations are recorded.

2. Begin the record of each field visit with a new page, with the date and time noted.

3. Use jotted notes only as a temporary memory aid, with key words or terms, or the first and last things said.

4. Use wide margins to make it easy to add to notes at any time. Go back and add to the notes if you remember something later.

5. Plan to type notes and keep each level of notes separate so it will be easy to go back to them later.

6. Record events in the order in which they occurred, and note how long they last (e.g., a 15-minute wait, a one-hour ride).

7. Make notes as concrete, complete, and comprehensible as possible.

8. Use frequent paragraphs and quotation marks. Exact recall of phrases is best, with double quotes; use single quotes for paraphrasing.

9. Record small talk or routines that do not appear to be significant at the time; they may become important later.

10. "Let your feelings flow" and write quickly without worrying about spelling or "wild ideas." Assume that no one else will see the notes, but use pseudonyms.

11. Never substitute tape recordings completely for field notes.

12. Include diagrams or maps of the setting, and outline your own movements and those of others during the period of observation.

13. Include the researcher's own words and behavior in the notes. Also record emotional feelings and private thoughts in a separate section.

14. Avoid evaluative summarizing words. Instead of "The sink looked disgusting," say, "The sink was rust-stained and looked as if it had not been cleaned in a long time. Pieces of food and dirty dishes looked as if they had been piled in it for several days."

15. Reread notes periodically and record ideas generated by the rereading.

16. Always make one or more backup copies, keep them in a locked location, and store the copies in different places in case of fire.

---

that the team was better than the Mets, who he thought had inferior infielders. He cited last week's game where the Cubs won against Boston by 8 to 3." A researcher notes who was present, what happened, where it occurred, when, and under what circumstances. New researchers may not take notes because "nothing important happened." An experienced researcher knows that events when "nothing happened" can reveal a lot. For example, members may express feelings and organize experience into folk categories even in trivial conversations.

Researcher Inference Notes. A field researcher listens to members in order to "climb into their skin" or "walk in their shoes." This involves a three-step process. The researcher listens without applying analytical categories; he or she compares what is heard to what was heard at other times and to what others say; then the researcher applies his or her own interpretation to infer or figure out what it means. In ordinary interaction, we do all three steps simultaneously and jump quickly to our own inferences. A field researcher learns to look and listen without inferring or imposing an interpretation. His or her observations without inferences go into *direct observation notes.*

A researcher records inferences in a separate section that is keyed to direct observations. People never see social relationships, emotions, or meaning. They see specific physical actions and hear words, then use background cultural knowledge, clues from the context, and what is done or said to assign social meaning. For example, one does not see *love* or *anger;* one sees and hears specific actions (red face, loud voice, wild gestures, obscenities) and draw inferences from them (the person is angry).

People constantly infer social meaning on the basis of what they see and hear, but not always correctly. For example, my niece visited me and accompanied me to a store to buy a kite. The clerk at the cash register smiled and asked her whether she and her "Daddy" (looking at me) were going to fly the kite that day. The clerk observed our interaction, then inferred a father/daughter, not an uncle/niece relationship. She saw and heard a male adult and a female child, but she inferred the social meaning incorrectly.

A researcher keeps inferred meaning separate from direct observation because the meaning of. actions is not always self-evident. Sometimes, people try to deceive others. For example, an unrelated couple register at a motel as Mr. and Mrs. Smith. More frequently, social behavior is ambiguous or multiple meanings are possible. For example, I see a White male and female, both in their late twenties, get out of a car and enter a restaurant together. They sit at a table, order a meal, and talk with serious expressions in hushed tones, sometimes leaning forward to hear each other. As they get up to leave, the woman, who has a sad facial expression and appears ready to cry, is briefly hugged by the male. They then leave together. Did I witness a couple breaking up, two friends discussing a third, two people trying to decide what to do because they have discovered that their spouses are having an affair with each other, or a brother and sister whose father just died?

Analytic Notes. Researchers make many decisions about how to proceed while in the field. Some acts are planned (e.g., to conduct an interview, to observe a particular activity, etc.) and others seem to occur almost out of thin air. Field researchers keep methodological ideas in analytic notes to record their plans, tactics, ethical and procedural decisions, and self-critiques of tactics.

Theory emerges in field research during data collection and is clarified when a researcher reviews field notes. Analytic notes have a running account of a researcher's attempts to give meaning to field events. He or she thinks out loud in the notes by suggesting links between ideas, creating hypotheses, proposing conjectures, and developing new concepts.

Analytic memos are part of the theoretical notes. They are systematic digressions into theory, where a researcher elaborates on ideas in depth, expands on ideas while still in the field, and modifies or develops more complex theory by rereading and thinking about the memos.

Personal Notes. As discussed earlier, personal feelings and emotional reactions become part of the data and color what a researcher sees or hears in the field. A researcher keeps a section of notes that is like a personal diary. He or she records personal life events and feelings in it ("I'm tense today. I wonder if it's because of the fight I had yesterday with Chris," "I've got a headache on this gloomy, overcast day").

Personal notes serve three functions: They provide an outlet for a researcher and a way to cope with stress; they are a source of data about personal reactions; and they give him or her a way to evaluate direct observation or inference notes when the notes are later reread. For example, if the researcher was in a good mood during observations, it might color what he or she observed (see Figure 11.2).

FIGURE 11.2   Types of Field Notes

Direct Observation	Inference	Analytic	Personal Journal
Sunday, October 4. Kay's Kafe 3:00 pm. Large White male in mid-40s, overweight, enters. He wears worn brown suit. He is alone; sits at booth #2. Kay comes by, asks, "What'll it be?" Man says, "Coffee, black for now." She leaves and he lights cigarette and reads menu. 3:15 pm. Kay turns on radio.	Kay seems friendly today, humming. She becomes solemn and watchful. I think she puts on the radio when nervous.	Women are afraid of men who come in alone since the robbery.	It is raining. I am feeling comfortable with Kay but am bored today.

Maps and Diagrams.   Field researchers often make maps and draw diagrams or pictures of the features of a field site. This serves two purposes: It helps a researcher organize events in the field and it helps convey a field site to others. For example, a researcher observing a bar with 15 stools may draw and number 15 circles to simplify recording (e.g., "Yosuke came in and sat on stool 12; Phoebe was already on stool 10"). Field researchers find three types of maps helpful: spatial, social, and temporal. The first helps orient the data; the latter two are preliminary forms of data analysis. A *spatial map* locates people, equipment, and the like in terms of geographical physical space to show where activities occur (Figure 11.3A). A *social map* shows the number or variety of people and the arrangements among them of power, influence, friendship, division of labor, and so on (Figure 11.3B). A *temporal map* shows the ebb and flow of people, goods, services, and communications, or schedules (Figure 11.3C).

Machine Recordings to Supplement Memory. Tape recorders and videotapes can be helpful supplements in field research. They never substitute for field notes or a researcher's presence in the field. They cannot be introduced into all field sites, and can be used only after a researcher develops rapport. Recorders and videotapes provide a close approximation to what occurred and a permanent record that others can review. They serve as "jotted notes" to help a researcher recall events and observe what is easy to miss. Nevertheless, these items can create disruption and an increased awareness of surveillance. Researchers who rely on them must address associated problems (e.g., ensure that batteries are fresh and there are enough blank tapes). Also, relistening to or viewing tapes can be time consuming. For example, it may take over 100 hours to listen to 50 hours recorded in the field. Transcriptions of tape are expensive and not always accurate; they do not always convey subtle contextual meanings or mumbled words. Duneier (1999) had a tape recorder on all the time in his study of New York City street vendors. He made others aware of the machine and took reponsibility for what behaviors he focused on, and he left the machine visible. The taping may have created some distortion but it also provided a record of everyday routines. He also had a collaborator who took a large collection of photographs of his field site and informants, which helped him to see things differently.

FIGURE 11.3   Types of Maps Used in Field Research

A Spatial Map

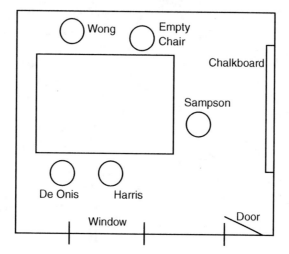

B Social Map

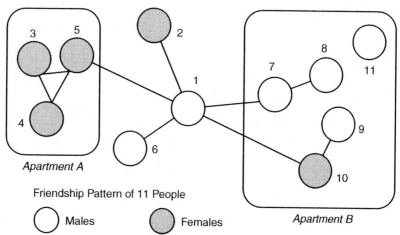

Friendship Pattern of 11 People

○ Males   ● Females

Apartment A

Apartment B

C Temporal Map

Day of Week, Buzz's Bar

	Mon	Tue	Wed	Thr	Fri	Sat
Open 10:00	Old Drunks	Old Drunks	Old Drunks	Old Drunks	Skip Work or Leave Early	Going to Fish
5:00						
	Football Watchers	Neighbors and Bridge Players	Softball Team (All-Male Night)	Young Crowd	Loud Music, Mixed Crowd	Loners and No Dates
Close 1:00						

Interview Notes.   If a researcher conducts field interviews (to be discussed), he or she keeps the interview notes separate.

Data Quality

Reliability in Field Research.   The reliability of field data addresses the question: Are researcher observations about a member or field event internally and externally consistent? *Internal consistency* refers to whether the data are plausible given all that is known about a person or event, eliminating common forms of human deception. In other words, do the pieces fit together into a coherent picture? For example, are a member's actions consistent over time and in different social contexts? *External consistency* is achieved by verifying or cross-checking observations with other, divergent sources of data. In other words, does it all fit into the overall context? For example, can others verify what a researcher observed about a person? Does other evidence confirm the researcher's observations?

Reliability in field research also includes what is not said or done, but is expected. Such omissions can be significant but are difficult to detect. For example, when observing a cashier end her shift, a researcher notices that the money in the cash drawer is not counted. He or she may notice the omission only if other cashiers always count the money at the end of the shift.

Reliability in field research depends on a researcher's insight, awareness, suspicions, and questions. He or she looks at members and events from different angles (legal, economic, political, personal) and mentally asks questions: Where does the money come from for that? What do those people do all day?

Field researchers depend on what members tell them. This makes the credibility of members and their statements part of reliability. To check member credibility, a researcher asks: Does the person have a reason to lie? Is she in a position to know that? What are the person's values and how might that shape what she says? Is he just

saying that to please me? Is there anything that might limit his spontaneity?

Field researchers take subjectivity and context into account as they evaluate credibility. They know that a person's statements or actions are affected by subjective perceptions. Statements are made from a particular point of view and colored by an individual's experiences. Instead of evaluating each statement to see if it is true, a field researcher finds statements useful in themselves. Even inaccurate statements and actions can be revealing from a researcher's perspective.

As mentioned before, actions and statements are shaped by the context in which they appear. What is said in one setting may differ in other contexts. For example, when asked "Do you dance?" a member may say no in a public setting full of excellent dancers, but yes in a semiprivate setting with few good dancers and different music. It is not that the member is lying but that the answer is shaped by the context.

Duneier (1999) has warned us to avoid the *ethnographic fallacy.* It occurs when a field researcher takes what he or she oberves at face value, does not question what people in a field site say, and focuses solely on the immediate concrete details of a field setting while ignoring larger social forces. Duneier noted that he tried to avoid the fallacy by being aware of larger social context and forces. Thus, he studied people who took responsibilty for their own failures (such as dropping out of school in the ninth grade) and blamed themselves. Duneier was fully aware from many other studies of the larger forces (e.g., family situation, violence, poor quality school, racial prejudice, joblessness) that often contributed to their experience of failure.[11]

Validity in Field Research.   Validity in field research is the confidence placed in a researcher's analysis and data as accurately representing the social world in the field. Replicability is not a criterion because field research is virtually impossible to replicate. Essential aspects of the field change: The social events and context change, the members are different, the individual researcher differs, and so on. There are four kinds of validity or tests of research accuracy: ecological validity, natural history, member validation, and competent insider performance.

- *Ecological validity.* Validity is achieved by describing the studied social world in a manner that matches what it would be without a research presence. Ecological validity suggests that events and interactions would occur the same without a researcher there and without being part of a research study.
- *Natural history.* Validity is achieved by offering a highly detailed description of how the research was conducted. Natural history offers readers a close-up view of a researcher's actions, assumptions, and procedures for evaluation.
- *Member validation.* Validity is achieved by asking members of a field site to review and verify the accuracy of the description of their intimate social world. Possible limitations of member validation are that different members may have conflicting perspectives, members may object to an unfavorable portrayal their social world, or members may not recognize parts of a description that go beyond their own narrow perspective.[12]
- *Competent insider performance.* Validity is achieved by a researcher interacting identically to or "passing" as an insider or member of the field site. This form of validity is reached when a researcher truly understands insider assumptions, knows and acts based on tacit local social rules or knowledge, and can tell and get insider jokes.

Focusing and Sampling

Focusing. The field researcher first gets a general picture, then focuses on a few specific problems or issues (see Figure 11.4). A researcher decides on specific research questions and develops hypotheses only after being in the field

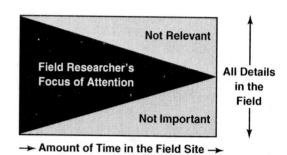

FIGURE 11.4   Focusing in Field Research

and experiencing it firsthand. At first, everything seems relevant; later, however, selective attention focuses on specific questions and themes.

Sampling. Field researchers often use nonprobability samples, such as snowball sampling. Many times the field research is sampling different types of units. A field researcher may take a smaller, selective set of observations from all possible observations, or sample times, situations, types of events, locations, types of people, or contexts of interest. For example, a researcher samples time by observing a setting at different times. He or she observes at all times of the day, on every day of the week, and in all seasons to get a full sense of how the field site stays the same or changes. It is often best to overlap when sampling (e.g., to have sampling times from 7:00 A.M. to 9:00 A.M., from 8:00 A.M. to 10:00 A.M., from 9:00 A.M. to 11:00 A.M., etc.).

A researcher often samples locations because one location may give depth, but a narrow perspective. Sitting or standing in different locations helps the researcher get a sense of the whole site. For example, the peer-to-peer behavior of school teachers usually occurs in a faculty lounge, but it also occurs at a local bar when teachers gather or in a classroom temporarily used for a teacher meeting. In addition, researchers trace the paths of members to various field locations.

Field researchers sample people by focusing their attention on different kinds of people (old-timers and newcomers, old and young, males and females, leaders and followers). As a researcher identifies types of people, or people with opposing outlooks, he or she tries to interact with and learn about all types. A field researcher also samples various kinds of events, such as routine, special, and unanticipated. Routine events (e.g., opening up a store for business) happen every day and should not be considered unimportant simply because they are routine. Special events (e.g., annual office party) are announced and planned in advance. They focus member attention and reveal aspects of social life not otherwise visible. Unanticipated events are those that just happen to occur while a researcher is present (e.g., unsupervised workers when the manager gets sick and cannot oversee workers at a store for a day). In this case, the researcher sees something unusual, unplanned, or rare by chance.

THE FIELD RESEARCH INTERVIEW

So far, you have learned how field researchers observe and take notes. They also interview members, but field interviews differ from survey research interviews. This section introduces the field interview.

The Field Interview

Field researchers use unstructured, nondirective, in-depth interviews, which differ from formal survey research interviews in many ways (see Table 11.1). The field interview involves asking questions, listening, expressing interest, and recording what was said. It is a joint production of a researcher and a member. Members are active participants whose insights, feelings, and cooperation are essential parts of a discussion process that reveals subjective meanings.

Field research interviews go by many names: unstructured, depth, ethnographic, open ended, informal, and long. Generally, they involve one or more people being present, occur in the field, and are informal and nondirective (i.e., the respondent may take the interview in various directions).

A field interview involves a mutual sharing of experiences. A researcher might share his or her background to build trust and encourage the informant to open up, but does not force answers or use leading questions. She or he encourages and guides a process of mutual discovery.

In field interviews, members express themselves in the forms in which they normally speak, think, and organize reality. A researcher retains members' jokes and narrative stories in their natural form and does not repackage them into a standardized format. The focus is on the members' perspectives and experiences. In order to stay close to a member's experience, the researcher asks questions in terms of concrete examples or situations—for example, "Could you tell me things that led up to your quitting in June?" instead of "Why did you quit your job?"

Field interviews can occur in a series over time. A researcher begins by building rapport and steering conversation away from evaluative or highly sensitive topics. He or she avoids probing inner feelings until intimacy is established, and even then, the researcher expects apprehension. After several meetings, he or she may be able to probe more deeply into sensitive issues and seek clarification of less sensitive issues. In later interviews, he or she may return to topics and check past answers by restating them in a nonjudgmental tone and asking for verification—for example, "The last time we talked, you said that you started taking things from the store after they reduced your pay. Is that right?"

The field interview is closer to a friendly conversation than the stimulus/response model found in a survey research interview. You are familiar with a friendly conversation. It has its own informal rules and the following elements: (1) a greeting ("Hi, it's good to see you again"); (2) the absence of an explicit goal or purpose (we don't say, "Let's now discuss what we did last weekend"); (3) avoidance of repetition (we don't say, "Could you clarify what you said about"); (4) question asking ("Did you see the race yesterday?"); (5) expressions of interest ("Really? I wish I could have been there!"); (6) expressions of ignorance ("No, I missed it. What happened?"); (7) turn taking, so the encounter is balanced (one person does not always ask questions and the other only answer); (8) abbreviations ("I missed the Derby, but I'm going to the Indy," not "I missed the Kentucky Derby horse race but I will go to the Indianapolis

500 automotive race"); (9) a pause or brief silence when neither person talks is acceptable; (10) a closing (we don't say, "Let's end this conversation"; instead, we give a verbal indicator before physically leaving: "I've got to get back to work now—see ya tomorrow").

The field interview differs from a friendly conversation. It has an explicit purpose—to learn about the informant and setting. A researcher includes explanations or requests that diverge from friendly conversations. For example, he or she may say, "I'd like to ask you about . . ." or "Could you look at this and see if I've written it

TABLE 11.1   Survey Interviews versus Field Research Interviews

Typical Survey Interview	Typical Field Interview
1. It has a clear beginning and end.	1. The beginning and end are not clear. The interview can be picked up later.
2. The same standard questions are asked of all respondents in the same sequence.	2. The questions and the order in which they are asked are tailored to specific people and situations.
3. The interviewer appears neutral at all times.	3. The interviewer shows interest in responses, encourages elaboration.
4. The interviewer asks questions, and the respondent answers.	4. It is like a friendly conversational exchange, but with more interviewer questions.
5. It is almost always with one respondent alone.	5. It can occur in group setting or with others in area, but varies.
6. It has a professional tone and businesslike focus; diversions are ignored.	6. It is interspersed with jokes, asides, stories, diversions, and anecdotes, which are recorded.
7. Closed-ended questions are common, with rare probes.	7. Open-ended questions are common, and probes are frequent.
8. The interviewer alone controls the pace and direction of interview.	8. The interviewer and member jointly control the pace and direction of the interview.
9. The social context in which the interview occurs is ignored and assumed to make little difference.	9. The social context of the interview is noted and seen as important for interpreting the meaning of responses.
10. The interviewer attempts to mold the framework communication pattern into a standard.	10. The interviewer adjusts to the member's norms and language usage.

Source: Adapted from Briggs (1986), Denzin (1989), Douglas (1985), Misher (1986), Spradley (1979a).

down right?" The field interview is less balanced. A higher proportion of questions come from the researcher, who expresses more ignorance and interest. Also, it includes repetition, and a researcher asks the member to elaborate on unclear abbreviations.

Kissane (2003) used depth interviews in her field study of low-income women in Philadelphia (discussed in Chapter 6). Interviews lasted from 30 minutes to three hours. Kissane noted that she asked the women what services they used, and then named specific agencies. Often a woman would then say she was aware of the named agency. She asked the women to describe their experiences with various agencies, when they had used them or if they would use services of various agencies, and what other social services they used. Open-ended interviewing allowed her to see the women's decision-making process.

Types of Questions in Field Interviews

Many field researchers ask three types of questions in a field interview: descriptive, structural, and contrast questions. All are asked concurrently, but each type is more frequent at a different stage in the research process (see Figure 11.5). During the early stage, a researcher primarily asks descriptive questions, then gradually adds

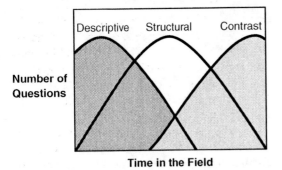

FIGURE 11.5   Types of Questions in Field Research Interviews

structural questions until, in the middle stage after analysis has begun, they make up a majority of the questions. Contrast questions begin to appear in the middle of a field research study and increase until, by the end, they are asked more than any other type.[13]

A *descriptive question* is used to explore the setting and learn about members. Descriptive questions can be about time and space—for example, "Where is the bathroom?" "When does the delivery truck arrive?" "What happened Monday night?" They can also be about people and activities: "Who is sitting by the window?" "What is your uncle like?" "What happens during the initiation ceremony?" They can be about objects: "When do you use a saber saw?" "Which tools do you carry with you on an emergency water leak job?" Questions asking for examples are descriptive questions—for example, "Could you give me an example of a great date?" "What were your experiences as a postal clerk?" Descriptive questions may ask about hypothetical situations: "If a student opened her book during the exam, how would you deal with it?" They also ask members about the argot of the setting: "What do you call a deputy sheriff?" (The answer is a "county Mountie.")

A researcher introduces a *structural question* after spending time in the field and starting to analyze data. It begins after a researcher organizes specific field events, situations, and conversations into conceptual categories. For example, a researcher's observations of a highway truck-stop restaurant revealed that the employees informally classify customers who patronize the truck stop. In a preliminary analysis, he or she creates a conceptual category of kinds of customers and has members verify the categories with structural questions. A common way to pose a structural question is to ask the members whether a category includes elements in addition to those already identified—for example, "Are there any types of customers other than regulars, greasers, pit stoppers, and long haulers?" In addition, a researcher asks for confirmation: "Is a greaser a type of customer that you serve?" "Would a pit stopper ever eat a three-course dinner?"

The *contrast question* builds on the analysis already verified by structural questions. Contrast questions focus on similarities or differences between elements in categories or between categories. The researcher asks members to verify the similarities and differences: "You seem to have a number of different kinds of customers come in here. I've heard you call some customers 'regulars' and others 'pit stoppers.' How are a regular and a pit stopper alike?" or "Is the difference between a long hauler and a greaser that the greaser doesn't tip?" or "Two types of customers just stop to use the restroom—entire families and a lone male. Do you call both pit stoppers?"

Informants

An informant or key actor in field research is a member with whom a field researcher develops a relationship and who tells about, or informs on, the field.[14] Who makes a good informant? The ideal informant has four characteristics:

1. The informant is totally familiar with the culture and is in position to witness significant events. He or she lives and breathes the culture and engages in routines in the setting without thinking about them.
2. The individual is currently involved in the field. Ex-members who have reflected on the field may provide useful insights, but the longer they have been away from direct involvement, the more likely it is that they have reconstructed their recollections.
3. The person can spend time with the researcher. Interviewing may take many hours, and some members are simply not available for extensive interviewing.
4. Nonanalytic individuals make better informants. A nonanalytic informant is familiar with and uses native folk theory or pragmatic common sense. This is in contrast to the analytic member, who preanalyzes the

setting, using categories from the media or education.

A field researcher may interview several types of informants. Contrasting types of informants who provide useful perspectives include rookies and old-timers, people in the center of events and those on the fringes of activity, people who recently changed status (e.g., through promotion) and those who are static, frustrated or needy people and happy or secure people, the leader in charge and the subordinate who follows. A field researcher expects mixed messages when he or she interviews a range of informants.

Interview Context

Field researchers recognize that a conversation in a private office may not occur in a crowded lunchroom. Often, interviews take place in the member's home environment so that he or she is comfortable. This is not always best. If a member is preoccupied or there is no privacy, a researcher will move to another setting (e.g., restaurant or university office).

The interview's meaning is shaped by its Gestalt or whole interaction of a researcher and a member in a specific context. For example, a researcher notes nonverbal forms of communication that add meaning, such as a shrug, a gesture, and so on.

LEAVING THE FIELD

Work in the field can last for a few weeks to a dozen years. In either case, at some point work in the field ends. Some researchers (e.g., Schatzman and Strauss, 1973) suggest that the end comes naturally when theory building ceases or reaches a closure; others feel that fieldwork could go on without end and that a firm decision to cut off relations is needed.

Experienced field researchers anticipate a process of disengaging and exiting the field. Depending on the intensity of involvement and the length of time in the field, the process can be disruptive or emotionally painful for both the researcher and the members. A researcher may experience the emotional pain of breaking intimate friendships when leaving the field. He or she may feel guilty and depressed immediately before and after leaving. He or she may find it difficult to let go because of personal and emotional entanglements. If the involvement in the field was intense and long, and the field site differed from his or her native culture, the researcher may need months of adjustment before feeling at home with his or her original cultural surroundings.

Once a researcher decides to leave—because the project reaches a natural end and little new is being learned, or because external factors force it to end (e.g., end of a job, gatekeepers order the researcher out, etc.)—he or she chooses a method of exiting. The researcher can leave by a quick exit (simply not return one day) or slowly withdraw, reducing his or her involvement over weeks. He or she also needs to decide how to tell members and how much advance warning to give.

The exit process depends on the specific field setting and the relationships developed. In general, a researcher lets members know a short period ahead of time. He or she fulfills any bargains or commitments that were made and leaves with a clean slate. Sometimes, a ritual or ceremony, such as a going-away party or shaking hands with everyone, helps signal the break for members. Maintaining friendships with members is also possible and is preferred by feminist researchers.

A field researcher is aware that leaving affects members. Some members may feel hurt or rejected because a close social relationship is ending. They may react by trying to pull a researcher back into the field and make him or her more of a member, or they may become angry and resentful. They may grow cool and distant because of an awareness that the researcher is really an outsider. In any case, fieldwork is not finished until the process of disengagement and exiting is complete.

FOCUS GROUPS

The *focus group* is a special qualitative research technique in which people are informally "interviewed" in a group-discussion setting.[15] Focus group research has grown over the past 20 years. The procedure is that a researcher gathers together 6 to 12 people in a room with a moderator to discuss a few issues. Most focus groups last about 90 minutes. The moderator is trained to be nondirective and to facilitate free, open discussion by all group members (i.e., not let one person dominate the discussion). Group members should be homogenous, but not include close friends or relatives. In a typical study, a researcher uses four to six separate groups. Focus group topics might include public attitudes (e.g., race relations, workplace equality), personal behaviors (e.g., dealing with AIDS), a new product (e.g., breakfast cereal), a political candidate, or a number of other topics. Researchers often combine focus groups with quantitative research, and the procedure has its own specific strengths and weaknesses (see Box 11.5).

Several years ago, I conducted an applied study on why parents and students chose to attend a private high school. In addition to collecting quantitative survey data, I formed six focus groups, each with 8 to 10 students from the high school. A trained college-student moderator asked questions, elicited comments from group members, and prevented one person from dominating discussions. The six groups were co-ed and contained members of either one grade level or two adjacent grades (e.g., freshmen and sophomores). Students discussed their reasons for attending the high school and whether specific factors were important. I tape-recorded the discussions, which lasted about 45 minutes, then analyzed the tapes to understand what the students saw as important to their decisions. In

Box 11.5 Advantages and Limitations of Focus Groups

Advantages

- The natural setting allows people to express opinions/ideas freely.
- Open expression among members of marginalized social groups is encouraged.
- People tend to feel empowered, especially in action-oriented research projects.
- Survey researchers are provided a window into how people talk about survey topics.
- The interpretation of quantitative survey results is facilitated.
- Participants may query one another and explain their answers to each other.

Limitations

- A "polarization effect" exists (attitudes become more extreme after group discussion).
- Only one or a few topics can be discussed in a focus group session.
- A moderator may unknowingly limit open, free expression of group members.
- Focus group participants produce fewer ideas than in individual interviews.
- Focus group studies rarely report all the details of study design/procedure.
- Researchers cannot reconcile the differences that arise between individual-only and focus group-context responses.

addition, the data helped when interpreting the survey data.

ETHICAL DILEMMAS OF FIELD RESEARCH

The direct personal involvement of a field researcher in the social lives of other people raises many ethical dilemmas. The dilemmas arise when a researcher is alone in the field and has little time to make a moral decision. Although he or she may be aware of general ethical issues before entering the field, they arise unexpectedly in the course of observing and interacting in the field. We will look at four ethical issues in field research: deception, confidentiality, involvement with deviants, and publishing reports.[16]

Deception

Deception arises in several ways in field research: The research may be covert; it may assume a false role, name, or identity; or it may mislead members in some way. The most hotly debated of the ethical issues arising from deception is that of covert versus overt field research. Some support it and see it as necessary for entering into and gaining a full knowledge of many areas of social life. Others oppose it and argue that it undermines a trust between researchers and society. Although its moral status is questionable, there are some field sites or activities that can only be studied covertly. Covert research is never preferable and never easier than overt research because of the difficulties of maintaining a front and the constant fear of getting caught.

Confidentiality

A researcher learns intimate knowledge that is given in confidence. He or she has a moral obligation to uphold the confidentiality of data. This includes keeping information confidential from others in the field and disguising members' names in field notes. Sometimes a field researcher cannot directly quote a person. One strategy is instead of reporting the source as an informant, the researcher can find documentary evidence that says the same thing and use the document (e.g., an old memo, a newspaper article, etc.) as if it were the source of the information.

Involvement with Deviants

Researchers who conduct field research on deviants who engage in illegal behavior face additional dilemmas. They know of and may sometimes be involved in illegal activity. This *guilty knowledge* is of interest not only to law-enforcement officials but also to other deviants.[17] The researcher faces a dilemma of building trust and rapport with the deviants, yet not becoming so involved as to violate his or her basic personal moral standards. Usually, the researcher makes an explicit arrangement with the deviant members.

Publishing Field Reports

The intimate knowledge that a researcher obtains and reports creates a dilemma between the right of privacy and the right to know. A researcher does not publicize member secrets, violate privacy, or harm reputations. Yet, if he or she cannot publish anything that might offend or harm someone, part of what the researcher learned will remain hidden, and it may be difficult for others to believe the report if a researcher omits critical details. Some researchers ask members to look at a report to verify its accuracy and to approve of their portrayal in print. For marginal groups (e.g., addicts, prostitutes, crack users), this may not be possible, but researchers must respect member privacy. On the other hand, censorship or self-censorship can be a danger. A compromise position is for a researcher to publish truthful but unflattering material after consideration and only if it is essential to the researcher's arguments.

CONCLUSION

In this chapter, you learned about field research and the field research process (choosing a site and gaining access, relations in the field, observing and collecting data, and the field interview). Field researchers begin data analysis and theorizing during the data collection phase.

You can now appreciate implications of saying that in field research, the researcher is directly involved with those being studied and is immersed in a natural setting. Doing field research usually has a greater impact on the researcher's emotions, personal life, and sense of self than doing other types of research. Field research is difficult to conduct, but it is a way to study parts of the social world that otherwise could not be studied.

Good field research requires a combination of skills. In addition to a strong sense of self, the best field researchers possess an incredible ability to listen and absorb details, tremendous patience, sensitivity and empathy for others, superb social skills, a talent to think very quickly "on one's feet," the ability see subtle interconnections among people and/or events, and a superior ability to express oneself in writing.

Field research is strongest when a researcher studies a small group of people interacting in the present. It is valuable for micro-level or small-group face-to-face interaction. It is less effective when the concern is macro-level processes and social structures. It is nearly useless for events that occurred in the distant past or processes that stretch across decades. Historical-comparative research, discussed in the next chapter, is better suited to investigating these types of concerns.

Key Terms

analytic memos
appearance of interest
attitude of strangeness
contrast question
descriptive question
direct observation notes
ecological validity
ethnography
ethnographic fallacy
ethnomethodology
external consistency
field site

focus group
go native
guilty knowledge
internal consistency
jotted notes
member validation
naturalism
normalize social research
structural question

Endnotes

1. For studies of these sites or topics, see Neuman (2000, 2003). On studies of children or schools, see Corsaro (1994), Corsaro and Molinari (2000), Eder (1995), Eder and Kinney (1995), Kelle (2000), and Merten (1999). On studies of homeless people, see Lankenau (1999), and on studies of female strippers, see Wood (2000).
2. Ethnography is described in Agar (1986), Franke (1983), Hammersley and Atkinson (1983), Sanday (1983), and Spradley (1979a:3–12, 1979b:3–16).
3. For a general discussion of field research and naturalism, see Adler and Adler (1994), Georges and Jones (1980), Holy (1984), and Pearsall (1970). For discussions of contrasting types of field research, see Clammer (1984), Gonor (1977), Holstein and Gubrium (1994), Morse (1994), Schwandt (1994), and Strauss and Corbin (1994).
4. See Lofland (1976:13–23) and Shaffir and colleagues (1980:18–20) on feeling marginal.
5. See Adler and Adler (1987:67–78).

6. See Hammersley and Atkinson (1983:42–45) and Lofland and Lofland (1995:16–30).
7. For more on gatekeepers and access, see Beck (1970:11–29), Bogdan and Taylor (1975:30–32), and Wax (1971:367).
8. Negotiation in the field is discussed in Gans (1982), Johnson (1975:58–59, 76–77), and Schatzman and Strauss (1973:22–23).
9. See Douglas (1976), Emerson (1981:367–368), and Johnson (1975:124–129) on the question of whether the researcher should always be patient, polite, and considerate.
10. For more on ways to record and organize field data, see Bogdan and Taylor (1975:60–73), Hammersley and Atkinson (1983:144–173), and Kirk and Miller (1986: 49–59).
11. See Duneier (1999:342–343) for detailed discussion.
12. For more on validity in field research, see Briggs (1986:24), Bogdan and Taylor (1975), Douglas (1976), Emerson (1981:361–363), and Sanjek (1990).
13. The types of questions are adapted from Spradley (1979a, 1979b).
14. Field research informants are discussed in Dean and associates (1969), Kemp and Ellen (1984), Schatzman and Strauss (1973), Spradley (1979a:46–54), and Whyte (1982).
15. For a discussion of focus groups, see Bischoping and Dykema (1999), Churchill (1983:179–184), Krueger (1988), Labaw (1980:54–58), and Morgan (1996).
16. See Lofland and Lofland (1995:26, 63, 75, 168–177), Miles and Huberman (1994:288–297), and Punch (1986).
17. Fetterman (1989) discusses the idea of guilty knowledge.

CHAPTER 12

Historical-Comparative Research

INTRODUCTION

Some students find historical-comparative research difficult and uninteresting because they do not know much about various countries or history, which is often necessary to appreciate this type of research and studies that use it. They may feel that historical-comparative studies are beyond their immediate daily experiences and not relevant. Yet, explaining and understanding major events in the world around them—an attack by terrorists, a nation going to war, the source of racism, large-scale immigration, violence based on religious hatred, urban decay—depend on historical-comparative research.

The classic social thinkers in the nineteenth century, such as Emile Durkheim, Karl Marx, and Max Weber, who founded the social sciences, used a historical and comparative method. This method is used extensively in a few areas of sociology (e.g., social change, political sociology, social movements, and social stratification) and has been applied in many others, as well (e.g., religion, criminology, sex roles, race relations, and family). Although much social research focuses on current social life in one country, historical and/or comparative studies have become more common in recent years.

Historical-comparative social research is a collection of techniques and approaches. Some blend into traditional history, others extend quantitative social research. The focus of this chapter is on the distinct type of social research that puts historical time and/or cross-cultural variation at the center of research—that is, the type of research that treats what is studied as part of the flow of history and situated in a cultural context.

Research Questions Appropriate for Historical-Comparative Research

Historical-comparative research is a powerful method for addressing big questions: How did major societal change take place? What fundamental features are common to most societies?

Why did current social arrangements take a certain form in some societies but not in others? For example, historical-comparative researchers have addressed the questions of what caused societal revolutions in China, France, and Russia (Skocpol, 1979); how major social institutions, such as medicine, have developed and changed over two centuries (Starr, 1982); how basic social relationships, such as feelings about the value of children, change (Zelizer, 1985); how recent changes in major cities, such as New York, London, and Tokyo, reveal the rise of a new global urban system (Sassen, 2001), and, as the study discussed in Chapter 2 by Marx (1998) asked, why Brazil, South Africa, and the United States developed different racial relations.[1]

Historical-comparative research is suited for examining the combinations of social factors that produce a specific outcome (e.g., civil war). It is also appropriate for comparing entire social systems to see what is common across societies and what is unique. An H-C researcher may apply a theory to specific cases to illustrate its usefulness. He or she brings out or reveals the connections between divergent social factors or groups. And, he or she compares the same social processes and concepts in different cultural or historical contexts. For example, Switzerland and United States have been compared in terms of the use of direct democracy and women's right to vote. Similar forms of lcoal government allowed direct democracy to spread in parts of both countries (Kriesi and Wisler, 1999). Although some U.S. states granted women to right to vote in the 1800s, the Swiss women did not get the right to vote until 1990 because, unlike the U.S. movement, the Swiss suffrage movement believed in consensus politics and local autonomy and relied on government parties for direction (Banaszak, 1996).

Researchers also use the H-C method to reinterpret data or challenge old explanations. By asking different questions, finding new evidence, or assembling evidence in a different way, the H-C researcher raises questions about old explanations and finds support for new ones by interpreting the data in its cultural-historical context.

Historical-comparative research can strengthen conceptualization and theory building. By looking at historical events or diverse cultural contexts, a researcher can generate new concepts and broaden his or her perspectives. Concepts are less likely to be restricted to a single historical time or to a single culture; they can be grounded in the experiences of people living in specific cultural and historical contexts.[2]

A difficulty in reading H-C studies is that one needs a knowledge of the past or other cultures to fully understand them. Readers who are familiar with only their own cultures or contemporary times may find it difficult to understand the H-C studies or classical theorists. For example, it is difficult to understand Karl Marx's *The Communist Manifesto* without a knowledge of the conditions of feudal Europe and the world in which Marx was writing. In that time and place, serfs lived under severe oppression. Feudal society included caste-based dress codes in cities and a system of peonage that forced serfs to give a large percent of their product to landlords. The one and only Church had extensive landholdings, and tight familial ties existed among the aristocracy, landlords, and Church. Modern readers might ask, Why did the serfs not flee if conditions were so bad? The answer requires an understanding of the conditions at the time. The serfs had little chance to survive in European forests living on roots, berries, and hunting. Also, no one would aid a fleeing serf refugee because the traditional societies did not embrace strangers, but feared them.

THE LOGIC OF HISTORICAL-COMPARATIVE RESEARCH

The terms used for H-C research can be confusing. Researchers may mean different things when they say *historical, comparative,* and *historical-comparative.* The key question is: Is

there a distinct historical-comparative method and logic?

The Logic of Historical-Comparative Research and Quantitative Research

Quantitative versus Historical-Comparative Research. One source of the confusion is that both positivist quantitatively oriented and interpretive (or critical) qualitatively oriented researchers study historical or comparative issues. Positivist researchers reject the idea that there is a distinct H-C method. They measure variables, test hypotheses, analyze quantitative data, and replicate research to discover generalizable laws that hold across time and societies. They see no fundamental difference between quantitative social research and historical-comparative research.

Most social research examines social life in the present in a single nation—that of the researcher. Historical-comparative research can be organized along three dimensions: Is the focus on what occurs in one nation, a small set of nations, or many nations? Is the focus on a single time period in the past, across many years, or a recent time period? Is the analysis based primarily on quantitative or qualitative data?

The Logic of Historical-Comparative Research and Interpretive Research

A distinct, qualitative historical-comparative type of social research differs from the positivist approach and from an extreme interpretive approach. Historical-comparative researchers who use case studies and qualitative data may depart from positivist principles. Their research is an intensive examination of a limited number of cases in which social meaning and context are critical. Case studies, even on one nation, can be very important. Case studies can elaborate historical processes and specify concrete historical details (see Box 12.1).

Scholars who adopt the positivist approach to social science criticize the historical-comparative

---

Box 12.1   Women of the Klan

In *Women of the Klan*, Kathleen Blee (1991) noted that, prior to her research, no one had studied the estimated 500,000 women in the largest racist, right-wing movement in the United States. She suggested that this may have been due to an assumption that women were apolitical and passive. Her six years of research into the unknown members of a secret society over 60 years ago shows the ingenuity needed in historical-sociological research.

Blee focused on the state of Indiana, where as many as 32 percent of White Protestant women were members of the Ku Klux Klan at its peak in the 1920s. In addition to reviewing published studies on the Klan, her documentary investigation included newspapers, pamphlets, and unpublished reports. She conducted library research on primary and secondary materials at over half a dozen college, government, and historical libraries. The historical photographs, sketches, and maps in the book give readers a feel for the topic.

Finding information was difficult. Blee did not have access to membership lists. She identified Klan women by piecing together a few surviving rosters, locating newspaper obituaries that identified women as Klan members, scrutinizing public notices or anti-Klan documents for the names of Klan women, and interviewing surviving women of the Klan.

To locate survivors 60 years after the Klan was active, Blee had to be persistent and ingenious. She mailed a notice about her research to every local newspaper, church bulletin, advertising supplement, historical society, and public library in Indiana. She obtained 3 written recollections, 3 unrecorded interviews, and 15 recorded interviews. Most of her informants were over age 80. They recalled the Klan as an important part of their lives. Blee verified parts of their memories through newspaper and other documentary evidence.

Membership in the Klan remains controversial. In the interviews, Blee did not reveal her opinions about the Klan. Although she was tested, Blee remained neutral and did not denounce the Klan. She stated, "My own background in Indiana (where I lived from primary school through college) and white skin led informants to assume—lacking spoken evidence to the contrary—that I shared their worldview" (p. 5). She did not find Klan women brutal, ignorant, and full of hatred. Blee got an unexpected response to a question on why the women had joined the Klan. Most were puzzled by the question. To them it needed no explanation—it was just "a way of growing up" and "to get together and enjoy."

---

approach for using a small number of cases. They believe that historical-comparative research is inadequate because it rarely produces probabilistic causal generalizations that they take as indicating a "true" (i.e., positivist) science.

Like interpretive field researchers, H-C researchers focus on culture, try to see through the eyes of those being studied, reconstruct the lives of the people studied, and examine particular individuals or groups. An extremist interpretive position says that an empathic understanding of the people being studied is the sole goal of social research. It takes a strict, idiographic, descriptive approach and rejects

causal statements, systematic concepts, or abstract theoretical models. In the extremist interpretive approach, each social setting is unique and comparisons are impossible.

A Distinct Historical-Comparative Approach

The distinct historical-comparative research method avoids the excesses of the positivist and extreme interpretive approaches. It combines a sensitivity to specific historical or cultural contexts with theoretical generalization. The logic and goals of H-C research are closer to those of field research than to positivist approaches. The following discussion describes similarities between H-C research and field research, and six more unique features of historical-comparative research (see Table 12.1).

Similarities to Field Research. First, both H-C research and field research recognize that the researcher's point of view is an unavoidable part of

research. Both involve interpretation, which introduces the interpreter's location in time, place, and worldview. Historical-comparative research does not try to produce a single, unequivocal set of objective facts. Rather, it is a confrontation of old with new or of different worldviews. It recognizes that a researcher's reading of historical or comparative evidence is influenced by an awareness of the past and by living in the present.

TABLE 12.1   Summary of a Comparison of Approaches to Research: The Qualitative versus Quantitative Distinction

Topic	Both Field and H-C	Quantitative
Researcher's perspective	Include as an intergral part of the research process	Remove from research process
Approach to data	Immersed in many details to acquire understanding	Precisely operationalize variables
Theory and data	Grounded theory, dialogue between data and concepts	Deductive theory compared with empirical data
Present findings	Translate a meaning system	Test hypotheses
Action/structure	People construct meaning but within structures	Social forces shape behavior
Laws/generalization	Limited generalizations that depend on context	Discover universal, context-free laws

Features of Distinct H-C Research Approach

Topic	Historical Comparative Researcher's Approach
Evidence	Reconstructs from fragments and incomplete evidence
Distortion	Guards against using own awareness of factors outside the social or historical context
Human role	Includes the consciousness of people in a context and uses their motives as causal factors
Causes	Sees cause as contingent on conditions, beneath the surface, and due to a combination of elements
Micro/macro	Compares whole cases and links the micro to macro levels or layers of social reality
Cross-contexts	Moves between concrete specifics in a context and across contexts for more abstract comparisons

Second, both field and H-C research examine a great diversity of data. In both, the researcher becomes immersed in data to gain an empathic understanding of events and people. Both capture subjective feelings and note how everyday, ordinary activities signify important social meaning.

The researcher inquires, selects, and focuses on specific aspects of social life from the vast array of events, actions, symbols, and words. An H-C researcher organizes data and focuses attention on the basis of evolving concepts. He or she examines rituals and symbols that dramatize culture (e.g., parades, clothing, placement of objects, etc.) and investigates the motives, reasons, and justifications for behaviors.

Third, both field and H-C researchers use *grounded theory.* Theory usually emerges during the process of data collection.

Next, in both field and H-C research the researcher's meaning system frequently differs from that of the people he or she studies, but he or she tries to penetrate and understand their point of view. Once the life, language, and perspective of the people being studied have been mastered, the researcher "translates" it for others who read his or her report.

Fifth, both field and H-C researchers focus on process and sequence. They see the passage of time and process as essential to how people construct social reality. This is related to how both are sensitive to an ever-present tension between agency—the active moving fluid side of people changing social reality—and structure—the fixed regularities and patterns that shape social life. For both types of research social reality simultaneously is what people create and something that imposes restrictions on human choice.[3]

Sixth, generalization and theory are limited in field and H-C research. Historical and cross-cultural knowledge is incomplete and provisional, based on selective facts and limited questions. Neither deduces propositions or tests hypotheses in order to uncover fixed laws. Likewise, replication is unrealistic because each researcher has a unique perspective and assembles a unique body of evidence. Instead, researchers offer plausible accounts and limited generalizations.

Unique Features of Historical-Comparative Research. Despite its many similarities to field research, some important differences distinguish H-C research. Research on the past and on an alien culture share much in common, and what they share distinguishes them from other approaches.

First, H-C research usually relies on limited and indirect evidence. Direct observation or involvement by a researcher is often impossible. An H-C researcher reconstructs what occurred from the evidence, but cannot have absolute confidence in the reconstruction. Historical evidence depends on the survival of data from the past, usually in the form of documents (e.g., letters and newspapers). The researcher is limited to what has not been destroyed and what leaves a trace, record, or other evidence behind.

Historical-comparative researchers must also interpret the evidence. Different people looking at the same evidence often ascribe different meanings to it, so a researcher must reflect on evidence. An understanding of it based on a first glance is rarely possible. To do this, a researcher becomes immersed in and absorbs details about a context. For example, a researcher examining the family in the past or a distant country needs to be aware of the full social context (e.g., the nature of work, forms of communication, transportation technology, etc.). He or she looks at maps and gets a feel for the laws in effect, the condition of medical care, and common social practices. For example, the meaning of "a visit by a family member" is affected by conditions such as roads of dirt and mud, the inability to call ahead of time, and the lives of people who work on a farm with animals that need constant watching.

A reconstruction of the past or another culture is easily distorted. Compared to the people being studied, a researcher is usually more aware of events occurring prior to the time studied, events occurring in places other than the location studied, and events that occurred after the period studied. This awareness gives the researcher a greater sense of coherence than was experienced by those living in the past or in an isolated social setting that he or she guards against in a reconstruction.

Historical-comparative researchers recognize the capacity of people to learn, make decisions, and act on what they learn to modify the course of events. For example, if a group of people are aware of or gain consciousness of their own past history and avoid the mistakes of the past, they may act consciously to alter the course of events. Of course, people will not necessarily learn or act on what they have learned, and if they do act they will not necessarily be successful. Nevertheless, people's capacity to learn introduces indeterminacy into historical-comparative explanations.

An H-C researcher wants to find out whether people viewed various courses of action as plausible. Thus, the worldview and knowledge of the people under study shaped what they saw as possible or impossible ways to achieve goals. The researcher asks whether people were conscious of certain things. For example, if an army knew an enemy attack was coming and so decided to cross a river in the middle of the night, the action "crossing the river" would have a different meaning than in the situation where the army did not know the enemy was approaching.

A historical-comparative researcher integrates the micro (small-scale, face-to-face interaction) and macro (large-scale social structures) levels. The H-C researcher describes both levels or layers of reality and links them to each other. For example, an H-C researcher examines the details of individual biographies by reading diaries or letters to get a feel for the individuals: the food they ate, their recreational pursuits, their clothing, their sicknesses, their relations with friends, and so on. He or she links this micro-level view to macro-level processes: increased immigration, mechanization of

production, proletarianization, tightened labor markets, and the like.

Historical-comparative researchers shift between details of specific context and making a general comparison. A researcher examines specific contexts, notes similarities and differences, then generalizes. Comparative researchers compare across cultural-geographic units (e.g., urban areas, nations, societies, etc.).[4] Historical researchers investigate past contexts, usually in one culture (e.g., periods, epochs, ages, eras, etc.), for sequence and comparison. Of course, a researcher can combine both to investigate multiple cultural contexts in one or more historical contexts. Yet, each period or society has its unique causal processes, meaning systems, and social relations, which may lack equivalent elements across the units. This produces a creative tension between the concrete specifics in a context and the abstract ideas a researcher uses to make links across contexts.

The use of transcultural concepts in comparative analysis is analogous to the use of transhistorical ones in historical research.[5] In comparative research, a researcher translates the specifics of a context into a common, theoretical language. In historical research, theoretical concepts are applied across time.

STEPS IN A HISTORICAL-COMPARATIVE RESEARCH PROJECT

In this section, we turn to the process of doing H-C research. Conducting historical-comparative research does not involve a rigid set of steps and, with only a few exceptions, it does not use complex or specialized techniques.

Conceptualizing the Object of Inquiry

An H-C researcher begins by becoming familiar with the setting and conceptualizing what is being studied. He or she may start with a loose model or a set of preliminary concepts and apply them to a specific setting. The provisional concepts contain implicit assumptions or organizing categories to "package" observations and guide a search through evidence.

If a researcher is not already familiar with the historical era or comparative settings, he or she conducts an orientation reading (reading several general works). This will help the researcher grasp the specific setting, assemble organizing concepts, subdivide the main issue, and develop lists of questions to ask. It is impossible to begin serious research without a framework of assumptions, concepts, and theory. Concepts and evidence interact to stimulate research. For example, Skocpol (1979) began her study of revolution with puzzles in macro-sociological theory and the histories of specific revolutions. The lack of fit between histories of revolutions and existing theories stimulated her research.

Locating Evidence

• Next, a researcher locates and gathers evidence through extensive bibliographic work. A researcher uses many indexes, catalogs, and reference works that list what libraries contain. For comparative research, this means focusing on specific nations or units and on particular kinds of evidence within each. The researcher frequently spends many weeks searching for sources in libraries, travels to several different specialized research libraries, and reads dozens (if not hundreds) of books and articles. Comparative research often involves learning one or more foreign languages.

As the researcher masters the literature and takes numerous detailed notes, he or she completes many specific tasks: creating a bibliography list (on cards or computer) with complete citations, taking notes that are neither too skimpy nor too extensive (i.e., more than one sentence but less than dozens of pages of quotes), leaving margins on note cards for adding themes later on, taking all notes in the same format (e.g., on cards, paper, etc.), and developing a file on themes or working

hypotheses. A researcher adjusts initial concepts, questions, or focus on the basis of what he or she discovers in the evidence and considers a range of research reports at different levels of analysis (e.g., general context and detailed narratives on specific topics).

Evaluating Quality of Evidence

The H-C researcher gathers evidence with two questions in mind: How relevant is the evidence to emerging research questions and evolving concepts? How accurate and strong is the evidence?

As the focus of research shifts, evidence that was not relevant can become relevant. Likewise, some evidence may stimulate new avenues of inquiry and a search for additional confirming evidence. An H-C researcher reads evidence for three things: the implicit conceptual frameworks, particular details, and empirical generalizations. He or she evaluates alternative interpretations of evidence and looks for "silences," or cases where the evidence fails to address an event, topic, or issue. For example, when examining a group of leading male merchants in the 1890s, a researcher finds that the evidence and documents about them ignore their wives and many servants.

Organizing Evidence

As a researcher gathers evidence and locates new sources, he or she begins to organize the data. Obviously, it is unwise to take notes madly and let them pile up haphazardly. A researcher begins a preliminary analysis by noting low-level generalizations or themes. Next, a researcher organizes evidence, using theoretical insights to stimulate new ways to organize data and for new questions to ask of evidence.

The interaction of data and theory means that a researcher goes beyond a surface examination of the evidence to develop new concepts by critically evaluating the evidence based on theory. For example, a researcher reads a mass of evidence about a protest movement. The preliminary analysis organizes the evidence into a theme: People who are active in protest interact with each other and develop shared cultural meanings. He or she examines theories of culture and movements, then formulates a new concept: "oppositional movement subculture." The researcher then uses this concept to reexamine the evidence.

Synthesizing

The next step is is to synthesize evidence. Once most of the evidence is in, the researcher refines concepts, creates new ones, and moves toward a general explanatory model. Concrete events in the evidence give meaning to new concepts. The researcher looks for patterns across time or units, and draws out similarities and differences with analogies. He or she organizes divergent events into sequences and groups them together to create a larger picture. Plausible explanations are then developed that subsume both concepts and evidence into a coherent whole. The researcher then reads and rereads notes and sorts and resorts them into piles or files on the basis of organizing schemes. He or she looks for links or connections while looking at the evidence in different ways.

Synthesis links specific evidence with an abstract model of underlying relations or causal mechanisms. Researchers may use metaphors. For example, mass frustration leading to a revolution is "like an emotional roller coaster drop" in which things seem to be getting better, and then there is a sudden letdown after expectations have risen very fast. The models are sensitizing devices.

Writing a Report

Assembling evidence, arguments, and conclusions into a report is always a crucial step, but more than in quantitative approaches, the careful crafting of evidence and explanation makes or breaks H-C research. A researcher distills mountains of evidence into exposition and prepares extensive footnotes. She or he must also weave together the evidence and arguments to communicate a coherent, convincing picture or "tell a story" to readers.

DATA AND EVIDENCE IN HISTORICAL CONTEXT

Types of Historical Evidence

First, some terms need clarification. *History* means the events of the past (e.g., it is *history* that the French withdrew troops from Vietnam), a record of the past (e.g., a *history* of French involvement in Vietnam), and a discipline that studies the past (e.g., a department of *history*). *Historiography* is the method of doing historical research or of gathering and analyzing historical evidence. Historical sociology is a part of historical-comparative research.

Researchers draw on four types of historical evidence or data: primary sources, secondary sources, running records, and recollections.[6] Traditional historians rely heavily on primary sources. H-C researchers often use secondary sources or the different data types in combination.

Primary Sources. The letters, diaries, newspapers, movies, novels, articles of clothing, photographs, and so forth of those who lived in the past and have survived to the present are *primary sources.* They are found in archives (a place where documents are stored), in private collections, in family closets, and in museums (see Box 12.2). Today's documents and objects (our letters, television programs, commercials, clothing, automobiles) will be primary sources for future historians. An example of a classic primary source is a bundle of yellowed letters written by a husband away at war to his wife and found in an attic by a researcher.

Published and unpublished written documents are the most important type of primary

Box 12.2 Using Archival Data

The archive is the main source for primary historical materials. Archives are accumulations of documentary materials (papers, photos, letters, etc.) in private collections, museums, libraries, or formal archives.

Location and Access

Finding whether a collection exists on a topic, organization, or individual can be a long, frustrating task of many letters, phone calls, and referrals. If the material on a person or topic does exist, it may be scattered in multiple locations. Gaining access may depend on an appeal to a family member's kindness for private collections or traveling to distant libraries and verifying one's reason for examining many dusty boxes of old letters. Also, the researcher may discover limited hours (e.g., an archive is open only four days a week from 10 A.M. to 5 P.M., but the researcher needs to inspect the material for 40 hours).

Sorting and Organization

Archive material may be unsorted or organized in a variety of ways. The organization may reflect criteria that are unrelated to the researcher's interests. For example, letters and papers may be in chronological order, but the researcher is interested only in letters to four professional colleagues over three decades, not daily bills, family correspondence, and so on.

Technology and Control

Archival materials may be in their original form, on microforms, or, more rarely, in an electronic form. Researchers may be allowed only to take notes, not make copies, or they may be allowed only to see select parts of the whole collection. Researchers become frustrated with the limitations of having to read dusty papers in one specific room and being allowed only to take notes by pencil for the few hours a day the archive is open to the public.

Tracking and Tracing

One of the most difficult tasks in archival research is tracing common events or persons through the materials. Even if all material is in one location, the same event or relationship may appear in several places in many forms. Researchers sort through mounds of paper to find bits of evidence here and there.

Drudgery, Luck, and Serendipity

Archival research is often painstaking slow. Spending many hours pouring over partially legible documents can be very tedious. Also, researchers will often discover holes in collections, gaps in a series of papers, or destroyed documents. Yet, careful reading and inspection of previously untouched material can yield startling new connections or ideas. The researcher may discover unexpected evidence that opens new lines of inquiry (see Elder et al., 1993, and Hill, 1993).

---

source. Researchers find them in their original form or preserved in microfiche or on film. They are often the only surviving record of the words, thoughts, and feelings of people in the past. Written documents are helpful for studying societies and historical periods with writing and literate people. A frequent criticism of written sources is that they were largely written by elites or those in official organizations; thus, the views of the illiterate, the poor, or those outside official social institutions may be overlooked. For example, it was illegal for slaves in the United States to read or write, and thus written sources on the experience of slavery have been indirect or difficult to find.

The written word on paper was the main medium of communication prior to the widespread use of telecommunications, computers, and video technology to record events and ideas. In fact, the spread of forms of communication that do not leave a permanent physical record (e.g., telephone conversations, computer records, and television or radio broadcasts), and which have largely replaced letters, written ledgers, and newspapers, may make the work of future historians more difficult.

Secondary Sources. Primary sources have realism and authenticity, but the practical limitation of time can restrict research on many primary sources to a narrow time frame or location. To get a broader picture, many H-C researchers use *secondary sources,* the writings of specialist historians who have spent years studying primary sources.

Running Records. *Running records* consist of files or existing statistical documents maintained by organizations. An example of a running record is a file in a country church that contains a record of every marriage and every death from 1910 to the present.

Recollections. The words or writings of individuals about their past lives or experiences based on memory are *recollections.* These can be in the form of memoirs, autobiographies, or interviews. Because memory is imperfect, recollections are often distorted in ways that primary sources are not. For example, Blee (1991) interviewed a woman in her late eighties about being in the Ku Klux Klan (see Box 12.1).

In gathering *oral history,* a type of recollection, a researcher conducts unstructured interviews with people about their lives or events in the past. This approach is especially valuable for nonelite groups or the illiterate. The oral history technique began in the 1930s and now has a professional association and scholarly journal devoted to it.

Research with Secondary Sources

Uses and Limitations. Social researchers often use secondary sources, the books and articles written by historians, as evidence of past conditions.[7] Secondary sources have limitations and need to be used with caution.

Limitations of secondary historical evidence include problems of inaccurate historical accounts and a lack of studies in areas of interest. Such sources cannot be used to test hypotheses. Post facto (after-the-fact) explanations cannot meet positivist criteria of falsifiability, because few statistical controls can be used and replication is impossible. Yet, historical research by others plays an important role in developing general explanations, among its other uses. For example, such research substantiates the emergence and evolution of tendencies over time.

Potential Problems. The many volumes of secondary sources present a maze of details and interpretations for an H-C researcher. He or she must transform the mass of descriptive studies into an intelligible picture that is consistent with the richness of the evidence. It also must bridge the many specific time periods or locales. The researcher faces potential problems with secondary sources.

One problem is that historians rarely present theory-free, objective "facts." They implicitly frame raw data, categorize information, and shape evidence using concepts. The historian's concepts are a mixture drawn from journalism, the language of historical actors, ideologies, philosophy, everyday language in the present, and social science. Most are vague, applied inconsistently, and not mutually exclusive nor exhaustive. For example, a historian describes a group of people in a nineteenth-century town as upper class, but never defines the term and fails to link it to any theory of social classes. The historian's implicit theories constrain the evidence and the social researcher may be looking for evidence for explanations that are contrary to ones implicitly being used by historians in secondary sources.

Historians also select some information from all possible evidence. Yet, the H-C researcher does not know how this was done. Without knowing the selection process, a historical-comparative researcher must rely on the historian's judgments, which can contain biases.[8] For example, a historian reads 10,000 pages of newspapers, letters, and diaries, then boils down this information into summaries and selected quotes in a 100-page book. An H-C researcher does not know whether information that the historian left out is relevant for his or her purposes.

The typical historian's research practice also introduces an individualist bias. A heavy reliance on primary sources and surviving artifacts combines with an atheoretical orientation to produce a narrow focus on the actions of specific people. This particularistic, micro-level view directs attention away from integrating themes or patterns. This emphasis on the documented activities of specific individuals is a type of theoretical orientation.[9]

Another problem is in the organization of the evidence. Tradional historians organize evidence as a *narrative history*. This compounds problems of undefined concepts and the selection of evidence. In the historical narrative, material is chronologically organized around a single coherent "story." Each part of the story is connected to each other part by its place in the time order of events. Together, all the parts form a unity or whole. Conjuncture and contingency are key elements of the narrative form—that is, if X (or X plus Z) occurred, then Y would occur, and if X (or X plus Z) had not occurred, something else would have followed. The contingency creates a logical interdependency between earlier and later events.

A difficulty of the narrative is that the primary organizing tool—time order or position in a sequence of events—does not denote theoretical or historical causality. In other words, the narrative meets only one of the three criteria for establishing causality—that of temporal order. Moreover, narrative writing frequently obscures causal processes. This occurs when a historian includes events in the narrative to enrich the background or context, to add color, but that have no causal significance. Likewise, he or she presents events with a delayed causal impact, or events that are temporarily "on hold" with a causal impact occuring at some unspecified later time.

Also, narratives rarely explicitly indicate how combination or interaction effects operate, or the relative size of different factors. For example, the historian discusses three conditions as causing an event. Yet, rarely do readers know which is most important or whether all three conditions must operate together to have a causal impact, but no two conditions alone, or no single condition alone, creates the same impact.[10]

The narrative organization creates difficulties for the researcher using secondary sources and creates conflicting findings. The H-C researcher must read though weak concepts, unknown selection criteria, and unclear casual logic. Theory may reside beneath the narrative but it remain implicit and hidden.

Two last problems are that a historian is influenced by when he or she is writing and historiographic schools. Various schools of historiography (e.g., diplomatic, demographic, ecological, psychological, Marxist, intellectual, etc.) have their own rules for seeking evidence and asking questions, and they give priority to certain types of explanatory factors. Likewise, a historian writing today will examine primary materials differently from how those writing in the past, such as 1920s, did.

Research with Primary Sources

The historian is the major issue when using secondary sources. When using primary sources, the biggest concern is that only a fraction of everything written or used in the past has survived into the present. Moreover, what survived is a nonrandom sample of what once existed.

Historical-comparative researchers attempt to read primary sources with the eyes and assumptions of a contemporary who lived in the past. This means "bracketing," or holding back knowledge of subsequent events and modern values. For example, when reading a source produced by a slave holder, moralizing against slavery or faulting the author for not seeing its evil is not worthwhile. The H-C researcher holds back moral judgments and becomes a moral relativist while reading primary sources.

Another problem is that locating primary documents is a time-consuming task. A researcher must search through specialized indexes and travel to archives or specialized libraries. Primary sources are often located in a dusty, out-of-the-way room full of stacked cardboard boxes containing masses of fading documents. These may be incomplete, unorganized, and in various stages of decay. Once the documents or other primary sources are located, the researcher evaluates them by subjecting them to external and internal criticism (see Figure 12.1).

External criticism means evaluating the authenticity of a document itself to be certain that it is not a fake or a forgery. Criticism involves asking: Was the document created when it is claimed to have been, in the place where it was supposed to be, and by the person who claims to be its author? Why was the document produced to begin with, and how did it survive?

Once the document passes as being authentic, a researcher uses *internal criticism*, an examination of the document's contents to establish credibility. A researcher evaluates whether what is recorded was based on what the author directly witnessed or is secondhand information. This requires examining both the literal meaning of what is recorded and the subtle connotations or intentions. The researcher notes other events, sources, or people mentioned in the document and asks whether they can be verified. He or she examines implicit assumptions or value positions, and the relevant conditions under which the document was produced is noted (e.g., during wartime or under a totalitarian regime). The researcher also considers language usage at the time and the context of statements within the document to distill a meaning.

In an H-C study of Chinese migrant networks in Peru, Chicago, and Hawaii early in the twentieth century, McKeown (2001) used both primary and secondary historical sources and running records. He considered events over nearly a century of history and in three nations, and everything from major international events and national laws to individual family biographies. He relied on secondary sources for major national or international events. Although his study was primarily historical and qualitative, he also examined quantitative data from running records and provided graphs, charts, and tables of statistics. His evidence also included geographic maps and photographs, quotes from 100-year-old telegrams, official government documents, original newspaper reports, and selections from personal letters in three languages. By comparing Chinese migrants over a long historical period and in divergent socialcultural settings, he could trace the formation and operation of transnational communities

FIGURE 12.1   Internal and External Criticism

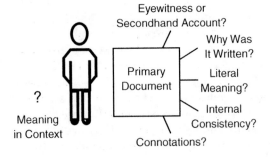

and social identities. He learned that networks with links back to villages in China and crossing several national borders helped to sustain a vibrant, interacting community. The network was held together by social relations from the village of origin, clan, family, business transactions, and shared language and customs. One of McKeown's major arguments is that a perspective based solely on nations can limit a researcher's ability to see a social community that is transnational and the hybrid of multiple cultures. Many aspects of the transnational community developed in reaction to specific interactions that occurred locally.

COMPARATIVE RESEARCH

Types of Comparative Research

A   Comparative   Method. Comparative research is more of a perspective or orientation than a separate research technique. In this section, we consider its strengths.

Problems in other types of research are magnified in a comparative study.[11] Holt and Turner (1970:6) said, "In principle, there is no difference between comparative cross-cultural research and research conducted in a single society. The differences lie, rather, in the magnitude of certain types of problems." A comparative perspective exposes weaknesses in research design and helps a researcher improve the quality of research. The focus of comparative research is on similarities and differences between units.

Comparative research helps a researcher identify aspects of social life that are general across units (e.g., cultures), as opposed to being limited to one unit alone. All researchers want to generalize to some degree. Positivist researchers are interested in discovering general laws or patterns of social behavior that hold across societies. But most positivist research is not comparative.

The comparative orientation improves measurement and conceptualization. Concepts developed by researchers who conduct research across several social units or settings are less likely to apply only to a specific culture or setting. It is difficult for a researcher to detect hidden biases, assumptions, and values until he or she applies a concept in different cultures or settings. Different social settings provide a wider range of events or behavior, and the range in one culture is usually narrower than for human behavior in general. Thus, research in a single culture or setting focuses on a restricted range of possible social activity. For example, two researchers, Hsi-Ping and Abdul, examine the relationship between the age at which a child is weaned and the onset of emotional problems. Hsi-Ping looks only at U.S. data, which show a range from 5 to 15 months at weaning, and indicate that emotional problems increase steadily as age of weaning increases. She concludes that late weaning causes emotional problems. Abdul looks at data from 10 cultures and discovers a range from 5 to 36 months at weaning. He finds that the rate of emotional problems rises with age of weaning until 18 months; it then peaks and falls to a lower level. Abdul arrives at more accurate conclusions: Emotional problems are likely for weaning between the ages of 6 and 24 months, but weaning either earlier or later reduces the chances of emotional problems. Hsi-Ping reached false conclusions about the relationship because of the narrow range of weaning age in the United States.

The way comparative research raises new questions and stimulates theory building is a major strength. For example, Lamont (2000) compared samples of blue-collar and lower–white-collar workers in France and the United States for their justifications and forms of argument used to explain racial differences. She drew random samples from telephone directories of Whites and Blacks in the suburbs of Paris and New York City and interviewed respondents for two hours. Lamont found that the arguments of racists and antiracists alike differed widely between France and the United States. People use arguments and rationales closely tied to the dominant cultural themes of their society. For example, in the United States, there is a long history of using biological inferiority to explain racial differences. This declined greatly but it still exists, yet such a rationale is absent in France. In the United States, the market has near-sacred status and both racist and antiracists frequently used the market and personal economic success in their arguments, but the market factor was absent in France because it is not viewed as a fair and efficient mechanism for allocating resources. The French use cultural arguments, egalitarianism, and the universality of all humans much more than Americans. In fact, the idea of a fundamental equality among all human beings was nearly absent among the justifications given in the United States. Such a discrepancy stimulates researchers to seek explanations for the relationship and to develop new research questions.

Comparative research also has limitations. It is more difficult, more costly, and more time consuming than research that is not comparative. The types of data that can be collected and problems with equivalence (to be discussed) are also frequent problems.

Another limitation is the number of cases. Comparative researchers can rarely use random sampling. Sufficient information is not available for all of the approximately 150 nations in the world. It is unavailable for a nonrandom subset (poor countries, nondemocratic countries, etc.). In addition, can a researcher treat all nations as equal units when some have over a billion people and others only 100,000? The small number of cases creates a tendency for researchers to particularize and see each case as unique, limiting generalization. For example, a researcher examines five cases (e.g., countries), but the units differ from each other in 20 ways. It is difficult to test theory or determine relationships when there are more different characteristics than units.

A third limitation is that comparative researchers can apply, not test, theory, and can make only limited generalizations. Despite the ability to use and consider cases as wholes in

H-C research, rigorous theory testing or experimental research is rarely possible. For example, a researcher interested in the effects of economic recessions cannot cause one group of countries to have a recession while others do not. Instead, the researcher waits until a recession occurs and then looks at other characteristics of the country or unit.

The Units Being Compared

Culture versus Nation.   For convenience, comparative researchers often use the nation-state as their unit of analysis. The nation-state is the major unit used in thinking about the divisions of people across the globe today. Although it is a dominant unit in current times, it is neither an inevitable nor a permanent one; in fact, it has been around for only about 300 years.

The nation-state is a socially and politically defined unit. In it, one government has sovereignty (i.e., military control and political authority) over populated territory. Economic relations (e.g., currency, trade, etc.), transportation routes, and communication systems are integrated within territorial boundaries. The people of the territory usually share a common language and customs, and there is usually a common educational system, legal system, and set of political symbols (e.g., flag, national anthem, etc.). The government claims to represent the interests of all people in the territory under its control.

The nation-state is not the only unit for comparative research. It is frequently a surrogate for culture, which is more difficult to define as a concrete, observable unit. *Culture* refers to a common identity among people based on shared social relations, beliefs, and technology. Cultural differences in language, customs, traditions, and norms often follow national lines. In fact, sharing a common culture is a major factor causing the formation of distinct nation-states.

The boundaries of a nation-state may not match those of a culture. In some situations, a single culture is divided into several nations; in other cases, a nation-state contains more than one culture. Over the past centuries, boundaries between cultures and distinct vibrant cultures have been destroyed, rearranged, or diffused as territory around the world was carved into colonies or nation-states by wars and conquest. For instance, European empires imposed arbitrary boundaries over several cultural groups in nations that were once colonies. Likewise, new immigrants or ethnic minorities are not always assimilated into the dominant culture in a nation. For example, one region of a nation may have people with a distinct ethnic backgrounds, languages, customs, religions, social institutions, and identities (e.g., the province of Quebec in Canada). Such intranational cultures can create regional conflict, since ethnic and cultural identities are the basis for nationalism.

The nation-state is not always the best unit for comparative research. A researcher should ask: What is the relevant comparative unit for my research question—the nation, the culture, a small region, or a subculture? For example, a research question is: Are income level and divorce related (i.e., are higher-income people less likely to divorce?)? A group of people with a distinct culture, language, and religion live in one region of a nation. Among them, income and divorce are not related; elsewhere in the nation, however, where a different culture prevails, income and divorce are related. If a researcher uses the nation-state as his or her unit, the findings could be ambiguous and the explanation weak. Instead of assuming that each nation-state has a common culture, a researcher may find that a unit smaller than the nation-state is more appropriate.

Galton's Problem.   The issue of the units of comparison is related to a problem named after Sir Francis Galton (1822–1911). When researchers compare units or their characteristics, they want the units to be distinct and separate from each other. If the units are not different but are actually the subparts of a larger unit, then researchers will find spurious relationships. For example, the units are the states and provinces in

Canada, France, and the United States; a researcher discovers a strong association between speaking English and having the dollar as currency, or speaking French and using the franc as currency. Obviously, the association exists because the units of analysis (i.e., states or provinces) are subparts of larger units (i.e., nations). The features of the units are due to their being parts of larger units and not to any relationship among the features. Social geographers also encounter this because many social and cultural features diffuse across geographic space.

Galton's problem is an important issue in comparative research because cultures rarely have clear, fixed boundaries. It is hard to say where one culture ends and another begins, whether one culture is distinct from another, or whether the features of one culture have diffused to another over time. Galton's problem occurs when the relationship between two variables in two different units is actually due to a common origin, and they are not truly distinct units (see Figure 12.2).

Galton's problem originated with regard to comparisons across cultures, but it applies to historical comparisons also. It arises when a researcher asks whether units are really the same or different in different historical periods. For example, is the Cuba of 1875 the same country as the Cuba of 2005? Do 130 years since the end of Spanish colonialism, the rise of U.S. influence, independence, dictatorship, and a communist revolution fundamentally change the unit?

Data in Cross-Cultural Research

Comparative Field Research.   Comparative researchers use field research and participant observation in cultures other than their own. Anthropologists are specially trained and prepared for this type of research. The exchange of methods between anthropological and field research suggests that there are small differences between field research in one's own society and in another culture. Field research in a different culture is usually more difficult and places more requirements on the researcher.

FIGURE 12.2   Galton's Problem

Galton's problem occurs when a researcher observes the same social relationship (represented by X) in different settings or societies (represented as A, B, and C) and falsely concludes that the social relationship arose independently in these different places. The researcher may believe he or she has discovered a relationship in three separate cases. But the actual reason for the occurrence of the social relation may be a shared or common origin that has diffused from one setting to others. This is a problem because the researcher who finds a relationship (e.g., a marriage pattern) in distinct settings or units of analysis (e.g., societies) may believe it arose independently in different units. This belief suggests that the relationship is a human universal. The researcher may be unaware that in fact it exists because people have shared the relationship across units.

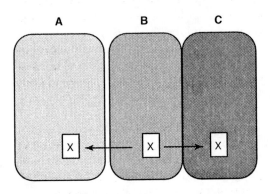

Existing Sources of Qualitative Data.   Comparative researchers can use secondary sources. For example, a researcher who conducts a comparative study of the Brazilian, Canadian, and Japanese educational systems can read studies by researchers from many countries, including Brazil, Canada, and Japan, which describe the education systems in the three nations.

There may have been 5,000 different cultures throughout human history; about 1,000 of them have been studied by social researchers. A valuable source of ethnographic data on different cultures is the *Human Relations Area Files (HRAF)* and the related *Ethnographic Atlas.*[12] The HRAF is a collection of field research reports that bring together information from ethnographic studies on various cultures, most of which are primitive or small tribal groupings. Extensive information on nearly 300 cultures has been organized by social characteristics or practices (e.g., infant feeding, suicide, childbirth, etc.). A study on a particular culture is divided up, and its information on a characteristic is grouped with that from other studies. This makes it easy to compare many cultures on the same characteristic. For example, a researcher interested in inheritance can learn that of 159 different cultures in which it has been studied, 119 have a patrilineal form (father to son), 27 matrilineal (mother to daughter), and 13 mixed inheritance.

Researchers can use the HRAF to study relationships among several characteristics of different cultures. For example, to find out whether sexual assault against women, or rape, is associated with patriarchy (i.e., the holding of power and authority by males), a researcher can examine the presence of sexual assault and the strength of patriarchy in many cultures.

Using the HRAF does have limitations, however. First, the quality of the original research reports depends on the initial researcher's length of time in the field, familiarity with the language, and prior experience, as well as on the explicitness of the research report. Also, the range of behavior observed by the initial researcher and the depth of inquiry can vary. In addition, the categorization of characteristics in the HRAF can be crude. Another limitation involves the cultures that have been studied. Western researchers have made contact with and conducted field research on a limited number of cultures prior to these cultures' contact with the outside world. The cultures studied are not a representative sample of all the human cultures that existed. In addition, Galton's problem (discussed earlier) can be an issue.

Cross-National Survey Research. Survey research was discussed in a previous chapter. This section examines issues that arise when a researcher uses the survey technique in other cultures. The limitations of a cross-cultural survey are not different in principle from those of a survey within one culture. Nevertheless, they are usually much greater in magnitude and severity.

Survey research in a different culture requires that the researcher possess an in-depth knowledge of its norms, practices, and customs. Without such an in-depth knowledge, it is easy to make serious errors in procedure and interpretation. Knowing another language is not enough. A researcher needs to be multicultural and thoroughly know the culture in addition to being familiar with the survey method. Substantial advance knowledge about the other culture is needed prior to entering it or planning the survey. Close cooperation with the native people of the other culture is also essential.

A researcher's choice of the cultures or nations to include in a cross-cultural survey should be made on both substantive (e.g., theoretical, research question) and practical grounds. Each step of survey research (question wording, data collection, sampling, interviewing, etc.) must be tailored to the culture in which it is conducted. One critical issue is how the people from the other culture experience the survey. In some cultures, the survey and interviewing itself may be a strange, frightening experience, analogous to a police interrogation.

Sampling for a survey is also affected by the cultural context. Comparative survey researchers must consider whether accurate sampling frames are available, the quality of mail or telephone service, and transportation to remote rural areas. They need to be aware of such factors as how often people move, the types of dwellings in which people live, the number of people in a dwelling, the telephone coverage, or typical rates of refusal. Researchers must tailor the sampling unit to the culture and consider how basic units, such as the family, are defined in that culture. Special samples or methods for locating people for a sample may be required.

Questionnaire writing problems in the researcher's own culture are greatly magnified when studying a different culture. A researcher needs to be especially sensitive to question wording, questionnaire length, introductions, and topics included. He or she must be aware of local norms and of the topics that can and cannot be addressed by survey research. For example, open questions about political issues, alcohol use, religion, or sexuality may be taboo. In addition to these cultural issues, translation and language equivalency often pose serious problems (see Equivalence in Historical-Comparative Research). Techniques such as back translation (to be discussed) and the use of bilingual people are helpful, but often it is impossible to ask the exact same question in a different language.

Interviewing requires special attention in cross-cultural situations. Selection and training of interviewers depends on the education, norms, and etiquette of the other culture. The interview situation raises issues such as norms of privacy, ways to gain trust, beliefs about confidentiality, and differences in dialect. For example, in some cultures, an interviewer must spend a day in informal discussion before achieving the rapport needed for a short formal interview.

Existing Sources of Quantitative Data. Quantitative data for many variables are available for different nations. In addition, large collections of quantitative data have been assembled. They gather information on many variables from other sources (e.g., newspaper articles, official government statistics, United Nations reports).

There are significant limitations on existing cross-national data, many of which are shared by other existing statistics. The theoretical definition of variables and the reliability of data collection can vary dramatically across nations.

Missing information is a frequent limitation. Intentional misinformation in the official data from some governments can be a problem. Another limitation involves the nations on which data are collected. For example, during a 35-year period, new nations come into existence and others change their names or change their borders.

The existing data are available in major national data archives in a form that computers can read, and researchers can conduct secondary analysis on international existing statistics data. For example, Sutton (2004) conducted a quantitative, statistical study on 15 nations between 1960 and 1990. Researchers have long observed that imprisonment rates do not closely follow changes in crime rates. Sutton tested the Rusche and Kirchheimer thesis. It says that unemployment rates cause a rise in imprisonment rates because imprisonment is a government attempt to control a surplus of unemployed working-class males in the population who could become unruly and dangerous to the social order. Basically, it predicts that prisons will be filled when many workers are out of work and will empty out when the economy is booming. Sutton gathered data from government statistical yearbooks of the 15 countries, from publications by international organizations such as the World Health Organization and the International Labor Organization, and from prior social science studies that identified features of several nations, such as their unionization pattern, political party structure, and so forth. Sutton found only limited support for the original thesis, but he documented a strong effect from several other factors. He argued that the effect of unemployment on imprisonment was probably spurious (see the discussion of a spurious relationship in Chapters 2, 4, and 10 of this book). Sutton found that specific features of the nation's political organization and labor market structure appeared to cause both specific unemployment patterns and different imprisonment policies. In short, when low-income people and workers were politically weak compared to wealthy people and corporation

owners, both unemployment and imprisonment rates rise compared to times when low-income people and workers have greater political power and influence.

EQUIVALENCE IN HISTORICAL-COMPARATIVE RESEARCH

The Importance of Equivalence

Equivalence is a critical issue in all research. It is the issue of making comparisons across divergent contexts, or whether a researcher, living in a specific time period and culture, correctly reads, understands, or conceptualizes data about people from a different historical era or culture. Without equivalence, a researcher cannot use the same concepts or measures in different cultures or historical periods, and this makes comparison difficult, if not impossible. It is similar to the problems that arise with measurement validity in quantitative research.

Types of Equivalence

The equivalence issue has implications for H-C research. A researcher might misunderstand or misinterpret events in a different era or culture. Assuming that the interpretation is correct, a researcher may find it difficult to conceptualize and organize the events to make comparisons across times or places. If he or she fully grasps another culture, a researcher may still find it difficult to communicate with others from his or her own time and culture. The equivalence issue can be divided into four subtypes: lexicon equivalence, contextual equivalence, conceptual equivalence, and measurement equivalence.

Lexicon Equivalence.   *Lexicon equivalence* is the correct translation of words and phrases, or finding a word that means the same thing as another word. This is clearest between two languages. For example, in many languages and cultures there are different forms of address and

pronouns for intimates (e.g., close friends and family members) and subordinates (e.g., younger persons and lower-status people) from
• those used in unknown or public settings or for persons of higher social status. There are no directly equal linguistic forms of speech in English, although the idea of close personal versus public relations exists in English-speaking cultures. In such languages, switching pronouns when saying, "How are you today?" might indicate a change in status or in the social relationship. One would have to indicate it in another, perhaps nonverbal, way if speaking in English. In cultures where age is an important status (e.g., Japan), many status-based words exist that are absent in English. One cannot say, for example, "my brother" without indicating whether one is speaking of an older or younger brother, and separate words are used for "my younger brother" or "my older brother."

Comparative researchers often use a technique called *back translation* to achieve lexicon equivalence. In back translation, a phrase or question is translated from one language to another and then back again. For example, a phrase in English is translated into Korean and then independently translated from Korean back into English. A researcher then compares the first and second English versions. For example, in a study to compare knowledge of international issues by U.S. and Japanese college students, the researchers developed a questionnaire in English. They next had a team of Japanese college faculty translate the questionnaire into Japanese. Some changes were made in the questionnaire. When they used back translation, they discovered "30 translating errors, including some major ones" (Cogan et al., 1988:285).

Back translation does not help when words for a concept do not exist in a different language (e.g., there is no word for *trust* in Hindi, for *loyalty* in Turkish, for *privacy* in Chinese, or for *good quarrel* in Thai). Thus, translation may require complex explanations, or a researcher may not be able to use certain concepts.

Lexicon equivalence can be significant in historical research because the meaning of words changes over time, even in the same language. The greater the distance in time, the greater the chance that an expression will have a different meaning or connotation. For example, today the word *weed* refers to unwanted plants or to marijuana, but in Shakespeare's era, the word meant clothing (see Box 12.3).

Contextual Equivalence. *Contextual equivalence* is the correct application of terms or concepts in different social or historical contexts. It is an attempt to achieve equivalence within specific contexts. For example, in cultures with different dominant religions, a religious leader (e.g., priest, minister, or rabbi) can have different roles, training, and authority. In some contexts, priests are full-time male professionals who are wealthy, highly esteemed, well-educated community leaders and also wield political power. In other contexts, a priest is anyone who rises above others in a congregation on a temporary basis but is without power or standing in

---

| Box 12.3 | Cross-Cultural Answers to Survey Questions |

The meaning of a statement or answer to a question often depends on the customs of a culture, the social situation, and the manner in which the answer is spoken. The manner of answering can reverse the different meanings of the same answer based on the manner in which the answer was spoken.

Manner in Which Answer Spoken	Answer to Question	
	Yes	*No*
Polite	No	Yes
Emphatic	Yes	No

Source: Adapted from Hymes (1970:329).

the community. Priests in such a context may be less well educated, have low incomes, and be viewed as foolish but harmless people. A researcher who asks about "priests" without noticing the context could make serious errors in interpretations.

Context also applies across historical eras. For example, *attending college* has a different meaning today than in a historical context in which only the richest 1 percent of the population attended college, most colleges had fewer than 500 students, all were private all-male institutions that did not require a high school diploma for entry, and a college curriculum consisted of classical languages and moral training. Attending college 100 years ago was not the same as it is today; the historical context has altered the meaning of attending college.

Conceptual Equivalence.   The ability to use the same concept across divergent cultures or historical eras is *conceptual equivalence*. Researchers live within specific cultures and historical eras. Their concepts are based on their experiences and knowledge from their own culture and era. Researchers may try to stretch their concepts by learning about other cultures or eras, but their views of other cultures or eras are colored by their current life situations. This creates a persistent tension and raises the question: Can a researcher create concepts that are simultaneously true reflections of life experiences in different cultures or eras and that also make sense to him or her?

The issue of a researcher's concept is a special case of a larger issue, because concepts can be incompatible across different time periods or cultures. Is it possible to create concepts that are true, accurate, and valid representations of social life in two or more cultural or historical settings that are very different? For example, the word *class* exists in many societies, but the system of classes (i.e., the role of income, wealth, job, education, status, relation to means of production), the number of classes, the

connotations of being in a particular class, and class categories or boundaries differ across societies, making the study of social class across societies difficult.

At times, the same or a very similar concept exists across cultures but in different forms or degrees of strength. For example, in many Asian societies, there is a marked difference between the outward, public presentation and definition of self and the private, personal presentation and the definition of self. What one reveals and shows externally is often culturally detached from true, internal feelings. Some languages mark this linguistically, as well. The idea of a distinct self for public, nonfamily, or nonprivate situations exists in Western cultures, as well, but it is much weaker and less socially significant. In addition, many Western cultures assume that the inner self is "real" and should be revealed, an assumption that is not always shared cross-culturally.

At other times, there is no direct cultural equivalent. For example, there is no direct Western conceptual equivalent for the Japanese *ie*. It is translated as family system, but this idea was created by outsiders to explain Japanese behavior. The *ie* includes a continuing line of familial descent going back generations and continuing into the future. Its meaning is closer to a European lineage "house" among the feudal nobility than the modern household or even an extended family. It includes ancestors, going back many generations, and future descendants, with branches created by noninheriting male offspring (or adopted sons). It can also include a religious identity and property-holding dimensions (as land or a business passed down for generations). It can include feelings of obligation to one's ancestors and feelings to uphold any commitments they may have made. The *ie* is also embedded in a web of hierarchical relationships with other *ie* and suggests social position or status in a community.

Conceptual equivalence also applies to the study of different historical eras. For example, measuring income is very different in a historical era with a largely noncash society in which most people grow their own food, make their own furniture and clothing, or barter goods. Where money is rarely used, it makes no sense to measure income by number of dollars earned. Counting hogs, acres of land, pairs of shoes, servants, horse carriages, and the like may be more appropriate.

Measurement Equivalence. *Measurement equivalence* means measuring the same concept in different settings. If a researcher develops a concept appropriate to different contexts, the question remains: Are different measures necessary in different contexts for the same concept? The measurement equivalence issue suggests that an H-C researcher must examine many sources of partial evidence in order to measure or identify a theoretical construct. When evidence exists in fragmentary forms, he or she must examine extensive quantities of indirect evidence in order to identify constructs.

ETHICS

Historical-comparative research shares the ethical concerns found in other nonreactive research techniques. The use of primary historical sources occasionally raises special ethical issues. First, it is difficult to replicate research based on primary material. The researcher's selection criteria for use of evidence and external criticism of documents places a burden on the integrity of the individual researcher.

Second, the right to protect one's privacy may interfere with the right to gather evidence. A person's descendants may want to destroy or hide private papers or evidence of scandalous behavior. Even major political figures (e.g., presidents) want to hide embarrassing official documents. Comparative researchers must be sensitive to cultural and political issues of cross-cultural interaction. They need to learn what is considered offensive within a culture. Sensitivity means showing respect for the traditions, customs, and meaning of privacy in a host country. For example, it may be taboo for a man to interview a married woman without her husband present.

In general, a researcher who visits another culture wants to establish good relations with the host country's government. He or she will not take data out of the country without giving something (e.g., results) in return. The military or political interests of the researcher's home nation or the researcher's personal values may conflict with official policy in the host nation. A researcher may be suspected of being a spy or may be under pressure from his or her home country to gather covert information.

Sometimes, the researcher's presence or findings may cause diplomatic problems. For example, a researcher who examines health care practices in a country, then declares that official government policy is to ignore treating a serious illness can expect serious controversy. Likewise, a researcher who is sympathetic to the cause of groups who oppose the government may be threatened with imprisonment or asked to leave the country. Social researchers who conduct research in any country should be aware of such issues and the potential consequences of their actions.

CONCLUSION

In this chapter, you have learned methodological principles for an inquiry into historical and comparative materials. The H-C approach is appropriate when asking big questions about macro-level change, or for understanding social processes that operate across time or are universal across several societies. Historical-comparative research can be carried out in several ways, but a distinct qualitative H-C approach is similar to that of field research in important respects.

Historical-comparative research involves a different orientation toward research more than it means applying specialized techniques. Some specialized techniques are used, such as the external criticism of primary documents, but the most vital feature is how a researcher approaches a question, probes data, and moves toward explanations.

Historical-comparative research is more difficult to conduct than research that is neither historical nor comparative, but the difficulties are present to a lesser degree in other types of social research. For example, issues of equivalence exist to some degree in all social research. In H-C research, however, the problems cannot be treated as secondary concerns. They are at the forefront of how research is conducted and determine whether a research question can be answered.

Key Terms

back translation
conceptual equivalence
contextual equivalence
external criticism
Galton's problem
Human Relations Area Files (HRAF)
internal criticism
lexicon equivalence
measurement equivalence
oral history
primary sources
recollections
running records
secondary sources

Endnotes

1. See Mahoney (1999) for major works of historical-comparative research.
2. See Calhoun (1996), McDaniel (1978), Przeworski and Teune (1970), and Stinchcombe (1978) for additional discussion.
3. For additional discussion, see Sewell (1987).
4. See Naroll (1968) for a discussion of difficulties in creating distinctions. Also see Whiting (1968).
5. Transhistorical concepts are discussed by others, such as Bendix (1963), Przeworski and Teune (1970), and Smelser (1976).
6. See Lowenthal (1985:187).
7. Bendix (1978:16) distinguished between the *judgments* of historians and the *selections* of sociologists.
8. Bonnell (1980:161), Finley (1977:132), and Goldthorpe (1977:189–190) discussed how historians use concepts. Selection in this context is discussed by Abrams (1982:194) and Ben-Yehuda (1983).
9. For introductions to how historians see their method, see Barzun and Graff (1970), Braudel (1980), Cantor and Schneider (1967), Novick (1988), or Shafer (1980).
10. The narrative is discussed in Abbott (1992), Gallie (1963), Gotham and Staples (1996), Griffin (1993), McLennan (1981:76–87), Runciman (1980), and Stone (1987:74–96).
11. For more on the strengths and limitations of comparative research, see Anderson (1973), Holt and Turner (1970), Kohn (1987), Ragin (1987), Smelser (1976), Vallier (1971a, 1971b), Walton (1973), and Whiting (1968).
12. For more on the *Human Relations Area File* and the *Ethnographic Atlas,* see Murdock (1967, 1971) and Whiting (1968).

Analysis of Qualitative Data

INTRODUCTION

Qualitative data come in the form of photos, written words, phrases, or symbols describing or representing people, actions, and events in social life. Qualitative researchers rarely use statistical analysis. This does not mean that qualitative data analysis is based on vague impressions. It can be systematic and logically rigorous, although in a different way from quantitative or statistical analysis. Over time qualitative data analysis has become more explicit, although no single qualitative data analysis approach is widely accepted.

This chapter is divided into four parts. First, the similarities and differences between qualitative and quantitative data analysis are discussed. Next is a look at how researchers use coding and concept/theory building in the process of analyzing qualitative data. Third is a review of some of the major analytic strategies researchers deploy and ways they think about linking qualitative data with theory. Last is a brief review of other techniques researchers use to manage and examine patterns in the qualitative data they have collected.

COMPARING METHODS OF DATA ANALYSIS

Similarities

Both styles of research involve researchers inferring from the empirical details of social life. To *infer* means to pass a judgment, to use reasoning, and to reach a conclusion based on evidence. In both forms of data analysis, the researcher carefully examines empirical information to reach a conclusion. The conclusion is reached by reasoning, simplifying the complexity in the data, and abstracting from the data, but this varies by the style of research. Both forms of data analysis anchor statements about the social world and are faithful to the data.

Qualitative as well as quantitative analysis involves a public method or process. Researchers systematically record or gather data and in so doing make accessible to others what they did. Both types of researchers collect large amounts of data, describe the data, and document how they collected and examined it. The degree to which the method is standardized and visible may vary, but all researchers reveal their study design in some way.

All data analysis is based on comparison. Social researchers compare features of the evidence they have gathered internally or with related evidence. Researchers identify multiple processes, causes, properties, or mechanisms within the evidence. They then look for patterns—similarities and differences, aspects that are alike and unlike. Both qualitative and quantitative researchers strive to avoid errors, false conclusions, and misleading inferences. Researchers are also alert for possible fallacies or illusions. They sort through various explanations, discussions, and descriptions, and evaluate merits of rivals, seeking the more authentic, valid, true, or worthy among them.

Differences

Qualitative data analysis differs from quantitative analysis in four ways. First, quantitative researchers choose from a specialized, standardized set of data analysis techniques. Hypothesis testing and statistical methods vary little across different social research projects. Quantitative analysis is highly developed and builds on applied mathematics. By contrast, qualitative data analysis is less standardized. The wide variety in qualitative research is matched by the many approaches to data analysis.

A second difference is that quantitative researchers do not begin data analysis until they have collected all of the data and condensed them into numbers. They then manipulate the numbers in order to see patterns or relationships. Qualitative researchers can look for patterns or relationships, but they begin analysis early in a research project, while they are still collecting data. The results of early data analysis guide subsequent data collection. Thus, analysis is less a distinct final stage of research than a dimension of research that stretches across all stages.

Another difference is the relationship between data and social theory. Quantitative researchers manipulate numbers that represent empirical facts to test theoretical hypotheses. By contrast, qualitative researchers create new concepts and theory by blending together empirical evidence and abstract concepts. Instead of testing a hypothesis, a qualitative analyst may illustrate or color in evidence showing that a theory, generalization, or interpretation is plausible.

The fourth difference is the degree of abstraction or distance from the details of social life. In all data analysis, a researcher places raw data into categories that he or she manipulates in order to identify patterns. Quantitative researchers assume that social life can be represented by using numbers. When they manipulate the numbers according to the laws of statistics, the numbers reveal features of social life. Qualitative analysis does not draw on a large, well-established body of formal knowledge from mathematics and statistics. The data are in the form of words, which are relatively imprecise, diffuse, and context-based, and can have more than one meaning.

Explanations and Qualitative Data

Qualitative explanations take many forms. A qualitative researcher does not have to choose between a rigid idiographic/nomothetic dichotomy—that is, between describing specifics and verifying universal laws. Instead, a researcher develops explanations or generalizations that are close to concrete data and contexts but are more than simple descriptions. He or she usually uses a lower-level, less abstract theory, which is grounded in concrete details. He or she may

build new theory to create a realistic picture of social life and stimulate understanding more than to test a causal hypothesis. Explanations tend to be rich in detail, sensitive to context, and capable of showing the complex processes or sequences of social life. The explanations may be causal, but this is not always the case. The researcher's goal is to organize specific details into a coherent picture, model, or set of interlocked concepts.

A qualitative researcher divides explanations into two categories: highly unlikely and plausible. The researcher is satisfied by building a case or supplying supportive evidence. He or she may eliminate some theoretical explanations from consideration while increasing the plausibility of others because only a few explanations will be consistent with a pattern in the data. Qualitative analysis can eliminate an explanation by showing that a wide array of evidence contradicts it. The data might support more than one explanation, but *all* explanations will not be consistent with it. In addition to eliminating less plausible explanations, qualitative data analysis helps to verify a sequence of events or the steps of a process. This temporal ordering is the basis of finding associations among variables, and it is useful in supporting causal arguments.

CODING AND CONCEPT FORMATION

Qualitative researchers often use general ideas, themes, or concepts as analytic tools for making generalizations. Qualitative analysis often uses nonvariable concepts or simple nominal-level variables.

Conceptualization

Quantitative researchers conceptualize and refine variables in a process that comes before data collection or analysis. By contrast, qualitative researchers form new concepts or refine concepts that are grounded in the data. Concept formation is integral to data analysis and begins during data collection. Conceptualization is how a qualitative researcher organizes and makes sense of the data.

A qualitative researcher organizes data into categories on the basis of themes, concepts, or similar features. He or she develops new concepts, formulates conceptual definitions, and examines the relationships among concepts. Eventually, he or she links concepts to each other in terms of a sequence, as oppositional sets (X is the opposite of Y) or as sets of similar categories that he or she interweaves into theoretical statements. Qualitative researchers conceptualize or form concepts as they read through and ask critical questions of data (e.g., field notes, historical documents, secondary sources, etc.). The questions can come from the abstract vocabulary of a discipline such as sociology—for example: Is this a case of class conflict? Was role conflict present in that situation? Is this a social movement? Questions can also be logical—for example: What was the sequence of events? How does the way it happened here compare to over there? Are these the same or different, general or specific cases? Researchers often conceptualize as they code qualitative data.

In qualitative data analysis, ideas and evidence are mutually interdependent. This applies particularly to case study analysis. Cases are not given preestablished empirical units or theoretical categories apart from data; they are defined by data and theory. By analyzing a situation, the researcher organizes data and applies ideas simultaneously to create or specify a case. Making or creating a case, called *casing*, brings the data and theory together. Determining what to treat as a case resolves a tension or strain between what the researcher observes and his or her ideas about it.

Coding Qualitative Data

A quantitative researcher codes after all the data have been collected. He or she arranges measures of variables, which are in the form of numbers, into a machine-readable form for statistical analysis.

Coding data has a different meaning in qualitative research. A researcher codes by organizing the raw data into conceptual categories and creates themes or concepts. Instead of a simple clerical task, coding is an integral part of data analysis guided by the research question. Coding encourages higher-level thinking about the data and moves a researcher toward theorical generalizations.

Coding is two simultaneous activities: mechanical data reduction and analytic data categorization. Coding data is the hard work of reducing mountains of raw data into manageable piles. In addition to making a large mass of data manageable, it is how a researcher imposes order on the data. Coding also allows a researcher to quickly retrieve relevant parts of the data. Between the moments of thrill and inspiration, coding qualitative data, or filework, can be wearisome and tedious.

Open Coding. *Open coding* is performed during a first pass through recently collected data. The researcher locates themes and assigns initial codes or labels in a first attempt to condense the mass of data into categories. He or she slowly reads field notes, historical sources, or other data, looking for critical terms, key events, or themes, which are then noted. Next, he or she writes a preliminary concept or label at the edge of a note card or computer record and highlights it with brightly colored ink or in some similar way. The researcher is open to creating new themes and to changing these initial codes in subsequent analysis. A theoretical framework helps if it is used in a flexible manner.

Open coding brings themes to the surface from deep inside the data. The themes are at a low level of abstraction and come from the researcher's initial research question, concepts in the literature, terms used by members in the social setting, or new thoughts stimulated by immersion in the data.

An example of this is found in LeMasters's (1975) field research study of a working-class tavern when he found that marriage came up in many conversations. If he open coded field notes, he might have coded a block of field notes with the theme *marriage*. Following is an example of hypothetical field notes that can be open coded with the theme *marriage*:

I wore a tie to the bar on Thursday because I had been at a late meeting. Sam noticed it immediately and said. "Damn it, Doc. I wore one of them things once—when I got married—and look what happened to me! By God, the undertaker will have to put the next one on." I ordered a beer, then asked him, "Why did you get married?" He replied, "What the hell you goin' to do? You just can't go on shacking up with girls all your life— I did plenty of that when I was single" with a smile and wink. He paused to order another beer and light a cigarette, then continued, "A man, sooner or later, likes to have a home of his own, and some kids, and to have that, you have to get married. There's no way out of it—they got you hooked." I said, "Helen [his wife] seems like a nice person." He returned, "Oh, hell, she's not a bad kid, but she's a goddamn woman and they get under my skin. They piss me off. If you go to a party, just when you start having fun, the wife says 'let's go home.' " (Adapted from LeMasters, 1975:36–37)

Historical-comparative researchers also use open coding. For example, a researcher studying the Knights of Labor, an American nineteenth-century movement for economic and political reform, reads a secondary source about the activities of a local branch of the movement in a specific town. When reading and taking notes, the researcher notices that the Prohibition party was important in local elections and that temperance was debated by members of the local branch. The researcher's primary interest is in the internal structure, ideology, and growth of the Knights movement. Temperance is a new and unexpected category. The researcher codes the notes with the label "temperance" and includes it as a possible theme.

Qualitative researchers vary in the units they code. Some code every line or every few words; others code paragraphs and argue that much of the data are not coded and are dross or left over. The degree of detail in coding depends on the research question, the "richness" of the data, and the researcher's purposes.

Open-ended coding extends to analytic notes or memos that a researcher writes to himself or herself while collecting data. Researchers should write memos on their codes (see the later discussion in Analytic Memo Writing).

Axial Coding. This is a "second pass" through the data. During open coding, a researcher focuses on the actual data and assigns code labels for themes. There is no concern about making connections among themes or elaborating the concepts that the themes represent. By contrast, in *axial coding,* the researcher begins with an organized set of initial codes or preliminary concepts. In this second pass, he or she focuses on the initial coded themes more than on the data. Additional codes or new ideas may emerge during this pass, and the researcher notes them; but his or her primary task is to review and examine initial codes. He or she moves toward organizing ideas or themes and identifies the axis of key concepts in analysis.

During axial coding, a researcher asks about causes and consequences, conditions and interactions, strategies and processes, and looks for categories or concepts that cluster together. He or she asks questions such as: Can I divide existing concepts into subdimensions or subcategories? Can I combine several closely related concepts into one more general one? Can I organize categories into a sequence (i.e., A, then B, then C), or by their physical location (i.e., where they occur), or their relationship to a major topic of interest? For example, a field researcher studying working-class life divides the general issue of marriage into subparts (e.g., engagement, weddings). He or she marks all notes involving parts of marriage and then relates marriage to themes of sexuality, division of labor in household tasks, views on children, and so on. When the theme reappears in different places, the researcher makes comparisons so he or she can see new themes (e.g., men and women have different attitudes toward marriage).

In the example of historical research on the Knights of Labor, a researcher looks for themes related to temperance. He or she looks for discussions of saloons, drinking or drunkenness, and relations between the movement and political parties that support or oppose temperance. Themes that cluster around temperance could also include drinking as a form of recreation, drinking as part of ethnic culture, and differences between men and women regarding drinking.

Axial coding not only stimulates thinking about linkages between concepts or themes but it also raises new questions. It can suggest dropping some themes or examining others in more depth. In addition, it reinforces the connections between evidence and concepts. As a researcher consolidates codes and locates evidences, he or she finds evidence in many places for core themes and builds a dense web of support in the qualitative data for them. This is analogous to the idea of multiple indicators described with regard to reliability and measuring variables. The connection between a theme and data is strengthened by multiple instances of empirical evidence.

Selective Coding.   By the time a researcher is ready for this last pass through the data, he or she has identified the major themes of the research project. *Selective coding* involves scanning data and previous codes. Researchers look selectively for cases that illustrate themes and make comparisons and contrasts after most or all data collection is complete. They begin after they have well-developed concepts and have started to organize their overall analysis around several

core generalizations or ideas. For example, a researcher studying working-class life in a tavern decides to make gender relations a major theme. In selective coding, the researcher goes through his or her field notes, looking for differences in how men and women talk about dating, engagements, weddings, divorce, extramarital affairs, or husband/wife relations. He or she then compares male and female attitudes on each part of the theme of marriage.

Likewise, the researcher studying the Knights of Labor decides to make the movement's failure to form alliances with other political groups a major theme. The researcher goes through his or her notes looking for compromise and conflict between the Knights and other political parties, including temperance groups and the Prohibition party. The array of concepts and themes that are related to temperance in axial coding helps him or her discover how the temperance issue facilitated or inhibited alliances.

During selective coding, major themes or concepts ultimately guide the researcher's search. He or she reorganizes specific themes identified in earlier coding and elaborates more than one major theme. For example, in the working-class tavern study, the researcher examines opinions on marriage to understand both the theme of gender relations and the theme of different stages of the life cycle. He or she does this because marriage can be looked at both ways. Likewise, in the Knights of Labor study, the researcher can use temperance to understand the major theme of failed alliances and also to understand another theme, sources of division within the movement that were based on ethnic or religious differences among members (see Figure 13.1).

Analytic Memo Writing

Qualitative researchers are compulsive notetakers. Their data are recorded in notes, they write comments on their research strategy in notes, and so on. They keep their notes

FIGURE 13.1   The Coding Process for Qualitative Data Analysis

Step 1: Open Coding

Carefully read and review all data notes, then create a code
that captures the idea, process, or theme in the data.

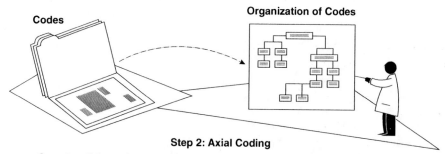

Step 2: Axial Coding

Organize all the codes created during open coding into a structure by separating
them into major or minor levels and showing relations among the codes.

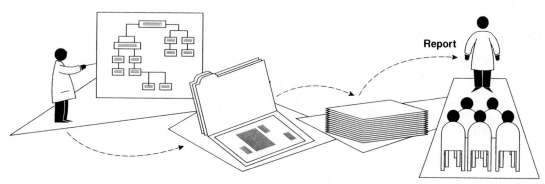

Step 3: Selective Coding

Take the organized codes from the axial coding process and review the codes in the original
data notes to select the best illustrations for entering them into a final report.

organized in files, and often have many files with different kinds of notes: a file on methodological issues (e.g., locations of sources or ethical issues), a file of maps or diagrams, a file on possible overall outlines of a final report or chapter, a file on specific people or events, and so on.

The *analytic memo* is a special type of note. It is a memo or discussion of thoughts and ideas about the coding process that a researcher writes to himself or herself. Each coded theme or concept forms the basis of a separate memo, and the memo contains a discussion of the concept or theme. The rough theoretical notes form the beginning of analytic memos.

The analytic memo forges a link between the concrete data or raw evidence and more abstract, theoretical thinking (see Figure 13.2). It contains a researcher's reflections on and thinking about the data and coding. The researcher adds to the memo and uses it as he or she passes through the data with each type of coding. The memos form the basis for analyzing data in the research report. In fact, rewritten sections from good-quality analytic memos can become sections of the final report.

The technology involved in writing analytic memos is simple: pen and paper, a few notebooks, computer files, and photocopies of notes. There are many ways to write analytic memos; each researcher develops his or her own style or method. Some researchers make multiple copies of notes, then cut them and place selections into an analytic memo file. This works well if the data files are large and the analytic memos are kept distinct within the file (e.g., on different-colored paper or placed at the beginning). Other researchers link the analytic memo file locations to the data notes where a theme appears. Then it is easy to move between the analytic memo and the data. Because data notes contain links or marked themes, it is easy to locate specific sections in the data. An intermediate strategy is to keep a running list of locations where a major theme appears in the raw data.

As a researcher reviews and modifies analytic memos, he or she discusses ideas with

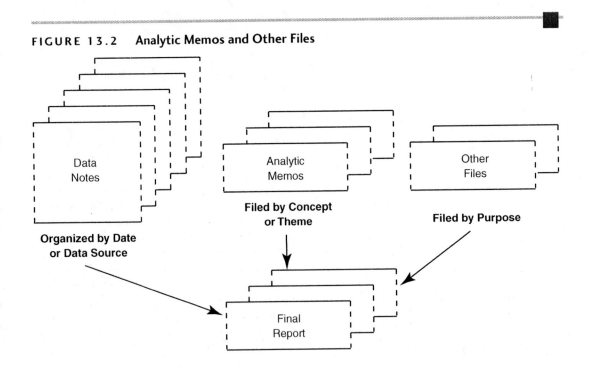

FIGURE 13.2   Analytic Memos and Other Files

colleagues, and returns to the literature with a focus on new issues. Analytic memos may help to generate potential hypotheses, which can be added and dropped as needed, and to develop new themes or coding systems.

ANALYTIC STRATEGIES FOR QUALITATIVE DATA

Techniques of coding and memo writing are approaches to the analysis of qualitative data. Most qualitative researchers use these techniques to some degree, often combined with a more specific strategy for the analysis of qualitative data. In this section you will learn about four strategies researchers use to analyze qualitative data: the narrative, ideal types, successive approximation, and the illustrative method.

Compared to the analysis of quantitative data, strategies for qualitative data are more diverse, less standardized, and less explicitly outlined by researchers. Only in the past decade have researchers started to explain and outline exactly how they analyze qualitative data.

In general, *data analysis* means a search for patterns in data—recurrent behaviors, objects, or a body of knowledge. Once a pattern is identified, it is interpreted in terms of a social theory or the setting in which it occurred. The qualitative researcher moves from the description of a historical event or social setting to a more general interpretation of its meaning.

The Narrative

You encountered the narrative in the last chapter on historical-comparative research. In field research, it is also called a *natural history* or *realist tale approach*. The narrative is a largely atheoretical description. The researcher–author "disappears" from the analysis and presents the concrete details in chronological order as if they were the product of a unique and "naturally unfolding" sequence of events. He or she simply "tells a story" of what occurred.

Some argue that the narrative approach is a presentation of data without analysis. There can be analysis in a narrative, but it is "light" and subtle. In the narrative method, a researcher assembles the data into a descriptive picture or account of what occurred, but he or she largely leaves the data to "speak for themselves." He or she interjects little in the form of new systematic concepts, external theories, or abstract models. The explanation resides not in abstract concepts and theories, but in a combination of specific, concrete details. The researcher presents or reveals the social reality as members in a field setting experience it, or the worldview of specific historical actors at a particular point in time. By using little commentary, a researcher tries to convey an authentic feel for life's complexity as experienced by particular people in specific circumstances, and does not derive abstract principles or identify generalizable analytic patterns.

In the narrative, data are "analyzed" or "explained" in the terminology and concepts of the people being studied. The analysis appears in how a researcher organizes the data for presentation and tells the story. It appears in a greater attention to particular people, events, or facts, and it relies on literary devices—the creative selection of particular words to tell a story, describe a setting, show character development, and present dramatic emphasis, intrigue, or suspense.

Researchers debate the usefulness of the narrative strategy. On the one hand, it provides rich concrete detail and clearly demonstrates the temporal ordering of processes or specific events. It captures a high degree of complexity and conveys a nuanced understanding of how particular events or factors mutually affect each other. The narrative allows the researcher to assemble very specific concrete details (i.e., the names, actions, and words of specific people and the detailed descriptions of particular events at specific times) that may be idiosyncratic but that contribute to a complete explanation. On the other hand, many researchers criticize the narrative approach for being too complex, particular, and idiosyncratic. It does not provide generalizations. The narrative may present an overwhelming array of particular details, but not provide a general explanation that researchers can apply to other people, situations, or time periods (see Box 13.1).

Ideal Types

Max Weber's *ideal type* is used by many qualitative researchers. Ideal types are models or mental abstractions of social relations or processes. They are pure standards against which the data

or "reality" can be compared. An ideal type is a device used for comparison, because no reality ever fits an ideal type. For example, a researcher develops a mental model of the ideal democracy or an ideal college beer party. These abstractions, with lists of characteristics, do not describe any specific democracy or beer party; nevertheless, they are useful when applied to many specific cases to see how well each case measures up to the ideal. This stage can be used with the illustrative method described earlier.

Weber's method of ideal types also complements John Stuart Mill's method of agreement.

 Box 13.1 The Narrative

Many qualitative researchers, especially feminist researchers, use the narrative because they believe it best enables them to retain a richness and authenticity from their original data sources (i.e., individual personal stories or events in ethnographies, or specific historical events). In simple terms, the narrative is story telling. In it, an author presents two or more events in temporal and causal sequences. Some narratives are complex, with elements such as (1) a summary statement of the entire story; (2) an orientation that identifies specific times, places, persons, and situations; (3) complicating actions or twists in the plot of "what happened"; (4) an evaluation or emotional assessment of the narrative's meaning or signifigance; (5) a resolution or what occured after a dramatic high point that resolves a suspenseful climatic event; and (6) a coda or signal that the narrative is ending.

People frequently tell one another stories in daily life. They usually structure or organize their narratives into one of several recognized patterns, often recounting it with visual clues, gestures, or voice intonations for dramatic emphasis. The structure may include plot lines, core metaphors, and rhetorical devices that draw on familiar cultural and personal models to effectively communicate meanings to others.

The narrative is found in literature, artistic expressions, types of therapy, judicial inquiries, social or political histories, biography and autobiography, medical case histories, and journalistic accounts. As a way to organize, analyze, and present qualitative social science data, the narrative shares many features with other academic and cultural communication forms, but it differs from the positivist model for organizing and reporting on data. The positivist model emphasizes using impersonal, abstract, "neutral" language and a standardized analytic approach.

Many qualitative researchers argue that researchers who adopt the positivist model are simply using an alternative form of narrative, one with specialized conventions. These conventions encourage formal analytic models and abstract theories, but such models or theories are not necessarily superior to a story-telling narrative. Positivist data analysis and reporting conventions have two negative effects. First, they make it easier for researchers to lose sight of the concrete actual events and personal experiences that comprise social science data. Second, they make it more difficult for researchers to express ideas and build social theories in a format that most people find to be familiar and comfortable.

With the method of agreement, a researcher's attention is focused on what is common across cases, and he or she looks for common causes in cases with a common outcome. By itself, the method of agreement implies a comparison against actual cases. This comparison of cases could also be made against an idealized model. A researcher could develop an ideal type of a social process or relationship, then compare specific cases to it.

Qualitative researchers have used ideal types in two ways: to contrast the impact of contexts and as analogy.

Contrast Contexts. Researchers who adopt a strongly interpretive approach may use ideal types to interpret data in a way that is sensitive to the context and cultural meanings of members. They do not test hypotheses or create a generalizable theory, but use the ideal type to bring out the specifics of each case and to emphasize the impact of the unique context.

Researchers making contrasts between contexts often choose cases with dramatic contrasts or distinctive features. For example, in *Work and Authority in Industry*, Reinhard Bendix (1956) compared management relations in very different contexts: Czarist Russia and industrializing England.

When comparing contexts, researchers do not use the ideal type to illustrate a theory in different cases or to discover regularities. Instead, they accentuate the specific and the unique. Other methods of analysis focus on the general and ignore peculiarities. By contrast, a researcher who uses ideal types can show how unique features shape the operation of general processes.

Analogies. Ideal types are used as analogies to organize qualitative data. An *analogy* is a statement that two objects, processes, or events are similar to each other. Researchers use analogies to communicate ideas and to facilitate logical comparisons. Analogies transmit information

about patterns in data by referring to something that is already known or an experience familiar to the reader. They can describe relationships buried deep within many details and are a shorthand method for seeing patterns in a maze of specific events. They also make it easier to compare social processes across different cases or settings. For example, a researcher says that a room went silent after person X spoke: "A chill like a cold gust of air" spread through the room. This does not mean that the room temperature dropped or that a breeze was felt, but it succinctly expresses a rapid change in emotional tone. Likewise, a researcher reports that gender relations in society Y were such that women were "viewed like property and treated like slaves." This does not mean that the legal and social relations between genders were identical to those of slave owner and slave. It implies that an ideal type of a slave-and-master relationship would show major similarities to the evidence on relations between men and women if applied to society Y.

The use of analogies to analyze qualitative data serves as a heuristic device (i.e., a device that helps one learn or see). It can represent something that is unknown and is especially valuable when researchers attempt to make sense of or explain data by referring to a deep structure or an underlying mechanism. Ideal types do not provide a definitive test of an explanation. Rather, they guide the conceptual reconstruction of the mass of details into a systematic format.

Successive Approximation

Successive approximation involves repeated iterations or cycling through steps, moving toward a final analysis. Over time, or after several iterations, a researcher moves from vague ideas and concrete details in the data toward a comprehensive analysis with generalizations. This is similar to the three kinds of coding discussed earlier.

A researcher begins with research questions and a framework of assumptions and concepts. He or she then probes into the data, asking questions of the evidence to see how well the concepts fit the evidence and reveal features of the data. He or she also creates new concepts by abstracting from the evidence and adjusts concepts to fit the evidence better. The researcher then collects additional evidence to address unresolved issues that appeared in the first stage, and repeats the process. At each stage, the evidence and the theory shape each other. This is called *successive approximation* because the modified concepts and the model approximate the full evidence and are modified over and over to become successively more accurate.

Each pass through the evidence is provisional or incomplete. The concepts are abstract, but they are rooted in the concrete evidence and reflect the context. As the analysis moves toward generalizations that are subject to conditions and contingencies, the researcher refines generalizations and linkages to reflect the evidence better. For example, a historical-comparative researcher believes that historical reality is not even or linear; rather, it has discontinuous stages or steps. He or she may divide 100 years of history into periods by breaking continuous time into discrete units or periods and define the periods theoretically. Theory helps the researcher identify what is significant and what is common within periods or between different periods.

The researcher cannot determine the number and size of periods and the breaks between them until after the evidence has been examined. He or she may begin with a general idea of how many periods to create and what distinguishes them but will adjust the number and size of the periods and the location of the breaks after reviewing the evidence. The researcher then reexamines the evidence with added data, readjusts the periodization, and so forth. After several cycles, he or she approximates a set of periods in 100 years on the basis of successively theorizing and looking at evidence.

The Illustrative Method

Another method of analysis uses empirical evidence to illustrate or anchor a theory. With the *illustrative method*, a researcher applies theory to a concrete historical situation or social setting, or organizes data on the basis of prior theory. Preexisting theory provides the *empty boxes*. The researcher sees whether evidence can be gathered to fill them. The evidence in the boxes confirms or rejects the theory, which he or she treats as a useful device for interpreting the social world. The theory can be in the form of a general model, an analogy, or a sequence of steps.

There are two variations of the illustrative method. One is to show that the theoretical model illuminates or clarifies a specific case or single situation. A second is the parallel demonstration of a model in which a researcher juxtaposes multiple cases (i.e., units or time periods) to show that the theory can be applied in multiple cases. In other cases, the researcher illustrates theory with specific material from multiple cases. An example of parallel demonstration is found in Paige's (1975) study of rural class conflict. Paige first developed an elaborate model of conditions that cause class conflict, and then provided evidence to illustrate it from Peru, Angola, and Vietnam. This demonstrated the applicability of the model in several cases. (See Box 13.2 for a summary of types.)

Box 13.2 A Summary of Four Strategies for Qualitative Data Analysis

1. *The narrative.* Tell a detailed story about a particular slice of social life.
2. *Ideal types.* Compare qualitative data with a pure model of social life.
3. *Successive approximation.* Repeatedly move back and forth between data and theory, until the gap between them shrinks or disappears.
4. *The illustrative method.* Fill the "empty boxes" of theory with qualitative data.

OTHER TECHNIQUES

Qualitative researchers use many analysis techniques. Here is a brief look at other techniques to illustrate the variety.

Network Analysis

The idea of social networks was discussed with network theory and with snowball sampling. Qualitative researchers often "map" the connections among a set of people, organizations, events, or places. Using sociograms and similar mapping techniques, they can discover, analyze, and display sets of relations. For example, in a company, Harry gives Sue orders, Sue and Sam consult and help one another. Sam gets materials from Sandra. Sandra socializes with Mary. Researchers find that networks help them see and understand the structure of complex social relations.

Time Allocation Analysis

Time is an important resource. Researchers examine the way people or organizations spend or invest time to reveal implicit rules of conduct or priorities. Researchers document the duration or amount of time devoted to various activities. Qualitative researchers examine the duration or amount of time devoted to activities. An analysis of how people, groups, or organizations allocate the valuable resources they control (such as time, space, money, prestige) can reveal a lot about their real, as contrasted with officially professed, priorities. Often, people are unaware of or do not explicitly acknowledge the importance of an activity on which they spent time. For example, a researcher notices that certain people are required to wait before seeing a person, whereas others do not wait. The researcher may analyze the amount of time, who waits, what they do while waiting, and whether they feel waiting is just. Or the researcher documents that people say that a certain celebration in a corporation is not important. Yet, everyone attends and spends two hours at the event. The collective allocation of two hours during a busy week for the celebration signals its latent or implicit importance in the culture of the corporation.

Flowchart and Time Sequence

In addition to the amount of time devoted to various activities, researchers analyze the order of events or decisions. Historical researchers have traditionally focused on documenting the sequence of events, but comparative and field researchers also look at flow or sequence. In addition to when events occur, researchers use the idea of a decision tree or flowchart to outline the order of decisions, to understand how one event or decision is related to others. For example, an activity as simple as making a cake can be outlined (see Figure 13.3). The idea of mapping out steps, decisions, or events and looking at their interrelationship has been applied to many settings.

Multiple Sorting Procedure

Multiple sorting is a technique similar to domain analysis that a researcher can use in field research or oral history. Its purpose is to discover how people categorize their experiences or classify items into systems of "similar" and "different." The multiple sorting procedure has been adopted by cognitive anthropologists and psychologists. It can be used to collect, verify, or analyze data. Here is how it works. The researcher gives those being studied a list of terms, photos, places, names of people, and so on, and asks them to organize the lists into categories or piles. The subjects or members use categories of their own devising. Once sorted, the researcher asks about the criteria used. The subjects are then given the items again and asked to sort them in other ways. There is a similarity to Thurstone scaling in that people sort items, but here, the number of piles and type of items differ. More significantly, the purpose of the sorting is not to create a uniform scale but to discover the variety of ways people

FIGURE 13.3   **Partial Flowchart of Cake Making**

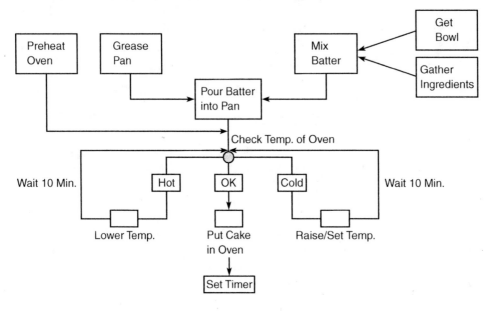

understand the world. For example (Canter et al., 1985:90), a gambler sorts a list of eight gambling establishments five times. Each sort has three to four categories. One of the sorts organized them based on "class of casino" (high to low). Other sorts were based on "frills," "size of stake," "make me money," and "personal preference." By examining the sorts, the researcher sees how others organize their worlds.

Diagrams

Qualitative researchers have moved toward presenting their data analysis in the form of diagrams and charts. Diagrams and charts help them organize ideas and systematically investigate relations in the data, as well as communicate results to readers. Researchers use spatial or temporal maps, typologies, or sociograms.

Quantitative researchers have developed many graphs, tables, charts, and pictorial devices to present information. Miles and Huberman (1994) argued that data display is a critical part

of qualitative analysis. In addition to taxonomies, maps, and lists, they suggested the use of flowcharts, organizational charts, causal diagrams, and various lists and grids to illustrate analysis (see Figure 13.4).

SOFTWARE FOR QUALITATIVE DATA

Quantitative researchers have used computers for nearly 40 years to generate tables, graphs, and charts to analyze and present numerical data. By contrast, qualitative researchers moved to computers and diagrams only in the past decade. A researcher who enters notes in a word-processing program may quickly search for words and phrases that can be adapted to coding data and linking codes to analytic memos. Word processing can also help a researcher revise and move codes and parts of field notes.

New computer programs are continuously being developed or modified, and most come

FIGURE 13.4   **Examples of the Use of Diagrams in Qualitative Analysis**

	EXAMPLE 1			
Person	Worked Before College	Part-Time Job in College	Pregnant Now	Had Own Car
John	Yes	Yes	N/A	No
Mary	Yes	DK	No	Yes
Martin	No	Yes	N/A	Yes
Yoshi	Yes	No	Yes	Yes

DK = don't know, N/A = not applicable

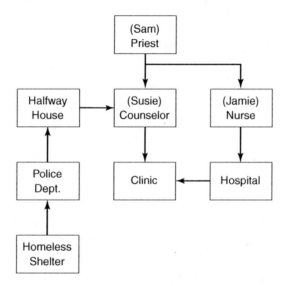

with highly detailed and program-specific user manuals. The review here does not go into detail about specific software. It covers only the major approaches to qualitative data analysis at this time.

Some programs perform searches of text documents. What they do is similar to the searching function available in most word-processing software. The specialized text retrieval programs are faster and have the capability of finding close matches, slight misspellings, similar-sounding words, and synonyms. For example, when a researcher looks for the keyword *boat,* the program might also tell whether any of the following appeared: *ship, battleship,* *frigate, rowboat, schooner, vessel, yacht, steamer, ocean liner, tug, canoe, skiff, cutter, aircraft carrier, dinghy, scow, galley, ark, cruiser, destroyer, flagship,* and *submarine.* In addition, some programs permit the combination of words or phases using logical terms *(and, or, not)* in what are called *Boolean searches.* For example, a researcher may search long documents for when the keywords *college student* and *drinking* and *smoking* occur within four sentences of one another, but only when the word *fraternity* is not present in the block of text. This Boolean search uses *and* to seek the intersection of *college student* with either of two behaviors that are connected by the logical term *or,* whereas the logical search word *not* excludes situations in which the term *fraternity* appears.

Most programs show the keyword or phrase and the surrounding text. The programs may also permit a researcher to write separate memos or add short notes to the text. Some programs count the keywords found and give their location. Most programs create a very specific index for the text, based only on the terms of interest to the researcher.

Textbase managers are similar to text retrieval programs. The key difference is their ability to organize or sort information about search results. They allow researchers to sort notes by a key idea or to add factual information. For example, when the data are detailed notes on interviews, a researcher can add information about the date and length of the interview, gender of interviewee, location of interview, and so on. The researcher can then sort and organize each interview or part of the interview notes using a combination of key words and added information.

In addition, some programs have *Hypertext* capability. Hypertext is a way of linking terms to other information. It works such that clicking the mouse on one term causes a new screen (one that has related information) to appear. The researcher can identify keywords or topics and link them together in the text. For example, a field researcher wants to examine the person Susan and the topic of hair (including haircuts, hairstyles, hair coloring, and hats or hair covering). The researcher can use Hypertext to connect all places Susan's name appears to discussions of hair. By the mouse clicking on Susan's name, one block of text quickly jumps to another in the notes to see all places where Susan and the hair topic appear together.

Code-and-retrieve programs allow a researcher to attach codes to lines, sentences, paragraphs, or blocks of text. The programs may permit multiple codes for the same data. In addition to attaching codes, most programs also allow the researcher to organize the codes. For example, a program can help a researcher make outlines or "trees" of connections (e.g., trunks, branches, and twigs) among the codes, and among the data to which the codes refer. The qualitative data are rearranged in the program based on the researcher's codes and the relations among codes that a researcher specifies.

CONCLUSION

In this chapter, you have learned how researchers analyze qualitative data. In many respects, qualitative data are more difficult to deal with than data in the form of numbers. Numbers have mathematical properties that let a researcher use statistical procedures. Qualitative analysis requires more effort by an individual researcher to read and reread data notes, reflect on what is read, and make comparisons based on logic and judgment.

Most forms of qualitative data analysis involve coding and writing analytic memos. Both are labor-intensive efforts by the researcher to read over data carefully and think about them seriously. In addition, you learned about methods that researchers have used for the analysis of qualitative data. They are a sample of the many methods of qualitative data analysis. You also learned about the importance of thinking about negative evidence and events that are not present in the data.

This chapter ends the section of the book on research design, data collection, and data analysis. Social research also involves preparing reports on a research project, which is addressed in the next chapter.

Key Terms

axial coding
empty boxes
illustrative method
narrative history
open coding
selective coding
successive approximation

Writing the Research Report

INTRODUCTION

The previous chapters have looked at how to design studies, gather data, and analyze the data. Yet, a research project is not complete until the researcher shares the results with others. Communicating results and how a study was conducted with others is a critical last step in the research process. It is usually in the form of a written report. Chapter 1 discussed how the scientific community emphasizes that researchers make public how they conducted their research and their findings. In this chapter, you will learn about writing a report on one's research.

THE RESEARCH REPORT

Why Write a Report?

After a researcher completes a project or a significant phase of a large project, it is time to communicate the findings to others through a research report. You can learn a lot about writing a research report by reading many reports and taking a course in scientific and technical writing.

A *research report* is a written document (or oral presentation based on a written document) that communicates the methods and findings of a research project to others. It is more than a summary of findings; it is a record of the research process. A researcher cannot wait until the research is done to think about the report; he or she must think ahead to the report and keep careful records while conducting research. In addition to findings, the report includes the reasons for initiating the project, a description of the project's steps, a presentation of data, and a discussion of how the data relate to the research question or topic.

The report tells others what you, the researcher, did, and what you discovered. In other words, the research report is a way of disseminating knowledge. As you saw in Chapter 1, the research report plays a significant role in binding together the scientific community. Other reasons for writing a report are to fulfill a class or job assignment, to meet an obligation to an organization that paid for the research, to persuade a professional group about specific aspects of a problem, or to tell the general public about findings. Communicating with the general public is rarely the primary method for communication of scientific results; it is usually a second stage of dissemination.

The Writing Process

Your Audience. Professional writers say: Always know for whom you are writing. This is because communication is more effective when it is tailored to a specific audience. You should write a research report differently depending on whether the primary audience is an instructor, students, professional social scientists, practitioners, or the general public. It goes without saying that the writing should be clear, accurate, and organized.

Instructors assign a report for different reasons and may place requirements on how it is written. In general, instructors want to see writing and an organization that reflect clear, logical thinking. Student reports should demonstrate a solid grasp of substantive and methodological concepts. A good way to do this is to use technical terms explicitly *when appropriate;* they should not be used excessively or incorrectly.

When writing for students, it is best to define technical terms and label each part of the report. The discussion should proceed in a logical, step-by-step manner with many specific examples. Use straight-forward language to explain how and why you conducted the various steps of the research project. One strategy is to begin with the research question, then structure the report as an answer.

Scholars do not need definitions of technical terms or explanations of why standard procedures (e.g., random sampling) were used. They are interested in how the research is linked to abstract theory or previous findings in the literature. They want a condensed, detailed description of research design. They pay close attention to how variables are measured and the methods of data collection. Scholars like a compact, tightly written, but extensive section on data analysis, with a meticulous discussion of results.

Practitioners prefer a short summary of how the study was conducted and results presented in a few simple charts and graphs. They like to see an outline of alternative paths of action implied by results with the practical outcomes of pursuing each path. Practitioners must be cautioned not to overgeneralize from the results of one study. It is best to place the details of research design and results in an appendix.

When writing for the general public, use simple language, provide concrete examples, and focus on the practical implications of findings for social problems. Do not include details of research design or of results, and be careful not to make unsupported claims when writing for the public. Informing the public is an important service, which can help nonspecialists make better judgments about public issues.

Style and Tone. Research reports are written in a narrow range of styles and have a distinct tone. Their purpose is to communicate clearly the research method and findings.

Style refers to the types of words chosen by the writer and the length and form of sentences or paragraphs used. *Tone* is the writer's attitude or relation toward the subject matter. For example, an informal, conversational style (e.g., colloquial words, idioms, clichés, and incomplete sentences) with a personal tone (e.g., these are my feelings) is appropriate for writing a letter to a close friend, but not for research reports. Research reports have a formal and succinct (saying a lot in few words) style. The tone expresses distance from the subject matter; it is professional and serious. Field researchers sometimes use an informal style and a personal tone, but this is the exception. Avoid moralizing and flowery language. The goal is to inform, not to advocate a position or to entertain.

A research report should be objective, accurate, and clear. Check and recheck details (e.g., page references in citations) and fully disclose how you conducted the research project. If readers detect carelessness in writing, they may question the research itself. The details of a research project can be complex, and such complexity means that confusion is always a danger. It makes clear writing essential. Clear writing can be achieved by thinking and rethinking the research problem and design, explicitly defining terms, writing with short declarative sentences, and limiting conclusions to what is supported by the evidence.

Organizing Thoughts. Writing does not happen magically or simply flow out of a person when he or she puts pen to paper (or fingers to keyboard) although many people have such an illusion. Rather, it is hard work, involving a sequence of steps and separate activities that result in a final product. Writing a research report is not radically different from other types of writing. Although some steps differ and the level of complexity may be greater, most of what a good writer does when writing a long letter, a poem, a set of instructions, or a short story applies to writing a research report.

First, a writer needs something about which to write. The "something" in the research report includes the topic, research question, design and measures, data collection techniques, results, and implications. With so many parts to write about, organization is essential. The most basic tool for organizing writing is the outline. Outlines help a writer ensure that all ideas are included and that the relationship between them is clear. Outlines are made up of topics (words or phrases) or sentences. Most of us are familiar with the basic form of an outline (see Figure 14.1).

Outlines can help the writer, but they can also become a barrier if they are used improperly. An outline is simply a tool to help the writer organize ideas. It helps (1) put ideas in a sequence (e.g., what will be said first, second,

FIGURE 14.1   Form of Outline

I. First major topic	One of the most important
A. Subtopic of topic I	Second level of importance
1. Subtopic of A	Third level of importance
a. Subtopic of 1	Fourth level of importance
b. Subtopic of 1	"
(1) Subtopic of b	Fifth level of importance
(2) Subtopic of b	"
(a) Subtopic of (2)	Sixth level of importance
(b) Subtopic of (2)	"
i. Subtopic of (b)	Seventh level of importance
ii. Subtopic of (b)	"
2. Subtopic of A	Third level of importance
B. Subtopic of topic I	Second level of importance
II. Second major topic	One of the most important

and third); (2) group related ideas together (e.g., these are similar to each other but they differ from those); and (3) separate the more general, or higher-level, ideas from more specific ideas, and the specific ideas from very specific details.

Some students feel that they need a complete outline before writing, and that once an outline is prepared, deviations from it are impossible. Few writers begin with a complete outline. The initial outline is sketchy because until you write everything down, it is impossible to put all ideas in a sequence, group them together, or separate the general from the specific. For most writers, new ideas develop or become clearer in the process of writing itself.

A beginning outline may differ from the final outline by more than degree of completeness. The process of writing may not only reveal or clarify ideas for the writer but it will also stimulate new ideas, new connections between ideas, a different sequence, or new relations between the general and the specific. In addition, the process of writing may stimulate reanalysis or a reexamination of the literature or findings. This does not mean beginning all over again. Rather, it means keeping an open mind to new insights and being candid about the research project.

Back to the Library.   Few researchers finish their literature review before completing a research project. The researcher should be familiar with the literature before beginning a project, but will need to return to the literature after completing data collection and analysis, for several reasons. First, time has passed between the beginning and the end of a research project, and new studies may have been published. Second, after completing a research project, a researcher will know better what is or is not central to the study and may have new questions in mind when rereading studies in the literature. Finally, when writing the report, researchers may find that notes are not complete enough or a detail is missing in the citation of a reference source (see Box 14.1). The visit to the library after data collection is less extensive and more selective or focused than that conducted at the beginning of research.

When writing a research report, researchers frequently discard some of the notes and sources that were gathered prior to completing the research project. This does not mean that the initial library work and literature review were a waste of time and effort. Researchers expect that some of the notes (e.g., 25 percent) taken before

Box 14.1 Formats for Reference Lists, Using American Sociological Association Style

Books

First-Edition Books

Eliasoph, Nina. 1998. *Avoiding Politics: How Americans Produce Apathy in Everyday Life.* New York: Cambridge University Press.

Glynn, Carroll J., Susan Herbst, Garrett J. O'Keefe and Robert Y. Shapiro. 1999. *Public Opinion.* Boulder, CO: Westview Press.

Later Editions of Books

Portes, Alejandro and Ruben G. Rumbaut. 1996. *Immigrant America: A Portrait, 2d ed.* Berkeley: University of California Press.

[Abbreviations are 2d ed., 3d ed., Rev. ed., 2 vols.]

One Volume of Multivolume Book

Marx, Karl. [1887] 1967. *Capital: Critique of Political Economy, Volume 1, The Process of Capitalist Production.* Translated by Frederick Engles. Reprint. New York: International Publishers.

Translated Books

Durkheim, Emile. 1933. *The Division of Labor in Society.* Translated by George Simpson. New York: Free Press.

Weber, Max. 1958. *The Protestant Ethic and the Spirit of Capitalism.* Translated by Talcott Parsons. New York: Charles Scribner's Sons.

Edited Books

Danziger, Sheldon and Peter Gottschalk, eds. 1993. *Uneven Tides: Rising Inequality in America.* New York: Russell Sage Foundation.

Republished Books

Mason, Edward S. [1957] 1964. *Economic Concentration and the Monopoly Problem.* Reprint. New York: Atheneum.

Articles from Books or Scholarly Journals

Wright, Erik Olin. 1997. "Rethinking, Once Again, the Concept of Class Structure." Pp. 41–72 in *Reworking Class,* edited by J. Hall. Ithaca: Cornell University Press.

Van Tubergen, Frank. 2005. "Self Employment of Immigrants: A Cross-National Study of 17 Western Societies." *Social Forces* 84:709–32.

[*Note:* Omit issue number except when each issue is renumbered beginning with page 1. Then give volume(issue):pages—for example, 84(2):709–33.]

Articles from Magazines and Newspapers

Janofsky, Michael. "Shortage of Housing for Poor Grows in the U.S." *New York Times* (April 29, 1998), p. A14.

Nichols, John. 1998. "How Al Gore Has It Wired" *Nation 267* (July 20, 1998): 11–16.

[It is not always necessary to include page numbers for newspapers].

Book Reviews

Academic Journals

Bergen, Raquel Kennedy. 1998. Review of *A Woman Scorned: Acquaintance Rape on Trial,* by Peggy Reeves Sanday. *Contemporary Sociology* 27:98–99.

Popular Magazines

Wolfe, Alan. 2001. Review of *Heaven Below: Early Pentacostals and American Culture,* by Grant Wacker. *New Republic, 225* (September 10):59–62.

Government Documents

U.S. Bureau of Census. 2006. *Statistical Abstract of the United States, 125th ed.* Washington DC: U.S. Government Printing Office.

Doctoral Dissertations and Theses

King, Andrew J. 1976. "Law and Land Use in Chicago: A Pre-History of Modern Zoning." Ph.D. dissertation, Department of Sociology, University of Wisconsin, Madison, WI.

Unpublished Papers, Policy Reports and Presented Papers

Haines, Herbert H. 1980. "Ideological Distribution and Racial Flank Effects in Social Movements"

BOX 14.1 Continued

Presented at the annual meeting of the American Sociological Association, August, New York City.

Internet Sources

[*Note:* The date retrieved is the date that the reader located and read the work on the Internet.]

Announcement or Personal Home Page
American Sociological Association 1999. *Journals and Newsletters.* Retrieved January 16, 1999. http://www.asanet.org/Pubs/publicat.html

On-Line Journal Article
Sosteric, Mike, Mike Gismondi and Gina Ratkovic. 1998. "The University, Accountability, and Market Discipline in the Late 1990s." *Electronic*

Journal of Sociology April 1988, Vol. 3. Retrieved January 16, 1999. http://www.sociology.org/content/vol003.003/sosteric.html

Newspaper Article
Lee, Don. 1999. "State's Job Growth Hits Unexpected Cold Spell." *Los Angeles Times* (January 16). Retrieved January 16, 1999. http://www.latimes.com/HOME/BUSINESS/topstory.html

Journal Abstract or Book Review
Stanbridge, Karen. 2005. Review of *The New Transnational Activism* by Sidney Tarrow. *Canadian Journal of Sociology Online.* Retrieved January 12, 2006. http://www.cjsonline.ca/reviews/transnatl.html.

---

completing the project will become irrelevant as the project gains focus. They do not include notes or references in a report that are no longer relevant, for they distract from the flow of ideas and reduce clarity.

Returning to the library to verify and expand references focuses ideas. It also helps avoid plagiarism. *Plagiarism* is a serious form of cheating, and many universities expel students caught engaging in it. If a professional ever plagiarizes in a scholarly journal, it is treated as a very serious offense. Take careful notes and identify the exact source of phrases or ideas to avoid unintentional plagiarism. Cite the sources of both directly quoted words and paraphrased ideas. For direct quotes, include the location of the quote with page numbers in the citation.

Using another's written words and failing to give credit is wrong, but paraphrasing is less clear. *Paraphrasing* is not using another's exact words; it is restating another's ideas in your own words, condensing at the same time. Researchers regularly paraphrase, and good paraphrasing requires a solid understanding of what is being paraphrased. It means more than replacing another's words with synonyms; paraphrasing is borrowing an idea, boiling it down to its essence, and giving credit to the source.

Steps in Writing

Writing is a process. The way to learn to write is by writing. It takes time and effort, and it improves with practice. There is no single correct way to write, but some methods are associated with good writing. The process has three steps:

1. *Prewriting.* Prepare to write by arranging notes on the literature, making lists of ideas, outlining, completing bibliographic citations, and organizing comments on data analysis.
2. *Composing.* Get your ideas onto paper as a first draft by freewriting, drawing up the bibliography and footnotes, preparing data for presentation, and forming an introduction and conclusion.

3. *Rewriting*. Evaluate and polish the report by improving coherence, proofreading for mechanical errors, checking citations, and reviewing voice and usage.

Many people find that getting started is difficult. Beginning writers often jump to the second step and end there, which results in poor-quality writing. *Prewriting* means that a writer begins with a file folder full of notes, outlines, and lists. You must think about the form of the report and audience. Thinking time is important. It often occurs in spurts over a period of time before the bulk of composing begins.

Some people become afflicted with a strange ailment called *writer's block* when they sit down to compose writing. It is a temporary inability to write when the mind goes blank, the fingers freeze, and panic sets in. Writers from beginners through experts occasionally experience it. If you experience it, calm down and work on overcoming it.

Numerous writers begin to compose by freewriting—that is, they sit down and write down everything they can as quickly as it enters the mind. Freewriting establishes a link between a rapid flow of ideas in the mind and writing. When you freewrite, you do not stop to reread what you wrote, you do not ponder the best word, you do not worry about correct grammar, spelling, or punctuation. You just put ideas on paper as quickly as possible to get and keep the creative juices or ideas flowing. You can later clean up what you wrote.

Writing and thinking are so intertwined that it is impossible to know where one ends and the other begins. This means that if you plan to sit and stare at the wall, the computer output, the sky, or whatever until all thoughts become totally clear before beginning, you may not get anything written. Writing itself can ignite the thinking process.

Rewriting. Perhaps one in a million writers is a creative genius who can produce a first draft that communicates with astounding accuracy and clarity. For the rest of us mortals, writing means that rewriting—and rewriting again—is necessary. For example, Ernest Hemingway is reported to have rewritten the end of *Farewell to Arms* 39 times. It is not unusual for a professional researcher to rewrite a report a dozen times. Do not become discouraged. If anything, rewriting reduces the pressure; it means you can start writing soon and get out a rough draft that you can polish later. Plan to rewrite a draft at least three or four times. A draft is a complete report, from beginning to end, not a few rough notes or an outline.

Rewriting helps a writer express himself or herself with a greater clarity, smoothness, precision, and economy of words. When rewriting, the focus is on clear communication, not pompous or complicated language. Rewriting means slowly reading what you have written and, if necessary, reading out loud to see if it sounds right. It is a good idea to share your writing with others. Professional writers often have others read and criticize their writing. New writers soon learn that friendly, constructive criticism is very valuable. Sharing your writing with others may be difficult at first because it means exposing your written thoughts and encouraging criticism. Yet, the purpose of the criticism is to clarify writing, and the critic is doing you a favor.

Rewriting involves two processes: revising and editing. *Revising* is inserting new ideas, adding supporting evidence, deleting or changing ideas, moving sentences around to clarify meaning, or strengthening transitions and links between ideas. *Editing* means cleaning up and tightening the more mechanical aspects of writing, such as spelling, grammar, usage, verb tense, sentence length, and paragraph organization. When you rewrite, go over a draft and revise it brutally to improve it. This is easier if some time passes between a draft and rewriting. Phrases that seemed satisfactory in a draft may look fuzzy or poorly connected after a week or two (see Box 14.2).

Even if you have not acquired typing skills, it is a good idea to type and print out at least one

> ### Box 14.2   Suggestions for Rewriting
>
> 1. *Mechanics.* Check grammar, spelling, punctuation, verb agreement, verb tense, and verb/subject separation with each rewrite. Remember that each time new text is added, new errors can creep in. Mistakes are not only distracting but they also weaken the confidence readers place in the ideas you express.
>
> 2. *Usage.* Reexamine terms, especially key terms, when rewriting to see whether you are using the exact word that expresses your intended meaning. Do not use technical terms or long words unnecessarily. Use the plain word that best expresses meaning. Get a thesaurus and use it. A *thesaurus* is an essential reference tool, like a dictionary, that contains words of similar meaning and can help you locate the exact word for a meaning you want to express. Precise thinking and expression requires precise language. Do not say *average* if you use the *mean*. Do not say *mankind* or *policeman* when you intend *people* or *police officer.* Do not use *principal* for *principle.*
>
> 3. *Voice.* Writers of research reports often make the mistake of using the passive instead of the active voice. It may appear more authoritative, but passive voice obscures the actor or subject of action. For example, the passive, *The relationship between grade in school and more definite career plans was confirmed by the data* is better stated as the active, *The data confirm the relationship between grade in school and more definite career plans.* The passive, *Respondent attitude toward abortion was recorded by an interviewer* reads easier in the active voice: *An interviewer recorded respondent attitude toward abortion.* Also avoid unnecessary qualifying language, such as *seems to* or *appears to.*
>
> 4. *Coherence.* Sequence, steps, and transitions should be logically tight. Try reading the entire report one paragraph at a time. Does the paragraph contain a unified idea? A topic sentence? Is there a transition between paragraphs within the report?
>
> 5. *Repetition.* Remove repeated ideas, wordiness, and unnecessary phrases. Ideas are best stated once, forcefully, instead of repeatedly in an unclear way. When revising, eliminate deadwood (words that add nothing) and circumlocution (the use of several words when one more precise word will do). Directness is preferable to wordiness. The wordy phrase, *To summarize the above, it is our conclusion in light of the data that X has a positive effect of considerable magnitude on the occurrence of Y, notwithstanding the fact that Y occurs only on rare occasions,* is better stated, *In sum, we conclude that X has a large positive effect on Y, but Y occurs infrequently.*
>
> 6. *Structure.* Research reports should have a transparent organization. Move sections around as necessary to fit the organization better, and use headings and subheadings. A reader should be able to follow the logical structure of a report.
>
> 7. *Abstraction.* A good research report mixes abstract ideas and concrete examples. A long string of abstractions without the specifics is difficult to read. Likewise, a mass of specific concrete details without periodic generalization also loses readers.
>
> 8. *Metaphors.* Many writers use metaphors to express ideas. Phrases like *the cutting edge, the bottom line,* and *penetrating to the heart* are used to express ideas by borrowing images from other contexts. Metaphors can be an effective method of communication, but they need to be used sparingly and with care. A few well-chosen, consistently used, fresh metaphors can communicate ideas quickly and effectively; however, the excessive use of metaphors, especially overused metaphors (e.g., the *bottom line*), is a sloppy, unimaginative method of expression.

draft before the final draft. This is because it is easier to see errors and organization problems in a clean, typed draft. Feel free to cut and paste, cross out words, or move phrases on the printed copy.

Good keyboarding skills and the ability to use a word processor are extremely valuable when writing reports and other documents. Serious professionals find that the time they invest into building keyboard skills and learning to use a word processor pays huge dividends later. Word processors not only make editing much easier but they also check spelling and offer synonyms. In addition, there are programs that check grammar. You cannot rely on the computer program to do all the work, but it makes writing easier. The speed and ease that a word processor offers is so dramatic that few people who become skilled at using one ever go back to writing by hand or typing.

One last suggestion: Rewrite the introduction and title after completing a draft so that they accurately reflect what is said. Titles should be short and descriptive. They should communicate the topic and the major variables to readers. They can describe the type of research (e.g., "An experiment on . . .") but should not have unnecessary words or phrases (e.g., "An investigation into the . . .").

The Quantitative Research Report

The principles of good writing apply to all reports, but the parts of a report differ depending on whether the research is quantitative or qualitative. Before writing any report, read reports on the same kind of research for models.

We begin with the quantitative research report. The sections of the report roughly follow the sequence of steps of a research project.

Abstract or Executive Summary.   Quantitative research reports usually begin with a short summary or abstract. The size of an abstract varies; it can be as few as 50 words (this paragraph has 90 words) or as long as a full page. Most scholarly

journal articles have abstracts that are printed on the first page of the article. The abstract has information on the topic, the research problem, the basic findings, and any unusual research design or data collection features.

Reports of applied research that are written for practitioners have a longer summary called the *executive summary.* It contains more detail than an article abstract and includes the implications of research and major recommendations made in the report. Although it is longer than an abstract, an executive summary rarely exceeds four or five pages.

Abstracts and executive summaries serve several functions: For the less interested reader, they tell what is in a report; for readers looking for specific information, they help the reader determine whether the full report contains important information. Readers use the abstract or summary to screen information and decide whether the entire report should be read. It gives serious readers who intend to read the full report a quick mental picture of the report, which makes reading the report easier and faster.

Presenting the Problem.   The first section of the report defines the research problem. It can be placed in one or more sections with titles such as "Introduction," "Problem Definition," "Literature Review," "Hypotheses," or "Background Assumptions." Although the subheadings vary, the contents include a statement of the research problem and a rationale for what is being examined. Here, researchers explain the significance of and provide a background to the research question. They explain the significance of the research by showing how different solutions to the problem lead to different applications or theoretical conclusions. Introductory sections frequently include a context literature review and link the problem to theory. Introductory sections also define key concepts and present conceptual hypotheses.

Describing the Methods.   The next section of the report describes how the researcher designed the study and collected the data. It goes by several names (e.g., "Methods," "Research Design," or "Data") and may be subdivided into other parts (e.g., "Measures," "Sampling," or "Manipulations"). It is the most important section for evaluating the methodology of the project. The section answers several questions for the reader:

1. What type of study (e.g., experiment, survey) was conducted?
2. Exactly how were data collected (e.g., study design, type of survey, time and location of data collection, experimental design used)?
3. How were variables measured? Are the measures reliable and valid?
4. What is the sample? How many subjects or respondents are involved in the study? How were they selected?
5. How were ethical issues and specific concerns of the design dealt with?

Results and Tables. After describing how data were collected, methods of sampling, and measurement, you then present the data. This section presents—it does not discuss, analyze, or interpret—the data. Researchers sometimes combine the "Results" section with the next section, called "Discussion" or "Findings."

Researchers make choices in how to present the data. When analyzing the data, they look at dozens of univariate, bivariate, and multivariate tables and statistics to get a feel for the data. This does not mean that every statistic or table is in a final report. Rather, the researcher selects the minimum number of charts or tables that fully inform the reader and rarely present the raw data itself. Data analysis techniques should summarize the data and test hypotheses (e.g., frequency distributions, tables with means and standard deviations, correlations, and other statistics).

A researcher wants to give a complete picture of the data without overwhelming the reader—not provide data in excessive detail nor present irrelevant data. Readers can make their own interpretations. Detailed summary statistics belong in appendixes.

Discussion. In the discussion section, researchers give the reader a concise, unambiguous interpretation of its meaning. The discussion is not a selective emphasis or partisan interpretation; rather, it is a candid discussion of what is in the "Results" section. The "Discussion" section is separated from the results so that a reader can examine the data and arrive at different interpretations.

Beginning researchers often find it difficult to organize the "Discussion" section. One approach is to organize the discussion according to hypotheses, discussing how the data relate to each hypothesis. In addition, researchers should discuss unanticipated findings, possible alternative explanations of results, and weaknesses or limitations.

Drawing Conclusions. Researchers restate the research question and summarize findings in the conclusion. Its purpose is to summarize the report, and it is sometimes titled "Summary."

The only sections after the conclusion are the references and appendixes. The "References" section contains only sources that were referred to in the text or notes of the report. Appendixes, if used, usually contain additional information on methods of data collection (e.g., questionnaire wording) or results (e.g., descriptive statistics). The footnotes or endnotes in quantitative research reports expand or elaborate on information in the text. Researchers use them sparingly to provide secondary information that clarifies the text but might distract from the flow of the reading.

The Qualitative Research Report

Compared to quantitative research, it is more difficult to write a report on qualitative social research. It has fewer rules and less structure. Nevertheless, the purpose is the same: to clearly communicate the research process and the data collected through the process.

Quantitative reports present hypotheses and evidence in a logically tight and condensed style. By contrast, qualitative reports tend to be longer, and book-length reports are common. The greater length is for five reasons:

1. The data in a qualitative report are more difficult to condense. Data are in the form of words, pictures, or sentences and include many quotes and examples.
2. Qualitative researchers try to create a subjective sense of empathy and understanding among readers in addition to presenting factual evidence and analytic interpretations. Detailed descriptions of specific settings and situations help readers better understand or get a feel for settings. Researchers attempt to transport the reader into the subjective world view and meaning system of a social setting.
3. Qualitative researchers use less standardized techniques of gathering data, creating analytic categories, and organizing evidence. The techniques applied may be particular to individual researchers or unique settings. Thus, researchers explain what they did and why, because it has not been done before.
4. Exploring new settings or constructing new theory is a common goal in qualitative research. The development of new concepts and the examination of relationships among them adds to the length of reports. Theory flows out of evidence, and detailed descriptions demonstrate how the researcher created interpretations.
5. Qualitative researchers may use more varied and literary writing styles, which increases length. They have greater freedom to employ literary devices to tell a story or recount a tale.

Field Research. Field research reports rarely follow a fixed format with standard sections, and theoretical generalizations and data are not separated into distinct sections. Generalizations are intertwined with the evidence, which takes the form of detailed description with frequent quotes.

Researchers balance the presentation of data and analysis to avoid an excessive separation of data from analysis, called the *error of segregation.* This occurs when researchers separate data from analysis so much that readers cannot see the connection.[1]

The tone of field research reports is less objective and formal, and more personal. Field research reports may be written in the first person (i.e., using the pronoun *I*) because the researcher was directly involved in the setting, interacted with the people studied, and was the measurement "instrument." The decisions or indecisions, feelings, reactions, and personal experiences of the researcher are parts of the field research process.

Field research reports often face more skepticism than quantitative reports do. This makes it essential to assess an audience's demands for evidence and to establish credibility. The key is to provide readers with enough evidence so that they believe the recounted events and accept the interpretations as plausible. A degree of selective observation is accepted in field research, so the critical issue is whether other observers could reach the same conclusion if they examined the same data.

Field researchers face a data reduction dilemma when presenting evidence. Most data are in the form of an enormous volume of field notes, but a researcher cannot directly share all the observations or recorded conversations with the readers. For example, in their study of medical students, *Boys in White,* Becker and colleagues (1961) had about 5,000 pages of single-spaced field notes. Field researchers include only about 5 percent of their field notes in a report as quotes. The remaining 95 percent is not wasted; there is just no room for it. Thus, writers select quotes and indirectly convey the rest of the data to readers.

There is no fixed organization for a field research report, although a literature review often appears near the beginning. There are many acceptable organizational forms. Lofland (1976) suggests the following:

1. Introduction
   a. Most general aspects of situation
   b. Main contours of the general situation
   c. How materials were collected
   d. Details about the setting
   e. How the report is organized
2. The situation
   a. Analytic categories
   b. Contrast between situation and other situations
   c. Development of situation over time
3. Strategies
4. Summary and implications

Devices for organizing evidence and analysis also vary a great deal. For example, writers can organize the report in terms of a *natural history,* an unfolding of events as you discovered them, or as a *chronology,* following the developmental cycle or career of an aspect of the setting or people in it. Another possibility is to organize the report as a *zoom lens,* beginning broadly and then focusing increasingly narrowly on a specific topic. Statements can move from universal statements about all cultures, to general statements about a specific cultures, to statements about a specific cultural scene, to specific statements about an aspect of culture, to specific statements about specific incidents.

Field researchers also organize reports by themes. A writer chooses between using abstract analytic themes and using themes from the categories used by the people who were studied. The latter gives readers a vivid description of the setting and displays knowledge of the language, concepts, categories, and beliefs of those being written about.[2]

Field researchers discuss the methods used in the report, but its location and form vary. One technique is to interweave a description of the setting, the means of gaining access, the role of the researcher, and the subject–researcher relationship into the discussion of evidence and analysis. This is intensified if the writer adopts what Van Maanen (1988:73) called a "confessional" style of writing.

A chronological, zoom lens, or theme-based organization allows placing the data collection method near the beginning or the end. In book-length reports, methodological issues are usually discussed in a separate appendix.

Field research reports can contain transcriptions of tape recordings, maps, photographs, or charts illustrating analytic categories. They supplement the discussion and are placed near the discussion they complement. Qualitative field research can use creative formats that differ from the usual written text with examples from field notes. Harper's (1982) book contains many photographs with text. The photographs give a visual inventory of the settings described in the text and present the meanings of settings in the terms of those being studied. For example, field research articles have appeared in the form of all photographs, a script for a play, or a documentary film.[3]

Direct, personal involvement in the intimate details of a social setting heightens ethical concerns. Researchers write in a manner that protects the privacy of those being studied and helps prevent the publication of a report from harming those who were studied. They usually change the names of members and exact locations in field reports. Personal involvement in field research leads researchers to include a short autobiography. For example, in the appendix to *Street Corner Society,* the author, William Foote Whyte (1955), gave a detailed account of the occupations of his father and grandfather, his hobbies and interests, the jobs he held, how he ended up going to graduate school, and how his research was affected by his getting married.

Historical-Comparative Research. There is no single way to write a report on historical-comparative research. Most frequently, researchers "tell a story" or describe details in general analytic categories. The writing usually goes beyond description and includes limited generalizations and abstract concepts.

Historical-comparative researchers rarely describe their methods in great detail. Explicit sections of the report or an appendix that describes the methods used are unusual. Occasionally, a book-length report contains a bibliographic essay that discusses major sources used. More often, numerous detailed footnotes or endnotes describe the sources and evidence. For example, a 20-page report on quantitative or field research typically has 5 to 10 notes, whereas an H-C research report of equal length may have 40 to 60 notes.

Historical-comparative reports can contain photographs, maps, diagrams, charts, or tables of statistics throughout the report and in the section that discusses evidence that relates to them. The charts, tables, and so forth supplement a discussion or give the reader a better feel for the places and people being described. They are used in conjunction with frequent quotes as one among several types of evidence. Historical-comparative reports rarely summarize data to test specific hypotheses as quantitative research does. Instead, the writer builds a web of meaning or descriptive detail and organizes the evidence itself to convey interpretations and generalizations.

There are two basic modes of organizing H-C research reports: by topic and chronologically. Most writers mix the two types. For example, information is organized chronologically within topics, or organized by topic within chronological periods. Occasionally other forms of organization are used—by place, by individual person, or by major events. If the report is truly comparative, the writer has additional options, such as making comparisons within topics. Box 14.3 provides a sample of some techniques used by historical-comparative researchers to organize evidence and analysis.

Some H-C researchers mimic the quantitative research report and use quantitative research techniques. They extend quantitative research rather than adopt a distinct historical-comparative research method. Their reports follow the model of a quantitative research report.

You learned about the narrative strategy of qualitative data analysis in Chapter 13. Researchers who use this strategy often adopt a narrative style of report writing. Researchers who use the narrative style organize their data chronologically and try to "tell a story" around specific individuals and events.

The Research Proposal

What Is the Proposal?   A research *proposal* is a document that presents a plan for a project to reviewers for evaluation. It can be a supervised project submitted to instructors as part of an educational degree (e.g., a master's thesis or a Ph.D. dissertation) or it can be a research project proposed to a funding agency. Its purpose is to convince reviewers that you, the researcher, are capable of successfully conducting the proposed research project. Reviewers have more confidence that a planned project will be successfully completed if the proposal is well written and organized, and if you demonstrate careful planning.

The proposal is similar to a research report, but it is written before the research project begins. A proposal describes the research problem and its importance, and gives a detailed account of the methods that will be used and why they are appropriate.

The proposal for quantitative research has most of the parts of a research report: a title, an abstract, a problem statement, a literature review, a methods or design section, and a bibliography. It lacks results, discussion, and conclusion sections. The proposal has a plan for data collection and analysis (e.g., types of statistics). It frequently includes a schedule of the steps to be undertaken and an estimate of the time required for each step.

Proposals for qualitative research are more difficult to write because the research process itself is less structured and preplanned. The

Box 14.3

Ten Features to Consider When Writing a Report on Historical-Comparative Research

1. *Sequence.* Historical-comparative researchers are sensitive to the temporal order of events and place a series of events in order to describe a process. For example, a researcher studying the passage of a law or the evolution of a social norm may break the process into a set of sequential steps.

2. *Comparison.* Comparing similarities and differences lies at the heart of comparative-historical research. Make comparisons explicit and identify both similarities and differences. For example, a researcher comparing the family in two historical periods or countries begins by listing shared and nonshared traits of the family in each setting.

3. *Contingency.* Researchers often discover that one event, action, or situation depends on or is conditioned by others. Outlining the linkages of how one event was contingent on others is critical. For example, a researcher examining the rise of local newspapers notes that it depended on the spread of literacy.

4. *Origins and consequences.* Historical-comparative researchers trace the origins of an event, action, organization, or social relationship back in time, or follow its consequences into subsequent time periods. For example, a researcher explaining the end of slavery traces its origins to many movements, speeches, laws, and actions in the preceding fifty years.

5. *Sensitivity to incompatible meaning.* Meanings change over time and vary across cultures. Historical-comparative researchers ask themselves whether a word or social category had the same meaning in the past as in the present or whether a word in one culture has a direct translation in another culture. For example, a college degree had a different meaning in a historical era when it was extremely expensive and less than 1 percent of the 18- to 22-year-old population received a degree compared to the late twentieth century, when college became relatively accessible.

6. *Limited generalization.* Overgeneralization is always a potential problem in historical-comparative research. Few researchers seek rigid, fixed laws in historical, comparative explanation. They qualify statements or avoid strict determination. For example, instead of a blanket statement that the destruction of the native cultures in areas settled by European Whites was the inevitable consequence of advanced technological culture, a researcher may list the specific factors that combined to explain the destruction in particular social-historical settings.

7. *Association.* The concept of association is used in all forms of social research. As in other areas, historical-comparative researchers identify factors that appear together in time and place. For example, a researcher examining a city's nineteenth-century crime rate asks whether years of greater migration into the city are associated with higher crime rates and whether those arrested tended to be recent immigrants.

8. *Part and whole.* It is important to place events in their context. Writers of historical-comparative research sketch linkages between parts of a process, organization, or event and the larger context in which it is found. For example, a researcher studying a particular political ritual in an eighteenth-century setting describes how the ritual fit within the eighteenth-century political system.

9. *Analogy.* Analogies can be useful. The overuse of analogy or the use of an inappropriate analogy is dangerous. For example, a researcher examines feelings about divorce in country X and describes them as "like feelings about death" in country Y. This analogy requires a description of "feelings about death" in country Y.

Box 14.3	*Continued*

10. *Synthesis.* Historical-comparative researchers often synthesize many specific events and details into a comprehensive whole. Synthesis results from weaving together many smaller generalizations and interpretations into coherent main themes. For example, a researcher studying the French Revolution synthesizes specific generalizations about changes in social structure, international pressures, agricultural dislocation, shifting popular beliefs and problems with government finances into a compact, coherent explanation. Researchers using the narrative form summarize the argument in an introduction or conclusion. It is a motif or theme embedded within the description. Thus, theoretical generalizations are intertwined with the evidence and appear to flow inductively out of the detailed evidence.

---

researcher prepares a problem statement, literature review, and bibliography. He or she demonstrates an ability to complete a proposed qualitative project in two ways. First, the proposal is well written, with an extensive discussion of the literature, significance of the problem, and sources. This shows reviewers familiarity with qualitative research and the appropriateness of the method for studying the problem. Second, the proposal describes a qualitative pilot study. This demonstrates motivation, familiarity with research techniques, and ability to complete a report about unstructured research.

Proposals to Fund Research. The purpose of a research grant is to provide the resources needed to help complete a worthy project. Researchers whose primary goal is to use funding for personal benefit or prestige, to escape from other activities, or to build an "empire" are less successful. The strategies of proposal writing and getting grants has become an industry called *grantsmanship.*

There are many sources of funding for research proposals. Colleges, private foundations, and government agencies have programs to award grants to researchers. Funds may be used to purchase equipment, to pay your salary or that of others, for research supplies, for travel to collect data, or for help with the publication of results. The degree of competition for a grant varies a great deal, depending on the source. Some sources fund more than 3 out of 4 proposals they receive, others fund fewer than 1 in 20.

The researcher needs to investigate funding sources and ask questions: What types of projects are funded—applied versus basic research, specific topics, or specific research techniques? What are the deadlines? What kind (e.g., length, degree of detail, etc.) of proposal is necessary? How large are most grants? What aspects (e.g., equipment, personnel, travel, etc.) of a project are or are not funded? There are many sources of information on funding sources. Librarians or officials who are responsible for research grants at a college are good resource people. For example, private foundations are listed in an annual publication, *The Foundation Directory. The Guide to Federal Funding for Social Scientists* lists sources in the U.S. government. In the United States, there are many newsletters on funding sources and two national computerized databases, which subscribers can search for funding sources. Some agencies periodically issue *requests for proposals (RFPs)* that ask for proposals to conduct research on a specific issue. Researchers need to learn about funding sources because it is essential to send the proposal to an appropriate source in order to be successful.

Researchers should show a track record of past success in the proposal, especially if they are going to be in charge of the project. The researcher in charge of a research project is the *principal investigator (PI)* or project director. Proposals usually include a curriculum vitae or academic resumé, letters of support from other researchers, and a record of past research. Reviewers feel safer investing funds in a project headed by someone who already has research experience than in a novice. One can build a track record with small research projects or by assisting an experienced researcher before seeking funding as a principal investigator.

The reviewers who evaluate a proposal judge whether the proposal project is appropriate to the funding source's goals. Most funding sources have guidelines stating the kinds of projects they fund. For example, programs that fund basic research have the advancement of knowledge as a goal. Programs that fund applied research often have improvements in the delivery of services as a goal. Instructions specify page length, number of copies, deadlines, and the like. Follow all instructions exactly.

Proposals should be neat and professional looking. The instructions usually ask for a detailed plan for the use of time, services, and personnel. These should be clearly stated and realistic for the project. Excessively high or low estimates, unnecessary add-ons, or omitted essentials will lower how reviewers evaluate a proposal. Creating a budget for a proposed project is complicated and usually requires technical assistance. For example, pay rates, fringe benefit rates, and so on that must be charged may not be easy to obtain. It is best to consult a grants officer at a college or an experienced proposal writer. In addition, endorsements or clearances of regulations are often necessary (e.g., IRB approval). Proposals should also include specific plans for disseminating results (e.g., publications, presentations before professional groups, etc.) and a plan for evaluating whether the project met its objectives.

The proposal is a kind of contract between researcher and the funding source. Funding agencies often require a final report, including details on how funds were spent, the findings, and an evaluation of whether the project met its objectives. Failure to spend funds properly, complete the project described in the proposal, or file a final report may result in a researcher being barred from receiving future funding or facing legal action. A serious misuse of funds may result in the banning of others at the same institution from receiving future funding.

The process of reviewing proposals after they are submitted to a funding source takes anywhere from a few weeks to almost a year, depending on the funding source. In most cases, reviewers rank a large group of proposals, and only highly ranked proposals receive funding. A proposal often undergoes a peer review in which the reviewers know the proposer from the vitae in the proposal, but the proposer does not know the reviewers. Sometimes a proposal is reviewed by nonspecialists or nonresearchers. Instructions on preparing a proposal indicate whether to write for specialists in a field or for an educated general audience.

If a proposal is funded, celebrate, but only for a short time. If the proposal is rejected, which is more likely, do not despair. Most proposals are rejected the first or second time they are submitted. Many funding sources provide written reviewer evaluations of the proposal. Always request them if they are provided. Sometimes, a courteous talk on the telephone with a person at the funding source will reveal the reasons for rejection. Strengthen and resubmit a proposal on the basis of the reviewer's comments. Most funding sources accept repeated resubmissions of revised proposals, and proposals that have been revised may be stronger in subsequent competitions.

If a proposal has been submitted to an appropriate funding source and all instructions are followed, reviewers are more likely to rate it high when:

- It addresses an important research question. It builds on prior knowledge and represents a substantial advance of knowledge for basic research. It documents a major social problem and holds promise for solutions for applied research.

■ It follows all instructions, is well written, and is easy to follow, with clearly stated objectives.

■ It completely describes research procedures that include high standards of research methodology, and it applies research techniques that are appropriate to the research question.

■ It includes specific plans for disseminating the results and evaluating whether the project has met its objectives.

■ The project is well designed and shows serious planning. It has realistic budgets and schedules.

■ The researcher has the necessary experience or background to complete the project successfully.

researcher, to be self-aware. Be aware of the place of the researcher in society and of the societal context of social research itself. Social researchers, and sociologists in particular, bring a unique perspective to the larger society.

Key Terms

- editing
- error of segregation
- executive summary
- grantsmanship
- paraphrasing
- plagiarism
- prewriting
- principal investigator
- request for proposals (RFPs)
- revising
- rewriting
- zoom lens

CONCLUSION

Clearly communicating results is a vital part of the larger scientific enterprise, as are the ethics and politics of social research.

I want to end this chapter by urging you, as a consumer of social research or a new social

Endnotes

1. The error of segregation is discussed in Lofland and Lofland (1984:146).
2. See Van Maanen (1988:13).
3. See Becker and associates (1989), Dabbs (1982), and Jackson (1978).

t, Chi, and *r* Critical Value Tables

TABLE A-1 t Distribution: Critical t Values

Degrees of Freedom	Area in One Tail				
	0.005	0.01	0.025	0.05	0.10
	Area in Two Tails				
	0.01	0.02	0.05	0.10	0.20
1	63.657	31.821	12.706	6.314	3.078
2	9.925	6.965	4.303	2.920	1.886
3	5.841	4.541	3.182	2.353	1.638
4	4.604	3.747	2.776	2.132	1.533
5	4.032	3.365	2.571	2.015	1.476
6	3.707	3.143	2.447	1.943	1.440
7	3.499	2.998	2.365	1.895	1.415
8	3.355	2.896	2.306	1.860	1.397
9	3.250	2.821	2.262	1.833	1.383
10	3.169	2.764	2.228	1.812	1.372
11	3.106	2.718	2.201	1.796	1.363
12	3.055	2.681	2.179	1.782	1.356
13	3.012	2.650	2.160	1.771	1.350
14	2.977	2.624	2.145	1.761	1.345
15	2.947	2.602	2.131	1.753	1.341
16	2.921	2.583	2.120	1.746	1.337
17	2.898	2.567	2.110	1.740	1.333
18	2.878	2.552	2.101	1.734	1.330
19	2.861	2.539	2.093	1.729	1.328
20	2.845	2.528	2.086	1.725	1.325
21	2.831	2.518	2.080	1.721	1.323
22	2.819	2.508	2.074	1.717	1.321
23	2.807	2.500	2.069	1.714	1.319
24	2.797	2.492	2.064	1.711	1.318
25	2.787	2.485	2.060	1.708	1.316
26	2.779	2.479	2.056	1.706	1.315
27	2.771	2.473	2.052	1.703	1.314
28	2.763	2.467	2.048	1.701	1.313
29	2.756	2.462	2.045	1.699	1.311
30	2.750	2.457	2.042	1.697	1.310
31	2.744	2.453	2.040	1.696	1.309
32	2.738	2.449	2.037	1.694	1.309
34	2.728	2.441	2.032	1.691	1.307
36	2.719	2.434	2.028	1.688	1.306
38	2.712	2.429	2.024	1.686	1.304
40	2.704	2.423	2.021	1.684	1.303
45	2.690	2.412	2.014	1.679	1.301
50	2.678	2.403	2.009	1.676	1.299
55	2.668	2.396	2.004	1.673	1.297
60	2.660	2.390	2.000	1.671	1.296
65	2.654	2.385	1.997	1.669	1.295
70	2.648	2.381	1.994	1.667	1.294
75	2.643	2.377	1.992	1.665	1.293
80	2.639	2.374	1.990	1.664	1.292
90	2.632	2.368	1.987	1.662	1.291
100	2.626	2.364	1.984	1.660	1.290
200	2.601	2.345	1.972	1.653	1.286
300	2.592	2.339	1.968	1.650	1.284
400	2.588	2.336	1.966	1.649	1.284
500	2.586	2.334	1.965	1.648	1.283
750	2.582	2.331	1.963	1.647	1.283
1000	2.581	2.330	1.962	1.646	1.282
2000	2.578	2.328	1.961	1.646	1.282
Large	2.576	2.326	1.960	1.645	1.282

TABLE A-2 Chi-Square (χ^2) Distribution

Area to the Right of the Critical Value

Degrees of Freedom	0.995	0.99	0.975	0.95	0.90	0.10	0.05	0.025	0.01	0.005
1	—	—	0.001	0.004	0.016	2.706	3.841	5.024	6.635	7.879
2	0.010	0.020	0.051	0.103	0.211	4.605	5.991	7.378	9.210	10.597
3	0.072	0.115	0.216	0.352	0.584	6.251	7.815	9.348	11.345	12.838
4	0.207	0.297	0.484	0.711	1.064	7.779	9.488	11.143	13.277	14.860
5	0.412	0.554	0.831	1.145	1.610	9.236	11.071	12.833	15.086	16.750
6	0.676	0.872	1.237	1.635	2.204	10.645	12.592	14.449	16.812	18.548
7	0.989	1.239	1.690	2.167	2.833	12.017	14.067	16.013	18.475	20.278
8	1.344	1.646	2.180	2.733	3.490	13.362	15.507	17.535	20.090	21.955
9	1.735	2.088	2.700	3.325	4.168	14.684	16.919	19.023	21.666	23.589
10	2.156	2.558	3.247	3.940	4.865	15.987	18.307	20.483	23.209	25.188
11	2.603	3.053	3.816	4.575	5.578	17.275	19.675	21.920	24.725	26.757
12	3.074	3.571	4.404	5.226	6.304	18.549	21.026	23.337	26.217	28.299
13	3.565	4.107	5.009	5.892	7.042	19.812	22.362	24.736	27.688	29.819
14	4.075	4.660	5.629	6.571	7.790	21.064	23.685	26.119	29.141	31.319
15	4.601	5.229	6.262	7.261	8.547	22.307	24.996	27.488	30.578	32.801
16	5.142	5.812	6.908	7.962	9.312	23.542	26.296	28.845	32.000	34.267
17	5.697	6.408	7.564	8.672	10.085	24.769	27.587	30.191	33.409	35.718
18	6.265	7.015	8.231	9.390	10.865	25.989	28.869	31.526	34.805	37.156
19	6.844	7.633	8.907	10.117	11.651	27.204	30.144	32.852	36.191	38.582
20	7.434	8.260	9.591	10.851	12.443	28.412	31.410	34.170	37.566	39.997
21	8.034	8.897	10.283	11.591	13.240	29.615	32.671	35.479	38.932	41.401
22	8.643	9.542	10.982	12.338	14.042	30.813	33.924	36.781	40.289	42.796
23	9.260	10.196	11.689	13.091	14.848	32.007	35.172	38.076	41.638	44.181
24	9.886	10.856	12.401	13.848	15.659	33.196	36.415	39.364	42.980	45.559
25	10.520	11.524	13.120	14.611	16.473	34.382	37.652	40.646	44.314	46.928
26	11.160	12.198	13.844	15.379	17.292	35.563	38.885	41.923	45.642	48.290
27	11.808	12.879	14.573	16.151	18.114	36.741	40.113	43.194	46.963	49.645
28	12.461	13.565	15.308	16.928	18.939	37.916	41.337	44.461	48.278	50.993
29	13.121	14.257	16.047	17.708	19.768	39.087	42.557	45.722	49.588	52.336
30	13.787	14.954	16.791	18.493	20.599	40.256	43.773	46.979	50.892	53.672
40	20.707	22.164	24.433	26.509	29.051	51.805	55.758	59.342	63.691	66.766
50	27.991	29.707	32.357	34.764	37.689	63.167	67.505	71.420	76.154	79.490
60	35.534	37.485	40.482	43.188	46.459	74.397	79.082	83.298	88.379	91.952
70	43.275	45.442	48.758	51.739	55.329	85.527	90.531	95.023	100.425	104.215
80	51.172	53.540	57.153	60.391	64.278	96.578	101.879	106.629	112.329	116.321
90	59.196	61.754	65.647	69.126	73.291	107.565	113.145	118.136	124.116	128.299
100	67.328	70.065	74.222	77.929	82.358	118.498	124.342	129.561	135.807	140.169

From Donald B. Owen, *Handbook of Statistical Tables*, ©1962 Pearson Addison-Wesley, an imprint of Pearson Education, Inc.

TABLE A-3	Critical Values of the Pearson Correlation Coefficient r	
n	$\alpha = .05$	$\alpha = .01$
4	.950	.999
5	.878	.959
6	.811	.917
7	.754	.875
8	.707	.834
9	.666	.798
10	.632	.765
11	.602	.735
12	.576	.708
13	.553	.684
14	.532	.661
15	.514	.641
16	.497	.623
17	.482	.606
18	.468	.590
19	.456	.575
20	.444	.561
25	.396	.505
30	.361	.463
35	.335	.430
40	.312	.402
45	.294	.378
50	.279	.361
60	.254	.330
70	.236	.305
80	.220	.286
90	.207	.269
100	.196	.256

NOTE: To test H_0: $\rho = 0$ against H_1: $\rho \neq 0$, reject H_0 if the absolute value of r is greater than the critical value in the table.

Following the definition, the number in parentheses indicates the chapter in which the term first appears in the text and is in the Key Terms section. Italicized terms refer to terms defined elsewhere in this glossary.

Abstract A term with two meanings in literature reviews: a short summary of a scholarly journal article that usually appears at its beginning, and a reference tool for locating scholarly journal articles. (4)

Accretion measures *Nonreactive measures* of the residue of the activity of people or what they leave behind. (9)

Action research study A type of *applied social research* in which a researcher treats knowledge as a form of power and abolishes the division between creating knowledge and using knowledge to engage in political action. (1)

Alternative hypothesis A *hypothesis* paired with a *null hypothesis* stating that the *independent variable* has an effect on a *dependent variable*. (4)

Analytic memo The written notes a qualitative researcher takes during data collection and afterwards to develop concepts, themes, or preliminary generalizations. (11)

Anonymity Research participants remain anonymous or nameless. (3)

Appearance of interest A technique in field research in which researchers maintain relations in a *field site* by pretending to be interested and excited by the activities of those studied, even though they are actually uninterested or very bored. (11)

Applied research Research that attempts to solve a concrete problem or address a specific policy question and that has a direct, practical application. (1)

Association A co-occurrence of two events, factors, characteristics, or activities, such that when one happens, the other is likely to occur as well. Many statistics measure this. (2)

Assumption Parts of social theories that are not tested, but act as starting points or basic beliefs about the world. They are necessary to make other theoretical statements and to build social theory. (2)

Attitude of strangeness A technique in *field research* in which researchers study a *field site* by mentally adjusting to "see" it for the first time or as an outsider. (11)

Attributes The categories or levels of a *variable*. (4)

Axial coding A second coding of *qualitative data* after *open coding*. The researcher organizes the codes, develops links among them, and discovers key analytic categories. (13)

Back translation A technique in comparative research for checking *lexicon equivalence*. A researcher translates spoken or written text from an original language into a second language, then translates the same text in the second language back into the original language, then compares the two original language texts. (12)

Bar chart A display of *quantitative data* for one variable in the form of rectangles where longer rectangles indicate more cases in a variable category. Usually, it is used with discrete data and there is a small space between rectangles. They can have a horizonal or vertical orientation. Also called bar graphs. (10)

Basic social research Research designed to advance fundamental knowledge about the social world. (1)

Bivariate statistics Statistical measures that involve two variables only. (10)

Blame analysis A counterfeit argument presented as if it were a theoretical explanation that substitutes attributing blame for a *causal explanation* and implies an intention or negligence, or responsibility for an event or situation. (2)

Body of a table The center part of a *contingency table*. It contains all the cells, but not the totals or labels. (10)

Bogardus social distance scale A *scale* that measures the distance between two or more social groups by having members of one group express the point at which they feel comfortable with various types of social interaction or closeness with members of the other group(s). (5)

Case study Research, usually qualitative, on one or a small number of cases in which a researcher carefully examines a large number of details about each case. (1)

Causal explanation A statement in social theory about why events occur that is expressed in terms of causes and effects. They correspond to associations in the empirical world. (2)

Cell of a table A part of the *body of a table*. In a *contingency table,* it shows the distribution of cases into categories of variables as a specific number or percentage. (10)

Central limit theorem A lawlike mathematical relationship that states: Whenever many *random samples* are drawn from a *population* and plotted, a *normal distribution* is formed, and the center of such a distribution for a variable is equal to its *population parameter*. (6)

Citation Details of a scholarly journal article's location that helps people find it quickly. (4)

Classical experimental design An *experimental design* that has *random assignment*, a *control group,* an *experimental group,* and *pretests* and *posttests* for each group. (8)

Classification Complex, multidimensional concepts that have subtypes. They are parts of social theories between one simple concept and a full theoretical explanation. (2)

Closed-ended questions A type of *survey research* question in which respondents must choose from a fixed set of answers. (7)

Cluster sampling A type of *random sample* that uses multiple stages and is often used to cover wide geographic areas in which aggregated units are randomly selected then *samples* are drawn from the sampled aggregated units, or clusters. (6)

Code sheets Paper with a printed grid on which a researcher records information so that it can be easily entered into a computer. It is an alternative to *direct-entry method* and using optical-scan sheets. (10)

Codebook A document that describes the procedure for coding variables and their location in a format for computers. (10)

Coding The process of converting raw information or data into another form for analysis. In *content analysis,* it is a means for determining how to convert symbolic meanings in *text* into another form, usually numbers (see *Coding system*); in *quantitative data* analysis, it is a means for assigning numbers; and in *qualitative data* analysis, it is a series of steps for reading raw notes and assigning codes or conceptual terms (see *Axial coding, Open coding, Selective coding*). (9)

Coding system A set of instructions or rules used in *content analysis* to explain how to systematically convert the symbolic content from *text* into *quantitative data*. (9)

Cohort study A type of *longitudinal research* in which a researcher focuses on a category of people who share a similar life experience in a specified time period. (1)

Computer-assisted telephone interviewing (CATI) *Survey research* in which the interviewer sits before a computer screen and keyboard and uses the computer to read questions that are asked in a telephone interview, then enters answers directly into the computer. (7)

Concept cluster   A collection of interrelated ideas that share common *assumptions,* belong to the same larger social theory, and refer to one another. (2)

Conceptual definition   A careful, systematic definition of a construct that is explicitly written to clarify one's thinking. It is often linked to other concepts or theoretical statements. (5)

Conceptual equivalence   In *historical-comparative research,* the issue of whether the same ideas or concepts occur or can be used to represent phenomena across divergent cultural or historical settings. (12)

Conceptual hypothesis   A type of *hypothesis* in which the researcher expresses variables in abstract, conceptual terms and expresses the relationship among variables in a theoretical way. (5)

Conceptualization   The process of developing clear, rigorous, systematic *conceptual definitions* for abstract ideas/concepts. (5)

Concurrent validity   *Measurement validity* that relies on a preexisting and already accepted measure to verify the indicator of a construct. (5)

Confidence interval   A range of values, usually a little higher and lower than a specific value found in a *sample,* within which a researcher has a specified and high degree of confidence that the *population parameter* lies. (6)

Confidentiality   Information with participant names attached, but the researcher holds it in confidence or keeps it secret from the public. (3)

Content analysis   Research in which one examines patterns of symbolic meaning within written text, audio, visual, or other communication medium. (9)

Content validity   *Measurement validity* that requires that a measure represent all the aspects of the conceptual definition of a construct. (5)

Context effect   An effect in *survey research* when an overall tone or set topics heard by a respondent

affects how he or she interprets the meaning of subsequent questions. (7)

Contextual equivalence   The issue in *historical-comparative research* of whether social roles, norms, or situations across different cultures or historical periods are equivalent or can be compared. (12)

Contingency cleaning   Cleaning data using a computer in which the researcher looks at the combination of categories for two variables for logically impossible cases. (10)

Contingency question   A type of *survey research* question in which the respondent next goes to one or another later question based on his or her answer. (7)

Contingency table   A table that shows the *cross-tabulation* of two or more variables. It usually shows *bivariate quantitative data* for variables in the form of percentages across rows or down columns for the categories of one variable. (10)

Continuous variable   Variables measured on a continuum in which an infinite number of finer gradations between variable *attributes* are possible. (5)

Contrast question   A type of interview question asked late in *field research* in which the researcher verifies the correctness of distinctions found among categories in the meaning system of people being studied. (11)

Control group   The group that does not get the *treatment* in *experimental research.* (8)

Control variable   A "third" variable that shows whether a *bivariate relationship* holds up to alternative explanations. It can occur before or between other variables. (10)

Covariation   The idea that two variables vary together, such that knowing the values in one variable provides information about values found in another variable. (10)

Cover sheet   One or more pages at the beginning of a *questionnaire* with information about an interview or respondent. (7)

Criterion validity   *Measurement validity* that relies on some independent, outside verification. (5)

Crossover design A design to reduce creating inequality; it is when a study group that gets no treatment in the first phase of the experiment becomes the group with the treatment in the second phase, and vice versa. (3)

Cross-sectional research Research in which a researcher examines a single point in time or takes a one-time snapshot approach. (1)

Cross-tabulation Placing data for two variables in a *contingency table* to show the number or percentage of cases at the intersection of categories of the two variables. (10)

Curvilinear relationship A relationship between two variables such that as the values of one variable increase, the values of the second show a changing pattern (e.g., first decrease then increase then decrease). It is not a *linear relationship*. (10)

Data The *empirical evidence* or information that a person gathers carefully according to established rules or procedures; it can be qualitative or quantitative. (1)

Debrief When a researcher gives a true explanation of the experiment to subjects after using *deception*. (8)

Deception When an experimenter lies to subjects about the true nature of an experiment or creates a false impression through his or her actions or the setting. (8)

Deductive approach An approach to inquiry or social theory in which one begins with abstract ideas and principles then works toward concrete, *empirical evidence* to test the ideas. (2)

Demand characteristics A type of *reactivity* in which the subjects in *experimental research* pick up clues about the *hypothesis* and alter their behavior accordingly. (8)

Dependent variable The effect variable that is last and results from the causal variable(s) in a *causal explanation*. Also the variable that is measured in the *pretest* and *posttest* and that is the result of the *treatment* in *experimental research*. (4)

Descriptive question A type of question asked early in *field research*. The researcher seeks basic information (e.g., who, what, when, where) about the *field site*. (11)

Descriptive research Research in which one "paints a picture" with words or numbers, presents a profile, outlines stages, or classifies types. (1)

Descriptive statistics A general type of simple statistics used by researchers to describe basic patterns in the data. (10)

Design notation The name of a symbol system used to discuss the parts of an experiment and to make diagrams of them. (8)

Deviant case sampling A type of *nonrandom sample,* especially used by qualitative researchers, in which a researcher selects unusual or nonconforming cases purposely as a way to provide greater insight into social processes or a setting. (6)

Diffusion of treatment A threat to *internal validity* that occurs when the *treatment* "spills over" from the *experimental group,* and *control group* subjects modify their behavior because they learn of the *treatment*. (8)

Direct-entry method A method of entering data into a computer by typing data without code or optical scan sheets. (10)

Direct observation notes Notes taken in *field research* that attempt to include all details and specifics of what the researcher heard or saw in a *field site*. They are written in a way that permits multiple interpretations later. (11)

Discrete variables Variables in which the *attributes* can be measured only with a limited number of distinct, separate categories. (5)

Double-barreled question A problem in *survey research* question wording that occurs when two ideas are combined into one question, and it is unclear whether the answer is for the combination of both or one or the other question. (7)

Double-blind experiment A type of *experimental research* in which neither the subjects nor the person who directly deals with the subjects for the experimenter knows the specifics of the experiment. (8)

Ecological fallacy Something that appears to be a *causal explanation* but is not. It occurs because of a confusion about *units of analysis*. A researcher has *empirical evidence* about an *association* for large-scale units or huge aggregates, but *overgeneralizes* to make theoretical statements about an *association* among small-scale units or individuals. (4)

Ecological validity A way to demonstrate the authenticity and trustworthiness of a *field research* study by showing that the researcher's descriptions of the field site matches those of the members from the site and that the researcher was not a major disturbance. (11)

Editing A step in the writing process that is part of *rewriting,* in which a writer cleans up and tightens the language and checks grammar, verb agreement, usage, sentence length, and paragraph organization to improve communication. (14)

Elaboration paradigm A system for describing patterns evident among tables when a *bivariate contingency table* is compared with *partials* after the *control variable* has been added. (10)

Empirical evidence The observations that people experience through their senses—touch, sight, hearing, smell, and taste; these can be direct or indirect. (1)

Empirical generalization A quasi-theoretical statement that summarizes findings or regularities in *empirical evidence*. It uses few if any abstract concepts and only makes a statement about a recurring pattern that researchers observe. (2)

Empirical hypothesis A type of *hypothesis* in which the researcher expresses variables in specific terms and expresses the *association* among the measured indicators of observable, *empirical evidence.* (5)

Empty boxes A name for conceptual categories in an explanation that a researcher uses as part of the *illustrative method* of *qualitative data analysis.* (13)

Equivalent time-series design An *experimental design* in which there are several repeated *pretests, posttests,* and *treatments* for one group often over a period of time. (8)

Erosion measures *Nonreactive measures* of the wear or deterioration on surfaces due to the activity of people. (9)

Error of segregation A mistake that can occur when writing qualitative research in which a writer separates concrete *empirical* details from abstract ideas too much. (14)

Ethnographic fallacy When a field researcher takes what is observed at face value, fails to question what members of a *field site* say, and only focuses on the immediate concrete details of a setting while ignoring larger social forces. (11)

Ethnography An approach to *field research* that emphasizes providing a very detailed description of a different culture from the viewpoint of an insider in that culture in order to permit a greater understanding of it. (11)

Ethnomethodology An approach to social science that combines philosophy, social theory, and method to study. (11)

Evaluation research study A type of *applied research* in which one tries to determine how well a program or policy is working or reaching its goals and objectives. (1)

Executive summary A summary of a research project's findings placed at the beginning of a report for an applied, nonspecialist audience. Usually a little longer than an *abstract.* (14)

Exhaustive attributes The principle that response categories in a *scale* or other measure should provide a category for all possible responses (i.e., every possible response fits into some category). (5)

Existing statistics research Research in which one examines numerical information from government documents or official reports to address new research questions. (1)

Experimental design Arranging the parts of an experiment and putting them together. (8)

Experimental group The group that receives the *treatment* in *experimental research*. (8)

Experimental research Research in which one intervenes or does something to one group of people but not to another, then compares results for the two groups. (1)

Explanation pattern A pattern in the *elaboration paradigm* in which the *bivariate contingency table* shows a relationship, but the *partials* show no relationship and the *control variable* occurs prior to the *independent variable*. (10)

Explanatory research Research that focuses on why events occur or tries to test and build social theory. (1)

Exploratory research Research into an area that has not been studied and in which a researcher wants to develop initial ideas and a more focused research question. (1)

External consistency A way to achieve *reliability* of data in *field research* in which the researcher cross-checks and verifies *qualitative data* using multiple sources of information. (11)

External criticism In historical research, a way to check the authenticity of *primary sources* by accurately locating the place and time of its creation (e.g., it is not a forgery). (12)

External validity The ability to generalize from *experimental research* to settings or people that differ from the specific conditions of the study. (5)

Face validity A type of *measurement validity* in which an indicator "makes sense" as a measure of a construct in the judgment of others, especially those in the scientific community. (5)

Factorial design A type of *experimental design* that considers the impact of several *independent variables* simultaneously. (8)

Fallacy of misplaced concreteness When a person uses too many digits in a quantitative measure in an attempt to create the impression that the data are accurate or the researcher is highly capable. (9)

Field experiment *Experimental research* that takes place in a natural setting. (8)

Field research A type of qualitative research in which a researcher directly observes the people being studied in a natural setting for an extended period. Often, the researcher combines intense observing with participation in the people's social activities. (1)

Field site The one or more natural locations where a researcher conducts *field research*. (11)

First-order interpretation In qualitative research, what the people who are being studied actually feel and think. (4)

Floaters Respondents who lack a belief or opinion, but who give an answer anyway if asked in a *survey research* question. Often, their answers are inconsistent. (7)

Focus groups A type of group interview in which an interviewer asks questions to the group, and answers are given in an open discussion among the group members. (11)

Frequency distribution A table that shows the distribution of cases into the categories of one variable (i.e., the number or percent of cases in each category). (10)

Frequency polygon A graph of connected points showing the distribution of how many cases fall into each category of a variable. (10)

Full-filter question A type of *survey research* question in which respondents are first asked whether they have an opinion or know about a topic, then only the respondents with an opinion or knowledge are asked a specific question on the topic. (7)

Functional theory A type of social theory based on biological analogies, in which the social world or its parts are seen as systems, with its parts serving the needs of the system. (2)

Funnel sequence A way to order *survey research* questions in a questionnaire from general ones to specific. (7)

Galton's problem In comparative research, the problem of finding correlations or *associations* among variables or characteristics in multiple cases or units, when the characteristics are actually diffused from a single unit or have a common origin. Thus, a researcher cannot really treat the multiple units (e.g., countries, cultures, etc.) as being wholly separate. (12)

General Social Survey (GSS) A survey of a *random sample* of about 1,500 U.S. adults that has been conducted in most years between 1972 and the present and is available for many researchers to analyze. (9)

Go native What happens when a researcher in *field research* gets overly involved and loses all distance or objectivity and becomes like the people being studied. (11)

Grantsmanship The strategies and skills of locating appropriate funding sources and preparing high-quality proposals for research funding. (14)

Grounded theory Social theory that is rooted in observations of specific, concrete details. (2)

Guilty knowledge When a researcher in *field research* learns of illegal, unethical, or immoral actions by the people in the *field site* that is not widely known. (11)

Guttman scaling A *scale* that researchers use after data are collected to reveal whether a hierarchical pattern exists among responses, such that people who give responses at a "higher level" also tend to give "lower-level" ones. (5)

Halo effect An error often made when people use personal experience as an alternative to science for acquiring knowledge. It is when a person overgeneralizes from what he or she accepts as being highly positive or prestigious and lets its strong reputation or prestige "rub off" onto other areas. (1)

Haphazard sampling A type of *nonrandom sample* in which the researcher selects anyone he or she happens to come across. (6)

Hawthorne effect An effect of *reactivity* named after a famous case in which subjects reacted to the fact that they were in an experiment more than they reacted to the *treatment*. (8)

Hidden populations People who engage in clandestine, deviant, or concealed activities and who are difficult to locate and study. (6)

Historical-comparative research Research in which one examines different cultures or periods to better understand the social world. (1)

History effects A threat to *internal validity* due to something that occurs and affects the *dependent variable* during an experiment, but which is unplanned and outside the control of the experimenter. (8)

Human Relations Area Files (HRAF) An extensive catalog and comprehensive collection of *ethnographies* on many cultures (mostly preliterate) that permits a researcher to compare across cultural units. (12)

Hypothesis The statement from a *causal explanation* or a *proposition* that has at least one *independent* and one *dependent variable,* but it has yet to be empirically tested. (4)

Ideal type A pure model about an idea, process, or event. One develops it to think about it more clearly and systematically. It is used both as a method of *qualitative data* analysis and in *social theory* building. (2)

Idiographic An approach that focuses on creating detailed descriptions of specific events in particular time periods and settings. It rarely goes beyond *empirical generalizations* to abstract social theory or *causal laws.* (2)

Illustrative method A method of *qualitative data* analysis in which a researcher takes the concepts of a *social theory* or explanation and treats them as *empty boxes* to be filled with *empirical* examples and descriptions. (13)

Independence The absence of a *statistical relationship* between two variables (i.e., when knowing the values on one variable provides no information about the values that will be found on another variable). There is no *association* between them. (10)

Independent variable The first variable that causes or produces the effect in a *causal explanation.* (4)

Index The summing or combining of many separate measures of a construct or variable. (5)

Inductive approach   An approach to inquiry or social theory in which one begins with concrete empirical details, then works toward abstract ideas or general principles. (2)

Inferential statistics   A branch of applied mathematics or statistics based on a *random sample*. It lets a researcher make precise statements about the level of confidence he or she has in the results of a *sample* being equal to the *population parameter*. (6)

Informed consent   An agreement by participants stating they are willing to be in a study after they learn something about what the research procedure will involve. (3)

Institutional Review Board   A committee of researchers and community members that oversees, monitors, and reviews the impact of research procedures on human participants and applies ethical guidelines by reviewing research procedures at a preliminary stage when first proposed. (3)

Interaction effect   The effect of two *independent variables* that operate simultaneously together. The effect of the variables together is greater than what would occur from a simple addition of the effects from each. The variables operate together on one another to create an extra "boost." (8)

Internal consistency   A way to achieve *reliability* of data in *field research* in which a researcher examines the data for plausibility and sees whether they form a coherent picture, given all that is known about a person or event, trying to avoid common forms of deception. (11)

Internal criticism   How historical researchers establish the authenticity and credibility of *primary sources* and determine its accuracy as an account of what occurred. (12)

Internal validity   The ability of experimenters to strengthen a *causal explanation's* logical rigor by eliminating potential alternative explanations for an *association* between the *treatment* and the *dependent variable* through an *experimental design*. (5)

Interpretation pattern   A pattern in the *elaboration paradigm* in which the *bivariate contingency table* shows a relationship, but the *partials* show no relationship and the *control variable* is intervening in the *causal explanation*. (10)

Interrupted time series   An *experimental design* in which the *dependent variable* is measured periodically across many time points, and the *treatment* occurs in the midst of such measures, often only once. (8)

Interval level of measurement   A *level of measurement* that identifies differences among variable *attributes*, ranks, and categories, and that measures distance between categories, but there is no true zero. (5)

Intervening variable   A variable that is between the initial causal variable and the final effect variable in a *causal explanation*. (4)

Interview schedule   The name of a *survey research questionnaire* when a telephone or face-to-face interview is used. (7)

Jotted notes   In *field research*, what a researcher inconspicuously writes while in the *field site* on whatever is convenient in order to "jog the memory" later. (11)

Laboratory experiment   *Experimental research* that takes place in an artificial setting over which the experimenter has great control. (8)

Latent coding   A type of *content analysis* coding in which a researcher identifies subjective meaning such as general themes or motifs in a communication medium. (9)

Latin square design   An *experimental design* used to examine whether the order or sequence in which subjects receive multiple versions of the *treatment* has an effect. (8)

Level of analysis   A way to talk about the scope of a *social theory, causal explanation, proposition, hypothesis,* or theoretical statement. The range of phenomena it covers, or to which it applies, goes from social psychological (*micro level*) to organizational (*meso level*) to large-scale social structure (*macro level*). (4)

Level of measurement   A system that organizes the information in the measurement of variables into four general levels, from *nominal level* to *ratio level*. (5)

Level of statistical significance   A set of numbers researchers use as a simple way to measure the degree to which a *statistical relationship* results from random factors rather than the existence of a true relationship among variables. (10)

Lexicon equivalence   Finding equivalent words or phrases to express the identical meaning in different languages or in the translation from one language to another (see *Back translation*). (12)

Likert scale   A *scale* often used in *survey research* in which people express attitudes or other responses in terms of several *ordinal-level* categories (e.g., agree, disagree) that are ranked along a continuum. (5)

Linear relationship   An *association* between two variables that is positive or negative across the attributes or levels of the variables. When plotted in a *scattergram,* the basic pattern of the *association* forms a straight line, not a curve or other pattern. (10)

Linear research path   Research that proceeds in a clear, logical, step-by-step straight line. It is more characteristic of a quantitative than a qualitative approach to social research. (4)

Literature review   A systematic examination of previously published studies on a research question, issue, or method that a researcher undertakes and integrates together to prepare for conducting a study or to bring together and summarize the "state of the field." (4)

Longitudinal research   Research in which the researcher examines the features of people or other units at multiple points in time. (1)

Macro-level theory   Social theories and explanations about more abstract, large-scale, and broad-scope aspects of social reality, such as social change in major institutions (e.g., the family, education, etc.) in a whole nation across several decades. (2)

Manifest coding   A type of *content analysis* coding in which a researcher first develops a list of specific words, phrases, or symbols, then finds them in a communication medium. (9)

Marginals   The totals in a *contingency table,* outside the *body of a table.* (10)

Matrix question   A type of *survey research* question in which a set of questions is listed in a compact form together, all questions sharing the same set of answer categories. (7)

Maturation   A threat to *internal validity* in *experimental research* due to natural processes of growth, boredom, and so on, that occur to subjects during the experiment and affect the *dependent variable.* (8)

Mean   A measure of central tendency for one variable that indicates the arithmetic average (i.e., the sum of all scores divided by the total number of scores). (10)

Measurement equivalence   In *historical-comparative research,* creating or locating measures that will accurately represent the same construct or variable in divergent cultural or historical settings. (12)

Measurement validity   How well an *empirical* indicator and the *conceptual definition* of the construct that the indicator is supposed to measure "fit" together. (5)

Median   A measure of central tendency for one variable indicating the point or score at which half the cases are higher and half are lower. (10)

Member validation   A way to demonstrate the authenticity and trustworthiness of a *field research* study by having the people who were studied (i.e., members) read and confirm as being true that which the *researcher* has reported. (11)

Meso-level theory   Social theories and explanations about the middle level of social reality between a broad and narrow scope, such as the development and operation of social organizations, communities, or social movements over a five-year period. (2)

Micro-level theory   Social theories and explanations about the concrete, small-scale, and narrow level of reality, such as face-to-face interaction in small groups during a two-month period. (2)

Mode A measure of central tendency for one variable that indicates the most frequent or common score. (10)

Mortality Threats to *internal validity* due to subjects failing to participate through the entire experiment. (8)

Multiple indicators Many procedures or instruments that indicate, or provide evidence of, the presence or level of a variable using *empirical evidence.* Researchers use the combination of several together to measure a variable. (5)

Mutually exclusive attributes The principle that response categories in a *scale* or other measure should be organized so that a person's responses fit into only one category (i.e., categories should not overlap). (5)

Narrative history A type of writing about a historical setting in which the writer attempts to "tell a story" by following chronological order, describing particular people and events, and focusing on many colorful details. (13)

Naturalism The principle that researchers should examine events as they occur in natural, everyday ongoing social settings. (11)

Negative relationship An *association* between two variables such that as values on one variable increase, values on the other variable fall or decrease. (2)

Nominal-level measurement The lowest, least precise *level of measurement* for which there is only a difference in type among the categories of a variable. (5)

Nomothetic An approach based on laws or one that operates according to a system of laws. (2)

Nonlinear research path Research that proceeds in a circular, back-and-forth manner. It is more characteristic of a qualitative than a quantitative style to social research. (4)

Nonrandom sample A type of sample in which the sampling elements are selected using something other than a mathematically random process. (6)

Nonreactive Measures in which people being studied are unaware that they are in a study. (9)

Normal distribution A "bell-shaped" frequency polygon for a distribution of cases, with a peak in the center and identical curving slopes on either side of the center. It is the distribution of many naturally occurring phenomena and is a basis of much statistical theory. (10)

Normalize social research Techniques in *field research* used by researchers to make the people being studied feel more comfortable with the research process and to help them accept the researcher's presence. (11)

Null hypothesis A *hypothesis* that says there is no relationship or *association* between two variables, or no effect. (4)

One-shot case study An *experimental design* with only an *experimental group* and a *posttest*, no *pretest*. (8)

Open coding A first coding of *qualitative data* in which a researcher examines the data to condense them into preliminary analytic categories or codes for analyzing the data. (13)

Open-ended question A type of *survey research* question in which respondents are free to offer any answer they wish to the question. (7)

Operational definition The definition of a variable in terms of the specific activities to measure or indicate it with *empirical evidence.* (5)

Operationalization The process of moving from the *conceptual definition* of a construct to a set of specific activities or measures that allow a researcher to observe it *empirically* (i.e., its *operational definition*). (5)

Oral history A type of *recollection* in which a researcher interviews a person about the events, beliefs, or feelings in the past that were directly experienced. (12)

Order effects An effect in *survey research* in which respondents hear some specific questions before others, and the earlier questions affect their answers to later questions. (7)

Ordinal-level measurement A *level of measurement* that identifies a difference among categories of a variable and allows the categories to be rank ordered. (5)

Overgeneralization An error that people often make when using personal experience as an alternative to science for acquiring knowledge. It occurs when some evidence supports a belief, but a person falsely assumes that it applies to many other situations, too. (1)

Panel study A powerful type of *longitudinal research* in which a researcher observes exactly the same people, group, or organization across multiple time points. (1)

Paradigm A general organizing framework for *social theory* and *empirical* research. It includes basic *assumptions*, major questions to be answered, models of good research practice and theory, and methods for finding the answers to questions. (2)

Parameter A characteristic of the entire *population* that is estimated from a *sample*. (6)

Paraphrasing When a writer restates or rewords the ideas of another person, giving proper credit to the original source. (14)

Partially open question A type of *survey research* question in which respondents are given a fixed set of answers to choose from, but in addition, an "other" category is offered so that they can specify a different answer. (7)

Partials In *contingency tables* for three variables, tables that show the *association* between the *independent* and *dependent variables* for each category of a *control variable*. (10)

Percentile A measure of dispersion for one variable that indicates the percentage of cases at or below a score or point. (10)

Pie chart A display of numerical information on one variable that divides a circle into fractions by lines representing the proportion of cases in the variable's *attributes*. (10)

Placebo A false *treatment* or one that has no effect in an experiment. It is sometimes called a "sugar pill" that a *subject* mistakes for a true *treatment*. (8)

Plagiarism A type of unethical behavior in which one uses the writings or ideas of another without giving proper credit. It is "stealing ideas." (3, 14)

Population The name for the large general group of many cases from which a researcher draws a *sample* and which is usually stated in theoretical terms. (6)

Positive relationship An *association* between two variables such that as values on one increase, values on the other also increase. (2)

Possible code cleaning Cleaning data using a computer in which the researcher looks for responses or answer categories that cannot have cases. (10)

Posttest The measurement of the *dependent variable* in *experimental research* after the *treatment*. (8)

Praxis An idea in critical social science that social theory and everyday practice interact or work together, mutually affecting one another. This interaction can promote social change. (2)

Prediction A statement about something that is likely to occur in the future. (2)

Predictive validity *Measurement validity* that relies on the occurrence of a future event or behavior that is logically consistent to verify the indicator of a construct. (5)

Preexperimental designs *Experimental designs* that lack *random assignment* or use shortcuts and are much weaker than the *classical experimental design*. They may be substituted in situations where an experimenter cannot use all the features of a *classical experimental design*, but have weaker *internal validity*. (8)

Premature closure An error that is often made when using personal experience as an alternative to science for acquiring knowledge. It occurs when a person feels he or she has the answers and does not need to listen, seek information, or raise questions any longer. (1)

Prestige bias A problem in *survey research* question writing that occurs when a highly respected group or individual is linked to one of the answers. (7)

Pretest The measurement of the *dependent variable* of an experiment prior to the *treatment*. (8)

Prewriting A very early step in the writing process, when one writes without worrying about word choice, spelling, or grammar, but tries to let "ideas flow" as quickly as possible to connect thinking processes with writing. (14)

Primary sources *Qualitative data* or *quantitative data* used in historical research. It is evidence about past social life or events that was created and used by the persons who actually lived in the historical period. (12)

Principal investigator (PI) The person who is primarily in charge of research on a project that is sponsored or funded by an organization. (14)

Principle of voluntary consent An ethical principle of social research that people should never participate in research unless they first explicitly agree to do so. (3)

Probability proportionate to size (PPS) An adjustment made in *cluster sampling* when each cluster does not have the same number of *sampling elements.* (6)

Probe A follow-up question or action in *survey research* used by an interviewer to have a respondent clarify or elaborate on an incomplete or inappropriate answer. (7)

Proposition A basic statement in social theory that two ideas or variables are related to one another. It can be true or false (e.g., most sex offenders were themselves sexually abused when growing up), conditional (e.g., if a foreign enemy threatens, then the people of a nation will feel much stronger social solidarity), and/or causal (e.g., poverty causes crime). (2)

Public sociology Social science that seeks to enrich public debates over moral and political issues by infusing them with social theory and research and tries to generate a conversation between researchers and public. Often uses *action research* and a *critical social science* approach with its main audience being nonexperts and practitioners. (3)

Purposive sampling A type of *nonrandom sample* in which the researcher uses a wide range of methods to locate all possible cases of a highly specific and difficult-to-reach *population.* (6)

Qualitative data Information in the form of words, pictures, sounds, visual images, or objects. (1)

Quantitative data Information in the form of numbers. (1)

Quasi-experimental designs *Experimental designs* that are stronger than *preexperimental designs.* They are variations on the *classical experimental design* that an experimenter uses in special situations or when an experimenter has limited control over the *independent variable.* (8)

Quasi-filter questions A type of *survey research* question including the answer choice "no opinion" or "don't know." (7)

Quota sampling A type of *nonrandom sample* in which the researcher first identifies general categories into which cases or people will be selected, then he or she selects a predetermined number of cases in each category. (6)

Random assignment Dividing subjects into groups at the beginning of *experimental research* using a random process, so the experimenter can treat the groups as equivalent. (8)

Random digit dialing (RDD) A method of randomly selecting cases for telephone interviews that uses all possible telephone numbers as a *sampling frame.* (6)

Random number table A list of numbers that has no pattern in them and that is used to create a random process for selecting cases and other randomization purposes. (6)

Random sample A type of *sample* in which the researcher uses a *random number table* or similar mathematical random process so that each *sampling element* in the *population* will have an equal probability of being selected. (6)

Range A measure of dispersion for one variable indicating the highest and lowest scores. (10)

Ratio-level measurement The highest, most precise *level of measurement* for which variable *attributes* can be rank ordered, the distance between the *attributes* precisely measured, and an absolute zero exists. (5)

Reactivity   The general threat to *external validity* that arises because subjects are aware that they are in an experiment and being studied. (8)

Recollections   The words or writings of people about their life experiences after some time has passed. The writings are based on a memory of the past, but may be stimulated by a review of past objects, photos, personal notes, or belongings. (12)

Recording sheet   Pages on which a researcher writes down what is coded in *content analysis.* (9)

Reductionism   Something that appears to be a *causal explanation,* but is not, because of a confusion about *units of analysis.* A researcher has *empirical evidence* for an association at the level of individual behavior or very small-scale units, but *overgeneralizes* to make theoretical statements about very large-scale units. (4)

Reliability   The dependability or consistency of the measure of a variable. (5)

Replication   The principle that researchers must be able to repeat scientific findings in multiple studies to have a high level of confidence that the findings are true. (2)

Replication pattern   A pattern in the *elaboration paradigm* in which the *partials* show the same relationship as in a *bivariate contingency table* of the *independent* and *dependent variable* alone. (10)

Request for proposal (RFP)   An announcement by a funding organization that it is willing to fund research and it is soliciting written plans of research projects. (14)

Research fraud   A type of unethical behavior in which a researcher fakes or invents data that he or she did not really collect, or fails to honestly and fully report how he or she conducted a study. (3)

Response set   An effect in *survey research* when respondents tend to agree with every question

in a series rather than thinking through their answer to each question. (7)

Revising   A step in the writing process that is part of *rewriting* in which a writer adds ideas or evidence, and deletes, rearranges, or changes ideas to improve clarity and better communicate meaning. (14)

Rewriting   A step in the writing process in which the writer goes over a previous draft to improve communication of ideas and clarity of expression. (14)

Running records   A special type of *existing statistics research* used in historical research because the files, records, or documents are maintained in a relatively consistent manner over a period of time. (12)

Sample   A smaller set of cases a researcher selects from a larger pool and generalizes to the *population.* (6)

Sampling distribution   A distribution created by drawing many *random samples* from the same *population.* (6)

Sampling element   The name for a case or single unit to be selected. (6)

Sampling error   How much a *sample* deviates from being representative of the *population.* (6)

Sampling frame   A list of cases in a *population,* or the best approximation of it. (6)

Sampling interval   The inverse of the *sampling ratio,* which is used in *systematic sampling* to select cases. (6)

Sampling ratio   The number of cases in the *sample* divided by the number of cases in the *population* or the *sampling frame,* or the proportion of the *population* in the *sample.* (6)

Scale   A type of *quantitative data* measure often used in *survey research* that captures the intensity, direction, level, or potency of a variable construct along a continuum. Most are at the *ordinal level* of measurement. (5)

Scattergram   A diagram to display the *statistical relationship* between two variables based on plotting each case's values for both of the variables. (10)

Scientific community   A collection of people who share a system of rules and attitudes that sustain the process of producing scientific knowledge. (1)

Scientific method   The process of creating new knowledge using the ideas, techniques, and rules of the *scientific community*. (1)

Scientific misconduct   When someone engages in *research fraud, plagiarism,* or other unethical conduct that significantly deviates from the accepted practice for conducting and reporting research within the *scientific community*. (3)

Secondary sources   *Qualitative data* and *quantitative data* used in historical research. Information about events or settings are documented or written later by historians or others who did not directly participate in the events or setting. (12)

Second-order interpretation   In qualitative research, what a researcher believes the people being studied feel and think. (4)

Selection bias   A threat to *internal validity* when groups in an experiment are not equivalent at the beginning of the experiment. (8)

Selective coding   A last pass at coding *qualitative data* in which a researcher examines previous codes to identify and select illustrative data that will support the conceptual coding categories that he or she developed. (13)

Selective observation   The tendency to take notice of certain people or events based on past experience or attitudes. (1)

Semantic differential   A *scale* in which people are presented with a topic or object and a list of many polar opposite adjectives or adverbs. They are to indicate their feelings by marking one of several spaces between two adjectives or adverbs. (5)

Sequential sampling   A type of *nonrandom sample* in which a researcher tries to find as many relevant cases as possible, until time, financial resources, or his or her energy are exhausted, or until there is no new information or diversity from the cases. (6)

Simple random sampling   A type of *random sample* in which a researcher creates a *sampling frame* and uses a pure random process to select cases. Each *sampling element* in the *population* will have an equal probability of being selected. (6)

Skewed distribution   A distribution of cases among the categories of a variable that is not *normal* (i.e., not a "bell shape"). Instead of an equal number of cases on both ends, more are at one of the extremes. (10)

Snowball sampling   A type of *nonrandom sample* in which the researcher begins with one case, then, based on information about interrelationships from that case, identifies other cases, and then repeats the process again and again. (6)

Social desirability bias   A bias in *survey research* in which respondents give a "normative" response or a socially acceptable answer rather than give a truthful answer. (7)

Social impact assessment study   A type of *applied social research* in which a researcher estimates the likely consequences or outcome of a planned intervention or intentional change to occur in the future. (1)

Social research   A process in which a researcher combines a set of principles, outlooks, and ideas with a collection of specific practices, techniques, and strategies to produce knowledge. (1)

Sociogram   A diagram or "map" that shows the network of social relationships, influence patterns, or communication paths among a group of people or units. (6)

Solomon four-group design   An *experimental design* in which *subjects* are randomly assigned to two *control groups* and two *experimental groups*. Only one *experimental group* and one *control group* receive a *pretest*. All four groups receive a posttest. (8)

Special populations   People who lack the necessary cognitive competency to give real informed consent or people in a weak position who might comprise their freedom to refuse to participate in a study. (3)

Specification pattern A pattern in the *elaboration paradigm* in which the *bivariate contingency table* shows a relationship. One of the *partial tables* shows the relationship, but other tables do not. (10)

Spuriousness A statement that appears to be a *causal explanation,* but is not because of a hidden, unmeasured, or initially unseen variable. The unseen variable comes earlier in the temporal order, and it has a causal impact on what was initially posited to be the *independent variable* as well as the *dependent variable.* (4)

Standard deviation A measure of dispersion for one variable that indicates an average distance between the scores and the *mean.* (10)

Standard-format question A type of *survey research* question in which the answer categories fail to include "no opinion" or "don't know." (7)

Standardization The procedure to statistically adjust measures to permit making an honest comparison by giving a common basis to measures of different units. (5)

Static group comparison An *experimental design* with two groups, no *random assignment,* and only a *posttest.* (8)

Statistic A numerical estimate of a *population parameter* computed from a *sample.* (6)

Statistical Abstract of the United States A U.S. government publication that appears annually and contains an extensive compilation of statistical tables and information. (9)

Statistical significance A way to discuss the likelihood that a finding or *statistical relationship* in a *sample* is due to the random factors rather than due to the existence of an actual relationship in the entire *population.* (10)

Stratified sampling A type of *random sample* in which the researcher first identifies a set of *mutually exclusive* and *exhaustive* categories, then uses a random selection method to select cases for each category. (6)

Structural question A type of question in *field research* interviews in which the researcher attempts to verify the correctness of placing terms or events into the categories of the meaning system used by people being studied. (11)

Structured observation A method of watching what is happening in a social setting that is highly organized and that follows systematic rules for observation and documentation. (9)

Subjects The name for people who are studied and participate in *experimental research.* (8)

Successive approximation A method of *qualitative data* analysis in which the researcher repeatedly moves back and forth between the *empirical data* and the abstract concepts, theories, or models. (13)

Suppressor variable pattern A pattern in the *elaboration paradigm* in which no relationship appears in a *bivariate contingency table,* but the *partials* show a relationship between the variables. (10)

Survey research Quantitative social research in which one systematically asks many people the same questions, then records and analyzes their answers. (1)

Systematic sampling A type of *random sample* in which a researcher selects every *k*th (e.g., 12th) case in the *sampling frame* using a *sampling interval.* (6)

Target population The name for the large general group of many cases from which a *sample* is drawn and which is specified in very concrete terms. (6)

Text A general name for symbolic meaning within a communication medium measured in *content analysis.* (9)

Third-order interpretation In qualitative research, what a researcher tells the reader of a research report that the people he or she studied felt and thought. (4)

Threatening questions A type of *survey research* question in which respondents are likely to cover up or lie about their true behavior or beliefs because they fear a loss of self-image or that they may appear to be undesirable or deviant. (7)

Time-series study Any research that takes place over time, in which different people or cases may be looked at in each time point. (1)

Treatment What the *independent variable* in *experimental research* is called. (8)

Type I error The logical error of falsely rejecting the *null hypothesis*. (10)

Type II error The logical error of falsely accepting the *null hypothesis*. (10)

Unidimensionality The principle that when using *multiple indicators* to measure a construct, all the indicators should consistently fit together and indicate a single construct. (5)

Unit of analysis The kind of empirical case or unit that a researcher observes, measures, and analyzes in a study. (4)

Univariate statistics Statistical measures that deal with one variable only. (10)

Universe The broad class of units that are covered in a *hypothesis*. All the units to which the findings of a specific study might be generalized. (4)

Unobtrusive measures Another name for *nonreactive measures*. It emphasizes that the people being studied are not aware of it because the measures do not intrude. (9)

Validity A term meaning truth that can be applied to the logical tightness of *experimental design,* the ability to generalize findings outside a study, the quality of measurement, and the proper use of procedures. (5)

Variable A concept or its *empirical* measure that can take on multiple values. (4)

Verstehen A German word that translates as understanding; specifically, it means an empathic understanding of another's worldview. (2)

Whistle-blower A person who sees ethical wrongdoing, tries to correct it internally but then informs an external audience, agency, or the media. (3)

Wording effects An effect that occurs when a specific term or word used in a *survey research* question affects how respondents answer the question. (7)

Zoom lens An organizational form often used by field researchers when writing reports that begin broadly then become narrow, focused, and specific. (14)

Z-score A way to locate a score in a distribution of scores by determining the number of *standard deviations* it is above or below the *mean* or arithmetic average. (10)

Abbott, Andrew. (1992). From causes to events. *Sociological Methods and Research,* 20:428–455.

Abrams, Philip. (1982). *Historical sociology.* Ithaca, NY: Cornell University Press.

Adams, Peter. (2004). "Gambling Impact Assessment" Centre for Gambling Studies, University of Auckland. www.waitakere.govt.nz/AbtCnl/pp/pdf/partoneintro.pdf, downloaded 08/15/05.

Adler, Patricia A., and Peter Adler. (1987). *Membership roles in field research.* Beverly Hills, CA: Sage.

Adler, Patricia A., and Peter Adler. (1993). Ethical issues in self-censorship. In *Research on sensitive topics,* edited by C. Renzetti and R. Lee, pp. 249–266. Thousand Oaks, CA: Sage.

Adler, Patricia A., and Peter Adler. (1994). Observational techniques. In *Handbook of qualitative research,* edited by N. Denzin and Y. Lincoln, pp. 377–392. Thousand Oaks, CA: Sage.

Agar, Michael. (1986). *Speaking of ethnography.* Beverly Hills, CA: Sage.

Alwin, Duane F., and Jon A. Krosnick. (1985). The measurement of values in surveys. *Public Opinion Quarterly,* 49:535–552.

American Sociological Association. (1997). *American Sociological Association style guide,* 2nd ed. Washington, DC: American Sociological Association.

Anderson, Barbara A., Brian D. Silver, and Paul R. Abramson. (1988). The effects of the race of interviewer on race-related attitudes of black respondents in SRC/CPS national election studies. *Public Opinion Quarterly,* 52:289–324.

Anderson, R. Bruce W. (1973). On the comparability of meaningful stimuli in cross-cultural research. In *Comparative research methods,* edited by D. Warwick and S. Osherson, pp. 149–186. Englewood Cliffs, NJ: Prentice-Hall.

Andolina, Molly W., and Jeremy Mayer. (2003). Demographic shifts and racial attitudes. *The Social Science Journal,* 40:19–31.

Andren, Gunnar. (1981). Reliability and content analysis. In *Advances in content analysis,* edited by K. Rosengren, pp. 43–67. Beverly Hills, CA: Sage.

Aronson, Elliot, and J. Merrill Carlsmith. (1968). Experimentation in social psychology. In *The handbook of social psychology, Vol. 2: Research methods,* edited by G. Lindzey and E. Aronson, pp. 1–78. Reading, MA: Addison-Wesley.

Babbie, Earl. (1989). *The practice of social research,* 5th ed. Belmont, CA: Wadsworth. (6th ed., 1992; 8th ed., 1998; 9th ed., 2001; 10th ed., 2004.)

Backstrom, Charles H., and Gerald Hursh-Cesar. (1981). *Survey research,* 2nd ed. New York: Wiley.

Bailey, Kenneth D. (1987). *Methods of social research,* 3rd ed. New York: Free Press.

Banaszak, Lee Ann. (1996). *Why movements succeed or fail.* Princeton NJ: Princeton University Press.

Barzun, Jacques, and Henry F. Graff. (1970). *The modern researcher,* rev. ed. New York: Harcourt, Brace and World.

Bauer, Raymond, ed. (1966). *Social indicators.* Cambridge, MA: MIT Press.

Beck, Bernard. (1970). Cooking welfare stew. In *Pathways to data,* edited by R. W. Habenstein, pp. 7–29. Chicago: Aldine.

Beck, Richard A. (1995). Publishing evaluation research. *Contemporary Sociology,* 24:9–12.

Becker, Howard S., Blanche Geer, Everett C. Hughes, and Anselm Strauss. (1961). *Boys in white: Student culture in medical school.* Chicago: University of Chicago Press.

Becker, Howard S., Michal M. McCall, and Lori V. Morris. (1989). Theatres and communities. *Social Problems,* 36:93–116.

Ben-Yehuda, Nachman. (1983). History, selection and randomness—Towards an analysis of social historical explanations. *Quality and Quantity,* 17:347–367.

Bendix, Reinhard. (1956). *Work and authority in industry.* New York: Wiley.

Bendix, Reinhard. (1963). Concepts and generalizations in comparative sociological studies. *American Sociological Review*, 28:91–116.

Bendix, Reinhard. (1978). *Kings or people: Power and the mandate to rule*. Berkeley: University of California Press.

Best, Joel. (2001). *Damned lies and statistics: Untangling numbers from the media, politicians, and activists*. Berkeley: University of California Press.

Bischoping, Katherine, and Jennifer Dykema. (1999). Toward a social psychological programme for improving focus group methods of developing questionnaires. *Journal of Official Statistics*, 15:495–516.

Bishop, George F. (1987). Experiments with the middle response alternative in survey questions. *Public Opinion Quarterly*, 51:220–232.

Blee, Kathleen M. (1991). *Women of the Klan: Racism and gender in the 1920s*. Berkeley: University of California Press.

Block, Fred, and Gene A. Burns. (1986). Productivity as a social problem: The uses and misuses of social indicators. *American Sociological Review*, 51:767–780.

Blum, Debra E. (1989). Dean charged with plagiarizing a dissertation for his book on Muzak. *Chronicle of Higher Education*, 35, A17.

Bogdan, Robert, and Steven J. Taylor. (1975). *Introduction to qualitative research methods: A phenomenological approach to the social sciences*. New York: Wiley.

Bond, Charles F., Jr., and Evan L. Anderson. (1987). The reluctance to transmit bad news: Private discomfort or public display? *Journal of Experimental Social Psychology*, 23:176–187.

Bonnell, Victoria E. (1980). The uses of theory, concepts and comparison in historical sociology. *Comparative Studies in Society and History*, 22:156–173.

Bradburn, Norman M. (1983). Response effects. In *Handbook of survey research*, edited by P. Rossi, J. Wright, and A. Anderson, pp. 289–328. Orlando, FL: Academic.

Bradburn, Norman M., and Seymour Sudman. (1980). *Improving interview method and questionnaire design*. San Francisco: Jossey-Bass.

Bradburn, Norman M., and Seymour Sudman. (1988). *Polls and surveys*. San Francisco: Jossey-Bass.

Brase, Gary L. and Jullian Richmond. (2004). The white-coat effect. *Journal of Applied Social Psychology* 34:2469–2483.

Braudel, Fernand. (1980). *On history*, trans. Sarah Matthews. Chicago: University of Chicago Press.

Brenner, Michael, Jennifer Brown, and David Canter, eds. (1985). *The research interview: Uses and approaches*. Orlando, FL: Academic Press.

Briggs, Charles L. (1986). *Learning how to ask*. New York: Cambridge University Press.

Broad, W. J., and N. Wade. (1982). *Betrayers of the truth*. New York: Simon and Schuster.

Broadhead, Robert, and Ray Rist. (1976). Gatekeepers and the social control of social research. *Social Problems*, 23:325–336.

Brody, Charles J. (1986). Things are rarely black or white. *American Journal of Sociology*, 92:657–677.

Burawoy, Michael. (2004). Public sociologies. *Social Forces*, 82:1603–1618.

Burawoy, Michael. (2005). For public sociology. *American Sociological Review* 70:4–28.

Calhoun, Craig. (1996). The rise and domestication of historical sociology. In *The historical turn in the human sciences*, edited by T. J. McDonald, pp. 305–337. Ann Arbor: University of Michigan Press.

Cannell, Charles F., and Robert L. Kahn. (1968). Interviewing. In *Handbook of social psychology*, 2nd ed., Vol. 2, edited by G. Lindzey and E. Aronson, pp. 526–595. Reading, MA: Addison-Wesley.

Canter, David, Jennifer Brown, and Linda Goat. (1985). Multiple sorting procedure for studying conceptual systems. In *The research interview: Uses and approaches*, edited by M. Brenner, J. Brown, and D. Canter, pp. 79–114. New York: Academic Press.

Cantor, Norman F., and Richard I. Schneider. (1967). *How to study history*. New York: Thomas Y. Crowell.

Carley, Michael. (1981). *Social measurement and social indicators*. London: George Allen and Unwin.

Carr-Hill, Roy A. (1984). The political choice of social indicators. *Quality and Quantity*, 18:173–191.

Catania, Joseph, D. Dinson, J. Canahola, L. Pollack, W. Hauck, and T. Coates. (1996). Effects of interviewer gender, interviewer choice and item wording on responses to questions concerning sexual behavior. *Public Opinion Quarterly*, 60:345–375.

Chafetz, Janet Saltzman. (1978). *A primer on the construction and testing of theories in sociology.* Itasca, IL: Peacock.

Channels, Noreen L. (1993). Anticipating media coverage. In *Research on sensitive topics,* edited by C. Renzetti and R. Lee, pp. 267–280. Thousand Oaks, CA: Sage.

Chavez, Leo R. (2001). *Covering immigration.* Berkeley: University of California Press.

Cherlin, Andrew J., Linda Burton, Tera Hurt, and Diane Purvin. (2004). The influence of physical and sexual abuse on marriage and cohabitation. *American Sociological Review* 69:768–789.

Chicago manual of style for authors, editors and copywriters, 13th ed., revised and expanded. (1982). Chicago: University of Chicago Press.

Church, Allan H. (1993). Estimating the effect of incentives on mail survey response rates: A meta analysis. *Public Opinion Quarterly,* 57:62–80.

Churchill, Gilbert A., Jr. (1983). *Marketing research,* 3rd ed. New York: Dryden.

Clammer, John. (1984). Approaches to ethnographic research. In *Ethnographic research: A guide to general conduct,* edited by R. F. Ellen, pp. 63–85. Orlando: Academic Press.

Cogan, Johan, Judith Torney-Purta, and Douglas Anderson. (1988). Knowledge and attitudes toward global issues: Students in Japan and the United States. *Comparative Education Review,* 32:283–297.

Cole, Stephen, and Linda Perlman Gordon. (1995). *Making sciencey.* Cambridge MA: Harvard University Press.

Converse, Jean M., and Stanley Presser. (1986). *Survey questions.* Beverly Hills, CA: Sage.

Converse, Jean M., and Howard Schuman. (1974). *Conversations at random.* New York: Wiley.

Cook, Thomas D., and Donald T. Campbell. (1979). *Quasi-experimentation.* Chicago: Rand McNally.

Corsaro, William. (1994). Discussion, debate, and friendship processes. *Sociology of Education,* 67:1–26.

Corsaro, William, and Luisa Molinari. (2000). Priming events and Italian children's transition from preschool to elementary school: Representations and action. *Social Psychology Quarterly,* 63:16–33.

Cotter, Patrick R., Jeffrey Cohen, and Philip B. Coulter. (1982). Race of interview effects in telephone interviews. *Public Opinion Quarterly,* 46:278–286.

Couper, Mick P., Eleanor Singer, et al. (1998). Participation in the 1990 decennial census. *American Politics Quarterly,* 26:59–81.

Craib, Ian. (1984). *Modern social theory: From Parsons to Habermas.* New York: St. Martin's Press.

Crane, Diana. (1972). *Invisible colleges.* Chicago: University of Chicago Press.

Crozat, Matthew. (1998). Are the times a-changin'? Assessing the acceptance of protest in Western democracies. In *The movement society,* edited by D. Meyer and S. Tarrow, pp. 59–81. Totowa, NJ: Rowman and Littlefield.

Dabbs, James M., Jr. (1982). Making things visible. In *Varieties of qualitative research,* edited by J. Van Maanen, J. Dabbs, Jr., and R. R. Faulkner, pp. 31–64. Beverly Hills, CA: Sage.

Dale, Angela, S. Arber, and Michael Procter. (1988). *Doing secondary analysis.* Boston: Unwin Hyman.

D'Antonio, William. (August 1989). Executive Office Report: Sociology on the move. *ASA Footnotes,* 17, p. 2.

Dasgupta, Nilanjana, and Shaki Asgari. (2004). Seeing is believing. *Journal of Experimental Social Psychology* 40:642–658.

Davis, Darren W. (1997). The direction of race of interviewer effects among African-Americans: Donning the black mask. *American Journal of Political Science,* 41:309–322.

Davis, James A., and Tom W. Smith. (1992). *The NORC General Social Survey: A user's guide.* Newbury Park, CA: Sage.

Dawes, R. M., and T. W. Smith. (1985). Attitude and opinion measurement. In *Handbook of social psychology,* 3rd ed., Vol. 1, edited by G. Lindzey and E. Aronson, pp. 509–566. New York: Random House.

Dean, John P., Robert L. Eichhorn, and Lois R. Dean. (1969). Fruitful informants for intensive interviewing. In *Issues in participant observation,* edited by G. McCall and J. L. Simmons, pp. 142–144. Reading, MA: Addison-Wesley.

De Heer, Wim. (1999). International response trends: Results from an international survey. *Journal of Official Statistics,* 15:129–142.

Denzin, Norman K. (1989). *The research act,* 3rd ed. Englewood Cliffs, NJ: Prentice-Hall.

deVaus, D. A. (1986). *Surveys in social research.* Boston: George Allen and Unwin.

Diener, Edward, and Rick Crandall. (1978). *Ethics in social and behavioral research.* Chicago: University of Chicago Press.

Dijkstra, Wil, and Johannes van der Zouwen, eds. (1982). *Response behavior in the survey interview.* New York: Academic Press.

Dillman, Don A. (1978). *Mail and telephone surveys: The total design method.* New York: Wiley.

Dillman, Don A. (1983). Mail and other self-administered questionnaires. In *Handbook of survey research,* edited by P. Rossi, J. Wright, and A. Anderson, pp. 359–377. Orlando, FL: Academic Press.

Dillman, Don A. (1991). The design and administration of mail surveys. *Annual Review of Sociology,* 17:225–249.

Dillman, Don A. (2000). *Mail and Internet surveys,* 2nd ed. New York: Wiley.

Dooley, David. (1984). *Social research methods.* Englewood Cliffs, NJ: Prentice-Hall.

Douglas, Jack D. (1976). *Investigative social research.* Beverly Hills, CA: Sage.

Douglas, Jack D. (1985). *Creative interviewing.* Beverly Hills, CA: Sage.

Downey, Liam. (2005). The unintended significance of race. *Social Forces,* 83:971–1008.

Draus, Paul J., Harvey Siegal, Robert Carlson, Russell Falck, and Jichuan Wang. (2005). Cracking in the heartland. *Sociological Quarterly* 46:165–189.

Duncan, Otis Dudley. (1984). *Notes on social measurement.* New York: Russell Sage Foundation.

Duncan, Otis Dudley, and Magnus Stenbeck. (1988). No opinion or not sure? *Public Opinion Quarterly,* 52:513–525.

Duneier, Mitchell. (1999). *Sidewalk.* New York: Farrar, Straus and Giroux.

Durkheim, Emile. (1938). *Rules of the sociological method,* trans. Sarah Solovay and John Mueller, edited by G. Catlin. Chicago: University of Chicago Press.

Durkheim, Emile. (1951). *Suicide.* (Translated from original 1897 work by John A. Spalding and George Simpson). New York: Free Press.

Dykema, Jennifer, and Nora Cate Schaeffer. (2000). Events, instruments, and reporting errors. *American Sociological Review,* 65:619–629.

Edelman, Lauren, Sally R. Fuller, and Iona Mara-Drita. (2001). Diversity rhetoric and the managerialization of law. *American Journal of Sociology,* 106:1589–1641.

Eder, Donna. (1995). *School talk.* New Brunswick, NJ: Rutgers University Press.

Eder, Donna, and David Kinney. (1995). The effect of middle school extracurricular activities on adolescents' popularity and peer status. *Youth and Society,* 26:298–325.

Elder, Glen H., Jr., Eliza Pavalko, and Elizabeth Clipp. (1993). *Working with archival data.* Thousand Oaks, CA: Sage.

Elder, Joseph W. (1973). Problems of crosscultural methodology. In *Comparative social research,* edited by M. Armer and A. D. Grimshaw, pp. 119–144. New York: Wiley.

Eliasoph, Nina. (1998). *Avoiding politics.* New York: Cambridge University Press.

Emerson, Robert M. (1981). Observational field work. *Annual Review of Sociology,* 7:351–378.

Felson, Richard. (1991). Blame analysis. *American Sociologist,* 22:5–24.

Felson, Richard, and Stephen Felson. (1993). Predicaments of men and women. *Society,* 30:16–20.

Fernandez, Roberto M. (2001). Skill-biased technological change and wage inequality. *American Journal of Sociology,* 107:273–321.

Fetterman, David M. (1989). *Ethnography: Step by step.* Newbury Park, CA: Sage.

Finkel, Steven E., Thomas M. Guterbock, and Marian J. Borg. (1991). Race-of-interviewer effects in a preelection poll: Virigina 1989. *Public Opinion Quarterly,* 55:313–330.

Finley, M. I. (Summer 1977). Progress in historiography. *Daedalus,* pp. 125–142.

Foddy, William. (1993). *Constructing questions for interviews and questionnaires.* New York: Cambridge University Press.

Foster, Gary S., Richard L. Hummel, and Donald J. Adamchak. (1998). Patterns of conception, natality and mortality from midwestern cemeteries. *Sociological Quarterly,* 39:473–490.

Fowler, Floyd J., Jr. (1984). *Survey research methods.* Beverly Hills, CA: Sage.

Fowler, Floyd J., Jr. (1992). How unclear terms can affect survey data. *Public Opinion Quarterly,* 56:218–231.

Fox, Richard, Melvin R. Crask, and Jonghoon Kim. (1988). Mail survey response rate. *Public Opinion Quarterly,* 52:467–491.

Franke, Charles O. (1983). Ethnography. In *Contemporary field research,* edited by R. M. Emerson, pp. 60–67. Boston: Little, Brown.

Franke, Richard H., and James D. Kaul. (1978). The Hawthorne experiments. *American Sociological Review*, 43:623–643.

Freeman, Howard, and Peter H. Rossi. (1984). Furthering the applied side of sociology. *American Sociological Review*, 49:571–580.

Frey, James H. (1983). *Survey research by telephone*. Beverly Hills, CA: Sage.

Gallie, W. B. (1963). The historical understanding. *History and Theory*, 3:149–202.

Gamson, William A. (1992). *Talking politics*. Cambridge: Cambridge University Press.

Gans, Herbert J. (1982). The participant observer as a human being: Observations on the personal aspects of fieldwork. In *Field research*, edited by R. G. Burgess, pp. 53–61. Boston: George Allen and Unwin.

Garza, Cecilia, and Michael Landeck. (2004). College freshmen at risk. *Social Science Quarterly*, 85:1390–1400.

George, Alexander, and Andrew Bennett. (2005). *Case studies and theory development in the social sciences*. Cambridge, MA: MIT Press.

Georges, Robert A., and Michael O. Jones. (1980). *People studying people*. Berkeley: University of California Press.

Gibelman, Margaret. (2001). Learning from the mistakes of others. *Journal of Social Work Education*, 37: 241–255.

Gillespie, Richard. (1988). The Hawthorne experiments and the politics of experimentation. In *The rise of experimentation in American psychology*, edited by J. Morawski, pp. 114–137. New Haven, CT: Yale University Press.

Gillespie, Richard. (1991). *Manufacturing knowledge*. New York: Cambridge University Press.

Goar, Carla, and Jane Sell. (2005). Using Task Definition to Modify Racial Inequality within Task Groups. *Sociological Quarterly*, 46:525–543.

Goldner, Jesse A. (1998). The unending saga of legal controls over scientific misconduct. *American Journal of Law & Medicine*, 24:293–344.

Goldthorpe, John. (1977). The relevance of history to sociology. In *Sociological research methods*, edited by M. Bulmer, pp. 178–191. London: Macmillan.

Gonor, George. (1977). "Situation" versus "frame": The "interactionist" and the "structuralist" analysis of everyday life. *American Sociological Review*, 42:854–867.

Gorden, Raymond. (1980). *Interviewing: Strategy, techniques and tactics*, 3rd ed. Homewood, IL: Dorsey Press.

Gorden, Raymond. (1992). *Basic interviewing skills*. Itasca, IL: Peacock.

Gordon, Phyllis, D. Feldman, J. Tantillo, and K. Perrone. (2004). Attitudes regarding interpersonal relationships with persons with mental illness and mental retardation. *Journal of Rehabilitation*, 70:50–56.

Gotham, Kevin Fox, and William G. Staples. (1996). Narrative analysis and the new historical sociology. *Sociological Quarterly*, 37:481–502.

Goyder, John C. (1982). Factors affecting response rates to mailed questionnaires. *American Sociological Review*, 47:550–554.

Graham, Sandra. (1992). Most of the subjects were white and middle class. *American Psychologist*, 47:629–639.

Griffin, Larry J. (1992). Comparative-historical analysis. In *Encyclopedia of sociology*, Vol. 1, edited by E. and M. Borgatta, pp. 263–271. New York: Macmillan.

Griffin, Larry J. (1993). Narrative, event structure analysis and causal interpretation in historical sociology. *American Journal of Sociology*, 98:1094–1133.

Groves, Robert M., and Robert L. Kahn. (1979). *Surveys by telephone*. New York: Academic Press.

Groves, Robert M., and Nancy Mathiowetz. (1984). Computer assisted telephone interviewing: Effects on interviewers and respondents. *Public Opinion Quarterly*, 48:356–369.

Gurney, Joan Neff. (1985). Not one of the guys: The female researcher in a male-dominated setting. *Qualitative Sociology*, 8:42–62.

Hage, Jerald. (1972). *Techniques and problems of theory construction in sociology*. New York: Wiley.

Hagstrom, Warren. (1965). *The scientific community*. New York: Basic Books.

Hammersley, Martyn, and Paul Atkinson. (1983). *Ethnography: Principles in practice*. London: Tavistock.

Harper, Douglas. (1982). *Good company*. Chicago: University of Chicago Press.

Harris, Sheldon H. (2002). *Factories of death*. New York: Taylor & Francis.

Hawkes, Daina, Charlene Senn, and Chantal Thorn. (2004). Factors that influence attitudes toward women with tattoos. *Sex Roles*, 50:593–604.

Hearnshaw, L. S. (1979). *Cyril Burt: Psychologist.* London: Holder and Stoughten.

Heberlein, Thomas A., and Robert Baumgartner. (1978). Factors affecting response rates to mailed questionnaires. *American Sociological Review,* 43:447–462.

Heberlein, Thomas A., and Robert Baumgartner. (1981). Is a questionnaire necessary in a second mailing? *Public Opinion Quarterly,* 45:102–107.

Herring, Lee, and Johanna Ebner. (May/June 2005). Sociologists' impact interpretation of federal welfare legislation. *American Sociological Association Footnotes,* 33, p. 3.

Hill, Michael R. (1993). *Archival strategies and techniques.* Thousand Oaks, CA: Sage.

Hindess, Barry. (1973). *The use of official statistics in sociology: A critique of positivism and ethnomethodology.* New York: Macmillan.

Hippler, Hans J., and Norbert Schwartz. (1986). Not forbidding isn't allowing. *Public Opinion Quarterly,* 50:87–96.

Hirschman, Albert O. (1970). *Exit, voice, and loyalty: Response to decline in firms, organizations and states.* Cambridge, MA: Harvard University Press.

Holden, Constance. (2000). Psychologist made up sex bias results. *Science,* 294:2457.

Holstein, James A., and Jaber F. Gubrium. (1994). Phenomenology, ethnomethodology and interpretative practice. In *Handbook of qualitative research,* edited by N. Denzin and Y. Lincoln, pp. 262–272. Thousand Oaks, CA: Sage.

Holsti, Ole R. (1968). Content analysis. In *Handbook of social psychology,* 2nd ed., Vol. 2, edited by G. Lindzey and E. Aronson, pp. 596–692. Reading, MA: Addison-Wesley.

Holsti, Ole R. (1969). *Content analysis for the social sciences and humanities.* Reading, MA: Addison-Wesley.

Holt, Robert T., and John E. Turner. (1970). The methodology of comparative research. In *The methodology of comparative research,* edited by R. Holt and J. Turner, pp. 1–20. New York: Free Press.

Holy, Ladislav. (1984). Theory, methodology and the research process. In *Ethnographic research: A guide to general conduct,* edited by R. F. Ellen, pp. 13–34. Orlando: Academic Press.

Horn, Robert V. (1993). *Statistical indicators for the economic and social sciences.* Cambridge: Cambridge University Press.

Hubbard, Raymond, and Eldon Little. (1988). Promised contributions to charity and mail survey responses: Replication with extension. *Public Opinion Quarterly,* 52:223–230.

Humphreys, Laud. (1975). *Tearoom Trade: Impersonal sex in public places.* Chicago: Aldine.

Hyman, Herbert H. (1975). *Interviewing in social research.* Chicago: University of Chicago Press.

Hyman, Herbert H. (1991). *Taking society's measure: A personal history of survey research.* New York: Russell Sage.

Hymes, Dell. (1970). Linguistic aspects of comparative political research. In *The methodology of comparative research,* edited by R. Holt and J. Turner, pp. 295–341. New York: Free Press.

Jackson, Bruce. (1978). Killing time: Life in the Arkansas penitentiary. *Qualitative Sociology,* 1:21–32.

Jackson, Bruce. (1987). *Fieldwork.* Urbana: University of Illinois Press.

Johnson, John M. (1975). *Doing field research.* New York: Free Press.

Jones, J. H. (1981). *Bad blood: The Tuskegee syphilis experiment.* New York: Free Press.

Jones, Wesley H. (1979). Generalizing mail survey inducement methods: Populations' interactions with anonymity and sponsorship. *Public Opinion Quarterly,* 43:102–111.

Junker, Buford H. (1960). *Field work.* Chicago: University of Chicago Press.

Juster, F. Thomas, and Kenneth C. Land, eds. (1981). *Social accounting systems: Essays on the state of the art.* New York: Academic Press.

Kalmijn, Matthijus. (1991). Shifting boundaries: Trends in religious and educational homogamy. *American Sociological Review,* 56:786–801.

Kane, Emily W., and Laura J. MacAulay. (1993). Interview gender and gender attitudes. *Public Opinion Quarterly,* 57:1–28.

Kaplan, Abraham. (1964). *The conduct of inquiry: Methodology for behavioral science.* New York: Harper & Row.

Karweit, Nancy, and Edmund D. Meyers, Jr. (1983). Computers in survey research. In *Handbook of survey research,* edited by P. Rossi, J. Wright, and A. Anderson, pp. 379–414. Orlando, FL: Academic Press.

Katzer, Jeffrey, Kenneth H. Cook, and Wayne W. Crouch. (1982). *Evaluating information: A guide for users of social science research,* 2nd ed. Reading, MA: Addison-Wesley.

Katzer, Jeffrey, Kenneth H. Cook, and Wayne W. Crouch. (1991). *Evaluating information: A guide for users of social science research,* 3rd ed. New York: McGraw-Hill.

Keeter, Scott, et al. (2000). Consequences of reducing non-response in a national telephone survey. *Public Opinion Quarterly,* 64:125–148.

Kelle, Helga. (2000). Gender and territoriality in games played by nine to twelve-year-old schoolchildren. *Journal of Contemporary Ethnography,* 29:164–197.

Kelman, Herbert. (1982). Ethical issues in different social science methods. In *Ethical issues in social science research,* edited by T. Beauchamp, R. Faden, R. J. Wallace, and L. Walters, pp. 40–99. Baltimore: Johns Hopkins University Press.

Kemp, Jeremy, and R. F. Ellen. (1984). Informants. In *Ethnographic research: A guide to general conduct,* edited by R. F. Ellen, pp. 224–236. Orlando: Academic Press.

Kercher, Kyle. (1992). Quasi-experimental research designs. In *Encyclopedia of sociology,* Vol. 3, edited by E. and M. Borgatta, pp. 1595–1613. New York: Macmillan.

Kidder, Louise H., and Charles M. Judd. (1986). *Research methods in social relations,* 5th ed. New York: Holt, Rinehart and Winston.

Kiecolt, K. Jill, and Laura E. Nathan. (1985). *Secondary analysis of survey data.* Beverly Hills, CA: Sage.

Kirk, Jerome, and Marc L. Miller. (1986). *Reliability and validity in qualitative research.* Beverly Hills, CA: Sage.

Kissane, Rebecca Joyce. (2003). What's need go to do with it? *Journal of Sociology and Social Welfare,* 30:137–148.

Kleg, Milton, and Kaoru Yamamoto. (1998). As the world turns. *Social Science Journal,* 35:183–190.

Knäuper, Bärbel. (1999). The impact of age and education on response order effects in attitude measurement. *Public Opinion Quarterly,* 63:347–370.

Kohn, Melvin L. (1987). Cross-national research as an analytic strategy. *American Sociological Review,* 52:713–731.

Koretz, Daniel. (Summer 1988). Arriving in Lake Wobegon. *American Educator,* 12:8–15.

Kriesi, Hanspeter, and Dominique Wisler. (1999). The impact of social movements on political institutions. In *How social movements matter,* edited by M. Giugni, D. McAdam, and Tilly, pp. 42–65. Minneapolis: University of Minnesota Press.

Krippendorff, Klaus. (1980). *Content analysis: An introduction to its methodology.* Beverly Hills, CA: Sage.

Krosnick, Jon. (1992). The impact of cognitive sophistication and attitude importance on response-order and question-order effects. In *Context effects,* edited by N. Schwarz and Sudman, pp. 203–218. New York: Springer-Verlag.

Krosnick, Jon, and Duane Alwin. (1988). A test of the form-resistant correlation hypothesis: Ratings, rankings, and the measurement of values. *Public Opinion Quarterly,* 52:526–538.

Krueger, Richard A. (1988). *Focus groups: A practical guide for applied research.* Beverly Hills, CA: Sage.

Kusserow, Richard P. (March 1989). *Misconduct in scientific research.* Report of the Inspector General of the U.S. Department of Health and Human Services. Washington, DC: Department of Health and Human Services.

Labaw, Patricia J. (1980). *Advanced questionnaire design.* Cambridge, MA: Abt Books.

Lamont, Michèle. (2000). The rhetorics of racism and anti-racism in France and the United States. In *Rethinking comparative cultural sociology,* edited by M. Lamont and L. Thèvenot, pp. 25–55. New York: Cambridge University Press.

Land, Kenneth. (1992). Social indicators. *Encyclopedia of sociology,* Vol. 4, edited by E. and M. Borgatta, pp. 1844–1850. New York: Macmillan.

Lang, Eric. (1992). Hawthorne effect. *Encyclopedia of sociology,* Vol. 2, edited by E. and M. Borgatta, pp. 793–794. New York: Macmillan.

Lankenau, Stephen E. (1999). Stronger than dirt. *Journal of Contemporary Ethnography,* 28:288–318.

Lauzen, Martha M., and David M. Dozier. (2005). Maintaining the double standard: Portrayals of age and gender in popular films. *Sex Roles,* 52:437–446.

LeMasters, E. E. (1975). *Blue collar aristocrats.* Madison: University of Wisconsin Press.

Lieberson, Stanley, Susan Dumais, and Shyon Baumann. (2000). The instability of androgynous names. *American Journal of Sociology,* 105:1249–1287.

Lifton, Robert J. (1986). *Nazi doctors.* New York: Basic Books.

Lofland, John. (1976). *Doing social life.* New York: Wiley.

Lofland, John, and Lyn H. Lofland. (1984). *Analyzing social settings,* 2nd ed. Belmont, CA: Wadsworth.

Lofland, John, and Lyn H. Lofland. (1995). *Analyzing social settings,* 3rd ed. Belmont, CA: Wadsworth.

Logan, John. (1991). Blaming the suburbs? *Social Science Quarterly,* 72:476–503.

Lowenthal, David. (1985). *The past is a foreign country.* New York: Cambridge University Press.

Lu, Shun, and Gary Alan Fine. (1995). The presentation of ethnic authenticity. *Sociological Quarterly,* 36:535–553.

MacKeun, Michael B. (1984). Reality, the press and citizens' political agendas. In *Surveying subjective phenomena,* Vol. 2, edited by C. Turner and E. Martin, pp. 443–473. New York: Russell Sage Foundation.

Mahoney, James. (1999). Nominal, ordinal, and narrative appraisal in macrocausal analysis. *American Journal of Sociology,* 104:1154–1196.

Maier, Mark H. (1991). *The data game.* Armonk, NY: M. E. Sharpe.

Markoff, John, Gilbert Shapiro, and Sasha R. Weitman. (1974). Toward the integration of content analysis and general methodology. In *Sociological methodology, 1974,* edited by D. Heise, pp. 1–58. San Francisco: Jossey-Bass.

Martin, Elizabeth. (1999). Who knows who lives here? *Public Opinion Quarterly,* 63:200–236.

Marx, Anthony W. (1998). *Making race and nation.* New York: Cambridge University Press.

Mastro, Dana E., and Charles Atkin. (2002). Exposure to alcohol billboards and beliefs and attitudes toward drinking among Mexican American high school students. *Howard Journal of Communications,* 13:129–151.

Mastro, Dana E., and Susannah Stern. (2003). Representations of race in television commercials. *Journal of Broadcasting and Electronic Media,* 47:638–647.

McCall, George. (1969). Quality control in participant observation. In *Issues in participant observation,* edited by G. McCall and J. L. Simmons, pp. 128–141. Reading, MA: Addison-Wesley.

McDaniel, Timothy. (1978). Meaning and comparative concepts. *Theory and Society,* 6:93–118.

McKelvie, Stuart J., and Linda A. Schamer. (1988). Effects of night, passengers and sex on driver behavior at stop signs. *Journal of Social Psychology,* 128:658–690.

McKeown, Adam. (2001). *Chinese migrants' networks and cultural change.* Chicago: University of Chicago Press.

McLennan, Gregor. (1981). *Marxism and the methodologies of history.* London: Verso.

Merten, Don E. (1999). Enculturation into secrecy among junior high school girls. *Journal of Contemporary Ethnography,* 28:107–138.

Merton, Robert K. (1957). *Social theory and social structure.* New York: Free Press.

Merton, Robert K. (1967). *On theoretical sociology.* New York: Free Press.

Merton, Robert K. (1970). *Science, technology and society in seventeenth century England.* New York: Harper & Row.

Merton, Robert K. (1973). *The sociology of science.* Chicago: University of Chicago Press.

Miles, Matthew B., and A. Michael Huberman. (1994). *Qualitative data analysis,* 2nd ed. Thousand Oaks, CA: Sage.

Milgram, Stanley. (1963). Behavioral study of obedience. *Journal of Abnormal and Social Psychology,* 6:371–378.

Milgram, Stanley. (1965). Some conditions of obedience and disobedience to authority. *Human Relations,* 18:57–76.

Milgram, Stanley. (1974). *Obedience to authority.* New York: Harper & Row.

Mishler, Elliot G. (1986). *Research interviewing.* Cambridge, MA: Harvard University Press.

Mitchell, Alison. (May 17, 1997). Survivors of Tuskegee study get apology from Clinton. *New York Times.*

Mitchell, Mark, and Janina Jolley. (1988). *Research design explained.* New York: Holt, Rinehart and Winston.

Molotch, Harvey, William Freudenburg, and Krista Paulsen. (2000). History repeats itself, but how? City character, urban tradition, and the accomplishment of place. *American Sociological Review,* 65:791–823.

Monaghan, Peter. (April 7, 1993a). Facing jail, a sociologist raises question about a scholar's right to protect sources. *Chronicle of Higher Education,* p. A10.

Monaghan, Peter. (May 26, 1993b). Sociologist is jailed for refusing to testify about research subject. *Chronicle of Higher Education,* p. A10.

Monaghan, Peter. (September 1, 1993c). Sociologist jailed because he "wouldn't snitch" ponders the way research ought to be done. *Chronicle of Higher Education,* pp. A8–A9.

Morgan, David L. (1996). Focus groups. *Annual Review of Sociology,* 22: 129–152.

Morse, Janice M. (1994). Designing funded qualitative research. In *Handbook of qualitative research,* edited by N. Denzin and Y. Lincoln, pp. 220–235. Thousand Oaks, CA: Sage.

Moser, C. A., and G. Kalton. (1972). *Survey methods in social investigation.* New York: Basic Books.

Mulkay, Michael. (1979). *Science and the sociology of knowledge.* London: George Allen and Unwin.

Mulkay, M. J. (1991). *Sociology of science.* Philadelphia: Open University Press.

Mullins, Nicholas C. (1971). *The art of theory: Construction and use.* New York: Harper & Row.

Murdock, George P. (1967). Ethnographic atlas. *Ethnology,* 6:109–236.

Murdock, George P. (1971). *Outline of cultural materials,* 4th ed. New Haven, CT: Human Relations Area Files.

Musick, Marc A., John Wilson, and William Bynum. (2000). Race and formal volunteering. *Social Forces,* 78:1539–1571.

Narayan, Sowmya, and John A. Krosnick. (1996). Education moderates some response effects in attitude measurement. *Public Opinion Quarterly,* 60:58–88.

Naroll, Raoul. (1968). Some thoughts on comparative method in cultural anthropology. In *Methodology in social research,* edited by H. Blalock and A. Blalock, pp. 236–277. New York: McGraw-Hill.

National Science Board. (2002). *Science and engineering indicators—2002.* Arlington, VA: National Science Foundation (NSB-02–1).

Neuman, W. Lawrence. (1992). Gender, race and age differences in student definitions of sexual harassment. *Wisconsin Sociologist,* 29:63–75.

Neuman, W. Lawrence. (2000). *Social research methods,* 4th ed. Boston: Allyn and Bacon.

Neuman, W. Lawrence. (2003). *Social research methods,* 5th ed. Boston: Allyn and Bacon.

Novick, Peter. (1988). *That noble dream.* New York: Cambridge University Press.

Oesterle, Sabrina, Monica Kirkpatrick Johnson, and Jeylan T. Mortimer. (2004). Volunteerism during the transition to adulthood. *Social Forces,* 82:1123–1149.

Ong, Andy S. J., and Colleen A. Ward. (1999). The effects of sex and power schemas, attitudes toward women, and victim resistance on rape attributions. *Journal of Applied Social Psychology,* 29:362–376.

Ostrom, Thomas M., and Katherine M. Gannon. (1996). Exemplar generation. In *Answering questions,* edited by N. Schwarz and S. Sudman, pp. 293–318. San Francisco: Jossey-Bass.

Pager, Devah, and Lincoln Quillian. (2005). Walking the talk? *American Sociological Review,* 70:355–380.

Paige, Jeffrey M. (1975). *Agrarian revolution.* New York: Free Press.

Parcel, Toby L. (1992). Secondary data analysis and data archives. *Encyclopedia of sociology,* Vol. 4, edited by E. and M. Borgatta, pp. 1720–1728. New York: Macmillan.

Patton, Michael Quinn. (2001). *Qualitative research and evaluation methods,* 3rd ed. Thousand Oaks, CA: Sage.

Pearsall, Marion. (1970). Participant observation as role and method in behavioral research. In *Qualitative methodology,* edited by W. J. Filstead, pp. 340–352. Chicago: Markham.

Phillips, Bernard. (1985). *Sociological research methods: An introduction.* Homewood, IL: Dorsey.

Piliavin, Irving M., J. Rodin, and Jane A. Piliavin. (1969). Good samaritanism: An underground phenomenon? *Journal of Personality and Social Psychology,* 13:289–299.

Pollner, Melvin, and Richard Adams. (1997). The effect of spouse presence on appraisals of emotional support and household strain. *Public Opinion Quarterly,* 61:615–626.

Presser, Stanley. (1990). Measurement issues in the study of social change. *Social Forces* 68:856–868.

Przeworski, Adam, and Henry Teune. (1970). *The logic of comparative inquiry.* New York: Wiley.

Punch, Maurice. (1986). *The politics and ethics of fieldwork.* Beverly Hills, CA: Sage.

Ragin, Charles C. (1987). *The comparative method.* Berkeley: University of California Press.

Ragin, Charles C. (1992). Introduction: Cases of "what is a case?" In *What is a case,* edited by C. Ragin and H. Becker, pp. 1–18. New York: Cambridge University Press.

Rampton, Sheldon, and John Stauber. (2001). *Trust us, we're experts.* New York: Putnam.

Rathje, William, and Cullen Murphy. (1992). *Rubbish: The archaeology of garbage.* New York: Vintage.

Reese, Stephen, W. Danielson, P. Shoemaker, T. Chang, and H. Hsu. (1986). Ethnicity of interview effects among Mexican Americans and Anglos. *Public Opinion Quarterly,* 50:563–572.

Reynolds, Paul Davidson. (1971). *A primer in theory construction.* Indianapolis: Bobbs-Merrill.

Reynolds, Paul Davidson. (1979). *Ethical dilemmas and social science research.* San Francisco: Jossey-Bass.

Reynolds, Paul Davidson. (1982). *Ethics and social science research.* Englewood Cliffs, NJ: Prentice-Hall.

Rind, Bruce, and David Strohmetz. (1999). Effect on restaurant tipping of a helpful message written on the back of customers' checks. *Journal of Applied Social Psychology,* 29:139–144.

Roethlisberger, F. J., and W. J. Dickenson. (1939). *Management and the worker.* Cambridge, MA: Harvard University Press.

Roscigno, Vincent J., and William Danaher. (2001). Media and mobilization: The case of Radio and Southern Textile Worker Insurgency, 1929–1934. *American Sociological Review,* 66:21–48.

Rosenberg, Morris. (1968). *The logic of survey analysis.* New York: Basic Books.

Rossi, Robert J., and Kevin J. Gilmartin. (1980). *The handbook of social indicators.* New York: Garland STPM Press.

Rueschemeyer, Dietrich, Evelyne Huber Stephens, and John D. Stephens. (1992). *Capitalist development and democracy.* Chicago: University of Chicago Press.

Runciman, W. G. (1980). Comparative sociology or narrative history. *European Journal of Sociology,* 21:162–178.

Sanday, Peggy Reeves. (1983). The ethnographic paradigm(s). In *Qualitative methodology,* edited by J. Van Maanen, pp. 19–36. Beverly Hills, CA: Sage.

Sanders, Jimy, Victor Nee, and Scott Sernau. (2002). Asian immigrants' reliance on social ties in a multiethnic labor market. *Social Forces,* 81:281–314.

Sanjek, Roger. (1978). A network method and its uses in urban anthropology. *Human Organization,* 37:257–268.

Sanjek, Roger. (1990). On ethnographic validity. In *Field notes,* edited by R. Sanjek, pp. 385–418. Ithaca, NY: Cornell University Press.

Sassen, Saskia. (2001). *The global city.* New York: Princeton University Press.

Schacter, Daniel L. (2001). *The seven deadly sins of memory.* Boston: Houghton Mifflin.

Schaffer, Nora Cate. (1980). Evaluating race-of-interviewer effects in a national survey. *Sociological Methods and Research,* 8:400–419.

Schatzman, Leonard, and Anselm L. Strauss. (1973). *Field research.* Englewood Cliffs, NJ: Prentice-Hall.

Schuman, Howard, and Jean M. Converse. (1971). Effects of black and white interviewers on black response in 1968. *Public Opinion Quarterly,* 65:44–68.

Schuman, Howard, and Stanley Presser. (1981). *Questions and answers in attitude surveys: Experiments on question form, wording and content.* New York: Academic Press.

Schwandt, Thomas A. (1994). Constructivist, interpretivist approaches to human inquiry. In *Handbook of qualitative research,* edited by N. Denzin and Y. Lincoln, pp. 118–137. Thousand Oaks, CA: Sage.

Scribner, Richard, and Deborah Cohen. (2001). The effect of enforcement on merchant compliance with the minimum legal drinking age law. *Journal of Drug Issues,* 31:857–867.

Sears, David O. (1986). College sophomores in the laboratory. *Journal of Personality and Social Psychology,* 51: 515–530.

Sewell, William H., Jr. (1987). Theory of action, dialectic, and history. *American Journal of Sociology,* 93:166–171.

Shafer, Robert Jones. (1980). *A guide to historical method,* 3rd ed. Homewood, IL: Dorsey.

Shaffir, William B., Robert A. Stebbins, and Allan Turowetz. (1980). Introduction. In *Fieldwork experience,* edited by W. B. Shaffir, R. Stebbins, and A. Turowetz, pp. 3–22. New York: St. Martin's Press.

Singer, Eleanor. (1988). Surveys in the mass media. In *Surveying social life: Papers in honor of Herbert H. Hyman,* edited by H. O'Gorman, pp. 413–436. Middletown, CT: Wesleyan University Press.

Singleton, Royce, Jr., B. Straits, Margaret Straits, and Ronald McAllister. (1988). *Approaches to social research.* New York: Oxford University Press.

Skidmore, William. (1979). *Theoretical thinking in sociology,* 2nd ed. New York: Cambridge University Press.

Skocpol, Theda. (1979). *States and social revolutions.* New York: Cambridge University Press.

Smelser, Neil J. (1976). *Comparative methods in the social sciences.* Englewood Cliffs, NJ: Prentice-Hall.

Smith, Mary Lee, and Gene V. Glass. (1987). *Research and evaluation in education and the social sciences.* Englewood Cliffs, NJ: Prentice-Hall.

Smith, Tom W. (1987). That which we call welfare by any other name would smell sweeter. *Public Opinion Quarterly,* 51:75–83.

Smith, Tom W. (1995). Trends in non-response rates. *International Journal of Public Opinion Research,* 7:156–171.

Snow, David, and Leon Anderson. (1991). Researching the homeless. In *A case for the case study,* edited by Joe R. Feagan, Anthony M. Orum, and Gideon Sjoberg, pp. 148–173. Chapel Hill: University of North Carolina Press.

Snow, David, and Leon Anderson. (1992). *Down on their luck.* Berkeley: University of California Press.

Snow, David, Sarah A. Soule, and Daniel M. Cress. (2005). Identifying the precipitants of homeless process across 17 U.S. cities, 1980–1990. *Social Forces,* 83:1183–1210.

Spector, Paul E. (1981). *Research designs.* Beverly Hills, CA: Sage.

Spradley, James P. (1979a). *The ethnographic interview.* New York: Holt, Rinehart and Winston.

Spradley, James P. (1979b). *Participant observation.* New York: Holt, Rinehart and Winston.

Stack, Steven, Ira Wasserman, and Roger Kern. (2004). Adult social bonds and use of Internet pornography. *Social Science Quarterly,* 85:75–88.

Starr, Paul. (1982). *The social transformation of American medicine.* New York: Basic Books.

Stevenson, Richard W. (October 16, 1996). U.S. to revise its estimate of layoffs. *New York Times.*

Stewart, David W. (1984). *Secondary research: Information sources and methods.* Beverly Hills, CA: Sage.

Stinchcombe, Arthur L. (1968). *Constructing social theories.* New York: Harcourt, Brace and World.

Stinchcombe, Arthur L. (1973). Theoretical domains and measurement, Part 1. *Acta Sociologica,* 16:3–12.

Stinchcombe, Arthur L. (1978). *Theoretical methods in social history.* New York: Academic Press.

Stone, Lawrence. (1987). *The past and present revisited.* Boston: Routledge and Kegan Paul.

Stone, Philip J., and Robert P. Weber. (1992). Content analysis. In *Encyclopedia of sociology,* Vol. 1, edited by E. and M. Borgatta, pp. 290–295. New York: Macmillan.

Strack, Fritz. (1992). "Order effects" in survey research. In *Context effects in social and psychological research,* edited by N. Schwarz and S. Sudman, pp. 23–24. New York: Springer-Verlag.

Strauss, Anselm. (1987). *Qualitative analysis for social scientists.* New York: Cambridge University Press.

Strauss, Anselm, and Juliet Corbin. (1990). *Basics of qualitative research.* Newbury Park, CA: Sage.

Strauss, Anselm, and Juliet Corbin. (1994). Grounding theory methodology. In *Handbook of qualitative research,* edited by N. Denzin and Y. Lincoln, pp. 273–285. Thousand Oaks, CA: Sage.

Sudman, Seymour. (1976). Sample surveys. *Annual Review of Sociology,* 2:107–120.

Sudman, Seymour. (1983). Applied sampling. In *Handbook of survey research,* edited by P. Rossi, J. Wright, and A. Anderson, pp. 145–194. Orlando, FL: Academic Press.

Sudman, Seymour, and Norman M. Bradburn. (1983). *Asking questions.* San Francisco: Jossey-Bass.

Sudman, Seymour, Norman M. Bradburn, and Norbert Schwarz. (1996). *Thinking about answers.* San Francisco: Jossey-Bass.

Suls, Jerry M., and Ralph L. Rosnow. (1988). Concerns about artifacts in psychological experiments. In *The rise of experimentation in American psychology,* edited by J. Morawski, pp. 153–187. New Haven, CT: Yale University Press.

Sutton, John R. (2004). The political economy of imprisonment in affluent western democrcies, 1960–1990. *American Sociological Review,* 69:170–189.

Taylor, Charles. (1979). Interpretation and the sciences of man. In *Interpretative social science: A reader,* edited by P. Rabinow and W. Sullivan, pp. 25–72. Berkeley: University of California Press.

Taylor, Steven. (1987). Observing abuse. *Qualitative Sociology,* 10:288–302.

Tourangeau, Roger, et al. (1997). Who lives here? *Journal of Official Statistics,* 13:1–18.

Turner, Charles, and Elizabeth Martin, eds. (1984). *Surveying subjective phenomena,* Vol. 1. New York: Russell Sage Foundation.

Turner, Stephen P. (1980). *Sociological explanation as translation.* New York: Cambridge University Press.

Tyldum, Guri, and Anette Brunovskis. (2005). Describing the unobserved. *International Migration,* 43:17–34.

Vallier, Ivan, ed. (1971a). *Comparative methods in sociology.* Berkeley: University of California Press.

Vallier, Ivan. (1971b). Empirical comparisons of social structure. In *Comparative methods in sociology,* edited by I. Vallier, pp. 203–263. Berkeley: University of California Press.

Van den Berg, Harry, and Cees Van der Veer. (1985). Measuring ideological frames of references. *Quality and Quantity,* 19:105–118.

Van Laar, Colette, Shana Levin, Stacey Sinclair, and Jim Sidanius. (2005). The effect of university roommate contact on ethnic attitudes and behavior. *Journal of Experimental Social Psychology,* 41:329–345.

Van Maanen, John. (1982). Fieldwork on the beat. In *Varieties of qualitative research,* edited by J. Van Maanen, J. Dabbs, Jr., and R. Faulkner, pp. 103–151. Beverly Hills, CA: Sage.

Van Maanen, John. (1988). *Tales of the field.* Chicago: University of Chicago Press.

Van Poppel, Frans, and L. Day. (1996). A test of Durkheim's theory of suicide—Without committing the "ecological fallacy." *American Sociological Review,* 61:500–507.

Vaquera, Elizabeth, and Grace Kao. (2005). Private and public displays of affection among interracial and intra-racial adolescent couples. *Social Science Quarterly,* 86:484–508.

Vidich, Arthur Joseph, and Joseph Bensman. (1968). *Small town in mass society,* rev. ed. Princeton, NJ: Princeton University Press.

Wade, Nicholas. (1976). IQ and heredity. *Science,* 194: 916–919.

Walton, John. (1973). Standardized case comparison. In *Comparative social research,* edited by M. Armer and A. Grimshaw, pp. 173–191. New York: Wiley.

Warwick, Donald P. (1982). Types of harm in social science research. In *Ethical issues in social science research,* edited by T. Beauchamp, R. Faden, R. J. Wallace, and L. Walters, pp. 101–123. Baltimore: Johns Hopkins University Press.

Warwick, Donald P., and Charles A. Lininger. (1975). *The sample survey.* New York: McGraw-Hill.

Wax, Rosalie H. (1971). *Doing fieldwork: Warnings and advice.* Chicago: University of Chicago Press.

Wax, Rosalie H. (1979). Gender and age in fieldwork and fieldwork education. *Social Problems,* 26:509–522.

Webb, Eugene J., Donald T. Campbell, Richard D. Schwartz, Lee Sechrest, and Janet Belew Grove.

(1981). *Nonreactive measures in the social sciences,* 2nd ed. Boston: Houghton Mifflin.

Weber, Robert P. (1983). Measurement models for content analysis. *Quality and Quantity,* 17:127–149.

Weber, Robert P. (1984). Computer assisted content analysis: A short primer. *Qualitative Sociology,* 7:126–149.

Weber, Robert P. (1985). *Basic content analysis.* Beverly Hills, CA: Sage.

Weeks, M. F., and R. P. Moore. (1981). Ethnicity of interviewer effects on ethnic respondents. *Public Opinion Quarterly,* 45:245–249.

Weinstein, Deena. (1979). Fraud in science. *Social Science Quarterly,* 59:639–652.

Weiss, Carol H. (1997). *Evaluation.* Englewood Cliffs, NJ: Prentice Hall.

Weiss, Janet A., and Judith E. Gruber. (1987). The managed irrelevance of educational statistics. In *The politics of numbers,* edited by W. Alonso and P. Starr, pp. 363–391. New York: Russell Sage Foundation.

Weitzer, Ronald, and Steven Tuch. (2004). Race and perceptions of police misconduct. *Social Problems,* 51:305–325.

Weitzer, Ronald, and Steven Tuch. (2005). Racially biased policing. *Social Forces,* 83:1009–1030.

Weitzman, Lenore, D. Eifler, E. Hokada, and C. Ross. (1972). Sex role socialization in picture books for preschool children. *American Journal of Sociology,* 77:1125–1150.

Whiting, John W. M. (1968). Methods and problems in cross-cultural research. In *The handbook of social psychology,* 2nd ed., edited by G. Lindzey and E. Aronson, pp. 693–728. Reading, MA: Addison-Wesley.

Whyte, William Foote. (1955). *Street corner society: The social structure of an Italian slum,* 2nd ed. Chicago: University of Chicago Press.

Whyte, William Foote. (1982). Interviewing in field research. In *Field research,* edited by R. G. Burgess, pp. 111–122. Boston: George Allen and Unwin.

Whyte, William Foote. (1984). *Learning from the field.* Beverly Hills: Sage.

Williams, Peter, and David Wallace. (1989). *Unit 731: Japan's secret biological warfare in World War II.* New York: Free Press.

Willimack, Diane K., Howard Schuman, Beth-Ellen Pennell, and James M. Lepkowski. (1995). Effects of prepaid non-monetary incentives on response rates and response quality in face-to-face survey. *Public Opinion Quarterly,* 59:78–92.

Wood, Elizabeth Anne. (2000). Working in the fantasy factory. *Journal of Contemporary Ethnography,* 29:5–32.

Zane, Anne, and Euthemia Matsoukas. (1979). Different settings, different results? A comparison of school and home responses. *Public Opinion Quarterly,* 43:550–557.

Zelizer, Viviana A. (1985). *Pricing the priceless child.* New York: Basic Books.

Ziman, John. (August 19, 1999). Social rules of the game in doing science. *Nature,* 400:721.

Zimbardo, Philip G. (1972). Pathology of imprisonment. *Society,* 9:4–6.

Zimbardo, Philip G. (1973). On the ethics of intervention in human psychological research. *Cognition,* 2:243–256.

Zimbardo, Philip G., et al. (April 8, 1973). The mind is a formidable jailer. *New York Times Magazine,* 122:38–60.

Zimbardo, Philip G., et al. (1974). The psychology of imprisonment: Privation, power and pathology. In *Doing unto others,* edited by Z. Rubin. Englewood Cliffs, NJ: Prentice-Hall.

NAME INDEX

A

Andolina, M., 19

B

Banaszak, L., 283
Bearman, P., 69
Becker, H., 331
Bendix, R., 315
Blee, K., 285, 292
Bond, C., 202, 207
Bradburn, N., 163–164
Brase, G., 193
Briggs, C., 275
Burawoy, M., 53
Burt, C., 37

C

Canter, D., 318
Chavez, L., 219
Cherlin, A., 17
Cogan, J., 301
Crozat, M., 125

D

Dasgupta, N., 205
Davis, J., 142, 146, 228
Denzin, N., 257, 275
DeVaus, D., 165
Diener, E., 46
Dillman, D., 172
Douglas, J., 275
Downey, L., 224–225

Draus, P., 46, 148
Duneier, M., 263–264, 270, 272, 294
Durkheim, E., 80, 85, 283

E

Edelman, L., 103
Elder, G., 291
Eliasoph, N., 259

F

Foster, G., 213
Fowler, F., 159
Freeman, H., 13

G

Galton, F., 297
Gamson, W., 131
Garza, C., 16
Goar, C., 91–92, 193
Gorden, D., 179
Gordon, P., 123
Gurney, J., 263

H

Harper, D., 332
Hawkes, D., 124, 194, 199, 200
Heberlein, T., 174
Hemingway, E., 327
Hill, M., 291
Holt, R., 295
Humphreys, L., 40–41, 45

Hyman, H., 183
Hymes, D., 301

J

Jeffreys, A., 11
Junker, B., 257

K

Katzer, J., 67
Kissane, R., 132, 276
Kleg, M., 121
Kriesi, H., 283

L

Lamont, M., 295
Lauzen, M., 91, 92, 216–218
LeMasters, E., 309
Lieberson, S., 232
Lofland, J., 332
Lu, S., 93–94

M

Marx, A., 283
Marx, K., 283–284
Mastro, D., 220
McKelvie, S., 213
Miles, M., 318
Milgram, S., 39, 40
Mill, J., 314
Misher, E., 275
Molotch, H., 93–94
Musick, M., 91–92

SUBJECT INDEX

Scholarly Journals in the Social Sciences in English

GENERAL SOCIAL SCIENCE

American Behavioral Scientist
Annals of the American Academy of Political
    and Social Science
Evaluation Practice (American
    Evaluation Association)
Evaluation Review
Human Relations
Public Opinion Quarterly (American
    Association for Public Opinion)
Rationality and Society
Social Science Journal (Western Social
    Science Association)
Social Science Quarterly (Southwestern Social
    Science Association)
Theory and Society

ANTHROPOLOGY

American Anthropologist (American
    Anthropological Association)
American Ethnologist (American Ethnological
    Society)
Critique of Anthropology
Ethnology
Human Organization (Society for
    Applied Anthropology)
Mankind Quarterly (Institute for the Study of Man)

CRIMINOLOGY/SOCIOLOGY OF LAW

Contemporary Crisis
Crime and Delinquency (National Council
    on Crime and Delinquency)
Crime, Law and Social Change
Criminal Justice and Behavior (American
    Association of Correctional Psychologists)
Criminology (American Society of Criminology)
Journal of Criminal Law and Criminology
Journal of Research in Crime and Delinquency
    (National Council on Crime and Delinquency)
Journal of Quantitative Criminology
Law and Social Inquiry (American Bar Association)
Law and Society Review (Law and Society Association)
Social Justice: A Journal of Crime, Conflict
    and World Order

RACE/ETHNIC RELATIONS

Ethnic Forum
Ethnic Groups
Ethnic and Racial Studies
Hispanic Journal of Behavioral Sciences
Journal of American Ethnic History
Journal of Black Studies
Negro Educational Review
Phylon: The Atlanta University Review
    of Race and Culture
Race and Class (Institute of Race Relations)
Review of Black Political Economy (National
    Economic Association)

COMPARATIVE-HISTORICAL RESEARCH

Comparative Political Studies
Comparative Studies in Society and History
Cross-Cultural Research
Development and Change
Economic Development and Cultural Change
International Journal of Comparative Sociology
International Journal of Contemporary Sociology
International Migration Review
Journal of Cross-Cultural Psychology
Review (Fernand Braudel Center)
Social Science History

POLITICAL SCIENCE/POLITICAL SOCIOLOGY

American Journal of Political Science (Midwest
    Political Science Association)
American Political Science Review (American
    Political Science Review)
American Politics Quarterly
British Journal of Political Science
Canadian Journal of Political Science (Canadian
    Political Science Association; also in French)
Journal of Conflict Resolution
Journal of Political and Military Sociology
Journal of Politics (Southern Political
    Science Association)
Political Methodology
Political Science Quarterly (Academy
    of Political Science)
Politics and Society

ue Sea

un sello de
V&R Editoras

ia Nápoles CP 03810,
, Ciudad de México
20-6620/6621

ergarariba.com.mx

gentina

Genevieve Tucholke.
V&R. 2016.

Fantásticas. I. Poch,

FF-497

ulo original: *Between the Devil and the Deep Bl*

Dirección editorial: Marcela Luza

‣ **Edición:** Leonel Teti con Erika Wrede
‣ **Coordinación de diseño:** Marianela Acuña
‣ **Diseño de interior:** Tomás Caramella
‣ **Arte de portada:** Kristin Smith
‣ **Foto de tapa:** Shutterstock.com

ARGENTINA:
San Martín 969 piso 10 (C1004AAS)
Buenos Aires
Tel./Fax: (54-11) 5352-9444
y rotativas
e-mail: editorial@vreditoras.com

MÉXICO:
Dakota 274, Colon
Del. Benito Juárez
Tel./Fax: (5255) 52
01800-543-4995
e-mail: editoras@v

ISBN: 978-987-747-169-4

Impreso en Argentina por Triñanes Gráfica · Printed in Ar
Septiembre de 2016

Tucholke, April Genevieve
Entre el demonio y el profundo mar azul / Apri
- 1a ed . - Ciudad Autónoma de Buenos Aires : V
352 p. ; 21 x 14 cm.

Traducción de: Silvina Poch.
ISBN 978-987-747-169-4

1. Literatura Juvenil Estadounidense. 2. Novelas
Silvina , trad. II. Título.
CDD 813.9283

APRIL GENEVIEVE TUCHOLKE

Entre el Demonio y el Profundo Mar Azul

Traducción: Silvina Poch

PARA TODOS LOS JÓVENES LECTORES

I should hate you,
But I guess I love you,
You've got me in between the devil and the deep blue sea.

CAB CALLOWAY

CAPÍTULO
1

—DEJAS DE TENERLE miedo al Demonio una vez que le tomas la mano.

Freddie me dijo eso cuando yo era pequeña.

Todos llamaban a mi abuela por su apodo, hasta mis padres, porque, como ella misma lo explicaba, su nombre era "Freddie, forma abreviada de Fredrikke", así lo explicaba. Ni madre ni abuela. Simplemente, Freddie.

Luego, me preguntó si quería a mi hermano.

—Luke es un maldito bravucón –respondí.

Recuerdo que estábamos subiendo juntas la antigua e imponente escalera y yo me había quedado observando el mármol rosado. Tenía vetas negras que se parecían a las venas azules y varicosas de las piernas blancas de Freddie.

Recuerdo haber pensado que la escalera se estaba volviendo vieja, como ella.

–Violet, no digas *maldito*.

–*Tú* también lo dices –y era cierto. Lo decía todo el tiempo–. Luke me empujó una vez por esta maldita escalera –dije sin despegar la mirada de los escalones de mármol. La caída no me mató, si es que esa había sido su intención, pero me rompí dos dientes y me hice un tajo en la frente que sangró una barbaridad–. No quiero a mi hermano –afirmé–. Y no me importa lo que piense el Demonio acerca de eso. Es la verdad.

Freddie me echó una mirada penetrante, sus ojos holandeses eran de un azul muy brillante, a pesar de la edad. Ella me había dado esos ojos azules, y también el cabello rubio.

Apoyó sus manos arrugadas sobre las mías.

–Violet, hay verdades y verdades. Y algunas malditas verdades no deberían decirse en voz alta, pues el Demonio puede escucharte y venir por ti. Amén.

Cuando Freddie era joven solía usar pieles, asistir a fiestas, beber cocteles y patrocinar artistas. Me contaba historias desenfrenadas, plagadas de alcohol, mujerzuelas, muchachos y problemas.

Pero algo sucedió. Algo de lo que Freddie nunca hablaba. Algo malo. Muchas personas tienen malas historias y, si se lamentan y lloran y le cuentan la historia a alguien que las escuche, todo se convierte en una estupidez. O, al menos, en media estupidez. Lo que *realmente* hiere a una persona, lo que casi la quiebra… es aquello de lo cual no habla. Nunca.

A veces, muy tarde en la noche, veía a Freddie escribiendo con rapidez y con fuerza, tanta que el papel se rasgaba debajo del bolígrafo… Pero no sabía si se trataba de un diario o de cartas a sus amigos.

Tal vez, fue el hecho de que su hija se ahogara siendo muy pequeña lo que la convirtió en una persona tan recta y religiosa. Tal vez, fue por otra cuestión. Fuera lo que fuese, Freddie comenzó a buscar algo para llenar el vacío que le había quedado. Y lo que encontró fue a Dios. A Dios y al Demonio: porque no existían uno sin el otro.

Ella hablaba todo el tiempo del Demonio, casi como si fuera su mejor amigo o un viejo amante. Pero a pesar de toda su charla sobre el Demonio, nunca la vi rezar.

Sin embargo, yo sí rezaba y rogaba.

A Freddie, después de que murió. Lo había hecho tan a menudo en los últimos cinco años, que se había transformado en algo inconsciente, como soplar la sopa cuando está muy caliente. Hablaba con ella y le contaba que mis padres se habían marchado, que se nos acababa el dinero y que, a veces, me sentía tan sola que el maldito ulular del viento a través de la ventana me parecía más cercano que el hermano que tenía en el piso de arriba.

Y le hablaba del Demonio. Le pedía que mantuviera mi mano lejos de la de él. Le rogaba que me mantuviera a salvo del mal.

No obstante, a pesar de todos mis ruegos, el Demonio igual me encontró.

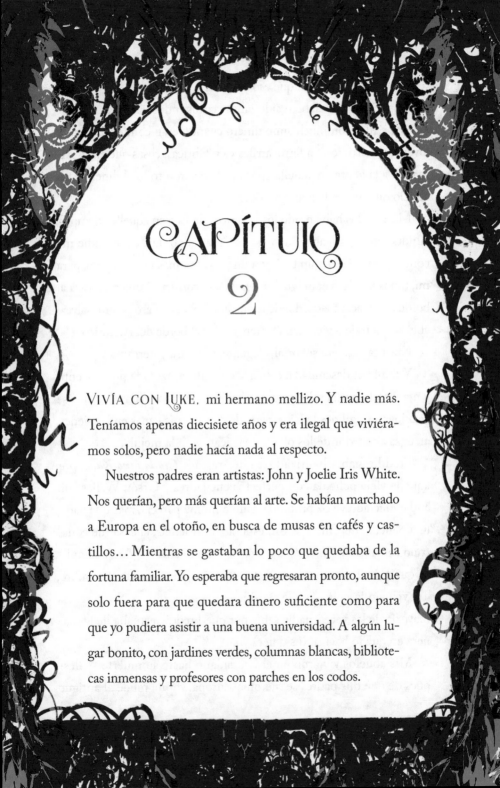

CAPÍTULO 2

VIVÍA CON LUKE, mi hermano mellizo. Y nadie más. Teníamos apenas diecisiete años y era ilegal que viviéramos solos, pero nadie hacía nada al respecto.

Nuestros padres eran artistas: John y Joelie Iris White. Nos querían, pero más querían al arte. Se habían marchado a Europa en el otoño, en busca de musas en cafés y castillos… Mientras se gastaban lo poco que quedaba de la fortuna familiar. Yo esperaba que regresaran pronto, aunque solo fuera para que quedara dinero suficiente como para que yo pudiera asistir a una buena universidad. A algún lugar bonito, con jardines verdes, columnas blancas, bibliotecas inmensas y profesores con parches en los codos.

Pero no contaba con que eso sucediera.

Mis bisabuelos habían sido empresarios industriales de la Costa Este e hicieron muchísimo dinero cuando eran condenadamente jóvenes. Invirtieron en ferrocarriles y en fábricas: cosas que entusiasmaban a la gente en aquella época. Y le dejaron todo el dinero a un abuelo que nunca llegué a conocer.

Mis abuelos habían sido los más ricos de Eco en aquellos tiempos, aunque no significaba mucho ser el "más" algo de Eco. Freddie me contó que los Glenship tuvieron una fortuna más grande, pero, para mí, todos los ricos eran iguales. Mi abuelo construyó una gran casa al borde de un acantilado, donde rompían las olas. Se casó con mi salvaje abuela y la trajo a vivir con él y tener hijos al borde del Atlántico.

Nuestra casa era señorial, elegante, inmensa y hermosa.

Y también descuidada, cubierta de maleza, azotada por el viento y manchada por la sal, como una bailarina de avanzada edad que se veía joven y ágil desde lejos, pero, de cerca, tenía canas en las sienes, arrugas alrededor de los ojos y una cicatriz en la mejilla.

Freddie había bautizado a nuestra casa *Ciudadano Kane*, por aquella vieja película con perfectos encuadres y Orson Welles con andar afectado y voz profunda. Pero a mí me parecía, más que nada, una película deprimente. Sin esperanza. Además, la casa fue construida en 1929 y *Ciudadano* recién se estrenó en 1941, lo que implica que Freddie se tomó unos cuantos años para pensar el nombre. Tal vez vio la película y le significó algo importante. No lo sé. La mayoría de las veces, nadie sabía por qué Freddie actuaba de la manera en que lo hacía. Ni siquiera yo.

Mis abuelos vivieron en el Ciudadano hasta su muerte. Y después de que mis padres se fueran a Europa, yo me mudé al antiguo dormitorio de Freddie en el primer piso. Dejé todo como estaba. Ni siquiera quité su ropa del vestidor.

Me encantaba mi habitación… El tocador con el espejo curvo, los silloncitos sin apoyabrazos, el biombo oriental de diseño elaborado. Me fascinaba estirar el cuerpo en el sofá de terciopelo, los libros apilados a mis pies, las polvorientas cortinas largas hasta el suelo corridas hacia los costados de las ventanas para poder ver el cielo. Por la noche, los bordes color violeta de las pantallas de las lámparas hacían que la luz se volviera de una tonalidad entre lila y cereza.

El dormitorio de Luke estaba en el segundo piso y creo que a los dos nos agradaba que hubiera espacio entre nosotros.

Ese verano se nos había acabado finalmente el dinero que nos dejaron nuestros padres cuando se marcharon a Europa en el otoño, muchos meses atrás. El Ciudadano necesitaba un techo nuevo, porque el viento del mar le daba unas buenas palizas, y Luke y yo necesitábamos comida. De modo que tuve la brillante idea de alquilar la casa de huéspedes. Sí, el Ciudadano tenía una casa de huéspedes, que había quedado de aquellos tiempos en que Freddie patrocinaba artistas muertos de hambre. Se mudaban durante unos meses, la pintaban a mi abuela y luego se mudaban a otro pueblo, con otra persona millonaria y otra botella de ginebra.

Pegué carteles en Eco, donde anunciaba que se alquilaba una casa de huéspedes, y pensé que no ocurriría nada.

Pero algo ocurrió.

Era uno de los primeros días de junio y soplaba una brisa templada, como si el verano estuviera dándole una palmada a la primavera. Se podía sentir el fuerte olor a sal en el aire. Me senté en los grandes escalones del frente, de cara a la carretera que corría a lo largo de la vasta franja de mar azul. Dos columnas de piedra enmarcaban la enorme puerta de entrada y, entre ellas, se extendían los peldaños. Desde donde me encontraba, nuestro jardín olvidado y enmarañado descendía hacia el camino sin asfaltar. Más allá, había una caída abrupta que terminaba en el fuerte oleaje.

De modo que me hallaba sentada allí, alternando entre leer de a ratos los cuentos de Nathaniel Hawthorne y mirar el cielo difuminado entre las olas lejanas, cuando un viejo auto ingresó a mi calle, pasó delante de la casa de Sunshine y se detuvo en la entrada circular de la casa. Digo viejo porque era de los años cincuenta, grande, hermoso y con aspecto de tener mucho kilometraje, pero estaba arreglado como si estuviese recién salido de la agencia, brillante como el rostro de un niño en Navidad.

El automóvil se detuvo y un chico se bajó. Tenía más o menos mi edad, pero aun así, no podía decir que fuera realmente un *hombre*. De modo que, sí, era un *chico*. Bajó del auto y me miró fijamente, como si yo hubiera pronunciado su nombre.

Pero no lo había hecho. Él no me conocía a mí y yo no lo conocía a él. No era alto (menos de un metro ochenta, tal vez), y era fuerte y esbelto. Tenía cabello castaño oscuro y grueso, con ondas y raya al costado… Hasta que la brisa del mar se lo levantó, lo hizo volar por la frente y le convirtió la cabeza en un revoltijo desgreñado. Su rostro me agradó de inmediato. También su piel tostada, que daba a entender que pasaba todo el día al sol. Y los ojos color café.

Nuestras miradas se encontraron.

–¿Eres Violet? –preguntó y no esperó mi respuesta–. Sí, creo que sí. Soy River. River West –agitó la mano delante de él–. Y esto debe ser el Ciudadano Kane.

Estaba observando mi casa, así que incliné la cabeza y la observé con él. En mi memoria, tenía brillantes columnas blancas de piedra, grandes ventanales cuadrados con molduras color azul turquesa, matorrales cuidados y delicadas estatuas desnudas en el centro de la gran fuente. Pero la fuente que veía ahora estaba sucia y cubierta de musgo, y a las pobres mujeres desvestidas les faltaban una nariz, un pecho y tres dedos. La pintura estaba descascarada y el azul intenso se había vuelto gris. Los matorrales ahora parecían una selva indómita de más de dos metros de altura.

No sentía vergüenza por el Ciudadano, porque todavía era una casa condenadamente maravillosa, pero ahora me preguntaba si tal vez no debería haber podado los arbustos, cepillado a las chicas desnudas de la fuente o pintado los marcos de las ventanas.

—Es un lugar un poco grande para una chica de cabello rubio y gusto por la lectura —dijo el chico que tenía delante de mí después de que ambos miramos la casa durante más de un minuto—. ¿Estás sola o tus padres andan por aquí?

Cerré el libro y me puse de pie.

—Mis padres están en Europa —hice una pausa—. ¿Y los *tuyos*?

—*Touché* —sonrió.

Nuestro pueblo era suficientemente pequeño como para que yo nunca llegara a desarrollar un saludable temor a los extraños. Para mí, eran como cosas emocionantes, envueltas para regalo y llenas de posibilidades. De ellos, emanaba el dulce aroma de un lugar desconocido, como un perfume. Por lo tanto, River West, un extraño, no me produjo ningún tipo de temor… sino una ola de emoción igual a la que sentía antes de que se desencadenara una gran tormenta, cuando la expectativa chisporroteaba en el aire.

Le sonreí.

—Vivo aquí con Luke, mi hermano mellizo. Él ocupa el segundo piso y no sale de ahí, por suerte —levanté la mirada, pero las ventanas del segundo piso estaban tapadas por el techo del pórtico. Volví la vista al muchacho—. ¿Y cómo sabes mi nombre?

—Lo vi en los carteles del pueblo, tonta —aclaró y sonrió—. *Se alquila casa de huéspedes. Ver a Violet en el Ciudadano Kane.* Anduve averiguando y unos lugareños me dieron tu dirección.

No dijo "tonta" como lo decía Luke mientras parpadeaba, los ojos entornados y la sonrisa altiva. River lo dijo como si fuera… un término cariñoso, lo cual me resultó ligeramente desconcertante. Me quité la sandalia del pie derecho y golpeé los dedos contra el escalón de piedra haciendo que la falda amarilla se balanceara sobre las rodillas.

—Bueno… Entonces, ¿quieres alquilar la casa de huéspedes?

—Sip —extendió el codo y se apoyó sobre su coche brillante. Llevaba pantalones negros de lino (de esos que yo pensaba que solo usaban los hombres españoles de barba incipiente en películas europeas que transcurrían junto al mar) y una camisa blanca. Habría resultado extraño en otra persona, pero en él quedaba perfectamente bien.

—De acuerdo. Tienes que darme el primer mes de alquiler por adelantado y en efectivo.

Asintió y metió la mano en el bolsillo trasero. Extrajo un tarjetero de cuero y lo abrió. En el interior había un grueso fajo de color verde. Tan grueso que, una vez que separó el dinero que necesitaba, le resultó difícil volver a cerrar la billetera. River West se acercó a mí, tomó mi mano y depositó en ella quinientos dólares.

—¿No quieres ver primero el lugar? —pregunté sin quitar los ojos de los billetes verdes. Cerré la mano sobre ellos y los apreté con fuerza.

—No.

Le lancé una amplia sonrisa. Cuando me la devolvió, noté que tenía la nariz recta y la boca torcida. Me agradó. Lo observé alejarse hacia la cajuela del automóvil contoneando la cadera (sí, contoneando la cadera) como una pantera. Luego, extrajo un par de maletas viejas, de esas con correas y hebillas en lugar de cremalleras. Volví a colocarme la sandalia en el pie derecho y eché a andar por el estrecho sendero de frondosos arbustos. Pasé por delante de las ventanas cubiertas de hiedra, por el garaje de madera a la vista y me dirigí a la parte trasera del Ciudadano.

Eché una mirada por encima del hombro solo una vez. Venía detrás de mí.

Lo conduje más allá de la derruida cancha de tenis y del viejo invernadero. Cada vez que los miraba, se veían peor. Todo se había venido abajo desde que Freddie murió, y no se debía solamente a la falta de dinero. Ella se las había ingeniado para mantener la casa sin dinero. Incansablemente, había arreglado las cosas por su cuenta, aprendido conocimientos rudimentarios de fontanería y carpintería, había limpiado, barrido y quitado el polvo día tras día. Pero no era nuestro caso. Nosotros no hacíamos nada, salvo pintar. Me refiero a telas, no paredes, ni cercas, ni marcos de ventanas.

Papá decía que esa clase de pintura era para Tom Sawyer y esos huérfanos sucios. No estaba muy segura de si lo había dicho en broma. Probablemente, no.

En la cancha de tenis, brotaba el césped verde y brillante en medio del cemento, y la red estaba en el suelo, deshecha y cubierta de hojas. ¿Quiénes habían sido los últimos en jugar al tenis? No podía recordarlo. El techo de vidrio del invernadero se había desplomado. Todavía había trozos de vidrio desparramados por el suelo y, por las vigas del edificio, crecían plantas exóticas en tonos de azul, verde y blanco que trepaban hacia el cielo. A veces, solía ir allí a leer. Tenía muchos lugares secretos de lectura en el Ciudadano. Habían sido lugares donde pintar, antes de que abandonara la pintura.

Al ir acercándonos a la casa de huéspedes, disminuimos el paso. Era un edificio de ladrillo rojo de dos habitaciones, cubierto de hiedra, como todo lo demás. Las tuberías eran decentes y la electricidad, espasmódica, y se encontraba en el ángulo derecho del Ciudadano. Si el mar fuera la boca, entonces nuestra casa sería la nariz blanca y ancha; la casa de huéspedes, el ojo derecho; el viejo y abandonado laberinto, el ojo izquierdo; y las canchas de tenis y el invernadero, dos lunares en la parte de arriba del pómulo derecho.

Entramos y examinamos el lugar. Estaba lleno de polvo, pero también resultaba acogedor y hasta tierno. Tenía una cocina abierta, tazas cachadas en armarios amarillos y mantas *patchwork* sobre los muebles de estilo art decó, y no tenía teléfono.

Varios meses atrás, Luke y yo nos habíamos quedado sin dinero para pagar la factura, de modo que tampoco teníamos teléfono de línea en el Ciudadano. Por ese motivo, no había puesto un número en el cartel de alquiler.

No podía recordar quién había sido la última persona que se había quedado en esa casa. Algunos amigos bohemios de mis padres, seguramente, mucho tiempo atrás. Aún había pomos secos de pintura al óleo apoyados en las repisas de las ventanas y pinceles olvidados en el fregadero, después de haber sido enjuagados. Mis padres tenían un taller del otro lado del laberinto, al que llamaban cobertizo, y siempre lo habían utilizado para sus tareas artísticas. Estaba lleno de telas a medio concluir y olía a aguarrás: un hedor que encontraba al mismo tiempo tranquilizador e irritante.

Al pasar, tomé los pinceles con la idea de arrojarlos a la basura, pero las cerdas que golpearon mi mano estaban húmedas. Por lo tanto, no pertenecían a antiguos amigos de mis padres: se habían utilizado recientemente.

Noté que River me observaba, pero no dijo nada. Volví a apoyar los pinceles donde los había encontrado e ingresé en la habitación principal, dejando lugar para que River pudiera arrojar las maletas encima de la cama. Siempre me había gustado ese dormitorio con las descoloridas paredes rojas, ahora rosadas, y las cortinas a rayas amarillas y blancas. River echó una mirada a su alrededor y captó todo con sus rápidos ojos café. Se dirigió hacia la cómoda, abrió la gaveta superior, miró el interior y la cerró nuevamente. Se desplazó hacia el otro lado de la habitación, corrió las cortinas y abrió las dos ventanas que daban al océano.

Una ráfaga de radiante y salado aire marino inundó el dormitorio y respiré profundamente. River hizo lo mismo y su pecho se ensanchó de modo tal que pude ver las costillas apretadas contra la camisa.

La casa de huéspedes estaba más alejada del mar que el Ciudadano, pero igual se podía ver una línea muy, muy azul por la ventana. Divisé un barco a lo lejos en el horizonte y me pregunté adónde se dirigiría o de dónde vendría. Generalmente, yo quería estar en esos barcos y navegar hacia un lugar frío y exótico. Pero, en ese momento, no tenía esa sensación impaciente y gitana.

River fue hasta la cama, se estiró y bajó la cruz negra de madera que colgaba arriba de las almohadas. La llevó a la cómoda, abrió la gaveta superior, colocó la cruz en el interior y la cerró con un leve golpe de la cadera.

—Mi abuelo construyó el Ciudadano Kane —expliqué—, pero fue mi abuela Freddie quien construyó esta cabaña. Se volvió religiosa de grande —mis ojos estaban clavados en la silueta color rojo intenso que había quedado en la pared, donde la cruz había protegido la pintura de los efectos decolorantes del sol—. Es probable que haya colgado esa cruz hace muchas décadas y quedó ahí desde entonces. ¿Eres ateo? ¿Es por eso que la descolgaste? Soy curiosa, por ende te hice la pregunta.

Me sobresalté. *¿Por ende?* Mi costumbre de leer más que relacionarme con la gente me hacía utilizar palabras raras e inoportunas impensadamente.

River no pareció percibirlo. Y con eso quiero decir que sí parecía percibir todo lo relacionado conmigo, y todo lo relacionado con la habitación, pero no pude distinguir si notó mi uso de *por ende* más que lo demás.

—No, no soy ateo. Soy simplemente una persona a la cual no le gusta dormir con una cruz arriba de la cabeza —volvió a mirarme—. ¿Y cuántos años tienes…? ¿Diecisiete?

—Sí —respondí—. Muy bien. Porque mi hermano dice que todavía parezco de doce.

—Entonces, tenemos la misma edad —una pausa—. Mis padres se fueron a Sudamérica hace unas semanas. Son arqueólogos. Y, hasta que regresen, me enviaron aquí. Tengo un tío que vive en Eco. Pero no quería vivir con él. Así que vi tu cartel y aquí estoy. Es más bien raro que nuestros padres se hayan marchado y nos hayan dejado, ¿no crees?

Asentí. Quería preguntarle quién era su tío; de dónde venía y cuánto tiempo pensaba quedarse en la casa de huéspedes. Pero se quedó mirándome de tal manera que no pude juntar la fuerza necesaria para hacerlo.

—¿Y dónde está ese hermano del que me has hablado? —se llevó los dedos al cabello y lo sacudió con fuerza. Me quedé observándolo a él y a su cabello alborotado hasta que me miró. Y entonces dejé de hacerlo.

—Está en el pueblo. Tendrás que esperar para conocerlo. Pero no me entusiasmaría mucho: no es tan agradable como yo —Luke se había dirigido a Eco después del desayuno con la intención de encontrar a una chica que conocía y tratar de toquetearla a plena luz del día en la cafetería donde trabajaba.

Señalé por la ventana.

—Si quieres ir al pueblo a hacer compras, hay un sendero que comienza en los manzanos, detrás del laberinto. Se une a las viejas vías del ferrocarril y termina justo en la calle principal. Lo que quiero decir es que, si quieres, puedes ir conduciendo, porque tienes auto, pero el camino es muy lindo si te agrada caminar. Corre junto a un viejo túnel del ferrocarril…

Comencé a retroceder hacia la puerta de la habitación. Empezaba a sentirme estúpida al estar hablando sin parar, como una chica tonta que abre la boca y deja salir todos sus pensamientos. Y, cuando me siento estúpida, mis mejillas se sonrojan. Y no tenía la menor duda de que ese chico observador que estaba junto a mí notaría que mis mejillas se ponían rojas, y era probable que adivinara el motivo.

—Ah, y la puerta del frente no tiene cerrojo —proseguí mientras me hundía en la bienvenida semioscuridad del pasillo y me llevaba las manos al rostro—. Si quieres, puedes hacerte una llave en la ferretería, pero nadie robará nada de aquí —hice una pausa—. Al menos, nadie lo ha hecho hasta ahora.

Me di vuelta y me marché sin esperar su respuesta. Salí de la casa de huéspedes, pasé por el derruido invernadero y las canchas de tenis, rodeé el Ciudadano y tomé por el angosto camino de grava hacia la única casa que había en mi calle: la de Sunshine.

Tenía que contarle a alguien que un chico con cuerpo de pantera se había instalado detrás de mi casa.

CAPÍTULO 3

SUNSHINE BLACK TENÍA el cabello castaño claro hasta la cintura y hoyuelos en los codos y las rodillas. Estaba sentada fuera de la cabaña, en la hamaca del porche. Una pierna flexionada colgaba del borde, mientras tomaba un vaso de té helado, la mirada perdida en el espacio. Teníamos la misma edad y, si bien no éramos realmente amigas, éramos las únicas vecinas. Y supongo que eso equivalía a serlo.

Me miró mientras subía los peldaños irregulares de madera (el papá de Sunshine había construido él mismo la cabaña), y luego movió las piernas para dejarme lugar a su lado.

—Hola, Violet. ¿Qué anda pasando en tu vida?

—En realidad, mucho.

Un cuervo graznó entre los árboles que estaban arriba de nosotras y aspiré el fuerte aroma de los pinos, que se captaba mejor en lo de Sunshine. Su casita estaba más retirada del océano, emplazada dentro del bosque. Al costado del porche había plantas de tomate, que también desprendían un suave aroma a tierra.

—¿Ah, sí? ¿Dónde está Luke? ¿Qué hace hoy?

—Luke está fastidiando a Maddy. Sabe cuánto detesto que la bese, y ella es demasiado estúpida como para rechazarlo. Él la manipula. Es un manipulador. Una vez dije que ella era dulce e inocente como una niña de un cuento de hadas, y entonces no pudo evitar corromperla. Pero ya basta de hablar de Luke. Tengo novedades.

Levemente interesada, Sunshine enarcó una ceja.

—Tengo un inquilino en la casa de huéspedes. Ya se mudó.

Los ojos de Sunshine se agrandaron un poco. Tenía ojos color café y entrecerrados, que le daban un aspecto seductor, tipo Marilyn Monroe, y era probable que eso provocara que los chicos imaginaran cómo se vería después de besarla. Mis ojos eran grandes y, según Luke, eran ojos que miraban fijo, de sabionda. Creo que eso significa que tengo una mirada penetrante, lo cual es posible que sea lo mismo, pero suena muchísimo mejor.

—¿Es viejo? ¿Degenerado? ¿Un asesino serial? ¿Te violará en medio de la noche? Te dije que no buscaras un inquilino. No entiendo por qué, si necesitas dinero, no consigues un trabajo y listo.

Le arrebaté el vaso de té helado de la mano y bebí un trago.

—No puedo conseguirme un trabajo. Si vienes de una familia de mucho dinero, tienes que gastarlo todo y luego embriagarte y morir en una zanja. No está permitido trabajar. De todas maneras, el tipo no es viejo ni asesino serial. Es joven, de nuestra edad. Sus padres lo dejaron, como los míos, y vino a vivir a Eco. Se suponía que debía quedarse con su tío, pero no quería. De modo que ahora está en el jardín trasero de mi casa.

Sunshine colocó el brazo alrededor de una de sus pálidas rodillas.

—Bueno, nuestro verano se ha vuelto más interesante. ¿Qué aspecto tiene?

—Está… está bien. Parece tener dinero, estilo retro. Tiene una buena sonrisa, medio torcida.

Mi vecina se mostró contenta.

—¿Cómo se llama?

—River West.

—¿En serio? Suena inventado.

—Mira quién habla, Sunshine Black —incliné el vaso para beber el final del té—. Tal vez sí lo inventó. No le pedí ninguna identificación.

Sunshine sacudió la cabeza con expresión de reprobación.

—Eso fue una estupidez, Violet. Eres tan ingenua. Mira, tendremos que conseguir su registro de conductor y fijarnos. Yo me encargo. ¿Luke todavía tiene ese vino de cerezo que hizo en el otoño?

—Supongo que sí —me encogí de hombros—. Creo que hay dos botellas en algún lugar de la bodega.

—Muy bien. Entonces todos nos embriagaremos y yo dejaré que el desconocido de tu casa de huéspedes me bese donde quiera. Mientras tanto, le robaré la cartera.

—O yo le pido que me deje ver su documento —no me gustó la idea de que Sunshine besara a River, o que hiciera cualquier otra cosa con él. Lo que fuera. La perspectiva de un verano entero con ellos dos transpirando y gimiendo en la casa de huéspedes me llenó de un terror helado. Además, River era mío. Y por mío, quiero decir que yo lo vi primero. Y por yo lo vi primero, quiero decir que no parecía ser el tipo de chico que se embriagaría con vino casero y trataría de besar a Sunshine.

Mi amiga se echó a reír.

—¿Y dónde está la diversión? Violet, estás frunciendo el ceño.

—No es cierto —dije, aunque estaba totalmente segura de que lo era. Oí pasos en la grava y levanté la vista.

Luke. Venía por el camino oscuro y flanqueado por árboles de la casa de Sunshine, los jeans caídos sobre su estrecha cadera y una camiseta que ajustaba demasiado los estúpidos músculos de su estúpido pecho, de una forma que, estoy segura, a Maddy le encantaba. Y a Sunshine, también.

Tenía los ojos castaño-verdosos de mi madre, pero, en líneas generales, se parecía a papá, con el cabello cobrizo, la frente amplia y el rostro cuadrado.

El cuervo graznó otra vez sobre nuestras cabezas y sopló un fuerte viento del mar, que atravesó violentamente los árboles y sacudió todas las pinochas verdes. Ese sonido siempre me erizaba la piel, de manera agradable. Era el sonido que escucha la institutriz de unos huérfanos en una novela, antes de que una mujer demente prenda fuego las cortinas de la cama.

—Hola, Sunshine. Hola, hermana.

Le lanzó a Sunshine una sonrisa de suficiencia, se echó el pelo hacia atrás y trató de lucir altanero y despreocupado. A mí me pareció que resultaba estúpido, pero a Sunshine, no. Ella bajó las pestañas, se estiró hacia atrás y deslizó el cabello largo por arriba del hombro para que se balanceara sobre las costillas de una manera que a ella le parecía sexy.

–Hola, Luke. ¿Cómo está Maddy? –Sunshine se corrió más cerca de mí para que Luke pudiera sentarse del otro lado.

–Huele a café. Pero eso es bueno, porque a mí me gusta el café. Violet, ¿por qué no vas a casa y me preparas un poco?

–Cállate la boca. *Tú* deberías hacerme café a mí. Acabo de conseguir dinero para que compremos comida. Y volvamos a tener teléfono –hice una pausa dramática–. Un desconocido contestó mi aviso y quiere alquilar la casa de huéspedes.

–Estás bromeando. ¿Esa idea tonta realmente funcionó? –levantó la mano y luego la dejó caer en el muslo de Sunshine, que sonrió.

Me estiré y le aparté la mano de un golpe.

Si Sunshine hubiese sido varón, mi hermano y ella habrían sido mejores amigos. Pero Luke nunca sería amigo de una mujer, aun cuando les gustaran las mismas cosas: como encerrarme en armarios con chicos brutos de la escuela o quemar los libros que estaba leyendo.

Luke y Sunshine habían andado juntos desde que ella se mudó aquí. Antes, había vivido en Texas, Oregón, Montana… Aparentemente, donde se necesitaran los servicios de sus padres bibliotecarios. Cinco años atrás, justo después de que murió Freddie, mis padres se quedaron sin un centavo y tuvieron que vender dos hectáreas y media de bosque de nuestras tierras. El padre de Sunshine había crecido aquí, de modo que compró la tierra, construyó una pequeña cabaña, se mudó a Eco con su familia y se encargó de manejar la biblioteca del pueblo con su mujer.

Sunshine se apretó más contra Luke y él volvió a apoyar la mano en el muslo de ella, todavía más arriba que antes.

—Termínenla. Los dos. Estoy sentada *al lado* de ustedes.

Luke rio.

—¿A quién le importa? Quiero saber quién es ese desconocido. ¿Viejo? ¿Joven? ¿Ya te pagó? ¿Dónde está el dinero?

—Sí, me pagó. Y no, no vas a ver ese dinero ni de cerca. Esta tarde compraré alimentos.

—Se llama River West —acotó Sunshine—. Y Violet decidió que se enamorará perdidamente de él.

—Eso no es ni remotamente cierto —dije lanzándole mi mirada penetrante de sabionda—. No puede estar más lejos de la verdad.

Pero Sunshine tenía toda la razón, y ambas lo sabíamos.

CAPÍTULO 4

REGRESAMOS LOS TRES al Ciudadano, apretujados en medio del sendero selvático que rodeaba la casa, tratando de que las ramas no nos rasguñaran los brazos y las piernas.

Sunshine había decidido que deberíamos ir a hacer las compras todos juntos e invitar a River para que nos acompañara. Por lo tanto, me dirigí a la casa de huéspedes y llamé a la puerta. Lo escuché gritar: "Pasa", y eso hice. Lo encontré en la cocina con las manos hundidas en agua jabonosa.

—Pensé que podía limpiar un poco. Los platos estaban llenos de polvo —miró a mi hermano—. ¿Tú eres

Luke? –retiró las manos del agua, abrió una gaveta y tomó una toalla blanca que tenía bordado un corderito sonriente.

Al observarlo secarse las manos, me pasó por la mente que la toalla que estaba utilizando debía tener miles de años, como el resto de la casa de huéspedes, y los dedos que cosieron la sonrisa roja en ese corderito ya no eran más que huesos bajo la tierra.

Los muertos nos rodean por todos lados, solía decir Freddie. *Así que no les tengas miedo, Violet. Y si no les tienes miedo a los muertos, entonces tampoco tendrás miedo de morir. Y si no tienes miedo de morir, a lo único que tendrás que temerle es al maldito Demonio. Y así debería ser.*

Extrañaba a mis padres. Extrañaba los dedos de mi mamá cubiertos de manchas de pintura y sus ojos adormilados, entre castaños y verdosos, que no tenían nada que ver con mis ojos, porque los míos, como dije, eran azules y de mirada penetrante. Extrañaba la forma en que mostraba demasiado los dientes al reír y que su nariz pareciera un poquito grande si la miraba de costado.

Y extrañaba a mi papá. Extrañaba pararme en la oscuridad de la puerta de servicio y observarlo mientras trasladaba una tela por todo el jardín trasero hasta encontrar la mejor luz. Extrañaba la forma en que suspiraba cuando miraba el derruido invernadero y luego sacudía la cabeza y regresaba a su pintura. Era mucho mayor que mi madre, y su cabello castaño rojizo estaba raleando. Extrañaba el brillo cobrizo que adquiría cuando se exponía directamente al sol. Extrañaba esa costumbre de beber jerez en la biblioteca después de la cena, y luego roncaba tan fuerte que podía escucharlo desde arriba. Extrañaba las arrugas de sus ojos y su frente amplia.

Pero eso no era nada comparado con el dolor que sentía adentro de mis entrañas por la maldita Freddie, la que siempre estaba presente, a diferencia de mis padres. Sí, siempre estaba presente hasta que murió, quiero decir. Extrañaba su cabello rubio y blanco, corto y ondeado, siempre igual desde los años treinta. Extrañaba las boinas de lana que usaba aunque hiciera calor, y que su ropa a veces oliera a limones y a veces a algún costoso perfume francés. Extrañaba la suave piel de su rostro, blanca y perfecta, sin arrugas. Algunas mujeres eran así: sus rostros se mantenían jóvenes y los ojos brillantes, sin importar la edad que tuvieran. Yo quería tener el aspecto de Freddie cuando llegara a las últimas décadas.

Luke se movía nerviosamente. Aparté los pensamientos tristes sobre cuánto extrañaba a Freddie y posé la mirada en River.

—Sí, este es mi hermano y ella es Sunshine, nuestra vecina. Vive en la cabaña que está un poco más abajo.

River le estrechó la mano. Me sorprendió que Luke midiera unos cuántos centímetros más, ya que recordaba que River era muy alto.

¿Realmente? No, cuando lo vi por primera vez, pensé que no era nada alto. Solamente en la última hora, River había crecido más de veinte centímetros dentro de mi mente.

Sunshine observó a River y después me miró por encima del hombro y se pasó la lengua por los labios. La ignoré y observé a Luke. Mi hermano trataba a todas las chicas más o menos de la misma manera, pero, cuando conocía a un chico, hacía una de dos cosas. Le hablaba de manera arrogante, utilizando un tono especial, condescendiente y odioso, muy propio de él. O lo veneraba con toda la vehemencia acumulada que solo un chico sin padre podía reunir.

—River, me alegra que hayas encontrado el cartel de Violet —hizo una pausa y se rascó el codo con forzada despreocupación y actitud falsamente relajada—. Será genial tenerte por aquí. Es agradable que haya otro hombre. En general, tengo que pasar el verano con estas dos –apuntó el mentón hacia Sunshine y hacia mí–. Necesito una persona que pueda beber whisky sin lloriquear. Y no me vendría mal alguien que me controle cuando hago pesas. Tengo un aparato en una de las habitaciones del segundo piso del Ciudadano. ¿Haces pesas?

De modo que sería veneración.

River le sonrió, pero no contestó.

–Iremos a hacer las compras. ¿Quieres venir? –Sunshine se deslizó delante de Luke, se acomodó el cabello y, de repente, pareció acaparar toda la atención.

–Sí, acabo de conectar el refrigerador y necesito alimentos. Por ende, los acompañaré al mercado –River me miró y me guiñó el ojo.

Me quedé mirándolo, luego me reí y él me lanzó su sonrisa torcida. Al notar que comenzaba a sonrojarme otra vez, me escabullí hacia la casa para buscar algunas bolsas de lona. Luego, los cuatro enfilamos hacia los manzanos. Las flores blancas volaban con la brisa del mar y, al pasar debajo de los árboles, varias cayeron en los hombros de River. Él las dejó, no se las quitó, y eso me agradó. Nuestros pies sacudieron el camino de tierra e iniciamos la marcha hacia Eco.

Luke le hacía constantes preguntas a River acerca de dónde venía y qué le gustaba hacer, pero él se las arreglaba para evitar darle respuestas directas de una manera que parecía trivial pero que, en realidad, era bastante brillante, si uno estaba prestando atención. Cosa que yo obviamente estaba haciendo.

Sunshine caminaba a mi lado con su cabello largo, su trasero redondo, sus muslos redondos y su habitual contoneo, deslizando un muslo contra el otro: estaba en la gloria al tener dos chicos bonitos con los cuales coquetear. El olor de la tierra, las hojas y todo lo relacionado con el bosque también me puso de buen humor.

Después de recorrer casi un kilómetro, nos topamos con el viejo túnel del ferrocarril, que acechaba entre los árboles verdes. Ya no circulaban los trenes por ahí, y no lo habían hecho desde hacía muchos años. Las vías habían desaparecido, pero el túnel permanecía en pie, negro como boca de lobo. Luego se adentraba en la colina de manera sinuosa durante un kilómetro y medio aproximadamente, donde, suponía, terminaba en una zona de derrumbe. Yo había ingresado unos veinte o treinta pasos en su interior, pero nunca reuní el valor suficiente para recorrerlo todo y descubrir qué había allí, en la oscuridad, en el final.

Siempre me había sorprendido que algunos adultos aguafiestas no hubieran intentado tapiar la entrada. Tal vez, el túnel estaba demasiado lejos del pueblo como para que un grupo de estúpidos adolescentes se perdiera allí dentro y muriera, o alguien se rompiera una pierna, o fumara marihuana o dejara embarazada a alguna alumna perfecta y encendiera en el pueblo las llamas de la convicción moral y el proselitismo antitúnel. O tal vez, la falta de interés por el túnel se debía a Blue Hoffman y los rumores. Todos nos detuvimos delante del túnel y nos quedamos mirando, como cuatro personas encarando a un viejo enemigo.

—Nadie sabe hasta dónde llega eso —dijo Luke—. Propongo que los hombres nos saltemos las compras y vayamos a investigar. ¿Qué piensas, River? ¿Enviamos a las chicas a comprar la comida mientras nosotros exploramos?

Sunshine se quejó.

–Claro. Yo soy una chica, de modo que me da mucho miedo entrar en el túnel. Vete al diablo, Luke.

–Dicen que ahí dentro vive un lunático –comenté volviéndome hacia River. Apoyé las manos en la cadera y las balanceé un poco para que la falda amarilla de Freddie se deslizara contra mis piernas de forma seductora. Después me di cuenta de que era algo propio de Sunshine y me detuve.

–Continúa –dijo River sonriendo. Sus ojos cafés se veían entretenidos y relajados, pero también impacientes y entusiasmados.

–La historia ha circulado desde que éramos niños, tal vez desde antes –expliqué–. Había un hombre llamado Blue Hoffman, que fue a la guerra y mató gente. Eso lo volvió loco. Regresó a su casa y después comenzaron a desaparecer niños. Finalmente, la policía fue a buscarlo pero, para entonces, él también había desaparecido. Nunca encontraron a los niños. Dicen que Blue vive en las profundidades del túnel y tiene a los chicos como esclavos, que nunca ven el sol, vuelan como murciélagos en la oscuridad, están casi ciegos, viven comiendo carne cruda de rata y están tan dementes como el Demonio.

Luke sacudió la cabeza.

–Violet, no puedo creer que recordaras todo eso. Yo dejé de creer en esa historia en el kínder.

Me encogí de hombros y me negué a sentirme estúpida.

–Es la leyenda urbana y personal de Eco. No importa que tú la creas o no. Solo hay que continuar transmitiendo la historia.

A pesar de que Luke dijera que no creía, yo sabía que el túnel le daba miedo. Era tan oscuro que una linterna apenas lograba penetrar la oscuridad. Y la idea de que hubiera un pobre niño desaparecido de piel blanca y sudorosa, ojos casi ciegos y blancuzcos siguiéndote mientras te tropezabas, esperando el momento indicado para arrastrar un dedo húmedo por tu cara antes de hundirte dos dientes filosos de murciélago en el cuello… Bueno, era suficiente como para mantener a cualquiera, incluso a mi hermano, lejos de ese túnel.

Sunshine, Luke y yo habíamos estado cinco veranos juntos, contando este, y habíamos pasado junto al túnel cientos de veces de camino al pueblo, pero ninguno había entrado más de tres metros y medio ni una sola vez. Ni siquiera el año pasado, cuando Sunshine me desafió a ir hasta el final y luego me amenazó con que besaría a Luke delante de mí si no lo hacía. Se habían dado un beso, largo y ruidoso, y *aun así*, no ingresé, aunque me retorcía de la vergüenza.

La cuestión es que ambos sabían que yo era pura y casta como una monja, y los dos imaginaron que era probable que prefiriera no serlo. Además, el hecho de que se besaran transformó la relación, súbitamente, en dos contra uno, en lugar de todos para uno y uno para todos.

Pero, dejando todo eso de lado, ahora River estaba observando, Luke estaba tratando de impresionarlo y el túnel se hallaba frente a nosotros.

River estiró un brazo y rodeó los hombros de Sunshine.

—¿Qué les parece si Sunshine y yo vamos a investigar mientras los mellizos nos esperan aquí y cuidan el fuerte? Sunshine, ¿qué dices? ¿Intentamos encontrar a este lunático come ratas?

Ella sonrió feliz y Luke se mostró disgustado. Yo tampoco estaba contenta. River condujo a Sunshine hasta la boca del túnel. Dieron un paso hacia adentro, después otro, y luego desaparecieron en la maldita oscuridad.

Luke caminó de un lado a otro con paso fuerte mientras la piel clara se le ponía rosada con el calor y el cabello castaño rojizo se volvía más rojo por el sol, como el de papá. Finalmente, se tumbó en el suelo y miró hacia el cielo.

Yo también me eché en el piso, en una zona de césped, al costado del sendero y cerca del túnel. Me quité las sandalias y me pregunté qué pretendía River al llevar a Sunshine adentro del túnel. Solos.

Luke giró y me lanzó una mirada enojada con sus ojos castaño-verdosos y pestañó.

—Veo que estás usando la falda de Freddie. ¿Por qué lo haces? Es extraño, hermanita. Es condenadamente extraño. Esa cosa parece tener cien años. Te da aspecto de demente.

Alisé la falda, deslicé los pulgares sobre los pliegues suaves y no le respondí. Había comenzado a usar la ropa de Freddie a principios de ese año, solo algunas de sus viejas faldas y algunos vestidos de cuando era joven. Finalmente había crecido lo suficiente como para que me quedaran bien. No era *tan* extraño.

Además, ya era verano otra vez, y el verano era la estación en que extrañaba a Freddie más intensa y profundamente que nunca. Y si quería usar sus viejos vestidos, lo haría.

¿Por qué mi hermano es así, Freddie? ¿Por qué no puede ser agradable conmigo de vez en cuando?

Tal vez lo es. La voz áspera de Freddie inundó mi mente. *Tal vez lo es pero tú estás demasiado empeñada en sentir antipatía por él como para notarlo.*

Miré a Luke.

—¿Sabes algo? Hay trajes del abuelo en uno de los armarios del primer piso. Podrías probarte sus chalecos, o usar una de sus corbatas o sus sombreros. Es... agradable ponerse ropa vieja y usada. ¿A quién le importa si te da aspecto de demente? Ya todos piensan que estamos locos porque papá y mamá desaparecieron y la casa es demasiado grande y tenemos antepasados ricos e ilustres.

Luke me observó durante unos segundos y luego sacudió la cabeza.

–No me sorprende que no tengas amigos, Vi. ¿Realmente llegaste a pensar alguna vez que yo voy a caminar por el pueblo contigo vestida con la ropa de nuestros "antepasados ilustres" y muertos?

Suspiré.

Transcurrieron unos minutos más. Comencé a preguntarme si River estaba besando a Sunshine en ese túnel, donde no llegaba el sol y si ella estaba tratando de robarle la cartera.

Me sentí algo triste.

Después oí el grito.

Volteé la cabeza abruptamente hacia la entrada del túnel. Ahí se encontraba Sunshine, a la sombra, la cabeza inclinada hacia atrás. Estaba gritando. Gritaba y gritaba mientras yo me levantaba y corría hacia ella. La alcancé en el momento en que se desplomaba en el suelo, la falda subida hasta la cintura y la ropa interior negra y transparente brillando contra las piernas blancas. Debería haberme arrodillado a su lado, bajarle la falda y tratar de despertarla. Pero no lo hice. Temía que si la tocaba, yo también me desvanecería y mi falda volaría hacia arriba mientras caía al suelo.

River salió a la luz. Luke y él se arrodillaron junto a Sunshine, le hablaron con susurros y trataron de despertarla. Pero yo no hice nada, absolutamente nada. Finalmente, River deslizó sus manos por debajo de ella y la levantó contra su pecho. Se alejó del túnel y la trasladó hacia la zona de césped. Los seguí, los brazos colgando a los costados. River la apoyó en el suelo y ella abrió los ojos.

—Lo vi, Violet —dijo con la mirada clavada en mí, sus adormilados ojos color café llenos de espanto y terror—. Vi a Blue.

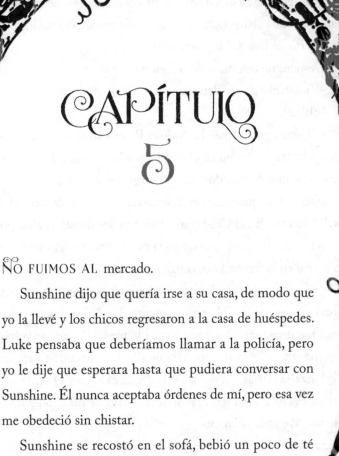

CAPÍTULO 5

NO FUIMOS AL mercado.

Sunshine dijo que quería irse a su casa, de modo que yo la llevé y los chicos regresaron a la casa de huéspedes. Luke pensaba que deberíamos llamar a la policía, pero yo le dije que esperara hasta que pudiera conversar con Sunshine. Él nunca aceptaba órdenes de mí, pero esa vez me obedeció sin chistar.

Sunshine se recostó en el sofá, bebió un poco de té helado y no me habló durante un rato largo. Observé un rayo de sol que se movía por el suelo y esperé.

Su casa era pequeña, especialmente si la comparaba con la mía. El Ciudadano era un inconexo laberinto de curvas, rincones, recovecos, escaleras, habitaciones vacías, grandes ventanales, terrazas deterioradas, armarios olvidados y sótanos con bodegas. Pero la cabaña de Sunshine era acogedora, de tamaño razonable y estaba abarrotada de cosas. Cada rincón era un lugar vívido y cubierto de libros. Me encantaba.

Después de dos vasos de té, por fin me miró.

—Violet, él está ahí dentro.

—¿Blue?

—Sí —hizo una pausa—. Es curioso, River y yo ni siquiera nos habíamos adentrado mucho en el túnel cuando lo vimos. Él tenía un encendedor, uno de esos dorados y recargables, ¿sabes de lo que hablo?

Asentí. Los que tenían el aspecto de haberse caído del bolsillo de Jack Kerouac. En el Ciudadano, había varios dando vueltas por ahí.

Sunshine secó con una mano la condensación del vaso y luego se lo apoyó en la frente. Estaba pálida.

—River levantó el viejo encendedor para que pudiéramos ver, pero igual estaba oscuro. Muy, muy oscuro. Lo único que se escuchaba eran nuestros pies resonando contra la piedra. El aire se volvía cada vez más frío y húmedo y pensé que River se detendría y me besaría. Yo lanzaba risitas nerviosas, sacudía el cabello y él tenía la mano en mi brazo. Finalmente, se detuvo y jaló de mi codo para darme vuelta. Me pasé la lengua por los labios porque pensé que sabía lo que venía.

Sunshine se estremeció. Estaba sentada bajo el sol directo y hacía calor, mucho, pero se estremeció.

—Creo que voy a enfermarme —dijo.

Metí la mano en mi té y tomé un cubo de hielo. Me arrodillé junto a ella y se lo apoyé en la frente.

–Tranquila, Sunshine. No tienes nada. Cuéntame lo que viste cuando River te hizo dar vuelta.

Sunshine parpadeó. El hielo derretido corrió por sus sienes y dejó una marca húmeda en el sofá.

–Me di vuelta y vi a un hombre encorvado cerca del suelo. Lo vi con toda claridad. Tenía ojos enormes, de un celeste pálido. Me sonrió con unos dientitos filosos que parecían peludos, como si hubiera estado comiendo piel –su voz brotaba con más rapidez. Se enderezó y colocó las rodillas debajo del mentón–. A esa altura, ya estaba gritando. Cuando lo vi, ya estaba gritando. Violet, había un niñito, o una niñita, entre los pies de Blue. Tenía una horrorosa piel blanca y orejas largas y puntiagudas. Y los mismos dientes peludos. Cada vez que pienso en eso, en esa cosa o ese niño blanco con dientes peludos, me...

Se llevó la mano a la boca, se incorporó de un salto y corrió al baño.

Llamé a la biblioteca y les pedí a sus padres que vinieran.

Cassandra y Sam no se parecían en nada a su hija. Eran muy delgados. Delgados adolescentes desgarbados, y no delgados como la gente grande que hacía mucho ejercicio o se mataba de hambre. Cassie se recogió el cabello atrás en un rodete, como las profesoras de ballet. Tenía lentes gruesos y redondos al estilo Aldous Huxley y le gustaba usar ropa gris con chalinas blancas. Tenía leves marcas alrededor de la boca y venas gruesas y azules en las manos. Sam, el padre de Sunshine, tenía una barba desaliñada y solía vestirse con prendas de corderoy. Tenía los ojos entrecerrados, como su hija.

Cerraron la biblioteca temprano y vinieron directamente a su casa. Les conté lo sucedido mientras Sunshine continuaba en el baño. Fui una vez a ver cómo estaba y la encontré con la mejilla apoyada en los mosaicos fríos y blancos del suelo, el cabello extendido a su alrededor como una chal de un suave color castaño. Me dijo que si se movía, vomitaría otra vez, de modo que la dejé ahí.

Después de que les hablé del túnel, de Blue y de Sunshine, Cassie fue a preparar té y Sam se quedó un instante con la mirada perdida, con aspecto perplejo y algo desconcertado. Era una expresión que le quedaba bien.

–Violet, tú sabes que la historia no es cierta –comentó finalmente–. Blue no era más que un hombre triste y confundido, y esos niños que se suponía que había secuestrado regresaron al pueblo una semana después. Resultó que habían leído *Tom Sawyer* en la escuela y eso les dio la idea –los dedos de Sam juguetearon con el puente de la nariz. No usaba lentes, pero tuve la impresión de que habría deseado hacerlo–. Se escaparon al bosque –continuó– y vivieron de bayas y sándwiches de manteca de maní. Ocho días después, aparecieron hambrientos, sucios y sorprendidos por el escándalo. Blue realmente desapareció, pero en una institución de enfermos mentales en el norte. Eso ocurrió hace treinta y pico de años, cuando yo era adolescente. No puedo creer que esa historia todavía esté vigente.

Primero asentí y después hice un movimiento negativo con la cabeza.

–Pero Sunshine no está mintiendo. Ella *realmente* vio algo. No cesaba de gritar. Era… era aterrador.

–¿El otro chico vio algo? –Cassie se dio vuelta y me alcanzó un sándwich de pepino. Era muy finito y no tenía corteza. Se había criado en Inglaterra y pensaba que los problemas se solucionaban con té y sándwiches de pepino. Lo cual era cierto, a veces. Cassie tomó un sándwich y comenzó a mordisquearlo, el codo flacucho levantado en el aire.

–Sí –agregó Sam. Su rostro delgado se veía todavía más delgado cuando alzaba las cejas–. El chico nuevo que se instaló en tu casita, ¿vio a un hombre en el túnel?

Abrí la boca y luego la cerré. Había olvidado preguntarle. Con toda la excitación del desmayo de Sunshine, me había olvidado por completo de preguntarle a River si *él* vio a Blue. Miré el pequeño emparedado triangular de pepino que tenía entre los dedos. La pesadilla del túnel se estaba desvaneciendo, rápidamente, como lo hacían las pesadillas, y la historia de Sunshine sonaba cada vez más delirante.

–No lo sé. Iré a preguntarle.

Se abrió la puerta del baño y Sunshine entró en la cocina, pálida y sudorosa, el cabello enmarañado. Sus ojos no tenían la usual expresión adormilada y medio aburrida. En su lugar, se veían frustrados y violentos: dos emociones que nunca antes había observado en ella. No era el tipo de chica que se dejaba invadir por la pasión. No de esa manera.

Sam se acercó a su hija y le dio un abrazo.

–Sunshine, yo siempre dije que albergabas una brillante imaginación. Tiene una curiosa manera de aparecer, pero yo sabía que lo haría tarde o temprano –Sam emitió una risa ahogada–. Violet les contó la leyenda de Blue, luego entraron al túnel y eso es lo que viste. Pero esa historia no es cierta. Tú sabes que no lo es, ¿verdad?

Sunshine no respondió.

—Está bien, Sunny —Cassie rodeó la cintura de su hija con su brazo largo y delgado, la estrechó con fuerza y sonrió. A diferencia de su cuerpo, los labios de Cassandra eran gruesos y carnosos, como los de una niñita hermosa, como los de Sunshine—. Todos vemos cosas a veces. Cuando tenía la edad de ustedes, me enamoré de tal manera de *Cumbres borrascosas* que me convencí de que Heathcliff realmente existía. En ese entonces, yo todavía vivía en Cambridge. Tomé un autobús hasta Yorkshire y comencé a buscarlo. Caminé durante más de treinta kilómetros por el páramo, siguiendo lo que yo pensaba que era la sombra de Heathcliff, que se extendía por los arbustos de brezo y me atraía hacia él. Terminé en un pub, horas más tarde, cansada, helada y avergonzada.

Sunshine me observó por arriba del hombro de su madre. Continuaba enojada, muy enojada. Y eso me perturbó.

—Voy a hablar con River —mascullé.

CAPÍTULO 6

Llamé a la puerta de la casa de huéspedes. Abrió Luke. Al verme, frunció el ceño, pero retrocedió para dejarme entrar. Sentí de inmediato el aroma a café. Olía a caramelo, a chocolate, a tierra negra y a la hora de despertarse en la mañana. Una gran cafetera italiana estaba humeando sobre la llama de la cocina. Mis padres tenían amigos artistas italianos y usaban esa cafetera para hacer café expreso. Se parecía a una mujer corpulenta con un vestido plateado y la mano en la cadera, y yo estaba ligeramente sorprendida de que River supiera utilizarla.

–Tomé un poco de café del Ciudadano –señaló.

Lo imaginé revisando los armarios de mi cocina, sin

permiso, buscando café… y descubrí que no me importaba. Hasta me gustó.

—¿Cómo supiste para qué servía la cafetera italiana? —pregunté—. ¿Estuviste en Italia?

River sonrió.

—De niño, pasé unos años en Nápoles. Vivía en un apartamento minúsculo en una calle bulliciosa, con una tía.

—¿En Italia? ¿En serio? —yo siempre quise viajar a Italia—. Di algo en italiano.

—*Io non parlo italiano* —me guiñó el ojo—. Significa que no hablo italiano.

—Sí, lo supuse. Pero estás mintiendo. Si viviste allí varios años, deberías hablarlo bastante bien. Di algo más.

No lo hizo.

—¿Y cómo está Sunshine? ¿Se encuentra bien?

—Realmente, no —quería hacerle más preguntas sobre Italia. Pero me observaba atentamente, con una media sonrisa, los ojos chispeantes, casi como si *quisiera* que le hiciera otra pregunta, para poder esquivarla nuevamente.

Me moví nerviosamente durante unos segundos bajo su atenta mirada.

—River, ¿viste a un hombre en el túnel? Sunshine dice que vio a Blue y a un niño pequeño. ¿Tú también los viste?

Tomó tres tazas del armario, limpió el interior con la toalla del corderito y las llenó con café expreso oscuro y cremoso. Le alcanzó una a Luke y a otra a mí, y luego bebió de la suya.

—No —respondió finalmente—. No vi nada. Caminábamos por el túnel oscuro y luego Sunshine comenzó a gritar. Después se fue corriendo hacia afuera y yo la seguí –hizo una pausa–. De manera que piensa que vio a Blue, ¿eh? Debe tener una imaginación infernal.

–Pero esa es la cuestión –bebí un sorbo de café. Estaba suave, caliente y muy bueno–. Sunshine no tiene imaginación. Bueno, al menos no una tan grande. No cree en fantasmas ni en monstruos ni en hadas. Ni siquiera lee. Cree en los terrores realistas como el calentamiento global y los asesinos seriales, pero no en leyendas urbanas ni en dientes peludos.

–¿Dientes peludos? –preguntó Luke–. ¿Qué diablos es eso?

–Eso dijo. El hombre que vio tenía dientes peludos, como si comiera animales con piel. Ella no pudo haber inventado un detalle semejante, de modo que sé que vio a alguien en ese túnel. Tenemos que entrar otra vez y verlo nosotros mismos. Si *realmente* hay un loco ahí dentro, tenemos que encontrarlo y contárselo a alguien.

River giró y se sirvió otro café. Pero antes de que volteara, alcancé a ver que sonreía. Fue rápido, tan rápido que casi pensé que no lo había visto, que tal vez parpadeé y lo vi dentro de mi mente. Estiré la taza para que me sirviera más café.

–Ay, Violet –Luke se pasó la mano por el mentón, cuya barba era todavía incipiente. Supongo que creía que le daba un aspecto inteligente. Pero no era así–. River ya dijo que no vio nada. Sería una pérdida de tiempo regresar al túnel. Sunshine está actuando como una típica mujer. Escuchó tu historia sobre Blue y se puso histérica.

–No pensabas lo mismo hace dos horas. Hace dos horas querías llamar a la policía.

Luke me ignoró. Apoyó la taza en la mesa, alzó las manos hacia el techo y se estiró. Los gruesos tendones de sus brazos se veían inflados, rígidos y estúpidos. Mientras que River, a su lado, era todo derecho, con líneas estilizadas. La camisa de Luke era dos números más ajustada y el jean, dos números más grande, mientras que las prendas de River caían perfectamente en las dos mitades de su cuerpo, como si las hubieran hecho especialmente para él. Cosa que tal vez había sido así.

—Viejo, me duelen los músculos —dijo Luke mientras se frotaba los pectorales con las dos manos, como para demostrar que tenía razón—. Esta mañana levanté realmente mucho peso.

—¿Sabes algo, Luke? Tus músculos son aburridos. Y no creas que no me di cuenta de que cambiaste de tema. Si quieres distraerme, te sugiero que hables de algo que no sea levantar pesas.

Esbozó una gran sonrisa, feliz de haberme hecho enfadar.

—Maddy no piensa que mis músculos sean aburridos. Maddy no piensa que mis músculos sean *nada* aburridos. Hablando de ella, su turno termina en media hora y si mis músculos y yo no estamos ahí esperándola, como un cachorrito de ojos grandotes, nuestra relación amorosa no pasará al segundo nivel. River, fue un placer. Estoy encantado de tenerte a bordo del Ciudadano. ¿Irás esta noche a ver la película?

—¿Una película? —preguntó River. Giró la cadera y se apoyó contra la mesa de la cocina—. ¿De qué película se trata?

—Durante el verano, pasan películas al aire libre en el parque —expliqué antes de que Luke pudiera responder—. Hoy, al anochecer, darán *Casablanca*. En general, yo preparo un picnic. Y nos gusta ir temprano para conseguir un buen lugar cerca de la pantalla.

—¿No tienes que ocuparte de Sunshine o algo por el estilo? —Luke giró la cadera y se apoyó contra la mesa en la misma posición que

River–. Estaba pensando en robar un poco de vodka de la casa de Maddy y beberlo durante la película. Me temo que suena muchísimo mejor que un estúpido picnic. ¿Qué piensas, River? ¿No crees que Violet debería quedarse en casa esta noche y dejar que los hombres vayan a jugar?

River pasó las manos por su cabello oscuro y sonrió.

–Violet, ¿por qué no acompañamos a Luke en su caminata al pueblo y esta vez realmente tratamos de hacer las compras? Sin detenernos en túneles y todo eso. Después podemos comprar cosas para un picnic. Y, Luke, si quieres, tengo una botella de coñac en la cajuela del auto. Yo no bebo, o, al menos, muy de vez en cuando. Lo estaba guardando para una ocasión especial, pero puedes quedártela.

Luke sacudió la cabeza. Estaba enojado con River por negarse a burlarse de mí y de mi tonta idea de hacer un picnic. Según la opinión de mi hermano, los verdaderos hombres bebían.

–No –dijo–. Está bien. Quédate con la botella. Yo tampoco bebo tanto. Solo quería hacerlo esta noche, porque siempre dan esas malditas películas viejas en blanco y negro, que son terriblemente lentas. Si no bebo, me quedo dormido.

–De hecho, *Casablanca* es una de mis películas preferidas –River me miró y hubo un leve temblor en la comisura de sus labios–. La vi unas doce veces, mi sobrio y querido amigo, y ni una sola vez me quedé dormido.

Luke refunfuñó y yo sonreí. Diablos, en realidad fue una sonrisa *resplandeciente*. River estaba poniéndose de mi lado en contra de Luke: Sunshine nunca hacía eso.

Tener a River cerca ya era mucho mejor que hablarle y rogarle a Freddie. Porque Freddie estaba muerta y River estaba vivito y coleando, haciéndole frente a Luke y a punto de acompañarme a hacer las compras. De repente, me sentí de maravillas.

Diez minutos después, cargando otra vez las bolsas, River y yo seguimos a un silencioso Luke por el sendero hacia el pueblo. Esta vez, cuando llegamos al túnel, no nos detuvimos. Los chicos siguieron de largo como si el túnel no significara nada, pero yo me estremecí como dice aquella antigua frase: "te estremeces cuando alguien camina por encima de tu tumba". Mantuve los ojos en el sendero, pues temía que, si levantaba la vista, vería a un hombre sucio sonriéndome desde la entrada, con dientes manchados y peludos que crujían y rechinaban como los de un perro salvaje.

El pueblo tenía un solo café y era muy bueno. Se encontraba justo en el centro, en la esquina de dos calles que delimitan la mitad de la plaza del pueblo, con su césped verde y sus robles. Si te colocabas en el centro y girabas, podías ver la biblioteca, la pizzería, el café, la Cooperativa Dandelion, la florería, *Jimmy the Popcorn Man* en su puesto de palomitas de maíz, la tienda de relojes antiguos, la ferretería y la librería anticuaria dirigida por el misterioso Nathan Keane, que tenía cien años, el cabello largo y despeinado, horarios muy extraños y ocultaba una historia de amor con final desdichado.

Eco tenía todos los rincones pintorescos que uno esperaría en cualquier pueblo de los más antiguos de Estados Unidos. Lucía limpio, tierno y atemporal, especialmente cuando brillaba el sol. Y mientras yo dedicaba una buena cantidad de tiempo a soñar que me marchaba, a veces, mi pueblo me resultaba bastante agradable.

El café pertenecía a la misma familia italiana que manejaba la pizzería, por lo tanto era realmente genuino. En los días lindos, podías sentarte fuera, en una de las mesas redondas de color negro, beber café italiano y observar al hermoso Gianni mientras vaporizaba la leche, y sentir que no estabas tan lejos de la civilización.

Yo había bebido café allí desde los doce años. El verano en que murió Freddie, me pasé casi todos los días yendo de la biblioteca a la cafetería, y supongo que se me podía ver a menudo con una taza de expreso en una mano y una hermana Brontë en la otra. A veces, los adultos pasaban a mi lado y me miraban, pero a mis padres no les habría importado que yo tomara café desde tan pequeña, aun cuando lo hubieran notado, lo cual no ocurrió. Freddie no me habría dejado, pero mis padres... a ellos no les gustaba entrometerse. Esa era una de sus características: no creían en las reglas. Especialmente si esas reglas interferían con lo que ellos consideraban que era una cuestión íntima y privada: como mi cuestión íntima y privada de consumir, si yo quería, un brebaje color caramelo que retrasaba mi normal crecimiento.

¿Regresarán?, preguntaba yo frecuentemente. *Freddie, ¿regresarán alguna vez?*

Sí, respondía siempre. *Sí, sí, sí. Tienes que esperar, Vi.*

Le pedimos a Maddy unos *lattes* para llevar, aunque acabábamos de beber café en la casa de huéspedes. Le sonreí, pero ella estaba mirando a Luke. Tenía mejillas redondas, pestañas largas y ojos negros y brillantes. Imagino que creía estar enamorada, o algo que se le parecía mucho.

Luke la señaló e hizo una mueca.

–¿Te estás portando bien?

Maddy rio.

–No.

–Esa es mi chica –y luego ella le sonrió, como si él fuera el sol en un día nublado.

–Puedes conseguir algo mejor –comenté, pero no lo suficientemente fuerte como para que ella escuchara. Freddie me dijo que las personas debían elegir sus propias batallas. Y supongo que esta no era la mía.

River y yo llevamos nuestros cafés afuera y yo lo fui bebiendo de a sorbos mientras meditaba acerca de lo bueno que era tomar café con una persona que te gustara. Y River me gustaba. Lo observé de reojo, de pie en la acerca con sus pantalones de lino, elegante, largo, con aspecto de ser el dueño del pueblo, pero de una forma positiva. Me gustaba cómo entornaba los ojos antes de beber el café, como si no supiera con qué se iba a encontrar.

Con River a mi lado, me dediqué a tomar café mientras echaba un vistazo a la bonita plaza principal de Eco, cuando un hombre demacrado de cabello gris muy finito dobló la esquina y tropezó con el césped. Se quedó en el lugar, levantó la vista y miró con furia hacia el cielo, como si el sol lo hubiera insultado. Era Daniel Leap, con el traje de lana color chocolate que siempre llevaba. Estaba ebrio. Siempre estaba ebrio. Normalmente, yo trataba de sentir pena por él. Pero, en ese momento, era una mancha oscura en lo que, de otra manera, constituía una bonita vista de mi pueblo, y, de repente, lo odié con esa furia fulminante que te provoca derramarte algo en un hermoso vestido o una mosca ahogada en un vaso de limonada fría y perfecta.

—Daniel Leap nos arruinó la vista —anuncié.

—¿Quién? —preguntó River.

—Daniel Leap. Sería el excéntrico del pueblo si ya no lo tuviéramos a Nathan Keane, el hombre con el corazón roto que es dueño de la librería. Por lo tanto, Daniel Leap es el alcohólico del pueblo.

—Me encantan los excéntricos de los pueblos —señaló River.

Y yo sonreí ante su comentario.

En ese instante, Daniel me divisó.

—Violet White —gritó a través de la plaza. No se acercó, sino que permaneció en el césped balanceándose y apuntándome con el dedo mientras mascullaba palabras ininteligibles, hasta que brotaron todas juntas, como la pintura goteando sobre una tela.

»Violet White —dijo otra vez— es una esnob que piensa que es mejor que el resto del pueblo como todos los White anteriores a ella, y también los Glenship, hasta que los expulsamos de Eco. Esnobs. Siempre lo fueron y siempre lo serán. Viven en esa gran mansión frente al mar, no saben nada y se comportan como si lo supieran todo, pero yo podría contarles un par de cosas…

Llevaba años haciendo lo mismo, cada vez que me veía a mí, a mi hermano o a mis padres; yo ya estaba acostumbrada. Su monólogo siempre tocaba los mismos temas: que nosotros éramos esnobs y que él podría contarnos un par de cosas. Una vez, le pregunté a mi padre por él, pues me pregunté si habría algún tipo de resentimiento entre él y mi familia. Pero se había limitado a tomar el pincel, encogerse de hombros y decir "Violet, ¿quién puede conocer cuáles son los motivos de la gente inferior?", antes de regresar a su pintura.

De modo que describirnos como esnobs no era algo tan descabellado.

Le di la espalda a Daniel Leap y decidí encaminarme hacia la Cooperativa Dandelion, el mercado que quedaba en la esquina. Pero alguien me sujetó el brazo y me detuve. Era River. Lo miré, pero él tenía la vista fija en Daniel Leap.

Estaba furioso. Tenía los ojos entrecerrados, las mejillas rojas y el cuerpo quieto. Me apretó el brazo con más fuerza.

—Está todo bien —dije y agité la mano libre como si estuviera espantando una mosca—. Siempre dice esas cosas cuando se encuentra con uno de nosotros. Estoy acostumbrada.

River sacudió la cabeza una vez, con rapidez.

—No deberías acostumbrarte a que alguien hable de ti de esa manera.

Daniel Leap dejó de señalarme. Se balanceó de un lado a otro y después se desplomó en el suelo.

—Mira —le dije—. Ahora quedó inconsciente. Vayamos a hacer las compras.

Finalmente, River apartó los ojos del alcohólico y me miró. Sonrió y pareció estar nuevamente relajado. Así, de golpe, la furia había desaparecido.

—De acuerdo. Te sigo.

La Cooperativa Dandelion vendía productos de la zona: verduras, leche de almendras y frutos secos y especias al por mayor. Los padres de Sunshine me habían convencido de las bondades de la comida natural. Cassie y Sam tenían un lindo jardincito detrás de la cabaña, en el único lugar que recibía mucho sol. Hacían helado de leche de coco, coliflor frito en aceite de oliva, pizzas con pesto y tantas cosas más. Desde que mis padres se marcharon, nos invitaban a Luke y a mí a pasar las fiestas con ellos. Y en la Navidad pasada, hasta nos hicieron regalos. Yo recibí una larga bufanda a rayas tejida a mano, que usé durante todo el invierno y Luke recibió un libro sobre artistas del Renacimiento italiano, que sorprendentemente leyó. Y nos habíamos divertido mucho, todos apretujados en la minúscula sala jugando a juegos de mesa hasta la medianoche mientras las agujas de pino del excesivo árbol de Navidad nos pinchaban a todos. Luke y Sunshine hasta se olvidaron de coquetear, por un rato.

Mis padres casi nunca cocinaban o hacían regalos. Supongo que querían emplear su dinero y ansias creativas en su arte y no malgastarlos en comprar regalos o en cocinar una comida que dos mocosos semiinconscientes consumirían en veinte minutos.

Comprar en la Cooperativa Dandelion me hacía sentir europea. Muy Audrey Hepburn en el personaje de Sabrina (esa película la dieron en el parque unas pocas semanas atrás). Para el picnic, River compró queso de cabra para untar en el crujiente pan francés, aceitunas, un envase de pimientos rojos asados, una barra de setenta por ciento de chocolate amargo y una botella de agua con gas. También compró algunas cosas para él: leche entera orgánica, otra baguette crujiente, café en grano (tostado por la familia de Gianni y vendido en todo el pueblo), plátanos, queso Parmesano, huevos gordos de color, aceite de oliva extra virgen y algunas especias a granel.

Lo observé mientras compraba. Con atención. Olió intensamente el increíble aroma tostado de los granos de café antes de molerlos él mismo. Abrió la caja de huevos, frotó las cáscaras de color y volvió a cerrarla. Deslizó sus dedos delgados en el barril de frijoles Borlotti, blancos y violetas, incapaz de resistir el deseo, igual que yo. Nunca podía dejar de hundir las manos en los bonitos frijoles manchados. Nunca.

Es increíble lo que se puede conocer de una persona con solo verla comprar alimentos. Pero es así. Luke compraba de manera salvaje, iba arrojando productos en una canasta como si los detestara. Sunshine compraba lenta e irreflexivamente, paseando de un pasillo a otro. Miraba los quesos importados durante veinte minutos y luego decidía comprar el primer paquete de pastas que podía manotear de camino a la caja. Ninguno de ellos había olido nunca café ni frotado huevos ni hundido las manos en los frijoles Borlotti. Ni una vez.

—¿Dónde aprendiste a comprar alimentos? —pregunté—. Eres bueno. Ni muy lento ni muy rápido.

—Fui a una escuela de gastronomía —respondió.

—No, no es cierto. Todavía estás en la escuela secundaria.

—¿En serio? —preguntó River.

Me sonrió, con esa sonrisa torcida, traviesa y hermosa.

—Sí, en serio —dije y luego fruncí ligeramente el ceño—. Se supone que todavía estás en la escuela, ¿no?

River solo sacudió la cabeza y rio.

Cuando regresamos al Ciudadano, me ayudó a guardar los comestibles. Nuestra cocina había pasado décadas sin ninguna renovación, pero los electrodomésticos todavía funcionaban bien. Era una habitación grande y sólida, con paredes de color azafrán, techos altos y una larga mesa de roble en el centro. Había cuatro ventanas en dos de sus lados y un viejo sofá amarillo en la pared más lejana, que recibía todo el sol de la tarde. Las ventanas tenían cortinas cuadriculadas y el suelo estaba revestido con mosaicos de color amarillo oscuro. A veces, yo dormía ahí dentro, en el sofá. Estar en la cocina por la noche me traía muchos recuerdos, como cuando horneaba galletas holandesas de Navidad con Freddie: el aroma a canela caliente me cubría como una manta y las migas azucaradas se derretían en mi boca como la nieve.

River se puso de rodillas y comenzó a examinar los armarios. Se le levantó la camisa en la espalda y me quedé mirando la piel tostada que asomaba por arriba de los pantalones de lino.

Tuve un deseo súbito de besarlo allí, en la parte inferior de la espalda. Para ser sincera, nunca antes había querido besar a un chico. A ninguno de esos chicos con los cuales Luke y Sunshine me encerraban en el vestidor, y a ninguno de los muchachos del pueblo, torpes, desconsiderados y tan poco parecidos a un héroe romántico estilo Lord Byron.

Pero River era... River era...

—¿Violet?

Parpadeé y moví los ojos hasta encontrarme con los de River. Estaba observando por encima del hombro, viendo cómo lo miraba.

—¿Sí?

—¿Tienes una sartén? No de teflón, las odio. ¿De hierro fundido? ¿O de acero inoxidable?

Le encontré una vieja sartén de hierro fundido en el armario que estaba junto al fregadero. La apoyé sobre las hornallas y me imaginé, por unos segundos, a Freddie joven, con un collar de perlas y un sombrero caído hacia un costado, utilizando esa misma sartén para hacer omelette después de una larga noche de bailes locos y geniales, propios de su época.

—Perfecta —comentó River. Encendió la hornalla y arrojó un poco de manteca en la sartén. Luego, cortó cuatro rebanadas de baguette, las frotó con un diente de ajo e hizo un hueco en cada una. Colocó el pan en la manteca y cascó un huevo sobre el pan para llenar el hueco. Las yemas eran de color anaranjado brillante y, según el padre de Sunshine, eso implicaba que, cuando pusieron los huevos, las gallinas estaban tan felices como un cielo azul.

—Huevos en canasta —River me sonrió.

Cuando los huevos ya estaban hechos, pero con la yema todavía líquida, los puso en dos platos, cortó un tomate en cuadraditos jugosos y los apiló arriba del pan. El tomate se había cultivado a unos kilómetros de Eco, en el invernadero de una persona tranquila, y era rojo como el pecado y maduro como el sol del mediodía. River roció los tomates con sal marina, un poquito de aceite de oliva y me extendió un plato.

Me relamí los labios, pero no como lo haría Sunshine. Lo hice en serio. Dejé el tenedor sobre la mesa, tomé el pan frito con la mano, mastiqué, tragué y me reí a carcajadas.

—Está muy bueno, River. Muy, pero muy bueno. ¿Dónde diablos aprendiste a cocinar? —el aceite de oliva y el jugo de tomate chorreaban por mi mentón y no me importó en absoluto.

—¿De verdad? Mi madre era cocinera —River tenía la media sonrisa en su boca torcida, traviesa, astuta—. Es una especie de bruschetta, pero con un huevo frito. De Estados Unidos pero vía Italia.

Comí otro bocado. Mi boca cantaba. Tragué, y estaba por atacar otra vez cuando recordé algo. Lo miré con una expresión dura.

—Creí que habías dicho que tu madre era arqueóloga.

Los labios de River brillaban por el aceite y sus ojos se estaban riendo de mí.

—¿En serio?

—Sí.

Se encogió de hombros.

–Entonces debo haber mentido. Pero el problema es cuál de las dos veces.

Sonreí y después largué una carcajada. River te arrinconaba y lanzaba su sonrisa torcida hasta que te sentías demasiado estúpida como para continuar haciéndole preguntas. Y luego actuaba como si todo importara menos que nada, y entonces uno también empezaba a creer lo mismo.

De repente, mientras mordía otra vez la bruschetta de huevo frito, me di cuenta de que hacía solamente un día que lo conocía. *Un día*. Esta mañana, no sabía que River existía. Mientras leía *Musgos de una vieja rectoría* de Hawthorne, ignoraba su existencia por completo. Ahora, hacía las compras con él y me gustaba que lo hiciera de la misma forma que yo. Y comía lo que él cocinaba, me lamía los labios y todo resultaba natural, alegre y maravillosamente único.

Pero la verdad era que yo no sabía nada de *nada* acerca de ese chico. Me pregunté qué habría dicho Freddie sobre el hecho de sentirse tan rápido tan cerca de alguien…

–Ahora permíteme preguntarte algo a *ti* –comentó River, interceptando mi mirada e interrumpiendo mis pensamientos. Sacudió el cabello bajo la luz del sol y vi asomar un mechón rubio entre el castaño oscuro. Luego volvió a acomodarse en el costado y su cabello quedó despeinado, pero lindo–. ¿Hace cuánto tiempo que tu hermano es así?

Enarqué las cejas.

–Así, ¿cómo?

–El sexismo, la inseguridad, la bebida. ¿Es debido a que tu padre se fue?

Apoyé la bruschetta en el plato de porcelana blanco y cachado.

—Sí y no. Luke siempre ha sido más bien... agresivo. Es más de lo que se ve a simple vista, es solo que no lo demuestra mucho. Necesita algo en lo cual creer. Al menos, eso es lo que mi Freddie, mi abuela, siempre decía.

—Me parece que Freddie era muy aguda —al hacer ese comentario, River no me estaba mirando, sino que tenía la vista perdida en la distancia, con una extraña expresión en el rostro. Y por extraña quiero decir que no era risueña y astuta, sino más bien sincera y ferviente. Y casi... severa.

—Ella era muchas cosas —desconcertada ante la extraña mirada de River, hice una pausa. Como no dijo nada, continué hablando—. Luke ha empeorado desde que nuestros padres se marcharon. Ellos siempre iban y venían mientras crecíamos, siempre ocupados con cuestiones artísticas, pero en esa época estaba Freddie para cuidarnos. Desde que murió, nunca se habían ido durante tanto tiempo como esta vez. Es como si hubiesen olvidado que todavía somos chicos, técnicamente.

No respondió. En su lugar, me alcanzó un vaso de agua con gas y hielo. Bebí un largo sorbo, que me resultó delicioso después de la comida salada. River se quitó los mocasines náuticos de lona. No llevaba calcetines y tenía lindos pies, especialmente para ser varón: fuertes, tostados, suaves y tan hermosos que casi no se podía seguir llamándolos pies. Bostezó, se dejó caer en el sofá amarillo del rincón y volvió a bostezar. Luego se inclinó hacia adelante y me tomó la mano.

—Oye, estuve conduciendo la mayor parte de la noche. Creo que es mejor que duerma una siesta antes de ir a ver la película.

—No tenemos que ir si no quieres —yo estaba concentrada en sus dedos, que cubrían a los míos. Era la primera vez que alguien me había sostenido la mano. Me refiero a un chico.

—No, quiero ver la película. *Casablanca* es una de mis preferidas. No dije eso solo para molestar a tu hermano —se detuvo y me dio un apretón en la mano. Al hacerlo, se le arrugó la frente, como si estuviera concentrado—. ¿Tienes que ir a ver cómo está Sunshine o crees que podrías acostarte aquí y dormir una siesta conmigo?

No le respondí. Ni siquiera lo pensé. Simplemente me deslicé en el sofá, apreté la espalda contra su pecho y dejé que me envolviera con los brazos. Aspiré su olor tibio y masculino, el aroma a hojas y aire de otoño, a medianoche, tomates y aceite de oliva. Apretó el rostro contra mi cabello y lo último que pensé antes de quedarme dormida era que hacía un maldito día que conocía a River, pero a quién diablos le importaba, a quién diablos realmente le importaba.

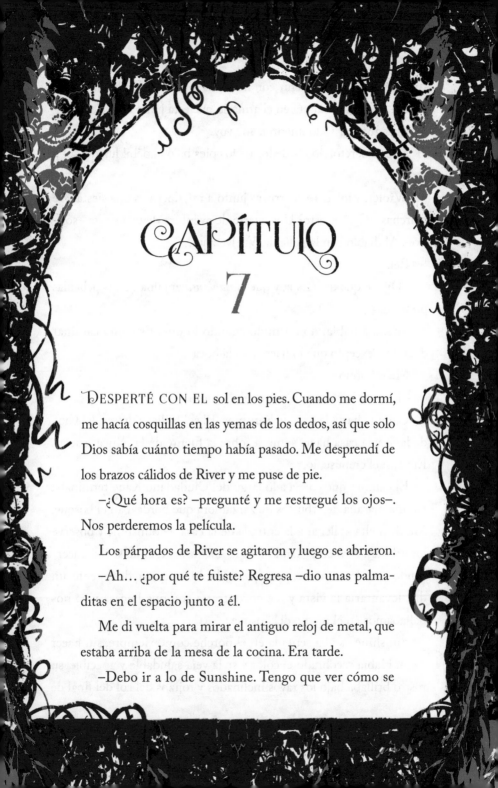

CAPÍTULO 7

DESPERTÉ CON EL sol en los pies. Cuando me dormí, me hacía cosquillas en las yemas de los dedos, así que solo Dios sabía cuánto tiempo había pasado. Me desprendí de los brazos cálidos de River y me puse de pie.

—¿Qué hora es? —pregunté y me restregué los ojos—. Nos perderemos la película.

Los párpados de River se agitaron y luego se abrieron.

—Ah… ¿por qué te fuiste? Regresa —dio unas palmaditas en el espacio junto a él.

Me di vuelta para mirar el antiguo reloj de metal, que estaba arriba de la mesa de la cocina. Era tarde.

—Debo ir a lo de Sunshine. Tengo que ver cómo se

encuentra y si quiere venir con nosotros a ver la película –hice una pausa–. Hay una canasta en el armario que está junto al refrigerador. ¿Podrás guardar todo mientras me voy?

Se estiró, retorció los dedos de los pies bajo la débil luz del sol y sonrió.

–Violet, Violet. Te acurrucas junto a mí, duermes una siesta y te marchas. ¿Qué es esto? Una suerte de aventura de una siesta –sonrió–. Al diablo con la película. Vuelve aquí.

Reí.

–Dijiste que querías ir, y que *Casablanca* era una de tus películas preferidas.

–Estaba hablando dormido cuando lo dije. Es como caminar dormido, excepto que lo haces con la boca.

Me reí otra vez.

–Prepara la canasta. Vuelvo en un momento.

Caminé hasta la casa de Sunshine. El sol brillaba detrás del Ciudadano y la casa hacía sombra sobre la fuente de las chicas sucias. Era casi el crepúsculo.

El camino que corría a lo largo del Ciudadano Kane terminaba en una maraña de arbustos de zarzamora que bordeaban el bosque. Me di vuelta al llegar a la entrada de la casa de Sunshine y observé los árboles. A veces, cuando caía la noche, sentía que se iban acercando muy lentamente, para que nadie lo notara. Y de repente, un día, levantaría la vista y me encontraría con que la casa y yo nos hallábamos en el medio del bosque.

Sunshine estaba sentada en el porche como siempre, sin hacer nada. Había recobrado el color y se la veía saludable y apacible, su rostro brillaba bajo los rayos inclinados y rojizos del sol del final de la tarde. No sabía cómo podía quedarse sentada ahí sin hacer nada mientras declinaba el día. Me gustara o no, tenía el temperamento artístico de mis padres y, si quedaban librados a su suerte, mis pensamientos comenzaban a ir de un lado a otro, a dar vueltas y enredarse. La cabeza de Sunshine debía funcionar de distinta forma. Tal vez, sus pensamientos ociosos eran más parecidos al hilito de agua de un arroyo. Un hilito de agua que corría junto a pájaros cantores, tazas de té rosadas, ardillas parlantes y casitas con techo de paja.

De pronto, le tuve envidia.

–Hola –saludé–. ¿Quieres venir a ver *Casablanca* con River y conmigo? Comienza en una hora.

Tomó un sándwich de tomate a medio comer del plato que tenía a sus pies y le dio un mordisco. Sin duda, la fruta había sido arrancada unos minutos antes de la planta de tomates en rama que se hallaba junto al porche. Cuando subí los peldaños, había notado que faltaba uno de los grandes y rojos.

–¿Luke va? –preguntó.

–Sí, pero Maddy también, así que no esperes que te ponga mucha atención. Robará un poco de vodka y espera pasar al segundo nivel de su relación, aunque ya no sé qué significa eso.

Sunshine levantó la mano y la agitó por encima de sus pechos.

–Creo que, en general, se refiere a estas chicas. Pero tal vez eso fue hace cien años, cuando nuestros padres eran chicos. Por lo que yo sé, el segundo nivel ahora significa recitar poesía juntos en una terraza, desnudos de la cintura para arriba.

Alcé las cejas.

Sunshine tragó otro bocado de su sándwich mientras negaba con la cabeza.

–No, Violet. Realmente no sé qué están haciendo los chicos hoy en día. ¿No notaste que paso la mayor parte del tiempo sentada en el porche o siguiéndolos a Luke y a ti a todas partes?

Sonrió levemente y yo hice lo mismo. Bebió el último sorbo del té helado y lo dejó en el borde del pasamanos.

–¿Y qué averiguaste del desconocido que vive ahora en tu casa de huéspedes?

–No le pedí que me mostrara el documento y no lo haré, porque ahora parecerá estúpido. Y es terrible para responder preguntas, así que casi sé menos de lo que sabía antes. ¿Sigues con la idea de embriagarlo y robarle la cartera?

Se reclinó en la hamaca y me miró. Sus ojos tenían una expresión aguda y sincera, algo raro en ella.

–No le gusto a River. Y que le gustara era una parte vital del plan –hizo una pausa–. ¿Le preguntaste si él también vio al sujeto de los dientes peludos?

Asentí.

–¿Y?

–Dijo que no vio nada.

–Lo imaginaba. No importa. Yo sé lo que vi –se quedó un momento en silencio–. Mira, vayan ustedes a ver la película. Yo me quedaré aquí. Quizás aparezca otro misterioso desconocido y quiera mudarse a *mi* casa de huéspedes.

Cuando regresé al Ciudadano, River ya tenía lista la canasta con el picnic. Tomamos el camino hacia el pueblo por tercera vez en las últimas ocho horas.

El parque estaba atestado de gente y el cielo, nublado, y oscurecía con rapidez. Llegamos tarde. Los primeros lugares estaban ocupados, pero la pantalla era lo suficientemente grande como para que se pudiera ver desde atrás de la plaza. Pasamos junto a un grupo de chicos de la escuela, pero ellos me ignoraron a mí y yo los ignoré a ellos. No se trataba de que nos odiáramos. No había suficiente pasión de ninguno de los dos lados como para que eso sucediera. Todos sabían que nuestros padres se habían marchado hacía mucho tiempo, pero no sabían si sentir lástima por nosotros, sin padres y ahora sin dinero, sentir envidia por nuestra libertad o burlarse de nosotros por tener problemas extraños, propios de los hijos de artistas. De modo que la gente no nos molestaba. Supongo que pensaban que éramos esnobs, como Daniel Leap.

A Luke le iba mejor que a mí, socialmente hablando. Era más atractivo y mucho menos sensible. Pero me parecía bien. De todas maneras, Freddie había sido la única persona con la cual me resultaba fácil hablar.

Y con River, descubrí de pronto. Con él, me sentía suficientemente cómoda.

Estiré la manta que traje de la casa en el suelo, bien lejos de mis compañeros de escuela. Distinguí a Gianni en medio del grupo. Era alto, moreno y había picardía en sus profundos ojos italianos, lo cual me gustaba. Cuando no estaba trabajando en la pizzería, a veces trabajaba con sus padres en el café y le agradaba hablarme de los granos de café de comercio justo, de *flat whites* y de la espuma perfecta para un capuchino. Solía perder la paciencia ante pedidos de sabores artificiales como chocolate blanco, y resultaba realmente encantador.

Gianni me pescó mirándolo, me saludó con la mano y sonrió. Le devolví la sonrisa.

A nuestra derecha, había un grupo de niñitos risueños: jugaban con un montón de yo-yos rojos y se divertían de esa manera tan espontánea que solo se puede encontrar en los niños. Me pregunté qué estarían haciendo en *Casablanca*. Supuse que sus padres los habrían echado de la casa después de cenar y ellos se habían encaminado hacia el centro del pueblo, el lugar donde estaba la acción. Me pregunté si se quedarían a ver la película y si conversarían durante toda la proyección. Pero luego decidí que realmente no me importaba.

River y yo atacamos las aceitunas, el queso y la baguette y observamos a los niños mientras comíamos. Eran seis varones, todos con yo-yos, y una niña con un aro tipo ula-ula. Reconocí a uno de los chicos. Tendría unos once años, cabello de un castaño rojizo oscuro y piel clara y pecosa. Lo había visto mucho por el pueblo y siempre me había impresionado lo serio que parecía, para ser un niño. A veces andaba con una banda de chicos pero, en general, andaba solo. Había comenzado a frecuentar la cafetería de vez en cuando y a beber café a muy temprana edad, como yo.

Después de unos minutos, un chico más grande emergió sigilosamente de la oscuridad, más allá de la plaza del pueblo, y comenzó a molestar a mis chicos con yo-yos. Tenía cabello oscuro y desgreñado y una expresión malvada en los ojos, como un perro salvaje y medio muerto de hambre. Tendría catorce años como máximo. Se burló de los chicos durante un rato, pero como ellos lo ignoraban, comenzó a empujarlos, a quitarles sus juguetes y mantenerlos fuera de su alcance.

River se llevó a la boca la última y jugosa aceituna Kalamata y luego se puso de pie. Se dirigió hacia el chico de cabello desgreñado y lo sujetó por su muñeca blanca y flacucha. El matón soltó el yo-yo que tenía en la mano. River le dijo algo y, súbitamente, el muchacho salió corriendo y se perdió en la noche sin decir una palabra.

River permaneció con el grupo y comenzó a enseñarles a los niños cómo funcionaba un yo-yo. Era bueno, lo usaba de manera fácil y natural, como si les hubiera hecho demostraciones a un millón de chicos y pudiera hacerlo con los ojos cerrados. Los niños escuchaban lo que decía con tanta atención que algunos hasta se inclinaban hacia él como para oír mejor.

Me quedé sentada observando a River y preguntándome distraídamente qué les estaría diciendo a los chicos, cuando la niña se acercó a mí y me extendió el aro. Era una niñita muy sonriente de ojos cafés y pelo negro y ensortijado. Me estiró el aro con una gran sonrisa y yo lo tomé y le devolví la sonrisa. Me metí dentro de él y lo hice girar alrededor de la cadera mientras movía el torso un poquito para un lado y un poquito para el otro, hasta que mi cuerpo empezó a recordar la sensación del ula-ula y giró por sí mismo.

La niña me observaba. Todos los demás tenían la vista fija sobre la pantalla, pues habían comenzado a pasar los títulos iniciales de la película. Mis caderas se movían y la falda amarilla se balanceaba y River me echó una mirada, el yo-yo en la mano. Los niños continuaban observándolo como si fuera la persona más genial del mundo, excepto mi muchacho de cabello cobrizo, que mantenía su expresión seria.

Le devolví el aro a la niña y le agradecí por permitirme usarlo. Sonrió y regresó con sus amigos.

River volvió, se sentó a mi lado y empezó a juguetear con algo entre las manos justo cuando divisé a Luke besando a Maddy, hacia un costado, debajo de un roble. Tenía una petaca en una mano y acariciaba la espalda de Maddy con la otra.

Ay, Luke. Eres una tremenda desilusión, pensé. Y luego me di cuenta de que era una estupidez, aunque lo hubiera dicho adentro de mi cabeza.

—Toma —susurró River, porque había comenzado la película. Sujetó mi mano, la dio vuelta, la palma hacia arriba y colocó algo encima—. Es un señalador, para tu Hawthorne.

Miré hacia abajo.

—No, no lo es —repuse con un susurro—. Es un billete de veinte dólares plegado con la forma de un elefante.

River sonrió.

—Me encanta el Origami.

Asentí.

—A mí también. Pero la mayoría de las personas pliega papel y no billetes de veinte.

Se encogió de hombros.

—No tenía papel. Mira, Violet, si alguna vez te quedas sin alimento o algo así, y yo no estoy cerca, puedes desplegarlo y usarlo. ¿De acuerdo?

—Está bien —susurré, porque no era muy orgullosa y guardé el señalador en el bolsillo de la falda.

River me miró e hizo un gesto de asentimiento, luego flexionó las rodillas, puso un brazo alrededor de ellas y se reclinó, listo para prestar atención a la película. Maldición. Era tan flexible y elegante. Yo todavía seguía atormentada por todos esos chicos de mi clase de gimnasia de los primeros años de la secundaria, con las rodillas demasiado grandes para las piernas blancas que asomaban de los shorts, los músculos de los muslos tan tensos desde los catorce años, que se movían como si alguien los hubiera desarmado y los hubiese vuelto a armar mal.

River era distinto a esos chicos. Hacía que mis entrañas se retorcieran y se deslizaran de esa forma tan agradable. River era algo… totalmente nuevo para mí.

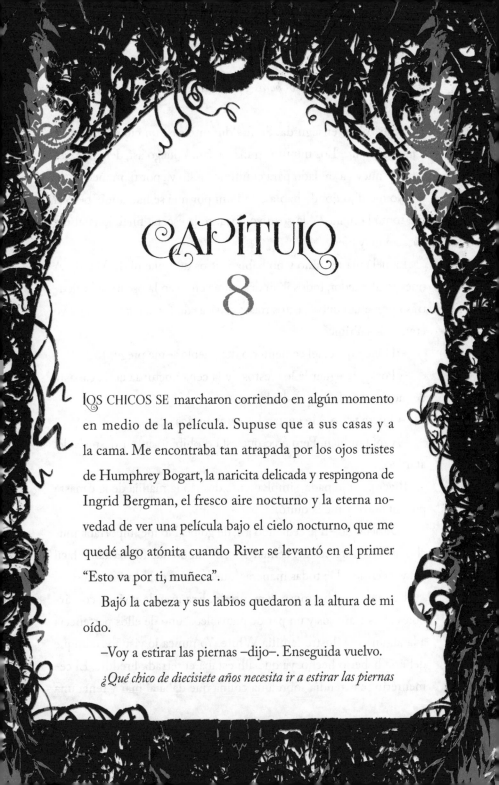

CAPÍTULO 8

LOS CHICOS SE marcharon corriendo en algún momento en medio de la película. Supuse que a sus casas y a la cama. Me encontraba tan atrapada por los ojos tristes de Humphrey Bogart, la naricita delicada y respingona de Ingrid Bergman, el fresco aire nocturno y la eterna novedad de ver una película bajo el cielo nocturno, que me quedé algo atónita cuando River se levantó en el primer "Esto va por ti, muñeca".

Bajó la cabeza y sus labios quedaron a la altura de mi oído.

—Voy a estirar las piernas —dijo—. Enseguida vuelvo.

¿Qué chico de diecisiete años necesita ir a estirar las piernas

durante una película de dos horas?, pensé mientras lo observaba cómo se marchaba.

Y no volvió enseguida. Se fue durante casi un cuarto de hora. *Tic-tac. Tic-tac.* Los minutos transcurrían. Y luego así, de golpe, estaba de nuevo a mi lado para el último "Esto va por ti, muñeca".

No me dijo dónde había estado ni por qué se había ido, pero sí me tomó la mano. Y la sostuvo durante la escena final, lo cual me pareció muy bien.

La película terminó y no había rastros de Luke ni de Maddy. A nuestro alrededor, todos iban desapareciendo en la oscuridad mientras se repetían unos a otros frases clásicas de *Casablanca*. River y yo éramos los últimos.

—¿Dónde queda el cementerio del pueblo? —me preguntó.

—¿Por qué? —guardé los restos de la cena nocturna en la canasta de picnic y me la colgué del brazo.

—Quiero verlo. Me gustan los cementerios.

—A mí también. Pero creo que está prohibido entrar después del atardecer.

River no dijo nada, simplemente deslizó la manija de la canasta por mi brazo y me la quitó.

—De acuerdo —dije cediendo así, de golpe. No me importaba mucho quebrar las leyes del cementerio, de modo que fue bastante fácil convencerme—. De todas maneras, queda cerca del camino a casa.

Eco tenía un hermoso cementerio. Era grande y viejo, con árboles altos y añosos y un par de mausoleos, uno de ellos pertenecía a la alguna vez ilustre familia White. Yo nunca lo visitaba, aunque debería haberlo hecho, ya que allí estaba enterrada Freddie. El cementerio se extendía sobre una colina que daba al mar y tenía una vista que rivalizaba con la del Ciudadano Kane. Era el tipo de lugar donde a alguien como Edgar Allan Poe le gustaría descomponerse… Hojas verdes y mojadas, y un silencio titilante y estrellado.

El cementerio estaba rodeado por una reja de hierro forjado, que pensé que estaría cerrada, pero no lo estaba. El portón estaba abierto de par en par. Entramos y River apoyó la canasta en la primera lápida que encontró. Luego se estiró y me tomó la mano. Sus dedos se entrelazaron con los míos y sentí un hormigueo ante el contacto de su piel.

—Me gustas, Violet —dijo en voz baja.

—Ni siquiera me conoces —repuse.

Me miró. Tenía su media sonrisa traviesa y torcida, que estaba volviéndose tan familiar.

—Sí, te conozco. Puedo enterarme de todo lo que necesito saber de una persona en dos minutos. Y nosotros ya hemos estado horas juntos —hizo una pausa—. Eres cauta, reflexiva, perceptiva. Más sincera que la mayoría. Odias la temeridad, pero eres impulsiva cuando te conviene. Odias a tu hermano y lo amas más que a nadie en el mundo. Desearías que tus padres regresaran, pero aprendiste a vivir sin ellos. Te gusta la paz, pero eres capaz de ejercer una bochornosa violencia si te presionan lo suficiente.

Hizo una pausa, otra vez, y me apretó la mano con tanta fuerza que casi me dolió.

—Pero lo que realmente me gusta (lo que te hace distinta) es que no quieres nada de mí. En absoluto.

—¿Eso crees?

—Sí. Y me resulta… tranquilizador.

No tenía respuesta para eso. Supuse que debería haberme puesto nerviosa, con eso de que ya supiera tanto de mí. Pero no fue así. Solo lo asimilé y traté de pensar la manera de disfrutarlo.

Trepamos una colina y nos detuvimos junto al mausoleo de los Glenship. Estaba cubierto de hiedra y era tan viejo que uno esperaba que las piedras se desmoronaran en cualquier momento y arrojaran al suelo una pila de huesos. La luna desapareció detrás de una nube y la oscuridad fue total. No podía ver nada, ni siquiera a River. Sin embargo, lo sentía cerca de mí. Lo escuchaba respirar. Sentía su calor…

Algo duro me golpeó la espalda. Me atraganté una vez, y otra más, caí, rodé y, de pronto, había sombras encima de mí, ahogándome, por todos lados, se movían y me sujetaban…

–*River* –grité. Manos frías aferraron la piel de mis piernas y unas palmas duras me oprimieron el estómago–. ¿Qué son? Están encima de mí, *Dios*…

–No pasa nada, Vi, no pasa nada. Son solo niños. Es un grupo de niños.

Dejé de retorcerme debajo de las manos y me quedé quieta. Contuve el aliento y abrí los ojos. Arriba, las nubes se abrieron. La luna brilló a través de ellas y distinguí a tres chicos. Los rostros eran blancos y lúgubres. Me miraban con furia, destellos de la pálida luz de luna se extendían por sus mejillas. Su aspecto era serio y horripilante, y no parecían niños en absoluto.

Sentí que un grito se agolpaba en mi garganta, un grito que no quería liberar. Yo no era una gritona, me negaba a serlo, eso quedaba para Sunshine y otras chicas, yo no iba a…

Otro rostro blanco brotó de la oscuridad y se inclinó sobre mí. Lo reconocí. Pertenecía a uno de los chicos del yo-yo del parque.

El que yo conocía. En su mano, una estaca improvisada de madera había reemplazado al yo-yo. Eran dos ramitas unidas en forma de cruz; los extremos, unas gruesas puntas afiladas y astilladas.

Miré las puntas y me estremecí.

—Por favor, no me apuñalen —exclamé mientras posaba la mirada en los ojos azules del muchacho, sabiendo que me había asustado como una estúpida por un grupo de niños y un par de ramitas. Sin embargo, no me importó, porque, diablos, estaba muerta de miedo.

—Dejen que se vaya —dijo el chico serio. Sacudió la cabeza con impaciencia y su cabello se agitó en el aire. Con los brazos cruzados y las piernas separadas, parecía un guerrero de *Los Siete Samuráis*.

»Yo les *dije*, el Demonio tiene ojos rojos que brillan en la oscuridad. ¿Miraron los ojos de ella? ¿Son rojos?

Tres chicos examinaron mi rostro y fruncieron el ceño.

—Muy bien —dijo el chico del yo-yo—. Sus ojos no son rojos. Así que déjenla ir.

Respiré profundamente mientras el niño que estaba sentado sobre mi estómago se levantaba. Los que estaban en mis piernas se pusieron de pie y se escabulleron en la oscuridad. Me enderecé, limpié la tierra de mi rostro y miré a River. Dos chicos apuntaban sus estacas hacia su garganta, pero las retiraron mientras yo observaba. River se levantó y se acercó a mí.

—¿Estás herida? —susurró.

Negué con un movimiento de cabeza y quité la hierba de mi falda. Me había rasguñado la pierna y unas gotitas de sangre brotaban de la piel de mi rodilla izquierda; salvo eso, estaba bien. River tomó mi mano y me ayudó a ponerme de pie.

El chico de cabello cobrizo nos miró fijamente.

—Soy Jack —dijo después de un momento. Tenía los ojos muy abiertos y no pestañaba. Me miró—. Te he visto antes en la cafetería. Eres Violet White, Luke es tu hermano y vives en la vieja mansión sobre el acantilado. Tu familia solía ser rica, pero ahora ya no lo es —se encogió de hombros—. Me compraste café una vez, cuando no me alcanzaba el dinero.

Asentí mientras recordaba.

—Sí, así fue —Jack entró un día al café con veintinueve centavos y trató de conseguir un café expreso. Pero yo me encontraba justo ahí y le compré un café expreso con crema, ya que, de todas maneras, no tenía dinero suficiente para ninguno de los dos.

—No deberían estar aquí —pronunció Jack en voz baja y seria, como la expresión de su rostro—. Estamos de patrulla. El Demonio robó a la hermana de Charlie hace un rato. Estaba jugando al lado de nosotros y luego el Demonio vino, le tomó la mano y desaparecieron. Y ahora, ella… *no está*.

Al decir eso, su voz se ahogó levemente. Le eché una mirada a River, pero su rostro se veía inexpresivo.

Jack se aclaró la garganta.

—Creo que volverá antes del amanecer para robar otro chico. El Demonio duerme todo el día, como los vampiros. Es por eso que tenemos estacas. Si duerme como un vampiro, se lo puede matar como a un vampiro. Con una estaca en el corazón.

Mientras Jack hablaba, los niños que nos atacaron comenzaron a formar un semicírculo alrededor de River y de mí. Se arrastraban desde las sombras, como lobos hambrientos.

—Quizá deberíamos clavarle una estaca, para estar seguros —dijo un niño bajito y delgado, de cabello negro y ensortijado, y una estaca que apuntaba a River–. Para ver si sangra. Yo escuché que el Demonio no sangra. Así que, de una manera u otra, lo descubriremos.

–Charlie, silencio. Yo estoy manejando esto –Jack señaló a dos de los chicos–. Danny, Ross y yo, los tres lo vimos. Isobel estaba jugando con el aro justo aquí, delante del mausoleo y él bajó rápidamente… y se la llevó –hizo una pausa y alzó la vista al cielo–. Tenía ojos rojos, ropa antigua y parecía un sujeto normal, salvo por los ojos rojos, la ropa de Acción de Gracias y el palo de serpiente. Pero yo me di cuenta de que era el Demonio.

–¿Ropa de Acción de Gracias? ¿Un palo de serpiente? –pregunté–. ¿Qué?

Jack me miró con los ojos entornados, tratando de decidir si yo le creía o no.

–Llevaba ropa antigua, como la que usan en Acción de Gracias, con capa y sombrero. Y tenía un palo, como un bastón, pero más alto.

–¿Como un bastón para caminar? –el que preguntó fue River.

–Sí, exactamente. Estaba tallado con la forma de una serpiente. Bajó rápidamente desde el cielo y… y se llevó a Isobel. Yo pensaba que el Demonio subiría desde debajo de la tierra, ya saben, desde el infierno, pero vino del cielo, como un ángel –Jack se detuvo y apretó sus puños pálidos y pecosos a ambos lados del cuerpo–. Y luego desapareció. Vamos a esperar aquí hasta que el Demonio vuelva. Y cuando vuelva, lo mataremos.

–Sí –dijeron los demás chicos–. Lo mataremos.

Era una especie de juego. Un juego infantil que había llegado demasiado lejos. Observé sus rostros serios, las estacas aferradas en cada mano, la forma antinatural en que cada uno se mantenía inmóvil y en silencio, algo raro en los niños. Me pregunté por la niñita, Isobel. ¿Acaso se habría ido a su casa sin avisarle a su hermano y el juego se originó a partir de allí? ¿O alguien realmente se la había llevado?

River se me acercó por detrás. Deslizó un brazo alrededor de mi cintura y me atrajo hacia él.

—Vámonos —susurró a mi oído—. Dejemos a los chicos con sus juegos. Solo se están divirtiendo. Estarán bien.

Sentí un cosquilleo en la piel del cuello donde River me rozó con su aliento. Lo ignoré. Me liberé de sus brazos y me arrodillé junto a Jack, que ahora estaba de rodillas y utilizaba un cuchillo para afilar el extremo de otra rama.

—Espero que encuentres a tu demonio. Ten cuidado, ¿sí? Se está haciendo tarde. Sería bueno que fueras pronto a tu casa. Es probable que tus padres se preocupen por ti.

—Tengo que hacer muchas más estacas —dijo sin levantar la vista—. Van a venir más chicos a ayudar. Isaac fue a buscarlos, a despertarlos. Le dije a Charlie que él podía ser el que apuñalara al Demonio, si... si su hermana está muerta. Dije que podía ser él.

Su voz se fue apagando a medida que se fue abstrayendo en su tarea. River me tomó de la cintura y nos alejamos hacia la reja. Le eché un último vistazo a Jack por encima del hombro. Estaba arrodillado en el suelo. No había existido ningún brillo de picardía, ni orgullo por la creación de su juego, ni júbilo nervioso por estar tan tarde fuera de su casa. Se había comportado con la misma seriedad de un joven soldado a punto de marchar a la guerra. Era inquietante, extraño. Me pregunté si debería contarle a alguien lo que estaba pasando. Intentar encontrar a algunos padres o llamar a la policía...

—Violet.

Me detuve y miré a River.

–Estarán bien. Es solo un juego.

No contesté.

River apoyó su cadera sobre la mía y mi espalda descansó contra el portón de hierro. Deslizó los dedos sobre la parte de atrás de mi cabeza y mis pensamientos... cesaron.

Me besó. Mis labios se encontraron con los suyos. Y. Dejé. De. Pensar. No pensé en que todavía era un extraño para mí. No pensé en el túnel, ni en Jack, ni en el Demonio, ni en nada. Mis labios se fundieron en mi corazón, que se fundió en mis piernas, que se fundió en la tierra que tenía debajo de mí.

Después, River me acompañó a casa bajo la luz de la luna. Ninguno habló.

Y todo fue casi perfecto.

CAPÍTULO 9

DORMÍ EN LA casa de huéspedes.

Había comenzado la noche en mi propia cama. Pero desperté en algún momento antes del amanecer y me encontré bajando descalza los fríos escalones de mármol de la imponente escalera, caminando por el césped cubierto de rocío que bordea el derruido invernadero hasta llegar a la cabaña y a la cama de River.

No sé por qué. Simplemente lo hice. River dijo que yo le gustaba y él me gustaba. Me hacía acordar a… mí, de alguna manera. Eso podrá sonar estúpido durante el día, pero en la noche, cuando estás semidormida, resulta completamente razonable.

Estaba echado de costado. Los ojos dormidos, la nariz recta y la boca torcida brillaban bajo la luz de la luna, que entraba por la ventana. Levanté las sábanas y me deslicé junto a él. Se despertó el tiempo suficiente como para acercarse a mí, rodearme con sus brazos y hundir el rostro en mi cuello.

Si lo sorprendió que yo me encontrara allí, estaba demasiado dormido como para demostrarlo.

De modo que pasé la noche con su cuerpo acurrucado junto al mío. Me dormí cerca de él y desperté junto a él. Dos veces en veinticuatro horas.

Ya era de día.

River era una de esas personas mágicas que dormía como una criatura del bosque o como si estuviera bajo un hechizo. Dulce, bonito y silencioso, con pestañas lustrosas y la boca en una leve trompita. Junto a él, yo me sentía arrugada, enredada y muy pero muy real. Salí de la cama y me dirigí a la ventana. Afuera, un día gris y tormentoso, olas grises y tormentosas, cielo gris y tormentoso. Las nubes eran oscuras, gruesas y malas, y el aire olía a sal y a esperanza.

No podía ver el horizonte a través de la densa neblina. Casi ni podía ver las olas. Algunas personas podrían sentirse atrapadas ante esta situación, supongo, pero yo no. Me había criado con el mar dentro del jardín. Era tan natural como una verja blanca de madera.

Al estirarme, el dolor se desató en la rodilla sobre la cual me había caído la noche anterior.

De niña había jugado a juegos nocturnos cuando venían mis primos a visitarnos. Jugábamos a "Quemen a la bruja" en los árboles de atrás del Ciudadano y mi corazón latía a toda velocidad hasta que encontraba un lugar donde esconderme. Y después venía la espera aterradora e interminable hasta que alguien me encontraba, y los gritos de "¡Bruja!" y "¡Quémenla!" resonaban en el aire frío y nocturno...

Aun así.

Estaba intranquila por esos chicos escalofriantes con las estacas y la extraña descripción del Demonio. Y la afirmación de que una niñita había desaparecido.

Me estiré otra vez y alisé el camisón de seda que llevaba. Era de Freddie. Lo había tomado de la cómoda unos días antes. En ese momento, todavía olía a perfume francés, pero ahora olía a River.

—¿Qué diablos sucedió aquí?

Me di vuelta y encontré a Luke, que me observaba desde la puerta de la habitación.

River despertó con el sonido de la voz de mi hermano. Se desperezó y sonrió.

—No pasó nada, Luke —contesté—, aunque no sea asunto tuyo. ¿No se te ocurrió golpear la puerta? Esta ya no es tu casa. River la alquiló y no puedes irrumpir cuando te da la gana.

—*Sí* golpeé, pero nadie respondió. Y esta mañana no te encontré, Violet. Empezaba a preocuparme. Si mi hermana melliza no está en su cama por primera vez en toda su vida —sus ojos se movieron velozmente alrededor de la habitación, se posaron un instante en River antes de regresar a mí—, entonces tengo derecho a ir a buscarla.

Sonreí ante el comentario.

—Luke, ¿acaso eso significa que te importo?

No me devolvió la sonrisa.

—No.

—Buen día —dijo River, relajado y tranquilo, como si hubiera estado esperando que mi hermano lo despertara. Y casi le agradara—. ¿Alguien quiere café? Ayer compré un buen expreso.

Luke asintió.

—Sí, sí. Quizá más tarde. Pero primero, tengo novedades. Esta mañana fui al pueblo porque Maddy tenía un turno temprano en la cafetería y, diablos, el lugar estaba en llamas. Se perdió una niñita. Desapareció anoche en el cementerio. Hay policías y grupos de búsqueda por todas partes. Y hasta algunos reporteros que vinieron de Portland. Es una locura.

Me llevé la mano al corazón. Isobel, la hermana de Charlie. Miré a River. Su rostro estaba calmo, la mirada interesada pero distante. Me volví a mi hermano.

—¿Una niñita? ¿Del cementerio? Anoche, River y yo…

Luke agitó la mano.

—Cállate, hermana. Ni siquiera llegué a la mejor parte. Parece que, aparentemente, unos chicos vieron al que se llevó a la niña. Y… aquí viene… esos chicos andan diciendo que fue el Demonio —echó a reír—. El *Demonio*. ¿Lo pueden creer? Uno de los reporteros que se encontraba en la cafetería era Jason Foster. Era el mejor corredor de la secundaria, Violet, ¿lo recuerdas? Corrió en las estatales y todo. Bueno, la cuestión es que ahora es reportero y, hombre, quedó encantado con esta historia. El Demonio. Qué pueblo que tenemos. Portland va a devorar esta noticia. *Chicos del insignificante y atrasado pueblo de Eco ven al príncipe de las tinieblas en el cementerio local.*

River se estiró lenta y prolongadamente, como un gato.

—Parece que desaparecen muchos niños en este pueblo —comentó en forma casual y despreocupada mientras se reclinaba con los brazos doblados detrás de la cabeza y una sonrisa en el rostro–. ¿Primero Blue y ahora el Demonio?

Abrí la boca para contarle a Luke acerca de Jack y su banda de chicos blandiendo estacas cuando Sunshine apareció en la puerta de la habitación, el cabello largo y castaño balanceándose sobre un vestido blanco de jersey que envolvía sus curvas de manera perfecta.

–Hola –saludó mientras echaba un vistazo a mi camisón arrugado y a River, el torso desnudo, todavía en la cama–. Como no había nadie en el Ciudadano, vine para acá. ¿Se enteraron de lo que está sucediendo en el pueblo? Fui a comprar leche de almendra para el desayuno y todos andaban corriendo y hablando de una niña que desapareció y comentando que el cementerio está lleno de chicos con estacas de madera que intentan matar al Demonio como si fuera un vampiro. ¿Acaso llegó el Apocalipsis y yo no me enteré?

Los cuatro fuimos a la cocina y River preparó café y omelettes. Estaba muy callado, totalmente concentrado en freír los huevos, de modo que yo fui quien le contó a Luke sobre nuestra visita al cementerio de la noche anterior. Pensé que Sunshine se enfadaría, considerando que había tenido alucinaciones con Blue en el túnel hacía menos de veinticuatro horas y que a él se lo acusaba de ser un ladrón de niños, pero ella parecía haber superado el asunto. Rio junto con Luke ante la idea de que Satán se encontrara en Eco.

–Como si el Demonio no tuviera un mejor lugar donde pasar el tiempo que nuestro cementerio –comentó–. Podría estar vagando por los sórdidos callejones de París o robando almas en alguna tumba de Nueva Orleans o correteando por el barrio rojo de Amsterdam. Pero no… el tonto elige Eco.

Luke sonrió mientras sus ojos percibían la forma en que los pechos, el segundo nivel de Sunshine, se balanceaban en su vestido cuando reía.

–Hablando de la Ciudad Luz –acoté–, Luke y yo vimos *Un americano en París* la semana pasada en la plaza del pueblo.

–Una estupidez –dijo Luke.

–Mentiroso –le alcancé un omelette–. Te encantó. Era la historia de un pintor pobre que vivía en París, y estabas fascinado. A propósito, vi que tu paquete con información sobre la Sorbonne llegó por correo hace unos días. Hermano, ¿estás pensando en enviar una solicitud de ingreso?

Luke fingió no escucharme.

Dibujé una sonrisa estilo River, muy pícara.

–Bueno… No sé por qué querrías estudiar en París de todas maneras, cuando Italia fue la verdadera cuna del arte. Papá siempre decía…

–Tú y el Renacimiento italiano, Vi. Eres igual a papá. Por más que digan lo que digan de Italia, los estilos de ambos evolucionaron a partir de la rapiña del Impresionismo francés. Mamá lo sabe. Yo lo sé. Fin de la discusión.

Sonreí, aunque esta vez sin picardía. Siempre me agradaba lograr que Luke hablara de arte. Ver el paquete de la Sorbonne me había emocionado hasta las lágrimas.

Comí un bocado de omelette. Estaba delicioso, salado y mantecoso, con la sorpresa y la fuerza de la cebolla picada y un poquito de Parmesano rallado.

Pensé que Luke podía estar enojado con River porque me encontró en su cama. El otoño pasado, me encerró en el vestidor de la habitación azul de huéspedes con Sean Fry, el chico arrogante de mentón cuadrado. Luke y Sunshine no cesaron de reírse mientras yo me movía a los tumbos arrojando perchas al suelo y esquivando los labios intrépidos y los brazos impacientes de Fry. Pero una vez que me dejó salir y Fry me arrinconó en la cocina y lo intentó nuevamente, mi hermano le dio un puñetazo en la cara.

Sin embargo, Luke no estaba enojado con River. Creo que le agradaba. Hasta le preguntó cómo cocinaba los huevos. Luke no tenía el menor interés en la cocina. Podía hacer un sándwich y eso era todo. De modo que lo tomé como una buena señal.

Luego del desayuno, regresé al Ciudadano Kane y me di una ducha en el enorme baño del primer piso, que quedaba frente al dormitorio de Freddie. De suelo a techo, las paredes estaban cubiertas con cerámicos cuadrados color verde esmeralda, que Freddie había elegido mucho tiempo atrás, y el polvoriento candelabro proyectaba fragmentos de luz a través del baño, que hacían bailar el polvo.

Me puse un viejo vestido de algodón con flores, que Freddie solía ponerse para cocinar. Me hacía sentir como si ella estuviera a mi lado haciendo limonada con jengibre y ahuyentando todas las cosas malas.

Sunshine habló conmigo mientras me cambiaba. Me hizo preguntas acerca de River y del hecho de que estuviera en su cama. Le contesté vagamente, al estilo River, mientras mi mente repasaba todo lo que había sucedido la noche anterior.

River. River. River.

Mientras me vestía, había decidido dirigirme al pueblo y ayudar en la búsqueda de Isobel. Y también quería encontrar a Jack y hablar con él. Estaba muy segura de que nadie lo tomaría en serio, y quería hacerle más preguntas acerca de lo que había visto.

Acerca del Demonio de ojos rojos.

Sunshine no tenía nada que hacer y quiso venir y, antes de que me diera cuenta, los cuatro nos dirigíamos al pueblo.

Eco era un caos. Las calles que rodeaban la plaza principal estaban atestadas de autos de policía y de gente. En la densa niebla que llegaba desde el mar, todos tenían aspecto grave, el ceño fruncido y expresión de derrota. Se movían en grupos, encorvados bajo los paraguas, aun cuando la lluvia era más bien una neblina inmóvil.

El café desbordaba de gente y la fila llegaba casi hasta la puerta, pero Sunshine y Luke entraron de todas maneras. River y yo nos quedamos afuera. Se había puesto una camisa y pantalones de lino limpios y, a pesar de la niebla, se veía relajado y hermoso como un mar turquesa en un día de sol. A mis espaldas, escuché fragmentos de una tensa conversación entre un grupo de policías:

—*Todo esto me produce escalofríos, todos esos niños con estacas…*

—*Las ideas pueden ser contagiosas, como la gripe…*

—*Se propagó con tanta rapidez. Creo que todos los chicos del pueblo están ahí…*

—*¿Se sabe algo de la niña?*

—*…alguien cuenta la historia de un secuestrador y, antes de que puedas reaccionar, tienes una epidemia en las manos. La ilusión colectiva es un hecho documentado.*

—*Blue Hoffman: esa historia todavía se mantiene viva…*

—*Lo que tenemos que hacer es ponerle las manos encima al que inició todo. Créanme, un solo niño es el responsable de lo ocurrido. Lo atrapamos y todo esto se cae a pedazos.*

Tomé la mano de River.

—Jack —dije, y él asintió.

El cementerio era peor que el centro del pueblo. Las personas formaban una fila del lado de afuera de la verja, apretadas como mosquitos en una noche húmeda, y el zumbido débil de las voces hacía que el aire pareciera tenso, como si estuviera atado con fuerza. River y yo nos deslizamos junto a una mujer de expresión preocupada, que sujetaba con fuerza la muñeca de un niño pequeño. El chico sostenía una estaca de ramitas, igual a la de Jack, y le rogaba a la mujer que lo soltara.

Al cruzar el portón, se me paralizó el corazón. Había niños por todos lados. *Por todos lados.* Niñas y niños arriba de los árboles y detrás de las lápidas, pequeñas sombras en la niebla. Todos empuñaban estacas. Y todos ignoraban el llamado de sus padres para que regresaran a su hogar. Los adultos deambulaban por el cementerio como ovejas aturdidas, gritando nombres como Zach, Ann, Jamie y Charlotte, mientras los niños entraban y salían velozmente de la neblina sin escucharlos.

Si la noche anterior los seis chicos se habían comportado en forma seria y espeluznante, como si no fuesen niños, bueno, eso no era nada comparado con observar todo un maldito *ejército* de críos blandiendo estacas como si fueran armas. Y el hecho de que todos se hubieran unido para cazar al Demonio resultaba escalofriante y estaba sencillamente *mal*. Cuando juegan, los niños tienden a dividirse en bandos. Algunos van a las hamacas, otros a las trepadoras, unos golpean a chicos menores y algunos fingen estar peleando con dragones en una cueva llena de oro. Pero, en este caso, *todos* los chicos estaban cazando al Demonio. Me pareció incomprensible.

Se me erizó la piel de los brazos. Miré a River. Su rostro estaba sombrío. Sombrío y tormentoso como el cielo. Pero lo peor era que tenía expresión… sorprendida, los ojos muy abiertos, más que de costumbre, y un poco… perdidos.

En él, resultaba un aspecto desconcertante.

Volteé hacia la izquierda y distinguí a una niñita escondida detrás de una gran lápida. Su cabello negro estaba encrespado en la neblina húmeda y sus ojos negros se movían de izquierda a derecha, de izquierda a derecha.

Me arrodillé junto a ella.

–Hola –le dije–. ¿Estás aquí para matar al Demonio?

Asintió.

–¿Sabes dónde está Jack? –le pregunté–. Necesito hablar con él.

Volvió a asentir.

–Está arriba, junto al mausoleo Glenship. Está ahí desde anoche –hablaba rápido y en voz baja, como si no quisiera que alguien la escuchara–. Él piensa que será el primer lugar adonde irá el Demonio, porque fue ahí donde lo vio por última vez. Pero hace horas que amaneció y yo ni siquiera sé qué se supone que estoy buscando. Lo único que dijo Jack es que tenía ojos rojos y estaba vestido como los peregrinos, ¿pero qué significa eso?

La niña levantó los ojos, observó el cielo gris y se estremeció.

Yo también observé el cielo gris. Me pregunté qué habría dicho Freddie si escuchaba que el Demonio era un hombre de ojos rojos, vestido de negro, volaba por el cielo nocturno y secuestraba niños.

94

No podía decidir si se hubiera reído de la historia o si la hubiese creído.

Tal vez la hubiese creído.

Dirigí la mirada hacia River, pero él estaba observando a un grupo de seis policías que ingresaba por el portón. Un hombre alto y rubio, de unos cuarenta y tantos años, se llevó un megáfono a la boca y comenzó a hablar.

—ESCUCHEN, CHICOS. TODOS TIENEN QUE IRSE A SUS CASAS. AHORA. ESTAMOS OCUPÁNDONOS DE UNA NIÑA QUE HA DESAPARECIDO Y NO QUEREMOS MÁS PROBLEMAS. SI ENCONTRAMOS A ALGUIEN MERODEANDO POR EL CEMENTERIO, LO ARRESTAREMOS. REPITO: VAYAN A SUS CASAS O LOS VAMOS A ESPOSAR Y LOS LLEVAREMOS A LA CÁRCEL.

Era una amenaza vacía, pero los chicos la creyeron.

Decenas de pequeñas siluetas comenzaron a salir de la niebla y dirigirse hacia la salida. Sin embargo, sus pequeños rostros se veían molestos y abatidos, y noté que se llevaron consigo las estacas cuando se marcharon.

Busqué a Jack, pero no lo vi. De todas maneras, era el menos indicado para creer el engaño del policía.

Se acercó una camioneta blanca y estacionó afuera del portón. Una mujer de baja estatura y cabello largo bajó de un salto. Atravesó el portón y nos apuntó con una cámara del EQUIPO DE NOTICIAS DEL CANAL 3.

—Diablos —dijo River—. Justo lo que necesitaba. Vamos, Vi. Larguémonos de acá.

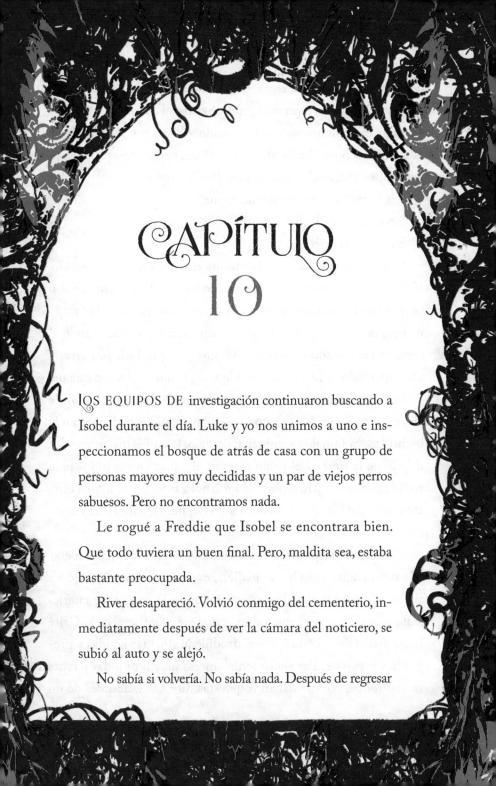

CAPÍTULO 10

LOS EQUIPOS DE investigación continuaron buscando a Isobel durante el día. Luke y yo nos unimos a uno e inspeccionamos el bosque de atrás de casa con un grupo de personas mayores muy decididas y un par de viejos perros sabuesos. Pero no encontramos nada.

Le rogué a Freddie que Isobel se encontrara bien. Que todo tuviera un buen final. Pero, maldita sea, estaba bastante preocupada.

River desapareció. Volvió conmigo del cementerio, inmediatamente después de ver la cámara del noticiero, se subió al auto y se alejó.

No sabía si volvería. No sabía nada. Después de regresar

de la búsqueda, me senté en los escalones del frente de la casa. No me dediqué a leer, solo a esperar. Esperar y rogarle a Freddie.

Luke me dijo que había ahuyentado a River con mi mirada de sabelotodo y por el hecho de ser una chica, pero, gracias a Dios, ya habíamos cobrado el alquiler en efectivo. Lo ignoré.

Las horas transcurrieron lentamente.

Sin noticias de Isobel.

Sin noticias de River.

Una vez que oscureció, los niños regresaron al cementerio. Volvieron furtivamente cuando sus padres estaban dormidos. Lo sé, porque yo también estaba ahí. Reuní uno por uno los fragmentos de valentía que encontré dentro de mí y fui caminando al cementerio cuando cayó la noche. Imaginé que Jack aún estaría ahí, esperando al Demonio. Pero lo que encontré, una vez que me deslicé sigilosamente por el portón del frente, fueron decenas de chicos otra vez en sus puestos, los rostros pálidos brillando en la oscuridad. Solo había sombras y silencio, los muertos enterrados debajo de la tierra y el ruido distante del mar en sus oídos para toda la eternidad. Me deslicé de un árbol a otro, de un niño a otro, manteniendo siempre el océano a mi izquierda, para saber dónde me encontraba.

Cada tanto, lo sentía a *él*, al Demonio, respirando en mi cuello. Me daba vuelta y no había nadie… excepto un niñito callado y sigiloso con dos ramas afiladas en las manos. Traté de preguntarles a algunos de ellos si sabían dónde podía encontrar a Jack. Grité hacia arriba de los árboles, me arrodillé junto a las lápidas y pregunté y pregunté. Pero ellos tenían ojeras muy profundas y tanta *concentración*. No me daban respuestas directas y, después de un rato, comencé a pensar que me estaban siguiendo. Acosándome. Asustándome deliberadamente.

El corazón empezó a golpearme el pecho con tanta fuerza que ahogó el sonido de las olas que chocaban abajo contra las rocas. Era hora de marcharme.

Y entonces oí algo detrás de mí. Pies. Piecitos sobre la piedra.

Volteé y ahí estaban. Dos niños y una niña en una hilera a tres metros de mí. Sostenían las ramas afiladas y me observaban.

—No tienes una estaca —dijo la niña—. El Demonio te llevará.

Se acercó un paso más y los otros niños la imitaron. Nos quedamos cara a cara, sin movernos, solamente observándonos. Una brisa me rozó la mejilla y me agitó el cabello. El viento salado era suave pero frío. *Frío*. Como nadar de noche en el mar. Como dedos húmedos y pegajosos trepándote por el cuello.

Me estremecí.

—¿Lo sientes? —preguntó la niña—. ¿Al Demonio?

Asentí.

—Es mejor que te escapes —repuso.

Escapé.

Cuando llegué a casa, cerré la enorme puerta del frente de un empujón y la trabé. Me deslicé hacia el suelo, la espalda contra la madera. Me sentía estúpida y avergonzada. Pero maldición, la imagen de esos niños en la oscuridad, con estacas en la mano, mirando fijamente el cielo, siguiéndome de una tumba a la otra…

Me dolían el pecho y los oídos, como si hubiera estado nadando bajo el agua a gran profundidad. Respiré tres veces y luego comencé la búsqueda.

Lo hacía de vez en cuando, después de que Freddie murió:

deambulaba por el Ciudadano Kane en la oscuridad. Ya había examinado su dormitorio infinitas veces, y la biblioteca, la cocina y el ático.

Esta vez, comencé por el sótano, revisé los rincones cubiertos de moho en busca de ladrillos sueltos y puertas trampa. Luego, subí a los dormitorios que no se habían utilizado en años y abrí cómodas y roperos y me arrastré debajo de las camas. Golpeé las paredes esperando escuchar un sonido hueco y volteé los cuadros. Había hecho eso antes muchas veces y volvería a hacerlo.

Dejé que se incrustaran en mi alma el polvo, las botellas de vino olvidadas, las alfombras raídas y las cortinas deshechas hasta que estuve tan paranoica y enardecida como Daniel Leap desvariando en la plaza del pueblo. Deseaba encontrar las antiguas cartas de Freddie, pero me habría contentado con cualquier cosa. Un diario, el comienzo de la trama de una historia de misterio y asesinato, fragmentos de mala poesía escritos en una servilleta amarillenta. Cualquier cosa que perteneciera a Freddie. Cualquier cosa que la reviviera, aunque fuera por un segundo.

Tenía que quedar *algo* más, aparte de la ropa que colgaba en el vestidor. Nadie vive toda una vida y no deja algún fragmento de ella cuando se va, además de un puñado de vestidos. ¿Acaso había quemado sus objetos personales en esas últimas semanas antes de morir? Me negaba a creerlo.

Tenía que haber algo.

Y había. Pero no era lo que yo quería, porque formulaba más preguntas y no daba ninguna respuesta.

El Ciudadano tenía un ático que abarcaba todo el largo de la casa. De pequeña, solía pasar horas allí arriba explorando todos los viejos y extraños arcones y baúles que eran vaya uno a saber de hacía cuánto. Ahí encontré el baúl negro, el que tenía la botella vacía de ginebra y una tarjetita roja que, al abrirla, decía: *Freddie, tú fuiste la primera en saber y la última en juzgar. Prometí que nunca te quemaría. Lo dije en serio entonces y lo digo en serio ahora. Pase lo que pase. Amor por siempre. Yo.*

Estaba escrito con la letra de un hombre elegante y educado. Debajo de la carta, había tres vestidos blancos de verano, doblados cuidadosamente, una cruz negra de madera y dos mechones de cabello: rubio claro y castaño. Pero no había cartas de Freddie. Ni una. Recordaba bien el baúl, porque lo había abierto una tarde calurosa de verano pocos días después de su muerte, pero el aire en el interior del baúl era fresco. Guardé la botella vacía y la tarjeta roja, empujé el baúl hacia el rincón más alejado y lo dejé en paz.

Pero a esta altura ya había intentado todo, así que pensé *qué más da.*

Estaba subiendo al desván cuando noté que había despertado a Luke con todo el ruido que estaba haciendo. Podía oír sus fuertes pisadas caminando por el piso de arriba. Me alcanzó en la tercera escalera, la que usaban los sirvientes antes de que yo naciera y cuando todavía teníamos sirvientes. Era angosta, con peldaños de madera gastados, y no tenía pasamanos. Luke echó una mirada hacia abajo, yo me encontraba en el descanso del primer piso. Tenía el cabello rojizo peinado hacia arriba, se veía cansado y más joven, más parecido al hermano de hacía cinco años, cuando Freddie murió.

–Violet –dijo parpadeando–, ¿por qué rayos andas corriendo por la casa y dando portazos a las tres de la madrugada?

–Explorando. Estoy explorando –subí al último escalón, me senté y suspiré.

—Estás explorando. Muy bien —se sentó a mi lado y acomodó su cuerpo en el angosto peldaño. Sus pies desnudos quedaron alineados junto a los míos, y brillaban con un color inquietante bajo el delgado rayo de luz de luna que ingresaba por la ventana de arriba: no dejaba ingresar mucha luz, porque la mitad estaba tapada por la desvencija-da escalera caracol que conducía al ático.

»Otra vez estabas buscando las cartas de Freddie. ¿Tan molesta estás con la partida de River? —preguntó al ver que yo no decía nada.

Apoyé las manos en las rodillas y dejé que el cabello me cayera sobre el rostro.

—No —mentí—. Estaba pensando dónde está la niñita —giré la ca-beza y lo miré—. Pero ahora que lo mencionas, es cierto que la parti-da de River me pone un poco furiosa.

Luke rio.

—¿Sabes algo? River dijo que yo era capaz de ejercer violencia si me presionaban lo suficiente. ¿Estás de acuerdo?

Tardó en contestar. Luego se encogió de hombros.

—Normalmente, querría moler a golpes a un tipo que comparte la cama contigo y luego se marcha. Pero River me gusta. Tiene algo especial.

—Así es —asentí.

Hice una pausa.

—Volví al cementerio —comenté—. Los niños estaban otra vez allí y me rodearon sigilosos con sus estacas y sus caritas fantasmales. Fue aterrador. No pude soportarlo y salí huyendo.

Luke volvió a reír. Fue una especie de risita ahogada que rara-mente le escuchaba.

—Hermana, esta ha sido una noche muy larga para ti.

Sonreí levemente, porque era cierto.

—¿Siempre eres tan amable en medio de la noche? Tal vez debería despertarte más seguido.

—Por favor, no. Algunos nos despertamos temprano —me sonrió y luego se puso de pie, bostezó y comenzó a caminar hacia su habitación—. Tarde o temprano, River regresará —comentó por encima del hombro—. Puedes estar segura.

Mi hermano tenía razón.

River entró con el coche en la temprana calma que antecedía al amanecer. Lo supe porque estaba despierta y esperándolo como una estúpida.

Se bajó del auto, caminó hacia mí con su clásico contoneo y esbozó su maldita sonrisa torcida. Sus ojos color café no se veían tan relajados y tranquilos como la última vez que se encontró conmigo en los escalones del frente. Y su cabello no tenía raya al medio, estilo retro… estaba hecho un revoltijo y enredado, como si hubiera estado pasando sus manos por él nerviosamente. Seguía siendo River, elegante y despreocupado, pero había algo extraño en su expresión, algo que no había estado ahí antes.

—Hola, Violet —dijo. Sin embargo, su voz brotó más despreocupada que nunca.

—Hola —repuse con la misma tranquilidad, aunque lo que quería hacer era ponerme de pie, inclinar la cabeza hacia atrás y gritarle al cielo por lo que había sucedido con los chicos, por lo del cementerio, por el Demonio, por la niña desaparecida, y por el hecho de que él se hubiese marchado sin decir una palabra cuando era el primer chico al que había besado y, maldición, eso te afecta.

Pero no quería permitir que River me viera tan… *conmovida*. Tenía la impresión de que le agradaría; le agradaría verme descontrolada. Además, él ya había notado la traicionera chispa de felicidad que había en mis ojos.

—¿Los niños regresaron al cementerio? —River no perdió el tiempo en charlas de cortesía. Me pareció bien, porque yo tampoco quería hacerlo.

—Sí, una vez que oscureció —no le expliqué cómo lo sabía.

Extendió la mano.

—Bueno, me parece que ya ha durado demasiado, ¿no crees? ¿Quieres ayudarme a terminar con esto?

Asentí y le tomé la mano.

Para cuando llegamos al portón del cementerio, todavía no le había preguntado adónde había ido y por qué. Y él no me brindó esa información. De todas formas, seguramente me habría mentido. Y ahora tenía su mano en la mía y sus largos dedos se entrelazaban con los míos mientras mis entrañas pasaban de blanco y negro a multicolor.

El amanecer se estaba desvistiendo, pateando sus rosados y violetas sobre el horizonte. Vi otra vez a la niña. La de cabello negro y rizado. Estaba acurrucada detrás de una lápida que pertenecía a un muchacho joven que se había *Ahogado en el mar* mucho tiempo atrás, las letras de su nombre caídas en el olvido por la erosión.

River se arrodilló junto a la niña, apoyó su mano en la de ella y le quitó suavemente la estaca del puño cerrado.

—Vete a tu casa —le dijo—. Nosotros encontraremos a Isobel. Tus padres se despertarán pronto y se preocuparán. Vete a casa. No hay un Demonio.

La pequeña se puso de pie, miró largamente a River y luego salió corriendo hacia el portón.

River partió en dos la estaca y la arrojó al bosque. Comenzamos a subir por la colina hacia el mausoleo. La temprana neblina matinal había empezado a soplar otra vez desde el mar, y en algunas partes era tan densa que parecía que caminábamos a través de un suéter de lana gris mojado. Nunca antes me había molestado la niebla, pero, por alguna razón, empecé a sentirme como si me estuvieran ahogando. Me concentré en respirar profundamente el aire marino y la sensación desapareció.

Al lado de la tumba había unos veinte chicos. Mientras nos aproximábamos, nos echaron miradas cansadas y fantasmales, como en una fotografía de refugiados de guerra en las páginas de un *National Geographic* cubierto de moho.

Seis horas antes, había buscado a Jack en el cementerio, pero no lo había encontrado. Sin embargo, ahora estaba ahí, de pie sobre el mausoleo Glenship, una pila de estacas a sus pies, la mirada dirigida hacia el cielo. River lo llamó y bajó la vista hacia nosotros, pero no se movió.

—Jack, ¿puedes bajar? —preguntó River—. Quiero hablar contigo.

Jack apuntó con el dedo a uno de los chicos.

—Danny, dejo mi puesto. Es tu turno de vigilar.

Sujetó un puñado de lianas y bajó balanceándose.

Danny, el muchacho de cabello rubio, trepó y ocupó el lugar de Jack, la cabeza inclinada hacia el cielo.

Jack se restregó los ojos y miró alrededor. Se veía pálido y cansado. Su pelo castaño cobrizo estaba enmarañado, tenía trocitos de hojas, como si hubiera estado rodando en la tierra. Había una mancha de tierra mezclada con las pequitas oscuras que cubrían su rostro y tenía los hombros caídos.

—Nick —dijo Jack mirando a un niñito de cabello castaño oscuro—, puedes reemplazar a Jenny en la esquina sudoeste. Logan, ¿podrías ir a ver cómo está Holly? Se asusta si se queda sola mucho tiempo.

Los chicos se alejaron rápidamente. Jack volvió a restregarse los ojos.

—Hola —dijo.

Lo saludé con una inclinación de cabeza. Me distraje con la montañita de estacas que había en la base del mausoleo. Eran decenas. Tal vez, cientos.

Jack se volvió hacia River.

—Eres el sujeto al que casi clavamos una estaca.

—Sí.

—El que nos enseñó a usar los yo-yos y el que nos dijo que fuéramos al cementerio a buscar al Demonio.

Levanté la cabeza abruptamente. Le eché una dura mirada a Jack y luego a River. Pero ninguno de los dos me devolvió la mirada.

—Bueno, ¿qué quieres? —preguntó Jack con voz suave y cansada—. ¿También intentarás convencernos de irnos a nuestras casas? No funcionará. La policía nos echó, pero regresamos.

River colocó las manos en las rodillas para poder mirar al niño directo a los ojos.

—Jack, ¿conoces la vieja casa del árbol? ¿La que está al lado del mar, detrás de la mansión Glenship?

Jack frunció el ceño.

–Sí. Todos la conocen. ¿Por qué?

–Ve ahí, Jack. Ahora. Y llévate a Charlie.

Se observaron durante tres, o quizá cuatro segundos. Luego Jack tembló y se dio vuelta.

–Díganles a todos que se vayan a sus casas –le gritó al grupo de chicos que se encontraba detrás de él–. Díganles que sé dónde está Isobel. Díganles… díganles que *no hay ningún Demonio*.

CAPÍTULO 11

LA NOTICIA SE propagó con rapidez. River y yo vimos caer los cuerpitos de los árboles y desaparecer en las sombras.

Quince minutos después, el cementerio estaba casi vacío. Solo quedaba un niño. Tenía cabello rubio y brazos muy delgados; permaneció inquieto junto al portón, como si no supiera si marcharse o no. Miró el cielo y los árboles y no se movió. Pero después River lo tomó del hombro y lo empujó gentilmente hacia la calle.

La niebla había aclarado y se podía ver el océano a lo lejos, debajo del cementerio. Estaba brillante, azul y lleno de promesas. River y yo nos quedamos mirándolo durante un rato.

Me pregunté cómo sabía dónde se hallaba la hermana de Charlie y cómo logró que Jack le creyera tan rápidamente.

Me pregunté qué quiso decir Jack cuando mencionó que River le había dicho que buscara al Demonio en el cementerio.

Me pregunté qué había sucedido con ese sentimiento hermoso, halagador y perturbador que abrigaba en presencia de River.

Porque ahora había desaparecido. Por completo.

River jaló de mi mano, salimos del cementerio y tomamos por un sendero que bordeaba la carretera principal. El bosque estaba oscuro y silencioso; el amanecer no lograba filtrarse a través de la densa arboleda. Los chicos entraban y salían zigzagueando por el sendero sombreado delante de nosotros, manteniendo siempre la distancia.

Siete minutos después nos encontrábamos en el centro de Eco. Doblé para ir a la cafetería, que abría condenadamente temprano, pero luego vi a un grupo de los chicos del cementerio caminando por una calle lateral con Jack a la cabeza. Estaban siguiendo las órdenes de River. Bajaban por la calle Glenship. Y la calle Glenship solo conducía a un lugar: a la mansión Glenship y a la casa del árbol.

Chester y Clara Glenship habían sido las personas ricas del pueblo a fines del siglo pasado, junto con los padres de mi abuelo. Ellos también construyeron una gran mansión sobre el océano, más cerca del pueblo que el Ciudadano Kane, y hacían fiestas muy divertidas para todos sus amigos de Boston y Nueva York, como los personajes de una novela de Scott Fitzgerald. Pero los Glenship se quedaron sin dinero antes que mi propia familia. Y, para empeorar las cosas, el hijo mayor de Chester y Clara, encantador y de ojos brillantes, llevó a su joven amante a la bodega y le cortó la garganta con una navaja. Por motivos desconocidos. Fue un caso sensacionalista, a los periódicos les encantó y la imponente mansión permaneció vacía y abandonada durante décadas, con la hiedra descuidada y las ventanas rotas, y un aire de lejana felicidad.

Cuando era más joven, albergaba la fantasía de que uno de los Glenship regresaría y arreglaría el lugar. Sería joven y hermoso, y nada demente como su antepasado que cortaba gargantas. Tendría el cabello peinado hacia atrás con gel, una educación de privilegio y una lengua afilada. Nos encontraríamos, pelearíamos, nos enamoraríamos, viviríamos, tendríamos hijos y envejeceríamos en la segunda mansión que tenía Eco junto al mar.

Cuando era más joven, era bastante estúpida.

Detrás de la casa y hasta la linde del bosque, se extendían los restos de las vastas tierras que conformaban la mansión. Durante las últimas y solitarias décadas, el parque había ido quedando en estado salvaje, con fuentes cubiertas de moho verde y matorrales gigantescos y descuidados. El Ciudadano tenía un aspecto ligeramente mejor. Pero no demasiado.

Hacia la parte trasera derecha del terreno, se encontraba la casa del árbol. Y no era una vieja casa del árbol cualquiera. Además de un hijo, Chester y Clara tenían una hija, a quien querían más que a su propia vida. De manera que no tuvo otra posibilidad que salir podrida hasta la médula o morir joven. Murió joven. Sus padres le construyeron una diminuta mansión en el árbol, donde ella jugaba bonita, malcriada e inconsciente, hasta que un día se cayó, se rompió el cuello y murió.

River y yo seguimos a Jack. Lo seguimos a él y a los otros chicos justo hasta la casita del árbol que mataba niños. La pintura había desaparecido hacía tiempo. Las tablas de madera estaban combadas y grises, y tenían clavos oxidados que sobresalían, deseosos de contagiar a alguien de tétanos. El techo a dos aguas estaba hundido en el centro, un solo viento fuerte le bastaría para ceder por completo.

Los chicos se dispersaron y formaron un círculo alrededor de Jack y del árbol. River y yo nos acercamos más y cerramos los bordes del círculo. Jack puso las dos manos en el árbol y trepó rápidamente por los restos de las tablas de madera, que habían sido clavados en el tronco como escalones. Todos lo observamos, los cuellos estirados hacia arriba. Jack le dio una patada a la deteriorada puerta de la casita y entró.

El corazón me latió una vez. Dos veces.

La puerta se abrió y ahí estaba él otra vez, con Isobel a su lado. Ella sonrió tímidamente y saludó con la mano al grupo de niños que estaban abajo, como si no sucediera nada. Como si fuera algo normal que una niña desapareciera y pasara dos largas noches en una magnífica y decrépita casa del árbol, comiendo Dios sabe qué, durmiendo en el suelo duro y preocupando mortalmente a todo el mundo.

Isobel bajó del árbol de un salto y se perdió entre la multitud de niños, que gritaban de alegría y la felicitaban por no estar secuestrada, probablemente muerta y en el infierno. Su hermano Charlie le dio un abrazo de oso, los rizos negros de ambos se fundieron hasta que no se sabía dónde terminaba uno y comenzaba el otro.

Pero Jack permaneció inmóvil, en la casita del árbol. Levanté la vista hacia él con los ojos entrecerrados y luego observé a River, y descubrí que se miraban mutuamente.

El corazón me latió una vez. Dos veces.

Dejamos a los niños, regresamos a la plaza del pueblo y nos detuvimos delante de la cafetería. Me quedé un rato sin decir nada y moviéndome nerviosamente. Luke y Sunshine estaban dentro; a través de la ventana, podía verlos al lado de la barra. Seguramente habían venido al pueblo mientras nosotros nos encontrábamos en el cementerio.

No me detuve cerca de River y él no se paró cerca de mí. Volteé para quedar mirando la plaza mientras él permanecía junto a la ventana. Un rayo de sol brilló a través del cielo gris, se movió súbitamente alrededor de una nube y me pegó de lleno en el rostro.

Silencio.

Silencio.

–Entonces, ¿ella estará bien?

–¿Quién?

–River, tú sabes quién. Isobel.

–Sí.

–¿Deberíamos avisarle a alguien, como la policía? ¿Avisarles que apareció?

–No. La noticia correrá con rapidez.

Hice una pausa.

–¿De modo que... no hay ningún Demonio?

–No.

Traté de captar la mirada de River, leer la expresión de su rostro, pero continuaba de frente al café y evitaba mirarme.

–¿Cómo supiste dónde estaba Isobel? ¿Cómo es posible que supieras dónde estaba? –me acerqué y le apoyé la mano en el brazo–. River. ¿Qué fue lo que Jack realmente vio en el cementerio? No mentía. Yo sé que no mentía. ¿Qué está sucediendo? ¿Y cómo pasaste a formar parte de todo esto? ¿Qué quiso decir Jack cuando mencionó que le indicaste que fuera al cementerio a buscar al Demonio?

Se limitó a mover la cabeza de un lado a otro y continuar con la mirada fija en la ventana de la cafetería.

–Mira, te lo contaré más tarde. Lo prometo. Pero, en este momento, lo único que quiero es buscar a Luke y a Sunshine y hacer una fogata junto al mar –hizo una breve pausa–. Sí, me parece que es una buena idea. Me gusta hacer una fogata después de que hayan ocurrido hechos excitantes. Eso calma a la gente –entonces me miró–. Yo incluido.

Bajé la vista hacia el vestido de Freddie. Me había puesto el floreado de color azul pálido. Sujeté la tela en la mano y la apreté con fuerza. Presionar a River solo me daría menos de lo que yo quería, y no más.

–Muy bien. Hagamos una fogata.

Me di vuelta y le hice un saludo con la mano a Sunshine, a través de la ventana del café. Luke y ella dejaron la barra y se encaminaron hacia afuera. Gianni estaba trabajando en lugar de Maddy y me hizo un leve saludo con la cabeza y me sonrió, y yo le devolví el saludo. Alcancé a distinguir un ejemplar de *Fresh Cup Magazine* en la barra, el último número, sin ninguna duda. Me pregunté si Gianni esperaba que yo entrara para hablarme sobre él.

–¿Se enteraron? –preguntó Sunshine mientras se ubicaba entre River y yo–. Parece que la chica desaparecida no había desaparecido en absoluto. Pasó las últimas noches en la casita del árbol de la mansión Glenship bebiendo rocío y comiendo únicamente fresas silvestres, según mis fuentes.

River me miró, una ceja levantada con arrogancia que, por un segundo, me recordó a Luke. Y, por eso, River me gustó un poquito menos.

–¿Cómo te enteraste de eso tan pronto, Sunshine? *Acaba* de ocurrir. River y yo estábamos ahí, nosotros…

Luke me interrumpió.

–Imagino que esos chicos inventaron todo eso del Demonio. La única oportunidad que tenía nuestro pueblo de hacerse famoso y la arruinamos. Quién iba a creerlo.

–Cállate, Luke. Tal vez esos niños realmente vieron al Demonio –hice una pausa–. Igual que Sunshine vio a Blue, en el túnel.

Ella me fulminó con la mirada por un segundo, pero entrecerró nuevamente los ojos al volverse hacia River.

–¿Y dónde estuviste? Luke dice que, desde que te marchaste, lo único que ha hecho Vi es vagar por la casa retorciendo las manos con preocupación y lamentándose.

Luke me echó una brillante sonrisa

A veces, detestaba a mi hermano.

–Luke está mintiendo –le dije a River–. Ni siquiera me di cuenta de que te habías ido.

River rio.

–Y yo que pensaba que era el único mentiroso en esta casa –se adelantó unos pasos y puso un brazo alrededor de los hombros de Sunshine y el otro alrededor de los de Luke–. Ya hablamos bastante de demonios, túneles y viajes misteriosos. El sol ya salió y decidí hacer una fogata en la playa. Están todos invitados –los ojos color café de River estaban encendidos, como las luciérnagas en pleno verano. El River serio y misterioso de antes había desaparecido. Por completo. Como si nunca hubiera existido.

Estaba preocupada. Realmente lo estaba. Sentí un agudo hormigueo en el fondo del estómago que me decía que las cosas no estaban bien, incluso mientras observaba el rostro sonriente de River y sus ojos de luciérnaga.

Pero él había regresado y la verdad era... que eso me hacía feliz. Tal vez no debía ser así, no lo sé. Pero, al fin y al cabo, ¿quién era yo para rechazar un poquito de alegría? Íbamos a hacer una fogata juntos en la playa y todo lo demás podía irse al infierno.

La fogata. Un sendero empinado conducía desde el camino de la casa de Sunshine hasta el mar; descendía serpenteando por el acantilado y terminaba en una ensenada pequeña y oculta. A unos dos kilómetros por la costa, había una playa mucho más grande, pero a mí me gustaba mi lugarcito privado porque no podía verse desde arriba y, por lo tanto, nadie sabía de su existencia. Yo iba a menudo allí sola, a leer, en la arena, mientras escuchaba las olas romper cerca de mí.

Luke, Sunshine y yo también íbamos a veces a nadar allí abajo. El océano era normalmente demasiado frío y feroz para hacerlo, pero en algunos días azules y calmos, estaba bastante bien y llevábamos una canasta con el picnic y chapoteábamos un rato. Sunshine tenía un maravilloso traje de baño blanco, que ella adoraba: destacaba sus curvas. Y yo, como era de esperar, usaba uno viejo y *vintage* de Freddie, que tenía un ribete marinero en blanco y un pequeño cinturón. Me cubría casi por completo, excepto los brazos y las piernas.

Me gustaban esos días en que nos bañábamos en el mar. Siempre teníamos frío y siempre nos reíamos. A veces, Luke me mantenía debajo del agua o besaba a Sunshine en la arena pero, sobre todo, lo pasábamos increíblemente bien. Luke se quejó con River de tener que pasar el verano con dos mujeres. Yo creo que, en verdad, le agradaba estar con nosotras. Al menos, nunca se molestó en buscar a alguien más.

Ahora no hacía calor suficiente para bañarse, pero el sol había apartado a las nubes y estaba otra vez azul y luminoso, y la tarde recién comenzaba. Luke desenterró una botella de oporto de la polvorienta bodega del Ciudadano, llamada El barril de amontillado, y se turnaban con Sunshine para beber de ella mientras River y yo hacíamos una pila de madera seca traída por el mar y encendíamos el fuego. Mientras Luke buscaba el vino, yo había encontrado en el sótano una vieja parrilla de campamento y River hizo, para el almuerzo, sándwiches calientes de queso, tomate y mostaza.

Sunshine había tomado algunas mantas del Ciudadano y, después de comer, las tendimos sobre la arena y los cuatro nos acurrucamos sobre ellas para observar cómo bailaban las llamas anaranjadas, amarillas y rojas contra el mar azul.

Yo tenía mi propia manta y River la suya. No nos sentamos cerca, y yo ni siquiera lo miré.

La mayor parte del tiempo.

River se encontraba boca arriba, las rodillas flexionadas, la mitad de sus bonitos pies desnudos hundidos en la arena. Debió haber sentido que lo observaba, porque giró la cabeza y me hizo un guiño, lento y distraído, como si supiera que yo había comenzado a desconfiar un poco de él y quisiera demostrarme que no le importaba mucho.

Dormir al lado de una persona tenía algo de… peligroso. Tal vez más peligroso que dormir *con* una persona. No es que yo supiera del tema. Pero estar junto a River, en la misma cama, y despertar al lado de él, le hacía mal a mi mente. Sentía como si *ya* lo conociera. De la misma manera que conocía a Sunshine, a Luke, a mis padres. Como conocía a Freddie.

Pero no era así. En absoluto. Y esa sensación de conocerlo, basada en nada, era peligrosa. Y, me parecía, algo carente de cordura.

—Violet, escucha esto.

Sunshine estaba totalmente acurrucada junto a mi hermano, el codo en el muslo de él, la mano en la botella de vino, el cabello largo y oscuro rozando la arena.

—¿Qué cosa? —le pregunté mientras empujaba su brazo del muslo de Luke.

—Anoche tuve un sueño. Un sueño con una jirafa.

Le quité la botella de la mano y la coloqué detrás de mi espalda. Estaba casi vacía.

—¿Una jirafa?

—Sí, una jirafa que era mi amiga. Verás, esa jirafa daba una fiesta y, al final, yo la ayudaba a limpiar. Nunca sueño con jirafas. ¿Acaso los niños pequeños sueñan con jirafas? Pero acá es donde se pone interesante. Leí la portada del periódico de Portland en el café y decía que ayer murió una jirafa en un zoológico. Y acabo de darme cuenta de que es probable que signifique algo. ¿No crees que signifique algo? Yo creo que sí.

Sunshine estaba ebria. De otra manera, nunca hubiera hablado de sus sueños. Odiaba lo que no era lógico, como los sueños, los cuentos de hadas y Salvador Dalí.

—Sunshine, estás ebria —le dije.

Levantó las cejas.

–¿No lo sabías, Violet? A los hombres les gustan las chicas ebrias –después de esa afirmación, se colocó de costado en la arena, levantó el brazo y lo dejó caer en un arco suave sobre la cadera. Luego se contoneó. Solo un poquito y en el lugar exacto.

Sunshine no cesaba de sorprenderme con su capacidad para atraer la atención para lo que ella consideraba que eran sus partes más interesantes. Sin esforzarse, aparentemente.

Luke se puso de pie, se estiró hacia mí y tomó de mis manos la botella de oporto.

–Tienes razón, Sunshine. *Claro* que nos gustan las chicas ebrias. ¿Qué piensas, River? Apuesto que has tenido tu buena cuota de chicas ebrias en su momento. Menos revuelo, digo yo –mi hermano hizo una pausa y bebió un trago–. Las mujeres siempre nos hacen las cosas difíciles a nosotros, los hombres, para que consigamos la única cosa que la naturaleza pretende que tengamos. Es realmente una pena.

De modo que Luke estaba otra vez hablando de lo mismo. Pensé que quizás abandonaría el discurso sobre el hombre y el amor delante de River, pero la bebida lo había traído de vuelta. River sacudió la cabeza ante el comentario de Luke y sonrió levemente. A veces, mi hermano decía cosas que estaban tan... *mal*, por tantos motivos, que era imposible hacer otra cosa que no fuera reír.

Luke le lanzó una enorme sonrisa a River y bebió el final del oporto de un largo trago. Llevó el brazo hacia atrás y arrojó la botella vacía a las danzantes olas del mar.

–Luke, ¿por qué hiciste eso? –apunté hacia el agua–. La botella se romperá y alguien caminará por la playa y se cortará los pies.

–Cállate, Vi. Solo nosotros conocemos este lugar.

–No puedo creer que pienses que arrojar una botella al mar te hace lucir atractivo. Es tan estúpido que ni siquiera tengo palabras para describir lo estúpido que es. Es indefiniblemente estúpido.

–Dejen de reñir, hermanos –Sunshine apoyó las manos en la arena y se impulsó para incorporarse–. El fuego está casi apagado y se está levantando el viento. Es hora de irnos. ¿Qué les parece si vamos a jugar al altillo del Ciudadano? Vamos, Violet, hace años que no lo hacemos. *Levántate* –me tomó del brazo y comenzó a jalar de él.

–Bueno, bueno –le dije y luego me volví hacia River–. ¿Quieres conocer el altillo? Es grande, polvoriento y aterrador.

–Sip –respondió.

De modo que los cuatro trepamos por el sendero, llegamos al camino y nos dirigimos a casa.

Jack nos estaba esperando.

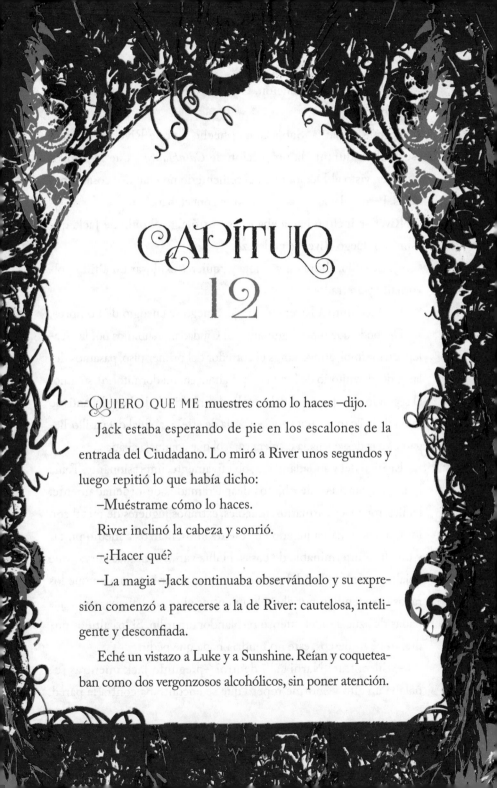

CAPÍTULO 12

—QUIERO QUE ME muestres cómo lo haces —dijo.

Jack estaba esperando de pie en los escalones de la entrada del Ciudadano. Lo miró a River unos segundos y luego repitió lo que había dicho:

—Muéstrame cómo lo haces.

River inclinó la cabeza y sonrió.

—¿Hacer qué?

—La magia —Jack continuaba observándolo y su expresión comenzó a parecerse a la de River: cautelosa, inteligente y desconfiada.

Eché un vistazo a Luke y a Sunshine. Reían y coqueteaban como dos vergonzosos alcohólicos, sin poner atención.

Pero yo sí ponía atención. Observé a River atentamente. Muy atentamente.

Porque yo sabía. Sabía que el hecho de que River se hubiera escabullido durante la proyección de *Casablanca* y que los chicos hubiesen visto al Demonio en el cementerio no eran dos cosas separadas. Pero todavía no sabía cómo se conectaban.

River se inclinó hacia abajo y susurró algo al oído de Jack, que asintió. Y luego River se enderezó.

–Jack –dijo, ahora en voz alta–, ¿quieres explorar un altillo polvoriento y aterrador?

El chico miró a River con enojo y luego se encogió de hombros.

De modo que todos ingresamos al Ciudadano, subimos por la escalera de mármol, atravesamos el corredor del primer piso, pasamos delante del dormitorio de Freddie (que ahora era mi dormitorio), subimos al segundo piso, pasamos delante del dormitorio de Luke y del antiguo salón de baile (que ahora era la galería de arte) y, al final del pasillo, llegamos a la desvencijada escalera caracol que conducía al ático.

El ático del Ciudadano era, objetivamente, impresionante. Tenía una gran cantidad de objetos desparramados desordenadamente: baúles, ropa vieja, armarios, muebles, extraños juguetes de metal con los que nadie había jugado en sesenta años, lienzos a medio pintar y una lista interminable de cosas. Había varias ventanas curvas que dejaban entrar la luz del sol y era un placer ver la forma en que los rayos se extendían por el suelo mientras el polvo bailaba, como las hadas de azúcar en el intenso resplandor amarillo. Si los altillos pudieran pedir deseos, este no tendría nada que pedir.

–¿Encontraré Narnia allí dentro? –preguntó Jack mientras señalaba un alto y enorme ropero que se encontraba contra la pared.

Llevaba jeans oscuros que eran muy grandes y una camiseta color chocolate descolorida. Encima de la camiseta, tenía una chaqueta verde de estilo militar, que también era muy grande pero le daba un aspecto interesante. Tenía muchos bolsillos, seguramente la razón por la cual le gustaba.

Sonriendo por el comentario del ropero, Jack giró hacia River y hacia mí, los labios finitos entreabiertos y las pecas agitándose con el movimiento.

–*Las crónicas de Narnia: El león, la bruja y el ropero* es un buen libro.

Así que, después de todo, había un niño pequeño adentro de Jack. Un niño pequeño al cual le gustaban los libros de fantasía y los roperos.

River sonrió.

–Es imposible que Narnia no esté allí dentro. Voy a entrar.

Comenzaron a volar tapados de piel comidos por las polillas mientras excavaban para llegar al fondo del armario alto y profundo. Yo me dirigí al antiguo gramófono a manivela del rincón y examiné con cuidado las fundas amarillentas de los discos, deteniéndome de vez en cuando para apartarme el cabello del rostro para poder inclinarme más. Para cuando las puntas del cabello estuvieron cubiertas de polvo, ya había encontrado lo que quería.

Coloqué el disco en el aparato y giré la púa. El crujiente sonido del blues de Robert Johnson llenó el ático.

Luego de que River y Jack desenterraron todos los viejos tapados del ropero de Narnia, este sirvió como cambiador. Sunshine se puso un vestido arrugado color azafrán, que era dos tallas más chico en el pecho y le quedaba muy bien. Mi hermano encontró un elegante traje a rayas, probablemente del abuelo. Cuando salió del ropero, yo quería decir que se veía muy bien, que debería vestirse siempre así y que, ey, es realmente increíble usar la ropa de tu pariente muerto… Pero no abrí la boca, porque temía que se quitara el traje.

Extraje de un arcón de madera un vestido negro de fiesta y un collar de perlas falsas (muy del estilo de *Desayuno en Tiffany's*) e ingresé al armario para ponérmelo. Cuando salí, River me miró y esbozó una sonrisa. Una agradable sonrisa de *admiración*.

—Tienes que recogerte el cabello —señaló.

Escarbé en una cajita de alhajas baratas hasta que reuní un puñado de horquillas. River apareció detrás de mí y, con sus dedos largos y bronceados, comenzó a levantarme el pelo, un mechón por vez, retorciéndolo y sujetándolo hasta que toda mi cabellera estuvo recogida con gracia arriba de mi cabeza. Tenía el cabello seco, lleno de sal por estar sentada en la playa y revuelto por el viento, pero River logró que se viera condenadamente elegante, teniendo en cuenta todos esos factores. Cuando terminó, fui a mirarme en uno de los grandes espejos de cuerpo entero, que estaba torcido y manchado por el tiempo, pero igual podía ver la mitad de mi rostro bastante bien.

—¿Cómo aprendiste a hacer esto? —le pregunté llevando la mano al cabello—. Espera… déjame adivinar. Tu madre es peluquera.

River rio, pero sus ojos no acompañaron la risa.

—No. Mi madre es… una persona con una gran vida social y asiste a muchas fiestas. Mientras se maquilla y elige las alhajas, conversamos. Me enseñó a arreglarle el cabello cuando era un niño. Así fue como aprendí.

Lo que River me estaba contando sonaba a algo privado… algo real. Como si no fuera una mentira. De modo que me sentí interesada y ardía en deseos de continuar haciéndole preguntas. Pero se alejó y comenzó a examinar un baúl rojo, que se encontraba junto al gramófono. Aparentemente, no pensaba hablar más.

Me toqué el cabello y di vueltas para poder examinarme otra vez en el espejo. Imaginé a River de niño, con su nariz recta y su sonrisa torcida, pero también con mejillas suaves, sin cabello, y un cuerpo de niño pequeño, como Jack. Me lo imaginé ayudando a su madre a sujetarse el cabello para una fiesta. Era una imagen muy dulce y, maldición, parecía que anulaba el sentimiento que me había embargado desde lo del cementerio.

Luke se acercó al espejo y me apartó para poder mirarse. Sonrió al ver cómo la tela a rayas le quedaba ceñida en el pecho y en los brazos. Y luego la sonrisa se desvaneció y los dedos volaron hacia la frente.

Mi hermano tenía entradas muy profundas y ya le preocupaba la idea de quedar calvo. A menudo lo encontraba mirándose en los espejos y en los vidrios de las ventanas, moviendo la cabeza de un lado a otro, tratando de decidir si las entradas eran cada vez más profundas.

—Mira, Vi —dijo señalándose la cabeza—. Mira. Se *movió*. Te juro que se movió.

—No, no es cierto —respondí sin mirar.

—¿Estás segura, Vi? No puedo quedar calvo. No puedo. No soy un tipo pelado. No me quedaría bien.

Suspiré y lancé una especie de risa.

—Tus entradas no se movieron. Están igual. Lo juro.

—Está bien —dijo Luke. Respiró hondo, largó el aire y se alejó del espejo—. Confío en ti.

Volví a reír y después me volví a mirar a River, que acababa de salir del ropero vestido con lo que parecía ser la ropa de un campesino italiano, que incluía un pañuelo rojo alrededor del cuello. Sin ninguna duda, era algo que había quedado de los amigos bohemios de mis padres. Hasta había conseguido un ukelele. Tomó asiento en uno de los destrozados sofás de terciopelo y se puso a rasguear los acordes de *Moon River* en honor a mi vestido.

Luego de hurgar un poco, Jack encontró un chaleco a cuadros y una gorra de tweed. Sonreía y creo que lo estaba pasando bien, pero se mantenía muy callado. Tuve la impresión de que estaba acostumbrado a permanecer quieto y en silencio. No provocaba la misma sensación que otros chicos, de temeridad, inocencia y picardía. Y me pregunté cuál sería la razón.

Jack se metió en el armario con su disfraz y, cuando salió, parecía un chico de la calle de una vieja película, que vendía periódicos en una esquina. Se veía condenadamente adorable. Y eso que yo no me considero particularmente susceptible a todo lo que sea adorable. Me asaltó el deseo de sentarme y pintarlo, ahí mismo. Y hacía mucho tiempo que no quería tomar los pinceles.

Luke y yo veníamos pintando desde mucho antes que comenzáramos a hablar y, mientras otros chicos tenían crayones, nosotros teníamos una caja de acrílicos. Pero después de ver durante tantos años a mis padres colocar el arte por encima de nosotros, me había hartado de eso. En el otoño, lo había dejado súbitamente y por completo, cuando mis padres se fueron a París. Por lo que yo sabía, Luke hacía años que había dejado de pintar, alrededor del momento en que Freddie murió. Y había sido mucho mejor que yo. Él era bueno, realmente bueno, como papá.

Recordé los pinceles húmedos en la casa de huéspedes.

–Luke, ¿has vuelto a pintar? –miré a mi hermano, que estaba sentado junto a Sunshine con su elegante traje encima de una pila de cojines de terciopelo, viejos y polvorientos. Me ignoró y comenzó a mordisquearle la oreja a Sunshine.

Le di una patada en la pierna.

–Solo dime si estás pintando otra vez. Me pondrá feliz.

Pero no me contestó y continuó besando a Sunshine. Tal vez consideraba que era algo demasiado importante como para hablar de ello. Le di otra patada, pero después lo dejé tranquilo.

Jack se sentó entre River y yo. Tener a ese chico cerca me hacía sentir maternal, aun cuando fuera más bien impasible y callado, y raramente se comportara como un niño. De todas maneras, me hacía reflexionar. Si yo fuera su madre, meditaba, no pasaría todas las tardes con mis amigos artistas hablando de Renoir y de Rodin ni me marcharía a Europa y desaparecería durante meses. No… Me sentaría con mi hijo, le haría un jugo de naranja y le contaría historias. No tendría que ser todo el tiempo, sino de vez en cuando, para que él supiera que me gustaba tenerlo cerca.

El chico comenzó a bostezar, lo cual era comprensible. Había pasado las últimas noches en un cementerio buscando al Demonio. Pensé en lo que Jack había dicho antes, delante del Ciudadano, eso de que quería que River le mostrara cómo lo hacía.

River sintió que lo estaba observando y volvió la vista hacia mí. Sus dedos continuaban en el ukelele y sus ojos estaban abiertos, felices y satisfechos.

Decidí imitar a Scarlett O'Hara y posponer el tema del demonio y del cementerio hasta el día siguiente.

Freddie me dijo una vez que yo era una obstinada de la peor clase, porque, en realidad, no era obstinada, sino paciente. Paciente, pero decidida. A una persona obstinada se la puede distraer o engañar, pero a mí, no. Yo insistía e insistía y no me daba por vencida hasta que conseguía lo que quería, mucho después de que los demás ya hubieran perdido el interés. No sé si lo que Freddie dijo era cierto. Tal vez, en ese momento, yo había hecho algo que la decepcionó.

Jack bostezó otra vez. Tenía pómulos altos que se proyectaban hacia afuera cuando abría mucho la boca y pensé que, cuando fuera más grande, sería un hombre de aspecto elegante, gallardo, como un George Sanders, estrella de cine de la década de 1940.

Cerró los ojos… y se durmió.

Giré la cabeza y miré por la ventana. Mis ojos vagaron por la habitación y siguieron a un rayo de sol hasta un rincón, donde cubría a un viejo baúl y hacía que el cuero negro se viera más claro, casi color chocolate. Me di cuenta de que se trataba del baúl de la botella de ginebra y la tarjeta roja. Había olvidado que quería hacer una nueva búsqueda allí dentro.

Y casi me levanté para hacerlo en ese mismo instante, pero Jack estaba apoyado sobre mí y se veía suave y dulce. No quería moverme y perder ese momento de paz disparando mi anhelo de Freddie una vez más.

Lo revisaría más tarde. Y, esta vez, no olvidaría hacerlo.

–Hay una historia de Faulkner, *Una rosa para Emily* –comenté en forma general una vez que River terminó la canción que estaba tocando y todo quedó en silencio, a excepción de la respiración suave de Jack, que dormía a mi lado. Sentí ganas de hablar, algo inusual en mí. Tenía muchos pensamientos dando vueltas por la cabeza, pero no quería reflexionar sobre ellos. De modo que abrí la boca y los dejé salir–. Trata sobre una mujer llamada Emily, que se enamora de un hombre, pero él no la quiere. Y un día él desaparece. Años después, cuando Emily muere, la gente del pueblo encuentra el cuerpo del hombre en estado de descomposición en la cama de ella, un largo mechón de cabello gris en la almohada, cerca de él –hice una pausa–. Emily lo envenenó con arsénico y luego lo colocó en su cama, para que yaciera allí para siempre.

Hice otra pausa.

–Sé que se supone que es una historia de horror, pero siempre pensé que toda la trama era más bien triste y de gran hermosura. Ella *realmente* quería a ese hombre. Eso es algo que se da muy raras veces, creo yo. Es más raro de lo que la gente cree. Todos pensaron que estaba demente, pero yo pienso que simplemente estaba muy, pero muy enamorada.

River dejó de juguetear con el ukelele y me miró.

Luego Luke estiró la pierna y me pateó en la canilla.

–*Dios*, Vi. Dime por favor que no andas por ahí contándole estupideces como esas a todo el mundo. No es de extrañar que nadie en el pueblo nos hable. En las familias ricas, siempre hay uno o dos dementes. ¿Ese es realmente el papel que quieres jugar?

–Nosotros ya no somos ricos, ¿recuerdas? Así que si estoy demente, a nadie le importa.

Luke se volvió hacia River.

–Dime, por favor, ¿qué diablos le ves a mi hermana? Siento curiosidad.

–Hermanos, dejen de reñir –Sunshine metió la mano en su vaso de té, tomó un cubito de hielo y se lo pasó por el cuello y la parte de arriba del pecho. Lentamente–. Hace demasiado calor aquí arriba para pelear.

–No hace calor –dije–. Ni remotamente. Hay dieciocho grados como máximo.

Sunshine dejó de mover el cubito, me sonrió francamente y después lo arrojó en su boca y comenzó a masticarlo.

Me levanté y puse el disco desde el principio.

–¿Saben que algunas personas piensan que a Robert Johnson lo envenenaron? –comenté–. Con estricnina. Tenía solamente veintisiete años cuando murió y nadie llegó a descubrir qué lo mató, así que, ¿quién sabe? La estricnina es un veneno malvado. La muerte es horrible y dolorosa. Alguien debe haberlo odiado mucho. De lo contrario, hubieran utilizado arsénico o cianuro. Si yo fuera a matar a alguien, usaría cianuro.

Cuando tenía catorce años, tuve una fuerte etapa Agatha Christie.

Luke me echó una mirada asesina.

–Ahora ya me estás enfureciendo. Vi, deja de hacerte la excéntrica. No te quedaba bien cuando eras más chica y ahora pareces simplemente trastornada. *Este* es el motivo por el cual no tienes ningún amigo.

–Hablando de eso –dije–. Luke, ¿podrías despejar el altillo de alguno de tus múltiples amigos? Hay demasiada gente.

River se reclinó en el sofá y colocó las manos detrás de la cabeza. Estaba riendo. Creo que mis peleas con Luke lo divertían, aunque yo me sentía un poco avergonzada. De todas maneras, eso no me detendría la próxima vez.

–¿No fue Robert Johnson el cantante de blues que llevó su guitarra a medianoche a un cruce de caminos y le vendió el alma al

Demonio a cambio de aprender a tocarla? –preguntó River unos segundos después.

–Sí, es ese –respondí–. El hombre hizo un pacto con el Diablo. Es un mito fáustico, un clásico. Aparentemente, Johnson dijo que era verdad. Pero supongo que el Demonio pasó a recolectar más temprano y arrastró a Johnson al infierno antes de que cumpliera treinta años.

–*Fausto*. Todos sabemos que eres una engreída tragalibros, hermana. Deja de presumir.

–Dejen de *pelear* –nos regañó Sunshine nuevamente–. Los dos. Interrumpen mi coqueteo.

–Desearía que la gente propagara un rumor fáustico acerca de mí –me incliné y aparté de un golpe la mano de Sunshine del cabello de Luke–. Un mito fáustico –repetí–. Es tanto más interesante que ser una chica rubia, nueva y pobre, que vive en una casa grande solamente con su hermano idiota, con abdominales más grandes que su cerebro. Sunshine, si alguna vez desaparezco, por favor dile a la gente que me fui tras el Demonio, para tratar de recuperar mi alma.

Sunshine me miró con sus ojos adormilados y parpadeó varias veces.

–Como quieras, Vi.

A mi lado, River le quitó la gorra a Jack y le revolvió el pelo. Jack abrió lentamente sus ojos azules.

–¿No deberías estar en algún lado? –le preguntó River–. Hace dos días que andas dando vueltas por un cementerio. ¿No hay nadie que se preocupe por ti?

Sin mirar a River, Jack se frotó un ojo.

—Mi madre se marchó cuando yo era un bebé. Y mi papá… está trabajando. A nadie le importa dónde estoy —en ese momento, levantó la mirada hacia River, su rostro pecoso estaba serio como siempre–. ¿Ahora me mostrarás cómo hiciste esa magia?

River se puso de pie.

—Es hora de llevar a este niño a su casa.

Asentí. River se inclinó hacia mí, me rodeó el cuello con los dedos y atrajo mi oído a sus labios.

—Cuando vuelva, te prepararé la cena, y después, responderé preguntas –susurró.

Me besó el lóbulo de la oreja. Sentí un cosquilleo en todo el cuerpo, algo exótico, desconocido, agridulce y como trascendente. Me dejó muda, como supongo que él sabía que sucedería.

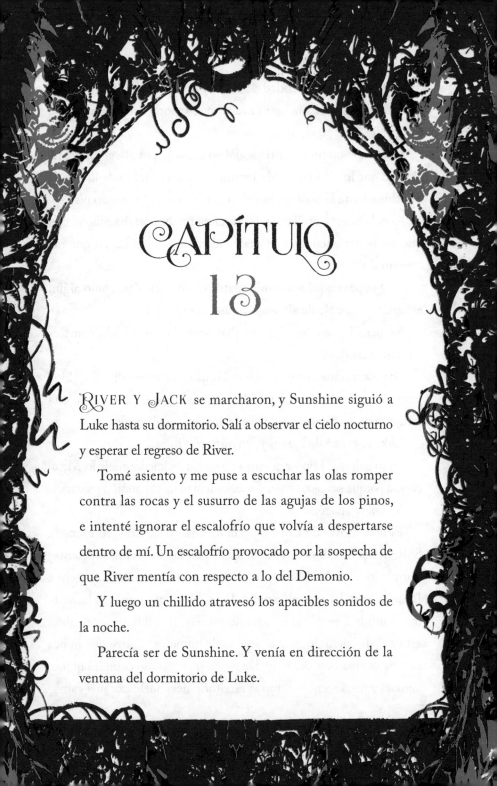

CAPÍTULO 13

RIVER Y JACK se marcharon, y Sunshine siguió a Luke hasta su dormitorio. Salí a observar el cielo nocturno y esperar el regreso de River.

Tomé asiento y me puse a escuchar las olas romper contra las rocas y el susurro de las agujas de los pinos, e intenté ignorar el escalofrío que volvía a despertarse dentro de mí. Un escalofrío provocado por la sospecha de que River mentía con respecto a lo del Demonio.

Y luego un chillido atravesó los apacibles sonidos de la noche.

Parecía ser de Sunshine. Y venía en dirección de la ventana del dormitorio de Luke.

Consideré la posibilidad de subir y ponerle fin a los chillidos, pero no me agradaba la idea de tener que soportar que mi hermano me gritara.

Pasaron los minutos. Mi escalofrío causado por River empeoró, al igual que los chillidos. Me levanté y seguí el sonido de la risa de Sunshine hasta la habitación de mi hermano en el segundo piso.

Abrí la puerta sin llamar. Ni siquiera me importaba mucho con qué me podía encontrar, lo cual evidenciaba el humor en que me encontraba.

—¿Qué pasa aquí adentro? —grité en voz bien alta, como algún estúpido personaje de alguna estúpida obra.

Silencio. Luke y Sunshine estaban sentados en el suelo, completamente vestidos.

—Encontramos un viejo tablero Ouija en el ático —dijo Sunshine y echó su cabello por arriba del hombro redondo—. Tu hermano está tratando de convencerme de que la casa está embrujada.

Luke se cruzó de brazos y me miró con furia.

—¿No golpeas? Hipócrita —pero no estaba realmente enojado. Me di cuenta porque sus ojos verdes-castaños tenían una expresión risueña.

Mi ira se apagó.

El dormitorio de Luke parecía un cuadro de Edward Hopper. Solía ser el estudio de mi abuelo. El Ciudadano tenía suficientes dormitorios vacíos (siete u ocho, nunca podía recordarlo), pero a Luke le gustaba más el estudio. Probablemente por su inherente masculinidad, entre los paneles de madera, las bibliotecas, el sillón art decó de cuero negro y el resabio de humo de cigarro que nunca parecía desaparecer del todo. De modo que, cuando cumplió quince años, él y papá reemplazaron el escritorio del abuelo por una cama.

Me senté entre Luke y Sunshine sobre la alfombra turca de color verde, justo debajo de una hilera de novelas de Dickens encuadernadas en cuero (que estoy segura de que Luke nunca había mirado) y frente a muchos lienzos en blanco, de diversos tamaños.

—¿En qué lugar del ático estaba? —observé el tablero Ouija.

—Al fondo de uno de los roperos —Sunshine se estremeció de manera obvia—. Contactamos a un espíritu. Es una niña. Se cayó al mar y se ahogó cuando tenía diez años, y ahora flota alrededor del Ciudadano y nos observa —los ojos entrecerrados de Sunshine se agrandaron—. Aterrador, ¿no?

—Sunshine, ¿desde cuándo crees en fantasmas? —pregunté dejando que se deslizara en mi voz más desprecio del que probablemente debería haber utilizado. Sunshine pensaba que a los chicos les gustaban las mujeres que se asustaban fácilmente. Diablos, tal vez tenía razón. Si un chico podía hacer chillar a una chica, tal vez ella se echaría en sus brazos en busca de consuelo. Y una vez que la tenía en sus brazos, era probable que pasar al segundo nivel fuera pan comido.

—Vi, ¿no hay en el salón de baile un cuadrito de uno de nuestros parientes muertos que es una niña de cabello rubio?

Observé a mi hermano.

—Sí. Se llamaba True. Era la hija de Freddie… la hermana más pequeña de papá. Freddie nunca hablaba de ella, pero papá me contó que se ahogó cuando era una niña —hice una pausa—. Papá también debe habértelo contado. Aparentemente.

Luke agitó las manos en el aire.

—Nunca había oído hablar de ella hasta ahora. Lo juro. Nos habló a través del tablero Ouija —lo empujó con la rodilla y el puntero se movió de una forma escalofriante.

Escruté a mi hermano de arriba abajo pero su expresión inocente se mantuvo firme.

—Está bien. Vayamos al salón.

El salón de baile era ahora la galería de arte familiar. Nadie había bailado en esos espléndidos suelos de madera en años, excepto aquella noche en que mis padres bajaron el tocadiscos del ático y decidieron enseñarnos a Luke y a mí algunos de los fluidos bailes de debutante que mi madre había aprendido en la época en que era una joven hermosa, elegante, peinada y maquillada, y no la madre artista de cabello largo que nunca usaba labial pero siempre tenía pintura debajo de las uñas y a Degas en la mente.

Nuestros padres empezaron enseñándonos los pasos pero terminaron bailando entre ellos, Luke y yo sentados en el suelo observándolos deslizarse a través de los pisos de madera del salón hasta el amanecer.

Ese era uno de mis buenos recuerdos.

—Está allá —indiqué, señalando el retrato que se encontraba en el rincón más lejano. Las paredes estaban tapizadas de cuadros. La mayoría habían sido pintados por mis padres o sus amigos artistas, pero unos pocos habían estado ahí desde los inicios. Rica, inteligente y encantadora, Freddie había conocido una buena cantidad de personas que se dedicaban a salpicar pintura. Había más de doce retratos de ella, realizados por varios hombres y mujeres. La mayoría la mostraba cuando era joven, sus radiantes ojos azules sonreían con audacia y daban la impresión de que brillarían para siempre.

Pero, por supuesto que eso no ocurrió.

Mi padre colgó los retratos de Freddie a gran altura, casi demasiado altos para que se pudieran ver. Probablemente porque estaba desnuda en casi todos, y a él no le agradaba ver a su madre desnuda día tras día.

Sunshine, Luke y yo contemplamos el retrato de True. Yo no había encendido las luces del salón porque hacía años que los tres candelabros no funcionaban, pero la luna se filtró por la ventana y Luke tenía una pequeña linterna en el bolsillo, que había encontrado en el altillo, de modo que podíamos verlo muy bien. El retrato era pequeño, de solo quince centímetros cuadrados, y estaba colocado entre una temprana pintura estilo Chagall de mi madre y un severo retrato de mi abuelo Lucas White, que incluía cigarro y solapa con flor. True era muy pequeña, una niña, de cabello muy pero muy rubio, como yo, piel clara, mejillas rosadas y una expresión lejana y de cuento de hadas en la mirada. Era un retrato al pastel, de estilo impresionista, incluso el vestido azul pálido, que combinaba perfectamente con sus ojos azules y contrastaba muy bien con las dos amapolas rojas que aferraba, una en cada mano.

—Dijo que los estaba cuidando —susurró Sunshine. Tomó la linterna de la mano de Luke y la apuntó hacia la pintura—. El tablero Ouija lo expuso con todas las letras. Claro como el agua. Dijo que los cuida a ti y a Luke.

Ahora se me había erizado la piel. Estaba más erizada que nunca. Diablos, yo creía más en la capacidad de Luke de inventar estupideces de lo que creía en fantasmas, pero aun así… Le eché una mirada a Luke y otra vez a Sunshine.

—¿El tablero dijo algo más?

A esta altura, River ya nos había encontrado. Entró sigilosamente en el salón de baile, como una sombra, y se me acercó por detrás.

—¿En qué andan? —preguntó.

Me recliné contra él, de modo que mi espalda tocó su pecho.

—Luke está tratando de asustar a Sunshine con un tablero Ouija. Típico de la adolescencia. Siento como si estuviera dentro de un misterio de Agatha Christie. Prepárense porque el tablero adivinará el próximo asesinato.

Luke giró y me miró con furia.

—No puedo creer que te lo estés tomando en broma, hermana —señaló la pintura—. True nos habló. Está tratando de advertirnos. Está por suceder algo malo.

Sunshine asintió, incapaz de apartar los ojos de la pintura.

—Sí. El tablero lo dijo con todas las letras: TENGAN CUIDA-DO. ALGUIEN VA A VENIR. Vi, eso fue justo antes de que entraras volando y gritando. Condenadamente aterrador.

Sunshine apartó la mirada del retrato y se estremeció otra vez. Luke la rodeó con sus brazos. Ella sonrió, se acurrucó más contra su hombro y me guiñó el ojo.

Lo miré a Luke.

—¿*Tengan cuidado*? ¿*Alguien va a venir*? Es demasiado vago como para resultar terrorífico. Buen trabajo, hermano.

Luke movió la cabeza de un lado a otro. Sus ojos se veían entusiasmados e inquietos.

—No fui yo, Vi. Creo que tenemos un fantasma aquí. En serio.

River bajó los ojos hacia mí.

—Tal vez *sí* tengan un fantasma, Vi. Creo que Luke está diciendo la verdad. Es mejor que vayamos a hablar otra vez con el tablero Ouija.

Asentí.

—De acuerdo. Ustedes ganan. Me siento intrigada. Hagámoslo —me di vuelta y me dirigí al dormitorio de Luke. Yo misma tenía un par de preguntas para hacerle. Quería saber cuán lejos estaba dispuesto Luke a llegar con eso.

River, Sunshine y Luke vinieron detrás de mí. Los cuatro nos sentamos junto al juego, River a mi lado. Pusimos los dedos sobre el puntero de madera.

Y esperamos.

Yo me moví inquieta. Sunshine emitió risitas nerviosas. Luke se había quitado el saco a rayas y comenzó a flexionar los músculos pectorales de la forma que yo detestaba. Con expresión entretenida, River permanecía sentado, un brazo delgado alrededor de una rodilla doblada. No ocurría nada. Desplacé el peso del cuerpo sobre la otra cadera y deseé que mi vestidito negro del ático fuera más largo. Alcé la vista hacia el techo, luego volví a mirar el tablero, después a Luke y le dije a Sunshine que dejara de reírse. Y seguía sin suceder nada.

—¿Eres True? —pregunté finalmente. Lo miré a Luke mientras lo decía, pero él estaba observando el tablero. El puntero se deslizó hacia el SÍ con tanta fuerza y rapidez que me caí sobre el codo.

Le eché una mirada asesina a Luke, pero él se mostró sorprendido. ¿Acaso mi hermano era tan buen actor?

—¿Eres la niña del cuadro? ¿La que se ahogó?

Eso lo dijo Luke.

Otra vez, el puntero se dirigió directamente al SÍ.

Transcurrieron unos segundos y el puntero se movió.

BÚSQUENME

CUANDO

SALGA

LA

LUNA

Se me erizaron los vellos del antebrazo.

Mientras iba diciendo las letras en voz alta, casi podía escuchar a la niña pronunciando las palabras: lenta y profundamente, como si las dijera debajo del agua.

El puntero comenzó a moverse otra vez.

ALGUIEN

VA

A

VENIR

Luke y Sunshine se quedaron en silencio, sin apartar la vista del tablero. River sonreía con su despreocupada sonrisa y daba la impresión de estar divirtiéndose mucho.

—¿Quién eres? —le pregunté al tablero por última vez—. ¿Quién eres?

El puntero se sacudió de un lado a otro debajo de nuestros dedos y luego se movió.

D

E

M

O

N

I

O

Apoyé las manos en el tablero Ouija, le di un empujón y salió volando contra la pared.

—¿Qué rayos te pasa, Vi? —Luke me dio un golpe en el brazo—. Ese juego es antiguo. Debe tener como ochenta años. Trátalo bien.

—Te pasaste de la raya, Luke. No hagas bromas con el Demonio.

Luke me sostuvo la mirada.

—No fui yo. Dios, Vi, con todo lo que decía Freddie, ¿crees que yo fingiría que el Demonio nos está hablando a través de un tablero Ouija?

Nos quedamos mirándonos durante un momento.

—Cálmense un poco, hermanos —dijo Sunshine, la voz relajada, como un ronroneo, y completamente inmune a lo que estaba sucediendo. Se reclinó sobre la espalda, levantó un pie y lo apoyó sobre la cama de Luke. El antiguo vestido amarillo trepó rápidamente hasta el interior de su muslo blanco, pero ella hizo como si no lo notara—. Es demasiado tarde para pelear.

—Está bien —dije.

—Está bien —repitió Luke.

Agité la mano hacia el muslo de Sunshine.

—Entonces te dejo con tu tablero, hermano.

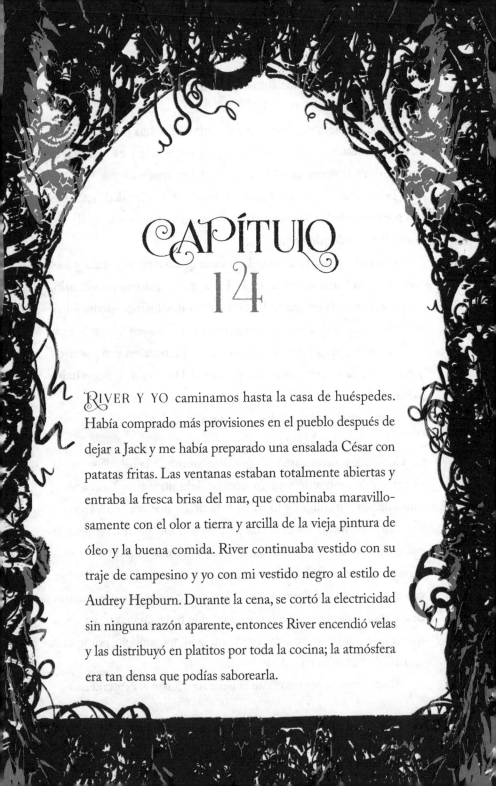

CAPÍTULO 14

RIVER Y YO caminamos hasta la casa de huéspedes. Había comprado más provisiones en el pueblo después de dejar a Jack y me había preparado una ensalada César con patatas fritas. Las ventanas estaban totalmente abiertas y entraba la fresca brisa del mar, que combinaba maravillo-samente con el olor a tierra y arcilla de la vieja pintura de óleo y la buena comida. River continuaba vestido con su traje de campesino y yo con mi vestido negro al estilo de Audrey Hepburn. Durante la cena, se cortó la electricidad sin ninguna razón aparente, entonces River encendió velas y las distribuyó en platitos por toda la cocina; la atmósfera era tan densa que podías saborearla.

River y yo estábamos solos por primera vez desde la casa del árbol.

Estaba inquieta por lo que iba a contarme… Las respuestas que había prometido en el ático. Y, para ser sincera, la rica comida, la dulce brisa y la densa atmósfera no ayudaban mucho.

—Te marchaste durante *Casablanca* –dije. Tenía los dedos aceitosos por la ensalada y las patatas fritas, y me los sequé en la toalla del corderito–. ¿Adónde fuiste?

Había esperado durante toda la cena que River empezara a hablar. Pero no había sucedido nada. Habría preferido no presionarlo, ya que eso parecía empeorar las cosas. Pero, diablos, necesitaba saber si el chico que acababa de prepararme la cena, el que vivía en la casa de huéspedes, era el tipo de chico que se metería en cementerios y convencería a unos niños de que era el Demonio. Y necesitaba saberlo pronto.

River juntó los platos y los puso en el fregadero.

—Más tarde, Vi. Más tarde.

Comenzó a hacer café y el agradable aroma de la bebida se sumó al agradable aroma de todo lo demás. Bebí un sorbo. Yo era noctámbula por naturaleza y lo había sido desde que era bebé. Uno de mis primeros recuerdos era estar sentada con mis padres, tarde en la noche, mientras ellos pintaban; a Luke lo habían llevado a la cama varias horas antes. Mis padres no eran perfectos aun cuando estaban cerca, pero hicieron algunas cosas bien, como dejar que me quedara despierta hasta tarde si yo tenía ganas. De todas maneras, yo sabía que el café por la noche empeoraría mi lado noctámbulo, por lo que andaba de puntillas cuando lo bebía.

—River, cuando abandonaste la película, ¿fuiste al cementerio?

Lo estaba presionando...

Se dio vuelta.

—¿Qué rayos estás haciendo? —exclamó ignorando mi pregunta y lanzándome una sonrisa burlona y torcida mientras yo andaba de un lado a otro en puntas de pie.

—Tratando de no beber mucho café —apoyé los talones en el suelo de madera de la cocina—. Es difícil beberlo de un trago cuando estás caminando de puntillas.

River levantó la taza y después los talones. Estaba descalzo otra vez. No le gustaba usar zapatos, lo cual me parecía bien, porque me agradaban sus pies. Se balanceó, bebió, apoyó los talones y me miró.

—Vi, eres rara. ¿Lo sabías?

Asentí.

—¿Pasabas mucho tiempo sola cuando eras pequeña?

Volví a asentir.

Me sonrió.

—Bueno, me gusta lo raro. La gente no es tan rara como uno quisiera. Todos somos bastante extraños de chicos y luego crecemos y...

—River, ¿estás cambiando de tema?

—Sí.

—No lo hagas —dije. Entrecerré los ojos y esperé que así pareciera que hablaba en serio.

—Antes de responder a tus preguntas, déjame contarte una historia —River miró su café, me miró a mí, suspiró y luego miró a la pared—. Cuando era más joven, había un chico con el cual me gustaba salir. Creo que podría decir que era mi mejor amigo. Siempre se metía en problemas, siempre peleaba, siempre hacía enfadar a algún otro chico mucho mayor que él y nunca pensaba antes de actuar.

River se detuvo y sus ojos se pusieron serios. Serios como la segunda vez que estuvimos en el cementerio. Esa expresión me asustaba, porque se veía tan extraña en su rostro travieso… pero también me producía cierta emoción.

–La gente no lo entendía –agregó unos segundos después–. No buscaba pelea, simplemente era sincero. Decía lo que pensaba, sin importarle las consecuencias –River no me miraba–. Yo le cubría las espaldas en las peleas. Pasé mi infancia cubierto de magullones. Eso enfurecía a mi padre. Recibía golpes en la pelea y cuando regresaba a casa.

Lanzó una suerte de risa y luego dejó de reír.

–¿Qué ocurrió?

–¿Qué? –preguntó después de un segundo.

–¿Qué le ocurrió a tu mejor amigo? Termina la historia, River.

–¿Qué le ocurrió al chico? –el cuerpo de River se puso tenso y su mandíbula se endureció tanto que se le formó un hoyuelo en el lado izquierdo. Tomó aire y exhaló–. Lo prendí fuego.

–*¿Qué?*

–Eso todavía me provoca pesadillas –River bebió el resto del café y colocó la taza en la mesa.

Coloqué la mano en su hombro. Finalmente me miró.

–Tonterías –dije.

Me apartó la mano.

–Lo hice en serio. Estábamos bromeando, haciendo una fogata en la playa. Estábamos jugando a un juego y yo me tropecé. Me caí contra él y… él se cayó dentro de la fogata.

–Pero fue un accidente. No lo hiciste a propósito.

–Bueno, de todas maneras sucedió, ¿no es cierto? Y yo fui la causa. *Murió quemado*, Violet.

Los ojos de River se humedecieron un poco. Se veía, no lo sé, como trágico.

Y, al verlo así, me sentí desesperada.

Me estiré y lo abracé. Primero se quedó muy quieto y luego se relajó.

—Lo siento —dije—. De verdad. No tienes que hablar más de eso si no quieres.

Sentí que las manos de River bajaban a mi cadera. Se inclinó y me besó. Despacio.

Era bueno besando. Suave. No era rudo y veloz como Sean Fry. Los besos de River parecían decir: "Tengo todo el tiempo del mundo porque sé que no te vas a ningún lado".

Y era así. Ese beso fue menos sorpresivo que el del cementerio. Aquella vez, me había quedado dura como una estatua del cuello para abajo. Pero ahora, no. Ahora me moví y yo también lo besé. No sabía lo que hacía, pero *sentía* que sí.

El beso de River sabía a café, a tormentas y a secretos.

Y despacio, despacio, comenzó a moverse más rápidamente, y después más todavía...

Y luego se detuvo.

Así como así, me soltó. Justo en el momento en que yo había olvidado quién era, justo en el momento en que había olvidado que ya no éramos dos personas distintas, sino un brillante y tembloroso océano de besos... me soltó. Retrocedió y respiró profundamente.

—¿Te quedarás aquí esta noche? —preguntó, con la respiración un tanto entrecortada como la mía. Se llevó la mano al cabello y se lo estiró hacia arriba de esa forma tan atractiva, lo cual me enojó un poco.

Miró por la ventana de la cocina el cielo negro y violeta y el mar negro y violeta.

—He tenido pesadillas desde que cumplí catorce años. Siempre. Pero dormí una siesta contigo hace unos días y, de repente, desaparecieron. Me voy por un día y, *bum*, regresan, así nomás —hizo una pausa—. ¿Sabes lo que significa eso, no?

Negué con la cabeza.

—Significa que tendrás que dormir a mi lado por el resto de mi vida.

Pasaron unos segundos. Luego puso una mano en mi cabello y la otra en la parte baja de mi espalda y me atrajo hacia él, con fuerza.

—¿River? —dije.

—¿Sí, Vi?

—¿A qué se refería Jack? ¿Qué quiso decir cuando te pidió que le mostraras cómo lo hacías?

Dejó caer los brazos. Sentí frío súbitamente y me pregunté si debería cerrar la ventana.

—Antes de contestarte, déjame hacerte una pregunta. ¿Has disfrutado los últimos días que pasamos juntos? ¿Has sido feliz?

Presintiendo que era una trampa, estudié su rostro.

—Sí, no. En general, no, creo. Tengo a un mentiroso viviendo en mi casa de huéspedes, que les dice a los niños que vayan a buscar al Demonio y luego desaparece después de que ellos lo encuentran. Mi vecina sufre alucinaciones en el túnel del pueblo y luego recibo un beso en el cementerio. Yo a eso no lo llamaría realmente *disfrutable*. Lo llamaría inquietante.

River se encogió de hombros.

—La ignorancia es felicidad. ¿Por qué no te relajas y aceptas lo que te sucede? Esa es *una* posibilidad, ¿sabes? Puedes ignorar todas esas preguntas que están ocupando lugar en esa cabecita rubia que tienes y venir a la cama conmigo. Déjame abrazarte y ambos dormiremos felices. E ignorantes. Yo, sin mis pesadillas y tú, sin tus respuestas.

Lo pensé. En serio. Pero solo durante unos pocos segundos.

—No. Quiero saber qué está ocurriendo. Realmente quiero.

River suspiró.

—De acuerdo. Pero recuerda que tú lo elegiste —sus ojos cafés se encontraron con mis ojos azules y se detuvieron—. Violet, tengo un secreto. Hay algo que yo puedo hacer y la demás gente no.

—Tienes toda mi atención.

—Es… Yo lo llamo el resplandor —dijo y sus ojos estaban abiertos e insondables, como antes en el altillo. Pero su boca tenía el mismo rictus travieso de siempre y no sabía a quién creer.

»Principalmente —continuó—, porque… porque es como si *resplandeciera* cuando lo uso. Por adentro. Por todos lados. Es como la sensación que tienes cuando duermes una siesta: tienes un sueño épico, fantástico, y luego te despiertas y el sol brilla, te estiras y sientes un cosquilleo en todo el cuerpo. Es algo así, pero mil veces mejor.

Vaciló unos segundos y luego prosiguió.

—Es la misma sensación que tengo cuando te beso, Vi. Y nada, pero *nada* me ha parecido mejor que el resplandor hasta ahora. Pensé que deberías saberlo.

Lo dijo rápido, como si sintiera vergüenza. Pero luego su rostro retomó tan rápidamente la expresión traviesa que no pude distinguir cuál de las dos partes era la verdadera. Además, mi mente continuaba atrapada con la palabra *resplandor*, y todos mis pensamientos se enredaban detrás de ella. Llevé las manos a la cabeza y apreté, porque sentía como si el cerebro fuera a escaparse del cráneo, como la pulpa de una ciruela muy madura apretada dentro del puño.

—¿El *resplandor*? ¿Qué es *eso*, River? ¿Qué diablos es eso?

Tomó mi mano y la acercó a su corazón. Dejé de hablar. Podía sentir los latidos, fuertes y ardientes y, sin mi consentimiento, eso me hizo sentir mejor.

—Mira, te mostraré —su mano oprimió la mía, que seguía oprimiendo su corazón. Me miró fijo, con fuerza.

Y entonces lo vi.

Al demonio de Jack.

Estaba detrás de River, un cuerpo alto que se cernía en la oscuridad, ojos rojos y filosos como cuchillos en su pálido rostro. Era delgado, demasiado delgado. Solo huesos y sombras debajo de un sombrero negro en punta. Sentí que de él emanaba maldad, como una colonia fuerte. No quería que me afectara. Sabía que debía moverme, pero el Diablo comenzaba a inclinarse sobre River, el labio superior curvado hacia atrás en una mueca de disgusto, el cuello blanco rozaba la oreja de River, los dientes blancos rechinaban mientras se acercaba cada vez más a su rostro…

Grité.

River no se movió. Ni siquiera se dio vuelta. El Demonio comenzó a desvanecerse de a poco hasta que quedé observando el rincón de la cocina, mirando nada más que la oscuridad.

—¿Sabes algo? Tú me diste la idea para eso —dijo River, la voz calma, casi alegre—. Cuando nos vimos por primera vez, estabas leyendo los cuentos de Hawthorne. El joven Goodman Brown ve al Demonio en el bosque. Muy buen cuento.

—Ropa de puritanos, a *eso* se refería Jack —al principio, no estaba segura de que había hecho ese comentario en voz alta porque había gritos dentro de mi mente y no alcanzaba a escuchar si las palabras salían de mi boca.

Pero River asintió.

—Yo quería que mi Demonio estuviera vestido de pecado, pero pensé que los chicos no podían saber qué aspecto tenía el pecado. De modo que lo hice como un típico personaje de Hawthorne: la ropa de *La letra escarlata*, y lo de la serpiente que está en el cuento. Yo agregué los ojos rojos. Pensé que sería más vívido —hizo una pausa—. Y Blue... eso también tuvo que ver contigo, Vi. La historia que nos contaste al lado del túnel me inspiró. Claro que tuve que improvisar, pues no tenía la más mínima idea del aspecto que podría tener un recluso demente que vivía en un túnel comiendo ratas. Por ende, le puse dientes peludos. Estaba orgulloso de eso. Un detalle simpático, ¿no crees?

Arranqué la mano de la de River y me alejé. Temblaba y veía puntos oscuros en los bordes de los ojos. Pensé en Sunshine, en los gritos y el desmayo. Supe exactamente, *exactamente* cómo se sintió. Eso era miedo. Un miedo penetrante, punzante, funesto, estridente y abrasador.

—¿Qué diablos eres? ¿Qué diablos eres, River? —sacudí la cabeza y me moví lentamente hacia la puerta mientras contenía el deseo ferviente de salir corriendo, porque parecería estúpido y, aun en ese momento, yo no quería parecer estúpida delante de River.

Se encogió de hombros.

—Un monstruo. Un santo. Ninguno de los dos. Algo intermedio. Dediqué mucho tiempo a pensar en eso y lo único que pude concluir es... que soy yo. River. Eso es todo. Desde que cumplí catorce, puedo hacer que la gente vea cosas y no sé por qué. Lo único que sé es que no soy malo –vaciló–. Tampoco sé si soy tan bueno. Soy simplemente yo. Y usar el resplandor en la gente me hace feliz. Es parecido a… una droga.

Apartó los ojos y volvió a mirar el mar.

–Una droga a la que debo tener adicción –confesó en voz baja, casi como si no quisiera que yo escuchara. Casi. Se volvió hacia mí–. Violet, pon tu mano otra vez sobre mi corazón.

Se adelantó hasta que estuvo frente a mí. Tomó mi mano temblorosa y volvió a colocarla sobre su pecho caliente.

–Mantén tu mano ahí unos segundos.

Extendió el otro brazo, me atrajo hacia él y me besó. El cuello, las mejillas, los labios. Bajo mi mano, su corazón aceleró los latidos y la piel se volvió caliente.

–¿Ves? –susurró a mi oído–. Besarte me perturba, igual que el resplandor. El corazón se acelera y la piel se calienta –hizo una pausa–. Así que parece que encontré otra cosa que no puedo abandonar.

Se echó hacia atrás para que pudiera leer su rostro y encontrar la verdad que estaba escrita allí. Pero no revelaba nada. Los ojos parecían genuinos y sinceros, pero la boca estaba torcida y tenía una expresión entre astuta y traviesa, de modo que no saqué nada en limpio.

–¿Cómo funciona? –le pregunté–. ¿Simplemente piensas en un monstruo y haces que alguien lo vea?

Se encogió de hombros.

–Algo así.

Medité durante unos segundos.

–Pero ¿por qué? ¿Por qué harías algo así?

–Porque puedo –hizo otra pausa y su rostro estaba inexpresivo, como el mar después de la tormenta–. Y porque necesito hacerlo.

–¿De modo que… asustas a todos esos chicos en el cementerio, a todo el pueblo (Jack, Isobel, Sunshine, a todos) solo porque puedes? ¿Solo porque el resplandor te hace sentir bien, como besar? ¿O lo haces porque realmente no puedes detenerte, como si fuera una droga? ¿Como el cigarrillo, el opio o la ginebra? ¿Cuál de los dos es?

Levantó los hombros.

–Por los dos motivos. No lo sé. Es complicado –dijo con una sonrisa amplia y, de repente, su rostro revivió nuevamente. Travieso y despreocupado como un niño con un secreto, recostado en un campo de flores bajo un cielo azul–. No voy a aburrirte con los detalles. Al menos, no todavía. Estoy demasiado lleno, feliz y dormido y, maldición, excitado. Ven a la cama conmigo, Vi.

Me quedé observando la piel morena que asomaba a través de un agujero en los pantalones de campesino y rehuí su mirada.

Monstruo.

Extraño.

Dios.

Esas eran las tres palabras que me vinieron a la mente mientras asimilaba lo que me había contado. Y me refiero a dios en el sentido romano. Tal vez River podía ser uno.

–¿Has hecho resplandecer a alguien más? –pregunté finalmente–. ¿Además de Sunshine y de Jack y sus amigos? ¿Has hecho ver algo a Luke?

–Todavía no. Con él, estoy abierto a lo que suceda.

–¿A quién más? ¿A quién más antes de venir a Eco?

–A todo el mundo.

Hice una mueca de dolor.

—¿A cuántos? ¿A cuántas personas?

—Cientos —hizo una pausa—. Miles.

—Oh —mi corazón comenzó a latir más rápido, más rápido que cuando River me besó. Rápido como una pesadilla, rápido como si me fuera la vida en ello.

—Pero a ti, no —dijo, como si me leyera la mente.

Y entonces se me ocurrió.

—River, ¿puedes leerme la mente? Porque si puedes entrar allí adentro para hacerme ver monstruos, sería lógico que…

—No, Violet —me interrumpió—. No estoy leyéndote la mente. No puedo leer la mente. Bueno, no *toda* la mente. A veces me llegan fragmentos muy pequeños. Pero es muy raro. Los niños son más fáciles. Como Jack. Pero no los adultos.

—Entonces ¿solo puedes hacer lo de los monstruos? ¿El resplandor solo hace que la gente vea monstruos?

River meneó la cabeza. Estiró los dedos y los colocó en el hueco de mi garganta, donde latía mi pulso. Respiré dos veces y luego… se desplazó y desapareció. Y, en su lugar, apareció mi madre, tan clara como el agua.

Los ojos se me llenaron de lágrimas. No pude evitarlo. Sabía que no era real, pero mis ojos, no. Estaba *ahí*, justo delante de mí, la piel perfecta, el cabello largo y lacio y la sonrisa demasiado amplia, entusiasmada y estresada como la última vez que la vi, justo antes de que se marchara con papá a París.

Y había pasado tanto tiempo. Meses y meses.

—Mamá —dije y la voz se me quebró.

Escuché una voz masculina que exclamaba *Maldición*.

Y luego River apareció otra vez frente a mí.

–Perdóname –se disculpó–. Debería haber imaginado que ver a tu madre te alteraría. Ves, es por *eso* que prefiero dedicarme a los monstruos.

Le eché una mirada asesina. Me caían las lágrimas y estaba muy enfadada.

–River, eso fue cruel. Ya había dejado de extrañarla y, ahora que la trajiste, la voy a extrañar otra vez.

Se acercó a mí y su brazo tocó el mío de una forma reconfortante. Sin embargo, no lo aparté como quería. Porque, con el contacto de nuestros brazos, me sentí de pronto un poquito mejor.

–No estés enojada conmigo –dijo–. No lo volveré a hacer. Solo lo hice para demostrarte que tenía razón. Es más fácil perdonar a alguien por asustarte que por hacerte llorar.

Nos quedamos un rato en silencio.

River miró por la ventana, como había estado haciendo durante toda la noche, las manos en los fríos cerámicos de la mesada de la cocina y el cabello sobre los ojos.

–Jack quería que yo lo hiciera otra vez –señaló sin mirarme–. Que le mostrara al Demonio. Le gustó mi pequeño truco. No sé cómo se dio cuenta ese chico de lo que estaba sucediendo, pero así fue. Antes de *Casablanca*, le dije que al Demonio le gustaba visitar el cementerio después del anochecer, y él fue para comprobarlo, como yo sabía que haría. Es un chico listo. Y luego yo llegué alegremente, hice aparecer al Demonio y, ya sabes, pura diversión.

–¿Y cómo fue lo de Isobel? –pregunté.

–Sí, Isobel –respondió aún sin mirarme–. Cuando fui al cementerio, la encontré en la entrada con su ula-ula. Le pregunté si conocía algún buen lugar donde esconderse y me habló de la casa del árbol. Luego le dije que fuera a esconderse ahí durante un rato. Le expliqué que era parte de un juego. No pensé que se quedaría tanto tiempo. Pensé que se ocultaría por unas pocas horas, como mucho, pero…

–¿Usaste el resplandor con *Isobel*? Pero ella es tan *pequeña*. ¿Hiciste que fuera a esa casita completamente sola? Las demás cosas, está bien, no son tan malas, y es probable que Sunshine se lo mereciera. ¿Pero Jack e *Isobel*? River, eso es una maldad. Es malo. Es algo propio del Demonio. Freddie diría…

En lo que dura un parpadeo, River me agarró. Sus brazos rodearon mi cuerpo, su rostro se hundió en mi cabello y fui recobrando la calma, calma, calma.

–Vi, Vi, shh. ¿Qué daño real produjo todo esto, incluida Isobel? –susurraba, los labios en mi frente y los dedos apretándome la espalda–. Tu vecina Sunshine vio a un loco dentro de un túnel en vez de recibir un beso, como esperaba. Tu pueblo tuvo el día más emocionante desde que un chico rico le cortó la garganta a su amante en una bodega… tu hermano estaba fascinado. Y nosotros dos tuvimos la posibilidad de ver niños corriendo por un brumoso cementerio con estacas en las manos. Es… diversión pura.

–¿Diversión pura?

–Sí.

Ahora estaba asustada. Realmente asustada. ¿Qué caos había estado provocando este chico en el mundo con su… con su *resplandor*, si pensaba que eso era diversión pura?

Pero, de todas maneras, no me desprendí de sus brazos.

Los dedos de su mano derecha jugaban con el extremo de la larga tira de perlas falsas que yo llevaba y sus nudillos no dejaban de rozar la parte de arriba de mi ombligo enviando oleadas de sensaciones agradables adentro de mí. Debería haberlo apartado. Debería haber gritado, supongo, o llorado o tratado de escapar. Pero no lo hice. Dejé que continuara.

Me besó otra vez. Nos besamos y nos besamos. Levanté las manos y las puse en su espalda y él subía y bajaba los dedos por las perlas, y sus nudillos tocaban lo que encontraban.

Llegamos a la cama.

Se quitó la camisa de campesino, pero se dejó el pañuelo rojo alrededor del cuello. Me sacó el collar de perlas y lo apoyó sobre la cómoda. Extrajo las horquillas de mi pelo suavemente, muy suavemente, y el cabello cayó más allá de los hombros. Luego se estiró hacia atrás y me bajó la cremallera del vestido, que se deslizó hacia el suelo. Estaba desnuda de la cintura hacia arriba, y abajo no llevaba demasiado. Me contempló durante unos segundos y me estremecí en la luz de la luna que entraba a través de la ventana. Respiré una vez. Dos veces. Y me rodeó con sus brazos.

No sabía qué sucedería a continuación y debo decir que no me importaba demasiado. Pero River solamente me llevó hasta la cama, nos metimos debajo de las sábanas, me besó la espalda desnuda, subió hasta el cuello y luego me susurró buenas noches al oído.

En unos segundos, ya estaba dormido.

Yo, no.

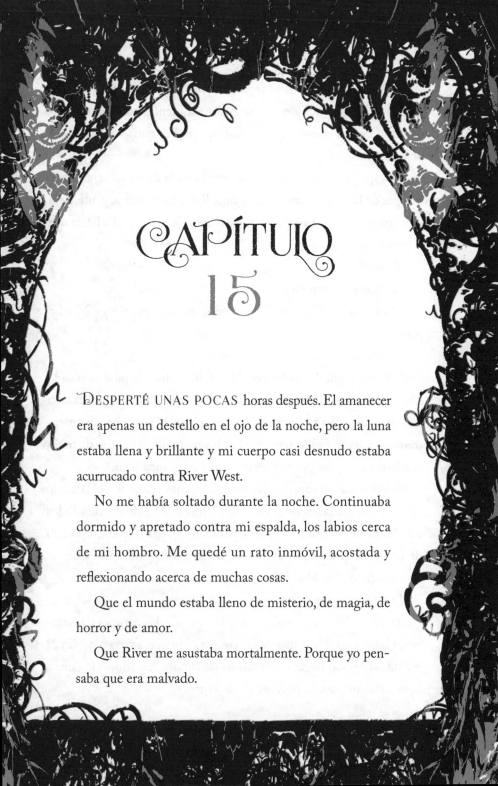

CAPÍTULO 15

DESPERTÉ UNAS POCAS horas después. El amanecer era apenas un destello en el ojo de la noche, pero la luna estaba llena y brillante y mi cuerpo casi desnudo estaba acurrucado contra River West.

No me había soltado durante la noche. Continuaba dormido y apretado contra mi espalda, los labios cerca de mi hombro. Me quedé un rato inmóvil, acostada y reflexionando acerca de muchas cosas.

Que el mundo estaba lleno de misterio, de magia, de horror y de amor.

Que River me asustaba mortalmente. Porque yo pensaba que era malvado.

Podía haber hecho cosas realmente malas con el resplandor. Era *muy probable* que hubiera hecho cosas realmente malas con el resplandor. Peores que asustar a Sunshine, peores que asustar a niños pequeños.

Y después, mientras estaba recostada en la cama escuchando el romper de las olas, se me ocurrió algo. River hacía que la gente viera monstruos y madres ausentes. ¿Qué más? ¿Qué más podía hacer que la gente viera?

¿O sintiera?

No quería pensar en eso.

Convertiría a River en algo… peor que un mentiroso. Mucho peor.

Y me convertiría a mí en una tonta.

Me desprendí de sus brazos. No se despertó. Me puse el vestido muy pero muy silenciosamente, caminé por el pasillo y salí de la casa de huéspedes. El aire frío de la noche me golpeó con fuerza y me estremecí. Atravesé el terreno, pasé el invernadero, la cancha de tenis, el laberinto y entré por la puerta trasera del Ciudadano.

Adentro de mi casa, no estaba mucho más cálido. Había dejado abiertas las ventanas de la cocina, y otras más. Subí corriendo los escalones de mármol, los pies desnudos se retorcieron por el frío de la piedra, y atravesé rápido el corredor del primer piso hasta el dormitorio de Freddie. *Mi* dormitorio.

Luke estaba sentado a los pies de mi cama.

Tenía los brazos cruzados sobre las rodillas, las manos en las sienes. Había encendido una de las lámparas, pero era vieja y débil y la luz difusa apenas llegaba más allá de las almohadas. Movió la cabeza bruscamente hacia la puerta cuando entré.

–¿Dónde estabas? Maldición, Vi. Hace horas que estoy aquí, esperándote.

Tomé una manta de uno de los sillones art decó y la arrojé sobre los hombros.

–Estaba con River. Pero supongo que ya lo sabías. ¿Por qué? ¿Sucede algo malo?

Me senté a su lado en la cama y extendí el extremo de la manta sobre sus pies desnudos. Luke se volvió hacia mí y noté que tenía miedo. Los ojos muy abiertos, a punto de entrar en pánico; mucho, mucho miedo.

–*Búsquenme cuando salga la luna.* Eso es lo que dijo. Y así es como vino.

–¿True? –pregunté. Y, de repente, tenía la piel erizada y sentía un cosquilleo adentro de la cabeza, como me ocurre a veces cuando tengo miedo.

–True –respondió Luke. Sacudió la cabeza y se estremeció–. En un momento, solo se veía la luz de la luna que entraba por la ventana y luego parpadeé y allí estaba. Una niña de unos diez años y cabello largo, y podías ver a través de ella como si fuera luz de luna, como si estuviera hecha de luz de luna, y me sonrió y creo que grité, quizá, pero después… –tragó saliva, su voz brotaba cada vez más rápido y también se quebraba–. Pero después estaba justo frente a mí y deslizaba sus deditos de luz de luna por mi mejilla y ya no pude gritar y me quedé mirándola y sus ojos no eran de luz de luna, sino negros como el cielo nocturno, sin bordes blancos ni color y entonces puso la mano sobre mi boca y fue como si derramara luz de luna por mi garganta y brotaba con tanta fuerza y con tanta rapidez, que estaba seguro de que me ahogaría.

Finalmente, Luke respiró. Su pecho subió y bajó mientras respiraba. Le tomé la mano y se la apreté mientras pensaba toda clase de cosas en las cuales no podía concentrarme en ese momento.

—Tosí —prosiguió Luke—, me atraganté y me ahogué con la luz de la luna, que sabía a manteca, acero, sal y neblina. Y luego, de golpe, justo cuando pensé que me iba a matar, que succionaría el aire de mis pulmones y me convertiría en un fantasma como ella, alzó la mano y… se desvaneció.

Inclinó la cabeza hacia mí y sus ojos castaño-verdosos tenían una expresión inocente, confiada y agobiada, como la de un niño pequeño.

—Vi, ¿no es cierto que fue un sueño? El sueño más aterrador del mundo, pero un sueño, ¿verdad?

Pensé en River, en lo que me había contado y eso que había dicho, *Estoy abierto a lo que suceda* con respecto a Luke, cuando, de hecho, ya había decidido lo que le haría a mi hermano y tal vez ya lo estaba haciendo en ese momento mientras hablaba conmigo.

Mentiroso.

Era un maldito mentiroso.

Miré a Luke, vi cuán asustado estaba, y, por un instante, sentí que no podía respirar. River. *River.*

Respira, Violet, por favor, respira.

Luke levantó la manta y la colocó sobre sus hombros, para que los dos estuviéramos metidos dentro.

—Desde que apareció River, han estado ocurriendo cosas insólitas. Es extraño, Vi, ¿no crees?

—Sí, lo es —concordé. Quería contarle. Acerca de River y el resplandor. En serio quería contarle. Pero si le contaba acerca del resplandor, acerca de los niños en el cementerio, acerca de Sunshine y Blue, y la razón por la cual un fantasma llamado True trató de ahogarlo con luz de luna mientras dormía… era probable que echara a River a patadas de la casa de huéspedes. Yo no confiaba en River. Hasta había comenzado a odiarlo. Pero tampoco quería que se marchara. No quería volver a estar sola con Luke y Sunshine: yo esperando mientras ellos se besaban. Todavía no sabía qué quería, pero no era eso.

A mi lado, Luke se estremeció otra vez.

–A veces, me asalta el deseo demente de perseguir a ese tipo con una horca hasta echarlo del pueblo. Pero, cuando vuelvo a verlo, ese deseo desaparece. Por completo. Y, por otro lado, tú estás haciendo cosas con él, y nunca antes demostraste interés por ningún chico y no sé qué pensar.

–¿Quieres dormir en el sofá? –pregunté. Y no era solamente por Luke. De repente, yo no quería estar sola en mi enorme habitación, en la maldita oscuridad.

»Yo solía dormir ahí cuando era el dormitorio de Freddie –le comenté a Luke–. Cada vez que tenía una pesadilla, venía corriendo aquí dentro, ella me daba una pila de mantas y yo dormía en el sofá y todo volvía a estar bien.

–Sí, lo recuerdo –dijo Luke. Parecía algo avergonzado y solemne al mismo tiempo–. No puedo volver a mi habitación esta noche. Realmente no puedo.

De modo que le di tres mantas viejas y uno de mis cojines y se durmió en lo que duran diez parpadeos. Pensé que le tomaría más tiempo, mucho más tiempo. Pero no fue así. Y luego, yo me eché sobre las sábanas y también caí muerta del sueño.

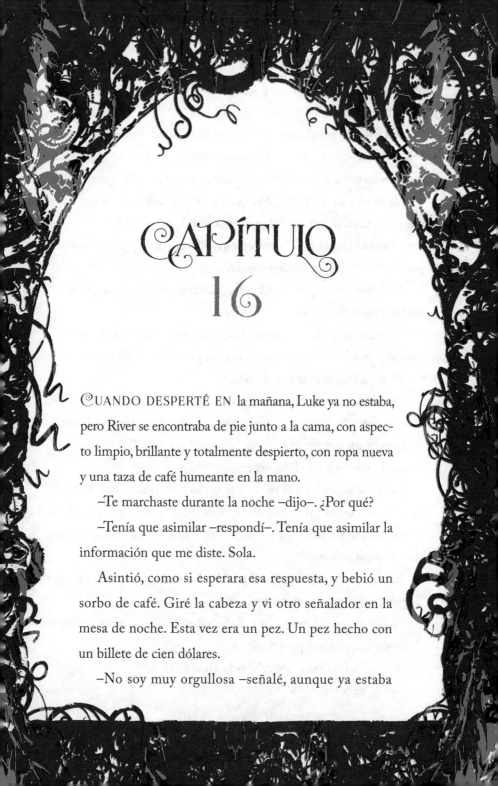

CAPÍTULO 16

CUANDO DESPERTÉ EN la mañana, Luke ya no estaba, pero River se encontraba de pie junto a la cama, con aspecto limpio, brillante y totalmente despierto, con ropa nueva y una taza de café humeante en la mano.

–Te marchaste durante la noche –dijo–. ¿Por qué?

–Tenía que asimilar –respondí–. Tenía que asimilar la información que me diste. Sola.

Asintió, como si esperara esa respuesta, y bebió un sorbo de café. Giré la cabeza y vi otro señalador en la mesa de noche. Esta vez era un pez. Un pez hecho con un billete de cien dólares.

–No soy muy orgullosa –señalé, aunque ya estaba

comenzando a sentirme un poco como si lo fuera–. No te obligaré a que te lo lleves.

–Es solo un señalador –dijo River encogiéndose de hombros y bebió el café–. ¿Crees que ya has asimilado lo suficiente como para acompañarme a Eco? Quiero ver cómo está Jack. Asegurarme de que desayune bien y tenga algo que hacer hoy. Como no tengo hermanos menores… me agrada ser responsable de alguien.

¿Acaso al Demonio le importaría que un chico serio y pelirrojo desayunara bien? ¿En serio le importaría?

Sí, disparó la voz de Freddie. *Especialmente si supiera que por eso te gustaría todavía más.*

–De acuerdo –repuse ignorando las palabras de la voz y sepultándolas profundamente en un rincón polvoriento de mi interior, donde podía olvidarlas por un rato.

River ya se había duchado y llevaba pantalones de lino color café, una camiseta blanca estilo James Dean, zapatos abotinados blancos y negros y un sombrero Panamá, que podía ser de él o haberlo encontrado en el altillo el día anterior.

Me puse el overol que mi madre usaba para pintar. Ella lo había encontrado en el invernadero después de que tuvo que decirle al jardinero que no viniera a trabajar más. Estaba cubierto de pintura de todos los colores.

River y yo nos dirigimos al pueblo. En el camino, justo cuando llegamos al túnel, me detuve y lo miré.

–Luke tuvo una pesadilla anoche –fue todo lo que dije, porque era todo lo que tenía para decir.

River rio. Inclinó la cabeza hacia atrás y *rio*.

–¿Y le agradó?

—Casi muere asfixiado por la luz de la luna, a manos de una niña muerta de diez años. Sí. No le agradó mucho —estaba comenzando a sentir el rostro tenso y contraído, como cuando me invadía el enojo (un enojo abrasador, al rojo vivo, como un fuego candente del infierno), y trataba de ocultarlo.

River se dio cuenta. Me puso las manos en la cintura y me atrajo hacia él.

—Lo siento —se disculpó y pareció que hablaba en serio, siempre teniendo en cuenta que su nivel de credibilidad no era muy alto—. No pude resistirme después de toda esa puesta en escena con el tablero Ouija. Era demasiado perfecto. Además, odio la manera en que te habla a veces. Fue agradable hacerle alguna maldad.

Levanté la vista hacia él. Su piel resplandecía bajo el sol matinal, y olía a limpio y a sal, como el mar, y tenía el cabello todavía húmedo de la ducha y se veía casi negro, y mi enojo se desvaneció.

—¿Así que esa es la razón por la cual lo hiciste? ¿Para castigarlo? Y entonces ¿qué pasa con Sunshine? ¿Por qué se lo hiciste a ella?

—Tampoco me gusta la forma en que te habla.

—River, ni siquiera la conocías cuando utilizaste el resplandor con ella en el túnel.

—Eso es cierto —afirmó y volvió a reír—. Mira, Vi, la cuestión es que yo sufro de una deplorable necesidad de justicia. Sí, me gusta sentir el resplandor en mí. Y sí, me está resultando muy difícil detenerlo. Pero tampoco puedo quedarme de brazos cruzados y contemplar a la gente que se porta mal con las personas que no se lo merecen. Es algo poderoso que llevo dentro. Quizá aún más poderoso que el resplandor —hizo una breve pausa y el brillo regresó a sus ojos—. Pero también soy fanático de las travesuras. Así que, entre los dos…

Mi expresión era más bien de odio, pero River fingió no notarlo.

—¿Y es por eso que utilizaste el resplandor con Jack y la pequeña Isobel? ¿Porque eres fanático de las travesuras?

Dejó de sonreír.

—De eso... de eso no estoy orgulloso. Sinceramente. Fui demasiado lejos. Lo sé.

Ni por un segundo le creí que estuviera arrepentido.

Pero *quería* creerle.

—No vuelvas a hacerlo otra vez. Nada de eso. Hablo en serio, River.

Asintió.

—No estaba en mis planes —acotó.

Entramos en la cooperativa y compramos plátanos y *pain au chocolat* para el desayuno. La mujer de la caja nos sonrió mientras River le pagaba. Fue una sonrisa agradable, genuina. Y River le sonrió a su vez. Y recordé lo que Luke había dicho en el altillo: que nadie nos hablaba. Y me pregunté, por primera vez, si tal vez no sería más por culpa nuestra que de ellos.

¿Acaso éramos esnobs? Vivíamos en una casa grande y teníamos antepasados interesantes, pero ya no teníamos dinero y era muy finito el hilo que nos mantenía aferrados al Ciudadano. Aun así, vivíamos apartados. Mis padres invitaban a sus amigos artistas de la ciudad, pero no se mezclaban con la gente de su propio pueblo. Mi padre dijo una vez que lo único que lo aburría eran las personas aburridas y que Eco estaba lleno de ellas.

Pensándolo bien, me pregunto si simplemente no sentiría vergüenza de que la mayoría de las veces no pudiéramos pagar la factura de la calefacción.

Respiré hondo y le lancé una sonrisa a la mujer, que me devolvió la sonrisa.

Me sentí bien.

River me mostró dónde vivía Jack. La casa estaba en una calle sin salida, cerca de la gran caja de ladrillos de odio que era mi escuela secundaria. Me permití un escalofrío al pasar junto a ella. Quería tomar clases en casa, como mi papá cuando era pequeño, pero no teníamos el dinero suficiente. No tenía muy claro cómo haría para enfrentar la vuelta a la escuela en el otoño, si mis padres no regresaban. Luke hacía deportes y eso le proporcionaba amigos, al menos, durante el año escolar. Lo único que yo tenía era a Sunshine... y Sunshine era Sunshine.

Tal vez debería haberme anotado en alguna actividad en la escuela, como... teatro. Y el club de apicultores. Tal vez no debería haberme pasado todo el tiempo libre entre libros. O siguiendo a una mujer de alrededor de noventa años a quien le agradaba hablar del Demonio.

De repente, me sentí vieja. Muy vieja. Vieja como Freddie. Me llevé las manos a la cara, pero las mejillas eran todavía suaves, todavía lisas, todavía jóvenes.

River me miró y bajé las manos. Habíamos llegado a la casa de Jack.

Era pequeña y la pintura saltada le daba un aire de tristeza, como un juguete olvidado bajo la lluvia. Fuimos hasta la puerta y golpeamos. Tenía la sonrisa preparada, esperando que el rostro solemne de Jack me recibiría en la puerta.

En su lugar, nos atendió un hombre. Era alto, delgado y huesudo. Tenía cabello finito y gris y huecos oscuros debajo de los ojos, como los que uno esperaría ver en un vagabundo medio muerto de hambre en los trenes en 1930. Pero sus rasgos rectos y parejos tenían una suave elegancia urbana, que todavía se podía distinguir a través de los huecos y los huesos. Debería haber sido guapo hacía mucho, mucho, mucho tiempo. Llevaba una sucia camisa amarilla y unos pantalones de lana color chocolate. La chaqueta que hacía juego estaba arrumbada en un revoltijo en el pasillo, a sus espaldas.

El hombre era Daniel Leap, el ebrio que vociferaba su opinión sobre mi familia desde cada una de las esquinas del pueblo, el hombre que había arruinado la vista que yo tenía adelante aquel primer día en que bebí café con River.

Y, súbitamente, comprendí. Comprendí por qué Jack estaba solo. Comprendí por qué era tan callado.

Daniel Leap sostenía un vaso con un líquido color ámbar en su mano de dedos largos. Whisky, imaginé. En la otra mano, tenía una aguja con una cola larga de hilo negro. Sus ojos eran grandes como los de Jack, excepto que, en vez de tener la melancolía penetrante del niño, parecían aturdidos y perdidos.

—¿Está Jack por ahí? —preguntó River. Su expresión era igual a la mía: sorpresa, confusión, preocupación.

—¿Qué quieren con él? —la voz del hombre era suave y susurrante, pero había en ella un atisbo de irritación.

Antes de que River pudiera responder, Jack apareció en la puerta.

—Hola, River —dijo—. Hola, Violet. Él es mi papá.

Daniel miró a su hijo, luego a River y finalmente a mí. Después se inclinó hacia el costado y empujó a Jack, solo un poquito. Solo lo suficiente.

—Cállate, Jack.

Se hizo una larga pausa. Daniel Leap bebió de su vaso y nosotros lo observamos sin decir nada.

–Entonces, ¿qué quieren con mi hijo? –preguntó otra vez y sonrió–. ¿Quieren comprarlo? A ustedes, los ricos, les gusta hacer eso, ¿no? –sus ojos se posaron en mí–. Sí, sé cómo eres, Violet White. Mi familia ha estado en Eco casi tanto tiempo como la tuya. Solo que nosotros no vivimos en mansiones frente al mar. No, mi gente vive y muere en una alcantarilla –rio. Su risa era suave y susurrante, como su voz–. Pero mira lo que estás haciendo ahora. Vienes a mi alcantarilla y tratas de comprar a mi hijo. Quieres alquilarlo como un compañero de juegos, como en ese libro de Charles Dickens, ¿verdad? Sí, lo leí. Sé leer.

Bebió un largo trago del whisky y me miró, de arriba abajo, de los pies hasta las cejas, hasta que comencé a moverme nerviosamente. ¿Estaba bromeando?

–No, no quiero comprar a tu hijo. Solo queremos…

Miré a Jack, que sonreía ligeramente, casi con cinismo, algo que no me esperaba. Estaba acostumbrado a que su padre hiciera el ridículo. Volví a mirar a Daniel Leap. Me pregunté si sabría lo inteligente que era su hijo. Me pregunté si sabría que su hijo no le tenía miedo.

Daniel empezó a mover torpemente la aguja. Trataba de coser un botón de su camisa mientras la tenía puesta, mientras sostenía un vaso con la otra mano y mientras las dos manos le temblaban.

–He estado toda la mañana tratando de coser este botón –dijo. Parecía haber olvidado, por el momento, todo lo relacionado con Dickens y el alquiler de compañeros de juego.

–¿Puedo sostenerle el vaso? –preguntó River, en forma educada y discreta.

El hombre se encogió de hombros y le alcanzó el vaso. River lo inclinó hacia arriba y bebió un largo trago. Levanté bruscamente las cejas. ¿Por qué querría River el whisky barato de Daniel Leap, si ni siquiera bebía?

Daniel, la mano derecha ahora libre, clavó la aguja en el centro del botón de su camisa amarilla. Me eché hacia atrás, pensando que iba a brotar sangre. Jack observó durante unos segundos, luego se estiró y tomó el hilo de los dedos de su padre. Lo condujo hasta una silla cerca de la puerta y lo sentó con un suave empujón.

Permanecimos ahí, sin decir nada. Luego Jack le echó una mirada dura a River, que dio vuelta el vaso de whisky y lo volcó en el suelo.

Cuando regresamos, fuimos a buscar a Luke. Yo quería que River le pidiera disculpas. Sin embargo, eso implicaba contarle a mi hermano acerca del resplandor de River y no sabía exactamente cómo le caería esa conversación.

Noté que la puerta del cobertizo estaba abierta. El cobertizo era más grande de lo que uno podría pensar, teniendo en cuenta que le decíamos "cobertizo". Era una pequeña construcción blanca con varias ventanas cuadradas. Adentro, había latas de pintura por todos lados, banquitos para sentarse, caballetes, pinceles, telas, materiales para naturalezas muertas: jarras, vasos, botellas de vino, frutas de utilería, velas y un cráneo humano.

Luke estaba adentro, pintando. Había dos telas armadas: una tenía una capa base de color blanco y la otra de color negro.

—Estoy haciendo un díptico —anunció sin levantar la vista de la caja de pinturas en la que estaba absorto—. Un toque de impresionismo con una veta de extravagancia victoriana. La tela negra —señaló sin mirar— será una niña de ojos profundos y cansados, en la playa, en una noche brillante con luz de luna. Llevará un traje de baño antiguo, esos que tienen shorts y un cinturón, como el que tú usas —alzó la vista hacia mí—. Desparramaré algunos objetos al azar, fuera de perspectiva, como algún pez, o una ballena o algo así. Y (esto es *fundamental*) ella estará sosteniendo su propia sombra, como si estuviera enferma y necesitara que ella la sostuviera. Haré la tela blanca con la misma niña en la playa, de día, con la misma sombra. Es una metáfora. Se entiende, ¿no? La niña siente que es una sombra, que no existe. La crisis existencial, etcétera, etcétera —me miró muy rápido y luego regresó a las pinturas—. Puedes ayudarme con la tela blanca, si quieres.

No dije nada. Pero estaba más contenta que unas castañuelas de que mi hermano hubiera vuelto a pintar, y River se dio cuenta pues me hizo un guiño a espaldas de Luke.

Eché una mirada a los rayos del sol que ingresaban a raudales por las ventanitas, a las telas sin terminar de mis padres, al suelo salpicado de pintura, a Luke, concentrado en el caballete que tenía delante. Tal vez había sido un error abandonar la pintura. Aspiré el leve olor amargo del aguarrás, el aroma aceitoso de la pintura, el perfume del aire fresco del mar.

Mis ojos se detuvieron ante un retrato inconcluso de mi madre. No era un autorretrato. Era la mano de mi padre la que había pintado esa larga nariz y esos ojos entrecerrados. Podía distinguirlo claramente. Sus trazos eran más definidos, más sólidos, sus colores, más oscuros que los de mi madre. Ella era Chagall, Renoir. Y mi padre era… bueno, era él mismo. De los dos, supuse, él era el verdadero pintor.

River recorría el lugar y miraba los viejos cuadros. Se veía esbelto, hermoso y sonriente. Pero, al observarlo, sentí que mi sensación de paz se esfumaba. Todavía me atormentaba la conversación de la noche anterior, que tapaba la luz del sol tan real y tibia que llenaba la habitación.

Volví a imaginarme al Demonio irguiéndose detrás de River con los ojos rojos. Sentí un hormigueo en la cabeza y me estremecí, como si tuviera frío, aunque no era así. River lo notó, sé que lo hizo, pero no dijo nada. Solo se inclinó, tomó una caja de acrílicos secos, la colocó debajo del brazo y luego señaló la tela más grande del cobertizo.

—¿Esa chica está disponible? Mi talento artístico es tan grande que solo puede contenerlo la tela más grande de todas. ¿Tela… lienzo? No conozco bien la jerga.

La enorme tela que quería River era supuestamente para un retrato familiar. Desde que era pequeña, mi madre había mencionado que quería pintarnos a los cuatro juntos. Había traído a casa esa tela muchos años atrás. Y todavía continuaba allí.

—Claro —contesté sin mirarlo a los ojos—. Puedes usarla.

Apoyó la caja de acrílicos y miró a su alrededor hasta que encontró una lata de pintura de interior, que mis padres utilizaban a veces para preparar la tela. Abrió la tapa, la mezcló bien y luego metió la mano, que salió con un puñado de amarillo.

—Jackson Pollock —dijo y me sonrió—. Es la única manera de pintar —arrojó el puño hacia la tela, lo abrió a último momento y la pintura amarilla salió volando.

Yo tomé un pincel.

CAPÍTULO 17

RIVER UTILIZÓ TRES latas enteras en su tributo a Pollock. La tela quedó cubierta de manchas azules, amarillas y negras. Mientras yo la observaba, apareció por detrás de mí y apoyó la mano, aún mojada con pintura, en la parte baja de mi espalda, agregándole más color al overol de mi madre.

–Te pinté a ti, Vi. Ojos azules, cabello amarillo y pensamientos negros.

–Por eso es tan feo –comentó Luke con una risa estrepitosa.

–No descargues tu odio a Pollock en el chico nuevo –repuse mientras me dirigía al pequeño fregadero del cobertizo para enjuagar los pinceles. Le eché una mirada a River por encima del hombro–. Luke cree que el impresionismo abstracto es, bueno, una estupidez. Mamá piensa lo mismo. Pero es el descendiente natural de…

–La pizza –Luke se puso de pie y se estiró–. Necesito un poco de pizza en el estómago antes de escuchar a Vi pontificar sobre el arte.

–Yo también –esto vino de Sunshine, que se encontraba en la puerta del cobertizo, un vaso de té helado en la mano.

–¿Dónde anduviste hoy? –pregunté–. Nosotros estuvimos aquí dentro creando grandes obras de arte –retrocedí y observé la pintura de Luke. Después miré la mía y fruncí el ceño. ¿Por qué mi hermano pintaba como yo, y yo como él? En todo lo demás éramos tan diferentes. Pero mis trazos iban por el mismo camino que los suyos, se afinaban, luego se engrosaban, eran iguales. Mis pinceladas también eran breves y rápidas como las de él. Eso… me molestaba. Me hacía pensar que Luke y yo éramos más parecidos de lo que yo había creído, como si… como si nos encamináramos en la misma dirección pero por caminos muy distintos.

–Mis padres me encargaron que me ocupara de la biblioteca ambulante –respondió Sunshine con voz lenta y susurrante, porque Luke estaba presente–. Un montón de viejas solteronas, que viven encerradas en sus casas, necesitaban sus horribles novelas románticas.

–Sunshine, eres la persona más generosa que conozco. ¿Alguna vez te lo he dicho?

Me lanzó una gran sonrisa y luego se dedicó a exclamar "Ooh" y "Aah" ante las pinturas de Luke.

–¿Y dónde se puede encontrar pizza en este pueblo? –me preguntó River.

—Hay un lugar muy bueno cerca de la plaza —respondí—. ¿Quieres ir?

—Sip —dijo y una chispa se encendió en sus ojos—. Será perfecto.

—¿Perfecto para qué?

—Ya verás —contestó y en su rostro se dibujó la sonrisa torcida.

Eco tenía una pizzería genial llamada Lucca, ubicada en la plaza principal, junto a la cafetería. Estaba dirigida por la misma familia italiana: Luciano, Graziella y sus tres hijos. Por lo que yo veía, los hombres de la familia eran los únicos que cocinaban y Graziella, principalmente, daba vueltas dando órdenes y diciendo *allora penso, allora penso*, una y otra vez. Una vez, le pregunté qué significaba esa expresión y me dijo que quería decir *entonces pienso*. Y, de acuerdo a eso, supuse que Graziella debía pensar mucho antes de hacer una pizza.

Llegamos temprano y el restaurante estaba vacío. Luke se ubicó en un box junto a los grandes ventanales que daban a la plaza; estaban medio abiertos y entraba una brisa agradable. Sunshine llevaba un vestido de verano rosado y hasta yo me había cambiado el overol de pintora y me había puesto una camisa negra de seda con una falda negra. Me sentía bonita. El sol de la tarde caía de esa forma oblicua que me resultaba romántica, especialmente porque daba sobre River y hacía brillar su cabello castaño oscuro.

Será perfecto, había dicho él.

Eché una mirada por el restaurante, luego observé la plaza a través de las ventanas y miré nuevamente a River. Estaba reclinado en el asiento, los brazos detrás de la cabeza como diciendo *Aquí no hay nada de qué preocuparse, Vi… soy el tipo más relajado del planeta… no hay nada en mi mente… no guardo ningún as bajo la manga…*

Su aire despreocupado era irritante. Realmente. Pero luego noté la pintura amarilla en el brazo derecho, y mi irritación… se derritió.

Pedí una pizza de pesto y una margarita, que llegaron en menos de veinte minutos. La masa era finita y tenía unas partes ennegrecidas por el fuego. Una delicia.

Graziella se acercó mientras comíamos e hizo un largo discurso en italiano que nadie entendió excepto River, que sí hablaba italiano, como yo había imaginado. Le respondió algo fluida y rápidamente, y Graziella rio. Luego gritó *"¡Gianni!"* y apareció su hijo de cabello oscuro. Lo envió a la cocina y regresó con un tazón de helado de pistacho para cada uno.

En sexto curso, al tomarnos la foto grupal, me colocaron junto a Gianni, y yo no podía quitar los ojos de su brazo largo y moreno al lado del mío, tan blanco. Aun cuando debíamos estar mirando a la cámara, yo no podía apartar la vista de él. Pero cuando notó que lo observaba, me sonrió, y me agradó desde ese momento. También ayudaba que siempre me saludara cuando los demás chicos de la clase no lo hacían.

Gianni se sentó en el banco junto a Sunshine y Luke, de modo que ellos tres quedaron un poco apretujados frente a River y a mí. Apoyó los codos sobre la mesa y Sunshine se acercó más a él mientras sonreía.

Pero Gianni me miraba a mí.

—Salió el nuevo número de *Fresh Cup Magazine* —comentó. Hablaba perfectamente nuestro idioma, ya que se había criado en Eco, pero su voz todavía conservaba el tono bajo y enfático de su Italia natal.

Asentí.

–Lo vi en el café. ¿Cuál es la última novedad?

Los ojos de Gianni se encendieron.

–El café de filtrado manual, todavía, *molto bene, molto bene*. Pero mamá no me deja servirlo en el local, aunque tostáramos granos de Kenia, jugosos y tropicales, que serían ideales para esa forma de hacer café. Solo podemos preparar café expreso, porque somos *italianos*. De todas maneras, ya encargué el hervidor especial, así que tienes que venir a probarlo alguna vez, fuera de horario. Debería llegar esta semana por correo, de modo que podríamos...

–Soy River –interrumpió mientras extendía la mano por arriba de la mesa–. Soy nuevo en el pueblo. Vivo con Violet.

–Él alquiló la casa de huéspedes –agregué, demasiado rápido.

Gianni dejó pasar la repentina grosería de River, se estiró hacia adelante y le estrechó la mano.

–Soy Gianni –hubo una pausa, River me miró y Gianni me miró y yo me volví hacia la ventana abierta y traté de no mirar a nadie.

Luke también miraba por la ventana. Tenía los dedos en la cabeza y observaba en el vidrio las entradas de su cabello cobrizo. Dejó de hacerlo cuando lo pesqué.

–¿Todos se enteraron de las noticias? –comentó Gianni después de unos segundos de silencio.

–¿Qué noticias? –preguntó Sunshine y se llevó la cuchara con helado a la boca y la sacó muy lentamente–. No me agrada leer los periódicos: me hacen doler la cabeza.

Le pateé la pierna por debajo de la mesa pero me ignoró.

—Sucedió algo extraño en Jerusalem Rock. Todos están hablando de eso, porque se parece a lo que sucedió aquí, con los chicos en el cementerio. Solo que peor.

—¿Dónde diablos queda Jerusalem Rock? —preguntó Luke.

—Es un pueblito al sur, que queda a dos horas de aquí —respondió Gianni y sus ojos tenían una expresión sombría e intraducible—. Dos días atrás, un grupo de personas se reunieron en un campo en las afueras de Jerusalem Rock y acusaron a una anciana de brujería. La amarraron a un poste y le arrojaron piedras hasta que se desmayó. Y luego la quemaron —Gianni hizo una pausa y respiró profundamente—. Dijeron que era una bruja porque tenía cabello rojo. *Cabello rojo*. ¿Qué le anda pasando a la gente de aquí últimamente? ¿Acaso alguien puso LSD en el pozo?

—¿Qué… qué le sucedió a la mujer? —pregunté en un susurro, porque me había quedado sin aire en los pulmones—. A la mujer pelirroja. ¿La salvaron? ¿Está bien?

Gianni me miró y negó con la cabeza.

—No, Violet. Murió. Y después ataron a una niñita pelirroja y le lanzaban acusaciones a los gritos. Tenían las manos llenas de piedras y estaban dispuestos a arrojarlas cuando finalmente llegó la policía. Tenía nueve años. Espeluznante, ¿no?

Ninguno de nosotros dijo nada. River continuaba observando a Gianni, y Gianni me miraba a mí con aspecto preocupado y yo miraba a River y, de repente, las manos me temblaron, me estremecí toda y sentí náuseas.

River. El resplandor. Él se marchó. Podría haber ido a Jerusalem Rock ese día en que desapareció, podría haberlo hecho, podría haber sido él, ¿quién más podría haber sido?

—Gianni —gritó Graziella desde adentro—. *In cucina, subito.*

Volvió a sacudir la cabeza de un lado a otro y se levantó.

—Lo único que les digo es que vayan pensando en conseguir unas botellas de San Pellegrino. Es mejor tomar precauciones y, por un tiempo, comprar agua de Italia.

Gianni desapareció por la puerta de la cocina. Sunshine y Luke comenzaron a hablar entre ellos, pero yo no pude poner atención en lo que decían. River se negaba a hacer contacto visual conmigo. Optó por darse vuelta y dedicarse a mirar por las ventanas. La parte de mi pierna que tocaba la suya, de pronto, se puso caliente, como si ardiera, de modo que me fui deslizando en el banco para alejarme de él.

River se puso tenso, echó los hombros hacia atrás y alzó súbitamente la cabeza. Me detuve y seguí su mirada.

Afuera, en la plaza, dos chicas de cabello oscuro estaban sentadas debajo de un árbol, una le leía un libro en voz alta a la otra. Un niño flacucho, de cabello rojo hasta los hombros y sombrero de vaquero estaba sentado en las hamacas y observaba a una madre que pasaba caminando con dos bebitos de unos dos años. *Jimmy the Popcorn Man* estaba sentado en su carrito de palomitas de maíz, el mentón contra el pecho, durmiendo. Era una escena alegre. Respiré hondo y me sentí un poquito mejor.

Y ahí fue cuando lo vi. A Daniel Leap. El padre de Jack. Estaba ebrio, muy ebrio. Con paso tambaleante, un inestable pie después del otro, caminó hasta el centro del césped y se quedó ahí, balanceándose de un lado a otro y arrebatándole toda la dulzura a mi pueblo.

Sentí que River se movía nerviosamente a mi lado. Él también estaba mirando al padre de Jack. Sus ojos entornados eran solo dos rayitas finitas, y su rostro se veía… impaciente y ansioso. A tal punto que tenía la mandíbula contraída.

Esa impaciencia y esa ansiedad me asustaron. Sentada a su lado en el banco, el miedo comenzó a cubrirme con sus garras como el agua a un hombre que se ahoga, hasta que se me estranguló la garganta y me ahogué. Algo estaba por suceder. Sunshine y Luke estaban ocupados con sus coqueteos y no prestaban atención. La mano de River sujetó la mía por debajo de la mesa, pero su piel estaba fría y mis dedos quedaron flojos entre los suyos. Observé al padre de Jack, que se balanceaba en la plaza. Observé mientras llevaba la mano al bolsillo y extraía un objeto plateado, que refulgió bajo el sol del atardecer.

Observé mientras lo levantaba hasta el cuello.

Y mientras se cortaba la garganta.

No ocurrió nada. Un segundo. Dos segundos. Tres.

Y luego brotó la sangre.

Cayó a borbotones por su camisa amarilla, que quedó húmeda y carmesí.

El papá de Jack se puso blanco, como un papel, en contraste con el rojo intenso de su camisa. Miró el objeto plateado que tenía en la mano, como si lo observara por primera vez, y lo arrojó lejos de sí. El objeto golpeó contra la acera y se deslizó varios centímetros.

La madre con los niñitos gritó. Las dos chicas de cabello oscuro gritaron. El padre de Jack cayó de rodillas. Un segundo. Dos. Y luego se inclinó hacia un costado y quedó inmóvil.

Ante el griterío, Sunshine se levantó del asiento y miró por las ventanas. Abrió la boca y un débil gemido se escurrió de sus labios. Luke se puso de pie de un salto. Siguió la mirada de Sunshine y sus manos se dirigieron a la mesa y la aferraron con fuerza.

Un hombre se mató delante de mí, delante del pueblo. Y River lo obligó a hacerlo. Lo sabía. De la misma manera que sabía que me encontraba cerca del mar por el gusto a sal en el aire. De la misma manera que sabía que era Luke quien deambulaba por el Ciudadano por el sonido de sus pasos. De la misma manera que sabía cuál era la sensación de tener los brazos de River alrededor de mi cuerpo cuando estaba profundamente dormido.

Sunshine continuaba profiriendo sus gemidos débiles y babosos y yo temblaba toda, los dedos, las piernas, la cabeza…

El rostro de River se veía inexpresivo. No parecía culpable ni avergonzado. En realidad, tenía cara de nada. Su mano todavía apretaba la mía por debajo de la mesa. La solté, me levanté del banco y salí corriendo del restaurante.

Me detuve cuando llegué hasta la mujer con los dos bebés, que había gritado. Ahora estaba callada, observaba en silencio y sus manos cubrían los ojos de los dos mellizos, para que no pudieran ver lo que había a sus pies.

Miré el gran tajo que el hombre tenía en la garganta, el frente de su camisa cubierto de sangre, el suelo debajo de él, también cubierto de sangre. El césped se había puesto negro.

Algo llamó mi atención hacia la izquierda.

Una navaja de afeitar.

Sunshine apareció a mi lado. Emitió otro grito débil. Una multitud comenzó a formarse alrededor del cuerpo: las dos chicas, el hombre de las palomitas de maíz, el chico vestido de vaquero, Luke, Graziella, Gianni.

Le eché otro vistazo al hombre que estaba echado en el suelo y luego volví al restaurante.

River continuaba sentado en el box. Me vio y sonrió, como si no ocurriera nada. Como si no ocurriera realmente *nada*.

Me marché. Tomé el sendero a través del bosque que conducía a casa. Pero cuando estaba por la mitad, me di vuelta y regresé.

Caminé por el pueblo. Pasé delante de mi escuela.

Encontré a Jack en su cocina sencilla y vacía, en la oscuridad, con la mirada perdida, como si estuviera esperando que algo malo ocurriera. Y había ocurrido.

—Decidí escaparme una vez que mi padre había estado ebrio durante una semana entera —dijo, después de que entré sin llamar. Estaba sentado en una silla desvencijada junto a una mesa barata de madera. Me pregunté si las luces estarían apagadas porque le gustaba o porque no habían pagado la factura de la electricidad. Las dos posibilidades me resultaban familiares.

»Primero, traté de fingir mi muerte, como Huckleberry Finn —prosiguió Jack—. Con sangre de cerdo. Hasta había ido a la carnicería y preguntado si me daban un poco. Pero el sujeto comenzó a hacerme un montón de preguntas, y me fui.

Eché un vistazo por la cocina. Sus paredes tristes estaban cubiertas de un empapelado descolorido, y se podía sentir el asqueroso optimismo de ese recargado estampado de flores rosadas, que ahora se desprendía en tiras. Había botellas de alcohol vacías en el fregadero, olor a humo, a polvo y a basura que nadie había desechado. Y la comparé con la cocina del Ciudadano, con los techos altos, los grandes ventanales, el sillón amarillo y, por primera vez en mucho tiempo, buena comida en el refrigerador.

—¿Quieres marcharte de aquí? —le pregunté.

Jack asintió. Se levantó y caminó por el corredor que salía de la cocina y retornó unos minutos después con una mochila. Me siguió hacia afuera de la casa.

Evitamos la plaza mientras resonaba en nuestros oídos la sirena de una ambulancia, y caminamos en silencio hasta el Ciudadano Kane.

Supuse que pronto se enteraría de lo de su padre. Seguramente, ya lo había imaginado. Fogonazos del rostro pálido y de la camisa empapada de sangre de Daniel Leap me golpeaban la mente como puñetazos. Yo no sabía mucho de niños. Especialmente si eran niños inteligentes que percibían todo y me miraban con grandes e inteligentes ojos azules debajo de su cabello rojizo. Todavía me temblaban las puntas de los dedos y el ritmo de los latidos de mi corazón era fuerte, irregular y *extraño*, como si toda mi agitación hubiera cambiado la posición de mi corazón y no consiguiera encontrar la forma de volver a donde estaba.

Llevé a Jack a la cocina del Ciudadano. Se sentó en el sillón amarillo y me observó mientras rallaba jengibre fresco en dos vasos de limonada casera. Freddie solía hacer lo mismo cuando yo estaba triste.

Tomamos asiento en el sillón amarillo de la cocina, en el débil sol del atardecer, y bebimos esa mezcla picante, dulce y agria, y nos sentimos mejor. O, al menos, yo me sentí mejor. Y no sé si fue el jengibre o el recuerdo de Freddie, pero mi miedo se disolvió un poquito. Tal vez no era algo bueno, pero así fue.

Después, conduje a Jack a uno de los dormitorios de huéspedes del primer piso. Había polvo, pero las sábanas estaban limpias... o habían estado alguna vez, cuando se hizo la cama, y esperé que eso no hubiera sido mucho tiempo atrás. Era una habitación más bien masculina, con empapelado verde oliva, alfombra y cortinas oscuras y una chimenea de ladrillos negros. Jack echó una mirada a su alrededor sin decir nada. Pero a mí me pareció que le gustó.

Apoyó la mochila en la cama y luego recostó su cuerpo delgado contra el engreído respaldo tallado de la cama.

—¿Era papá? —preguntó mirándome directamente a los ojos, los labios finitos apretados con fuerza.

—Sí —respondí.

—¿Está muerto?

Escruté sus ojos azul oscuro.

—Sí.

Fui hasta la vieja lámpara que se encontraba junto a la cama y la encendí. La luz era densa y amarilla e inundó el dormitorio de una agradable calidez. Ahora podía ver las pecas oscuras en la nariz y las mejillas de Jack. Y sus ojos secos. Limpié el polvo de la mesa de noche con la mano.

—¿Fue River quien lo hizo?

El corazón se me detuvo y luego volvió a latir.

—¿Qué quieres decir, Jack?

—¿Usó el resplandor para hacer que papá se matara?

Tragué saliva y tomé aire. *¿River le había hablado del resplandor?*

—No. Sí. Mayormente, sí, supongo.

No habló durante unos minutos, solo se quedó mirando la chimenea, aunque no había fuego.

Alcé los ojos hacia el techo. Todas las habitaciones del Ciudadano tenían techos altos y, en general, eso le otorgaba a la casa una sensación de aire y espacio. Sin embargo, esa noche, el techo no parecía suficientemente alto. Ese dormitorio con su viejo cubrecama de satín, su gran cama de madera y sus seis ventanas cubiertas, resultaba sofocante.

—Lo siento, Jack —dije finalmente—. Haré que River abandone la casa de huéspedes. Haré que se marche muy lejos. De verdad.

Aun mientras lo decía, sabía que era una mentira.

Yo no haría nada parecido.

—River solo estaba cuidándome —respondió.

—Eso no justifica lo que hizo —comenté con un poco de dureza, pero luego apoyé la mano en su pequeño hombro—. ¿Qué te contó acerca de su… acerca de lo que puede hacer? ¿Qué te contó sobre el resplandor?

Se encogió de hombros y el cabello se agitó alrededor de sus orejas.

—No mucho. Solo que puede hacer cosas, como hacer que la gente vea monstruos. Sin embargo, yo no creo que esa sea toda la historia —Jack me miró directamente a los ojos—. River es un mentiroso.

—Sí —dije—. Lo sé.

Jack comenzó a desempacar la mochila. Había traído muchas cosas, probablemente porque esperaba no regresar. Y yo esperaba lo mismo. Lo ayudé a guardar sus pertenencias y le busqué pasta de dientes y esas cosas. Cuando llegó al fondo del bolso, extrajo un cuadrito que tendría unos veintitrés centímetros.

—Era de mi abuelo —explicó mientras lo apoyaba contra la pared, encima de la mesa de noche—. Mi padre vendió el resto de sus cuadros, porque quería estar ebrio todo el día en vez de trabajar. Pero yo salvé este.

El cuadro estaba hecho con óleo y era un autorretrato. El pintor se había pintado a sí mismo, delante de una tela, el pincel en alto, mientras una mujer rubia estaba recostada en un sofá a su derecha. El pintor se parecía a alguien. A alguien conocido. Tal vez se parecía a Daniel Leap, sin todo el alcohol encima.

O tal vez, no.

Y la mujer recostada era exactamente igual a Freddie.

Arropé a Jack y bajé a la cocina a esperar a River.

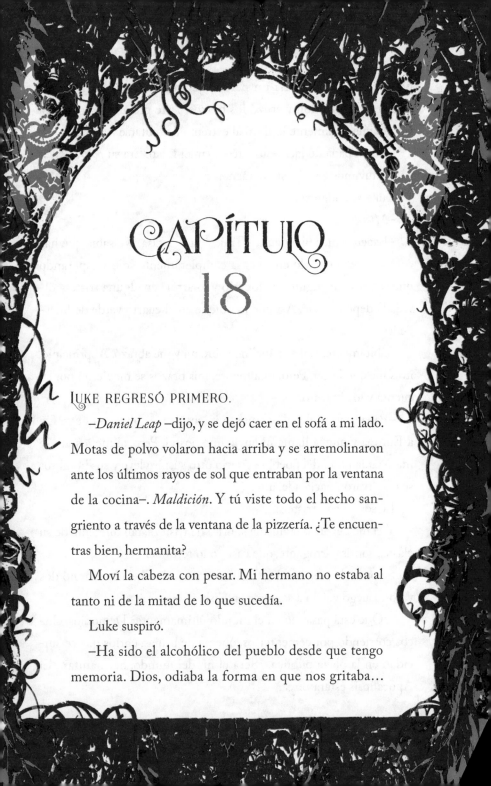

CAPÍTULO 18

LUKE REGRESÓ PRIMERO.

–*Daniel Leap* –dijo, y se dejó caer en el sofá a mi lado. Motas de polvo volaron hacia arriba y se arremolinaron ante los últimos rayos de sol que entraban por la ventana de la cocina–. *Maldición*. Y tú viste todo el hecho sangriento a través de la ventana de la pizzería. ¿Te encuentras bien, hermanita?

Moví la cabeza con pesar. Mi hermano no estaba al tanto ni de la mitad de lo que sucedía.

Luke suspiró.

–Ha sido el alcohólico del pueblo desde que tengo memoria. Dios, odiaba la forma en que nos gritaba…

pero aun así... Era casi un personaje emblemático de Eco —se arrellanó en el sillón y cruzó los brazos—. Me pregunto qué habrá sido lo que finalmente lo llevó al extremo de quitarse la vida.

—Era el papá de Jack —susurré—. Daniel Leap. Era su *padre*. River y yo estuvimos con él esta mañana.

Luke se enderezó.

—*Mierda*.

—Exacto —hice una pausa—. Traje a Jack a casa. No sabía qué hacer. No podía dejarlo en su casa completamente solo y esperando que se presente algún funcionario y lo arroje en alguna triste y olvidada dependencia. Así que lo ubiqué en el cuarto verde de huéspedes.

Súbitamente, Luke se inclinó sobre mí y me abrazó. Al principio, no supe qué hacer. Pero, finalmente, mis brazos se movieron por su cuenta y lo abrazaron.

—Papá es un imbécil —comentó mientras me soltaba— que se fue a Europa y nunca llama ni envía una postal. Pero, al menos, no se mató en la plaza del pueblo —emitió otro suspiro leve y sus hombros se encorvaron hacia adelante.

Le sonreí con tristeza.

Y él me devolvió la misma sonrisa de tristeza, tan diferente de su clásica sonrisa arrogante, que casi no lo reconocí.

Se puso de pie, fue al refrigerador, sacó el té helado y sirvió dos vasos. Luego volvió a sentarse en el sofá.

—¿Qué está pasando en el mundo últimamente? Demonios, chicos corriendo por cementerios, quema de brujas, ebrios que se suicidan en la plaza pública. ¿Será el fin del mundo, hermanita? ¿El Apocalipsis estará cerca?

Luke bebió un largo sorbo de té y sacudió la cabeza con pesar.

–Como dije anoche, todo comenzó cuando llegó River. Podría ser una coincidencia, como la mayoría de las cosas de la vida. Pero qué casualidad que un hombre se mate en el centro del pueblo *y* ustedes lo observan desde un asiento en la primera fila *y* el hijo del suicida estaba con ustedes en el ático el día anterior. *Dios mío.* No podré quitarme de la mente la imagen de la camisa llena de sangre en *muchos* años.

Me estremecí. Fue el estremecimiento más fuerte y completo, de esos que comienzan en la cabeza, se extienden por las piernas y llegan hasta los dedos de los pies.

Sin embargo, lo que me estaba haciendo estremecer no era la imagen de la camisa ensangrentada de Daniel Leap ni el enorme tajo en su garganta. Era River con expresión de impaciencia y ansiedad mientras Daniel se llevaba la navaja al cuello.

Los últimos destellos de luz se escurrieron de la ventana y la luz azul del crepúsculo se instaló en la cocina.

–Jack tiene un cuadro –señalé–. Lo vi cuando desempacó. Es de Freddie. Dijo que pertenecía a su abuelo.

Las cejas de Luke se alzaron bruscamente.

–Sí –asentí.

Se levantó del sillón y se estiró.

–Bueno, puedes agregar ese misterio a la larga lista. Mira, me iré a dormir. Es probable que Jack despierte temprano. Y como parece que se mudó a esta casa, tendremos que ocuparnos de él.

Como debe ser, decía su rostro, *no como nuestros padres.*

Salió de la cocina y, un minuto después, oí sus pies moviéndose por el piso de arriba. Seguramente iba a corroborar si Jack se encontraba bien.

Me quedé en la cocina vacía bebiendo mi té. Ya estaba oscuro. La mayor parte de la habitación estaba en penumbras. Las ventanas se encontraban totalmente abiertas y, de repente, tuve la sensación de que alguien me observaba, desde afuera, oculto por la oscuridad...

La puerta del frente se abrió de un golpe. Oí pisadas que atravesaban el vestíbulo, pasaban junto a la escalera de mármol, por delante del comedor formal que nunca usábamos y se detenían en la entrada de la cocina. Hice tintinear los cubitos de hielo del fondo del vaso y levanté los ojos.

River.

Me quedé sentada mirándolo y él también me miró. Y al mirarlo tuve un deseo, un deseo *apremiante*, de empujarlo por la puerta del Ciudadano Kane y arrojarlo al suelo y patearle la cara hasta que se le borrara del rostro esa expresión despreocupada.

Tal vez él tenía razón, sobre mí y mi bochornosa violencia.

—Violet, ¿recuerdas cuando dormimos la siesta en este sofá? —se sentó a mi lado.

—De hecho, sí, lo recuerdo. Fue el lunes —giré y observé el enorme y malvado cuchillo de carnicero que se encontraba sobre la mesa de la cocina. Luke lo utilizaba para cortar el pan, aunque yo le había dicho más de una vez que, en su lugar, utilizara el cuchillo dentado. Pensé en tomar ese cuchillo y en la sensación que me provocaría clavárselo en medio de las costillas. Dejé que mi mente se detuviera por un momento en esa sensación, dejé que se revelara la parte bochornosa de mí.

—¿El lunes? Parece que pasó toda una vida.

Lo ignoré.

—Bien, dime cómo lo hiciste. Y trata de no mentir, mentiroso.

Dejó de reír, pero su rostro estaba tranquilo.

–Hice que pensara que la navaja era un bolígrafo plateado. Y luego hice que trazara con él una línea a través de la garganta –emitió una risa ahogada.

Escuchar a River admitir lo que hizo, decirlo en voz alta y volverlo cierto y real, hizo que mi corazón se paralizara, como si alguien le estuviera clavando las uñas.

Había mentido cuando me dijo que no planeaba volver a utilizar el resplandor. En mi propia cara.

Lo odiaba.

Una parte de mí lo odiaba.

La otra parte… Esa parte no importaba.

Lo cual me asustaba mortalmente.

River tomó mi mano y la acercó a su pecho. Me desprendí violentamente, pero él la volvió a sujetar… y un segundo después, mi furia desapareció, rápido, como el agua fría por la garganta en un día calcinante.

–River, que no hayas empuñado el arma, no significa que no fuera asesinato.

Continuó sosteniendo mi mano. Traté de soltarme, con poco entusiasmo, y él me sujetó con más fuerza.

Busqué en mi interior. Intenté recuperar mi indignación previa, pero no encontré nada. Sentía el calor de la mano de River sobre la mía y me resultaba agradable y ya estaba agotada.

–No te preocupes, Vi. No estoy en peligro. Esa es la maravilla de poder hacer algo que nadie más puede hacer. Nadie lo creería. No hay forma de que me atrapen.

–*Maldición*, no me refería a eso –aparté su mano de la mía y me puse de pie con dificultad, para quedar por encima de él–. El tema aquí no es que te atrapen, sino que cometiste un asesinato. Un *asesinato*. ¿No piensas que hubo algo malo en lo que hiciste? Daniel era alcohólico, me insultaba a los gritos y no cuidaba a su hijo, pero también era patético y estaba triste y confundido. No se asesina así a la gente, River. No se asesina a *nadie*. Se les demuestra compasión, por el amor de Dios.

Vamos, Vi. Enfurécete. Él se lo merece. Hasta parece que lo desea. *Esa mirada despreocupada… es un desafío… Tienes que estar a la altura de ese desafío…*

River se encogió de hombros.

–¿Quién tiene tiempo para eso? Un asesinato es algo bastante ambiguo, moralmente hablando. Vi, sé un poco más filosófica. ¿Qué clase de persona sería yo si dejara que Daniel Leap siguiera vivo? La forma en que te habló aquel día en la plaza… eso estuvo realmente mal. Y Jack llevaba una vida miserable con él. Uno podría afirmar que Daniel *quería* morir. Si no, ¿por qué otro motivo se embriagaría tan seguido? Y yo podía ayudarlo a conseguir lo que quería, con tan solo pensarlo. Así de fácil. Algunas personas no merecen vivir. Y, para ir un paso más allá, algunas personas *tienen* que morir. ¿Por qué nací yo con este don si no es para hacer del mundo un lugar mejor? Por supuesto que hago lo de los monstruos para divertirme y porque me gusta sentir el resplandor en mí. Pero lo del padre de Jack… eso no fue para divertirme. Lo hice por Jack. Y por ti. Sí, podrás decir que fue un poco desordenado y estuvo lejos de ser perfecto. Pero, bueno, los dos están mejor ahora –se llevó la mano a la boca y bostezó. La conversación lo aburría–. No puedes negarlo, Vi.

Me quedé ahí de pie, en silencio.

—Sí, puedo —dije finalmente. Pero River... River estaba empezando a sonar razonable. Al menos, lo que decía, resultaba *lógico*. Una parte de mí, una parte aguda y crítica de mí, no lo aceptaba. No por completo. Algo estaba... mal.

¿No es cierto?

River se estiró, colocó las manos en mi cintura y me atrajo hacia él.

—No me arrepiento de nada. Lo único que desearía es que no se estuviera volviendo cada vez más difícil predecir los resultados del resplandor. Yo lo hacía muy bien, incluso hasta hace pocos meses. Pero, últimamente, es como si no pudiera dejar de utilizarlo, y, cuando lo hago, no sale de acuerdo a lo planeado.

—Perdón, ¿*cómo*? ¿No puedes predecir los resultados? ¿Qué diablos significa eso? —intenté liberarme de los brazos de River, pero sin mucha convicción, y me ignoró.

—No, no es nada. Solo siento como si estuviera perdiendo un poco el control. Es algo sorprendente, eso es todo. Es como si pensara por sí mismo, casi como si me controlara, en vez de ser al revés. De todas maneras, estoy seguro de que no es importante.

Dejé de retorcerme, comenzaba a sentirme mejor. River tenía razón. Algunas personas *realmente* merecían morir. Un resplandor incontrolable *no era* algo importante.

—¿Sabes algo, Violet? Cuando estoy a tu lado, puedo captar algunos leves destellos de lo que está sucediendo en tu gran cerebro. Por ejemplo, sé que detestas la remolacha. En tu cabeza, la idea de una remolacha está rodeada de un desagradable humo oscuro. Lo vi cuando las levanté en la tienda. No hace falta decir que las dejé donde estaban. A diferencia de los tomates, que tienen un agradable halo rosado a su alrededor.

Me llevé las manos instintivamente a la cabeza, como si pudiera impedir que River recibiera los destellos que se escapaban. Pero luego me sentí estúpida y las bajé.

—¿Qué otra cosa puedes ver? —pregunté.

—Puedo ver que te gusto, a tu pesar —River sonrió y una parte de mí se derritió ante la sonrisa, como chocolate en la boca y hielo bajo el sol.

Pero la otra parte deseaba tener un ladrillo en la mano para poder golpearlo justo en el medio de su boca hermosa y torcida, hasta que la sangre fluyera a raudales y le cubriera la camisa, como a Daniel Leap.

—Vi, deberías haber visto la nube negra que había esta mañana en tu cabeza alrededor de Daniel Leap. Guau. Y yo que pensaba que odiabas la remolacha. Tenías a ese cabrón en un agujero negro. En un *abismo*.

—Existe una diferencia abismal entre desear que alguien esté muerto y matarlo, River.

En ese instante, se me cruzó un pensamiento. Un pensamiento negro, oscuro y malvado. ¿Y si para River no existía ninguna diferencia? ¿Era eso lo que quiso decir cuando mencionó que le estaba costando predecir los resultados del resplandor? ¿Acaso todo su discurso sobre la ambigüedad moral no era más que una forma de justificar algo que no podía controlar?

Y luego recordé lo que dijo Gianni acerca de la pobre mujer pelirroja. La bruja. Lo había olvidado, con todo el horror que vino después, lo había olvidado…

—River, ¿adónde fuiste el día que no estuviste aquí?

Se encogió de hombros. Levantó el borde de mi camisa con una mano y comenzó a besarme el estómago. Tenía las manos cubiertas de pintura seca.

—¿Acaso fuiste… a Jerusalem Rock? —*concéntrate*. *Si dejas que haga desaparecer tu ira, si no sientes ira, entonces no eres mejor que él.*

River seguía acariciándome el torso con la nariz.

—¿Dónde queda Jerusalem Rock?

—Es el pueblo del cual Gianni estuvo hablando, donde quemaron a una mujer. Fuiste tú, ¿verdad? —al decir eso, no sentí nada. Solo los besos suaves de River en mi piel, como una brisa fresca en un día de calor.

—Yo —beso—. No tengo —beso—. La menor idea de qué estás hablando —beso, beso, beso.

—¿De modo que no fuiste a Jerusalem Rock? —se me estaba haciendo muy difícil concentrarme. Los besos de River… De repente, me sentí tan bien, tan serena, tan feliz—. Entonces ¿a dónde fuiste?

—A otro lugar. Tenía que marcharme por un tiempo. Conduje hacia el sur. No recuerdo bien adónde me dirigí.

—River, eso suena a mentira. Eres tan misterioso, siempre misterioso, es cierto que me gusta, pero quiero… quiero saber si… —*concentración*—. Pero has… alguna vez has… —*maldita sea*—. ¿Alguna vez mataste a alguien más? Digo, ¿alguna vez hiciste que otra persona se matara, como con Daniel Leap?

—Sí —masculló contra mi piel.

—¿Cuántos?

Entre sus manos, River me dio vuelta y comenzó a besarme la parte baja de la espalda.

—Muchos, Vi.

—¿Cuántos son "muchos"? —mis ojos se cerraron.

—No lo sé. Tantos como era necesario que murieran. Quizá doce, supongo. Quizá muchos más. Tendría que pensarlo. Hace cuatro años que tengo el resplandor.

—¿Así que… ni siquiera sabes, sin pensarlo mucho, a cuántos has asesinado?

River se puso de pie. Sus manos acariciaban mi espalda con lentitud y confianza. Me apoyó la cabeza en el cuello.

—No —respondió—. Una vez que está hecho, ya no pienso más en eso.

Sus labios siguieron la línea de mi mentón. Su cabello olía a arena y a sal, como si hubiera estado nadando. Tal vez el mío también. Era algo normal al vivir al lado del mar.

De inmediato, ya estábamos besándonos. Los besos eran largos y profundos. Sentí que eso que él hacía comenzaba a correr dentro de mí, como la primera vez en el cementerio. Fluía y fluía, como el agua bajando por una montaña. Como fluía el tiempo en un día de verano. Como fluía la sangre por un cuello cortado por una navaja.

—River, ¿estás utilizando el resplandor conmigo? —pregunté.

—Quizá —hizo una pausa—. ¿Te importa?

No me importaba. O, en caso de importarme, no lo sabría hasta después.

—Al diablo —susurré, y volví a unir mis labios a los suyos.

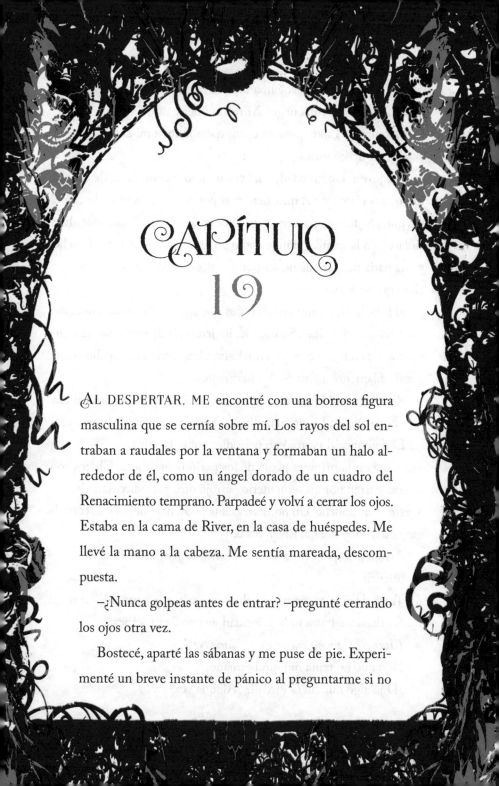

CAPÍTULO 19

AL DESPERTAR, ME encontré con una borrosa figura masculina que se cernía sobre mí. Los rayos del sol entraban a raudales por la ventana y formaban un halo alrededor de él, como un ángel dorado de un cuadro del Renacimiento temprano. Parpadeé y volví a cerrar los ojos. Estaba en la cama de River, en la casa de huéspedes. Me llevé la mano a la cabeza. Me sentía mareada, descompuesta.

—¿Nunca golpeas antes de entrar? —pregunté cerrando los ojos otra vez.

Bostecé, aparté las sábanas y me puse de pie. Experimenté un breve instante de pánico al preguntarme si no estaría desnuda, pero eché una mirada hacia abajo y vi que todavía llevaba puesta mi ropa negra. Miré a mi hermano.

Pero no era Luke quien se encontraba junto a mi cama.

Era un desconocido.

Era joven. De mi edad, o tal vez un año menor. Alto, de cabello rubio más claro que el mío, pero más por haberse decolorado con el sol que por tener una abuela holandesa. Tenía un difuso magullón violáceo en la mejilla, grande como un puño, debajo del ojo derecho, y una nariz perfecta de no ser por una ligera torcedura que dejaba en claro que se había roto.

–Hola, hola, ¿cómo andan todos por aquí? –dijo el desconocido y sonrió con picardía–. Siento mucho irrumpir de esta manera y encontrarme con… lo que sea esto. Estaba buscando a… –se dio vuelta y miró fijamente a River–. Mi hermano.

River se sentó lentamente en la cama, se estiró y rascó su cabeza.

–Hola, Neely. Lindo magullón. ¿Cómo me encontraste esta vez?

El desconocido arrojó un periódico sobre la cama.

–Está en la primera plana de los periódicos, idiota. Chicos con estacas corren por un cementerio –arrojó otro periódico. Uno local–. Y este es de anoche. Un hombre va a la plaza del pueblo y se corta la garganta. Muy buena, River. Sutil.

Arrojó otro periódico más. *El Boletín de Jerusalem Rock*.

Silencio.

Traté de acomodarme el cabello y estirar la ropa mientras mi mente daba vueltas a toda velocidad dentro de mi cabeza.

River tiene un hermano que se llama Neely.

Dijo que no tenía ningún hermano.

¿Dijo algo que fuera verdad? ¿Alguna vez?

Noté que River y Neely me miraban. Respiré profundamente. Si no me calmaba, y rápido, mis mejillas se pondrían rojas y todo lo que sentía se dibujaría en mi rostro.

—Ella es Violet —dijo River—. Vive en la casa grande con su hermano Luke. Pero imagino que eso ya lo sabes.

Neely volvió a lanzarme su amplia sonrisa de picardía. Era la misma sonrisa torcida de River. Era raro verla en el rostro de este extraño. Los ojos de Neely eran azules, y no color café como los de su hermano, pero tenían el mismo brillo. Ese que decía *No ando en nada bueno*. Sin embargo, el brillo de los ojos de River era despreocupado y arrogante. El de Neely era… no lo sé. Afable, enérgico, travieso, como un niñito obstinado o un maldito Jack Russell.

—Conocí a Luke en Eco. Yo estaba en la cafetería preguntando por mi hermano y alguien me señaló a Luke. Me dijo que River se encontraba aquí, en la casa de huéspedes, y el auto de *American Graffiti* de la entrada me lo confirmó. Sin embargo, olvidó mencionar que podría haber una chica bonita en la cama con él —me apuntó con el pulgar, pero no me miró.

Maldita sea, las mejillas se me estaban sonrojando y no podía hacer nada al respecto.

—Sí —repuse—. Yo estaba aquí, en la cama de River. Pero no sucedió nada. Aunque no lo hayas preguntado. Solo estábamos durmiendo juntos. Uno *al lado* del otro. Anoche yo estaba enojada y luego River me tranquilizó, y él tiene pesadillas, así que…

Mi voz se fue apagando. No estaba segura de lo que había sucedido la noche anterior después de que River y yo comenzamos a besarnos en la cocina del Ciudadano. Recordaba haberlo odiado por lo que le hizo al papá de Jack, odiarlo en serio, y después el odio…

desapareció. Y luego ya estábamos en la casa de huéspedes, y luego la cama…

A Neely se le borró la sonrisa. Miró a su hermano y su expresión se tornó dura.

—Dime que no lo utilizaste con ella. Dios mío, River. Caíste otro escalón más. No creía que eso fuera posible.

Con un suspiro, River se levantó de la cama, tomó su camisa del suelo y la deslizó por la cabeza.

—Violet sabe todo acerca del resplandor. Se lo conté. Y si lo usé anoche, fue solo de manera recreativa —le echó una mirada fugaz a Neely y apartó la vista rápido, casi (*casi*) como si, por un segundo, estuviera avergonzado—. Lo que hayamos hecho es algo entre Violet y yo, nadie más, ¿está claro?

Neely miró fijamente a su hermano, pero no dijo nada.

—Mira —prosiguió River, nuevamente tranquilo y despreocupado—, pasemos a la cocina y prepararé el desayuno. No tiene sentido mantener una "conversación importante" con el estómago vacío. Y contigo, Neely, toda conversación es "importante".

Los tres entramos a la cocina. Nadie habló. El único sonido era el repiqueteo de las ollas y las sartenes, y los suspiros de irritación del hermano de River. Luego de unos minutos, decidí que podría ser una actitud sensata de mi parte dejarlos solos un rato, de modo que me marché.

Volví al Ciudadano para ver cómo estaba Jack, pero se había ido. Maldición. Debería haberme despertado más temprano, como dijo Luke. No debería haberme metido otra vez en la cama de River. Maldición. No podía pensar bien. Alrededor de River, yo no era yo. Y eso me asustaba. Pero, en realidad, últimamente todo me asustaba, aunque nunca me había considerado una cobarde.

Volví a salir y vi a Luke pintando en el cobertizo, la puerta abierta para que entrara más luz. Estaba inclinado sobre el caballete, el rostro decidido pero satisfecho. Era una expresión inusual en él.

—Hola —lo saludé mientras me acercaba a la puerta—. ¿Sabes dónde está Jack?

Señaló la mesa del rincón sin levantar la vista. Jack estaba allí, inclinado sobre una tela, aplicando acrílico negro y blanco en líneas finitas e irregulares.

Vi ojos rojos y manos pequeñas aferrando lápidas. Estaba pintando al Demonio en el cementerio.

—Tiene un talento natural —comentó Luke—. Me dijo que nunca había pintado antes, pero es tan bueno como lo éramos nosotros a su edad. Tiene ojo para el color y la atmósfera... y para las dimensiones... —la voz de Luke se fue apagando y los ojos regresaron a su trabajo.

Jack alzó la mirada, se apartó el cabello cobrizo del rostro pecoso y lanzó una gran sonrisa.

—Supongo que viene de familia.

Le devolví la sonrisa.

—Sí, en la nuestra también.

Y, entonces, algo se iluminó dentro de mi cabeza. Algo importante. Algo a lo que yo sabía que debía prestar atención...

—¿El hermano de River los encontró? —Luke apoyó el pincel y volteó hacia mí.

—Sí. En la cama, con River.

Cuando dije eso, Jack volvió a alzar la mirada, luego se inclinó otra vez sobre su pintura.

Luke bajó la voz.

—¿Qué te anda pasando, Vi? ¿No muestras ningún interés por los chicos, de no ser por una charlita de café con Gianni, y, de repente, pasas todas las noches en la cama con un desconocido?

Tenía razón. Toda la razón. ¿Qué me estaba *pasando*?

River. El resplandor. Eso era. Aun así, no tenía ganas de que me regañara un hermano que se pasaba el verano intentando pasar torpemente al segundo nivel de una relación amorosa con una camarera del café de mejillas redondas, o tocándole los muslos a nuestra vecina de al lado.

—Pero mira quién habla —exclamé con un tono que sonó amargo, y me odié por eso—. Maddy, Sunshine. *Tú* no puedes quedarte con las manos quietas.

—Es distinto —dijo Luke, moviendo la cabeza—. Tú eres… Tú tienes que ser más cuidadosa que yo. Y no, antes de que me interrumpas, no es porque seas mujer. Es porque eres… apasionada. Más que Maddy, Sunshine y yo juntos. River te romperá el corazón. Puedes estar segura.

—No lo hará.

Me miró directamente a los ojos.

—No lo hará. A veces, parece una persona agradable, cuando es bueno con Jack, me prepara la cena o me cuenta historias tiernas de su pasado. Y me gusta que sea diferente. Me gusta que sea… misterioso. Pero, generalmente, no confío en él. En absoluto. Es solo que… a veces lo olvido. No dejo que se acerque a mi maldito corazón, Luke. No lo dejo.

Luke suspiró.

—¿Y qué quería su hermano? Veo que dejó su BMW estacionado en la entrada. Debe ser un tipo rudo. ¿Qué chico conduce un BMW nuevo?

—Imagino que quería ver a River.

—¿Acaso nuestro chico BMW también se mudará aquí? Porque entonces podemos cobrarles más alquiler.

Hice un gesto de desaliento.

—Es mejor que vuelvas a tu pintura, hermano.

Luke frunció el ceño. Y ahí, delante de una tela con un pincel en la mano, se parecía tanto a papá, que me molestó. Paseé la mirada entre él y Jack. El cabello rojo de ambos brillaba bajo el sol mientras se inclinaban sobre sus pinturas. Ambos sostenían el pincel de la misma extraña manera, apretado entre el pulgar y el dedo del medio; por el centro, no por la base.

Me marché. Entré en la casa de huéspedes sin llamar. River estaba cocinando seis huevos y Neely bebía una taza de café humeante. Ninguno hablaba. El ambiente era denso e incómodo. Permanecí en la puerta, preguntándome qué debía decir.

Finalmente, River colocó un plato de huevos en mi mano y los tres nos sentamos a la mesa para comer. En silencio. Mojé el pan tostado caliente en las líquidas yemas de color amarillo anaranjado y traté de no notar la embarazosa calma. Neely era un importante bebedor de café, como su hermano, y, para cuando terminó el desayuno, ambos se habían bajado tres tazas de expreso. Lo bebían sosteniendo la taza en la palma de la mano, en lugar de sujetar el asa. Los dos entornaban los ojos antes de beber un sorbo. Bebían como hermanos.

Una vez que terminamos de comer, River y Neely daban vueltas por la cocina acomodando todo, pero seguían sin hablarse.

Los observé fascinada. Neely era por lo menos quince centímetros más alto que River y levemente más delgado. Pero tenía el mismo bronceado ligero y saludable y llevaba la misma ropa de aspecto costoso y no muy normal: pantalones oscuros de lino de tiro bajo combinados con una chaqueta blanca tipo rompevientos, con la cremallera subida hasta el mentón. Yo nunca hubiera pensado que una chaqueta de ese tipo pudiera lucir costosa, pero la de él, lo hacía.

Neely era más o menos igual de hermoso que River, con un rostro que se veía dulce y abierto en las partes donde el de River lucía oscuro y reservado. Cuando bebían café, parecían mellizos. Pero cuando se movían por la cocina, parecían desconocidos. Los gestos de River eran lentos y despreocupados. Los de Neely, rápidos y ágiles. Sin embargo, los dos arrugaban el entrecejo de la misma manera: justo en el centro de su frente bronceada.

—River me dijo que no tenía ningún hermano —señalé, al decidir romper el silencio llamándolo mentiroso a River. Me hizo bien decirlo.

»¿Tus padres son realmente arqueólogos? —le pregunté a Neely.

El hermano de River echó la cabeza hacia atrás y rio. Rio *en serio*. Era algo que valía la pena escuchar. Una risa profunda y contagiosa. Lo miró a River.

—Si comparamos la cantidad de veces que mientes con la cantidad de veces que papá tiene una aventura pasajera, tú ganas. Y eso es mucho decir.

River se encogió de hombros.

—Mentir hace que la vida sea más interesante, por no mencionar más fácil, en casi todo.

Neely volvió a reír. Y luego sus ojos se encontraron con los míos.

—River piensa que la vida debería ser fácil. Pero luego arma más problemas en una sola noche de lo que el Demonio arma en diez.

Y creo que al final todo le sale bien porque tiene un hermanito que aparece y le arregla todo.

Neely se acercó más a mí y bajó el rostro hacia mi oído.

–¿Puedo contarte un secreto? – me susurró–. Son puras tonterías. River alardea cuando está asustado, como nuestro padre. La pregunta es… ¿a qué le teme? ¿Ya lo has descubierto?

Neely se apartó. Me froté la oreja a la que había estado susurrándome. River me observaba atentamente, pero no lo miré.

–¿Qué dijiste, Neely? ¿Qué le contaste?

River se veía preocupado, lo cual me alegró.

Neely apoyó las manos en la mesa y se inclinó hacia adelante.

–Ningún hermano. Qué estupidez. Por lo que nosotros sabemos, tenemos al menos dos hermanastros y una hermanastra. Como dije, a nuestro padre le gusta tener aventuras pasajeras. Por suerte, todavía son niños, así que es probable que aún no sepan lo que es formar parte de nuestra familia. Con el tiempo se enterarán.

–¿Una hermana? –la expresión preocupada de River se desvaneció y fue reemplazada por otra de leve sorpresa–. Nadie me habló de ella.

–Acabo de enterarme, idiota. Estaba examinando algunas cuentas y descubrí que papá estaba manteniendo a alguien más, en algún lugar de Colorado. ¿Y por qué te preocupas? Papá nunca los adoptará legalmente y tú me dijiste, textual, "No quiero conocer nunca al fruto de las tramposas entrañas de papá".

Todo esbelto y elegante, River se encogió de hombros.

–Quizá mentí.

–Cállate, River –Neely me miró–. Violet, ¿llegó a contarte cuál es su apellido?

–West –respondí–. Dijo que se llamaba River West.

Neely se echó a reír y el cabello rubio se sacudió sobre sus ojos.

—El apellido de River (mi apellido) es Redding —hizo una pausa para que yo asimilara la información—. Neely es una abreviatura de Cornelius. Y River es un apodo. Su verdadero nombre es William.

Parpadeé. Miré a Neely, después a River y luego volví a Neely. La expresión del rostro de River era esquiva y evitaba mirarme, pero los ojos de su hermano estaban posados directamente sobre los míos, todavía abiertos y sonrientes. Una enorme sonrisa se dibujó en su rostro, como si supiera que yo sabía lo que eso significaba.

Y tenía razón. Los Redding eran una de las grandes y tradicionales familias de la Costa Este. Si mis parientes fueron en una época acaudalados empresarios industriales con lujosas mansiones en la Costa Este, no eran nada, *nada*, comparado con los Redding. Ellos tenían residencias a lo largo y a lo ancho de las trece colonias originales. Eran dueños de barcos, de ferrocarriles y de presidentes. Tenían lazos con la mafia, los masones y los Beatles.

Freddie había mencionado a los Redding en sus historias. Una vez, cuando yo tenía unos diez años, me mostró una joya: un collar de esmeraldas que vendimos luego de su muerte. Contó que lo usó para una depravada fiesta de los Redding cuando era joven.

De modo que había estado durmiendo con un Redding. *Al lado* de un Redding.

—De modo que he estado durmiendo con un Redding —dije—. *Al lado* de un Redding —mis pensamientos brotaban por mi boca—. Oí hablar de tu familia —dirigí la vista hacia River—. Freddie contó que, una vez, fue a una alocada fiesta de los Redding en Nueva York.

—Eso suena a mi familia —contestó River y me echó una extraña mirada, que no alcancé a descifrar bien.

Neely se frotaba el brazo hacia arriba y hacia abajo, con un gesto pensativo.

—Eco. Qué lindo nombre para un pueblo. Es perfecto. El eco de todas las cosas que sucedieron antes de él. ¿Qué número de lugar es este? ¿Octavo, noveno? —Neely notó lo que estaba haciendo con la mano y se detuvo—. River, ¿cuándo dejarás de fugarte? Porque estoy pensando que, si no terminas pronto con tus escapadas, tendré que golpearte. Mucho. Con los puños. Y preferiría no hacerlo.

—Son ocho, ocho pueblos. A menos que cuentes Archer, cosa que no deberías hacer pues esa vez ni siquiera murió alguien.

Neely volvió a reír, era una risa más oscura, con una veta amarga.

—De modo que los pueblos sin muertes ni siquiera se registran. Es bueno saberlo. Dios, River. No sé si matarte o venerarte.

Así que River ya había escapado otras veces. Y también había muerto gente. Sentí un dolor muy profundo en mi interior, como si me hubiera azotado un frío intenso y glacial… aunque la mañana era suficientemente calurosa. Miré una y otra vez a los dos chicos y me pregunté en qué diablos me había metido.

River se estiró y apoyó la mano en el brazo de Neely.

—Esta vez, tengo todo bajo control. Lo prometo.

Neely apartó la mano de su hermano bruscamente.

—Siempre dices lo mismo —se le sonrojaron las mejillas. El color había comenzado con una manchita a cada lado cuando River dijo que Archer no contaba, pero ahora estaba ruborizado desde el cuello hasta el cuero cabelludo.

La boca de River se puso tensa y vi el hoyuelo en el mentón, que estaba muy apretado. Y sus ojos… la última vez que entrecerró los ojos de esa manera, un hombre se mató en la plaza del pueblo.

—Cornelius, no busques pelear conmigo. No terminará bien.

—Papá es la única persona que puede llamarme Cornelius —dijo Neely. Su voz estaba tensa y la risa había desaparecido de sus ojos. Me sentí incómoda al ser testigo de esa pelea entre hermanos, como si fuera una fisgona.

—¿Y cómo *anda* papá últimamente? ¿Cómo es eso de hacer siempre de hijo bueno? ¿Alguna vez se torna aburrido? —River y Neely se miraron fijamente durante unos segundos—. Estoy tratando de terminar con esto, Neely —dijo River finalmente—. En serio. Si regreso a casa, todo volverá a comenzar. Y no soy tan bueno como solía ser. El resplandor está cambiando...

—¿Estás tratando de terminar con el resplandor? —Neely soltó una risa corta—. Lo estás haciendo muy bien, River. En cada sitio al que vas, se desencadena el caos a las pocas horas —cerró los ojos y apoyó los dedos en las sienes sonrojadas. Luego los abrió y me miró—. Pregúntale sobre Rattlesnake Albee.

—River, ¿qué sucedió en Rattlesnake Albee? —inquirí en voz baja y, en medio de la pregunta, me di cuenta de que no quería escuchar la respuesta. Quería cruzar la puerta, ir a caminar junto al mar y no regresar hasta que hubiera descubierto la forma de resucitar a Freddie.

Sin mirarme, River desenroscó la cafetera italiana y comenzó a llenar con café el pequeño recipiente del interior.

—No ocurrió nada en Rattlesnake Albee. Neely, estás haciendo una montaña de un grano de arena, como siempre. Es solo un pueblito en la campiña con el que me topé en una ocasión. Pensé que sería divertido para algunos de sus ciudadanos creer que estaban en el medio de un ataque indio, como en la época de los colonizadores.

¿Cómo podía imaginar que todos los habitantes del pueblo tenían escopeta?

Neely le echó una mirada asesina a su hermano.

—Los veintitrés habitantes del pueblo. Muertos. En una hora. ¿Cómo es eso de que estoy haciendo una montaña de un grano de arena? ¿Dónde está la exageración?

—Mira, no murieron personas inocentes. Todos los habitantes del pueblo se habían jubilado hacía rato y eran tan malvados como los villanos de una obra de Shakespeare. Yo había estado solo cinco minutos en el pueblo y vi a un hombre pegarle a su caballo con un látigo y a una mujer arrojar un gato por la ventana de un primer piso. En la iglesia, había un letrero que decía: *Todas las mujeres son las concubinas del Demonio, todos los niños, sus vástagos.* El pueblo realizaba una celebración anual en honor a la peste negra por librar al mundo de la basura. ¿Es necesario que continúe? Le hice un favor al mundo.

—No —dijo Neely—. Te pusiste en el lugar de Dios.

—Yo soy un dios.

Neely agitó el brazo en el aire.

—Bueno, ahí tienes. ¿Qué le puedo decir? ¿Cómo razono con un *dios*?

—¿Cómo no me enteré de algo así? Un pueblo entero se mató. ¿Cómo no llegó a los canales de noticias? —me ubiqué entre medio de River y Neely. Un terror negro y áspero comenzó a crecer dentro de mi estómago. River no mataría a un pueblo *entero*. Eso no sería simplemente picardía ni venganza. Eso era maldad. Maldad *demoníaca*.

—Porque Rattlesnake estaba en el medio de la nada, de modo que a nadie le importó –River hizo una pausa–. Y porque mi padre y yo nos *aseguramos* de que a nadie le importara.

Sobrevino un largo silencio.

–¿Sabes algo? Papá y tú son más parecidos de lo que piensan –señaló Neely–. Las cosas te resultarían mucho más fáciles si lo entendieras de una vez.

River desvió rápidamente la mirada hacia su hermano.

–Y te preguntas por qué sigo escapándome. ¿No crees que ya sé cuánto me parezco a él? ¿Y no crees que eso me provoca un miedo mortal? Vete a casa, Neely. No tienes nada que hacer aquí.

Él no se movió, y pestañeó varias veces.

–Leí acerca de esos adolescentes. Lo que les hiciste. Hacerles creer que se estaban quemando durante dos horas. Dos *horas* de alaridos. Retorciéndose de dolor mientras sus padres los contemplaban impotentes –Neely señaló el magullón junto a su ojo–. Después de leer eso, me metí en un bar de universitarios y peleé con uno de esos cretinos niños de mamá. Y cada vez que mi puño le golpeaba la cara, deseaba que fueras tú.

River retrocedió un paso y levantó las manos.

–¿Chicos quemándose? Neely, ¿de qué estás hablando?

–Los adolescentes en el parque, en Texas, unas semanas atrás. Tengo el periódico en el auto. ¿Creíste que no me enteraría?

–Nunca estuve en Texas.

Neely golpeó el puño con fuerza sobre la mesa.

–*No mientas más.*

–Neely, te juro que no tengo idea de qué estás hablando. Nunca. Estuve. En Texas. Neely, eres mi *hermano*. Si tú ya no me crees, ¿entonces quién lo hará?

—*Quiero* creerte, River. No tienes idea de cuánto quiero creerte. Yo te quiero. Te quiero más que a nadie en el mundo. Pero. Me. Estás. Matando. Odio las cosas que haces. Las *odio*. Las odio tanto que tengo que golpear a desconocidos para no enloquecer. Me estoy volviendo demente. *Demente.* A veces siento que estoy perdiendo el control, en serio… y me da miedo, River. Tengo *miedo*.

River miró a su hermano, luego a mí y volvió a él, y su mirada se veía herida, amargada y filosa como la navaja que le cortó la garganta a Daniel Leap.

—¿Saben algo? —dijo después de un instante—. Váyanse al infierno. Los dos.

Y se marchó.

Hice un intento de salir detrás de él, pero Neely me cortó el paso.

—River necesita estar solo un rato. Volverá a ser el de siempre en unas horas. Al principio, cuando nos encontramos, siempre sucede lo mismo.

Me apoyé contra el marco de la puerta y observé a River hasta que se perdió en el bosque.

—Sí, yo también tengo un hermano —eché una mirada hacia el cobertizo—. Sé lo que es pelear.

Luego Neely me miró, me miró de verdad y sonrió. El color rojo ya se estaba esfumando de su rostro y noté otra vez que tenía la nariz rota.

—Hola, Violet White —dijo—. Es un placer conocerte. Yo soy Cornelius Redding, de los Redding de la Costa Este, tengo un hermano mágico y asesino, y un carácter infernal —rio.

Yo también me reí y nos quedamos ahí mirándonos y riendo luego de todo lo ocurrido, y entró el viento del océano y pude sentir el olor de Neely. Shampoo de manzanilla, ropa limpia, tierra, bosque y medianoche.

No… medianoche, no. Mediodía. Las doce en punto.

Sol, y no estrellas.

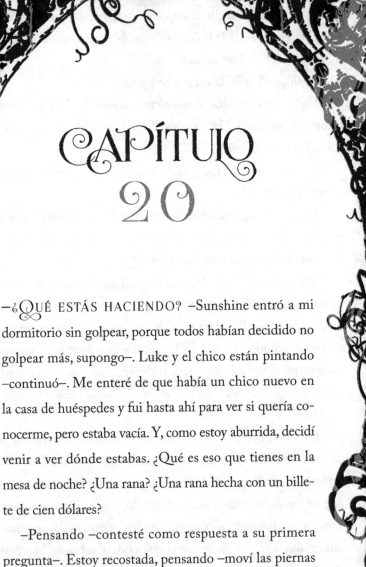

CAPÍTULO 20

—¿QUÉ ESTÁS HACIENDO? —Sunshine entró a mi dormitorio sin golpear, porque todos habían decidido no golpear más, supongo—. Luke y el chico están pintando —continuó—. Me enteré de que había un chico nuevo en la casa de huéspedes y fui hasta ahí para ver si quería conocerme, pero estaba vacía. Y, como estoy aburrida, decidí venir a ver dónde estabas. ¿Qué es eso que tienes en la mesa de noche? ¿Una rana? ¿Una rana hecha con un bille-te de cien dólares?

—Pensando —contesté como respuesta a su primera pregunta—. Estoy recostada, pensando —moví las piernas para que Sunshine pudiera sentarse en mi cama, pero, en su lugar, se dirigió al espejo de cuerpo entero para admirar sus pechos y su largo cabello castaño–. Y sí. Es una rana hecha en Origami. River me las deja todo el tiempo. No me siento muy orgullosa.

Al decirlo, se vuelve verdad.

Sunshine sacudió la cabeza con pesar.

–Violet, en estos días, estoy escuchando toda clase de cosas acerca de ti. Duermes en la cama de River, y ahora esto –agitó la mano hacia la rana–. Guau.

–Le preocupa que me quede sin dinero y no pueda comprar alimentos, o algo así.

–Es una preocupación entendible –echó el cabello hacia atrás y se colocó frente a mí–. Pero dejarte una rana hecha con dinero en la mesa de noche sigue siendo… raro.

Pero yo no quería hablar de River. Las risas con Neely habían liberado algo. No estaba segura de qué, pero me sentía… mejor. Más despejada. Y sin River en mi cabeza, podía pensar en otras cosas, como en Freddie, en que Jack pintaba y en lo que se removió en mi interior al ver a Luke y Jack trabajando juntos en el cobertizo, y volvió a removerse cuando vi a River y a Neely bebiendo café.

Me incorporé.

–Una vez, Freddie me dijo algo. Se estaba preparando para la cena de Navidad (habíamos preparado nosotros la comida porque tuvimos que despedir al cocinero unos meses antes) y se había puesto un viejo vestido negro y ceñido, y se veía triste y abstraída. Y no era porque nos estuviéramos quedando sin dinero, que no le importaba. Era porque pensaba que podría ser su última Navidad. Y lo fue.

Me detuve unos segundos y parpadeé rápido, varias veces.

—Estaba cepillándose el cabello frente a ese espejo. Yo observaba su reflejo mientras admiraba la forma en que su vestido negro combinaba con la cruz que se encontraba a sus espaldas y pensaba en lo bien que se verían alineados contra la pared verde musgo. Me pregunté si debería tratar de pintarlos. Pero luego dejó el cepillo, se volvió hacia mí y dijo: "Esconde tus cartas, Vi. Esconde tus cartas, pero no tan bien que tus seres queridos no puedan encontrarlas después de que mueras".

Las cejas oscuras y finitas de Sunshine se arquearon. Se acercó y tomó asiento en la cama, a mi lado.

—Desde entonces, he estado buscando esas cartas —expliqué—. Tengo que encontrarlas, Sunshine. Pronto. Por alguna razón, siento que es… importante.

—Bueno, no tengo nada mejor que hacer —se levantó, se dirigió a mi cómoda y comenzó a quitar las gavetas y examinar la parte de atrás.

Sonreí. A veces, Sunshine era una buena chica.

Vaciamos las dos cómodas de la habitación. Nada. Examinamos detrás de los siete cuadros, esperando encontrar algo pegado detrás. Nada. Hurgamos en el vestidor y debajo de la cama. Ya había hecho todo eso antes, pero lo hice otra vez.

Y seguía sin encontrar nada.

Hasta que me imaginé a Freddie nuevamente dentro de mi mente. La imaginé alejándose del espejo con su vestido negro, captando mi mirada sobre ella y luego desviando la mirada hacia…

Me acerqué a la cruz de madera oscura de la pared y la descolgué. Era más pesada de lo que parecía: tenía cinco centímetros de grosor y la forma simple de un monje medieval. La di vuelta, oprimí la parte de atrás con el pulgar y se movió.

La madera se deslizó y se abrió. Había un compartimento negro y vacío de unos treinta centímetros de largo y más de siete de ancho. Volví a colgar la cruz en su lugar.

—Sígueme —dije, y Sunshine vino detrás de mí.

Nos encaminamos a la casa de huéspedes. No había nadie, como Sunshine había dicho. Era probable que Neely hubiera ido a buscar a River.

Entré en la habitación de River y abrí la gaveta superior de la cómoda. La cruz continuaba allí, justo donde lo había visto colocarla. La tomé, la di vuelta y oprimí con los pulgares en el mismo lugar.

El panel posterior se deslizó.

—Aquí vamos —dijo Sunshine, porque mientras se abría el panel, cayeron dos hojas de papel doblado y se deslizaron hasta nuestros pies.

Sonreí.

21 de junio de 1947
Freddie:
Lo de anoche fue un error.

He estado enamorado de ti desde el primer momento en que te vi, desde el momento en que me mudé a tu casa de huéspedes, desde el momento en que chasqueaste los dedos y luego te quitaste toda la ropa delante de mí, libre y desvergonzada, como las chicas que bailaban el hoochie coochie en los salones de Europa.

Amé pintarte, amé trazar la afilada curva de tu codo con carbonilla, amé darle vida al brillo rosado de tu piel en la tela, amé mezclar el azul perfecto para tus ojos. Te amé cuando te estirabas sobre mi sofá vistiendo solo

tu piel blanca, relajada como una gatita al sol. Amé la forma en que bebías licor de endrinas de una petaca, como un vaquero en una droguería. Amé que nunca quisieras saber quién era yo o de dónde venía, porque no te importaba. Lo único que te importaba era lo que tenías delante de ti. Y te gustó. Te gusté, creo.

Pero tienes esposo. Y yo... yo no tengo nada. Nada más que un puñado de pinceles y el deseo de pintar en los dedos.

Ahora estoy empacando todas mis cosas. Y para cuando despiertes, para cuando regrese el decente e impasible Lucas, ya habré vuelto a la ciudad. Te dejé dos de mis pinturas. Eran tus preferidas.

John

Lo sabía. Lo sabía aun antes de leer la carta.

27 de febrero de 1950

Freddie:

Ha pasado mucho tiempo. Creo que se cumplieron tres años este verano. Podrías habérmelo dicho hace mucho tiempo. Deberías habérmelo dicho hace mucho tiempo. Pero te perdono. Supongo que pensaste que regresaría y causaría problemas... que me pondría a aullar en medio de la noche o provocaría un duelo. Pero deberías haber sabido que ese no es mi estilo. Nunca tuve el fogoso temperamento artístico que llevó a mis colegas pintores a la notoriedad.

Me casé recientemente con una muchacha de Eco. Ann Marie Thompson; sí, la chica rubia y bonita que trabajó en tu casa como mucama, hace algún tiempo. *Nos encontramos en una fiesta en Nueva York hace unos meses. Ella es muy buena bailarina. Freddie. Nunca lo creerías. Es casi tan buena como tú.*

En las próximas semanas, nos mudaremos a Eco. Como dije, no te causaré problemas. Seremos como extraños.

Pero me haría feliz ver al niño, de vez en cuando, solo de pasada.

John

P.D.: Le pusiste mi nombre. Fue un gesto amable.

—¿Acaso esto significa lo que yo creo que significa? —Sunshine y yo habíamos caminado en silencio hasta mi dormitorio. Ahora estábamos sentadas en la cama, nos pasábamos las cartas mutuamente y las leíamos una y otra vez.

—Sí, eso creo —respondí, pero no tenía bien la voz. Me aclaré la garganta.

—Tu padre se llama John —dijo Sunshine. Me miraba atentamente, tratando de deducir qué haría yo: si me pondría a dar vueltas por la habitación con paso fuerte, arrojar objetos o qué, aunque yo sabía que ella sabía que no lo haría.

—Sí, Sunshine, ya sé cómo se llama mi papá.

—Y este "John" era artista, y tu padre es artista y Luke y tú son artistas.

—Sí, lo *sé*. ¿Y con eso qué?

Sunshine alzó los brazos en el aire.

—Ah, los ricos.

Le eché una mirada de soslayo y supuse que mi expresión "Y con eso qué" había brotado cargada de sensibilidad, porque se puso de pie y se dirigió a la puerta sin decir una palabra más.

Pero luego se detuvo, se dio vuelta y su rostro estaba... triste... y pensativo, y muy distinto a la Sunshine de siempre.

–Vi... Creo que sería bueno que averiguaras si Freddie no escondió más cartas –me observó durante un instante.

Asentí.

Se marchó.

A veces, Freddie me había mirado de la misma manera: triste y pensativa. Principalmente cuando estaba preocupada porque Luke me pegaba o porque yo lo odiaba o porque mis padres tardaban mucho tiempo en regresar.

Fui al salón de baile y me senté debajo del cuadro de mi abuelo Lucas hasta que se puso el sol. Me dediqué a pensar en todas estas cosas y sentí que podía echarme a llorar si me lo permitía.

Pero no lo hice.

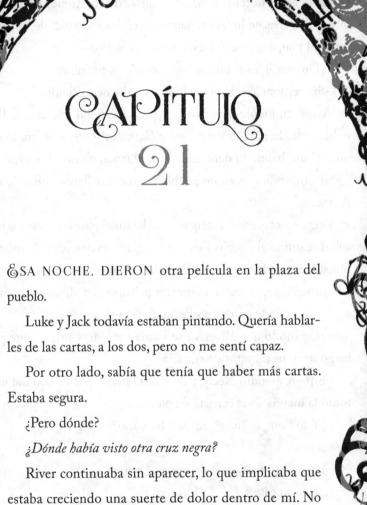

CAPÍTULO 21

ESA NOCHE, DIERON otra película en la plaza del pueblo.

Luke y Jack todavía estaban pintando. Quería hablarles de las cartas, a los dos, pero no me sentí capaz.

Por otro lado, sabía que tenía que haber más cartas. Estaba segura.

¿Pero dónde?

¿Dónde había visto otra cruz negra?

River continuaba sin aparecer, lo que implicaba que estaba creciendo una suerte de dolor dentro de mí. No sabía qué significaba ni por qué estaba allí. Y traté de ignorarlo.

Sunshine nos invitó a cenar. Sus padres habían cocinado pollo al horno con patatas alargadas a la crema. Luke y Jack fueron, pero yo me quedé. No tenía ganas de charlar de cuestiones triviales. Lo que tenía ganas de hacer era sentarme en los escalones de adelante y mirar el mar, que es como Neely me encontró.

—¿Quieres ir a ver una película vieja? –le pregunté.

—Sí –respondió–. Es justo lo que estaba necesitando.

Armé un picnic para Neely y para mí, igual que el que River había armado para él y para mí y *Casablanca*. Pero no era lo mismo. Ahora había un demonio, un fantasma, un hombre asesinado y veintitrés muertos en un pueblo inexistente llamado Rattlesnake Albee.

Pensé en contarle a Neely acerca del túnel cuando pasamos junto a él de camino al pueblo. Pensé en contarle lo que River le mostró a Sunshine cuando estaban los dos adentro. Pero, al final, no dije nada. Me pareció que se reiría o buscaría pelearse con alguien. No estaba segura de cuál de las dos posibilidades era peor.

—¿De modo que River ya se había escapado antes? –pregunté luego de unos minutos de silencio.

—Sip –respondió Neely, y deslizó el brazo por debajo del mío y tomó la manija de la canasta de picnic.

—¿Y tú siempre tienes que ir a buscarlo?

—Sip.

—Y luego se pelean, él desaparece por un tiempo y luego ambos regresan a su casa.

—Así funciona –Neely me miró–. Él no se quedará, Violet. No sé qué te dijo, pero no se quedará. Nunca se ha quedado en ningún lugar, no por mucho tiempo. Ni siquiera en casa.

Traté de aparentar que no me importaba. Sentía una suerte de odio por River, así que debería haberlo hecho mejor.

–Si te sirve de consuelo, tú eres la primera chica –dijo al notar mi expresión. Se detuvo, me tomó la mano y la dio vuelta. Después se inclinó y me besó la palma de la mano.

Atónita, contuve la respiración. Lo había hecho tan fácil y naturalmente como sonreír.

Y yo había pensado que River era un galán.

Neely sonrió al ver mi expresión.

–Nunca antes había encontrado a River durmiendo con alguien. Mira, no hay duda de que te ha contado algunas mentiras. Es lo que River hace. Mi hermano tiene… problemas. Pero, por lo que yo sé, tú eres la primera chica a la que ha prestado atención. Y tiene que ser algo bueno. Así que… gracias.

–¿Me besaste la mano para agradecerme?

–Sip.

Había pasado los últimos días con un chico rico que tenía un resplandor que no podía evitar utilizar y una inclinación hacia los justicieros como el personaje de *Operación Masacre*. Pero en lo único que pude pensar durante el resto del camino era en que todavía sentía el beso de Neely en la palma de la mano.

Una vez que llegamos, eché una mirada alrededor del parque y mantuve los ojos bien abiertos por si aparecía River. Pero no vi nada.

La noche se había puesto fresca y alcanzaba a sentir el calor que emanaba de Neely, sentado sobre la manta junto a mí. En la pantalla, pasó un tren y empezó a sonar Rachmaninoff. La película era *Breve Encuentro*. Ya la había visto el verano pasado en la plaza: nítidos acentos británicos y un maldito final desgarrador.

A mi izquierda, dos chicas se susurraban al oído mientras un niño pequeño compartía un cono de helado derretido con un educado Border Collie. A mi derecha, un chico alto y flaco, de cabello rojo intenso –casi violeta bajo la luz tenue– cortó una manzana en trozos con un cuchillito finito y le ofreció a una chica rubia que estaba sentada cerca con su familia. Un hombre de barba pasó por encima de una pila de tierra y arrojó una manta justo al lado. Yo sabía por qué había allí una pila de tierra. Alguien había cavado el césped manchado de sangre donde cayó… Daniel Leap.

–¿Eres un colibrí? –le pregunté a Neely por lo bajo mientras la antipática mujer charlatana con la caja de sombreros interrumpía a los amantes condenados en la pantalla frente a nosotros.

–¿Un qué? –susurró mientras me lanzaba una mirada entre divertida y desconcertada.

–Un hombre… que tiene muchas aventuras amorosas.

La risa de Neely estalló en medio de la quietud de la noche de cine. La gente giró para mirarnos, pero él continuó riendo por un rato.

Mi cara se puso roja, menos mal que estaba oscuro.

–Ahora caigo en la cuenta –dijo en un susurro después del estallido–. River. Tú. Ya caigo. River siempre fue muy selectivo con las mujeres. Pero esto –me señaló a mí–, esto es coherente. *Tú* eres coherente.

Y luego me sonrió con la sonrisa torcida de su hermano y pensé que, pocos días antes, había estado sentada con River en ese mismo lugar y haciendo lo mismo.

En la mitad de la película, justo después de la escena del bote de remos, sentí una mano en el codo. Al levantar la vista, me encontré con los ojos oscuros de Gianni.

–Ven, Violet –fue todo lo que dijo–. Tengo que hablar contigo.

–Bueno –susurré. Sentí curiosidad, pero no preocupación. Seguramente solo quería mostrarme su nuevo aparato para hacer café de filtrado manual.

Me puse de pie. Neely alzó los ojos hacia mí con las cejas levantadas, pero yo simplemente señalé a Gianni y me encogí de hombros.

–Neely, él es Gianni –susurré–. Voy a hablar con él.

Con el ceño fruncido, Neely lo miró y después a mí.

–Vuelve rápido –susurró.

Seguí a Gianni fuera de la plaza. Se detuvo debajo del resplandor amarillo opaco del farol, cerca de la Tienda de Libros Antiguos y apartó un rizo negro del ojo. Tenía un rasguño en la mejilla derecha, que parecía recién hecho.

–Gianni, ¿cómo te lastimaste el rostro? –pregunté.

Me ignoró.

–Violet, quiero que veas algo.

Súbitamente, me golpeó una fresca brisa marina y me abotoné el cárdigan amarillo.

—De acuerdo. Pero ¿no puedes esperar hasta que termine la película?

—No. Tienes que verlo ahora.

Era extraño. Realmente lo era. Y si yo no hubiera estado tan distraída pensando en River, Neely, el Demonio, el suicidio, Jack, las cartas y el resplandor, lo habría notado en ese momento. Pero, en su lugar, dejé que Gianni deslizara sus dedos entre los míos y me arrastrara calle abajo. Abajo, abajo, hacia el oscuro callejón sin salida.

Debería haberle contado a alguien que seguía a Gianni hacia lo desconocido. Como, por ejemplo, a Neely, al hombre de barba, al chico con la manzana, a cualquiera. Pero no lo hice. Confié en él. Diablos, lo conocía desde sexto curso.

De modo que dejé que me condujera calma y serena como una monja diciendo sus oraciones.

Nos detuvimos en la calle de la mansión Glenship. Gianni la señaló.

—Lo que tengo que mostrarte está allí dentro.

Finalmente, el primer destello de miedo se encendió dentro de mí.

—Pero la casa está tapiada. No podemos entrar y no quiero hacerlo. Hace años que nadie entra ahí. Debe haber ratas, murciélagos, fantasmas… y otras cosas más.

Normalmente, yo no era tan cobarde. Pero la noche era oscura y la mansión Glenship se veía enorme, negra, imponente y embrujada como nunca. Y Gianni me observaba de una manera rara. Sus ojos brillantes y oscuros parecían diferentes bajo la luz de la luna… como apagados y vacíos. Hundió la mano en el bolsillo del jean y extrajo un pequeño martillo.

—Ven —dijo.

Me condujo hasta la casa y sus dedos no soltaron los míos ni por un segundo. Noté que había dos tablas de madera en el suelo. Uno de los grandes ventanales estaba descubierto y divisé una luz tenue que titilaba en el piso del interior. Gianni arrancó otra tabla con una mano y la arrojó al suelo. La ventana estaba rota, pero se aseguró de que no quedaran vidrios rotos antes de ayudarme a entrar, después de él.

Dejó el martillo y tomó la lámpara. Era de las que funcionaban con aceite. Utilizando la luz de la luna que ingresaba a raudales por la ventana ahora descubierta, encontró la perilla a un costado y la giró. La habitación se llenó de luz.

Me encontraba en la biblioteca polvorienta y en ruinas. El empapelado levantado, un solitario sillón de cuero rasgado y deshecho, ningún libro, los estantes desnudos y vacíos. Luché contra un deseo irresistible de largarme a correr y a explorar. No había querido ingresar, pero, de repente, deseé haber entrado a Glenship muchos años antes. Me moría por compararla con el Ciudadano, ver qué cosas habían quedado, examinar las gavetas, ah, todo tipo de cosas. Gianni seguía observándome de manera extraña, pero, maldita sea, yo quería recorrer las habitaciones, la cocina y el sótano donde asesinaron a la niña. Freddie dijo una vez que Glenship tenía una piscina subterránea, seis pasadizos secretos y…

Gianni jaló de mi mano.

—Ven, Violet. Él está arriba —hizo un gesto con la lámpara hacia la escalera.

Mis ojos dejaron de recorrer la habitación y se posaron en él.

—¿Quién está arriba, Gianni?

Los dedos aún aferrados con fuerza a los míos, me miró y parpadeó, los ojos conservaban esa mirada escalofriante y sin vida.

—El brujo, por supuesto.

Aun en ese momento, después de que dijo *eso*, yo no estaba realmente asustada. Pensé que estaba bromeando. Una broma pésima y de mal gusto, después de la historia de Jerusalem Rock. Pero aun así. Dejé que me sacara de la biblioteca y me llevara por un suelo de mosaicos blancos y negros hasta la imponente escalera, tan parecida a la del Ciudadano. Subimos al primer piso, al segundo. La escalera se volvía más y más estrecha y, a continuación, llegamos al ático.

Se me cortó el aliento. El ático de Glenship se parecía tanto a mi propio y querido ático que, por un instante, olvidé dónde me encontraba. Los espejos de cuerpo entero, los armarios, los baúles, las telarañas.

¿Quién había abandonado todas estas cosas? ¿Había alguien todavía vivo para reclamarlas?

Sentí un deseo ardiente de hurgar en el polvo y ver qué podía encontrar; imaginé fotografías, discos viejos y hasta una posible mención de Freddie en una carta...

Jack.

Su cabello cobrizo estaba desgreñado y sucio, pegoteado con polvo y vaya uno a saber qué más. Los brazos flacuchos estaban levantados por arriba de la cabeza; las manos amarradas con cuerdas colgaban de la viga que atravesaba el techo inclinado. Solo llevaba jeans, y los pies desnudos se veían pequeños y blancos, como la porcelana contra las sucias tablas de madera del suelo.

El rostro pecoso estaba vuelto hacia el costado. Había huellas de lágrimas en medio de la suciedad.

—Ayuda —exclamó con voz entrecortada—. Insiste en que soy un brujo. ¿Qué quiere decir con eso? ¿Qué le ocurre? —jaló de la cuerda que tenía encima de la cabeza. Apretadas una contra la otra debajo de los nudos, sus muñecas se veían increíblemente pequeñas.

Me volví hacia Gianni. Todo el miedo que antes no había venido, me atravesó violentamente.

—¿Gianni? ¿Qué es esto? ¿Qué estás haciendo? —pero, mientras hablaba, la garganta se me cerró y la voz se fue apagando de a poco hasta que fue solo un susurro.

Sonrió y me dio un golpecito con el codo.

—Alguien me avisó que habías acorralado a un brujo en el Ciudadano. Así que fui a tu casa y lo tenté para que saliera de tu guarida. ¿Qué piensas, Violet? *Mira ese cabello rojo.* Cuánta maldad. Es un monstruo pelirrojo que ama al Demonio —hizo una pausa, se inclinó y recogió algo—. Tenía que mostrártelo. Solo una extraña clase de chica podía apreciar lo que estoy a punto de hacer. Y tú eres extraña, Vi.

—¿*Qué vas a hacer, Gianni?*

Ahí fue cuando mis ojos vieron lo que tenía en la mano derecha. Me estiré, le arranqué la lámpara de la mano izquierda e iluminé el altillo.

Hacia mi izquierda, había una pila de piedras en las sombras. Junto a una lata de gasolina del color rojo de las carretillas.

Gianni me miró con sus ojos muertos.

—Hacerlo confesar, obviamente. Puedes mirar o, si quieres, ayudar. Tengo las piedras allá. Pero si no dan resultado, encontré una vieja navaja oxidada en el sótano. Eso seguro que servirá. Tenemos que asegurarnos de dejar un poco de gasolina en él, al final. Es necesario que sienta las llamas. Escuché que a los brujos hay que sacarles el Demonio con fuego, quemándolos, y no puedes hacer eso si ya están muertos antes de ponerlos en la hoguera.

A esta altura, Jack ya estaba gritando. Se retorcía contra las cuerdas y gritaba.

Y, por encima de sus gritos, alcancé a escuchar a alguien más. Alguien detrás de mí que reía en la oscuridad. Levanté la lámpara, pero no logré penetrar los rincones más alejados. Risas, risas y risas.

—¿River? —exclamé, mi voz un susurro que no podía atravesar los gritos de Jack—. Por favor, que no sea River —rogué a nadie, porque nadie estaba escuchando.

Freddie, ayúdame, Gianni lo va a quemar, ¿qué debo hacer? ¿Qué debo hacer? Le ocurre algo malo, está muy raro y creo que conozco la razón, Freddie, ayúdame, por favor, Freddie, ayúdame...

Gianni levantó la lata de gasolina.

—Más vale tenerlo bien empapado antes de la confesión. Ahorra tiempo.

Y levantó la lata sobre la cabeza de Jack.

Freddie no iba a ayudarme. ¿Cómo podría hacerlo?

Estaba muerta.

Me lancé sobre el costado de Gianni. Emitió un extraño grito gutural y dejó caer la lata, que rodó por el suelo. El aire se llenó de densos vapores.

Gianni se puso de pie de un salto, su hermoso rostro estaba apretado y retorcido. Aullaba mientras me sacudía el brazo y yo dejé caer la lámpara...

Y luego llegaron las llamas. Y luego llegó Neely.

Había humo y vapor por todos lados y no veía nada, pero escuché risas, y después Gianni se restregaba los ojos a mi lado mientras gritaba *¿Dónde estoy?* y el humo cedía un poco y Neely arrojaba mantas viejas y ropa sobre el fuego hasta que se extinguió por completo, y yo intenté soltar a Jack y finalmente el último nudo quedó desatado y Neely nos empujó fuera de la habitación, hacia las escaleras.

Atravesamos la ventana rota de la biblioteca y todo no era más que desorden y confusión y mi rodilla chocó contra el alféizar de la ventana y caí al suelo, y sentí la hierba bajo las manos. Me puse de pie sin dejar de mirar a Gianni, que ya no parecía enfadado sino confundido, aterrorizado y, maldita sea, tan perdido.

Jack puso sus brazos alrededor de mí y lo estreché con fuerza. Gianni continuaba restregándose los ojos.

—Gianni —dijo Neely, la voz baja y dura—. Mírame.

—¿Qué hago aquí? ¿Qué sucedió? —preguntó apartando las manos de su rostro.

Neely estiró la mano y aferró la camiseta blanca de Gianni con el puño. Lo sacudió, no con fuerza pero tampoco con suavidad.

—Cálmate. Cálmate, maldición.

—¿Yo inicié el fuego? —no dejaba de pasear la vista entre Jack y las ventanas del altillo de Glenship—. ¿Qué... qué me sucede? Yo...

Neely le dio un golpe a Gianni en la mandíbula y éste se desplomó en la tierra. Se quedó tumbado sin moverse. Luego Neely extendió la mano y lo ayudó a ponerse de pie.

—Gianni, *concéntrate*.

El labio de Gianni sangraba y le chorreaba por el mentón. Pero sus ojos se encontraron con los de Neely y asintió.

—Esto es lo que harás —dijo—. Olvidarás todo lo sucedido. No pensarás en ello ni harás preguntas —metió la mano en el bolsillo y extrajo un fajo de billetes—. Toma esto y mantén la boca cerrada.

Gianni se quedó observándolo con la boca abierta. Neely sujetó su mano y colocó los billetes en ella.

–Vete a tu casa. Alguien puede haber visto el fuego y es probable que la policía esté en camino. Así que, *vete*. Sal de aquí. Ahora.

Cerró la mano sobre el dinero. Asintió. Volteó. Echó una mirada a Neely por encima del hombro y luego sus ojos se encontraron con los míos. Me sostuvo la mirada. La apartó. Salió corriendo y se perdió en la oscuridad.

Neely me sujetó el brazo.

–Nosotros también tenemos que marcharnos, Violet.

–Pero él está allá arriba, en el ático. Tenemos que regresar…

Una sirena de policía rasgó el aire inmóvil. Neely tironeó de mi brazo. Tomé la mano de Jack y echamos a correr.

CAPÍTULO 22

—GIANNI DIJO QUE estabas buscándome —Jack y yo nos hallábamos sentados frente a la chimenea del dormitorio verde. Cuando regresé a casa, junté algunos troncos y encendí el fuego; pensé que un poco de calor podía ayudar después de todo lo sucedido, si es que algo podía hacerlo.

Jack se había mantenido cerca de mí mientras lo preparaba, como si no quisiera perderme de vista. Había estado temblando y se veía pálido debajo de la suciedad que todavía cubría su rostro. Pero ya estaba mejor, el temblor había desaparecido. Le había dado un viejo suéter negro de Luke para que se pusiera y tenía las mejillas rojas por el fuego. Al menos tenía calor.

–Me había ido de la casa de Sunshine, pero Luke seguía allí, y Gianni me encontró solo en mi habitación y dijo que me estabas esperando en el ático de la mansión Glenship –continuó–. Era extraño y él actuaba de manera extraña, pero no sé… le creí. Fue una estupidez. La próxima vez no caeré en la trampa. La próxima vez, seré más inteligente.

Retorcía las manos una y otra vez.

–Me obligó a quitarme la camisa y los zapatos. Amarró mis manos y dijo que me quemaría vivo.

Puse los brazos alrededor de Jack y lo abracé.

–Yo también escuché las risas –levantó la mirada–. ¿Era River?

No respondí, y nos quedamos callados durante un rato.

–Hoy encontré algo –dije, pensando que, al fin y al cabo, ese era un momento tan bueno como cualquier otro–. Unas cartas. ¿Viste el cuadro que tienes ahí, encima de la mesa de noche? Bueno…

–¿Tiene que ver con mi abuelo?

Suspiré.

–De modo que ya lo sabes.

Jack se movió y se puso de pie. Fue hasta la mesa de noche y tomó la pintura.

–Es ella, ¿verdad? ¿Tu abuela? Papá me contaba cosas, cuando no estaba ebrio. Cosas que mi abuelo le contaba.

–Sí, es ella. Y ese es John Leap, tu abuelo. Se parece a tu papá –me detuve y respiré hondo–. Y al mío.

Nos miramos durante uno o dos segundos.

–Descubrí los cuadros de tu abuela en el salón de baile –dijo Jack y volvió a colocar la tela sobre la mesa de noche–. Y ahí fue cuando supe con seguridad que era cierto.

–Muéstramelos.

Seguí a Jack por el pasillo y subimos la escalera de mármol hasta el segundo piso. Al pasar delante del dormitorio de Luke, quise detenerme, pero escuché las risas de Sunshine en el interior.

Jack caminó hasta el extremo izquierdo del salón, junto a los ventanales, y señaló dos cuadritos con desnudos, ambos de Freddie, ambos perdidos entre la multitud de telas más grandes y voluminosas que cubrían las paredes.

Al observarlos atentamente por primera vez, pude notar que las pinturas de John Leap estaban hechas en la casa de huéspedes. El mismo sofá, el mismo empapelado... hasta había latas de pintura en las repisas de las ventanas. Freddie lucía blanca, desnuda y radiante.

Jack y yo nos quedamos mirando los cuadros durante un rato, y luego regresamos al dormitorio verde. Tomé las cartas de Freddie, que había llevado todo el día en el bolsillo, y se las entregué a Jack. Las leyó junto al fuego.

Cuando terminó, sus ojos azules se encontraron con los míos y sonrió.

–Así que nuestros padres eran... hermanos.

–Hermanastros –asentí–, al parecer.

–¿Entonces ahora puedo vivir aquí, porque somos parientes?

–Si mi opinión y la de Luke tienen alguna importancia, entonces... sí.

Y volvió a reír. Aun después de la noche que había tenido, Jack todavía podía reír.

Me quedé con él hasta que se durmió. Me senté al lado de su cama y le leí *Las crónicas de Narnia: El león, la bruja y el ropero* hasta que se le cerraron los ojos. Pero después lo desperté antes de irme para que cerrara la puerta una vez que yo me hubiera ido. Y le pedí que me prometiera que no dejaría entrar a nadie, excepto a Luke y a mí, por ningún motivo.

Fui hasta mi habitación, cerré la puerta y me senté en la cama. Ahora que estaba nuevamente sola, me sentía vacía en lo más profundo de mi ser. Tan vacía como Montana, que había escuchado que era el vacío mismo, junto con Wyoming. Me acerqué a una de las ventanas. Estaban negras con la noche negra, y hacían juego con mi ánimo vacío y negro.

En el suelo, había una pila de libros con un pingüino de origami encima.

Bajé a la cocina.

Neely se encontraba ahí, en el mismo lugar donde lo había dejado cuando regresamos de la mansión Glenship. Había encendido las velas de la mesa y la atmósfera parecía medieval. Estaba sentado en el sofá silbando Rachmaninoff.

—Neely, ¿tú nos seguiste a Gianni y a mí hasta Glenship? —pregunté.

—Sí.

—¿Por qué?

Neely no respondió.

—¿Alguna señal de River? —inquirí.

Meneó la cabeza.

—¿Por qué golpeaste a Gianni?

—Porque tenía que hacerlo. Se nos estaba acabando el tiempo y necesitaba que me prestara atención.

—¿De modo que golpeas a la gente así nomás? ¿A eso te dedicas?

Neely esbozó una gran sonrisa.

—No, soy un colibrí. Me dedico a… picar flores.

Reí, aunque no quería hacerlo. Señalé el refrigerador.

—¿Quieres limonada con jengibre?

—Obviamente —respondió.

Hice otra tanda del jugo para sentirse bien de Freddie mientras Neely observaba y después serví dos vasos. Bebió un sorbo y suspiró.

—Me siento mal por haberle pegado a Gianni. Lo que le ocurrió no fue su culpa. No me malinterpretes, me encantan las buenas peleas. Pero eso fue… el mal necesario —se llevó la mano al cabello y lo agitó.

Se parecía tanto a River que contuve la respiración por unos segundos.

Bajó la mano y el cabello le quedó hecho un revoltijo.

—Es que, la sola idea de que lastimara a un niño, de que te lastimara a ti, a quien fuera, me hizo perder el control… —su voz se fue apagando.

Me apoyé contra la mesa.

—River no se siente tan arrepentido por lo que hace.

—Mi hermano no es tan malo como parece —Neely levantó la vista hacia mí. Bajo la luz de la vela, el magullón se veía morado oscuro, como si hubiera empeorado durante el día, en vez de mejorar.

—Ya lo sé —respondí.

—Convive con un don. Un don muy poderoso. Y está solo. No tiene con quién hablar del tema, nadie que lo ayude a distinguir lo que está bien de lo que está mal.

Bebí la limonada y no dije nada. Me llevé la mano a la nuca, me había asaltado otra vez ese hormigueo, el que había sentido antes en la cocina, por la noche, ese que me decía que *alguien me estaba observando*. Me di vuelta. Nadie. Miré la noche por las ventanas oscuras de la cocina. En el vidrio, solo vi el reflejo de Neely y mío.

Recordé las risas en el ático de Glenship y me estremecí.

Neely se levantó y se quitó la chaqueta blanca. Llevaba una camiseta negra debajo, pero no fue eso lo que llamó mi atención. Tenía una larga cicatriz rosada que se extendía desde el cuello a lo largo de todo el brazo derecho.

—*Maldición* —exclamé y, de inmediato, deseé poder retractarme. Aun así, quería estirar la mano y tocar la cicatriz. Quería quitársela con las uñas para ver la piel suave y limpia que tenía que haber debajo. Tuve que controlarme para no hacerlo.

—Está bien —dijo y sonrió—. A veces, también me quedo sin aliento cuando me miro al espejo. Si quieres, puedes tocarla.

Lo hice. Deslicé los dedos por el cuello y después por el brazo. La cicatriz terminaba en la muñeca, y la pálida piel de esa zona no tenía vellos y era muy suave. Más suave de lo que debería haber sido.

—Es todo un desafío mantenerla oculta —señaló—. Especialmente cuando uno es un niño mimado al que le gusta navegar y quitarse la camisa cuando está al sol, como cualquiera.

—¿Cómo ocurrió?

Neely rio. Aunque muy leve, igual fue una risa.

—River tenía catorce años —dijo, las comisuras de sus labios continuaban temblando—, y yo acababa de cumplir trece. Mi hermano todavía no sabía lo del resplandor. Sin embargo, ya comenzaba a sospechar algo. Estaba empezando a sospechar que era… diferente. Un día, estábamos los dos en la playa haciendo una fogata. A River le gusta hacerlo cada vez que está enojado por algo. Y, al poco rato, nos pusimos a pelear. Cuando no estaba peleándome con otros chicos, estaba peleándome con River —Neely hizo una pausa y sonrió ligeramente—. Yo y mis peleas. En general, River sabía manejarme, cómo calmarme mientras esquivaba mis puños. Pero esa vez, perdió el control.

Yo conocía esa historia. Sabía lo que venía a continuación. Cerré los ojos. De modo que River no había mentido. A veces, no mentía. No del todo.

La mano de Neely rozó mi brazo.

—No fue su culpa. Esa vez, de veras no lo fue. Estaba furioso y pensó algo malo de mí. Todos lo hacemos, pensar cosas malas de una persona cuando estamos enojados con ella. Pero los pensamientos de River no son simplemente pensamientos: son *armas*. Estábamos peleando en la arena, yo lo tenía inmovilizado y... él me hizo ver algo. El cadáver ensangrentado de una niña flotando en el océano a mis pies. Un estilo propio de River, muy macabro. No lo hizo intencionadamente. Simplemente lo pensó y... sucedió. Pero yo me asusté y eché a correr. Luego tropecé y me caí... justo en medio de la fogata.

Abrí los ojos.

Neely se tocó la cicatriz y meneó la cabeza.

—Caí en medio de las llamas, Violet. Me prendí fuego. River me empujó al suelo y me arrojó arena para que dejara de arder. Gritaba mi nombre y lloraba. Después me desmayé y eso es todo lo que recuerdo. Pasé el mes siguiente en el hospital. Los médicos más costosos del mundo hicieron lo que pudieron. Esto es lo que quedó.

Neely se miró el brazo. Todavía había una ligera sonrisa en su rostro, pero la expresión de sus ojos era más oscura.

Apoyé los dedos en el antebrazo de Neely, en esa piel arrugada, de color rosado y blanquecino.

—Lo siento —dije, porque no se me ocurrió otra cosa que decir.

—Mira, yo sé que River ha hecho... cosas malas —hizo una pausa—.

Conozco la historia del vinatero, las mellizas españolas, la niñita escocesa. Conozco todas esas historias. Y odio lo sucedido. Lo odio tanto. Pero River es mi hermano. Siempre estuvo a mi lado cuando yo era un niño y decía cosas que no debía, cada vez que mi carácter me dominaba y, súbitamente, me encontraba peleando con tres chicos al mismo tiempo, todos más grandes que yo. Nunca retrocedió, nunca escapó, nunca le contó a papá, ni siquiera me pidió que me detuviera o tratara de cambiar. Se rompió la mano derecha seis veces. Siempre estuvo a mi lado cuando lo necesité. Siempre.

Quería preguntarle por el vinatero, las mellizas y la niña escocesa. Quería saber más de River cuando era un niño, antes del resplandor.

—Yo escuché risas —dije, cuando abrí la boca. Largué una bocanada de aire que no me había dado cuenta que estaba conteniendo—. Escuché risas en el ático, antes de que llegaras. No era Gianni. Había alguien atrás, en la sombra, que miraba y reía. Y no estaba en su sano juicio, era una risa histérica, aterradora, y...

—Ey, olvídate de todo eso —me tomó la muñeca por un segundo y después la soltó—. Deja de pensar en eso. Llevaré a casa a mi hermano y todo esto se acabará. ¿De acuerdo? River... no se está comportando con normalidad.

Se sentó otra vez en el sillón y apoyó la cabeza contra la pared.

—Creo que se ha vuelto adicto al resplandor, como si fuera una suerte de droga. Vive escapando y quizá *realmente* sea porque quiere dejar de utilizarlo. No lo sé. Pero mi hermano se aburre o conoce a alguien que no le agrada o se enardece ante alguna injusticia y... —me miró y sonrió. Pero esta vez había tristeza. Era una sonrisa triste y torcida que hacía juego con su nariz torcida, y le quedaba bien—. Y hay gente que termina muerta. Siempre.

Me senté en el sofá junto a él y nuestros brazos se tocaron, y nos quedamos así por un rato. Olí el mar, como siempre lo hacía, y el olor de Neely, a mediodía, y me sentí... mejor.

Y luego sentí otra vez el hormigueo en la nuca.

De pronto, deseé poder ver. Los rincones de la cocina estaban llenos de sombras y no había encendido ninguna luz. ¿Acaso afuera se encontraba River, observándonos en la noche? ¿O yo todavía estaba asustada? Tal vez había imaginado las risas del ático.

Tal vez el terror me había enloquecido.

¿Era eso posible?

Sospechaba que sí.

Pero no... Jack también había escuchado las risas.

—No sé qué otra cosa puedo hacer salvo llevarlo a casa —concluyó Neely finalmente—. Aunque escapará otra vez.

Evité mirarlo. No le conté acerca del estúpido y maldito dolor que sentía al pensar en la partida de River, porque no podía confiar en lo que sentía.

—Violet, tengo que pedirte un favor —dijo Neely. Volvió a ponerse de pie, se colocó la chaqueta y la cerró hasta el mentón.

—Bueno...

—Creo que es genial lo que ocurre entre ustedes dos. Entre River y tú —me miró y supe por el brillo de sus ojos que estaba pensando en la primera vez que me vio en la cama de River, con la ropa toda arrugada—. Pero, creo que ya no debes permitir que River te toque. Escúchame. Tengo una sensación, una intuición. Creo que la única forma de que River se ponga mejor es que deje de usar el resplandor, excepto cuando es absolutamente necesario. Así que no debes permitir que te toque. ¿Puedes hacer eso por él?

Moví la cabeza de un lado a otro.

–Neely, estoy confundida. ¿Qué tiene que ver que River me toque con el resplandor?

Neely me miró fijamente.

–¿Quieres decir que no lo sabes? ¿No te lo dijo? –dio un puñetazo en la mesa, rápido, duro, fuerte. Una de las velas se cayó y se apagó. La mitad de la cocina quedó en penumbras. Yo seguía sentada en el sofá y él se cernía sobre mí. Me puse de pie y *continuaba* cerniéndose sobre mí. Era tan *alto*. Hasta su voz sonaba alta–. River necesita tocar a las personas para usar el resplandor. No puede hacerte ver algo a menos que haya tenido algún tipo de contacto en el pasado reciente. Ese contacto duraba una o dos horas, pero actualmente, a veces, puede hacer que se prolongue durante días. Su resplandor está… cambiando. Volviéndose más fuerte, o más débil. Quién sabe.

Golpeó la mesa otra vez y se apagó la otra vela. Ahora la cocina estaba a oscuras. Todavía podía ver a Neely, pero no muy bien.

–No puedo *creer* que no te lo haya dicho. Te tuvo en la cama, te tocó, te hizo ver, te hizo sentir… no sé qué clase de cosas, ¿y ni siquiera te contó cómo funcionaba su resplandor? –inclinó la cabeza hacia atrás y pensé que reiría nuevamente. Pero, en cambio, emitió una especie de aullido de angustia y frustración. Me eché hacia atrás, sorprendida.

El aullido de Neely disparó mis pensamientos de manera vertiginosa…

River rodeando a Sunshine con el brazo. Mostrándole a Jack cómo usar el yo-yo, la mano apoyada sobre su hombro. River abrazándome en el cementerio, besándome, estrechándole la mano a Gianni en la pizzería; River tomando el vaso de whisky; los dedos de River junto a los de Luke

en el puntero del tablero Ouija; River besándome, tocándome, tocándome, tocándome...

—Está mal, Violet. No es bueno para ti. Puede hacerte pensar cosas, cosas que no son ciertas. Yo lo quiero, pero seré el primero en decir que es inestable y peligroso. Más peligroso que cualquier persona que yo haya conocido o que vaya a conocer. *No debes permitir que te toque más.*

Pero apenas lo escuchaba, porque mi mente estaba hecha pedazos y mis pensamientos estaban destrozados, rotos y ensangrentados por el suelo. Y sabía que Neely lo percibía, que percibía la sensación de tristeza y de malestar que emanaba de mí. Pero no me importó. No me importó que lo viera.

Odié a River.

Lo odié *de verdad.*

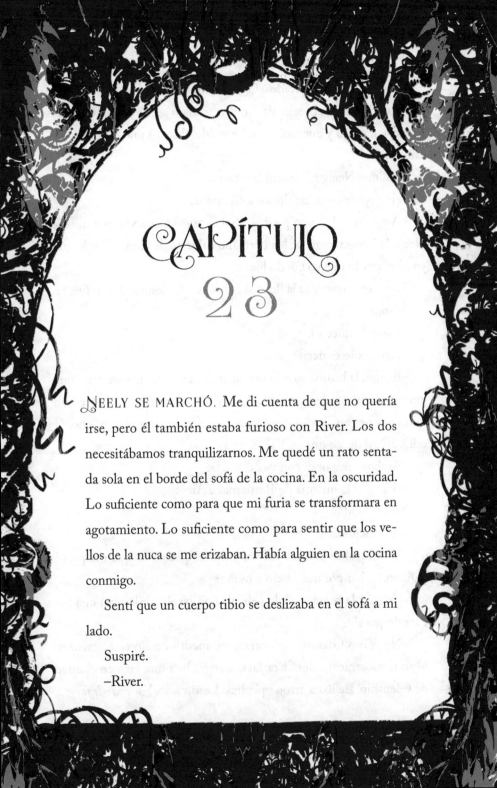

CAPÍTULO 23

Neely se marchó. Me di cuenta de que no quería irse, pero él también estaba furioso con River. Los dos necesitábamos tranquilizarnos. Me quedé un rato sentada sola en el borde del sofá de la cocina. En la oscuridad. Lo suficiente como para que mi furia se transformara en agotamiento. Lo suficiente como para sentir que los vellos de la nuca se me erizaban. Había alguien en la cocina conmigo.

Sentí que un cuerpo tibio se deslizaba en el sofá a mi lado.

Suspiré.

—River.

Alivio y furia. Mezclados. Quería empujarlo fuera del sofá, que se golpeara contra el suelo. Pero mis manos no se movían. Y después River se levantó y encendió una vela. Me observó unos segundos y asintió.

—Así que Neely te mostró la cicatriz.

—¿Estuviste escuchándonos a escondidas?

—Algo así —hizo una pausa—. ¿Sabes algo? Cada vez que miro a Neely, la imagen regresa. Mi hermano cubierto de llamas. Por lo que yo hice, por lo que yo puedo hacer.

Tomó mi mano y se la llevó al corazón. Me desprendí con fuerza. Suspiró.

—Estoy herido, Vi.

—¿Qué quieres decir?

—Bueno, la bruma rosada que aparecía en tu mente siempre que pensabas en mí, desapareció. Ahora mi color es rojo sangre con manchas negras. Y eso, según mi experiencia, significa miedo. U odio. ¿Cuál de los dos es, Vi?

—Ambos —respondí con voz cansada.

—¿Fue por la historia de Rattlesnake Albee?

No respondí.

—¿El suicidio?

—River, ¿sabes adónde estuve anoche? ¿Sabes lo que me pasó? ¿Quieres saber por qué huelo a humo?

—Fuiste a la plaza a ver la película con Neely. ¿Hicieron una fogata después?

—No. Vino Gianni a buscarme en medio de *Breve Encuentro*. Quería mostrarme algo. Era Jack, amarrado a una viga en el ático de Glenship. Le iba a arrojar piedras. Lastimarlo. *Y prenderle fuego.*

Me puse de pie. Hablar de Jack atado y asustado me hacía perder la apatía. Tenía las mejillas enrojecidas y mi enojo estaba retornando, fuerte, alto y renovado.

—Sal de aquí, River. Vete. *Hablo en serio.*

No se movió. Por una vez, sus ojos se veían mortalmente serios y heridos, y hasta un poquito... traicionados. ¿Acaso sus ojos podían mentir? ¿Podían mentir tanto como su boca?

—Violet, ese no era yo. Nunca usaría el resplandor para lastimar a un niño inocente. ¿Cómo puedes pensar que soy capaz de algo así?

—Hiciste que Jack viera al Demonio. E hiciste que su padre se cortara la garganta en la plaza del pueblo.

—Es verdad —dijo y levantó las manos en el aire, como si estuviera alejando la verdad—. Tienes razón. Maldita sea. Mira, no estoy seguro de lo que ocurrió en la mansión Glenship y no sé qué le sucede a Gianni, pero no tiene nada que ver conmigo. ¿Te encuentras bien, Vi? ¿Y Jack?

—*River, te escuché reír* —mis mejillas ardían y la furia inundaba mi cuerpo—. En el ático. Te *escuché.* Y luego me enteré por Neely que tenías que tocar a las personas para hacerlas resplandecer. ¿Cuántas mentiras me contaste, River? ¿Cuán fuera de control está tu resplandor? Porque una parte de mí piensa que debería salvar al mundo y enterrarte en el sótano. Y todavía no he decidido si lo voy a hacer. Más vale que digas algo convincente, y pronto.

River apoyó la espalda contra el marco de la puerta de la cocina y suspiró. De repente, se veía distinto. Ni pícaro ni con aspecto felino. Simplemente joven, triste y algo desesperado, lo cual me desconcertó, porque ese *no* era River.

—¿Quieres saber por qué quiero a Neely? —preguntó—. Nosotros peleamos una y otra vez, sin embargo, el color con el que piensa en mí nunca cambia. Siempre soy amarillo brillante, sin importar lo que haga. Y he hecho mucho. Nunca me tuvo miedo ni me odió. A una persona así hay que quererla. Una devoción incondicional es algo que solo sucede muy rara vez.

Lo observé durante unos segundos y no contesté.

—¿Quieres subir al ático conmigo? —preguntó por fin, con voz suave—. Dejaré de mentir —agregó—. Y comenzaré a hablar.

—De acuerdo —dije, así nomás. Porque... qué diablos. River se marchaba y eso era lo mejor. Una última noche de charla no le haría mal a nadie. Además, había una parte de él, la que no usaba el resplandor, que todavía me gustaba, a pesar de todo... la fogata, el ponerse de mi parte en contra de Luke, que cocinara bien, los animales de Origami y dormir entre sus brazos...

Diez minutos después, River y yo estábamos sentados en el ático, en los extremos opuestos del viejo sofá de terciopelo, escuchando a Robert Johnson. Adoraba el crujido de la estática que se escuchaba en el fondo de todas esas viejas grabaciones. Respiré hondo y olí la sal de la brisa y, por debajo, el hedor a humo que todavía emanaba de mi cabello. El viento del mar soplaba a través de las ventanas curvas, que se abrían de costado como una moneda girando sobre el canto, y hacía titilar las velas al ritmo de los latidos del corazón.

River deslizó dentro de su boca varias uvas color negro violáceo. Yo había traído algo de comida de la cocina, sabiendo que probablemente no había comido en todo el día. Y sabiendo que no debería importarme. Pero, maldición, me importaba igual. River tomó el triángulo de Gouda, cortó un trozo y me lo alcanzó. Lo tomé con sumo cuidado para que nuestros dedos no se tocaran. Después colocó los brazos detrás de la cabeza y se reclinó en el sofá.

—Escuché que Neely te dijo que no me tocaras.

Lo miré.

—River, yo no recuerdo qué ocurrió anoche. No recuerdo nada después de que nos besamos en la cocina. Esta mañana desperté mareada en tu cama, sin siquiera saber si llevaba algo de ropa puesta. No confío en ti. En serio. Eres un mentiroso y un adicto —hice una pausa—. ¿Por qué no puedo recordar el momento en que me dormí? ¿O cualquier cosa que pudo haber sucedido antes de eso?

Se encogió de hombros.

—Mira, sí, es cierto, al principio usé el resplandor contigo, para calmarte. Estabas enojada por lo de Daniel Leap. Te estaba *ayudando*. No era mi intención que olvidaras lo que sucedió. A veces, el resplandor hace eso.

Asimilé esa información durante un minuto.

—Así que primero me confesaste que te estaba costando controlar tu don. Y luego Gianni *se volvió demente y secuestró a Jack esa noche y yo escuché esa risa y tú dices que no eras tú* —apreté los dientes y me calmé—. Bueno, supongo que tengo que creerte. Eres un mentiroso, pero tengo que creerte. Si no te creo, tendré que hacer algo al respecto. Como embriagarte y después ahogarte en el mar antes de que hagas que Jack se mate.

Levantó una mano brillante de aceite de oliva, la metió dentro del cabello y me miró.

—Más o menos así es como están las cosas, Vi.

—*Amarás a tu retorcido prójimo con tu retorcido corazón* —dije.

—¿Qué?

—Es de un poema de Auden. Algo que Freddie solía decir a veces.

—¿Qué significa?

–Que nadie es perfecto, supongo.

–Bueno –repuso–. Esa es la verdad más grande que se ha dicho hoy en todo el mundo.

Nos quedamos sentados uno al lado del otro, sin hablar y sin tocarnos. Robert Johnson comenzó a cantar *Between the Devil and the Deep Blue Sea*. Cantaba la canción con lentitud y melancolía, no se parecía en nada a la versión original de Cab Calloway.

Lo miré a River y escuché el rugido de las olas que golpeaban abajo e imaginé que Robert me cantaba directamente a mí, en ese mismo instante.

El aire se tornó pesado y los truenos irrumpieron en la quietud, como un redoble de tambores. Estaba por comenzar una tormenta. El disco terminó, el viento se volvió todavía más frío y la atmósfera del ático cambió. En lo que le lleva al corazón latir cien veces, el lugar se tornó gélido y negro. Era como un sueño transformándose en una pesadilla. A mí me gustaban las tormentas, pero, en ese momento, no estaba de humor para disfrutarla.

–De todas maneras, Neely tiene razón –dijo River. Al desatarse la tormenta, su rostro se había vuelto oscuro e intenso, y me pregunté si podía confiar en esa expresión–. Neely tiene razón, yo debería mantener mis manos resplandecientes lejos de ti. Siempre tiene razón, el muy cabrón. Violet, ¿puedo contarte algo?

–Sí.

Se escuchó el rugido de un trueno. River se sobresaltó.

–Odio las tormentas. Hace unos meses, abandoné mi estricta escuela privada y huí a Nuevo México. No llovió, ni una vez. No soñé que prendía fuego a Neely. No soñé nada. No había dormido tan bien hasta que… hasta que llegué aquí. Y te conocí.

»Mi madre no era arqueóloga ni cocinera –continuó después de unos segundos de silencio–. Era una señora de la alta sociedad con un gran corazón, que murió cinco años atrás. Se ahogó en el mar, como el personaje de un poema. Se cayó de un velero en medio de una tormenta. Yo estaba ahí. Vi cuando se cayó del borde, se hundió en el agua negra y desapareció.

Freddie también murió cinco años atrás. Yo sabía lo que era perder a alguien y sabía lo que era la muerte.

–Lo siento –murmuré, y hablaba en serio.

–Ella solía decirme que yo no debía ser como él. Como papá. Decía que debería ser compasivo, aun con aquellos que no lo merecían. Pero Neely se parece a ella en eso. Yo no. Él... a él le cayó muy mal la muerte de mamá. Ahí fue cuando comenzó a pelear, a pelear de verdad. Durante un tiempo, fue algo cotidiano –se pasó las manos por la cabellera y se recostó otra vez en el sofá–. Pero no lo castigaban a él, sino a mí.

No dije nada. No lo toqué ni dejé que me tocara.

–Un año después de que muriera mi madre, descubrí que tenía el resplandor –relató River, los ojos cerrados–. Y después hice algo estúpido. Tenía las mejores intenciones, pero ya sabes lo que se dice de ellas.

Abrió los ojos, suspiró y volvió a cerrarlos.

–Era el cumpleaños de mi padre. Él, bueno, él había amado a mi madre. La había amado *realmente*, a pesar de todas sus aventuras amorosas. A pesar de todas las veces que se distrajo con las modelitos bonitas que se arrojaban sobre él, por el dinero que tenía. Mis padres habían sido mejores amigos desde chicos, y novios en la secundaria. La muerte de mamá lo destruyó. De modo que se me ocurrió lo que yo pensé, como un niño estúpido, que era una idea brillante como regalo de cumpleaños. Lo encontré en su oficina, sentado al sol y con la mirada fija en la pared. Me acerqué a William Redding II, apoyé mi mano en la suya y le permití que viera a mi madre. Le dejé que la viera por... un largo rato. Hasta que se echó a llorar. Y entonces retiré la mano.

Estalló un trueno y River se sobresaltó otra vez. Se inclinó hacia adelante y colocó los codos sobre las rodillas.

–Una vez que entendió lo ocurrido, me pegó –prosiguió–. Papá tomó un pisapapeles del escritorio y me golpeó con él hasta que me rompió dos costillas.

River explicó esto sin una pizca de autocompasión, como si estuviera leyendo una receta o dando indicaciones.

Podía escuchar el sonido de las gotas de lluvia martillando contra el techo, como tratando de ingresar.

–Y a pesar de la gran paliza que me dio mi padre, me obligó a hacerlo de nuevo –explicó–. Me hizo repetirlo una y otra vez hasta que se volvió medio demente al ver a mi madre delante de él, llena de vida como el día previo a su muerte. Y no se detuvo. De ahí en más, si alguien no estaba de acuerdo con él, me llamaba para que arreglara las cosas. Yo hacía lo que podía. Como dije antes, cuando era más joven, controlaba mejor el resplandor. Pero no era suficiente. Nunca lo era. Maté al primer hombre porque mi padre me lo exigió. O, al menos, hizo que se matara. Solo porque tuvo la osadía de rechazar la oferta de un Redding. A papá le gusta un buen pinot y quería comprar el viñedo de ese hombre. El sujeto era italiano y trajo las vides desde su país de origen cuando era un niño. Se negaba a vender. Bueno, ¿adivina, al final, quién ganó? El viejo vinatero, amable y testarudo, cayó, y mi padre, William Redding II, tiene ahora su propia bodega. Y, maldito sea yo que le ayudé a conseguirla.

Eché los brazos alrededor de River. No lo pensé. No pensé en el resplandor, simplemente lo hice. Permanecimos así durante un rato largo, enredados uno en el otro, hasta que la tormenta se desvaneció y el viento se aplacó.

Entonces se secó los ojos con la manga de la camisa y parpadeó con rapidez.

—Papá quiere que regrese porque se ha vuelto adicto a lo que yo puedo hacer. Tiene que seguir viendo a mi madre aun cuando eso lo esté volviendo demente. No puede dejarla ir. Te lo juro, es peor que una droga. Sé que Neely cree que yo tengo un problema, pero mi padre está mucho peor. ¿La historia que nos contaste se llamaba *Una rosa para Emily*?

Asentí.

—He estado pensando mucho en eso. En Emily y en que no podía dejar ir al hombre que amaba y eso la volvió demente. No creo que mi padre esté completamente... cuerdo —River acercó la cabeza a mi cuello. Tenía las manos en mi espalda, los dedos alineados con mi columna—. Neely es el pacificador, lo cual resulta muy cómico teniendo en cuenta la cantidad de peleas en las que se mete. Él cree que puede convencer a papá de que cambie, de que se detenga. O que, al menos, permita que yo me detenga. Pero está equivocado, mi hermano no sabe a lo que se enfrenta. Además, nunca deja de pelearse el tiempo suficiente como para poder ayudarnos —sacudió la cabeza—. Neely parece abierto y dulce, y lo es, la mayor parte del tiempo. Pero tiene mal genio, igual que papá.

—Y que tú —agregué.

–Y que yo –concordó.

Nos quedamos un rato más abrazados, ya habíamos terminado de hablar. Al poco tiempo, comenzó a deslizar el pulgar por la parte interna de mi brazo, piel contra piel. En mi mente, resonaba la voz de Neely que me decía que lo detuviera, pero la ignoré. Quería ver qué sucedía.

River ya tenía las manos en mis mejillas. El cosquilleo en la piel me advirtió que comenzaba ese efecto que River provocaba en mí. Esa sensación placentera que fluía a través de mí y me calmaba.

Me pregunté en lo profundo de mi mente si River utilizaba el resplandor en mí mucho más de lo que había admitido. Me pregunté si, de hecho, lo utilizaba cada vez que me tocaba.

Y me había tocado mucho.

Y hasta era probable que yo me estuviera volviendo adicta a esa sensación, como él y como su padre.

Tal vez no podía contenerse. Tal vez él realmente quería tocarme y no sabía que estaba utilizando el resplandor. Pero eso no cambiaba nada. Tal vez lo empeoraba.

Apoyé las dos manos en el pecho de River y lo empujé. Abrió los ojos y me miró. Su rostro estaba rojo y supuse que el mío también. Me levanté, y luego River también se levantó y nos quedamos los dos de pie, mirándonos, los rostros enrojecidos.

–Daniel Leap era mi tío –comenté, porque en algún momento tenía que decírselo–. Mi medio tío. Y tú lo mataste antes de que descubriera quién era realmente. Esa cruz que descolgaste en tu habitación tenía cartas ocultas en su interior, escritas por mi abuelo, que no era Lucas White sino John Leap. Un pintor.

River sacudió la cabeza, se veía desconcertado.

—Déjame leerlas —pidió. Estaba serio, tan serio como cuando habló de su padre y del pisapapeles—. Ahora.

Extraje las cartas del bolsillo de mi falda y se las entregué. Las leyó, dos veces, y me las devolvió.

—Lo siento —dijo con simpleza—. No lo sabía. Era un alcohólico que te insultaba y descuidaba a su hijo. No podía soportarlo.

—Sí, lo sé, River. Pero en algún momento, tendrás que aprender a enfrentar la injusticia como el resto de nosotros, los que no fuimos dotados con el resplandor. Es parte de la vida. No puedes castigar a todo el mundo.

—Puedo intentarlo.

—Bueno, tal vez puedes pensar en alguna forma que no implique personas matándose mutuamente. O que se corten la garganta en la plaza del pueblo. La vida no es una descarnada novela del salvaje oeste, River. Aquí tratamos de actuar civilizadamente y tú te comportas como si esto fuera la serie *Deadwood*.

River rio.

—Eso es porque desearía que lo fuera.

No compartí su risa. Pero, maldición, sabía a qué se refería. Había leído suficientes novelas de Zane Grey y McMurtry, había visto suficientes películas de Sergio Leone como para que las palabras *pistolero solitario* y *justiciero* causaran dentro de mí un dulce estallido de excitación.

—¿Hay más cartas? —preguntó al ver que me quedaba en silencio—. ¿Estas son las únicas cartas de Freddie que encontraste? Yo... —vaciló y apareció en su rostro esa extraña expresión, la que había visto antes—. Porque me gustaría mucho leer cualquier cosa que encuentres —concluyó en voz baja y suave.

—No, no encontré nada más —respondí mirándolo atentamente—. ¿Por qué? ¿Por qué quieres saber qué encontré?

Y luego la expresión extraña de River se desvaneció y lanzó una especie de risa suave y amable, como una brisa de verano. Y esa risa era muy distinta de la del ático, completamente distinta en todo sentido. No podía haber sido River el que estaba allí arriba.

Pero entonces... ¿quién?

Y un pensamiento asomó en mi mente, un pensamiento tan grande que empujó a todos los demás —como las cartas, Daniel Leap y esa manera de actuar de River propia de una serie del lejano oeste— hacia un costado.

¿Por qué River no había sentido ninguna curiosidad por saber quién era realmente el que estaba en el ático utilizando el resplandor sobre Gianni y riendo? No había hecho ninguna pregunta ni había especulado con alguna respuesta. ¿Por qué?

En mi interior, una vocecita terrible y cruel me decía que existía una buena razón por la cual no sentía curiosidad. River dijo que, a veces, el resplandor hacía que la gente olvidara cosas. Si me había hecho olvidar cosas a mí, también podría hacerle olvidar cosas a él.

Él ya sospechaba de sí mismo, y era por eso que no quería hablar del tema.

De pronto, me sentí cansada. Vieja, gastada, usada y apta para ser quemada como en una novela barata a la que le faltaran páginas y fuera, básicamente, mala, de todas maneras. Ahí estaba yo, lidiando con River y el resplandor, con demonios y un Jack amarrado en un ático, cuando, pocos días antes, mi vida no había sido más que té helado en el porche de Sunshine y tratar de conseguir algo de dinero para comprar alimentos.

Esa Violet ahora parecía estar muy, muy lejos.

—Esta noche dormiré en mi habitación —anuncié con una vocecita frágil y delicada que odiaba—. Y, maldición, River, estoy siendo muy buena contigo, así que no toques a nadie. No toques a Luke, ni a Sunshine, ni a Jack. Solo vete a la casa de huéspedes y duérmete. Hablo en serio.

—No, Violet —dijo—. Por favor, no te vayas. La tormenta…

Pero me fui. Me di vuelta y abandoné el ático.

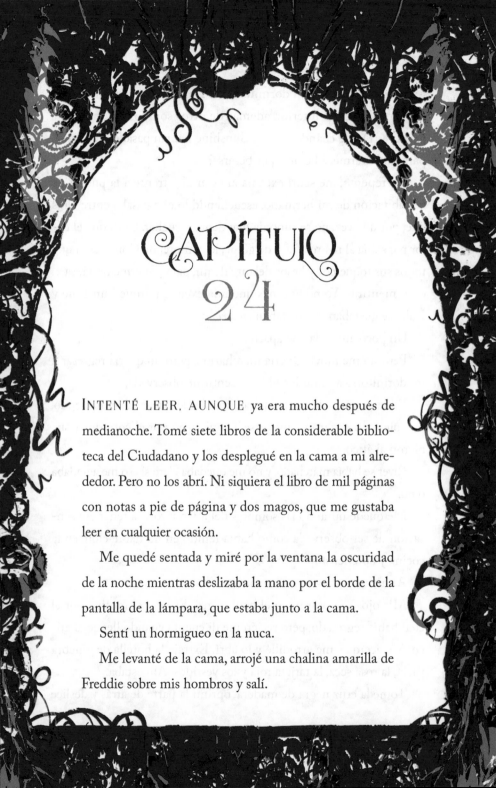

CAPÍTULO 24

INTENTÉ LEER, AUNQUE ya era mucho después de medianoche. Tomé siete libros de la considerable biblioteca del Ciudadano y los desplegué en la cama a mi alrededor. Pero no los abrí. Ni siquiera el libro de mil páginas con notas a pie de página y dos magos, que me gustaba leer en cualquier ocasión.

Me quedé sentada y miré por la ventana la oscuridad de la noche mientras deslizaba la mano por el borde de la pantalla de la lámpara, que estaba junto a la cama.

Sentí un hormigueo en la nuca.

Me levanté de la cama, arrojé una chalina amarilla de Freddie sobre mis hombros y salí.

Pasé por delante del dormitorio de Luke. Todavía se oía la voz de Sunshine en el interior, además de otros sonidos de crujidos y pisadas. ¿Desde cuándo Luke y Sunshine habían pasado de besarse para molestarme, a besarse por besarse?

De repente, me sentí extraña al estar ahí, frente a la puerta de la habitación de mi hermano, escuchando lo que pasaba entre ellos que, por una vez, no se suponía que debía escuchar. Sentí que el calor me subía al rostro. Y así, de golpe, lo comprendí. Comprendí que todos sus toqueteos y besos delante de mí, para ponerme nerviosa… eran mentiras. Yo no era más que una excusa, porque Sunshine y Luke se gustaban. Se gustaban *en serio*.

Un poco aturdida, me aparté.

Pero no me moví. Quería marcharme, pero no quería regresar a mi dormitorio a mirar los libros y sentirme observada.

Y luego, antes de que pudiera entender lo que estaban haciendo, mis pies comenzaron a moverse. Caminaron por el corredor y subieron al ático.

River se había marchado, y no me quedaba claro si eso me agradaba o no.

Me quedé mirando las sombras del ático y volví a tener esa sensación de ser observada como había tenido en mi habitación, en la cocina y en Glenship.

Al menos, esta vez, no había risas.

Mis ojos se posaron en el baúl negro. Ese era el motivo por el cual había regresado, pero recién me di cuenta cuando llegué al ático. Me acerqué, me arrodillé y lo abrí. Extraje la botella de ginebra vacía, la rosa seca, la tarjeta roja y los vestidos. Allí estaba.

Tomé la cruz negra de madera, oprimí la parte de atrás y deslicé el panel. Al girarlo, cayeron al suelo unas hojas de papel arrugadas. Eran cinco en total. Cinco hojas. Cinco cartas.

Mis ojos bajaron hasta el final de la primera. Esperaba encontrar otra vez el nombre de John. Pero la primera carta estaba firmada por una persona distinta. Fui pasando las cinco hojas mientras leía con mucha rapidez…

11 de enero de 1928
Querida Freddie:

¿Cómo puedes decir que te casarás con él? No hablas en serio. Lucas es bueno y estable, pero no es para ti. Y sí, ya sé que te está construyendo una gran casa junto al mar, pero tú nunca vivirás allí. No puede suceder. No va a suceder. Todavía eres tan joven. Todos lo somos. Somos chicos.

No crezcas, Freddie.

Una súplica de un amigo,
Will

18 de febrero de 1928
Freddie.
Cásate conmigo.

Tú me conoces mejor que nadie. Estabas ahí cuando ocurrió por primera vez. El primer fuego.

Nos entregamos mutuamente nuestra inocencia en ese sótano de Manhattan mientras arriba estallaba la fiesta. Hasta el día de hoy, cada vez que escucho pisadas en el techo, pienso en ti.

Nos contamos todo. Nos hemos entregado todo.

Sé lo que dirás. Lo que siempre dices.

Así que, está bien, no te cases conmigo. Pero, si no te casas conmigo, cásate con Chase. Él, al menos, tiene pasión, coraje, corazón. Ha viajado. Puede defenderse en una conversación e intentó leer a Joyce. Sus padres te adoran. Ellos ya no son los mismos desde que Alexandra se cayó de aquella casa del árbol y murió.

A su familia le vendría bien un poco de tu encanto natural, tu risa, tus ganas de vivir. Por favor, no te cases con Lucas. Te aburrirás y le serás infiel. Ahórraselo a él y ahórratelo a ti.

Con amor,
Will

10 de junio de 1929
Querida Freddie:

No es lo que piensas.

Estaba mejor. Lo tenía controlado. Me hiciste prometerte que no lo utilizaría nunca, después de que se quemó la iglesia. Y lo intenté. En serio. Se suponía que esa sería la única vez.

Rose. Y Chase. Estoy seguro de que lo sabías. Nuestras familias se han visitado durante años, y Rose había estado enamorada de él desde que llevaba trenzas. Supongo que tenía que suceder. Debería haberlo adivinado. Y luego encontrarlos, de la manera en que lo hice, en el dormitorio de él... fue una conmoción. Ella tenía solamente dieciséis años. Ellos... no eran el uno para el otro.

Rose es demasiado sensible e inocente para un playboy como Chase. Yo no podía creer que la hubiera seducido. Estaba enfadado, muy enfadado. Solo quería asustarlo un poco, hacer que pensara que ella le era infiel, para que no la molestara más y la dejara ir libremente...

No se suponía que sucediera de esa manera. Yo pensé que solo lograría que él dejara de amarla...

Yo le di esa navaja a él cuando cumplió catorce años. Era para nuestras excursiones de pesca. Para cortar redes, carnada, pescado y esas cosas.

En cambio, la usó para cortar la garganta de mi hermana.

Renuncio. Todo terminó. Para siempre.

¿Recuerdas aquella vez en que fumamos opio en el ático de Glenship? Chase dijo que no te atreverías y tuviste que demostrarle que estaba equivocado. Bueno, esto que yo tengo es peor que el opio, Freddie. Muchísimo peor. Es probable que tenga que marcharme por un tiempo. Pero lo voy a superar.

Te amo, Freddie. Por siempre jamás,

William

15 de diciembre de 1942
Querida Freddie:
Eres la única persona que me comprende. Eres la única que lo sabe, además de mi familia. Tu silencio de estos últimos años ha sido... insoportable.

Algún día, es probable que tenga mis propios hijos, hijos que tengan mi mismo color de cabello, mi egoísmo y mi fuego. *Eso me preocupa, Freddie. ¿Recuerdas cuán asustados estábamos cuando te tomé la mano por primera vez y te hice ver a tu hermano mayor con su uniforme de teniente? Me pegaste tan fuerte que la nariz me sangró durante una hora.*

Y después me tomaste entre tus brazos delgados y me repetiste una y otra vez que todo estaría bien.

Hace cinco años fui a Eco, solo para verlo otra vez. No le conté a nadie que iría. Un día me subí al coche y fui a la mansión Glenship. Está toda tapiada y va camino a convertirse en una ruina. Casi se me parte el corazón. Una noche tarde hicimos el amor en la biblioteca, detrás de las cortinas de terciopelo verde. ¿Recuerdas?

También fui a ver a Rose. Hiciste que la enterraran en el mausoleo de tu familia para que pudiera descansar para siempre en el pueblo que amaba. Nunca te lo agradecí.

El otro día vi Ciudadano Kane. *Me hizo pensar en ti.*

Freddie, eres mi Rosebud,
Will

13 de marzo de 1958
Freddie:

John me contó que True se ahogó. Sí, te hago vigilar por uno de tus antiguos amantes. No lo culpes. Aún está enamorado.

John dijo que dejaste de usar maquillaje, de beber, de patrocinar artistas, de hacer fiestas y todas las cosas que tanto adorabas. Todas las cosas que te daban vida. Dijo

que te encerraste en tu mansión y que te pasas el día mirando el mar o el cielo.

Las personas mueren, Freddie. Hasta los niños mueren, a veces. No es tu culpa. Dios no te está castigando por tus locuras. De la misma manera que no me está castigando a mí por... las cosas que hice. La vida es así.

Cuando éramos jóvenes, siempre decías que yo llevaba al Demonio dentro de mí. Pero las personas pueden cambiar. Yo cambié. No soy el Demonio, Freddie.

Escríbeme, por favor,
Will

Me vestí y fui a la casa de huéspedes. Caminé con cuidado por el césped oscuro y húmedo y me estremecí con cada ráfaga de viento que venía del mar. River todavía estaba despierto, sentado en la cocina bebiendo café. Si le sorprendió verme, no lo demostró. Le pedí que fuera a despertar a Neely porque tenía algo que mostrarles. Sin decir una palabra, se levantó, caminó por el pasillo e hizo lo que le había pedido.

Tomé por el sendero que conducía al pueblo, River y Neely detrás de mí, nada nos separaba de la noche oscura excepto el rayo blanco y líquido de la linterna que yo llevaba. Había dejado de llover, pero el sendero estaba enlodado y resbaladizo.

—¿Adónde estamos yendo, Vi? —preguntó River finalmente, después de que pasamos el túnel. Neely todavía no había pronunciado una sola palabra.

—A buscar una prueba —respondí—. En el mausoleo de los White.

—¿Una prueba de qué? —indagó River, y me pareció agradable que, por una vez, fuera él quien hiciera las preguntas.

Lo ignoré.

–Jack estaba arriba del mausoleo de los Glenship cuando buscaba al Demonio. Pero el mausoleo White está más lejos, escondido entre los árboles. Sin embargo, es más grande y tiene columnas góticas y una frase enigmática grabada sobre la entrada. Les gustará.

–Estoy seguro de ello –River tropezó con una piedra en el camino, pero recuperó el equilibrio y no cayó–. ¿No podría gustarme de la misma manera por la mañana? ¿Cuando hace calor y podemos ver dónde estamos pisando?

–No –dije.

Neely rio.

La luna estaba comenzando a asomar la cara en el cielo nocturno cuando llegamos al cementerio, y el viento del mar era más suave, ahora que, supongo, la hora de las brujas había quedado atrás. La puerta de hierro estaba abierta. Los tres nos deslizamos por el hueco.

Me quedé quieta y traté de absorber la sensación de calma y soledad del cementerio. Y luego conduje a River y a Neely al mausoleo White.

La bóveda familiar estaba sola, en la parte trasera del cementerio junto a algunas tumbas de los primeros suicidas y a la abandonada cabaña del cuidador, una construcción que escupía ladrillos viejos y le confería al lugar una atmósfera de misterio. Freddie estaba enterrada ahí, también mi abuelo, un tío demente y dos pobres bebés que habían nacido muertos, que Freddie dio a luz antes de que naciera papá.

Al mausoleo Glenship se lo podaba y se le cortaba el césped de vez en cuando porque estaba cerca de la entrada del cementerio. Pero al nuestro, no. Las enredaderas brotaban del techo de piedra como si fueran dueñas y señoras del lugar, y los arbustos de moras cubrían las paredes como si fueran sanguijuelas con espinas. Estar ahí, frente a nuestro mausoleo, me hizo sentir un tanto conmocionada por el brutal abandono. Era palpable, casi opresivo. No podía recordar cuándo había sido la última vez que lo había visitado, que *alguien* lo había visitado. ¿Fue cuando Freddie murió? ¿Había pasado tanto tiempo?

Sentí que la punzada amarga de la culpa se encendía dentro de mí. ¿Por qué no me había preocupado por la tumba de Freddie?

Tal vez había absorbido la desidia de mis padres, junto con el arte y el esnobismo.

Está bien, Violet, brotó la voz de Freddie en mi cabeza. *Me gusta que mi tumba esté así. Olvidada y silenciosa.*

Y era verdad. A Freddie siempre le habían gustado las cosas abandonadas y quietas. Como los pueblos fantasmas, los automóviles herrumbrosos en los depósitos de chatarra y los molinos de viento rotos donde solía haber una granja.

Tenía una colección de llaves de edificios de Eco que se habían incendiado. Eran once, todas muy parecidas, excepto la llave grande que había pertenecido a una antigua iglesia de madera, reducida a cenizas por un sacerdote que se había vuelto loco. Las guardaba en un pañuelo rosado y me las mostró una noche de verano en que ambas no podíamos dormir. Recuerdo las luciérnagas y que el pañuelo de Freddie olía a pétalos de rosa, y el aire húmedo de la noche, la limonada de jengibre y las manos suaves, queridas y arrugadas.

Me estiré y jalé de una rama de la enredadera, que había estado ocultando las palabras grabadas en la piedra, arriba de la puerta. Las letras descendían, se enroscaban y refulgían bajo la luz de la luna, como si pertenecieran a la Tierra Media.

—¿Está en élfico? —preguntó River ni dos segundos después de que la asociación con Tolkien diera vueltas por mi cabeza.

—*Mea culpa. Por ese pecado cayeron los ángeles. Exuro, Exuro, Exuro* —me puse de puntillas y tracé las palabras con los dedos—. *Mea culpa* supongo que ya saben qué quiere decir. La segunda frase es de *Enrique VIII* de Shakespeare y el final quiere decir *Me quemo, Me quemo, Me quemo*. Freddie lo hizo grabar allí arriba, varias décadas atrás y nunca quiso decirme qué significaba. Finalmente, tuve que ir a la biblioteca a investigar. Traduje el latín pero, con respecto a lo que Freddie pretendía decir con eso...

—Estaba arrepentida —dijo Neely hablando por primera vez desde que River lo había despertado. Tenía un aspecto tierno y desaliñado con sus pantalones de lino arrugados y su chaqueta rompevientos—. Estaba arrepentida por los pecados que cometió. Y el fuego son las llamas del infierno.

—No lo creo —respondí. Freddie no se estaba quemando en el infierno. Al menos de eso sí estaba segura.

Le di unos golpecitos al candado oxidado de la puerta del mausoleo y cayeron virutas de metal en el suelo. Pensé que podría romperlo con una piedra si quisiera. Además, quién rayos sabía dónde se encontraba la llave.

Un momento.

Los nombres podrían estar del lado de afuera, sepultados bajo las hojas verdes.

Fui al otro lado de la tumba y aparté la enredadera.

El primer nombre que apareció fue True White, mi tía, la niñita que se ahogó. El fantasma que River había convocado para asustar a Luke. La hija que condujo a Freddie a los brazos de Dios, y del Demonio.

Pero el nombre que todos estábamos observando, no era el de True.

ROSE REDDING
Amada hija y amada hermana
Asesinada en su cumpleaños número 16
8 de junio de 1929

Tomé la tarjeta roja y las cinco cartas que guardaba en el bolsillo. Le entregué la linterna a River. Leyó todo, en silencio. Y después le pasó las cartas a Neely.

—¿Lo sabías? —le pregunté a River, después de varios tramos largos de silencio—. ¿Tu abuelo te hablaba de Freddie y de Eco, y es por eso que viniste aquí? ¿Sabías que él también tenía el resplandor?

River hizo una pausa y sus ojos se encontraron con los míos. Después se reclinó sobre el tejido de enredadera que cubría el mausoleo y asintió.

—Mi abuelo lo llamaba el *fuego*. Y sí, unos años antes de su muerte, comenzó a hablar conmigo. Esa fue la primera vez que me enteré de que lo que yo tenía, ese resplandor, era de familia. Papá no lo tenía, pero mi abuelo sí. Y me enteré de que existía una mujer llamada Freddie, que era la única mujer a la que Will Redding había amado. Me habló de un pueblo llamado Eco, donde perdió el control de su fuego, y eso mató a su hermana. Antes de morir, él trató de advertirme. Pero era demasiado tarde. Papá ya me hacía trabajar para él, y yo ya había llegado demasiado lejos. Ya me había vuelto adicto. Pensé que… tal vez, si venía aquí, a Eco, podría… no sé. Podría ayudarme.

—Pero no fue así —señaló Neely.

Y yo estaba pensando lo mismo.

River me miró con ojos suplicantes.

—Llegué a Eco y descubrí que Freddie tenía una nieta que era exactamente igual a ella. Y esa nieta estaba buscando a alguien que quisiera alquilar la casa de huéspedes. Parecía demasiado bueno para ser verdad. Pensé que era el destino. Pensé... pensé que ibas a salvarme, Vi.

—Lo estoy *intentando* —repuse.

—Lo *sé* —admitió y se estiró hacia mí... y luego se detuvo y bajó las manos—. Pero no fue por eso, Vi. No tiene que ver con Freddie ni con mi abuelo. Tampoco con el resplandor. Tiene que ver contigo, con que el hecho de que te sientes en esos magníficos escalones y leas bajo el sol. Tiene que ver con la forma en que bebes café de puntillas. Tiene que ver con que eres directa y tímida al mismo tiempo, y comprensiva y excéntrica y algo esnob. Es todo eso —dejó de hablar durante unos segundos, pero sus ojos no se apartaron de los míos—. Antes nunca hubo nadie. Ninguna chica. No sé qué es lo que estoy haciendo. Vi. Vi, mírame. ¿Me crees? ¿Crees lo que te estoy diciendo?

La última parte la dijo rápido, muy rápido, como si tal vez le diera vergüenza.

—No. Eres un mentiroso —pero no brotó con la dureza que yo pretendía.

Neely rio.

—Tiene razón, River. Te dije que todas esas mentiras tendrían sus consec...

Un grito. Un grito de un niño. Casi un alarido. Vino desde el mausoleo Glenship.

Nos miramos los tres y luego salimos disparando en dirección hacia el sonido. Al acercarnos a la vieja tumba, vi a dos chicos que se movían en las sombras. Uno era alto, delgado y de cabello negro. El otro era más pequeño y se encontraba en el suelo, encogido de miedo junto a una lápida, cubriéndose la cara con las manos porque el chico mayor le estaba dando una gran paliza. Sus gemidos impregnaban el aire nocturno; eran como hilos de telarañas, fantasmales, débiles, patéticos y desgarradores.

—No, River, yo me encargo. No lo toques —gritó Neely, pero era demasiado tarde. River golpeó al chico con el hombro y lo estampó contra el mausoleo. Sujetó al matón de la camisa y jaló de él hasta ponerlo de pie. Luego le puso la mano en la garganta y lo empujó contra el muro cubierto de enredadera. Con fuerza.

La cabeza del chico se sacudió hacia atrás y chocó contra la piedra.

—River, *déjalo* —exclamé. Era el mismo chico de unos días atrás. El bravucón. El de *Casablanca* y los yo-yos—. Es un niño. *Déjalo*.

River me ignoró.

—¿Pegarle a un chico que tiene la mitad de tu tamaño? —gritó River—. ¿Te parece *justo*? ¿Te parece *bien*?

El matón se retorció debajo de la mano de River. Luego levantó un brazo y lo apuntó hacia el niño, que estaba desparramado en el suelo.

—Vine aquí buscando un lugar donde fumar y ese chico tuvo los cojones de decirme que me marchara a causa del Demonio. Del Demonio. Esos mocositos mentirosos le contaron a todo el mundo que vieron al maldito demonio y nos hicieron quedar a todos como estúpidos. Y después viene uno de ellos a decirme *a mí* que me vaya del cementerio. Esa *mierdita*.

Me arrodillé junto al niño que estaba en el suelo. Lo reconocí. Era el chico rubio que había vacilado junto a la verja, cuando los demás chicos abandonaban el cementerio. Estaba sucio y tenía la ropa hecha jirones y le salía sangre de la boca y la nariz. Se pasó la mano por los ojos y le echó una mirada asesina al chico de cabello negro.

—No soy mentiroso. El Demonio estuvo aquí. Lo vimos. Todos lo vimos.

El bravucón luchaba entre las manos de River.

—*Mentiroso de mierda.* Te voy a patear hasta que se te parta el pecho y tu corazoncito mentiroso quede estrujado entre las costillas…

Neely corrió hacia adelante y arrancó las manos de River del matón. El chico se quedó congelado durante un instante —los ojos fijos y blancos miraban más allá de las sombras— y luego salió disparando entre los árboles, como un ciervo.

Las manos de Neely temblaban. Noté cómo aparecían y desaparecían bajo la luz de la luna. Respiraba con rapidez y apretaba las temblorosas manos en un puño.

—¿Es cierto, River? ¿Lo hiciste? ¿Usaste el resplandor en ese chico? —la voz de Neely había cambiado. Era baja y más bien impaciente, como si *quisiera* que River dijera que sí.

River se llevó las manos a las sienes.

—Yo… no lo sé. Tenía las manos en su garganta, y estaba tan furioso, y yo…

Neely llevó el puño derecho hacia atrás, el de las cicatrices que terminaban en la muñeca, y le dio un golpe a River justo en medio de la cara.

La cabeza de River se sacudió de costado y él retrocedió trastabillando. Se llevó la mano a la mejilla y miró a su hermano.

–Gracias –fue todo lo que le dijo. Sacudió la cabeza para apartar el cabello de la frente, con algo de arrogancia. Casi, *casi*, como si estuviera invitando a Neely a pegarle nuevamente.

–Vamos –dijo y ahora su voz sonaba tensa y excitada. Rodeó a River durante unos segundos y luego volvió a lanzarle un puñetazo, ágil, fuerte y veloz.

River lo esquivó con destreza, como si fuera lo más natural del mundo. Neely adelantó la cabeza y chocó su cuerpo con fuerza contra el costado del River. Ambos cayeron al suelo y rodaron. Neely quedó arriba pero River lo tenía sujeto del cuello y no le permitía moverse.

–¿Ya terminaste? –preguntó River–. ¿*Ya terminaste?*

–*Sí, sí, maldita sea* –contestó Neely en un susurro porque tenía la parte interna del codo de su hermano en la garganta.

River lo soltó y se puso de pie, y lo mismo hizo Neely. River miró a su hermano, después me miró a mí y comenzó a bajar la colina.

Me volví hacia el niño rubio.

–¿Estás herido? –le pregunté estúpidamente.

–Un poco –respondió, la mano derecha oprimía las costillas y la izquierda limpiaba la sangre que salía de la boca–. Pero estaré bien.

Le moví la mano y palpé su pequeño pecho para ver si había algo roto.

–A ver, déjame a mí –Neely se arrodilló a mi lado. Todavía respiraba agitado pero parecía más… calmo, después de la pelea–. Hice entrenamiento de primeros auxilios. Fui voluntario durante un verano como técnico de emergencias médicas.

Neely revisó al niño. Tenía sangre en los nudillos: podía ser por pegarle a River o de pegarse contra el suelo, pero no dio muestras de dolor mientras movía las manos. Era gentil y eficiente, y no se sintió ni remotamente perturbado por los ojos oscuros y penetrantes del niño, como me sentí yo.

–Tienes suerte –dijo Neely, después de unos minutos–. No hay huesos rotos, solo magullones. Es mejor que vayas a tu casa y dejes que tu madre les ponga hielo.

El chico apoyó las manos en la tierra húmeda y se puso de pie.

Neely le puso la mano en el hombro.

–No deberías volver aquí. No hay ningún demonio y nunca lo hubo, ¿de acuerdo? Prométeme que te mantendrás alejado del cementerio.

–Lo intentaré –contestó mientras miraba a Neely con ojos parpadeantes y la mano en las costillas. Se dio vuelta y echó a andar por el sendero.

Lo observé hasta que la noche negra y obstinada se lo devoró.

Y después sentí que unos dedos tibios se entrelazaban con los míos. Neely me había tomado la mano y permanecimos hombro con hombro, frente al bosque. Podía sentir la sangre seca bajo las yemas de los dedos.

–Más tarde, iré a buscar al otro chico –señaló–. No sé qué fue lo que River le hizo ver con el resplandor, pero… no puede haber sido algo bueno. Tendré que ir a limpiar y ordenar.

Asentí. Y, a continuación, regresamos al Ciudadano escuchando a las criaturas nocturnas cantar sus canciones nocturnas. Los dedos de Neely se mantuvieron apretados alrededor de los míos, hasta que los solté.

Cuando llegamos a la casa de huéspedes, todavía no había rastros de River. Neely fue a buscarlo por los alrededores. Era tarde. Faltaban pocas horas para que amaneciera. El césped estaba cubierto de rocío y el aire estaba húmedo y fresco, casi frío. La luna brillaba y todo estaba en calma, salvo el océano. Hasta los grillos estaban en silencio.

Me fui a casa, escarbé en el frízer y encontré un poco de hielo. Tomé dos toallitas para secar los platos, coloqué cuatro cubitos en cada una y salí. Me senté en los escalones del porche, en el lugar donde la luz del vestíbulo se desparramaba a través de los ventanales del frente.

Neely apareció unos minutos después. No había señales de River.

—Aquí tienes —dije alcanzándole una de las toallitas.

Sonrió y el magullón que tenía debajo del ojo sobresalió con más fuerza por un segundo. Puso el hielo en la mano inflamada.

—Gracias, cariño. No resultaría difícil acostumbrarse a esto: a que te cuiden después de una pelea.

—Lo del matón se arreglará —mentí, porque a veces una chica tiene que mentir—. Estoy segura de que River le hizo ver a Cthulhu o algo parecido, cuando regresaba a su casa.

—Sí, es posible —rio Neely—. Yo no debería haber... Mi hermano me pone *realmente* loco. Así que... —alzó la mano herida y señaló el magullón de la cara—. Lamento que hayas tenido que ver eso.

—Está bien. Yo misma he querido pegarle a River unas cuantas veces.

—Él provoca eso en la gente —suspiró Neely y vi otra vez esa sonrisa triste, la de antes—. Sé que parece que no me tomo en serio sus problemas, pero no es así. Estoy preocupado por él. Constantemente. Creo que deberías saberlo.

—Lo sé.

Y volvió a sonreír.

—Vi, ¿hay algo que se te escape?

Me encogí de hombros y pensé en Luke y en Sunshine, en las cartas ocultas de Freddie, en el secreto de Daniel Leap.

—Sí, muchas cosas.

Rio.

—Bueno, iré a caminar. No quiero estar aquí cuando River regrese arrepentido, porque es probable que le pegue otra vez. Volveré pronto, ¿de acuerdo?

—De acuerdo.

Neely se marchó. Los cuatro cubitos de hielo que había guardado para River se derritieron en mi mano y chorrearon al suelo. Deslicé el dedo por la falda roja que llevaba (de Freddie) y pensé en la sangre en la boca del niño rubio, en Rose Redding con la garganta cortada, en las cartas y en River.

Él apareció unos veinte minutos después. Subió los escalones del Ciudadano con su habitual contoneo y me lanzó su maldita sonrisa angelical.

—Creo que hace mucho tiempo que Neely tenía ganas de hacer esto —rio mientras se llevaba los dedos a la mejilla, que estaba hinchada, con un aspecto horrendo y comenzaba a formarse un magullón. Hermanos con sonrisas y magullones haciendo juego.

Entré y me dirigí a la cocina, River vino detrás de mí. Saqué unos cubitos de hielo nuevos del frízer, los puse en una toallita y se la alcancé sin decir una palabra. Al ver su rostro sonriente y magullado, un sentimiento se despertó dentro de mí, y era fuerte, violento y amargo, como el café quemado, sin leche ni azúcar.

—Deja de sonreír, River. Ni siquiera sabes si utilizaste el resplandor en ese chico. ¿Entiendes el peligro que representas? ¿Entiendes lo que eso significa?

Apretó el hielo contra la cara y el brillo arrogante de sus ojos se volvió más tenue.

—¿No podríamos hablar de esto más tarde? Me duele la cara. Mañana podemos decidir qué hacer conmigo. Empacaré, me marcharé a casa, me meteré en problemas y me escaparé otra vez —hizo una pausa—. Sin embargo, en el próximo pueblo, no estarás tú. Lo cual me fastidia mucho cuando lo pienso.

Y sonaba medio sincero, lo cual ya era algo. Lo observé durante unos segundos.

—Lo que dijiste en el cementerio, antes de que escucháramos los gritos del niño, eso de que no había existido otra chica antes que yo. Estabas diciendo la verdad, ¿no?

River miró a la pared y se movió nerviosamente de manera tal que Neely se hubiera reído de haberlo visto.

—Sí. Sí. Era verdad.

—¿Estás mintiendo?

—Sí.

—¿Acabas de mentir, otra vez?

—Sí.

River emitió un prolongado suspiro y el último resto de arrogancia titiló y se apagó. De pronto, pareció más joven.

—Vi, ¿podrías dormir esta noche a mi lado? ¿Por favor?

—De acuerdo —dije, porque sería la última vez. Además, las cosas que dijo en el cementerio me resultaron bastante creíbles.

Fuimos a la casa de huéspedes, abrimos las ventanas del dormitorio para que entrara la brisa del mar y nos metimos debajo de las mantas. River hizo una mueca de dolor cuando su mejilla inflamada tocó la almohada. No lo besé ni me besó, pero me dormí con sus brazos alrededor del cuerpo y su rostro en mi cabello.

Y soñé.

Soñé con cementerios, con un túnel y con un hombre con dientes peludos y un tajo en el cuello. Soñé con el Demonio, que se parecía a River, excepto por el cabello rojo y los ojos rojos e inyectados en sangre. Pero no era el Demonio ni River. Era Neely, el cabello rubio estaba rojo por la luz del atardecer, el rostro rojo de pelear. De pelear con River que, de repente, me besaba y yo me sentía tan bien, tan bien, porque River me besaba el cuello y luego los hombros y yo me quitaba la ropa y él me ayudaba y después yo lo ayudaba a él y estábamos desnudos, y no me importaba, y solo quería que River continuara besándome por toda la eternidad, amén, y todo era tan natural y yo sabía que era el momento y yo lo quería, ah, cómo lo quería...

Una puerta se cerró violentamente.

Me desperté de una sacudida.

Respiré hondo y abrí los ojos.

Ya casi amanecía, la luz era de un inquietante gris oscuro y azulino. Había dormido solamente unas pocas horas. Y estaba en la cama de River. Había estado soñando, solo soñando. Un sueño tan bueno.

Maldita sea esa puerta que se cerró violentamente.

Un momento. Algo había cambiado. Estaba tibia. Incluso caliente. Sentí un cosquilleo en la piel. Me moví.

Y descubrí súbitamente qué había cambiado. Estaba desnuda.

Y River también.

Nuestros cuerpos estaban apretados uno contra otro, muy apretados. El sueño. *El sueño había sido real.* El cuerpo desnudo de River estaba acurrucado contra el mío, y resultaba tan natural, como en el sueño...

—¿Violet? —susurró River.

—¿Sí? —dije en voz muy baja. Respiré profundamente otra vez, mi pecho se hinchó contra el cuerpo de River. Dejé salir el aire y nuestros ojos se encontraron. Movió las manos y las apoyó en la parte inferior de mi espalda.

—Me parece que... utilicé el resplandor mientras dormía. Ni siquiera sabía que podía hacerlo. Ay, diablos. Nosotros, nosotros casi... Dios, lo siento, Vi. No sé qué me pasa...

No me moví.

—Neely tiene razón —agregó y su voz sonó insegura y tensa, muy distinta a la de siempre—. Perdí el control.

—Sí —respondí y, aun así, no me moví.

—Violet, ya no estoy seguro —dijo finalmente—. *Tú no estás segura conmigo.* Deberías irte. Vi, *vete de aquí, ahora.*

Mi corazón se detuvo, se estremeció y volvió a latir. Me deslicé fuera de los brazos de River y fuera de la cama. Mi ropa estaba desparramada por el suelo, mezclada con la de él. Me vestí y me marché.

Después di media vuelta, caminé por el pasillo y volví a entrar al dormitorio.

—River, tienes que irte de Eco —susurré. Me quedé junto a la cama, las manos en el corazón, y esperé. River giró, las mantas se resbalaron de su cuerpo y dejaron a la vista la cadera desnuda hasta el muslo—. Mañana. Y no quiero verte antes de que te marches, ¿de acuerdo?

–Violet, vete de aquí –fue todo lo que me dijo.

Y eso fue lo que hice. Me marché.

Neely se hallaba en la cocina de la casa de huéspedes. Bebía café de una tacita rosada que tenía una quebradura. Estaba de espaldas a la ventana y el sol comenzaba a salir detrás de él.

–Neely, no sé cómo puedes beber tanto café –la voz brotó ligeramente entrecortada. Sujeté la taza y bebí de un sorbo lo que quedaba. Me sentí un poco mejor con ese brebaje quemándome la garganta.

Él me miró. Sonreía, pero sus ojos me taladraban.

–¿Estás bien, Vi?

–Sip. Totalmente –pero mis manos todavía temblaban y Neely sabía que mentía, como lo hacía su hermano.

–Muy bien –repuso–. Dejaré eso por el momento. ¿Quieres saber dónde estuve?

No quería.

–Traté de localizar al chico al que River le aplicó el resplandor –continuó Neely ante mi silencio–. Regresé al cementerio y seguí el sendero entre los árboles durante un rato, pero no encontré nada. Estoy preocupado por él.

Miré por la ventana para evitar los ojos de Neely.

–Yo también –mustié. Neely me echó una mirada penetrante.

–¿Y por qué estás despierta? –preguntó–. ¿Por qué no estás todavía durmiendo en la cama de mi hermano, envuelta entre sus brazos, rompiendo la promesa de que no permitirías que te tocara?

Sacudí la cabeza y no respondí.

–¿Qué sucedió? –inquirió Neely en voz baja–. Violet, ¿qué pasó?

Observé su mano derecha, la que estaba inflamada. La que golpeó a su hermano en medio de la cara.

–¿Me prometes que no comenzarás a pelearte otra vez?

–No –hizo una pausa y se pasó la mano por el cabello igual que River–. Sí, sí, lo prometo. Lo juro por Dios, Vi.

–River usó el resplandor conmigo. Mientras dormía. No fue intencional… pero lo hizo de todas maneras. Y las cosas estaban sucediendo y los dos dejábamos que sucedieran, pero después escuché que se abría la puerta del frente y eso me despertó. A tiempo –agregué ese último dato solo porque los ojos de Neely se estaban poniendo nerviosos e impacientes como antes, un segundo antes de que golpeara a River.

Neely respiró hondo y me tomó la mano. La apretó con tanta fuerza que las costras de las heridas se abrieron y comenzaron a sangrar nuevamente. Y nos quedamos ahí, en silencio, en la cocina de la casa de huéspedes, mientras amanecía y la brisa del mar se colaba por las ventanas.

CAPÍTULO 25

Alguien pronunciaba mi nombre con voz suave. Parpadeé varias veces ante el sol brillante de la mañana y volteé para ver quién había decidido despertarme. ¿Luke? ¿Sunshine? ¿Neely? Me estiré y me di cuenta de que no había nadie junto a mí en la cama.

River.

Me incorporé y me froté los ojos. Y luego, los recuerdos de la noche anterior inundaron mi mente y me despertaron más rápido que una cubeta de agua fría. River se marchaba. Estaba en problemas. Había perdido el control. El resplandor. Las cartas…

—¿Violet?

Era Jack. Estaba parado en un rayo de sol al pie de la cama, con la expresión seria de siempre.

–Jack. Hola. Estaba durmiendo, sola –*concéntrate Violet*–. ¿Qué sucede?

–Esta mañana fui a caminar –dijo–. Quería encontrar el árbol perfecto y pintarlo. Pero encontré… otra cosa. En la zanja, junto a las vías.

Lo miré sin comprender.

–Necesito que vengas conmigo –prosiguió–. Ahora.

–De acuerdo –asentí.

Me cepillé el cabello y los dientes, me puse una falda verde y una camisa ligera de manga larga que mi mamá solía utilizar para pintar. Jack me esperó afuera. No le avisé a nadie que me iba, ni a Luke, ni a Neely, ni a… River. Le había dicho que no quería verlo antes de que se marchara. Y ya no estaba muy segura de si todavía pensaba lo mismo.

Maldición.

Seguí a Jack por el camino hacia Eco, más allá del túnel y del cementerio. El sol brillaba en el cielo y el rocío de la hierba hacía que mis pies resbalaran dentro de las sandalias.

Sonó el silbato del tren en la distancia y los pequeños hombros de Jack se pusieron rígidos delante de mí. Habíamos pasado el centro del pueblo y transitábamos junto al campo vacío que llevaba a la calle Glenship, y todavía Jack no había dicho una sola palabra. Estaba comenzando a ponerme nerviosa.

–Por el amor de Dios, Jack, ¿qué viste?

Pero no hizo más que sacudir la cabeza de un lado a otro. Caminamos un par de minutos más. Ya se podía oír el arroyo que rodeaba el pueblo y, unos kilómetros después, desembocaba en el mar. Le di un manotazo a un mosquito e hice una mueca ante la mancha de sangre que me dejó en el brazo.

Al levantar la vista, noté que Jack se había detenido y apuntaba hacia las vías.

Los trenes todavía llegaban a Eco. Las vías cercanas al Ciudadano habían desaparecido hacía mucho tiempo, pero todavía existía una vía activa que circulaba por las afueras del pueblo y transportaba cargamentos y, con menor frecuencia, pasajeros, hasta Canadá. Jack señalaba un tramo de esas vías, rodeado de árboles.

Escurrió su mano dentro de la mía y juntos pisamos los rieles. Agucé el oído para ver si se acercaba un tren, pero lo único que alcancé a escuchar fueron los arrullos de las palomas torcazas, con su típico tono grave y melancólico. Jack jaló de mi mano y nos deslizamos por la zanja, mitad caminando y mitad resbalando, al otro lado de las vías.

Cuando llegamos al fondo, lo miré a Jack, desconcertada. Su cabello castaño rojizo refulgía bajo el sol. Tenía el semblante pálido.

Y entonces lo vi.

A él.

Cabello negro enmarañado y pegoteado con sangre seca. Eso fue lo primero que noté. El resto del cuerpo del muchacho estaba oculto en las sombras que proyectaban los árboles. Pero su rostro estaba a la luz. Tropecé hacia el costado y casi pisé la mano del chico muerto. Un ruido brotó de mi boca, una mezcla de grito y de gemido, y el resto de mí se estremeció ante el sonido.

—Supongo que lo atropelló un tren —dijo Jack—. Es probable que el conductor ni siquiera lo haya oído. Rebotó y... rodó.

No dije nada, solo miraba los ojos del chico muerto. Esos ojos que habían estado tan enojados en el cementerio, la mano de River apretándole el cuello, ahora estaban muy abiertos y fijos. Y muertos. Muertos, muertos, muertos. Eso era distinto que ver a Daniel Leap cortándose la garganta en la plaza del pueblo. El cuerpo que tenía delante había pertenecido a un niño. Y tenía la cabeza retorcida de manera horrenda y antinatural, la piel violeta y gris, y el cabello negro estaba sucio y lleno de hojas y de sangre y, diablos, estaba viendo a un niño muerto tan de cerca que podía tocar su desdichado cuerpo de niño muerto...

–Violet, ¿fue River? ¿Fue él quien lo hizo pararse delante del tren? No le conté a nadie más. No quiero que se meta en problemas. Le iba a contar a la policía, pero después pensé, ¿y si fue River?

Solté la mano de Jack, volteé hacia el costado y vomité.

Jack me palmeó la espalda y yo continué vomitando sin parar. Y cuando ya no me quedaba nada más, devolví una vez más mientras las arcadas secas retorcían mi cuerpo y me hacían temblar, al igual que las hojas de los árboles que impedían que el cuerpo del muchacho muerto quedara expuesto a la luz.

Por fin, por fin, me enderecé. Caminé hacia el arroyo, apoyé las rodillas desnudas en la orilla enlodada y me arrojé agua fría en el rostro. Me sequé la boca y después regresé con Jack y el cuerpo.

–River está fuera de control, Jack. El del ático era él. Estoy segura. Es peligroso. Para mí, para ti, para todos. Entonces... esto es lo que haremos. Irás al café o a la biblioteca y te quedarás allí hasta que yo vaya a buscarte. No quiero que te mezcles en esto. Iré a lo de Sunshine, utilizaré su teléfono y llamaré a la estación de policía de Portland –me pasé el dorso de la mano por la frente. Tenía la cara fría, pero no sabía si era debido al agua del arroyo o por la sensación fría y húmeda que me había quedado después de vomitar.

»Vete al pueblo –exclamé al ver que Jack me miraba y no atinaba a moverse.

–¿Tú no vienes conmigo? –preguntó, y su tono era dulce, serio y preocupado.

–No, esperaré aquí unos minutos. No quiero que nadie nos vea entrando juntos al pueblo. No quiero que nadie sepa que estás mezclado en... esto.

Jack me observó durante unos segundos, asintió y se marchó.

Sonó el arrullo de las torcazas y el graznido de un cuervo arriba de un árbol. Las sombras danzaron a mi alrededor mientras las nubes pasaban delante del sol. Ahora todo el cuerpo del muchacho ya estaba en la oscuridad. Yo quería ayudarlo. Quería moverlo para que se viera más cómodo, quería...

–Hola.

Por un segundo, un segundo de locura y de terror, pensé que era el muchacho muerto quien me hablaba. Pensé que había revivido. Pensé que me había vuelto loca. Con la mano en el corazón, me incliné sobre él y observé atentamente la boca y los ojos esperando que se movieran.

Y después sentí un cosquilleo en la nuca.

Me di vuelta.

Un chico. Un chico que no estaba muerto. Se encontraba a menos de tres metros en la oscuridad, debajo de la densa arboleda. Catorce años, tal vez, pero más alto que yo. Vagamente familiar. ¿Acaso lo conocía? Era flacucho, puro huesos, codos y piernas. Y el cabello. Tenía el cabello largo por los hombros, y rojo. Rojo como el cielo mañanero, aviso para el marinero. Rojo como el fuego. Rojo como la sangre.

Llevaba botas negras de vaquero, jeans negros ajustados de aspecto costoso y una camiseta blanca lisa. Tenía ojos verdes, muy abiertos y sorprendidos.

Señaló el cuerpo con la cabeza.

—Sí, señora. Es una ima… una imagen impactante —dijo con voz entrecortada. Tenía acento sureño, pero no del Sur Profundo sino el acento sureño de McMurtry. Tal vez de Texas—. Me tropecé con él mientras miraba pasar los trenes. Así es como llegué hasta aquí —hizo un gesto con la cabeza hacia las vías—. En tren. Me gusta mirarlos y, a veces, viajar en ellos.

Lo miré fijo. Traté de no temblar, de no entrar en pánico.

—¿Cuánto tiempo llevas parado ahí?

Por favor, Dios, no permitas que haya escuchado lo que dije acerca de River, por favor, pensé. Aun cuando no importara, ya que había decidido hablar con la policía de todas maneras.

—Solo unos cinco segundos, señora. Vivo en Eco. Me dirigía al pueblo a buscar ayuda cuando los vi venir a usted y al otro muchacho, así que me escondí entre los árboles hasta saber qué se traían entre manos —estiró la mano—. Brodie es mi nombre.

Le estreché la mano; era delgada, pero fuerte. Sus dedos sujetaron los míos… y luego los soltaron.

—¿Brodie? No creo que… ¿Nos hemos visto antes? ¿Acabas de mudarte al pueblo?

Asintió con rapidez. Con el movimiento, el cabello rojo se le dividió en dos y asomaron las puntas de las orejas. Sobresalieron un poco e hicieron que pareciera todavía más joven.

—Hace pocos días que estoy en Eco —se estiró hacia abajo y recogió algo junto a sus pies. Era un sombrero negro de vaquero. Se lo calzó con rapidez y algo del rojo desapareció de un fogonazo, como una bombilla que se apaga—. Soy de Texas.

Yo había visto ese sombrero antes. El chico sentado en la hamaca cuando Daniel Leap se mató... llevaba un sombrero como ese.

Las nubes se desplazaron y el sol apareció otra vez. La cara del chico muerto quedó nuevamente a la luz. Y entonces me di cuenta de que había mantenido una conversación con un chico texano que no conocía, a treinta centímetros de un cadáver.

—De Texas, claro... —dije distraídamente. En lo único que estaba pensando otra vez era en River, en entregarlo, en lo que le harían a él y en lo que eso me haría a mí—. Tengo que hacer una llamada telefónica, de modo que... no puedo hablar ahora. Tengo que irme a mi casa y...

—Señora, ¿le importaría que la acompañara? —Brodie se quitó el sombrero y lo sostuvo al costado del cuerpo—. ¿Va a llamar a la policía, verdad? Bueno, puedo esperar con usted y luego contarles lo que vi. Me gustaría ayudarla. Se la ve un poco pálida, para ser sincero. Yo ya he visto a un muchacho muerto. Hay muchos cadáveres en Texas. De modo que no me afecta mucho.

Pero mi mente estaba a millones de kilómetros de distancia y no le respondí. Y cuando comencé a caminar en dirección al pueblo, Brodie me siguió. La parte de mí que aún podía percibir lo que estaba sucediendo, lo percibió. ¿Pero qué podía cambiar? ¿Qué podía cambiar que él me acompañara y les contara a los policías su parte de la historia?

Al llegar al pueblo, tomamos un camino alternativo para rodear la plaza. No quería tener que explicarle a nadie por qué tenía las piernas cubiertas de lodo, por qué tenía el cabello empapado con agua del arroyo, por qué tenía aspecto de enferma y por qué caminaba junto a un chico llamado Brodie. Estaba segura de que, si una persona se detenía a preguntarme qué me sucedía, abriría la boca y confesaría todo: el resplandor, River, el Demonio, el muchacho muerto. Todo.

Si Brodie habló en el camino a casa, ya no podía recordarlo.

En el Ciudadano, todo estaba en silencio. Fui al cobertizo, pero Luke no estaba pintando. La casa de huéspedes parecía deshabitada. Cuando apoyé el oído en la puerta y traté de captar los sonidos del desayuno, el café chisporroteando en la cafetera italiana, los huevos cocinándose en la sartén, Neely y River peleando, no escuché nada.

Me quedé en el jardín trasero y me dieron escalofríos. Había una desagradable sensación en el aire, como si se estuviera por levantar una tormenta. Pero el cielo estaba diáfano, el sol brillaba y hacía calor. Sin embargo, algo me hacía erizar la piel. *Algo* me estaba dando la sensación de que me vigilaban.

Eché un vistazo a mi alrededor. Nadie. No había nadie por ningún lado.

—No sé dónde están todos —dije—. Es… extraño.

Brodie se limitó a encogerse de hombros y sonreír.

Empecé a flaquear. Me dirigí hacia los escalones del frente del Ciudadano y consideré la idea de volver a meterme en la cama y olvidar lo que había visto. Olvidar al chico muerto, el cabello lleno de sangre. Olvidar a Daniel Leap deslizando la navaja por su garganta. Olvidar todo.

Pero después miré a Brodie, con su cabello rojo, su sombrero negro y sus "señoras".

Él también había visto el cuerpo.

No había forma de olvidarlo, de taparlo.

—Quédate ahí —dije de manera poco cortés y no me importó—. Voy a ir a lo de mi vecina para utilizar el teléfono. Es más fácil si te quedas aquí, ¿de acuerdo?

Brodie alzó el sombrero negro en un gesto de aprobación y después apuntó hacia el suelo bajo sus pies como diciendo *No me despego de acá.*

Respiré hondo y eché a andar por el camino hacia la casa de Sunshine.

No estaba afuera sentada en la hamaca. *También debe estar dormida,* pensé. Me pregunté qué maldita hora de la mañana sería. Sunshine era madrugadora, como Luke, y no sabía qué hacían los madrugadores: cuándo se levantaban, cuándo tomaban el desayuno o qué hacían a esa hora tan temprana. Nunca había sido una de ellos, excepto esas veces en que me despertaban unos chicos serios apenas daban las siete de la mañana para mostrarme cadáveres junto a las vías del tren.

La puerta principal de la casa de Sunshine estaba abierta. Golpeé el mosquitero, pero entré sin esperar a que me respondieran.

Vi a los padres de Sunshine. Sam y Cassie estaban de pie, uno al lado del otro, en la sala. Sam con su habitual expresión perdida y su ropa de corderoy; Cassie con el cabello negro y los lentes. Miraban algo que estaba en el suelo con suma atención.

Lo que se encontraba en el suelo era Sunshine. Estaba tumbada boca abajo y sangraba. La sangre manaba de un magullón húmedo cerca de la sien, se deslizaba por su rostro y formaba un charquito en el suelo, a su lado.

Al verme, abrió la boca. Trató de decirme algo, pero lo único que brotó fue saliva y más sangre. Tosió y la sangre se desparramó entre sus dientes.

—Quizás tengas que golpearla otra vez —dijo Cassie—. Mira, trata de moverse.

Sam tenía un bate en una mano. No lo había notado. *¿Por qué no había notado que tenía un bate? ¿Desde cuándo tenían un bate los padres lectores de Sunshine?* Mi amiga estiró la mano y me tocó el pie, y yo quería ayudarla, yo quería ayudarla, pero no podía moverme. Estaba completamente inmóvil y petrificada, trataba de gritar pero no emitía ningún sonido, y Sunshine ya no se movía y el bate de Sam tenía sangre y cabello pegoteado, y por qué no lo había visto cuando entré; Sunshine, la sangre, el bate, yo temblaba y emitía un grito silencioso…

Y Cassie finalmente me vio.

Sonrió. Sus ojos tenían una mirada extraña, penetrante, parecida a la del muchacho muerto junto a las vías.

—Hola, Violet. ¿Quieres un té? Hemos tenido una mañana tremenda. Entró una rata, pero Sam la mató con su bate. Mírala, ahí junto a tus pies. ¿No es repugnante? Es probable que tenga rabia. Sam la llevará atrás y la quemará. Violet, te ves disgustada. ¿Sucede algo?

A continuación, Sam levantó la vista. Me miró y alzó el bate en el aire.

—Te dije que habría más de una, Cassie. Las ratas vienen en hordas. Apártate que tengo que matar a esta también…

Balanceó el bate y me incliné. La madera dura rebotó en mi sien y retrocedí a los tumbos. No me caí, pero Sam levantó el bate nuevamente y, Dios mío, yo no quería dejar a Sunshine, pero podía oír el sonido del bate rasgando el aire y...

Corrí. Crucé la puerta, me tropecé, bajé los escalones a toda velocidad, me tropecé otra vez, pasé delante de los árboles, del mar, entré por la verja y me dirigí directamente al Ciudadano Kane.

Brodie me estaba esperando. Se encontraba junto a la fuente. Me vio venir corriendo y no pareció sorprendido. En absoluto. Estaba frotando con una mano las mujeres desnudas y sucias de la fuente mientras sonreía.

–¿Cómo está Sunshine? –preguntó en forma agradable y lenta cuando me detuve frente a él, sudando y enferma porque todo mi maldito mundo se estaba cayendo a pedazos–. ¿Ya está muerta la zorrita?

Luego me miró fijo y me guiñó el ojo.

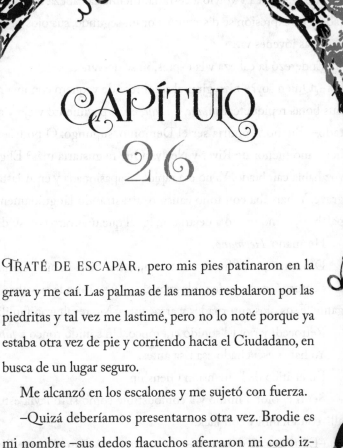

CAPÍTULO 26

TRATÉ DE ESCAPAR, pero mis pies patinaron en la grava y me caí. Las palmas de las manos resbalaron por las piedritas y tal vez me lastimé, pero no lo noté porque ya estaba otra vez de pie y corriendo hacia el Ciudadano, en busca de un lugar seguro.

Me alcanzó en los escalones y me sujetó con fuerza.

—Quizá deberíamos presentarnos otra vez. Brodie es mi nombre —sus dedos flacuchos aferraron mi codo izquierdo y me hizo bajar al suelo de un empujón—. Y tú debes ser Violet.

Me soltó, como si supiera que no iba a escapar. Y no lo hice.

—¿Qué quieres? —pregunté, aunque no deseaba saberlo—. ¿Quién eres?

Abrió la boca y volvió a cerrarla. Inclinó la cabeza hacia un costado y su expresión se distendió. Por un segundo, sus ojos se volvieron más jóvenes y...

Enderezó la cabeza y la expresión se desvaneció.

—¿Quién soy? —hizo girar el sombrero de vaquero con una mano. Sus botas repiquetearon, *tac, tac, tac*, en el pavimento viejo y agrietado—. Bueno... podría ser el Demonio, supongo. O podría ser el hermano menor de River y Neely. ¿Qué te gustaría más? Elige —su voz había cambiado. Ya no era rápida ni apasionada y entusiasta. Era grave. Y hablaba con tono cansino, arrastrando lánguidamente las palabras, como reacio a dejarlas ir, igual que un avaro con su dinero.

Hermano. *Hermano*.

Dio unos pasos hacia mí. Sus ojos también habían cambiado. Los entornó, como si le molestara el sol, y su mirada se volvió arrogante. Esos ojos entornados y arrogantes. Me resultaron familiares.

Retrocedí y rio. El sonido era ronco. Un sonido ronco y *familiar*. Yo había escuchado esa risa antes.

En el ático de la mansión Glenship.

Sentí el olor a humo y a combustible como si todavía estuviera allí, con Gianni y con Jack.

—Entonces no dejarás que me acerque a ti, claro. Porque River te habló del resplandor. Mis dos hermanos son muy charlatanes, pero de los dos, creo que River es el peor. ¿Y tú?

No respondí. Apoyé las manos contra el corazón y apreté las palmas con fuerza para desacelerar los latidos.

Brodie volvió a reír y dio un paso hacia mí.

—Oye, no tienes que preocuparte. Yo no resplandezco como River. No por contacto. Yo me enciendo, arrojo chispas. Y necesito sangre para hacerlo —hizo una pausa. Sus ojos entrecerrados adquirieron otra vez esa expresión extraña, como antes: se volvieron intensamente verdes y con la mirada... perdida. Luego su semblante se suavizó y se tornó casi agradable—. Si yo no fuera un joven tan violento, seguramente me habría llevado años descubrirlo. ¿Y acaso no habría sido eso una pena? Mira esto.

Brodie deslizó la mano dentro de la bota y extrajo algo, un instrumento de plata, delgado, de diez centímetros, con mango de nácar. Un cuchillo.

Yo había visto ese cuchillo antes: cortaba una manzana para darle a un niño durante la proyección de *Breve Encuentro*, en la plaza.

—Lo mandé a hacer especialmente —dijo mientras lo agitaba delante de mis ojos—. Para mi novia. Ella era una cosita dulce, dulce como el azúcar, dulce e inocente como un potrillo de un día de vida. Me gustaba cortarla. Me gustaba verla llorar.

Escurrió el cuchillo nuevamente en la bota.

—Maldita sea. Acabamos de conocernos y, sin embargo, ya estoy conversando contigo como si nos conociéramos desde hace años. Debe ser porque te pareces a Sophie. Mi pequeña Sophie. Cabello rubio, piel blanca, miedo insípido en tus ojos azules e insípidos. Mmm... me gustaría cortarte alguna vez. Verte llorar. Creo que te agradaría. *Sé* que a mí, sí.

Vaciló y los dedos de su mano derecha golpetearon las puntas de su cabello rojo.

—Veamos, ¿dónde estaba? Ah, sí. Vivo en Texas, o al menos solía vivir. Para ser sincero, soy el único medio hermano de River y

Neely. De diferentes madres. Papá no me servía de mucho. Pagaba las cuentas y venía a la ciudad de vez en cuando por asuntos de Redding Oil en Abilene, y para procurarse un poco de la dulzura de Texas. Esto fue así hasta que mamá enloqueció. Ahora se está pudriendo en algún manicomio y no la he visto desde entonces —el cuerpo de Brodie se quedó inmóvil, nada de repiqueteos de botas ni golpeteos de dedos. Lo único que se movía era su cabello intensamente rojo, agitado por la brisa que venía del mar—. Ella solía llamarme Mestizo. ¿Lo sabías?

Negué con la cabeza.

Sus ojos se movieron hacia el costado durante un segundo y no me miraron.

—Bueno, está encerrada con los que gritan y se babean, y le llegó lo que se merecía, ¿verdad? Pero volvamos a nuestro tema. La última vez que papá Redding vino de visita, tuvimos una extraña charla. William Redding II es frío como un témpano en el infierno, de modo que, cuando comenzó a hablarme del resplandor y a hacerme preguntas sobre si mis pensamientos se volvían realidad y conseguían que la gente hiciera cosas con solo pensarlo… bueno. Yo le puse atención.

Moví bruscamente la cabeza tratando de divisar a River, a Neely o a Luke. A *alguien*. ¿Dónde estaban? ¿Acaso Brodie ya los había encontrado? ¿Ya había…?

—No te distraigas, Violet —de repente, la voz de Brodie era dura y sus palabras, rápidas—. No me gusta que me ignoren. Mírame a los ojos. *Mírame a los ojos.*

Posé la vista en él. Sus ojos estaban muy verdes y entornados y llenos de demencia, y sentí que yo también me volvería loca si los miraba fijamente por mucho más tiempo. Pero apreté los puños y no aparté la mirada.

—Bien, así está mejor —dijo, la voz lenta y lánguida otra vez—. Como decía, hace unos meses, estaba usando mi cuchillito con Sophie y, bueno, intenté lograr que ella hiciera algo, utilizando mi mente. Antes nunca había funcionado. Había estado intentando, de vez en cuando, después de que papá y yo mantuvimos esa charla. Pero, en ese momento, funcionó. Ah, diablos si funcionó. A partir de ahí, querida Sophie, ya no hubo posibilidad de que te salvaras. Yo lo tomé de ti y tú estuviste feliz de entregarlo, ya lo creo que sí.

Abrió la boca y se pasó la lengua por el labio inferior.

—Sunshine —susurré—. ¿Qué le hiciste a Sunshine?

Encogió sus hombros estrechos, que desaparecieron bajo el cabello rojo.

—Nada. Ella me enseñó esos pechos, blancos y atractivos como un envase de crema fresca, que asomaban por el escote de ese vestido rojo de prostituta. Así que le pregunté por ti y me dijo que ibas camino al pueblo con el huerfanito. La seguí hasta su casa y conocí a sus padres. Y ellos conocieron a mi cuchillito. Soy bastante rápido con él. Te sorprenderías. Y les corté las palmas de sus manos flacuchas con la misma facilidad con que les estreché las manos. Y te encontré a ti diez minutos después y Jack nos llevó a los dos hasta el cuerpo. Soy muy silencioso cuando tengo que serlo. No oíste nada.

Las lágrimas corrían por mis mejillas. Resbalaban de mis ojos y me dejaban una huella húmeda por todo el cuello. River no era el Demonio. Nunca lo había sido. El chico pelirrojo que estaba frente a mí con un cuchillo era el verdadero Demonio. En carne y hueso. Lo reconocí de la misma forma en que reconocía el olor de la pintura secándose en una tela. De la misma forma en que reconocía el latido de mi corazón dentro de mi propio pecho.

—Pero... el padre de Sunshine le dio un golpe en la cabeza con un bate. Un *bate* —mi voz brotó con un fuerte tono de súplica, que odié—. Ella está herida...

—Bravo, papá Sam —Brodie clavó los pulgares en los bolsillos de su jean y luego deslizó su mirada por mi cuerpo—. ¿Quieres que te cuente un secreto, Violet?

Negué con la cabeza.

—Claro que quieres. Yo, Brodie Redding, llevo tres días en este abandonado pueblo de mierda. Puedo ver por tu expresión que estás sorprendida, Violet. Como yo lo estaba... Localizo a un hermano y el otro también aparece. Por supuesto que los dos son demasiado estúpidos como para notar que estoy aquí. Si existe alguien más tedioso que tú y River, con sus charlas sobre el resplandor y sus besos, ese es Neely. Siempre peleando como un maldito salvaje. Este viaje resultó aburrido de principio a fin. Tuve que quemar a una bruja por el camino solo para no volarme los sesos del aburrimiento.

Brodie sonrió, como si le agradara pensar en eso.

—Pero volvamos a la cuestión, Vi. Los estuve observando. A ti, a River, a Jack, a Luke y a la chica rata. Comiendo pizza, pintando, durmiendo. Sí, señora. Todas las ventanas de la casa de huéspedes están abiertas de par en par y a simple vista, y he estado entrando y saliendo del Ciudadano muchas más veces de las que recuerdo. He visto todo. He escuchado todo. ¿Nunca se te ha ocurrido cerrar las puertas de la casa de vez en cuando? He estado yendo y viniendo a gusto durante estos últimos días, y los he observado pintar juntos, besarse, adoptar huérfanos pelirrojos al azar que ni siquiera… que ni siquiera pueden… –hizo una pausa.

»De todas maneras, fue demasiado fácil. Y las cosas fáciles, maldita sea, me aburren. Estoy aburrido. Aburrido, Violet.

–Eras tú –susurré–. Las risas en el ático. El matón. River no lo olvidó, él no lo hizo, tal como dijo –me sentí sucia, expuesta, débil y asustada, y lo único que quería era volver a dormirme y despertarme, *excepto que no era una pesadilla. Sunshine realmente estaba herida, el chico estaba realmente muerto y todo iba a ponerse mucho peor de lo que ya estaba.*

–Veamos, Violet. Debes reconocer cuál fue la participación exacta de River. Yo le arrojé chispas a tu pizzero italiano, es verdad. Una vez que encontré esa mansión en ruinas, supe que tenía que utilizarla como escenario de alguna travesura. Qué buen lugar para prender fuego a alguien. Y todo estaba yendo tan bien hasta que Neely metió la nariz, ese idiota lanzador de puñetazos. Pero ese muchachito muerto junto a las vías fue todo de River. Sí, señora. Neely estaba rondando en busca del niño, tratando de salvarlo, ese papanatas sentimental. Pero ahora sabemos que el muchachito ya estaba tumbado en la zanja, lleno de sangre, hinchado y muerto como una viuda de la cintura para abajo.

Lanzó un silbido grave y prolongado.

Había estado aquí, todo este tiempo. Era cierto. Había estado enfrente de nosotros, riendo, espiándonos y tramando maldades. La cabeza me zumbaba y me ardía la garganta, como si estuviera tragando humo.

Iba a matarme. A mí y a nosotros. A todos.

–¿Por qué? –fue todo lo que dije. Y luego lo repetí–. *¿Por qué?*

Brodie continuaba silbando los primeros compases de alguna tonada triste y sencilla.

–Bueno, tal vez deberíamos ir a ver en qué andan mis hermanos –dijo finalmente–. ¿Mmm? No sacudas la cabeza, querida. Vámonos.

Me lancé hacia adelante. Iba a correr. Correr hasta Eco, buscar ayuda, *irme, escapar…*

Y mi cabeza se sacudió. El dolor se extendió por arriba del cráneo. El chico pelirrojo había sujetado mi cabello en el puño y me atrajo a su lado de un tirón.

Los ojos verdes de Brodie me observaban desde arriba, me atravesaban, como si intentaran abrir un camino hasta mi alma.

–Jugarás un papel en mi plan, te guste o no. Así que es mejor que me ahorres tiempo y hagas lo que te digo.

Un grito. Venía desde el bosque. Era Jack. Corría y gritaba *Déjala ir, déjala ir* y llegó hasta nosotros…

Vi un destello plateado.

Y Jack cayó.

En la tierra, los ojos azules estaban cerrados y un hilo de sangre se abría paso a través de las pecas de la mejilla.

Brodie se inclinó sobre el cuerpo duro como una roca de Jack. Tomó un poco de su cabello y lo retorció entre dos dedos.

–Ni siquiera es rojo puro –señaló–. Es solo este color oxidado y terroso de mierda. Francamente, no le veo el atractivo.

Se puso de pie y deslizó la punta de la bota debajo del cuerpo de Jack. De una patada rápida, lo dio vuelta y lo dejó boca abajo, para que su cara quedara metida en la tierra. Me apartó bruscamente, se inclinó y le levantó la camisa. La piel blanca de la espalda de Jack brilló bajo los rayos brillantes del sol.

–Te gustará ver esto –dijo Brodie–. Lo voy a cortar. Esta vez, lo haré más despacio –se pasó la lengua por el labio inferior–. Estás pensando en salir corriendo a pedir ayuda, ¿verdad, Vi? Siempre me doy cuenta cuando mis víctimas están a punto de echar a correr. Pero si lo haces, en vez de cortar a Jack, lo mataré. No –levantó la mirada hacia mí–. No irás a ningún lado, Violet White. Tengo grandes planes para ti. Haré que sangres. Te cortaré y te cortaré y te haré sangrar y sangrar.

Cuando Sunshine se desmayó, pensé que tenía miedo. Cuando vi al Demonio arriba de los hombros de River, pensé que tenía miedo. Cuando vi a Jack amarrado en el ático, el chico muerto junto a las vías, la cabeza ensangrentada de Sunshine y Sam con el bate, pensé que no podía tener más miedo. Pero eso era solo el principio. El principio y el medio. Y todo conducía al chico pelirrojo que se encontraba frente a mí.

Este era el fin.

CAPÍTULO 27

ME ARRASTRÓ HASTA la casa de huéspedes, una mano me jalaba de la camisa y la otra se hundía en mi cabello como una garra. Sus dedos finos y duros se retorcieron y se sacudieron hasta que sus uñas se llenaron de sangre.

Traté de darme vuelta, traté de gritarle a Jack –él continuaba inmóvil en el suelo, la piel entrecruzada por líneas rojas–, pero las uñas se hundieron con más fuerza.

Brodie abrió la puerta y me empujó hacia adentro. Lo primero que vi fue a River, arrodillado en el suelo de la cocina. Neely estaba parado detrás, sosteniendo un cuchillo de cocina en su garganta. La cabeza de River estaba echada hacia atrás y el borde de la hoja se hundía tan profundamente contra la piel suave cercana a la nuez que sus latidos hacían que el cuchillo temblara levemente.

La habitación comenzó a girar. Vi puntos negros a los costados de los ojos. Iba a vomitar otra vez y no quería hacerlo delante del chico pelirrojo. *Vi, no vomites…*

—Neely —susurré—. Neely, *detente*. Brodie te tiene engañado. Se trata de un truco. *Baja el cuchillo.*

Él estaba sangrando. Una línea roja y finita chorreaba por su mejilla izquierda, igual que a Jack.

Neely me miró cuando pronuncié su nombre, pero sus ojos tenían una expresión extraña y vacía, como la de Cassie y Sam. Y la de Gianni.

—Violet —dijo—. Atrapé a este chico intentando colarse sin permiso en el Ciudadano. Iba a secuestrarte, llevarte con sus hombres y violarte. Él y su banda han estado provocando un infierno en esta zona durante años. Pero ahora ya lo tengo atrapado. ¿Podrías ir a la prisión y traer al alguacil? No logro mover los brazos. Tengo que mantener el cuchillo en su garganta, ¿ves? De lo contrario, duele…

Extendí la mano.

—Neely, baja el cuchillo. Es River, tu hermano, *tienes que bajar el cuchillo*…

Brodie me sujetó. Los dedos finitos me envolvieron la muñeca y me sacudió la mano hacia atrás.

—No te aconsejo hacer eso, querida —las palabras se arrastraban fuera de su boca como la melaza—. Las personas a las cuales enciendo tienden a responder muy violentamente si las interrumpes en mitad de la acción.

Grité, pero Brodie no me soltó el brazo. River me observaba por encima del cuchillo. Sus ojos no estaban vacíos como los de Neely, sino vivaces y brillantes como siempre.

—Vi, no hagas ninguna tontería —dijo. Al hablar, la hoja del cuchillo se hundió todavía más en la piel de su cuello. La sangre comenzó a brotar de la herida y cayó en el cuello de la camisa, donde se abrió como una flor.

Me desplomé. Mis rodillas, todavía enlodadas de la orilla del arroyo, golpearon contra el suelo de la cocina con un estrepitoso chasquido. Moví la cabeza hacia atrás para poder mirar hacia arriba. Las puntas de mi cabello rubio barrieron los mosaicos negros y blancos, y me topé con los ojos de Brodie.

—Entonces anula lo que hiciste —dije.

Brodie se quedó mirándome. Los segundos pasaron. Inspiró y exhaló. Luego sonrió ampliamente.

—Tu degradación me divierte —comentó finalmente y se encogió de hombros.

Oí el ruido del cuchillo al chocar contra el suelo a mis espaldas. Me levanté y me di vuelta. Neely se frotaba los ojos. River se puso de pie, lentamente. Se llevó una mano al cuello, donde había estado el cuchillo, y se limpió la sangre. Luego se estiró y me ayudó a levantarme. Pero no me miró. Ni siquiera lo miró a Neely. Sus ojos estaban clavados en Brodie.

—¿Cómo hiciste eso? —preguntó, y su voz tembló. Solo un poquito, pero fue suficiente. River nunca había perdido la calma desde que lo conocí. Esa era una característica de él. Era tranquilo. Tranquilo como un día de verano. Tranquilo como una agradable siesta bajo el sol. Aun cuando las niñas se desmayaran y los hombres se cortaran la garganta delante de uno. Se había sentido mal por las tormentas y por su madre muerta, y al no saber que había estado usando el resplandor conmigo mientras dormía, pero nunca había sentido miedo, no de esta manera.

Y si River –*River*– tenía miedo…

–*Dime cómo lo hiciste* –River extendió el brazo, como si fuera a sujetar a Brodie del cuello, pero se apartó, suavemente, de puntillas, con las rodillas flexionadas como una marioneta flacucha y libidinosa.

–¿Qué cosa? ¿Retirar la chispa? –Brodie se llevó la la mano a la barbilla afilada y la frotó–. Bueno, tarde o temprano, mis víctimas se libran de la chispa por sí mismos, pero puede llevar horas. De lo contrario, la arranco de sus cabezas manualmente, por decirlo de alguna manera. Es tan fácil como arrancar manzanas de un árbol, viejo. Y soy bastante bueno para eso –miraba el rostro de River con atención, con *suma* atención–. Si quisieras, podría mostrarte cómo lo hago.

River se quedó en silencio sin dejar de mirarlo.

Brodie se quitó el sombrero de vaquero y lo apoyó sobre la mesa. Se pasó la mano por el cabello rojo y me recordó tanto a River y a Neely que se me hizo un nudo tirante en el estómago. Un gusto desagradable me llenó la boca, rancio y fétido.

No cabía duda de que eran hermanos.

–Supongo que ya es hora de presentarnos –continuó Brodie al darse cuenta de que River no iba a hablar–. Temo haberme comportado de manera grosera. Llegué aquí, le hice unos cortes a Neely con mi cuchillo y ni una sola vez le dije *Hola, soy tu hermano Brodie. Nuestro padre embarazó a mi demente madre y luego regresó a sus verdaderos*

hijos, que son ustedes. Y aquí estamos. Encantado de conocerte. Me distraje con esa regordeta meretriz que caminaba por el jardín. Salí corriendo sin decir una palabra. Y después seguí a Violet y a un mocosito hasta un cadáver. Pensaba volver antes. Como ya dije: fui grosero. Bueno, presentémonos como corresponde –extendió la mano.

En los ojos de River, apareció un brillo travieso y estiró la mano. El corazón me dio un salto y pensé *Aquí vamos*, pero Brodie dejó caer el brazo rápidamente hacia el costado del cuerpo y rio.

–Ja. Ni lo sueñes, River. Sé cómo funciona. Sé cómo funciona tu resplandor. Papá me puso al corriente de todo, mucho antes de que llegara acá y tuviera que escuchar la cháchara incesante de ustedes tres sobre el tema. Pareces sorprendido. Estuve rondando el lugar todo este tiempo, escuchando en secreto, más aburrido que chupar clavos. ¿Qué? ¿Sigues sorprendido? ¿Acaso no sabías que tenías un hermano, River? ¿Acaso nadie te habló de mí?

–Se suponía que eras más chico –comentó Neely, la voz apagada, débil y extraña–. Es probable que papá tenga decenas de hijos mitad Redding, pero son pequeños. Se suponía que tú eras pequeño.

Brodie rio con su risa grave y ronca.

–Exactamente. *Mitad* Redding. Los chicos crecen, Neely. Sí, el viejo Redding no podía mantener la bragueta cerrada. Dejó embarazada a mi pobre madre cuando tenía solo diecisiete años. La conoció en una de esas ridículas fiestas al aire libre que les gusta hacer a los inútiles y ricachones para aburrirse como la mierda. Por supuesto que tardó en enterarse de que la familia de mi madre tenía su propia maldición.

Hizo una pausa, una mano en la cadera, la otra en el aire, y giró sobre el tacón de una bota.

—Tendemos a volvernos locos. Locos de arrancarnos los pelos y de rodar por la tierra. Ah, cómo me gusta pensar en mamá, descalza, el cabello rojo hasta la cintura, aullando en el manicomio, rasguñando las piedras con las uñas. Espero que las ratas le muerdan los dedos de los pies. Mestizo, mestizo. Ja. Ja. Jajajajajaja. Mis abuelos trataron de criarme bien después de que la encerraron, pero, bueno, ellos son viejos y yo tengo mucha energía. No funcionó muy bien.

Mientras Brodie hablaba, River apoyó las manos sobre mí y me empujó hacia atrás de él.

—Y, al poco tiempo, leo en el periódico una historia tan rematadamente loca que se extendió desde la Costa Este hasta el otro lado del país. Era la historia de unos chicos que habían visto el Demonio en un cementerio. Y pensé… ey, eso me suena familiar. Como mi chispa. *Diantres*. Subí a un tren y aquí estoy. ¿Qué piensas, River? ¿Estás impresionado? ¿Te gusta lo que viste hasta ahora?

—¿Eras tú, verdad? —ahora Neely estaba quieto. Congelado, sin moverse ni respirar—. Los chicos en el parque. Texas. La quema de la bruja. El ático. Y ahora estás aquí. Nos encontraste. ¿Qué quieres?

En el semblante de Brodie se dibujó una sonrisa de suficiencia.

—Lo notaste. Austin. Esa ciudad está llena de cerdos y prostitutas. Pasé por delante de un grupo de jóvenes con cara de ratas que andaban dando vueltas con aires de superioridad. Los desafié a pelear al estilo Neely, con los puños, pero se rieron. Se *rieron*. Así que pensé, ya saben, qué diablos, les prenderé fuego.

Neely dejó de frotarse los ojos. Apretó los puños súbitamente y le pegó. En la mejilla izquierda, justo en el medio. Tan rápido que ni siquiera Brodie pudo esquivarlo.

Brodie no hizo nada. Simplemente lo recibió y sonrió levemente.

–Pelea –exclamó Neely, su rostro rojo como un ladrillo, los ojos brillantes–. Aquí mismo. Sin resplandor.

–Chispa –lo interrumpió Brodie mientras se tocaba la mejilla magullada y no dejaba de sonreír–. Yo lo llamo chispa.

Neely lo ignoró.

–Quemaste gente, hiciste que le pusiera un cuchillo en la garganta a mi hermano. Yo lo culpé a River por lo que sucedió en la mansión Glenship. Trató de negarlo pero no quise escucharlo, no le creí…

El puño de Neely salió volando. Pero, esta vez, Brodie logró esquivarlo, rápido y ágil, como si fuera demasiado fácil y no se esforzara mucho.

El rostro de Neely estaba rojo como la sangre. Rojo como el cabello de Brodie.

River puso la mano en el brazo de su hermano.

–Ya está.

Neely lo apartó de un empujón.

–Debería haberme dado cuenta –a esta altura, Neely casi gritaba–. Pensé que eras simplemente un pequeño ranchero al que papá quería tratar correctamente. Pero era obvio que tenías el resplandor. ¿Qué otro motivo podría tener él para mantener un vástago flacucho de Texas?

Brodie rio francamente.

–Apuesto a que te contó que todos los otros bastardos Redding también son pequeños. Que ni siquiera tienen la edad suficiente como para tener la chispa. ¿Y tú le creíste?

Neely daba vueltas y caminaba de un lado a otro, tratando de acercarse más a Brodie. River se estiró y le sujetó el brazo.

—No lo hagas, Neely —dijo en voz baja—. Te va a cortar.

—Qué aburrimieeeento —la voz de Brodie arrastró las palabras. Se sentó a la mesa de la cocina y puso un brazo alrededor de la rodilla. La otra pierna se balanceaba libremente y el tacón de la bota golpeaba contra la pata de la mesa—. Esto es *tan* aburrido. Neely, *cállate*. Y tú también, River. Me estoy cagando de aburrimiento. Miren, hice este largo viaje para ver cómo era mi hermano legítimo, no mestizo, con chispa. Quería que estableciéramos un vínculo, como hermanos. Ver si él quería que formáramos un equipo y nos divirtiéramos en serio. Hasta me permití fantasear sobre eso mientras venía hacia aquí: nosotros dos, enfrentando al mundo, destruyendo a nuestros enemigos, celebrando nuestras victorias, cortando mujeres… Pero hasta el momento, River, no me has impresionado… Pienso que es porque Neely, el buen samaritano, es una mala influencia —Brodie volteó y observó a su otro hermano. Y, mientras lo observaba, sus ojos se entornaron, lentamente. Después volvió a enfrentar a River y rio ampliamente—. ¿Alguna reflexión?

Escuché un ruido, pero no aparté los ojos de Brodie. Ninguno lo hizo.

Esperé que no fuera Jack. Recé para que no lo fuera. No sabía qué le había hecho Brodie con el cuchillo. Tal vez lo había dormido para que no se interpusiera en su camino.

Por favor, Jack, espero que estés inconsciente.

Brodie inclinó la cabeza y miró hacia la puerta.

—Bueno, bueno, bueno. Tú debes ser el hermano mellizo. Sunshine te mencionó, es decir, antes de que su padre la matara con un bate.

Seguí la mirada de Brodie. Luke estaba de pie junto a la puerta, con rostro de preocupación. Dirigió la vista hacia mí.

–¿Qué demonios le ocurrió a Jack? Está afuera, tumbado en el suelo inconsciente y sangrando. Tenemos que llamar a una ambulancia. *Ya* –y entonces vio a Brodie–. Vi, ¿quién es este vaquero que está en nuestra mesa?

Luke indicó a Brodie con un movimiento de cabeza. Sin embargo, no se acercó a él ni intentó estrecharle la mano. Una parte profunda e instintiva le advirtió que en Brodie había algo que no estaba bien.

Algo incorrecto.

Malo.

–Corre –le dije a Luke. Pero tenía la boca seca y no proferí ningún sonido. Tosí y tragué–. *Corre* –susurré.

Y, esa vez, me escuchó. Retrocedió, se dio vuelta…

Pero Brodie fue más rápido. Se levantó volando de la mesa y aterrizó con los pies en el piso, con suavidad, las botas tintinearon levemente en el suelo. Por el rabillo del ojo, vi que algo destellaba en la luz que entraba por las ventanas. Y después, mi hermano estaba sangrando. Cuentas húmedas y redondas bajaban formando un hilo por su mejilla izquierda. Los ojos de Luke pasaron de la sorpresa a la conmoción y al enojo.

Y a la nada.

Di un paso adelante y estiré los brazos como para ayudarlo, tomarlo entre mis brazos y sacudir ese vacío que teñía sus ojos, pero River me retuvo. Recordé el motivo y me quedé inmóvil.

Luke entró en la cocina. Se inclinó y levantó el cuchillo de la cocina, de donde había caído al suelo. Volteó y arrojó su cuerpo contra Neely, que salió volando y se estampó contra la pared de la cocina. Y, a continuación, ya tenía el cuchillo en la garganta. El cuello de Neely estaba tenso; mi hermano tenía una mano en el mango negro y la otra en el mentón de Neely, obligándolo a mantenerlo levantado.

Brodie aplaudió.

–Veamos. El primer punto de la agenda es deshacerse de Neely de una forma más permanente. Él no puede lanzar chispas y, aunque pudiera, no lo querría tener cerca. No tiene tu… naturaleza moralmente ambigua, River. Tú y yo, somos iguales, hermano. Solo que todavía no lo sabes.

River lo ignoró.

–Luke. Baja el cuchillo. Baja ese cuchillo.

–No puedo –respondió Luke, la voz forzada y los ojos clavados en el cuello de Neely–. El cabrón iba a prender fuego a mi hermana. Tengo que mantener el cuchillo acá para que no escape.

–Luke –dije una y otra vez mientras mis manos aferraban la falda y retorcían la tela–. *Luke, Luke, Luke, Luke.*

River volvió a intentarlo.

–No, Luke, no tienes que hacerlo. Es un truco. Baja el cuchillo.

Mi hermano negó con la cabeza.

–No puedo. Me produce dolor.

Quería gritarle a Luke como le había gritado a Neely. Quería caer de rodillas y rogarle a Brodie que lo dejara ir, como lo había hecho con River, pero sabía que no iba a funcionar otra vez.

–*Detente, Brodie, detente. Detente de una vez* –grité de todas maneras.

–Te mataré –susurró Neely–. Te voy a destrozar la cara con mis puños. Intenta reír cuando estés ahogándote con tus propios dientes, cabrón demente –mientras él hablaba, el cuchillo se hundía en su cuello, como había sucedido con River. Una mancha roja se formó debajo de la hoja plateada. River la vio y soltó un gemido fuerte y furioso que le hizo estallar el pecho.

Luego sujetó el brazo de mi hermano con las manos y comenzó a jalar.

—Suelta el cuchillo, Luke —aulló—. *Suéltalo*.

El brazo de Luke empezó a descender y después él comenzó a gritar. Gritó y gritó. Gritó como aquella vez en que se cayó de una de las ventanas del Ciudadano cuando tenía diez años, y aterrizó con la pierna torcida y rota debajo del cuerpo, gritos y gritos y gritos.

River lo soltó y se alejó. El brazo de Luke se levantó violentamente, el cuchillo regresó a la garganta de Neely y los gritos de mi hermano se apagaron.

—Te avisé —dijo Brodie—. No interrumpas a mis víctimas. No les agrada.

River apartó la mirada de Luke y de la sangre que comenzaba a chorrear por el cuello de Neely y empapaba su camisa. Miró a Brodie, y en sus ojos se veía un dolor profundo y oscuro, furia y horror.

Apoyó la mano en el corazón.

—¿Sabes algo, Brodie? Yo puedo ver colores. Los colores de las personas. No estoy seguro si papá te lo contó.

Brodie asintió.

—Me lo contó, pero me importó una mierda, porque yo no puedo hacerlo y, de todas maneras, no sirve para nada —se encogió de hombros y miró hacia otro lado.

—Bueno, la mayoría de las personas están hechas de colores brillantes —continuó River, como si no lo hubiera escuchado—. Rosa, amarillo, azul, verde. Pero tú, no. Tú eres negro. Negro como el café derramado a través de un cielo nocturno. Yo... nunca había visto antes algo así...

Los ojos de River estaban asustados.

Brodie sonrió. Fue una sonrisa torcida, como la de River y la de Neely.

—Soy bastante especial, ¿no creen? Siempre lo he dicho, pero ahora también lo dirán todos los demás. River, te pido por favor que me mires cuando te estoy hablando. Puedo ver que estás tratando de usar el resplandor. Puedo sentirlo, como una corriente eléctrica que corre de tu cuerpo al de Luke. Pero tú no ejercitas tu locura. Eres demasiado, demasiado, demasiado cuerdo. Estás débil y agotado. Lo único que puedes hacer es ignorarme y observar a Luke deseando poder lograr algo con tu resplandor. Pero no puedes. No puedes, River. Mis chispas giran alrededor de las tuyas. ¿No te molesta eso? Eres el Redding legal y verdadero y, sin embargo, te derroté sin tener que esforzarme. No debería ser así. Déjame ayudarte, hermano. Déjame mostrarte cómo se hace realmente.

Brodie agitó el brazo, formó un círculo por arriba de la cabeza y luego golpeó los tacones de las botas uno contra otro, como Dorothy en *El mago de Oz*.

—Diablos, *esto* es solo el principio —sus ojos se movían enloquecidamente y estaban verdes como el vidrio de mar—. Espera a ver todo lo que puedo hacer. Puedes estar seguro de que esto será un viaje infernal. Y al llegar al final, serás mi mayor admirador. Créelo, hermano. Nuestro momento ha llegado.

Nos quedamos quietos. No dijimos una sola palabra.

Brodie miró atentamente a River, cerró los ojos un segundo y luego los abrió.

—Después de todo, River, yo soy el único que sabe lo que es tener una chispa, un resplandor. El imbécil de Neely que está ahí, no lo sabe. No lo sabrá nunca. Pero yo sí. Hermano, somos nosotros contra ellos.

River seguía quieto y sin decir nada.

Brodie movió el cuerpo lentamente hasta quedar encorvado.

—Pucha, estoy aburrido —dijo, despacio, tranquilo y suave. Y su tono era suficientemente convincente, pero sus hombros se desplomaron hacia adelante.

Y ahí fue cuando lo vi.

Un atisbo.

Debajo del cuchillo, del chico alto, flaco, pelirrojo, aburrido, loco.

Un atisbo de chico solitario y no deseado como Jack.

Y, debajo de eso…

Furia.

Una furia negra como el cielo nocturno, vacía como Montana, amarga como el café quemado, funesta, escalofriante, ensordecedora.

Ver eso, sabiendo lo que significaba… me perturbó. Profundamente, hasta los huesos.

Tal vez, Brodie no estaba loco.

Tal vez, estaba enojado. Muy, muy, muy enojado.

Y eso era… muchísimo peor.

Transcurrieron unos segundos y después se enderezó repentinamente en el asiento, como si se le acabara de ocurrir algo.

Me miró.

Y comencé a ver puntos negros otra vez.

—Violet —dijo—. Ven aquí.

Cerré los ojos y sacudí la cabeza de un lado a otro.

—Violet, ven aquí. Me vas a ayudar a convencer a River. Ven aquí. Ahora.

Algo centelleó en la luz.

River se arrojó delante de mí, pero Brodie se apartó de un giro y sentí una punzada aguda en la mejilla. Me llevé la mano a la cara.

Y entonces todo comenzó.

CAPÍTULO 28

RIVER HABÍA UTILIZADO el resplandor conmigo. Probablemente, muchas veces. Lo utilizó para hacerme ver el demonio de Jack y a mi madre. Lo utilizó para calmarme después de haber visto el cadáver de Daniel Leap. Pero el resplandor de River era suave, seductor; se deslizaba sobre mí como el crepúsculo y se convirtió en una parte tan importante de mí que lo extrañé cuando desapareció, como el sol al final del día. La magia de River podrá haber sido mala, pero la sensación era tan… *buena*.

No era igual con la de Brodie. Sentí que una mano, dura como el acero, aferraba mi cerebro en un puño. Sus dedos me apretaban como una abrazadera, cada vez más fuerte.

Qué dolor, por Dios, qué dolor.

Me defendí y la abrazadera me sujetó con tanta fuerza que mi mente quedó como papilla, una papilla espesa, aceitosa, supurante.

Dejé de pelear.

Incliné la cabeza y me miré la camisa. Parecía muy lejana, como si perteneciera a otra persona. Mis manos se dirigieron a los botones de la suave camisa que mi madre usaba para pintar. De pronto, sentí que la tela me producía escozor y calor, como si me quemara. Como si todos sus hilitos me rasguñaran y chisporrotearan sobre mi piel, como para prenderme fuego. Manoteé los botones. Tenía que quitarme la camisa de inmediato. Apreté los dientes del dolor. Marcas rojas y arrugadas brotaban en todo mi cuerpo. Desgarré la tela y alcancé a escuchar a River gritar mi nombre, pero estaba muy lejos y me di vuelta y la desgarré y *por fin* me la quité y cayó al suelo, donde debía estar.

Di un resoplido de alivio al ver la camisa en el piso. La picazón se detuvo, la abrazadera cedió, mi mente dejó de gotear a través de los dedos de acero y pude pensar otra vez. Mientras hiciera lo que la mano quería, yo estaba bien. Mientras *creyera* lo que la mano quería, el dolor se detendría.

La parte superior de mi cuerpo estaba desnuda, excepto por una fina enagua negra que había encontrado en el ropero de Freddie el verano pasado. Me la había puesto para dormir la noche anterior y no me había molestado en cambiarme antes de ir con Jack a ver al chico muerto. Solo llevaba un camisón transparente, la falda verde y las rodillas enlodadas. Quería poner los brazos alrededor de mi cuerpo y escurrirme sigilosamente hacia el rincón.

Pero la mano no me lo permitía. De modo que no hice nada.

Podía oír la voz ronca de Brodie. Sonaba hueca, profunda y como si estuviera a miles de kilómetros. Decía: "Chicos, todavía no han visto nada. Desnudarla es solo el principio. Voy a cortarla, lenta y suavemente, como se desliza un cuchillo por la manteca. Observa esto, River. Te encantará".

–Brodie, déjala ir –dijo River y sus palabras navegaban hacia mí, como lo habían hecho las de Brodie, y sonaban cansadas, suplicantes y tristes, como si ya hubieran renunciado a combatir–. Retira la chispa y te prestaré atención. Te… seguiré. Haré lo que quieras. No presentaré pelea. Ni siquiera tendrás que usar tu resplandor. Me mostraré tan tranquilo como un corderito recién nacido.

Brodie rio.

–Está bien, hermano. Así me gusta más.

Y, súbitamente, la mano de acero desapareció. Mi mente tembló y se expandió. Llevé las palmas de las manos a los ojos y los froté con fuerza. Los froté hasta borrar la mano de acero de mi mente, froté y borré mientras respiraba profundamente. Después abrí los ojos…

Entonces River saltó hacia adelante, sujetó a Brodie y lo arrojó de costado contra la mesa. Una botella de aceite de oliva cayó al suelo y se hizo añicos. Brodie y River se trenzaron, jalaron y forcejearon hasta caer al piso, justo arriba de los fragmentos de vidrio verde. Brodie no dejaba de reír. Golpeaba las botas contra el suelo y reía a más no poder. River tenía la mano de Brodie, la del cuchillo, inmovilizada detrás de su espalda, y yo pensé: *Este es el final. River ganará, River nos salvará…* Pero nada de eso sirvió. Brodie volteó la cabeza hacia el costado y hundió sus dientes blancos y filosos en el antebrazo de River.

Cuando despegó los dientes, estaban llenos de sangre.

Los brazos de River se desplomaron hacia el suelo y sus ojos se apagaron.

Brodie se puso de pie de un salto, sigiloso y rápido como un gato.

Maldito sea, ¿por qué es tan ágil?, pensé en el fondo de mi mente. *¿Cómo logra ser tan ágil? ¿Es así como se mueve el Demonio?*

Brodie pasó por encima del cuerpo inmóvil de River, fue hasta el fregadero y escupió sangre.

—¿Ves, Violet? —dijo, después de limpiarse la boca con la toalla del corderito—, es por *eso* que uso el cuchillo. Es mucho más limpio. Me gusta ser ordenado. Supongo que algunos podrán llamarlo vanidad, pero ahí tienes. No me gusta morder a la gente. No es civilizado.

Mientras hablaba, yo no lo miraba, aunque sabía que eso lo hacía enfadar. Estaba mirando la sangre que goteaba del antebrazo de River. Por la sangre, ni siquiera podía ver las marcas de los dientes de Brodie. Y ahora sus ojos estaban vacíos. Y ese vacío era todavía más desagradable en sus ojos que en los de Neely y Luke.

River fue hasta la cocina, tomó la tetera y la llenó de agua. Encendió el quemador y colocó la tetera encima.

Luego puso los brazos a los costados del cuerpo y se quedó ahí, frente al fuego. Esperando.

—¿Qué está haciendo? —la naturaleza benigna de los movimientos de River me preocupaba más que si tuviera un cuchillo en la mano. La habitación daba vueltas. Me restregué nuevamente los ojos para que dejara de girar—. ¿Qué diablos está haciendo?

Brodie alzó los brazos y se estiró, como si se levantara de una larga siesta.

—River hervirá esa agua y después la verterá sobre la cabeza de Neely. Es infantil, pero estaba presionado por el tiempo. Y matará dos pájaros de un tiro, por así decirlo. River entenderá quién soy y mostrará un poco de respeto por mí y por lo que quiero hacer. Unirá su resplandor a mi chispa. Empezará a comprender que Neely es un idiota sin chispa, que no puede impedir que le hiervan la cara. Yo seré un mestizo bastardo de Texas con una madre loca, pero a River no le importará, no después de esto —hizo una pausa y vi otra vez esa misma expresión, la que hacía que sus ojos verdes parecieran enormes, profundos y jóvenes. Pero solo duró un segundo. Movió la cabeza de un lado a otro y esbozó una gran sonrisa—. Y luego tiene un beneficio agregado y es que, de cualquiera de las dos maneras, me permitirá terminar de jugar contigo.

Se acercó a mí, estiró un dedo y fue recorriendo mi cuerpo por arriba de la enagua. Desde el cuello, por el medio de mis pechos, hasta el ombligo. Luego se inclinó, metió la mano dentro de la bota y tomó su cuchillito.

—Tienes tiempo hasta que comience a hervir el agua —la voz de Brodie era grave y vieja. Vieja como el tiempo. Vieja como las montañas. Vieja como las estaciones y los océanos. Y buena y mala—. Haz lo que yo quiero, y hazlo bien. Después quizá, *quizá*, liberaré a River antes de que derrita la bonita cara de nuestro hermano.

Me quedé callada y quieta. *De acuerdo, Violet. Hazlo. Haz lo que él quiera y evitarás que River lastime a Neely. Esa es la tarea que tienes aquí y vas a hacerla. No, no puedes comenzar otra vez a ver manchas. No puedes desmayarte, porque entonces no podrás salvarlos. No lo pienses, simplemente asiente con la cabeza. ASIENTE CON LA CABEZA, VI.*

Asentí.

Brodie extendió el cuchillo y lo puso contra mi vientre. Podía sentir la hoja afilada a través de la fina seda negra. Contuve la respiración.

–Relájate –me ordenó.

Dejé salir el aire.

–¿Estás acostándote con él? ¿Estás acostándote con River? ¿Eso es lo que estás haciendo? –la voz de Brodie era cantarina, ligera, como si le hablara a un bebé.

Negué con la cabeza, los ojos clavados en el cuchillo plateado apretado contra mí.

–Sophie se mató, sabes. Mi novia, Sophie. Se cortó las muñecas justo antes de que me marchara de Texas. Era una chica… llena de problemas –hizo una pausa–. A veces lamento haber tenido que usar la chispa en ella antes de que permitiera que estuviéramos juntos. Carnalmente hablando. Sophie fue criada como una buena católica y creía en Dios, en el infierno, en las vírgenes y en las prostitutas. Nada funcionaba con ella, ni siquiera que la cortara, hasta que usé la chispa. ¿River también tuvo que usar el resplandor en ti? ¿O te metiste en su cama por propia voluntad?

No se te ocurra intentar escapar, Violet. No hagas nada salvo quedarte quieta y soportarlo; no corras; ni siquiera te muevas, o lastimará a River, a Neely, a Luke y a Jack, con toda tranquilidad…

Brodie deslizó el cuchillo a través de mi vientre. Cortó la enagua y la piel. Hizo un tajo superficial. Al principio, apenas sangró. Aun así, cerré los ojos. No podía permitirme desmayarme. La sangre golpeaba dentro de mi cabeza y me resultaba difícil oír el agua en la tetera. Agucé el oído. Nada. Todavía nada. ¿Cuánto tiempo tardaba el agua en hervir? ¿Qué podía hacerme antes de que eso ocurriera?

—*Ah. Sí, así.*

Abrí los ojos.

La boca de Brodie estaba ligeramente abierta y realizaba breves inspiraciones a través de los dientes. Tenía la vista posada en mi estómago, en la herida que escupía gruesos círculos rojos...

Aguanta, Vi. El agua tiene que hervir pronto y luego Brodie hará que todo se detenga. Solo se está divirtiendo. Se aburrirá pronto. Aguanta, no te desmayes, eso lo volvería loco. Más loco de lo que está. Aguanta. No, ese no es el silbido de la tetera, es la sangre en tus oídos, aguanta, aguanta...

—Sophie, dime que me amas —susurró. Ahora sus ojos estaban posados en los míos, verdes, intensos y brillantes de lágrimas y *locos, locos, locos*—. Dime que me amas.

—Te amo —dije, pero estaba llorando, y las lágrimas se deslizaban entre mis labios mientras hablaba, haciendo que mis palabras sonaran falsas y forzadas.

Tomó mi brazo izquierdo, lo extendió y lo elevó en el aire. Luego apretó su cuerpo contra el mío con fuerza, con más fuerza, con toda la fuerza del mundo. Con tanta fuerza que apenas podía respirar. Con tanta fuerza que la sangre del estómago se escurrió entre nosotros y comenzó a gotear por los costados de mi cuerpo.

—Te voy a cortar otra vez, Sophie. Te voy a cortar en serio. River, ¿oíste? Voy a lastimarla y no puedes hacer nada al respecto. Todavía. Pero te enseñaré. Te enseñaré a hacerte el demente. Te enseñaré a cortar. Te encantará. Lo prometo.

River no giró. Continuaba con la vista fija en la tetera, como si fuera lo único que existiera en el mundo.

El cuchillo de Brodie lanzó un destello y, esta vez, fue más profundo. Me cortó la muñeca izquierda, la soltó y cortó la derecha.

La sangre brotó.

Era caliente, espesa, húmeda y, Dios mío, fluía con gran rapidez. ¿Por qué salía con tanta rapidez? Vi las manchas, la habitación giró y el cerebro se desplazó fuera de mí...

Dobla, dobla, hierve y borbotea. Arde, fuego y borbotea el caldero. Me estaba volviendo loca, esforzándome por escuchar la tetera y tratando de no desmayarme. *Aun cuando la sangre saliera a borbotones y pareciera papilla y mi falda estuviera negra y empapada ¿y cómo podía haber tanta sangre dentro de mí?*

Mis ojos giraron dentro de mi cabeza y finalmente se posaron en River, que continuaba de pie frente al fuego. El agua emitía ese ruido hueco y caliente. *Pronto, pronto...*

–Bésame, Sophie.

Brodie se inclinó y apoyó su boca sobre la mía. Traté de resistirme y lo aparté, pero repentinamente me sentí muy débil, muy, pero muy débil...

Colocó las manos en mis hombros y me sacudió.

–Bésame como si *realmente* lo desearas, Sophie. O mataré a tu hermano y después buscaré a ese mocosito pelirrojo y haré que beba su propia sangre.

Lo hice. Juro por Dios que lo hice. Puse mis brazos ensangrentados alrededor de él y deslicé mi boca sobre la suya. Se me revolvieron las entrañas y la bilis trepó por mi garganta. Pero nada de eso, *nada de eso* llegó a mis labios. Lo besé como si yo fuera un desierto y él la lluvia fresca de primavera. Como si yo estuviera siete años en el mar y él fuera la primera visión de tierra.

Lo besé como si fuera River.

Los ojos de Brodie se cerraron.

Entonces me incliné, me estiré hacia el suelo y tomé un fino fragmento de vidrio verde y aceitoso.

Grité de dolor y de alegría mientras mis dedos se cerraban sobre la esquirla.

Llevé el brazo hacia atrás, lo lancé hacia adelante y se lo clavé en el pecho. La sangre borboteó en la herida y comenzó a chorrear por su camisa. Abrió los ojos, miró la sangre y echó a reír. La camisa se iba empapando de rojo, como la de Daniel Leap, y él reía más y más. Colocó los dedos alrededor del trozo de vidrio y lo arrancó. Se escuchó un agudo sonido metálico cuando golpeó contra el suelo. Y entonces la sangre salió a borbotones. Brodie gritó. Gritó al mismo tiempo que gritó la tetera.

Y después todo se volvió negro.

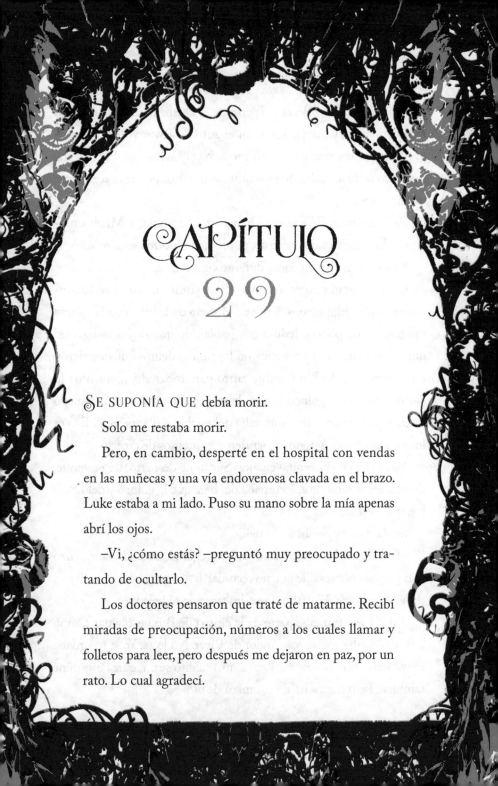

CAPÍTULO 29

Se suponía que debía morir.

Solo me restaba morir.

Pero, en cambio, desperté en el hospital con vendas en las muñecas y una vía endovenosa clavada en el brazo. Luke estaba a mi lado. Puso su mano sobre la mía apenas abrí los ojos.

—Vi, ¿cómo estás? —preguntó muy preocupado y tratando de ocultarlo.

Los doctores pensaron que traté de matarme. Recibí miradas de preocupación, números a los cuales llamar y folletos para leer, pero después me dejaron en paz, por un rato. Lo cual agradecí.

Perdí mucha sangre. *Mucha*. Estaba casi muerta. Se suponía que estaba muerta. Pero River despertó de la chispa de Brodie, y luego también Luke, y me pusieron en el auto de River y llené de sangre los asientos retro, pero no morí. Neely sabía qué hacer y me mantuvo con vida durante esos últimos minutos que eran realmente importantes.

Para entonces, Brodie ya se había ido hacía mucho. Mucho, mucho. A los confines del infierno, por lo que nosotros sabíamos.

Sunshine estuvo en coma durante cuatro días.

Cassie y Sam despertaron, se restregaron los ojos y se encontraron con su hija inconsciente en el suelo de la sala, con la cabeza sangrando. La policía dedujo que había sido uno de los indigentes que saltaron del tren y provocaron los únicos delitos que ocurrieron en nuestro pueblo. Un hombre entró para robar algo, Sunshine lo sorprendió y él la golpeó con un bate que encontró por ahí. Luego se trepó al siguiente tren que salía del pueblo y desapareció. Eso es lo que dedujeron. Y todos se sintieron contentos de creerlo.

Yo estaba en el hospital cuando Sunshine despertó. Le pregunté, de manera amable, qué recordaba del bate que la golpeó y del hombre que lo sostenía.

Se dio vuelta y se hizo un ovillo.

–Cállate –fue todo lo que dijo. Y agregó–: La policía ya me hizo esas preguntas y les dije que no recordaba. Así que ahora te lo digo a ti: *No lo recuerdo, Vi*. ¿Ahora puedes traerme té helado?

Tal vez eso formaba parte de la chispa de Brodie, olvidar. Como a veces sucedía con el resplandor de River. No lo sé. Yo sí recordaba muy bien lo que Brodie me hizo a mí, maldito sea. Y quizá Sunshine también. Pero nunca habló conmigo de eso.

Unos pocos días después de que ella saliera del hospital, pasamos delante de unos chicos de camino al pueblo. Llevaban el equipo de las ligas infantiles de béisbol y, uno de ellos, un niño flacucho pelirrojo, arrojaba un bate de una mano a la otra. Cada vez que el bate golpeaba la palma de su mano, Sunshine se estremecía y vi que sus ojos se llenaban de lágrimas. Pero no dije nada. Y ella no dijo nada. Y luego entramos a la cafetería y enseguida estaba sonriendo y coqueteando con Gianni, que se hallaba detrás del mostrador, y la vida continuó como siempre.

Después del incendio, Gianni dejó de hablarme. Ni siquiera me miraba a los ojos cuando me traía el café. Supuse que tenía miedo; que yo le recordaba la noche en que se volvió loco... la noche en que Neely le pagó para que mantuviera la boca cerrada.

Me pregunté si, a la larga, cambiaría de actitud. Me pregunté qué sucedería si River y Neely se marcharan, si entonces volvería a mirarme otra vez. Me pregunté cuánto deseaba yo que lo hiciera.

Los policías encontraron al chico muerto cuando buscaban en las vías del tren rastros del hombre que atacó a Sunshine. Un accidente. Un chico anda por las vías, no oye al tren que se acerca, lo atropella y cae en la zanja. ¿Qué otra cosa podría ser?

En el fondo de mi mente, yo pensaba que sucedería algo. Que habría reuniones municipales y que la gente se congregaría en los sótanos y juraría buscar respuestas, localizar a los culpables y tratar de entender el extraño verano de Eco de niños con estacas, demonios secuestradores, chicas golpeadas con bates y niños muertos al costado de las vías del tren.

Pero no sucedió nada. La gente siguió adelante con su vida, igual que Sunshine.

A veces, yo pensaba que ella estaba… distinta, después de Brodie. En sus ojos había algo que antes no estaba. Ya no se sentaba tanto en el porche, tomando té y no haciendo nada. Comenzó a leer libros sobre medioambiente y la supervivencia en tierras salvajes. Dijo que quería ir de campamento, nosotras dos solas, y yo le dije que estaba de acuerdo. Una vez fui a la playa, a leer en el lugar secreto y la encontré nadando. Estaba sola en medio de las olas, con su ajustado traje de baño blanco, y no logré entender si nadaba hacia algo o se alejaba de algo, o tal vez ambas cosas.

Me gustaba la nueva Sunshine, y también a Luke. Pero creo que, de alguna manera, los dos también extrañábamos a la de antes.

Estaba observando a River mientras empacaba sus maletas vintage de cuero, unas pocas semanas después de lo de Brodie. Acababa de quitarme las últimas vendas de la muñeca y las cicatrices estaban rojas y tenían un aspecto desagradable. Las detestaba. Froté las marcas hinchadas y enrojecidas mientras River arrojaba las últimas prendas en la segunda maleta, bajaba la tapa de un golpe y cerraba las cuatro hebillas con chasquidos. Me estremecí cada vez que el metal chocó contra el metal y se trabó. Era un sonido tan específico.

Un sonido como de *final*.

Se puso de pie, una maleta en cada mano. Lucía igual que la primera vez que lo había visto. Salvo por la marca de la mordida en el antebrazo, que todavía se estaba curando. Salvo por la expresión de su mirada.

Sus ojos ya no eran solamente arrogantes, seguros, indiferentes y observadores. Ahora había algo nuevo. Algo... *más*. Y me pregunté si yo tendría algo que ver.

Eso esperaba.

La gente decía que el tiempo era relativo, y supongo que eso explicaba por qué mi vida antes de River me parecía que solo había sido un puñado de segundos: breves destellos de pequeños sucesos que sumaban muy poco. Pero mi vida después de River era una saga de tres volúmenes. Épica. Con búsquedas, villanos, asesinatos, soluciones insatisfactorias y personas desgarradas.

—¿Quieres un café? –preguntó.

Aunque lo que en realidad quiso decir fue: *¿Quieres un café antes de que lleve las maletas al auto, me marche y no regrese nunca más?*

—Sí –respondí.

Así que hizo una última jarra de café expreso en la cafetera italiana y lo bebimos, hirviendo, junto al fregadero.

Y lo observé mientras bebía y entornaba los ojos. Miré su cuerpo de perfil, largo y esbelto. Ya no me parecía misterioso ni exótico ni lleno de secretos. Solo parecía River.

Y eso era suficiente.

—Solo pareces River –comenté.

Y me miró de soslayo, la taza a mitad de camino hacia los labios.

—Eso es bueno –dijo, mitad en serio y mitad riéndose–, porque *soy* River.

Y, a continuación, River West William Redding III volvió a levantar las maletas y yo lo seguí hacia afuera. Neely ya estaba esperando, y también Jack y Luke. Los cuatro formamos un semicírculo alrededor del auto nuevo-viejo de River, los asientos aún manchados de sangre.

River miró a su hermano.

—¿Tú sabes por qué tengo que hacer esto, no?

Neely rio.

—Sí, lo sé. Ve a controlar tu resplandor para que así podamos perseguir a Brodie y darle una buena paliza. Si todavía está vivo.

—Lo está —afirmó River.

Negué con la cabeza.

—Yo lo apuñalé, en el pecho. Vi la sangre. Lo *escuché* gritar —había dicho eso antes. Lo había dicho tantas veces que había empezado a repetirlo como si fuera una oración.

River no dijo nada. Jack interceptó mi mirada.

—Salió corriendo, mientras yo todavía estaba en el suelo, después de cortarme. Yo no podía mover los brazos ni las piernas, pero podía ver. Abandonó la casa de huéspedes y echó a correr.

Jack tenía razón. Habíamos hablado una y otra vez acerca de ese tema y la conversación siempre terminaba con Jack diciendo que había visto a Brodie salir corriendo y nosotros sabiendo lo que eso significaba. Brodie sobrevivió. Se fue sin dejar rastro. Y habíamos buscado, cuidadosamente.

Luke le dio a River una suerte de abrazo relajado y masculino. Después, River se inclinó y atrajo a Jack contra su pecho. Ese abrazo no fue relajado y masculino, sino fuerte y genuino.

—Le voy a conseguir un café a este chico —dijo Luke finalmente—. Jack, ¿no deberíamos ir a ver qué sucede en el pueblo? Quizás algunos chicos vieron a una banda de zombis en la plaza. Me parece que estamos justo a tiempo.

Jack sonrió. Se separó de River y, sin mirar atrás, siguió a Luke por el sendero que conducía a Eco.

Solo quedábamos River, Neely y yo.

River se pasó la mano por el cabello y se reclinó contra el auto.

—Mi abuelo me contó algo una vez. Neely, ¿recuerdas cuando lo visité en los Alpes franceses? Estábamos sentados mirando cómo caía el sol detrás de las cumbres montañosas. Mi abuelo ya no estaba tan sagaz como siempre y su mente solía vagar sin rumbo. En general hablaba de Freddie y de las cosas que les sucedieron cuando eran jóvenes. Pero, esa vez, me miró directamente a los ojos. *Tienes que abstenerte*, dijo. *Si comienza a volverse incontrolable, tienes que abstenerte. Es la única forma.*

Sobrevino un momento de silencio, mientras todos pensábamos en esas palabras. Escuché el rumor de las hojas agitándose en los árboles y las olas rompiendo abajo contra las rocas. Escuché cómo mi corazón se quebraba, volvía a armarse y crecía, porque ya no era pequeño ni estaba reseco ni hambriento.

—Si voy a perseguir a Brodie —prosiguió River después de un minuto—, tengo que abstenerme. Tengo que estar solo. Completamente solo. De lo contrario… no confío en poder lograrlo.

—Brodie dijo que tenías que enloquecer para que el resplandor te obedeciera —deslicé la mano en la de River y le di un apretón—. ¿Qué pasaría si tu abuelo estuviera equivocado? ¿Si detenerte no ayudara y Brodie se volviera cada vez más fuerte?

River se encogió de hombros.

—Tengo que intentarlo, Violet. Puedo detenerme o continuar hasta terminar demente como él. ¿Qué te parece mejor?

Neely sacudió la cabeza y echó a reír.

—Yo estaría dispuesto a volverme loco si eso significara que puedo matar a ese vaquerito. Lo mataría con tantas ganas…

River abrazó a su hermano. Luego lo soltó y me sujetó a mí. Nos abrazamos fuerte, lo más fuerte que pudimos, y River acercó los labios a mi oído.

—Voy a desaparecer —susurró—. Si arruino todo y uso el resplandor, Neely me encontrará. Pero si no me encuentra, es que estoy haciendo algo bien. Deja que me mantenga oculto. Y cuando regrese, seré más fuerte. Mejor.

Sus dedos se deslizaron por mi cabello y me acercó todavía más a él. Continuó hablando:

—Brodie pensó que morirías. ¿Qué hará cuando descubra que no fue así? Quizá no le importe, pero no quiero correr más riesgos. Neely se quedará en la casa de huéspedes. Se quedará hasta que yo vuelva.

Asentí y mi mejilla se movió contra su camisa. No mencioné que Neely no había sido capaz de impedir que Brodie tratara de matarme.

Me besó la mejilla, la frente y el lóbulo de la oreja. Neely observaba y sonreía, pero a River no le importó y tampoco a mí.

—¿Cómo voy a hacer para dormir sin ti? —murmuró en mi cuello—. Vi, nunca le tuve miedo a nadie en toda mi vida, pero mi hermano pelirrojo y vaquero me da un miedo infernal. Pero no me importa. No me importa si tengo que venderle el alma al Diablo. No me importa si Brodie *es* el Diablo. Voy a matarlo, como él trató de matarte a ti. Para que no vuelva a repetirlo. Lo juro por Dios.

Y después me besó, en los labios. *Intensamente.* Cerré los ojos, me hundí en el beso y traté de volver a experimentar esa sensación en que me derretía, que había sentido antes en el cementerio, la primera vez.

Pero comenzaron a dolerme las cicatrices de las muñecas y vi un destello de cabello rojo. Y después, *de golpe*, sentí los labios de Brodie sobre los míos mientras mi sangre nos empapaba la ropa.

Me separé. Y, por la expresión de los ojos de River, me di cuenta de que no tenía que decir nada, ni una maldita palabra, porque él comprendía.

Hurgó en el bolsillo y sacó otro señalador. Era un billete de cien dólares doblado en forma de estrella. Lo colocó en mi mano.

Luego se subió al auto.

Y se alejó.

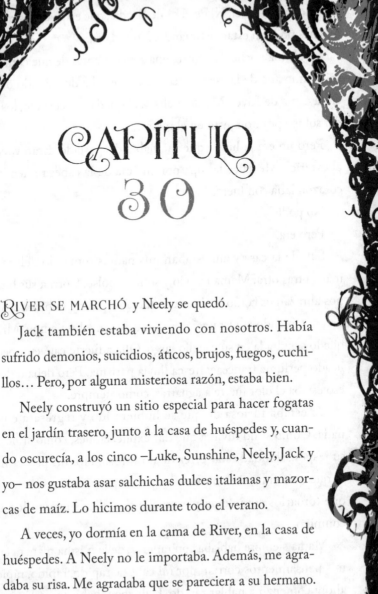

CAPÍTULO 30

RIVER SE MARCHÓ y Neely se quedó.

Jack también estaba viviendo con nosotros. Había sufrido demonios, suicidios, áticos, brujos, fuegos, cuchillos… Pero, por alguna misteriosa razón, estaba bien.

Neely construyó un sitio especial para hacer fogatas en el jardín trasero, junto a la casa de huéspedes y, cuando oscurecía, a los cinco –Luke, Sunshine, Neely, Jack y yo– nos gustaba asar salchichas dulces italianas y mazorcas de maíz. Lo hicimos durante todo el verano.

A veces, yo dormía en la cama de River, en la casa de huéspedes. A Neely no le importaba. Además, me agradaba su risa. Me agradaba que se pareciera a su hermano.

No hablábamos de River, y ambos dejamos de leer los periódicos. No queríamos saber. Ni de él ni de Brodie, qué estaban haciendo y a quiénes podrían estar lastimando. No todavía.

La última noche de agosto, una semana antes de que comenzara mi último año de la escuela secundaria, estaba durmiendo otra vez en la cama de River. Me di vuelta y, al quedar de costado, los rayos del sol me pegaron justo en el rostro.

Pero no era la luz lo que me había despertado. Eran voces, en el exterior. Me calcé la ropa por encima de la cabeza mientras mi corazón latía con fuerza.

No podía ser.

Pero era.

Salí de la casa y ahí estaban mis padres tomando del taxi una maleta tras otra. Mamá me vio y soltó el bolso. Corrí a sus brazos y nos abrazamos como si abrazarse fuera respirar y hubiéramos estado conteniendo la respiración por mucho, mucho tiempo. Mi nariz quedó sepultada en su cabello largo. Olía a fuerte café europeo, delicado perfume francés y fresca lluvia parisina. Pero debajo de todo eso estaba el olor fuerte a aguarrás, como siempre.

Yo estaba furiosa de que se hubiera ido y regresara como si nada. Como si no tuviera que dar explicaciones, como si no fuera su responsabilidad estar cerca de nosotros. Pero mis padres harían lo que quisieran, sin importar lo que yo pensara al respecto. Tenía que tomarlos como eran y esperaba que ellos hicieran lo mismo conmigo.

Mamá siempre hablaba con rapidez, de la misma manera en que mis pensamientos corrían por mi cabeza, rápido, rápido, rápido. Y ahora comenzó a hablar rápido. Hablaba y hablaba de Europa, de museos, de una exposición en París y solo la escuché por la mitad porque estaba abrazando a mi padre y disfrutando el momento.

—Violet, ¿me escuchaste? —mamá apoyó la mano en mi brazo—. Papá vendió todos los cuadros de una exposición en París, y ¿qué crees que significa eso? Significa que finalmente tenemos algo de dinero para gastar, eso es lo que significa. Ah, acá está *Luke*.

A esa altura, Luke ya estaba afuera y bajaba corriendo los escalones. Derramó algunas lágrimas, lo cual me resultó extraño pues nunca lo había visto llorar. Papá tenía esa expresión distante en la mirada mientras Luke lo abrazaba, una expresión que, descubrí súbitamente, había extrañado como loca. Luego aparecieron Neely y Jack e hicimos las presentaciones del caso. Las presentaciones llevaron a hablar de arte, lo cual nos llevó al cobertizo y luego a la casa de huéspedes, y les contamos todo lo que había ocurrido desde que ellos se marcharon, que era casi nada, porque no les hablamos de River, de Brodie, de las cartas de Freddie, de que la sangre lo había llamado a Jack, de Sunshine, el bate, del niño junto a las vías y de que yo había estado a las puertas de la muerte, había apuñalado al Demonio en el corazón y de lo que ocultaba bajo las mangas largas que llevaba en un día de calor.

Unas horas después, esa misma tarde, estaba sentada sola en los escalones preguntándome otra vez en qué olvidado rincón estaría oculto River. La noche caía sobre uno de los últimos días de verano y me invadió la añoranza de River, como solía sucederme cerca del atardecer. Podía oír las risas de Neely y Luke mientras juntaban ramas y troncos. Íbamos a pasar la noche de campamento en el jardín trasero. Papá estaba armando una carpa verde y polvorienta que había encontrado en el sótano y mamá pintaba en el cobertizo con la puerta abierta de par en par para poder observarnos a todos. Jack batía helado en una vieja máquina de manivela y Sunshine estaba sentada a su lado, los ojos entrecerrados en la luz tenue, tratando de leer un viejo manual de la biblioteca, de los Niños Exploradores, sobre cómo encender una fogata.

Yo me preguntaba si River tenía el resplandor bajo control. Si se sentía solo y me extrañaba como yo lo extrañaba a él. Pero después Neely apareció frente a mí con una ramita con un malvavisco y exigió que me uniera a la diversión. Y eso hice. Asé malvaviscos, comí helado casero, pinté a la luz de la luna y dormí en el suelo en una bolsa de dormir. Y la noche se convirtió en una gran llamarada difusa de todo y de nada. Me sentía segura y contenta, a pesar de cuánto añoraba a River.

Le eché una mirada a Neely, tumbado de costado junto al fuego. Pensé que estaba dormido, pero abrió los ojos y me miró, como si supiera en qué estaba pensando, y esbozó una gran sonrisa. Y esa sonrisa me atravesó profundamente.

Freddie a menudo me decía que uno tiene que ser feliz mientras puede, porque la vida no esperará a que te tomes el tiempo necesario para ser feliz. Y tenía razón. Lo había aprendido por las malas. Mi abuela era humana y había cometido errores. Pero, en el camino, había aprendido a aferrarse a su felicidad. Le rezaba a Dios y se aferraba a ella.

Resbalé los dedos por las cicatrices de las muñecas. Sin River, la vida era más segura. Y menos. Menos impresionante. Menos aterradora. Menos estimulante. Menos... todo.

Maldición. Realmente te extraño, River.

Tal vez eran los restos del resplandor los que me hacían sentir así. Tal vez era el resplandor lo que me causaba esa añoranza… pero parecía real. Y mis sentimientos, puros o no, eran lo único que tenía para seguir adelante. River había manipulado gente. Y asesinado. Era malvado. No tanto como Brodie, pero… igual era malvado. Era mejor que se hubiera ido, que estuviera fuera de mi vida. Lógicamente, yo sabía eso. Sin embargo, lo que *sentía* en lo más profundo y en lo más oscuro de mi corazón, era que me importaba un bledo que River fuera malo. Igual me gustaba. Tal vez hasta lo amaba.

Y tal vez eso me volvía malvada a mí también.

AGRADECIMIENTOS

A Nate.

A Joanna Volpe. Mi agente, fanática de Stephen King, compañera de andanzas nocturnas. Por mí, miraste *Diabolique*. Estoy en deuda contigo.

A Jessica Garrison. Sabías exactamente cómo extraer la bondad de mi librito de demonios. Si alguna vez quieres escapar de coyotes, yo conozco un lugar.

A todos los demás de Dial y Penguin, a Kristin Smith en especial, por esa cubierta impresionantemente hermosa.

A Simon Alander, por la increíble tipografía.

A Sandra, por permitirme quedarme despierta leyendo hasta la hora que quisiera. A Jason, por su activa imaginación: siempre me gustó eso de ti. A Erin y Todd, por jugar conmigo a *Egypt Game* esa noche de verano. A Loren, por la casa del árbol.

A Joelie Hicks, por tu amor por los libros.

A Erin Bowman, por estar siempre cerca.

A Elsie Chapman.

A Lucky 13s.

A Friday the Thirteeners, por el hilo sobre unicornios.

Y al chico pelirrojo, por la calavera.

Sobre la autora

April Genevieve Tucholke es la autora de *Entre el demonio y el profundo mar azul* y de *Wink Poppy Midnight*. También fue la curadora de una antología de terror llamada *Slasher Girls & Monster Boys*.

Sus novelas fueron elegidas por la Junior Library Guild, Kids' Indie Next picks y YALSA Teens Top Ten.

Cuando no está escribiendo, a April le gusta caminar en el bosque con sus dos perros, explorar casas abandonadas y tomar café.

ROMA

¿Y si Ana Bolena y el Rey Enrique se conocieran en pleno siglo XXI?

ANNE & HENRY - *Dawn Ius*

¿Y si el villano se enamora de su presa...?

FIRELIGHT - *Sophie Jordan*

Personajes con poderes especiales

SKY - *Joss Stirling*

Dos jóvenes que desafían las reglas...

NIGHT OWLS - *Jenn Bennett*

NCE

Un amor que nace del milagro de la Navidad

NOCHE DE LUZ -
Jay Asher

En una convención de cómics todo es posible, incluso el amor

LA IMPROBABLE TEORÍA
DE ANA Y ZAK - *Brian Katcher*

Una historia de amor tan oscura como apasionante

SI EL AMOR ES UNA ISLA -
Esther Sanz

ENTRE EL DEMONIO
Y EL PROFUNDO MAR AZUL
- *Joss Stirling.*

STRUCK - *Joss Stirling.*

Un misterio que acrecienta la pasión...

¡QUEREMOS SABER QUÉ TE PARECIÓ LA NOVELA!

Nos puedes escribir a **vrya@vreditoras.com**
con el título de esta novela en el asunto.

Encuéntranos en

 facebook.com/vreditorasya

 twitter.com/vreditorasya

 instagram.com/vreditorasya

COMPARTE
tu experiencia con
este libro con el hashtag

#entreeldemonio